Our Problem

Everyone is destined to die, but life does not end with death. The Bible says that after death there will be a judgment where each person will give an account of his life to God (Hebrews 9:27). When God created Adam and Eve in His own image in the Garden of Eden, He gave them an abundant life, and the freedom to choose between good and evil. They chose to disobey God and go their own way. As a consequence, death was introduced into the human race, not only physical death, but also spiritual death. For this reason, all people are separated from God. "For all have sinned and fall short of the glory of God." Romans 3:23

We have tried to overcome this separation in many ways: by doing good, through religion or philosophy, or by attempting to live morally and justly. However, none of these things is enough to cross the barrier of separation between God and humanity, because God is holy and people are sinful.

HOLY GOD

S E P A R A T I O N

GOOD WORKS — RELIGION — PHILOSOPHY — MORALITY

SINFUL PEOPLE

This spiritual separation has become our natural and normal condition, and because of this we are condemned: "The one who believes in Him is not judged; the one who does not believe has been judged already, because he has not believed in the name of the only Son of God." John 3:18

There is only one solution to our problem: Jesus responded and said to him, "Truly, truly, I say to you, unless someone is born again he cannot see the kingdom of God." (John 3:3); that is, it is necessary to be born again in the spiritual sense. God Himself has provided the means that makes it possible for anyone to be born again, and this is the plan that He has for us because He loves us.

God's Plan: Salvation

"For God so loved the world, that He gave His only Son, so that everyone who believes in Him will not perish, but have eternal life." John 3:16

(Jesus said)... "I came so that they would have life, and have it abundantly." (A full and meaningful life.) John 10:10

"The one who believes in the Son has eternal life; but the one who does not obey the Son will not see life, but the wrath of God remains on him." John 3:36

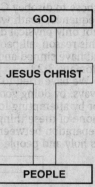

(Jesus said)... "I am the way, and the truth, and the life; no one comes to the Father except through Me." John 14:6

"And there is salvation in no one else; for there is no other name under heaven that has been given among mankind by which we must be saved." Acts 4:12

When Jesus Christ died on the cross, He substituted Himself for our sins and bridged the separation of people from God. Because of this sacrifice, every person who is born again can have true fellowship with God.

Jesus Christ is alive today

After Jesus Christ died on the cross at Calvary, where He received the punishment that we deserved, the Bible says that He was buried in a tomb. But He did not remain there: He resurrected! For all those who believe in Jesus Christ, the resurrection is a guarantee that they will also be resurrected to eternal life in the presence of God. This is very good news! (Gospel of Salvation!)

"Now I make known to you, brothers and sisters, the gospel which I preached to you, which you also received, in which you also stand, by which you also are saved, if you hold firmly to the word which I preached to you, unless you believed in vain.

For I handed down to you as of first importance what I also received, that Christ died for our sins according to the Scriptures, and that He was buried, and that He was raised on the third day according to the Scriptures, and that He appeared to Cephas, then to the twelve." 1 Corinthians 15:1-5

How to receive God's love and plan

In His mercy, God has determined that salvation is free. To receive it, you need to only do this:

1. Admit your problem: being separated from God by sin. Recognize that you have sinned, need God's solution, and repent.

2. Believe that Jesus Christ died for your sins on the cross, was buried, and rose from the dead.

3. Ask Jesus Christ to come into your heart and He will give you salvation and the Holy Spirit to guide your life.

4. Receive Jesus Christ now as your personal Lord, God, and Savior of your life.

In Romans 10:9 and 13 the Bible tells us "that if you confess with your mouth Jesus as Lord, and believe in your heart that God raised Him from the dead, you will be saved...Everyone who calls on the name of the Lord will be saved."

A Suggested prayer to receive Jesus Christ

Dear Lord Jesus, I know that I have sinned against You and that I am not living within your plan. For this I repent and ask You to forgive me. I believe that You died and rose again for me and in doing so, You paid the penalty for my sins. I am willing to turn from my sins, and now I ask You to come into my heart and life as my personal Lord, God, and Savior. Send Your Holy Spirit and Help me now to change, to follow and obey You and to find Your perfect will for my life. Amen.

My personal decision

On (date) _____, I,

_____ repented of my sins, believed, confessed, and received Jesus Christ as my personal Lord, God, and Savior. Amen.

You Have Eternal Life

When you called upon the Lord, He listened. Your sins have all been forgiven (Colossians 1:14), you became a child of God (John 1:12), you are born again (John 3:3) you will not be judged (John 5:24), you now have eternal life (John 3:16).

Do not be concerned with your feelings, for they may change sometimes under the pressure of daily life. Place your trust in your Heavenly Father "having cast all your anxiety on Him, because He cares about you." 1 Peter 5:7

"If we confess our sins, He is faithful and righteous, so that He will forgive us our sins and cleanse us from all unrighteousness." 1 John 1:9

His Promise Fulfilled

(Jesus said)... "If you continue in My word, then you are truly My disciples; and you will know the truth, and the truth will set you free. ...So if the Son sets you free, you really will be free." John 8:31-32, 36

"The one who has the Son has the life; the one who does not have the Son of God does not have the life. These things I have written to you who believe in the name of the Son of God, so that you may know that you have eternal life." 1 John 5:12-13

"But the Helper, the Holy Spirit whom the Father will send in My name, He will teach you all things, and remind you of all that I said to you." John 14:26

This is the beginning of the abundant life that Jesus Christ came to offer, because God desires to restore what was lost in the Garden of Eden. Now you are saved and you will be with Him in Heaven forever!

"Therefore if anyone is in Christ, this person is a new creation; the old things passed away; behold, new things have come." 2 Corinthians 5:17

What Should I do Now?

Pray and read the Bible daily to stay in contact with the Lord, starting with the Gospel of John in this New Testament. Attend a Bible preaching and teaching Christian church, get involved with a Bible study, fellowship with Christian friends so that you may strengthen one another, and witness to others about Jesus Christ.

"They were continually devoting themselves to the apostles' teaching and to fellowship, to the breaking of bread and to prayer. ...Praising God and having favor with all the people. And the Lord was adding to their number day by day those who were being saved." Acts 2:42, 47

FOREWORD

SCRIPTURAL PROMISE

"The grass withers, the flower fades,
but the word of our God stands forever."
Isaiah 40:8

The New American Standard Bible has been produced with
the conviction that the words of Scripture as originally penned
in the Hebrew, Aramaic, and Greek were inspired by God. Since
they are the eternal Word of God, the Holy Scriptures speak
with fresh power to each generation, to give wisdom that leads
to salvation, that people may serve Christ to the glory of God.

The NASB strives to adhere as closely as possible to the
original languages of the Holy Scriptures and to make the translation in a fluent and readable style according to current English
usage.

THE FOURFOLD AIM
OF
THE LOCKMAN FOUNDATION

1. These publications shall be true to the original Hebrew, Aramaic, and Greek.
2. They shall be grammatically correct.
3. They shall be understandable.
4. They shall give the Lord Jesus Christ His proper place, the place which the Word gives Him; therefore, no work will ever be personalized.

PREFACE TO THE
NEW AMERICAN STANDARD BIBLE

In the history of English Bible translations, the King James Version is the most prestigious. This time-honored version of 1611, itself a revision of the Bishops' Bible of 1568, became the basis for the English Revised Version appearing in 1881 (New Testament) and 1885 (Old Testament). The American counterpart of this last work was published in 1901 as the American Standard Version. The ASV, a product of both British and American scholarship, has been highly regarded for its scholarship and accuracy. Recognizing the values of the American Standard Version, The Lockman Foundation felt an urgency to preserve these and other lasting values of the ASV by incorporating recent discoveries of Hebrew and Greek textual sources and by rendering it into current English. Therefore, in 1959 a new and original translation project was launched, based on the time-honored principles of translation used for the ASV and KJV to produce an accurate and readable English text. The result is the New American Standard Bible.

This edition of the NASB represents updates according to modern English usage and refinements recommended over the last several years as well as updates based on current research of the ancient manuscripts.

PRINCIPLES OF TRANSLATION

MODERN ENGLISH USAGE: The goal is to render the grammar and terminology in contemporary English. When it was felt that the word-for-word literalness was unacceptable to the modern reader, a change was made in the direction of a more current English idiom. In editions that include the full set of translator's notes, in the instances where this has been done, a more literal rendering is indicated by "Lit" notes when necessary. These notes provide the "literal" meaning of the word or phrase in question, or as more technically known, its formal equivalent in the immediate context. Almost all words have a range of meanings, and a "Lit" note supplies the literal or formal meaning for that particular context. There are a few exceptions to this procedure. Punctuation is a relatively modern invention, and ancient writers often linked most of their sentences with "and" or other connectives, which are sometimes omitted at the beginning of sentences for better English.

GENDER ACCURACY: In past editions it was common practice to translate the Greek word *anthropoi* as "men." The same was true for singulars, as masculine. This was never intended to be gender-exclusive when the context indicated that women were included; it was assumed at that time that readers inferred the inclusion of women. Gender accuracy is important, however, so in this edition Greek words that are not actually exclusive in gender as they are used in a given context are rendered by inclusive terms, such as "people." Just as important, when the words in the original languages are in fact referring only to males or females, the distinction is maintained in English.

THE WORD BRETHREN: This word was used in past editions of the NASB as the plural of the Greek "brothers" (*adelphoi*) because it can still be used in a formal setting to address members of a profession, society, or church, regardless of gender. However, most people today would seldom use "brethren" informally and not often in most churches. This created the challenge of choosing a replacement that would have the same meaning that led to the original usage of "brethren," and only "brothers" was deemed adequate. To be gender-accurate, when it is clear that the author or speaker is referring to women as well as men, "*and sisters*" is added in italic for accuracy and clarity. The italic is necessary to indicate that the addition is implied in the meaning of *adelphoi* for the context, and the addition is not in the Greek text itself.

LET'S FOR ACTION: In most places the phrase "let us" has been replaced with "let's" when a proposal is being made by one or more persons within a group to engage in an action. Such a proposal is common not only in English, but also in the ancient languages of the Bible; however, it is expressed in the ancient languages grammatically rather than by using an auxiliary, "helping" verb such as "let." It is common today for readers to understand "let us" to mean "allow us," so in effect, "let us" has become unintentionally misleading to most readers. Therefore, the simple contraction "let's" has emerged as the clearest expression because this form reflects the nuance of meaning in the original languages–that is, a proposal to do something. However, in some situations "Let Us" is retained for intimate discourse within the Godhead, as in Gen 1:26. "Let us" is also kept when there is a request for permission, and in some other select cases.

ALTERNATIVE READINGS: In addition to the more literal renderings explained under MODERN ENGLISH USAGE, notations have been made to include alternate translations, readings of variant manuscripts, and explanatory equivalents of the text. Only such notations have been used as have been felt justified in assisting the reader's comprehension of the terms used by the original author.

NAMES IN THE NEW TESTAMENT: The Greek versions of Hebrew names found in the New Testament, such as "Zacharias," are usually given in their original Hebrew forms, as in "Zechariah" for "Zacharias." Exceptions occur when the person is very commonly known by another name in English versions of the Bible. One of the most notable of such names is "James." An accurate translation would render this name "Jacob." Unfortunately, many would find it confusing to suddenly change the name "James" to "Jacob." There are other special cases where we do not follow the pattern outlined above, and these are often noted. The name "Jesus" itself is a special case, based on the Greek, from an abbreviated form of "Joshua." In fact, in two cases in the New Testament the Greek name refers instead to the famous Joshua of the Old Testament (Acts 7:45; Heb 4:8).

GREEK TEXT: Consideration was given to the latest available manuscripts with a view to determining the best Greek text. In most instances the 28th edition of the Nestle-Aland NOVUM TESTAMENTUM GRAECE was followed. For Acts and the General Epistles, the Editio Critica Maior (ECM) was followed in most instances. However, the apparatuses provided by both editions are intended to enable scholars to make informed decisions about readings, and sometimes alternate readings with better support to those chosen by the editors were preferred.

GREEK TENSES: A careful distinction has been made in the treatment of the Greek aorist tense (usually translated as the

English past, "He did") and the Greek imperfect tense (normally rendered either as English past progressive, "He was doing"; or, if inceptive, as "He began to do" or "He started to do"; or else if customary past, as "He used to do"). "Began" is italicized if it is added to translate an imperfect tense, in order to distinguish it from the Greek verb for "begin." In some contexts the difference between the Greek imperfect and the English past is conveyed better by the choice of vocabulary or by other words in the context, and in such cases the Greek imperfect may be rendered as a simple past tense (e.g. "had an illness for many years" would be preferable to "was having an illness for many years" and the first option would be common in English).

Not all aorist tenses have been rendered as English pasts ("He did"), because some of them are clearly to be rendered as English perfects ("He has done"), or even as past perfects ("He had done"), judging from the context in which they occur. Such aorists have been rendered as perfects or past perfects in this translation.

As for the distinction between aorist and present imperatives, these have usually been rendered as imperatives in the customary way, rather than attempting any fine distinction such as "Begin to do!" (for the aorist imperative), or, "Continually do!" (for the present imperative).

As for the sequence of tenses, care was taken to follow English rules rather than Greek in translating Greek presents, imperfects, and aorists. For example where English says, "We knew that he was doing," Greek puts it, "We knew that he does"; similarly, "We knew that he had done" is the English for "We knew that he did." Likewise, the English, "When he had come, they met him," is represented in Greek by, "When he came, they met him." In all cases a consistent transition has been made from the Greek tense in the subordinate clause to the appropriate tense in English. In the rendering of negative questions introduced by the Greek particle *mē* (which always expects the answer "No") the wording has been altered from a mere, "Will he not do this?" to a more accurate, "He will not do this, will he?"

EXPLANATION OF GENERAL FORMAT

FOOTNOTES are listed by the chapter and verse numbers to which they refer. This edition contains a smaller set of footnotes.

PARAGRAPHS are designated by boldfaced verse numbers or letters.

CAPITALIZED WORDS are used to provide helpful information. Personal pronouns are capitalized when pertaining to Deity. The word "Law" is capitalized when pertaining to Mosaic Law.

ITALICS are used in the text to indicate words that are not found in the original Hebrew, Aramaic, or Greek but are implied by it, or are sometimes necessary for correct English. Italics are used in the marginal notes to signify alternate readings for the text. Roman text in these marginal alternate readings is the same as italics in the Bible text. There are also special cases of italics referring to words that actually are in the original text. Italic "began" mentioned in GREEK TENSES is one example, where "began" communicates the grammatical tense of a verb. Another is italic possessive pronouns for Greek articles ("the" in Greek) used as possessive pronouns, a common feature in the Greek language. "*His* good pleasure," literally: "the good pleasure" in Phil 2:13 is an example. The purpose of the italic in this case is to inform the reader that the expected Greek word (the Greek possessive pronoun) is not found in the original text, but is represented by another word (the article) in the original text.

SMALL CAPS in the New Testament are used in the text to indicate Old Testament quotations or references to Old Testament texts. Variations of Old Testament wording are found in New Testament citations depending on whether the New Testament writer translated from a Hebrew text, used existing Greek or Aramaic translations, or paraphrased the material. It should be noted that modern rules for the indication of direct quotation were not used in biblical times, and the ancient writer would use exact quotations or references to quotation without any specific indication of them.

ASTERISKS are used to mark verbs that are historical presents in the Greek grammar and have been translated with an English past tense in order to conform to modern usage. The translators recognized that in some contexts the present tense seems more unexpected and unjustified to the English reader than a past tense would have been. But Greek authors frequently used the present tense for the sake of heightened vividness, thereby transporting their readers in imagination to the actual scene at the time of occurrence. However, the translators felt that it would be wise to change these historical presents to English past tenses.

ABBREVIATIONS AND SPECIAL MARKINGS:

Aram = Aramaic; DSS = Dead Sea Scrolls; Gr = Greek;
Heb = Hebrew; Lat = Latin; LXX = Greek translation of O.T.
(Septuagint); MT = Masoretic Text; Lit = A literal translation
(formal equivalent); Or = An alternate translation justified by
the original language; Ancient versions = O.T. manuscripts
that are not Hebrew; [[ ]] = In text, double brackets indicate
words very likely not in the original manuscripts; [ ] = In text,
brackets indicate words probably not in the original manuscripts; [ ] = In notes, brackets indicate references to a name,
place, or thing similar to, but not identical with that in the
text; ch = chapter; cf. = compare; ff = following verses;
ms, mss = manuscript(s); v, vv = verse(s)

THE NEW TESTAMENT

The Gospel According to
MATTHEW

The Genealogy of Jesus the Messiah

1 The record of the genealogy of Jesus the Messiah, the son of David, the son of Abraham:

2 Abraham fathered Isaac, Isaac fathered Jacob, and Jacob fathered ¹Judah and his brothers. 3 Judah fathered Perez and Zerah by Tamar, Perez fathered Hezron, and Hezron fathered Ram. 4 Ram fathered Amminadab, Amminadab fathered Nahshon, and Nahshon fathered Salmon. 5 Salmon fathered Boaz by Rahab, Boaz fathered Obed by Ruth, and Obed fathered Jesse. 6 Jesse fathered David the king.

David fathered Solomon by ¹her *who had been the wife* of Uriah. 7 Solomon fathered Rehoboam, Rehoboam fathered Abijah, and Abijah fathered Asa. 8 Asa fathered Jehoshaphat, Jehoshaphat fathered Joram, and Joram fathered Uzziah. 9 Uzziah fathered Jotham, Jotham fathered Ahaz, and Ahaz fathered Hezekiah. 10 Hezekiah fathered Manasseh, Manasseh fathered Amon, and Amon fathered Josiah. 11 Josiah fathered Jeconiah and his brothers, at the time of the deportation to Babylon.

12 After the deportation to Babylon: Jeconiah fathered Shealtiel, and Shealtiel fathered Zerubbabel. 13 Zerubbabel fathered Abihud, Abihud fathered Eliakim, and Eliakim fathered Azor. 14 Azor fathered Zadok, Zadok fathered Achim, and Achim fathered Eliud. 15 Eliud fathered Eleazar, Eleazar fathered Matthan, and Matthan fathered Jacob. 16 Jacob fathered Joseph the husband of Mary, by whom Jesus was born, who is called the Messiah.

17 So all the generations from Abraham to David are fourteen generations; from David to the deportation to Babylon, fourteen generations; and from the deportation to Babylon to the Messiah, fourteen generations.

Conception and Birth of Jesus

18 Now the birth of Jesus the Messiah was as follows:

1:2 ¹Gr *Judas;* a name of a person in the Old Testament is given in its Old Testament form   1:6 ¹I.e., Bathsheba when His mother Mary had been ¹betrothed to Joseph, before they came together she was found to be pregnant by the Holy Spirit. ¹⁹ And her husband Joseph, since he was a righteous man and did not want to disgrace her, planned to ¹send her away secretly. ²⁰ But when he had thought this over, behold, an angel of the Lord appeared to him in a dream, saying, "Joseph, son of David, do not be afraid to take Mary as your wife; for the Child who has been conceived in her is of the Holy Spirit. ²¹ She will give birth to a Son; and you shall name Him Jesus, for He will save His people from their sins." ²² Now all this took place so that what was spoken by the Lord through ¹the prophet would be fulfilled: ²³ "BEHOLD, THE VIRGIN WILL CONCEIVE AND GIVE BIRTH TO A SON, AND THEY SHALL NAME HIM IMMANUEL," which translated means, "GOD WITH US." ²⁴ And Joseph awoke from his sleep and did as the angel of the Lord commanded him, and took *Mary* as his wife, ²⁵ but kept her a virgin until she gave birth to a Son; and he named Him Jesus.

The Visit of the Magi

2 Now after Jesus was born in Bethlehem of Judea in the days of Herod the king, behold, ¹magi from the east arrived in Jerusalem, saying, ² "Where is He who has been born King of the Jews? For we saw His star in the east and have come to worship Him." ³ When Herod the king heard *this,* he was troubled, and all Jerusalem with him. ⁴ And gathering together all the chief priests and scribes of the people, he inquired of them where the Messiah was to be born. ⁵ They said to him, "In Bethlehem of Judea; for this is what has been written by ¹the prophet:

6   'AND YOU, BETHLEHEM, LAND OF JUDAH,
     ARE BY NO MEANS LEAST AMONG THE LEADERS OF JUDAH;
     FOR FROM YOU WILL COME FORTH A RULER
     WHO WILL SHEPHERD MY PEOPLE ISRAEL.'"

⁷ Then Herod secretly called for the magi and determined from them the exact time the star appeared. ⁸ And he sent them to Bethlehem and said, "Go and search

---

1:18 ¹ Unlike engagement, a betrothed couple was considered married, but did not yet live together   1:19 ¹ Or *divorce her*
1:22 ¹ I.e., Isaiah   2:1 ¹ A caste of educated men specializing in astronomy, astrology, and natural science   2:5 ¹ I.e., Micah

the barn, but He will burn up the chaff with
unquenchable fire."

The Baptism of Jesus

13 Then Jesus *arrived from Galilee at the Jordan,
coming to John to be baptized by him. **14** But John tried
to prevent Him, saying, "I have *the* need to be baptized
by You, and *yet* You are coming to me?" **15** But Jesus,
answering, said to him, "Allow *it* at this time; for in this
way it is fitting for us to fulfill all righteousness." Then
he *allowed Him. **16** After He was baptized, Jesus came
up immediately from the water; and behold, the heavens
were opened, and he saw the Spirit of God descending as
a dove *and* settling on Him, **17** and behold, a voice from
the heavens said, "This is My beloved Son, with whom I
am well pleased."

The Temptation of Jesus

4 Then Jesus was led up by the Spirit into the wilderness to be tempted by the devil. **2** And after He had
fasted for forty days and forty nights, He then became
hungry. **3** And the tempter came and said to Him, "If You
are the Son of God, command that these stones become
bread." **4** But He answered and said, "It is written: 'MAN
SHALL NOT LIVE ON BREAD ALONE, BUT ON EVERY WORD THAT COMES
OUT OF THE MOUTH OF GOD.'"

5 Then the devil *took Him along into the holy city and
had Him stand on the pinnacle of the temple, **6** and he
*said to Him, "If You are the Son of God, throw Yourself
down; for it is written:

'HE WILL GIVE HIS ANGELS ORDERS CONCERNING YOU';
and

'ON *THEIR* HANDS THEY WILL LIFT YOU UP,
SO THAT YOU DO NOT STRIKE YOUR FOOT AGAINST A STONE.'"
7 Jesus said to him, "On the other hand, it is written:
'YOU SHALL NOT PUT THE LORD YOUR GOD TO THE TEST.'"

8 Again, the devil *took Him along to a very high
mountain and *showed Him all the kingdoms of the
world and their glory; **9** and he said to Him, "All these
things I will give You, if You fall down and worship me."
10 Then Jesus *said to him, "Go away, Satan! For it is
written: 'YOU SHALL WORSHIP THE LORD YOUR GOD, AND SERVE
HIM ONLY.'" **11** Then the devil *left Him; and behold,
angels came and *began to* serve Him.

Jesus Begins His Ministry

12 Now when Jesus heard that John had been taken into custody, He withdrew into Galilee; **13** and leaving Nazareth, He came and settled in Capernaum, which is by the sea, in the region of Zebulun and Naphtali. **14** *This happened* so that what was spoken through Isaiah the prophet would be fulfilled:

15 "THE LAND OF ZEBULUN AND THE LAND OF NAPHTALI,
  BY THE WAY OF THE SEA, ON THE OTHER SIDE OF THE JORDAN,
    GALILEE OF THE [1]GENTILES—
16 THE PEOPLE WHO WERE SITTING IN DARKNESS SAW A GREAT
      LIGHT,
    AND THOSE WHO WERE SITTING IN THE LAND AND SHADOW OF
      DEATH,
    UPON THEM A LIGHT DAWNED."

17 From that time Jesus began to preach and say, "Repent, for the kingdom of heaven is at hand."

The First Disciples

18 Now as *Jesus* was walking by the Sea of Galilee, He saw two brothers, Simon, who was called Peter, and his brother Andrew, casting a net into the sea; for they were fishermen. **19** And He *said to them, "Follow Me, and I will make you fishers of people." **20** Immediately they left their nets and followed Him. **21** Going on from there He saw two other brothers, James the *son* of Zebedee, and his brother John, in the boat with their father Zebedee, mending their nets; and He called them. **22** Immediately they left the boat and their father, and followed Him.

Ministry in Galilee

23 Jesus was going about in all of Galilee, teaching in their synagogues and proclaiming the gospel of the kingdom, and healing every disease and every sickness among the people. **24** And the news about Him spread throughout Syria; and they brought to Him all who were ill, those suffering with various diseases and severe pain, demon-possessed, people with epilepsy, and people who were paralyzed; and He healed them. **25** Large crowds followed Him from Galilee and *the* Decapolis, and Jerusalem, and Judea, and *from* beyond the Jordan.

4:15 [1] Lit *nations*, usually non-Jewish

The Sermon on the Mount; The Beatitudes

5 Now when Jesus saw the crowds, He went up on the mountain; and after He sat down, His disciples came to Him. 2 And He opened His mouth and *began* to teach them, saying,

3 "Blessed are the poor in spirit, for theirs is the kingdom of heaven.

4 "Blessed are those who mourn, for they will be comforted.

5 "Blessed are the 'gentle, for they will inherit the earth.

6 "Blessed are those who hunger and thirst for righteousness, for they will be satisfied.

7 "Blessed are the merciful, for they will receive mercy.

8 "Blessed are the pure in heart, for they will see God.

9 "Blessed are the peacemakers, for they will be called sons of God.

10 "Blessed are those who have been persecuted for the sake of righteousness, for theirs is the kingdom of heaven.

11 "Blessed are you when *people* insult you and persecute you, and falsely say all kinds of evil against you because of Me. 12 Rejoice and be glad, for your reward in heaven is great; for in this same way they persecuted the prophets who were before you.

Disciples and the World

13 "You are the salt of the earth; but if the salt has become tasteless, how can it be made salty *again?* It is no longer good for anything, except to be thrown out and trampled underfoot by people.

14 "You are the light of the world. A city set on a hill cannot be hidden; 15 nor do *people* light a lamp and put it under a basket, but on the lampstand, and it gives light to all who are in the house. 16 Your light must shine before people in such a way that they may see your good works, and glorify your Father who is in heaven.

17 "Do not presume that I came to abolish the Law or the Prophets; I did not come to abolish, but to fulfill. 18 For truly I say to you, until heaven and earth pass

away, not the smallest letter or stroke of a letter shall pass from the Law, until all is accomplished! **19** Therefore, whoever nullifies one of the least of these command-ments, and teaches others *to do* the same, shall be called least in the kingdom of heaven; but whoever keeps and teaches *them,* he shall be called great in the kingdom of heaven.

20 "For I say to you that unless your righteousness far surpasses *that* of the scribes and Pharisees, you will not enter the kingdom of heaven.

Personal Relationships

21 "You have heard that the ancients were told, 'YOU SHALL NOT MURDER,' and 'Whoever commits murder shall be answerable to the court.' **22** But I say to you that everyone who is angry with his brother shall be answerable to the court; and whoever says to his brother, '[1]You good-for-nothing,' shall be answerable to [2]the supreme court; and whoever says, 'You fool,' shall be guilty *enough to go* into the [3]fiery hell. **23** Therefore, if you are presenting your offering at the altar, and there you remember that your brother has something against you, **24** leave your offering there before the altar and go; first be reconciled to your brother, and then come and present your offering. **25** Come to good terms with your accuser quickly, while you are with him on the way *to court,* so that your accuser will not hand you over to the judge, and the judge to the officer, and you will not be thrown into prison. **26** Truly I say to you, you will not come out of there until you have paid up the last [1]quadrans.

27 "You have heard that it was said, 'YOU SHALL NOT COMMIT ADULTERY'; **28** but I say to you that everyone who looks at a woman with lust for her has already committed adultery with her in his heart. **29** Now if your right eye is causing you to sin, tear it out and throw it away from you; for it is better for you to lose one of the parts of your *body,* than for your whole body to be thrown into hell. **30** And if your right hand is causing you

---

5:22 [1] Or *You empty-head; Gr Raka (Raca)* from Aramaic *reqa*
5:22 [2] Lit *the Sanhedrin;* i.e., Jewish High Court   5:22 [3] Lit *Gehenna of fire*   5:26 [1] A small Roman copper coin, worth about 1/64 of a laborer's daily wage

to sin, cut it off and throw it away from you; for it is better for you to lose one of the parts of your *body,* than for your whole body to go into hell.

31 "Now it was said, 'WHOEVER SENDS HIS WIFE AWAY IS TO GIVE HER A CERTIFICATE OF DIVORCE'; **32** but I say to you that everyone who divorces his wife, except for *the* reason of sexual immorality, makes her commit adultery; and whoever marries a divorced woman commits adultery.

33 "Again, you have heard that the ancients were told, 'YOU SHALL NOT MAKE FALSE VOWS, BUT SHALL FULFILL YOUR VOWS TO THE LORD.' **34** But I say to you, take no oath at all, neither by heaven, for it is the throne of God, **35** nor by the earth, for it is the footstool of His feet, nor by Jerusalem, for it is THE CITY OF THE GREAT KING. **36** Nor shall you take an oath by your head, for you cannot make a single hair white or black. **37** But make sure your state-ment is, 'Yes, yes' *or* 'No, no'; anything beyond these is of evil *origin.*

38 "You have heard that it was said, 'EYE FOR EYE, and TOOTH FOR TOOTH.' **39** But I say to you, do not show opposi-tion against an evil person; but whoever slaps you on your right cheek, turn the other toward him also. **40** And if anyone wants to sue you and take your ¹tunic, let him have your ²cloak also. **41** Whoever forces you to go one mile, go with him two. **42** Give to him who asks of you, and do not turn away from him who wants to borrow from you.

43 "You have heard that it was said, 'YOU SHALL LOVE YOUR NEIGHBOR and hate your enemy.' **44** But I say to you, love your enemies and pray for those who persecute you, **45** so that you may prove yourselves to be sons of your Father who is in heaven; for He causes His sun to rise on *the* evil and *the* good, and sends rain on *the* righteous and *the* unrighteous. **46** For if you love those who love you, what reward do you have? Even the tax collectors, do they not do the same? **47** And if you greet only your brothers *and sisters,* what more are you doing *than others?* Even the Gentiles, do they not do the same? **48** Therefore you shall be perfect, as your heavenly Father is perfect.

5:40 ¹A long shirt worn next to the skin   5:40 ²Or *outer garment*

Charitable Giving to the Poor and Prayer

6 "Take care not to practice your righteousness in the sight of people, to be noticed by them; otherwise you have no reward with your Father who is in heaven.

2 "So when you give to the poor, do not sound a trumpet before you, as the hypocrites do in the synagogues and on the streets, so that they will be praised by people. Truly I say to you, they have their reward in full. 3 But when you give to the poor, do not let your left hand know what your right hand is doing, 4 so that your charitable giving will be in secret; and your Father who sees *what is done* in secret will reward you.

5 "And when you pray, you are not to be like the hypocrites; for they love to stand and pray in the synagogues and on the street corners so that they will be seen by people. Truly I say to you, they have their reward in full. 6 But as for you, when you pray, go into your inner room, close your door, and pray to your Father who is in secret; and your Father who sees *what is done* in secret will reward you.

7 "And when you are praying, do not use thoughtless repetition as the Gentiles do, for they think that they will be heard because of their many words. 8 So do not be like them; for your Father knows what you need before you ask Him.

The Lord's Prayer

9 "Pray, then, in this way:
'Our Father, who is in heaven,
    Hallowed be Your name.
10 'Your kingdom come.
    Your will be done,
    On earth as it is in heaven.
11 'Give us this day our daily bread.
12 'And forgive us our debts, as we also have forgiven
        our debtors.
13 'And do not lead us into temptation, but deliver us
        from evil.'"

14 For if you forgive *other* people for their offenses, your heavenly Father will also forgive you. 15 But if you do not

---

6:13 1 Late mss add *For Yours is the kingdom and the power and the glory forever. Amen* forgive *other* people, then your Father will not forgive your offenses.

Fasting; The True Treasure; Wealth

16 "Now whenever you fast, do not make a gloomy face as the hypocrites *do,* for they distort their faces so that they will be noticed by people when they are fasting. Truly I say to you, they have their reward in full. **17** But as for you, when you fast, anoint your head and wash your face, **18** so that your fasting will not be noticed by people but by your Father who is in secret; and your Father who sees *what is done* in secret will reward you.

19 "Do not store up for yourselves treasures on earth, where moth and rust destroy, and where thieves break in and steal. **20** But store up for yourselves treasures in heaven, where neither moth nor rust destroys, and where thieves do not break in or steal; **21** for where your treasure is, there your heart will be also.

22 "The eye is the lamp of the body; so then, if your eye is clear, your whole body will be full of light. **23** But if your eye is bad, your whole body will be full of darkness. So if the light that is in you is darkness, how great is the darkness!

24 "No one can serve two masters; for either he will hate the one and love the other, or he will be devoted to one and despise the other. You cannot serve God and 'wealth.

The Cure for Anxiety

25 "For this reason I say to you, do not be worried about your life, *as to* what you will eat or what you will drink; nor for your body, *as to* what you will put on. Is life not more than food, and the body more than clothing? **26** Look at the birds of the sky, that they do not sow, nor reap, nor gather *crops* into barns, and *yet* your heavenly Father feeds them. Are you not much more important than they? **27** And which of you by worrying can add a single day to his life's span? **28** And why are you worried about clothing? Notice how the lilies of the field grow; they do not labor nor do they spin *thread for cloth,* **29** yet I say to you that not even Solomon in all his glory

---

6:24 ¹ Gr *mamonas,* for Aramaic *mamon* (mammon); i.e., wealth etc. personified as an object of worship

clothed himself like one of these. **30** But if God so clothes the grass of the field, which is *alive* today and tomorrow is thrown into the furnace, *will He* not much more *clothe* you? You of little faith! **31** Do not worry then, saying, 'What are we to eat?' or 'What are we to drink?' or 'What are we to wear for clothing?' **32** For the Gentiles eagerly seek all these things; for your heavenly Father knows that you need all these things. **33** But seek first His kingdom and His righteousness, and all these things will be provided to you.

34 "So do not worry about tomorrow; for tomorrow will worry about itself. Each day has enough trouble of its own.

Judging Others

7 "Do not judge, so that you will not be judged. **2** For in the way you judge, you will be judged; and by your standard of measure, it will be measured to you. **3** Why do you look at the speck that is in your brother's eye, but do not notice the log that is in your own eye? **4** Or how can you say to your brother, 'Let me take the speck out of your eye,' and look, the log is in your own eye? **5** You hypocrite, first take the log out of your own eye, and then you will see clearly to take the speck out of your brother's eye!

6 "Do not give what is holy to dogs, and do not throw your pearls before pigs, or they will trample them under their feet, and turn and tear you to pieces.

Prayer and the Golden Rule

7 "Ask, and it will be given to you; seek, and you will find; knock, and it will be opened to you. **8** For everyone who asks receives, and the one who seeks finds, and to the one who knocks it will be opened. **9** Or what person is there among you who, when his son asks for a loaf of bread, will give him a stone? **10** Or if he asks for a fish, he will not give him a snake, will he? **11** So if you, *despite* being evil, know how to give good gifts to your children, how much more will your Father who is in heaven give good things to those who ask Him!

12 "In everything, therefore, treat people the same way you want them to treat you, for this is the Law and the Prophets.

The Narrow and Wide Gates

13 "Enter through the narrow gate; for the gate is wide and the way is broad that leads to destruction, and there are many who enter through it. **14** For the gate is narrow and the way is constricted that leads to life, and there are few who find it.

A Tree and Its Fruit

15 "Beware of the false prophets, who come to you in sheep's clothing, but inwardly are ravenous wolves. **16** You will know them by their fruits. Grapes are not gathered from thorn *bushes,* nor figs from thistles, are they? **17** So every good tree bears good fruit, but the bad tree bears bad fruit. **18** A good tree cannot bear bad fruit, nor can a bad tree bear good fruit. **19** Every tree that does not bear good fruit is cut down and thrown into the fire. **20** So then, you will know them by their fruits.

21 "Not everyone who says to Me, 'Lord, Lord,' will enter the kingdom of heaven, but the one who does the will of My Father who is in heaven *will enter.* **22** Many will say to Me on that day, 'Lord, Lord, did we not prophesy in Your name, and in Your name cast out demons, and in Your name perform many miracles?' **23** And then I will declare to them, 'I never knew you; LEAVE ME, YOU WHO PRACTICE LAWLESSNESS.'

The Two Foundations

24 "Therefore, everyone who hears these words of Mine, and acts on them, will be like a wise man who built his house on the rock. **25** And the rain fell and the floods came, and the winds blew and slammed against that house; and *yet* it did not fall, for it had been founded on the rock. **26** And everyone who hears these words of Mine, and does not act on them, will be like a foolish man who built his house on the sand. **27** And the rain fell and the floods came, and the winds blew and slammed against that house; and it fell—and its collapse was great."

28 When Jesus had finished these words, the crowds were amazed at His teaching; **29** for He was teaching them as one who had authority, and not as their scribes.

Jesus Cleanses a Man with Leprosy

8 When Jesus came down from the mountain, large crowds followed Him. 2 And a man with [1]leprosy came to Him and bowed down before Him, and said, "Lord, if You are willing, You can make me clean." 3 Jesus reached out with His hand and touched him, saying, "I am willing; be cleansed." And immediately his leprosy was cleansed. 4 And Jesus *said to him, "See that you tell no one; but go, show yourself to the priest and present the offering that Moses commanded, as a testimony to them."

The Centurion's Faith

5 And when Jesus entered Capernaum, a centurion came to Him, begging Him, 6 and saying, "Lord, my servant is lying paralyzed at home, terribly tormented." 7 Jesus *said to him, "I will come and heal him." 8 But the centurion replied, "Lord, I am not worthy for You to come under my roof, but just say the word, and my servant will be healed. 9 For I also am a man under authority, with soldiers under me; and I say to this one, 'Go!' and he goes, and to another, 'Come!' and he comes, and to my slave, 'Do this!' and he does *it.*" 10 Now when Jesus heard *this,* He was amazed and said to those who were following, "Truly I say to you, I have not found such great faith with anyone in Israel. 11 And I say to you that many will come from east and west, and [1]recline *at the table* with Abraham, Isaac, and Jacob in the kingdom of heaven; 12 but the sons of the kingdom will be thrown out into the outer darkness; in that place there will be weeping and gnashing of teeth." 13 And Jesus said to the centurion, "Go; it shall be done for you as you have believed." And the servant was healed at that *very* moment.

Peter's Mother-in-law and Many Others Healed

14 When Jesus came into Peter's home, He saw his mother-in-law lying sick in bed with a fever. 15 And He touched her hand, and the fever left her; and she got up and waited on Him. 16 Now when evening came, they brought to Him many who were demon-possessed; and

---

8:2 [1]I.e., leprosy or a serious, unspecified skin disease, and so throughout the ch; see Lev 13   8:11 [1]I.e., to dine

He cast out the spirits with a word, and healed all who were ill. **17** *This happened* so that what was spoken through Isaiah the prophet would be fulfilled: "HE HIMSELF TOOK OUR ILLNESSES AND CARRIED AWAY OUR DISEASES."

Discipleship Tested

18 Now when Jesus saw a crowd around Him, He gave orders to depart to the other side *of the sea.* **19** Then a scribe came and said to Him, "Teacher, I will follow You wherever You go." **20** And Jesus *said to him, "The foxes have holes and the birds of the sky *have* nests, but the Son of Man has nowhere to lay His head." **21** And another of the disciples said to Him, "Lord, allow me first to go and bury my father." **22** But Jesus *said to him, "Follow Me, and let the dead bury their own dead."

Jesus Calms the Storm

23 When He got into the boat, His disciples followed Him. **24** And behold, a violent storm developed on the sea, so that the boat was being covered by the waves; but *Jesus* Himself was asleep. **25** And they came to *Him* and woke Him, saying, "Save *us,* Lord; we are perishing!" **26** He *said to them, "Why are you afraid, you men of little faith?" Then He got up and rebuked the winds and the sea, and it became perfectly calm. **27** The men were amazed, and said, "What kind of a man is this, that even the winds and the sea obey Him?"

Jesus Sends Demons into Pigs

28 And when He came to the other side into the country of the Gadarenes, two demon-possessed men confronted Him as they were coming out of the tombs. *They were* so extremely violent that no one could pass by that way. **29** And they cried out, saying, "What business do You have with us, Son of God? Have You come here to torment us before the time?" **30** Now there was a herd of many pigs feeding at a distance from them. **31** And the demons begged Him, saying, "If You *are going to* cast us out, send us into the herd of pigs." **32** And He said to them, "Go!" And they came out and went into the pigs; and behold, the whole herd rushed down the steep bank into the sea and drowned in the waters. **33** And the herdsmen ran away, and went to the city and reported everything, including what had happened to the demon-possessed men. **34** And behold, the whole city came out to meet Jesus; and when they saw Him, they pleaded with Him to leave their region.

A Paralyzed Man Healed

9 Getting into a boat, *Jesus* crossed over *the Sea of Galilee* and came to His own city.

2 And they brought to Him a paralyzed man lying on a stretcher. And seeing their faith, Jesus said to the man who was paralyzed, "Take courage, son; your sins are forgiven." **3** And some of the scribes said to themselves, "This man is blaspheming!" **4** And Jesus, perceiving their thoughts, said, "Why are you thinking evil in your hearts? **5** For which is easier, to say, 'Your sins are forgiven,' or to say, 'Get up and walk'? **6** But so that you may know that the Son of Man has authority on earth to forgive sins"—then He *said to the paralyzed man, "Get up, pick up your stretcher and go home." **7** And he got up and went home. **8** But when the crowds saw *this,* they were awestruck, and they glorified God, who had given such authority to men.

Matthew Called

9 As Jesus went on from there, He saw a man called Matthew sitting in the tax collector's office; and He *said to him, "Follow Me!" And he got up and followed Him. **10** Then it happened that as Jesus was reclining *at the table* in the house, behold, many tax collectors and sinners came and *began* dining with Jesus and His disciples. **11** And when the Pharisees saw *this,* they said to His disciples, "Why is your Teacher eating with the tax collectors and sinners?" **12** But when *Jesus* heard *this,* He said, "*It is* not those who are healthy who need a physician, but those who are sick. **13** Now go and learn what this means: 'I DESIRE COMPASSION, RATHER THAN SACRIFICE,' for I did not come to call the righteous, but sinners."

The Question about Fasting

14 Then the disciples of John *came to Him, asking, "Why do we and the Pharisees fast, but Your disciples do not fast?" **15** And Jesus said to them, "The attendants of the groom cannot mourn as long as the groom is with them, can they? But the days will come when the groom is taken away from them, and then they will fast. 16 But no one puts a patch of unshrunk cloth on an old garment; for the patch pulls away from the garment, and a worse tear results. 17 Nor do *people* put new wine into old wineskins; otherwise the wineskins burst, and the wine pours out and the wineskins are ruined; but they put new wine into fresh wineskins, and both are preserved."

Miracles of Healing

18 While He was saying these things to them, behold, a *synagogue* official came and bowed down before Him, and said, "My daughter has just died; but come and lay Your hand on her, and she will become alive again." 19 Jesus got up *from the table* and *began to* accompany him, along with His disciples.

20 And behold, a woman who had been suffering from a hemorrhage for twelve years came up behind Him, and touched the border of His cloak; 21 for she was saying to herself, "If I only touch His cloak, I will get well." 22 But Jesus, turning and seeing her, said, "Daughter, take courage; your faith has made you well." And at once the woman was made well.

23 When Jesus came into the official's house and saw the flute players and the crowd in noisy disorder, 24 He said, "Leave; for the girl has not died, but is asleep." And they *began* laughing at Him. 25 But when the crowd had been sent out, He entered and took her by the hand, and the girl got up. 26 And this news spread throughout that land.

27 As Jesus went on from there, two men who were blind followed Him, crying out, "Have mercy on us, Son of David!" 28 And after He entered the house, the men who were blind came up to Him, and Jesus *said to them, "Do you believe that I am able to do this?" They *said to Him, "Yes, Lord." 29 Then He touched their eyes, saying, "It shall be done for you according to your faith." 30 And their eyes were opened. And Jesus sternly warned them, saying, "See that no one knows *about this!*" 31 But they went out and spread the news about Him throughout that land.

32 And as they were going out, behold, a demon-possessed man who was unable to speak was brought to Him. 33 And after the demon was cast out, the man who

was *previously* unable to speak talked; and the crowds were amazed, *and were* saying, "Nothing like this has ever been seen in Israel." **34** But the Pharisees were saying, "He casts out the demons by the ruler of the demons."

35 Jesus was going through all the cities and villages, teaching in their synagogues and proclaiming the gospel of the kingdom, and healing every disease and every sickness.

36 Seeing the crowds, He felt compassion for them, because they were distressed and downcast, like sheep without a shepherd. **37** Then He *said to His disciples, "The harvest is plentiful, but the workers are few. **38** Therefore, plead with the Lord of the harvest to send out workers into His harvest."

The Twelve Disciples; Instructions for Service

10 *Jesus* summoned His twelve disciples and gave them authority over unclean spirits, to cast them out, and to heal every disease and every sickness.

2 Now the names of the twelve apostles are these: The first, Simon, who is called Peter, and his brother Andrew; and James the son of Zebedee, and his brother John; **3** Philip and Bartholomew; Thomas and Matthew the tax collector; James the son of Alphaeus, and Thaddaeus; **4** Simon the Zealot, and Judas Iscariot, the one who also betrayed Him.

5 These twelve Jesus sent out after instructing them, saying, "Do not go on a road to Gentiles, and do not enter a city of Samaritans; **6** but rather go to the lost sheep of the house of Israel. **7** And as you go, preach, saying, 'The kingdom of heaven has come near.' **8** Heal *the* sick, raise *the* dead, cleanse those with leprosy, cast out demons. Freely you received, freely give. **9** Do not acquire gold, or silver, or copper for your money belts, **10** or a bag for *your* journey, or even two ¹tunics, or sandals, or a staff; for the worker is deserving of his support. **11** And whatever city or village you enter, inquire who is worthy in it, and stay at his house until you leave *that city.* **12** As you enter the house, give it your greeting. **13** If the house is worthy, *see that* your *blessing of* peace comes upon it. But if it is not worthy, take back your *blessing of* peace.

---

14 And whoever does not receive you nor listen to your words, as you leave that house or city, shake the dust off your feet. **15** Truly I say to you, it will be more tolerable for *the* land of Sodom and Gomorrah on the day of judgment, than for that city.

A Hard Road Ahead of Them

16 "Behold, I am sending you out as sheep in the midst of wolves; so be as wary as serpents, and as innocent as doves. **17** But be on guard against people, for they will hand you over to *the* courts and flog you in their synagogues; **18** and you will even be brought before governors and kings on My account, as a testimony to them and to the Gentiles. **19** But when they hand you over, do not worry about how or what you are to say; for what you are to say will be given you in that hour. **20** For it is not you who are speaking, but *it is* the Spirit of your Father who is speaking in you.

21 "Now brother will betray brother to death, and a father *his* child; and children will rise up against parents and cause them to be put to death. **22** And you will be hated by all because of My name, but it is the one who has endured to the end who will be saved.

23 "But whenever they persecute you in one city, flee to the next; for truly I say to you, you will not finish *going through* the cities of Israel until the Son of Man comes.

The Meaning of Discipleship

24 "A disciple is not above his teacher, nor a slave above his master. **25** It is enough for the disciple that he may become like his teacher, and the slave like his master. If they have called the head of the house Beelzebul, how much more *will they insult* the members of his household!

26 "So do not fear them, for there is nothing concealed that will not be revealed, or hidden that will not be known. **27** What I tell you in the darkness, tell in the light; and what you hear *whispered* in *your* ear, proclaim on the housetops. **28** And do not be afraid of those who kill the body but are unable to kill the soul; but rather fear Him who is able to destroy both soul and body in ¹hell. 29 Are two sparrows not sold for an ¹assarion? And *yet* not one of them will fall to the ground apart from your Father. 30 But even the hairs of your head are all counted. 31 So do not fear; you are more valuable than a great number of sparrows.

32 "Therefore, everyone who confesses Me before people, I will also confess him before My Father who is in heaven. 33 But whoever denies Me before people, I will also deny him before My Father who is in heaven.

34 "Do not think that I came to bring peace on the earth; I did not come to bring peace, but a sword. 35 For I came to TURN A MAN AGAINST HIS FATHER, AND A DAUGHTER AGAINST HER MOTHER, AND A DAUGHTER-IN-LAW AGAINST HER MOTHER-IN-LAW; 36 and A PERSON'S ENEMIES *WILL BE* THE MEMBERS OF HIS HOUSEHOLD.

37 "The one who loves father or mother more than Me is not worthy of Me; and the one who loves son or daughter more than Me is not worthy of Me. 38 And the one who does not take his cross and follow after Me is not worthy of Me. 39 The one who has found his life will lose it, and the one who has lost his life on My account will find it.

The Reward for Service

40 "The one who receives you receives Me, and the one who receives Me receives Him who sent Me. 41 The one who receives a prophet in *the* name of a prophet shall receive a prophet's reward; and the one who receives a righteous person in the name of a righteous person shall receive a righteous person's reward. 42 And whoever gives one of these little ones just a cup of cold *water* to drink in the name of a disciple, truly I say to you, he shall by no means lose his reward."

John's Questions

11 When Jesus had finished giving instructions to His twelve disciples, He went on from there to teach and preach in their cities.

2 Now *while* in prison, John heard about the works of Christ, and he sent *word* by his disciples, 3 and said to Him, "Are You the Coming One, or are we to look for

---

10:28 ¹Gr *Gehenna*   10:29 ¹A Roman copper coin, worth about 1/16 of a laborer's daily wage

someone else?" 4 Jesus answered and said to them, "Go and report to John what you hear and see: 5 *those who are* BLIND RECEIVE SIGHT and *those who* limp walk, *those* with leprosy are cleansed and *those who are* deaf hear, *the* dead are raised, and *the* POOR HAVE THE GOSPEL PREACHED TO THEM. 6 And blessed is any person who does not take offense at Me."

Jesus' Tribute to John

7 As these *disciples of John* were going *away,* Jesus began speaking to the crowds about John: "What did you go out into the wilderness to see? A reed shaken by the wind? 8 But what did you go out to see? A man dressed in soft *clothing?* Those who wear soft *clothing* are in kings' palaces! 9 But what did you go out to see? A prophet? Yes, I tell you, and *one who is* more than a prophet. 10 This is the one about whom it is written:

'BEHOLD, I AM SENDING MY MESSENGER AHEAD OF YOU,
    WHO WILL PREPARE YOUR WAY BEFORE YOU.'

11 Truly I say to you, among those born of women there has not arisen *anyone* greater than John the Baptist! Yet the one who is least in the kingdom of heaven is greater than he. 12 And from the days of John the Baptist until now the kingdom of heaven has been treated violently, and violent men take it by force. 13 For all the Prophets and the Law prophesied until John. 14 And if you are willing to accept *it, John* himself is Elijah who was to come. 15 The one who has ears to hear, let him hear.

16 "But to what shall I compare this generation? It is like children sitting in the marketplaces, who call out to the other *children,* 17 and say, 'We played the flute for you, and you did not dance; we sang a song of mourning, and you did not mourn.' 18 For John came neither eating nor drinking, and they say, 'He has a demon!' 19 The Son of Man came eating and drinking, and they say, 'Behold, a gluttonous man and a heavy drinker, a friend of tax collectors and sinners!' And *yet* wisdom is vindicated by her deeds."

The Unrepenting Cities

20 Then He began to reprimand the cities in which most of His miracles were done, because they did not repent. 21 "Woe to you, Chorazin! Woe to you, Bethsaida! For if the miracles that occurred in you had occurred in

Tyre and Sidon, they would have repented long ago in sackcloth and ashes. 22 Nevertheless I say to you, it will be more tolerable for Tyre and Sidon on *the* day of judgment than for you. 23 And you, Capernaum, will not be exalted to heaven, will you? You will be brought down to Hades! For if the miracles that occurred in you had occurred in Sodom, it would have remained to this day. 24 Nevertheless I say to you that it will be more tolerable for the land of Sodom on *the* day of judgment, than for you."

Come to Me

25 At that time Jesus said, "I praise You, Father, Lord of heaven and earth, that You have hidden these things from *the* wise and intelligent, and have revealed them to infants. 26 Yes, Father, for this way was well pleasing in Your sight. 27 All things have been handed over to Me by My Father; and no one knows the Son except the Father; nor does anyone know the Father except the Son, and anyone to whom the Son determines to reveal *Him.*

28 "Come to Me, all who are weary and burdened, and I will give you rest. 29 Take My yoke upon you and learn from Me, for I am gentle and humble in heart, and YOU WILL FIND REST FOR YOUR SOULS. 30 For My yoke is comfortable, and My burden is light."

Sabbath Questions

12 At that time Jesus went through the grainfields on the Sabbath, and His disciples became hungry and began to pick the heads *of grain* and eat. 2 Now when the Pharisees saw *this,* they said to Him, "Look, Your disciples are doing what is not lawful to do on a Sabbath!" 3 But He said to them, "Have you not read what David did when he became hungry, he and his companions— 4 how he entered the house of God, and they ate the consecrated bread, which was not lawful for him to eat nor for those with him, but for the priests alone? 5 Or have you not read in the Law that on the Sabbath the priests in the temple violate the Sabbath, and *yet* are innocent? 6 But I say to you that *something* greater than the temple is here. 7 But if you had known what this means: 'I DESIRE COMPASSION, RATHER THAN SACRIFICE,' you would not have condemned the innocent.

Lord of the Sabbath

8 For the Son of Man is Lord of the Sabbath."

9 Departing from there, He went into their synagogue. **10** And a man *was there* whose hand was withered. And they questioned Jesus, asking, "Is it lawful to heal on the Sabbath?"—so that they might bring charges against Him. **11** But He said to them, "What man is there among you who has a sheep, and if it falls into a pit on the Sabbath, will he not take hold of it and lift it out? **12** How much more valuable then is a person than a sheep! So then, it is lawful to do good on the Sabbath." **13** Then He *said to the man, "Stretch out your hand!" He stretched it out, and it was restored to normal, like the other. **14** But the Pharisees went out and conspired against Him, *as to* how they might destroy Him.

15 But Jesus, aware of *this,* withdrew from there. Many followed Him, and He healed them all, **16** and warned them not to tell who He was. **17** *This happened* so that what was spoken through Isaiah the prophet would be fulfilled:

18 "Behold, My Servant whom I have chosen;
      My Beloved in whom My soul delights;
      I will put My Spirit upon Him,
      And He will proclaim justice to the Gentiles.
19 "He will not quarrel, nor cry out;
      Nor will anyone hear His voice in the streets.
20 "A bent reed He will not break *off,*
      And a dimly burning wick He will not extinguish,
      Until He leads justice to victory.
21 "And in His name the Gentiles will hope."

The Pharisees Rebuked

22 Then a demon-possessed man *who was* blind and unable to speak was brought to Jesus, and He healed him so that the man who was unable to speak talked and could see. **23** And all the crowds were amazed and were saying, "This man cannot be the Son of David, can he?" **24** But when the Pharisees heard *this,* they said, "This man casts out demons only by Beelzebul the ruler of the demons."

25 And knowing their thoughts, *Jesus* said to them, "Every kingdom divided against itself is laid waste; and no city or house divided against itself will stand. **26** And if Satan is casting out Satan, he has become divided against himself; how then will his kingdom stand? 27 And if by Beelzebul I cast out the demons, by whom do your sons cast *them* out? Therefore, they will be your judges. 28 But if I cast out the demons by the Spirit of God, then the kingdom of God has come upon you. 29 Or, how can anyone enter the strong man's house and carry off his property, unless he first ties up the strong *man?* And then he will plunder his house.

The Unpardonable Sin

30 The one who is not with Me is against Me; and the one who does not gather with Me scatters.

31 "Therefore I say to you, every sin and blasphemy shall be forgiven people, but blasphemy against the Spirit shall not be forgiven. 32 And whoever speaks a word against the Son of Man, it shall be forgiven him; but whoever speaks against the Holy Spirit, it shall not be forgiven him, either in this age or in the *age* to come.

Words Reveal Character

33 "Either assume the tree *to be* good as well as its fruit good, or assume the tree *to be* bad as well as its fruit bad; for the tree is known by its fruit. 34 You offspring of vipers, how can you, being evil, express *any* good things? For the mouth speaks from that which fills the heart. 35 The good person brings out of *his* good treasure good things; and the evil person brings out of *his* evil treasure evil things. 36 But I tell you that *for* every careless word that people speak, they will give an account of it on *the* day of judgment. 37 For by your words you will be justified, and by your words you will be condemned."

The Desire for Signs

38 Then some of the scribes and Pharisees said to Him, "Teacher, we want to see a sign from You." 39 But He answered and said to them, "An evil and adulterous generation craves a sign; and *so* no sign will be given to it except the sign of Jonah the prophet; 40 for just as JONAH WAS IN THE STOMACH OF THE SEA MONSTER FOR THREE DAYS AND THREE NIGHTS, so will the Son of Man be in the heart of the earth for three days and three nights. 41 The men of Nineveh will stand up with this generation at the judgment, and will condemn it because they repented at the

preaching of Jonah; and behold, *something* greater than Jonah is here. **42** *The* Queen of *the* South will rise up with this generation at the judgment and will condemn it, because she came from the ends of the earth to hear the wisdom of Solomon; and behold, *something* greater than Solomon is here.

43 "Now when the unclean spirit comes out of a person, it passes through waterless places seeking rest, and does not find *it*. **44** Then it says, 'I will return to my house from which I came'; and when it comes, it finds *it* unoccupied, swept, and put in order. **45** Then it goes and brings along with it seven other spirits more wicked than itself, and they come in and live there; and the last *condition* of that person becomes worse than the first. That is the way it will also be with this evil generation."

Changed Relationships

46 While He was still speaking to the crowds, behold, His mother and brothers were standing outside, seeking to speak to Him. **47** [¹Someone said to Him, "Look, Your mother and Your brothers are standing outside, seeking to speak to You."] **48** But Jesus replied to the one who was telling Him and said, "Who is My mother, and who are My brothers?" **49** And extending His hand toward His disciples, He said, "Behold: My mother and My brothers! **50** For whoever does the will of My Father who is in heaven, he is My brother, and sister, and mother."

Jesus Teaches in Parables

13 On that day Jesus had gone out of the house and was sitting by the sea. **2** And large crowds gathered to Him, so He got into a boat and sat down, and the whole crowd was standing on the beach.

3 And He told them many things in parables, saying, "Behold, the sower went out to sow; **4** and as he sowed, some *seeds* fell beside the road, and the birds came and ate them up. **5** Others fell on the rocky places, where they did not have much soil; and they sprang up immediately, because they had no depth of soil. **6** But after the sun rose, they were scorched; and because they had no root, they withered away. **7** Others fell among the thorns, and the thorns came up and choked them out. **8** But others

---

12:47 ¹ This verse is not found in early mss

fell on the good soil and yielded a crop, some a hundred, some sixty, and some thirty *times as much.* 9 The one who has ears, let him hear."

An Explanation for Parables

10 And the disciples came up and said to Him, "Why do You speak to them in parables?" 11 And Jesus answered them, "To you it has been granted to know the mysteries of the kingdom of heaven, but to them it has not been granted. 12 For whoever has, to him *more* shall be given, and he will have an abundance; but whoever does not have, even what he has shall be taken away from him. 13 Therefore I speak to them in parables; because while seeing they do not see, and while hearing they do not hear, nor do they understand. 14 And in their case the prophecy of Isaiah is being fulfilled, which says,

'YOU SHALL KEEP ON LISTENING, BUT SHALL NOT UNDERSTAND;
AND YOU SHALL KEEP ON LOOKING, BUT SHALL NOT PERCEIVE;
15 FOR THE HEART OF THIS PEOPLE HAS BECOME DULL,
WITH THEIR EARS THEY SCARCELY HEAR,
AND THEY HAVE CLOSED THEIR EYES,
OTHERWISE THEY MIGHT SEE WITH THEIR EYES,
HEAR WITH THEIR EARS,
UNDERSTAND WITH THEIR HEART, AND RETURN,
AND I WOULD HEAL THEM.'

16 But blessed are your eyes, because they see; and your ears, because they hear. 17 For truly I say to you that many prophets and righteous people longed to see what you see, and did not see *it,* and to hear what you hear, and did not hear *it.*

The Sower Explained

18 "Listen then to the parable of the sower. 19 When anyone hears the word of the kingdom and does not understand *it,* the evil *one* comes and snatches away what has been sown in his heart. This is the one sown *with seed* beside the road. 20 The one sown *with seed* on the rocky places, this is the one who hears the word and immediately receives it with joy; 21 yet he has no *firm* root in himself, but is *only* temporary, and when affliction or persecution occurs because of the word, immediately he falls away. 22 And the one sown *with seed* among the thorns, this is the one who hears the word, and the anxiety of the world and the deceitfulness of

wealth choke the word, and it becomes unfruitful. **23** But the one sown *with seed* on the good soil, this is the one who hears the word and understands it, who indeed bears fruit and produces, some a hundred, some sixty, and some thirty *times as much.*"

Weeds among Wheat

24 Jesus presented another parable to them, saying, "The kingdom of heaven is like a man who sowed good seed in his field. **25** But while his men were sleeping, his enemy came and sowed ¹weeds among the wheat, and left. **26** And when the wheat sprouted and produced grain, then the weeds also became evident. **27** And the slaves of the landowner came and said to him, 'Sir, did you not sow good seed in your field? How then does it have weeds?' **28** And he said to them, 'An enemy has done this!' The slaves *said to him, 'Do you want us, then, to go and gather them up?' **29** But he *said, 'No; while you are gathering up the weeds, you may uproot the wheat with them. **30** Allow both to grow together until the harvest; and at the time of the harvest I will say to the reapers, "First gather up the weeds and bind them in bundles to burn them; but gather the wheat into my barn."'"

The Mustard Seed

31 He presented another parable to them, saying, "The kingdom of heaven is like a mustard seed, which a person took and sowed in his field; **32** and this is smaller than all the *other* seeds, but when it is *fully* grown, it is larger than the garden plants and becomes a tree, so that THE BIRDS OF THE SKY come and NEST IN ITS BRANCHES."

The Leaven

33 He spoke another parable to them: "The kingdom of heaven is like leaven, which a woman took and hid in three ¹sata of flour until it was all leavened."

34 All these things Jesus spoke to the crowds in parables, and He did not speak anything to them without a parable. **35** *This was* so that what was spoken through the prophet would be fulfilled:

13:25 ¹Prob. *darnel*, a weed resembling wheat   13:33 ¹A Gr term for a Heb measure, totaling about 48 lb. or 22 kg of flour

"I WILL OPEN MY MOUTH IN PARABLES;
I WILL PROCLAIM THINGS HIDDEN SINCE THE FOUNDATION OF
    THE WORLD."

The Weeds Explained

36 Then He left the crowds and went into the house.
And His disciples came to Him and said, "Explain to us
the parable of the weeds of the field." **37** And He said,
"The one who sows the good seed is the Son of Man,
38 and the field is the world; and *as for* the good seed,
these are the sons of the kingdom; and the weeds are
the sons of the evil *one;* **39** and the enemy who sowed
them is the devil, and the harvest is the end of the age;
and the reapers are angels. **40** So just as the weeds are
gathered up and burned with fire, so shall it be at the
end of the age. **41** The Son of Man will send forth His
angels, and they will gather out of His kingdom all stumbling blocks, and those who commit lawlessness, **42** and
they will throw them into the furnace of fire; in that
place there will be weeping and gnashing of teeth.
43 Then THE RIGHTEOUS WILL SHINE FORTH LIKE THE SUN in the
kingdom of their Father. The one who has ears, let him
hear.

Hidden Treasure

44 "The kingdom of heaven is like a treasure hidden in
the field, which a man found and hid *again;* and from joy
over it he goes and sells everything that he has, and buys
that field.

A Costly Pearl

45 "Again, the kingdom of heaven is like a merchant
seeking fine pearls, **46** and upon finding one pearl of great
value, he went and sold everything that he had and
bought it.

A Dragnet

47 "Again, the kingdom of heaven is like a dragnet that
was cast into the sea and gathered *fish* of every kind;
48 and when it was filled, they pulled it up on the beach;
and they sat down and gathered the good *fish* into containers, but the bad they threw away. **49** So it will be at
the end of the age: the angels will come forth and
remove the wicked from among the righteous, **50** and

they will throw them into the furnace of fire; in that place there will be weeping and gnashing of teeth. **51** "Have you understood all these things?" They *said to Him, "Yes." **52** And Jesus said to them, "Therefore every scribe who has become a disciple of the kingdom of heaven is like a head of a household, who brings out of his treasure new things and old."

Jesus Revisits Nazareth

53 When Jesus had finished these parables, He departed from there. **54** And He came to His hometown and *began* teaching them in their synagogue, with the result that they were astonished, and said, "Where *did* this man *acquire* this wisdom and *these* miraculous powers? **55** Is this not the carpenter's son? Is His mother not called Mary, and His brothers, James, Joseph, Simon, and Judas? **56** And His sisters, are they not all with us? Where then *did* this man *acquire* all these things?" **57** And they took offense at Him. But Jesus said to them, "A prophet is not dishonored except in his hometown and in his *own* household." **58** And He did not do many miracles there because of their unbelief.

John the Baptist Beheaded

14 At that time Herod the tetrarch heard the news about Jesus, **2** and said to his servants, "This is John the Baptist; he himself has been raised from the dead, and that is why miraculous powers are at work in him."

3 For when Herod had John arrested, he bound him and put him in prison because of Herodias, the wife of his brother Philip. **4** For John had been saying to him, "It is not lawful for you to have her." **5** Although Herod wanted to put him to death, he feared the crowd, because they regarded John as a prophet.

6 But when Herod's birthday came, the daughter of Herodias danced before *them* and pleased Herod, **7** so *much* that he promised with an oath to give her whatever she asked. **8** And after being prompted by her mother, she *said, "Give me the head of John the Baptist here on a platter." **9** And although he was grieved, the king commanded *it* to be given because of his oaths and his dinner guests. **10** He sent *word* and had John beheaded in the prison. **11** And his head was brought on a platter and given to the girl, and she brought *it* to her mother. [12] John's disciples came and took away the body and buried it; and they went and reported to Jesus.

Five Thousand Men Fed

[13] Now when Jesus heard *about John,* He withdrew from there in a boat to a secluded place by Himself; and when the people heard *about this,* they followed Him on foot from the cities. [14] When He came ashore, He saw a large crowd, and felt compassion for them and healed their sick.

[15] Now when it was evening, the disciples came to Him and said, "This place is secluded and the hour is already past *to eat;* send the crowds away, so that they may go into the villages and buy food for themselves." [16] But Jesus said to them, "They do not need to go; you give them *something* to eat!" [17] They *said to Him, "We have nothing here except five loaves and two fish." [18] And He said, "Bring them here to Me." [19] And ordering the crowds to sit down on the grass, He took the five loaves and the two fish, and looked up toward heaven. He blessed *the food* and breaking the loaves, He gave them to the disciples, and the disciples *gave them* to the crowds. [20] And they all ate and were satisfied, and they picked up what was left over of the broken pieces: twelve full baskets. [21] There were about five thousand men who ate, besides women and children.

Jesus Walks on the Water

[22] Immediately *afterward* He compelled the disciples to get into the boat and to go ahead of Him to the other side, while He sent the crowds away. [23] After He had sent the crowds away, He went up on the mountain by Himself to pray; and when it was evening, He was there alone. [24] But the boat was already *a long distance from the land, battered by the waves; for the wind was contrary. [25] And in the *fourth watch of the night He came to them, walking on the sea. [26] When the disciples saw Him walking on the sea, they were terrified, and said, "It is a ghost!" And they cried out in fear. [27] But immediately Jesus spoke to them, saying, "Take courage, it is I; do not be afraid."

14:24 [1] Lit *many stadia from;* a Roman stadion perhaps averaged 607 ft. or 185 m   14:25 [1] I.e., 3-6 a.m.

28 Peter responded and said to Him, "Lord, if it is You, command me to come to You on the water." **29** And He said, "Come!" And Peter got out of the boat and walked on the water, and came toward Jesus. **30** But seeing the wind, he became frightened, and when he began to sink, he cried out, saying, "Lord, save me!" **31** Immediately Jesus reached out with His hand and took hold of him, and *said to him, "You of little faith, why did you doubt?" **32** When they got into the boat, the wind stopped. **33** And those who were in the boat worshiped Him, saying, "You are truly God's Son!"

34 When they had crossed over, they came to land at Gennesaret. **35** And when the men of that place recognized Him, they sent *word* into all that surrounding region and brought to Him all who were sick; **36** and they pleaded with Him that they might just touch the border of His cloak; and all who touched *it* were cured.

Tradition and Commandment

15 Then *some* Pharisees and scribes *came to Jesus from Jerusalem and said, **2** "Why do Your disciples break the tradition of the elders? For they do not wash their hands when they eat bread." **3** And He answered and said to them, "Why do you yourselves also break the commandment of God for the sake of your tradition? **4** For God said, 'HONOR YOUR FATHER AND MOTHER,' and, 'THE ONE WHO SPEAKS EVIL OF FATHER OR MOTHER IS TO BE PUT TO DEATH.' **5** But you say, 'Whoever says to *his* father or mother, "Whatever I have that would help you has been given *to God*," **6** he is not to 'honor his father *or mother*.' And *by this* you have invalidated the word of God for the sake of your tradition. **7** You hypocrites, rightly did Isaiah prophesy about you, by saying:

8   'THIS PEOPLE HONORS ME WITH THEIR LIPS,
         BUT THEIR HEART IS FAR AWAY FROM ME.
9   'AND IN VAIN DO THEY WORSHIP ME,
         TEACHING AS DOCTRINES THE COMMANDMENTS OF MEN.'"

10 After Jesus called the crowd to Him, He said to them, "Hear and understand! **11** *It is* not what enters the mouth *that* defiles the person, but what comes out of the mouth, this defiles the person."

12 Then the disciples came and *said to Him, "Do You

15:6 ¹I.e., by supporting them with it

know that the Pharisees were offended when they heard this statement?" 13 But He answered and said, "Every plant which My heavenly Father did not plant will be uprooted. 14 Leave them alone; they are blind guides [1] of blind people. And if a person who is blind guides *another* who is blind, both will fall into a pit."

The Heart of Man

15 Peter said to Him, "Explain the parable to us." 16 Jesus said, "Are you also still lacking in understanding? 17 Do you not understand that everything that goes into the mouth passes into the stomach, and is eliminated? 18 But the things that come out of the mouth come from the heart, and those things defile the person. 19 For out of the heart come evil thoughts, murders, *acts of* adultery, *other* immoral sexual acts, thefts, false testimonies, *and* slanderous statements. 20 These are the things that defile the person; but to eat with unwashed hands does not defile the person."

The Faith of a Canaanite Woman

21 Jesus went away from there, and withdrew into the region of Tyre and Sidon. 22 And a Canaanite woman from that region came out and *began* to cry out, saying, "Have mercy on me, Lord, Son of David; my daughter is severely demon-possessed." 23 But He did not answer her *with even* a word. And His disciples came up and urged Him, saying, "Send her away, because she keeps shouting at us!" 24 But He answered and said, "I was sent only to the lost sheep of the house of Israel." 25 But she came and *began* to bow down before Him, saying, "Lord, help me!" 26 Yet He answered and said, "It is not good to take the children's bread and throw it to the dogs." 27 And she said, "Yes, Lord; *but please help,* for even the dogs feed on the crumbs that fall from their masters' table." 28 Then Jesus said to her, "O woman, your faith is great; it shall be done for you as you desire." And her daughter was healed at once.

Healing Crowds

29 Departing from there, Jesus went along the Sea of Galilee, and after going up on the mountain, He was

---

15:14 [1] Later mss add *of blind people*

sitting there. [30] And large crowds came to Him bringing with them *those who were* limping, had impaired limbs, *were* blind, *or were* unable to speak, and many others, and they laid them down at His feet; and He healed them. [31] So the crowd was astonished as they saw those who were unable to speak talking, those with impaired limbs restored, those who were limping walking around, and those who were blind seeing; and they glorified the God of Israel.

Four Thousand Men Fed

[32] Now Jesus called His disciples to Him and said, "I feel compassion for the people, because they have remained with Me now for three days and have nothing to eat; and I do not want to send them away hungry, for they might faint on the way." [33] The disciples *said to Him, "Where would we get so many loaves in *this* desolate place to satisfy such a large crowd?" [34] And Jesus *said to them, "How many loaves do you have?" And they said, "Seven, and a few small fish." [35] And He directed the people to sit down on the ground; [36] and He took the seven loaves and the fish; and after giving thanks, He broke them and started giving them to the disciples, and the disciples *gave them* to the crowds. [37] And they all ate and were satisfied, and they picked up what was left over of the broken pieces, seven large baskets full. [38] And those who ate were four thousand men, besides women and children.

[39] And sending away the crowds, Jesus got into the boat and came to the region of Magadan.

Pharisees and Sadducees Test Jesus

16 The Pharisees and Sadducees came up, and putting *Jesus* to the test, they asked Him to show them a sign from heaven. [2] But He replied to them, "When it is evening, you say, '*It will be* fair weather, for the sky is red.' [3] And in the morning, '*There will be* a storm today, for the sky is red and threatening.' You know how to discern the appearance of the sky, but are you unable *to discern* the signs of the times? [4] An evil and adulterous generation wants a sign; and *so* a sign will not be given to it, except the sign of Jonah." And He left them and went away.

[5] And the disciples came to the other side *of the sea,*

but they had forgotten to bring *any* bread. 6 And Jesus said to them, "Watch out and beware of the leaven of the Pharisees and Sadducees." 7 They began to discuss *this* among themselves, saying, "*He said that* because we did not bring *any* bread." 8 But Jesus, aware *of this,* said, "You men of little faith, why are you discussing among yourselves *the fact* that you have no bread? 9 Do you not yet understand nor remember the five loaves of the five thousand, and how many baskets you picked up? 10 Nor the seven loaves of the four thousand, and how many large baskets you picked up? 11 How *is it that* you do not understand that I did not speak to you about bread? But beware of the leaven of the Pharisees and Sadducees." 12 Then they understood that He did not say to beware of the leaven of bread, but of the teaching of the Pharisees and Sadducees.

Peter's Confession of Christ

13 Now when Jesus came into the region of Caesarea Philippi, He was asking His disciples, "Who do people say that the Son of Man is?" 14 And they said, "Some *say* John the Baptist; and others, Elijah; and *still* others, Jeremiah, or one of the *other* prophets." 15 He *said to them, "But who do you yourselves say that I am?" 16 Simon Peter answered, "You are the Christ, the Son of the living God." 17 And Jesus said to him, "Blessed are you, Simon Barjona, because flesh and blood did not reveal *this* to you, but My Father who is in heaven. 18 And I also say to you that you are Peter, and upon this rock I will build My church; and the gates of Hades will not overpower it. 19 I will give you the keys of the kingdom of heaven; and whatever you bind on earth shall have been bound in heaven, and whatever you loose on earth shall have been loosed in heaven." 20 Then He gave the disciples strict orders that they were to tell no one that He was the Christ.

Jesus Foretells His Death

21 From that time Jesus began to point out to His disciples that it was necessary for Him to go to Jerusalem and to suffer many things from the elders, chief priests, and scribes, and to be killed, and to be raised up on the third day. 22 And *yet* Peter took Him aside and began to rebuke Him, saying, "God forbid it, Lord! This shall

never happen to You!" 23 But He turned and said to Peter, "Get behind Me, Satan! You are a stumbling block to Me; for you are not setting your mind on God's purposes, but men's."

Discipleship Is Costly

24 Then Jesus said to His disciples, "If anyone wants to come after Me, he must deny himself, take up his cross, and follow Me. 25 For whoever wants to save his life will lose it; but whoever loses his life for My sake will find it. 26 For what good will it do a person if he gains the whole world, but forfeits his soul? Or what will a person give in exchange for his soul? 27 For the Son of Man is going to come in the glory of His Father with His angels, and WILL THEN REPAY EVERY PERSON ACCORDING TO HIS DEEDS.

28 "Truly I say to you, there are some of those who are standing here who will not taste death until they see the Son of Man coming in His kingdom."

The Transfiguration

17 Six days later, Jesus *took with Him Peter and James, and his brother John, and *led them up on a high mountain by themselves. 2 And He was transfigured before them; and His face shone like the sun, and His garments became as white as light. 3 And behold, Moses and Elijah appeared to them, talking with Him. 4 Peter responded and said to Jesus, "Lord, it is good that we are here. If You want, I will make three tabernacles here: one for You, one for Moses, and one for Elijah." 5 While he was still speaking, a bright cloud overshadowed them, and behold, a voice from the cloud said, "This is My beloved Son, with whom I am well pleased; listen to Him!" 6 When the disciples heard *this,* they fell face down to the ground and were terrified. 7 And Jesus came to *them* and touched them and said, "Get up, and do not be afraid." 8 And raising their eyes, they saw no one except Jesus Himself alone.

9 When they were coming down from the mountain, Jesus commanded them, saying, "Tell the vision to no one until the Son of Man has risen from the dead." 10 And His disciples asked Him, "Why then do the scribes say that Elijah must come first?" 11 And He answered and said, "Elijah is coming and will restore all things; 12 but I say to you that Elijah already came, and

they did not recognize him, but did to him whatever they wanted. So also the Son of Man is going to suffer at their hands." **13** Then the disciples understood that He had spoken to them about John the Baptist.

The Demon-possessed Boy

14 When they came to the crowd, a man came up to Jesus, falling on his knees before Him and saying, **15** "Lord, have mercy on my son, because he has seizures and suffers terribly; for he often falls into the fire and often into the water. **16** And I brought him to Your disciples, and they could not cure him." **17** And Jesus answered and said, "You unbelieving and perverse generation, how long shall I be with you? How long shall I put up with you? Bring him here to Me." **18** And Jesus rebuked him, and the demon came out of him, and the boy was healed at once.

19 Then the disciples came to Jesus privately and said, "Why could we not cast it out?" **20** And He *said to them, "Because of your meager faith; for truly I say to you, if you have faith the size of a mustard seed, you will say to this mountain, 'Move from here to there,' and it will move; and nothing will be impossible for you.¹"

22 And while they were gathering together in Galilee, Jesus said to them, "The Son of Man is going to be handed over to men; **23** and they will kill Him, and He will be raised on the third day." And they were deeply grieved.

The Temple Tax

24 Now when they came to Capernaum, those who collected the ¹two-drachma *tax* came to Peter and said, "Does your teacher not pay the two-drachma *tax?*" **25** He *said, "Yes." And when he came into the house, Jesus spoke to him first, saying, "What do you think, Simon? From whom do the kings of the earth collect customs or ¹poll-tax, from their sons or from strangers?" **26** When *Peter* said, "From strangers," Jesus said to him, "Then the sons are exempt. **27** However, so that we do

---

17:20 ¹Late mss add (traditionally v 21): *But this kind does not go out except by prayer and fasting*   17:24 ¹Equivalent to about two denarii or two days' wages for a laborer, paid as a temple tax   17:25 ¹I.e., a tax on each person in the census

not offend them, go to the sea and throw in a hook, and take the first fish that comes up; and when you open its mouth, you will find a [1]stater. Take that and give it to them for you and Me."

Rank in the Kingdom

18 At that time the disciples came to Jesus and said, "Who then is greatest in the kingdom of heaven?" **2** And He called a child to Himself and set him among them, **3** and said, "Truly I say to you, unless you change and become like children, you will not enter the kingdom of heaven. **4** So whoever will humble himself like this child, he is the greatest in the kingdom of heaven. **5** And whoever receives one such child in My name, receives Me; **6** but whoever causes one of these little ones who believe in Me to [1]sin, it is better for him that a heavy millstone be hung around his neck, and that he be drowned in the depths of the sea.

Stumbling Blocks

7 "Woe to the world because of *its* stumbling blocks! For it is inevitable that stumbling blocks come; but woe to the person through whom the stumbling block comes! **8** "And if your hand or your foot is causing you to sin, cut it off and throw it away from you; it is better for you to enter life maimed or without a foot, than to have two hands or two feet and be thrown into the eternal fire. **9** And if your eye is causing you to sin, tear it out and throw it away from you. It is better for you to enter life with one eye, than to have two eyes and be thrown into the [1]fiery hell. **10** "See that you do not look down on one of these little ones; for I say to you that their angels in heaven continually see the face of My Father who is in heaven.[1]

Ninety-nine Plus One

12 "What do you think? If any man has a hundred sheep, and one of them goes astray, will he not leave the ninety-nine on the mountains, and go and search for the

---

17:27 [1] A silver four-drachma Greek coin   18:6 [1] Or *stumble,* and so throughout the ch   18:9 [1] Lit *Gehenna of fire*   18:10 [1] Late mss add (traditionally v 11): *For the Son of Man has come to save that which was lost*

one that is lost? **13** And if it turns out that he finds it, truly I say to you, he rejoices over it more than over the ninety-nine that have not gone astray. **14** So it is not *the* will of your Father who is in heaven for one of these little ones to perish.

Discipline and Prayer

15 "Now if your brother sins[1], go and show him his fault in private; if he listens to you, you have gained your brother. **16** But if he does not listen *to you,* take one or two more with you, so that ON THE TESTIMONY OF TWO OR THREE WITNESSES EVERY MATTER MAY BE CONFIRMED. **17** And if he refuses to listen to them, tell it to the church; and if he refuses to listen even to the church, he is to be to you as a Gentile and a tax collector. **18** Truly I say to you, whatever you bind on earth shall have been bound in heaven; and whatever you loose on earth shall have been loosed in heaven.

19 "Again I say to you, that if two of you agree on earth about anything that they may ask, it shall be done for them by My Father who is in heaven. **20** For where two or three have gathered together in My name, I am there in their midst."

Forgiveness

21 Then Peter came up and said to Him, "Lord, how many times shall my brother sin against me and I *still* forgive him? Up to seven times?" **22** Jesus *said to him, "I do not say to you, up to seven times, but up to seventy-seven times.

23 "For this reason the kingdom of heaven is like a king who wanted to settle accounts with his slaves. **24** And when he had begun to settle *them,* one who owed him [1] ten thousand talents was brought to him. **25** But since he did not have *the means* to repay, his master commanded that he be sold, along with his wife and children and all that he had, and repayment be made. **26** So the slave fell *to the ground* and prostrated himself before him, saying, 'Have patience with me and I will repay you everything.' **27** And the master of that slave felt compassion, and he released him and forgave him the debt. **28** But that slave

---

18:15 [1] Late mss add *against you*   18:24 [1] By one estimate, a debt of 60 million working days for a laborer

went out and found one of his fellow slaves who owed him a hundred 'denarii; and he seized him and *began* to choke *him,* saying, 'Pay back what you owe!' **29** So his fellow slave fell *to the ground* and *began* to plead with him, saying, 'Have patience with me and I will repay you.' **30** But he was unwilling, and went and threw him in prison until he would pay back what was owed. **31** So when his fellow slaves saw what had happened, they were deeply grieved and came and reported to their master all that had happened. **32** Then summoning him, his master *said to him, 'You wicked slave, I forgave you all that debt because you pleaded with me. **33** Should you not also have had mercy on your fellow slave, in the same way that I had mercy on you?' **34** And his master, moved with anger, handed him over to the torturers until he would repay all that was owed him. **35** My heavenly Father will also do the same to you, if each of you does not forgive his brother from your heart."

Concerning Divorce

19 When Jesus had finished these words, He left Galilee and came into the region of Judea beyond the Jordan; **2** and large crowds followed Him, and He healed them there.

3 *Some* Pharisees came to Jesus, testing Him and asking, "Is it lawful *for a man* to divorce his wife for any reason *at all?*" **4** And He answered and said, "Have you not read that He who created *them* from the beginning MADE THEM MALE AND FEMALE, **5** and said, 'FOR THIS REASON A MAN SHALL LEAVE HIS FATHER AND HIS MOTHER AND BE JOINED TO HIS WIFE, AND THE TWO SHALL BECOME ONE FLESH'? **6** So they are no longer two, but one flesh. Therefore, what God has joined together, no person is to separate." **7** They *said to Him, "Why, then, did Moses command to GIVE *HER* A CERTIFICATE OF DIVORCE AND SEND HER AWAY?" **8** He *said to them, "Because of your hardness of heart Moses permitted you to divorce your wives; but from the beginning it has not been this way. **9** And I say to you, whoever divorces his wife, except for sexual immorality, and marries another woman 'commits adultery²."

18:28 ¹ The denarius was a day's wages for a laborer   19:9 ¹ One early ms *makes her commit adultery*   19:9 ² One early ms adds *and he who marries a divorced woman commits adultery*

¹⁰ The disciples *said to Him, "If the relationship of the man with his wife is like this, it is better not to marry." ¹¹ But He said to them, "Not all men *can* accept this statement, but *only* those to whom it has been given. ¹² For there are eunuchs who were born that way from their mother's womb; and there are eunuchs who were made eunuchs by people; and there are *also* eunuchs who made themselves eunuchs for the sake of the kingdom of heaven. The one who is able to accept *this,* let him accept *it.*"

Jesus Blesses Little Children

¹³ Then *some* children were brought to Him so that He would lay His hands on them and pray; and the disciples rebuked them. ¹⁴ But Jesus said, "Leave the children alone, and do not forbid them to come to Me; for the kingdom of heaven belongs to such as these." ¹⁵ After laying His hands on them, He departed from there.

The Rich Young Ruler

¹⁶ And someone came to Him and said, "Teacher, what good thing shall I do so that I may obtain eternal life?" ¹⁷ And He said to him, "Why are you asking Me about what is good? There is *only* One who is good; but if you want to enter life, keep the commandments." ¹⁸ *Then* he *said to Him, "Which ones?" And Jesus said, "You shall not commit murder; You shall not commit adultery; You shall not steal; You shall not give false testimony; ¹⁹ Honor your father and mother; and You shall love your neighbor as yourself." ²⁰ The young man *said to Him, "All these I have kept; what am I still lacking?" ²¹ Jesus said to him, "If you want to be complete, go *and* sell your possessions and give to *the* poor, and you will have treasure in heaven; and come, follow Me." ²² But when the young man heard this statement, he went away grieving; for he was one who owned much property.

²³ And Jesus said to His disciples, "Truly I say to you, it will be hard for a rich person to enter the kingdom of heaven. ²⁴ And again I say to you, it is easier for a camel to go through the eye of a needle, than for a rich person to enter the kingdom of God." ²⁵ When the disciples heard *this,* they were very astonished and said, "Then who can be saved?" ²⁶ And looking at *them,* Jesus said to

them, "With people this is impossible, but with God all things are possible."

The Disciples' Reward

27 Then Peter responded and said to Him, "Behold, we have left everything and followed You; what then will there be for us?" **28** And Jesus said to them, "Truly I say to you, that you who have followed Me, in the ¹regeneration when the Son of Man will sit on His glorious throne, you also shall sit upon twelve thrones, judging the twelve tribes of Israel. **29** And everyone who has left houses or brothers or sisters or father or mother ¹or children or farms on account of My name, will receive many times as much, and will inherit eternal life. **30** But many *who are* first will be last; and *the* last, first.

Laborers in the Vineyard

20 "For the kingdom of heaven is like a landowner who went out early in the morning to hire laborers for his vineyard. **2** When he had agreed with the laborers for a ¹denarius for the day, he sent them into his vineyard. **3** And he went out about the ¹third hour and saw others standing idle in the marketplace; **4** and to those he said, 'You go into the vineyard also, and whatever is right, I will give you.' And *so* they went. **5** Again he went out about the ¹sixth and the ninth hour, and did the same thing. **6** And about the ¹eleventh *hour* he went out and found others standing *around;* and he *said to them, 'Why have you been standing here idle all day long?' **7** They *said to him, 'Because no one hired us.' He *said to them, 'You go into the vineyard too.'

8 "Now when evening came, the owner of the vineyard *said to his foreman, 'Call the laborers and pay them their wages, starting with the last *group* to the first.' **9** When those *hired* about the eleventh hour came, each one received a ¹denarius. **10** And *so* when those *hired* first came, they thought that they would receive more; but each of them also received a denarius. **11** When they received it, they grumbled at the landowner,

---

19:28 ¹Or *renewal;* i.e., the new world   19:29 ¹One early ms adds *or wife*   20:2 ¹The denarius was a day's wages for a laborer   20:3 ¹I.e., 9 a.m.   20:5 ¹I.e., noon and 3 p.m.   20:6 ¹I.e., 5 p.m.   20:9 ¹The denarius was a day's wages for a laborer

12 saying, 'These who *were hired* last worked *only* one hour, and you have made them equal to us who have borne the burden of the day's *work* and the scorching heat.' 13 But he answered and said to one of them, 'Friend, I am doing you no wrong; did you not agree with me for a denarius? 14 Take what is yours and go; but I want to give to this last person the same as to you. 15 Is it not lawful for me to do what I want with what is my own? Or is your eye envious because I am generous?' 16 So the last shall be first, and the first, last."

Death, Resurrection Foretold

17 As Jesus was about to go up to Jerusalem, He took the twelve *disciples* aside by themselves, and on the road He said to them, 18 "Behold, we are going up to Jerusalem, and the Son of Man will be handed over to the chief priests and scribes, and they will condemn Him to death, 19 and they will hand Him over to the Gentiles to mock and flog and crucify, and on the third day He will be raised up."

Request for Preferred Treatment

20 Then the mother of the sons of Zebedee came to Jesus with her sons, bowing down and making a request of Him. 21 And He said to her, "What do you desire?" She *said to Him, "Say that in Your kingdom these two sons of mine shall sit, one at Your right, and one at Your left." 22 But Jesus replied, "You do not know what you are asking. Are you able to drink the cup that I am about to drink?" They *said to Him, "We are able." 23 He *said to them, "My cup you shall drink; but to sit at My right and at *My* left is not Mine to give, but *it is for those* for whom it has been prepared by My Father."

24 And after hearing *this,* the *other* ten *disciples* became indignant with the two brothers. 25 But Jesus called them to Himself and said, "You know that the rulers of the Gentiles domineer over them, and those in high position exercise authority over them. 26 It is not this way among you, but whoever wants to become prominent among you shall be your servant, 27 and whoever desires to be first among you shall be your slave; 28 just as the Son of Man did not come to be served, but to serve, and to give His life as a ransom for many."

Sight for Those Who Are Blind

29 As they were leaving Jericho, a large crowd followed Him. **30** And two people who were blind, sitting by the road, hearing that Jesus was passing by, cried out, "Lord, have mercy on us, Son of David!" **31** But the crowd sternly warned them to be quiet; yet they cried out all the more, "Lord, Son of David, have mercy on us!" **32** And Jesus stopped and called them, and said, "What do you want Me to do for you?" **33** They *said to Him, "Lord, *we want* our eyes to be opened." **34** Moved with compassion, Jesus touched their eyes; and immediately they regained their sight and followed Him.

The Triumphal Entry

21 When they had approached Jerusalem and had come to Bethphage, at the Mount of Olives, Jesus then sent two disciples, **2** saying to them, "Go into the village opposite you, and immediately you will find a donkey tied *there* and a colt with it. Untie them and bring them to Me. **3** And if anyone says anything to you, you shall say, 'The Lord needs them,' and he will send them on immediately." **4** Now this took place so that what was spoken through the prophet would be fulfilled:

5 "SAY TO THE DAUGHTER OF ZION,
    'BEHOLD YOUR KING IS COMING TO YOU,
    HUMBLE, AND MOUNTED ON A DONKEY,
    EVEN ON A COLT, THE FOAL OF A DONKEY.' "

6 The disciples went and did just as Jesus had instructed them, **7** and brought the donkey and the colt, and laid their cloaks on them; and He sat on the cloaks. **8** Most of the crowd spread their cloaks on the road, and others were cutting branches from the trees and spreading them on the road. **9** Now the crowds going ahead of Him, and those who followed, were shouting,

    "Hosanna to the Son of David;
    BLESSED IS THE ONE WHO COMES IN THE NAME OF THE LORD;
    Hosanna in the highest!"

10 When He had entered Jerusalem, all the city was stirred, saying, "Who is this?" **11** And the crowds were saying, "This is Jesus the prophet, from Nazareth in Galilee."

Cleansing the Temple

12 And Jesus entered the temple *area* and drove out all those who were selling and buying on the temple *grounds,* and He overturned the tables of the money changers and the seats of those who were selling doves. 13 And He *said to them, "It is written: 'MY HOUSE WILL BE CALLED A HOUSE OF PRAYER'; but you are making it a DEN OF ROBBERS."

14 And *those who were* blind and *those who* limped came to Him in the temple *area,* and He healed them. 15 But when the chief priests and the scribes saw the wonderful things that He had done, and the children who were shouting in the temple *area,* "Hosanna to the Son of David," they became indignant, 16 and they said to Him, "Do You hear what these *children* are saying?" And Jesus *said to them, "Yes. Have you never read, 'FROM THE MOUTHS OF INFANTS AND NURSING BABIES YOU HAVE PREPARED PRAISE FOR YOURSELF'?" 17 And He left them and went out of the city to Bethany, and spent the night there.

The Barren Fig Tree

18 Now in the early morning, when He was returning to the city, He became hungry. 19 And seeing a lone fig tree by the road, He came to it and found nothing on it except leaves alone; and He *said to it, "No longer shall there ever be *any* fruit from you." And at once the fig tree withered.

20 Seeing *this,* the disciples were amazed and asked, "How did the fig tree wither *all* at once?" 21 And Jesus answered and said to them, "Truly I say to you, if you have faith and do not doubt, you will not only do what *was done* to the fig tree, but even if you say to this mountain, 'Be taken up and cast into the sea,' it will happen. 22 And whatever you ask in prayer, believing, you will receive it all."

Authority Challenged

23 When He entered the temple *area,* the chief priests and the elders of the people came to Him while He was teaching, and said, "By what authority are You doing these things, and who gave You this authority?" 24 But Jesus responded and said to them, "I will also ask you one question, which, if you tell Me, I will also tell you by what authority I do these things. 25 The baptism of John was from what *source:* from heaven or from men?" And they *began* considering *the implications* among

themselves, saying, "If we say, 'From heaven,' He will say to us, 'Then why did you not believe him?' **26** But if we say, 'From men,' we fear the people; for they all regard John as a prophet." **27** And answering Jesus, they said, "We do not know." He also said to them, "Neither am I telling you by what authority I do these things.

Parable of Two Sons

28 "But what do you think? A man had two sons, and he came to the first and said, 'Son, go work today in the vineyard.' **29** But he replied, 'I do not want to.' Yet afterward he regretted it and went. **30** And *the man* came to his second *son* and said the same thing; and he replied, 'I *will,* sir'; and *yet* he did not go. **31** Which of the two did the will of his father?" They *said, "The first." Jesus *said to them, "Truly I say to you that the tax collectors and prostitutes will get into the kingdom of God before you. **32** For John came to you in the way of righteousness and you did not believe him; but the tax collectors and prostitutes did believe him; and you, seeing *this,* did not even have second thoughts afterward so as to believe him.

Parable of the Landowner

33 "Listen to another parable. There was a landowner who PLANTED A VINEYARD AND PUT A FENCE AROUND IT, AND DUG A WINE PRESS IN IT, AND BUILT A TOWER, and he leased it to vine-growers and went on a journey. **34** And when the harvest time approached, he sent his slaves to the vine-growers to receive his fruit. **35** And the vine-growers took his slaves and beat one, killed another, and stoned another. **36** Again, he sent other slaves, more than the first; and they did the same things to them. **37** But afterward he sent his son to them, saying, 'They will respect my son.' **38** But when the vine-growers saw the son, they said among themselves, 'This is the heir; come, let's kill him and take possession of his inheritance!' **39** And they took him and threw him out of the vineyard, and killed him. **40** Therefore, when the owner of the vineyard comes, what will he do to those vine-growers?" **41** They *said to Him, "He will bring those wretches to a wretched end and lease the vineyard to other vine-growers, who will pay him the fruit in the *proper* seasons."

42 Jesus *said to them, "Did you never read in the Scriptures,

'A STONE WHICH THE BUILDERS REJECTED,
THIS HAS BECOME THE CHIEF CORNERSTONE;
THIS CAME ABOUT FROM THE LORD,
AND IT IS MARVELOUS IN OUR EYES'?

43 Therefore I say to you, the kingdom of God will be taken away from you and given to a people producing its fruit. 44 And the one who falls on this stone will be broken to pieces; and on whomever it falls, it will crush him."

45 When the chief priests and the Pharisees heard His parables, they understood that He was speaking about them. 46 And *although* they sought to arrest Him, they feared the crowds, since they considered Him to be a prophet.

Parable of the Marriage Feast

22 Jesus spoke to them again in parables, saying, 2 "The kingdom of heaven is like a king who held a wedding feast for his son. 3 And he sent his slaves to call those who had been invited to the wedding feast, and they were unwilling to come. 4 Again he sent other slaves, saying, 'Tell those who have been invited, "Behold, I have prepared my dinner; my oxen and my fattened cattle are *all* butchered and everything is ready. Come to the wedding feast!"' 5 But they paid no attention and went their *separate* ways, one to his own farm, another to his business, 6 and the rest seized his slaves and treated them abusively, and *then* killed them. 7 Now the king was angry, and he sent his armies and destroyed those murderers and set their city on fire. 8 Then he *said to his slaves, 'The wedding feast is ready, but those who were invited were not worthy. 9 So go to the main roads, and invite whomever you find *there* to the wedding feast.' 10 Those slaves went out into the streets and gathered together all whom they found, both bad and good; and the wedding hall was filled with dinner guests.

11 "But when the king came in to look over the dinner guests, he saw a man there who was not dressed in wedding clothes, 12 and he *said to him, 'Friend, how did you get in here without wedding clothes?' And the man was speechless. 13 Then the king said to the servants, 'Tie his

hands and feet, and throw him into the outer darkness;
there will be weeping and gnashing of teeth in that
place.' 14 For many are called, but few *are* chosen."

Poll-tax to Caesar

15 Then the Pharisees went and plotted together how
they might trap Him in what He said. 16 And they *sent
their disciples to Him, along with the Herodians, saying,
"Teacher, we know that You are truthful and teach the
way of God in truth, and do not care what anyone
thinks; for You are not partial to anyone. 17 Tell us then,
what do You think? Is it permissible to pay a 'poll-tax to
Caesar, or not?" 18 But Jesus perceived their malice, and
said, "Why are you testing Me, you hypocrites? 19 Show
Me the coin *used* for the poll-tax." And they brought
Him a denarius. 20 And He *said to them, "Whose image
and inscription is this?" 21 They *said to Him, "Caesar's."
Then He *said to them, "Then pay to Caesar the things
that are Caesar's; and to God the things that are God's."
22 And hearing *this,* they were amazed; and they left Him
and went away.

Jesus Answers the Sadducees

23 On that day *some* Sadducees (who say there is no
resurrection) came to Jesus and questioned Him, 24 saying, "Teacher, Moses said, 'If a man dies having no children, his brother as next of kin shall marry his wife, and
raise up children for his brother.' 25 Now there were
seven brothers among us; and the first married and died,
and having no children, he left his wife to his brother.
26 *It was* the same also *with* the second *brother,* and the
third, down to the seventh. 27 Last of all, the woman
died. 28 In the resurrection, therefore, whose wife of the
seven will she be? For they all had her *in marriage.*"

29 But Jesus answered and said to them, "You are mistaken, since you do not understand the Scriptures nor
the power of God. 30 For in the resurrection they neither
marry nor are given in marriage, but are like angels in
heaven. 31 But regarding the resurrection of the dead,
have you not read what was spoken to you by God: 32 'I
AM THE GOD OF ABRAHAM, THE GOD OF ISAAC, AND THE GOD OF
JACOB'? He is not the God of the dead, but of the living."

22:17 1 I.e., a tax on each person in the census

33 When the crowds heard *this,* they were astonished at His teaching.

34 But when the Pharisees heard that *Jesus* had silenced the Sadducees, they gathered together. **35** And one of them, ¹a lawyer, asked Him a question, testing Him: **36** "Teacher, which is the great commandment in the Law?" **37** And He said to him, " 'YOU SHALL LOVE THE LORD YOUR GOD WITH ALL YOUR HEART, AND WITH ALL YOUR SOUL, AND WITH ALL YOUR MIND.' **38** This is the great and foremost commandment. **39** The second is like it, 'YOU SHALL LOVE YOUR NEIGHBOR AS YOURSELF.' **40** Upon these two commandments hang the whole Law and the Prophets."

41 Now while the Pharisees were gathered together, Jesus asked them a question: **42** "What do you think about the Christ? Whose son is He?" They *said to Him, "*The son* of David." **43** He *said to them, "Then how does David in the Spirit call Him 'Lord,' saying,

44   'THE LORD SAID TO MY LORD,
    "SIT AT MY right hand,
      UNTIL I PUT YOUR enemies UNDER YOUR feet" '?
45 Therefore, if David calls Him 'Lord,' how is He his son?" **46** No one was able to offer Him a word in answer, nor did anyone dare from that day *on* to ask Him any more questions.

Hypocrisy Exposed

23 Then Jesus spoke to the crowds and to His disciples, **2** saying: "The scribes and the Pharisees have seated themselves in the chair of Moses. **3** Therefore, whatever they tell you, do and comply with it all, but do not do as they do; for they say *things* and do not do *them.* **4** And they tie up heavy burdens and lay them on people's shoulders, but they themselves are unwilling to move them with *so much as* their finger. **5** And they do all their deeds to be noticed by *other* people; for they broaden their ¹phylacteries and lengthen the tassels *of their garments.* **6** And they love the place of honor at banquets, and the seats of honor in the synagogues, **7** and personal greetings in the marketplaces, and being called Rabbi by the people. **8** But as for you, do not be called

---

22:35 ¹I.e., an expert in the Mosaic Law   23:5 ¹I.e., small pouches containing Scripture texts, worn on the left forearm and forehead for religious purposes

Rabbi; for *only* One is your Teacher, and you are all brothers *and sisters.* 9 And do not call *anyone* on earth your father; for *only* One is your Father, He who is in heaven. 10 And do not be called leaders; for *only* One is your Leader, *that is,* Christ. 11 But the greatest of you shall be your servant. 12 Whoever exalts himself shall be humbled, and whoever humbles himself shall be exalted.

Eight Woes

13 "But woe to you, scribes and Pharisees, hypocrites, because you shut the kingdom of heaven in front of people; for you do not enter *it* yourselves, nor do you allow those who are entering to go in.¹

15 "Woe to you, scribes and Pharisees, hypocrites, because you travel around on sea and land to make one proselyte; and when he becomes *one,* you make him twice as much a son of ¹hell as yourselves.

16 "Woe to you, blind guides, who say, 'Whoever swears by the temple, *that* is nothing; but whoever swears by the gold of the temple is obligated.' 17 You fools and blind men! Which is more important, the gold or the temple that sanctified the gold? 18 And *you say,* 'Whoever swears by the altar, *that* is nothing; but whoever swears by the offering that is on it is obligated.' 19 You blind men, which is more important, the offering or the altar that sanctifies the offering? 20 Therefore, the one who swears by the altar, swears *both* by the altar and by everything on it. 21 And the one who swears by the temple, swears *both* by the temple and by Him who dwells in it. 22 And the one who swears by heaven, swears *both* by the throne of God and by Him who sits upon it.

23 "Woe to you, scribes and Pharisees, hypocrites! For you tithe mint and dill and cumin, and have neglected the weightier provisions of the Law: justice and mercy and faithfulness; but these *are the things* you should have done without neglecting the others. 24 You blind guides, who strain out a gnat and swallow a camel!

25 "Woe to you, scribes and Pharisees, hypocrites! For

23:13 ¹ Late mss add (traditionally v 14): *Woe to you, scribes and Pharisees, hypocrites, because you devour widows' houses even while for appearances' sake you make long prayers; therefore you will receive greater condemnation* (as v 14); cf. Mark 12:40; Luke 20:47
23:15 ¹ Gr *Gehenna*

you clean the outside of the cup and of the dish, but inside they are full of robbery and self-indulgence. 26 You blind Pharisee, first clean the inside of the cup and of the dish, so that the outside of it may also become clean.

27 "Woe to you, scribes and Pharisees, hypocrites! For you are like whitewashed tombs which on the outside appear beautiful, but inside they are full of dead men's bones and all uncleanness. 28 So you too, outwardly appear righteous to people, but inwardly you are full of hypocrisy and lawlessness.

29 "Woe to you, scribes and Pharisees, hypocrites! For you build the tombs for the prophets and decorate the monuments of the righteous, 30 and you say, 'If we had been *living* in the days of our fathers, we would not have been partners with them in *shedding* the blood of the prophets.' 31 So you testify against yourselves, that you are sons of those who murdered the prophets. 32 Fill up, then, the measure *of the guilt* of your fathers. 33 You snakes, you offspring of vipers, how will you escape the sentence of hell?

34 "Therefore, behold, I am sending you prophets and wise men and scribes; some of them you will kill and crucify, and some of them you will flog in your synagogues, and persecute from city to city, 35 so that upon you will fall *the guilt of* all the righteous blood shed on earth, from the blood of righteous Abel to the blood of Zechariah, the son of Berechiah, whom you murdered between the temple and the altar. 36 Truly I say to you, all these things will come upon this generation.

Grieving over Jerusalem

37 "Jerusalem, Jerusalem, who kills the prophets and stones those who have been sent to her! How often I wanted to gather your children together, the way a hen gathers her chicks under her wings, and you were unwilling. 38 Behold, your house is being left to you desolate! 39 For I say to you, from now on you will not see Me until you say, 'BLESSED IS THE ONE WHO COMES IN THE NAME OF THE LORD!'"

Signs of Christ's Return

24 Jesus left the temple *area* and was going *on His way* when His disciples came up to point out the temple buildings to Him. 2 But He responded and said to

them, "Do you not see all these things? Truly I say to you, not *one* stone here will be left upon another, which will not be torn down."

3 And as He was sitting on the Mount of Olives, the disciples came to Him privately, saying, "Tell us, when will these things happen, and what *will be* the sign of Your coming, and of the end of the age?"

4 And Jesus answered and said to them, "See to it that no one misleads you. 5 For many will come in My name, saying, 'I am the Christ,' and they will mislead many people. 6 And you will be hearing of wars and rumors of wars. See that you are not alarmed, for *those things* must take place, but *that* is not yet the end. 7 For nation will rise against nation, and kingdom against kingdom, and there will be famines and earthquakes in various places. 8 But all these things are *merely* the beginning of birth pains.

9 "Then they will hand you over to tribulation and kill you, and you will be hated by all nations because of My name. 10 And at that time many will fall away, and they will betray one another and hate one another. 11 And many false prophets will rise up and mislead many people. 12 And because lawlessness is increased, most people's love will become cold. 13 But the one who endures to the end is the one who will be saved. 14 This gospel of the kingdom shall be preached in the whole world as a testimony to all the nations, and then the end will come.

Perilous Times

15 "Therefore when you see the ABOMINATION OF DESOLATION which was spoken of through Daniel the prophet, standing in the holy place—let the 'reader understand— 16 then those who are in Judea must flee to the mountains. 17 Whoever is on the housetop must not go down to get things out of his house. 18 And whoever is in the field must not turn back to get his cloak. 19 But woe to those women who are pregnant, and to those who are nursing babies in those days! 20 Moreover, pray that when you flee, it will not be in the winter, or on a Sabbath. 21 For then there will be a great tribulation, such as has not occurred since the beginning of the world

---

24:15 1 I.e., the reader of Daniel

until now, nor ever will *again*. ²² And if those days had not been cut short, no life would have been saved; but for the sake of the elect those days will be cut short. ²³ Then if anyone says to you, 'Behold, here is the Christ,' or '*He is over* here,' do not believe *him*. ²⁴ For false christs and false prophets will arise and will provide great signs and wonders, so as to mislead, if possible, even the elect. ²⁵ Behold, I have told you in advance. ²⁶ So if they say to you, 'Behold, He is in the wilderness,' do not go out; *or,* 'Behold, He is in the inner rooms,' do not believe *them*. ²⁷ For just as the lightning comes from the east and flashes as far as the west, so will the coming of the Son of Man be. ²⁸ Wherever the corpse is, there the vultures will gather.

The Glorious Return

²⁹ "But immediately after the tribulation of those days THE SUN WILL BE DARKENED, AND THE MOON WILL NOT GIVE ITS LIGHT, AND THE STARS WILL FALL from the sky, and the powers of the heavens will be shaken. ³⁰ And then the sign of the Son of Man will appear in the sky, and then all the tribes of the earth will mourn, and they will see the SON OF MAN COMING ON THE CLOUDS OF THE SKY with power and great glory. ³¹ And He will send forth His angels with A GREAT TRUMPET BLAST, and THEY WILL GATHER TOGETHER His elect from the four winds, from one end of the sky to the other.

Parable of the Fig Tree

³² "Now learn the parable from the fig tree: as soon as its branch has become tender and sprouts its leaves, you know that summer is near; ³³ so you too, when you see all these things, recognize that He is near, *right* at the door. ³⁴ Truly I say to you, this generation will not pass away until all these things take place. ³⁵ Heaven and earth will pass away, but My words will not pass away.

³⁶ "But about that day and hour no one knows, not even the angels of heaven, nor the Son, but the Father alone. ³⁷ For the coming of the Son of Man will be just like the days of Noah. ³⁸ For as in those days before the flood they were eating and drinking, marrying and giving in marriage, until the day that Noah entered the ark, ³⁹ and they did not understand until the flood came and took them all away; so will the coming of the Son of Man

be. **40** At that time there will be two *men* in the field; one will be taken and one will be left. **41** Two *women* will be grinding at the mill; one will be taken and one will be left.

Be Ready for His Coming

42 "Therefore be on the alert, for you do not know which day your Lord is coming. **43** But be sure of this, that if the head of the house had known at what time of the night the thief was coming, he would have been on the alert and would not have allowed his house to be broken into. **44** For this reason you must be ready as well; for the Son of Man is coming at an hour when you do not think *He will.*

45 "Who then is the faithful and sensible slave whom his master put in charge of his household slaves, to give them their food at the proper time? **46** Blessed is that slave whom his master finds so doing when he comes. **47** Truly I say to you that he will put him in charge of all his possessions. **48** But if that evil slave says in his heart, 'My master is not coming for a long time,' **49** and he begins to beat his fellow slaves, and he eats and drinks with those habitually drunk; **50** *then* the master of that slave will come on a day that he does not expect, and at an hour that he does not know, **51** and he will cut him in two and assign him a place with the hypocrites; in that place there will be weeping and gnashing of teeth.

Parable of Ten Virgins

25 "Then the kingdom of heaven will be comparable to ten virgins, who took their lamps and went out to meet the groom. **2** Five of them were foolish, and five were prudent. **3** For when the foolish took their lamps, they did not take *extra* oil with them; **4** but the prudent ones took oil in flasks with their lamps. **5** Now while the groom was delaying, they all became drowsy and *began* to sleep. **6** But at midnight there finally was a shout: 'Behold, the groom! Come out to meet *him.*' **7** Then all those virgins got up and trimmed their lamps. **8** But the foolish *virgins* said to the prudent ones, 'Give us some of your oil, because our lamps are going out.' **9** However, the prudent ones answered, '*No,* there most certainly would not be enough for us and you *too;* go instead to the merchants and buy *some* for yourselves.' **10** But while they were on their way to buy *the oil,* the groom came, and those who were ready went in with him to the wedding feast; and the door was shut. **11** Yet later, the other virgins also came, saying, 'Lord, lord, open up for us.' **12** But he answered, 'Truly I say to you, I do not know you.' **13** Be on the alert then, because you do not know the day nor the hour.

Parable of the Talents

14 "For *it is* just like a man *about* to go on a journey, *who* called his own slaves and entrusted his possessions to them. **15** To one he gave five ¹talents, to another, two, and to another, one, each according to his own ability; and he went on his journey. **16** The one who had received the five talents immediately went and did business with them, and earned five more *talents.* **17** In the same way the one who *had received* the two *talents* earned two more. **18** But he who received the one *talent* went away and dug *a hole in the* ground, and hid his master's money.

19 "Now after a long time the master of those slaves *came and *settled accounts with them. **20** The one who had received the five talents came up and brought five more talents, saying, 'Master, you entrusted five talents to me. See, I have earned five more talents.' **21** His master said to him, 'Well done, good and faithful slave. You were faithful with a few things, I will put you in charge of many things; enter the joy of your master.'

22 "Also the one who *had received* the two talents came up and said, 'Master, you entrusted two talents to me. See, I have earned two more talents.' **23** His master said to him, 'Well done, good and faithful slave. You were faithful with a few things, I will put you in charge of many things; enter the joy of your master.'

24 "Now the one who had received the one talent also came up and said, 'Master, I knew you to be a hard man, reaping where you did not sow, and gathering where you did not scatter *seed.* **25** And I was afraid, so I went away and hid your talent in the ground. See, you *still* have what is yours.'

26 "But his master answered and said to him, 'You worthless, lazy slave! Did you know that I reap where I

25:15 ¹ A talent was worth about fifteen years' wages for a laborer

did not sow, and gather where I did not scatter *seed?*
27 Then you ought to have put my money in the bank,
and on my arrival I would have received my *money* back
with interest. **28** Therefore: take the talent away from
him, and give it to the one who has the ten talents.'

29 "For to everyone who has, *more* shall be given, and
he will have an abundance; but from the one who does
not have, even what he does have shall be taken away.
30 And throw the worthless slave into the outer darkness;
in that place there will be weeping and gnashing of
teeth.

The Judgment

31 "But when the Son of Man comes in His glory, and
all the angels with Him, then He will sit on His glorious
throne. **32** And all the nations will be gathered before
Him; and He will separate them from one another, just as
the shepherd separates the sheep from the goats; **33** and
He will put the sheep on His right, but the goats on the
left.

34 "Then the King will say to those on His right,
'Come, you who are blessed of My Father, inherit the
kingdom prepared for you from the foundation of the
world. **35** For I was hungry, and you gave Me *something*
to eat; I was thirsty, and you gave Me *something* to
drink; I was a stranger, and you invited Me in; **36** naked,
and you clothed Me; I was sick, and you visited Me; I
was in prison, and you came to Me.' **37** Then the
righteous will answer Him, 'Lord, when did we see You
hungry, and feed You, or thirsty, and give You *something*
to drink? **38** And when did we see You *as* a stranger, and
invite You in, or naked, and clothe You? **39** And when did
we see You sick, or in prison, and come to You?' **40** And
the King will answer and say to them, 'Truly I say to you,
to the extent that you did *it* for one of the least of these
brothers *or sisters* of Mine, you did *it* for Me.'

41 "Then He will also say to those on His left, 'Depart
from Me, you accursed people, into the eternal fire
which has been prepared for the devil and his angels;
42 for I was hungry, and you gave Me nothing to eat; I
was thirsty, and you gave Me nothing to drink; **43** I was a
stranger, and you did not invite Me in; naked, and you
did not clothe Me; sick, and in prison, and you did
not visit Me.' **44** Then they themselves also will answer,

'Lord, when did we see You hungry, or thirsty, or *as* a stranger, or naked, or sick, or in prison, and did not take care of You?' [45] Then He will answer them, 'Truly I say to you, to the extent that you did not do *it* for one of the least of these, you did not do *it* for Me, either.' [46] These will go away into eternal punishment, but the righteous into eternal life."

The Plot to Kill Jesus

26 When Jesus had finished all these words, He said to His disciples, [2] "You know that after two days the Passover is coming, and the Son of Man is *to be* handed over for crucifixion."

[3] At that time the chief priests and the elders of the people were gathered together in the courtyard of the high priest named Caiaphas; [4] and they plotted together to arrest Jesus covertly and kill Him. [5] But they were saying, "Not during the festival, otherwise a riot might occur among the people."

The Precious Ointment

[6] Now when Jesus was in Bethany, at the home of Simon 'the Leper, [7] a woman came to Him with an alabaster vial of very expensive perfume, and she poured it on His head as He was reclining *at the table.* [8] But the disciples were indignant when they saw *this,* and said, "Why this waste? [9] For this *perfume* could have been sold for a high price and *the money* given to the poor." [10] But Jesus, aware of this, said to them, "Why are you bothering the woman? For she has done a good deed for Me. [11] For you always have the poor with you; but you do not always have Me. [12] For when she poured this perfume on My body, she did it to prepare Me for burial. [13] Truly I say to you, wherever this gospel is preached in the whole world, what this woman has done will also be told in memory of her."

Judas' Bargain

[14] Then one of the twelve, named Judas Iscariot, went to the chief priests [15] and said, "What are you willing to give me to betray Him to you?" And they set *out* for him

---

26:6 [1] I.e., a nickname; the man no doubt was cured

thirty pieces of silver. **16** And from then on he looked for a good opportunity to betray Jesus.

17 Now on the first *day* of 'Unleavened Bread the disciples came to Jesus and asked, "Where do You want us to prepare for You to eat the Passover?" **18** And He said, "Go into the city to a certain man, and say to him, 'The Teacher says, "My time is near; I am keeping the Passover at your house with My disciples." ' " **19** The disciples did as Jesus had directed them; and they prepared the Passover.

The Last Passover

20 Now when evening came, Jesus was reclining *at the table* with the twelve. **21** And as they were eating, He said, "Truly I say to you that one of you will betray Me." **22** Being deeply grieved, they began saying to Him, each one: "Surely it is not I, Lord?" **23** And He answered, "He who dipped his hand with Me in the bowl is the one who will betray Me. **24** The Son of Man is going away just as it is written about Him; but woe to that man by whom the Son of Man is betrayed! It would have been good for that man if he had not been born." **25** And Judas, who was betraying Him, said, "Surely it is not I, Rabbi?" Jesus *said to him, "You have said *it* yourself."

The Lord's Supper Instituted

26 Now while they were eating, Jesus took *some* bread, and after a blessing, He broke *it* and gave *it* to the disciples, and said, "Take, eat; this is My body." **27** And when He had taken a cup and given thanks, He gave *it* to them, saying, "Drink from it, all of you; **28** for this is My blood of the covenant, which is being poured out for many for forgiveness of sins. **29** But I say to you, I will not drink of this fruit of the vine from now on until that day when I drink it with you, new, in My Father's kingdom."

30 And after singing a hymn, they went out to the Mount of Olives.

31 Then Jesus *said to them, "You will all 'fall away because of Me this night, for it is written: 'I WILL STRIKE THE SHEPHERD, AND THE SHEEP OF THE FLOCK WILL BE SCATTERED.' **32** But after I have been raised, I will go ahead of you to

---

26:17 'I.e., Passover week   26:31 'I.e., have a lapse in faith

Galilee." 33 But Peter replied to Him, "*Even* if they all fall away because of You, I will never fall away!" 34 Jesus said to him, "Truly I say to you that this *very* night, before a rooster crows, you will deny Me three times." 35 Peter *said to Him, "Even if I have to die with You, I will not deny You!" All the disciples said the same thing as well.

The Garden of Gethsemane

36 Then Jesus *came with them to a place called Gethsemane, and *told His disciples, "Sit here while I go over there and pray." 37 And He took Peter and the two sons of Zebedee with Him, and began to be grieved and distressed. 38 Then He *said to them, "My soul is deeply grieved, to the point of death; remain here and keep watch with Me."

39 And He went a little beyond *them,* and fell on His face and prayed, saying, "My Father, if it is possible, let this cup pass from Me; yet not as I will, but as You *will.*" 40 And He *came to the disciples and *found them sleeping, and He *said to Peter, "So, you *men* could not keep watch with Me for one hour? 41 Keep watching and praying, so that you do not come into temptation; the spirit is willing, but the flesh is weak."

42 He went away again a second time and prayed, saying, "My Father, if this *cup* cannot pass away unless I drink *from* it, Your will be done." 43 Again He came and found them sleeping, for their eyes were heavy. 44 And He left them again, and went away and prayed a third time, saying the same thing once more. 45 Then He *came to the disciples and *said to them, "Are you still sleeping and resting? Behold, the hour is at hand and the Son of Man is being betrayed into the hands of sinners. 46 Get up, let's go; behold, the one who is betraying Me is near!"

Jesus' Betrayal and Arrest

47 And while He was still speaking, behold, Judas, one of the twelve, came accompanied by a large crowd with swords and clubs, *who came* from the chief priests and elders of the people. 48 Now he who was betraying Him gave them a sign *previously,* saying, "Whomever I kiss, He is *the one;* arrest Him." 49 And immediately *Judas* went up to Jesus and said, "Greetings, Rabbi!" and kissed Him. 50 But Jesus said to him, "Friend, *do* what you have

come for." Then they came and laid hands on Jesus and arrested Him.

51 And behold, one of those who were with Jesus reached and drew his sword, and struck the slave of the high priest and cut off his ear. **52** Then Jesus *said to him, "Put your sword back into its place; for all those who take up the sword will perish by the sword. **53** Or do you think that I cannot appeal to My Father, and He will at once put at My disposal more than twelve ¹legions of angels? **54** How then would the Scriptures be fulfilled, *which say* that it must happen this way?"

55 At that time Jesus said to the crowds, "Have you come out with swords and clubs to arrest Me as *you would* against a man inciting a revolt? Every day I used to sit within the temple *grounds* teaching, and you did not arrest Me. **56** But all this has taken place so that the Scriptures of the prophets will be fulfilled." Then all the disciples left Him and fled.

Jesus before Caiaphas

57 Those who had arrested Jesus led Him away to Caiaphas, the high priest, where the scribes and the elders were gathered together. **58** But Peter was following Him at a distance, as far as the courtyard of the high priest, and he came inside and sat down with the officers to see the outcome.

59 Now the chief priests and the entire Council kept trying to obtain false testimony against Jesus, so that they might put Him to death. **60** They did not find *any,* even though many false witnesses came forward. But later on two came forward, **61** and said, "This man stated, 'I am able to destroy the temple of God and to rebuild it in three days.'" **62** The high priest stood up and said to Him, "Do You offer no answer for what these men are testifying against You?" **63** But Jesus kept silent. And the high priest said to Him, "I place You under oath by the living God, to tell us whether You are the Christ, the Son of God." **64** Jesus *said to him, "You have said *it* yourself. But I tell you, from now *on* you will see the Son of Man sitting at the right hand of power, and coming on the clouds of heaven."

65 Then the high priest tore his robes and said, "He

26:53 ¹A legion equaled 6,000 troops

has blasphemed! What further need do we have of witnesses? See, you have now heard the blasphemy; **66** what do you think?" They answered, "He deserves death!"

67 Then they spit in His face and beat Him with their fists; and others slapped Him, **68** and said, "Prophesy to us, You Christ; who is the one who hit You?"

Peter's Denials

69 Now Peter was sitting outside in the courtyard, and a slave woman came to him and said, "You too were with Jesus the Galilean." **70** But he denied *it* before them all, saying, "I do not know what you are talking about." **71** When he had gone out to the gateway, another *slave woman* saw him and *said to those who were there, "This man was with Jesus of Nazareth." **72** And again he denied *it,* with an oath: "I do not know the man." **73** A little later the bystanders came up and said to Peter, "You really are *one* of them as well, since even the way you talk gives you away." **74** Then he began to curse and swear, "I do not know the man!" And immediately a rooster crowed. **75** And Peter remembered the statement that Jesus had made: "Before a rooster crows, you will deny Me three times." And he went out and wept bitterly.

Judas' Remorse

27 Now when morning came, all the chief priests and the elders of the people conferred together against Jesus to put Him to death; **2** and they bound Him and led Him away, and handed Him over to Pilate the governor.

3 Then when Judas, who had betrayed Him, saw that He had been condemned, he felt remorse and returned the thirty pieces of silver to the chief priests and elders, **4** saying, "I have sinned by betraying innocent blood." But they said, "What *is that* to us? You shall see *to it* yourself!" **5** And he threw the pieces of silver into the temple sanctuary and left; and he went away and hanged himself. **6** The chief priests took the pieces of silver and said, "It is not lawful to put them in the temple treasury, since it is money paid for blood." **7** And they conferred together and with the money bought the Potter's Field as a burial place for strangers. **8** For this reason that field has been called the Field of Blood to this day. **9** Then that which was spoken through Jeremiah the prophet was fulfilled: "AND THEY TOOK THE THIRTY PIECES OF SILVER, THE PRICE OF THE ONE WHOSE PRICE HAD BEEN SET by the sons of Israel; 10 AND THEY GAVE THEM FOR THE POTTER'S FIELD, JUST AS THE LORD DIRECTED ME."

Jesus before Pilate

11 Now Jesus stood before the governor, and the governor questioned Him, saying, "*So* You are the King of the Jews?" And Jesus said to him, "*It is as* you say." 12 And while He was being accused by the chief priests and elders, He did not offer any answer. 13 Then Pilate *said to Him, "Do You not hear how many things they are testifying against You?" 14 And *still* He did not answer him in regard to even a single charge, so the governor was greatly amazed.

15 Now at *the Passover* Feast the governor was accustomed to release for the people *any* one prisoner whom they wanted. 16 And at that time they were holding a notorious prisoner called Barabbas. 17 So when the people gathered together, Pilate said to them, "Whom do you want me to release for you: Barabbas, or Jesus who is called Christ?" 18 For he knew that *it was* because of envy *that* [1]they had handed Him over.

19 And while he was sitting on the judgment seat, his wife sent him *a message,* saying, "*See that you have nothing to do* with that righteous Man; for last night I suffered greatly in a dream because of Him." 20 But the chief priests and the elders persuaded the crowds to ask for Barabbas, and to put Jesus to death. 21 And the governor said to them, "Which of the two do you want me to release for you?" And they said, "Barabbas." 22 Pilate *said to them, "Then what shall I do with Jesus who is called Christ?" They all *said, "Crucify Him!" 23 But he said, "Why, what evil has He done?" Yet they kept shouting all the more, saying, "Crucify Him!"

24 Now when Pilate saw that he was accomplishing nothing, but rather that a riot was starting, he took water and washed his hands in front of the crowd, saying, "I am innocent of this Man's blood; you yourselves shall see." 25 And all the people replied, "His blood *shall be* on us and on our children!" 26 Then he released Barabbas for

---

27:18 [1]I.e., the Jewish leaders

them; but after having Jesus flogged, he handed Him over to be crucified.

Jesus Is Mocked

27 Then the soldiers of the governor took Jesus into the ¹Praetorium and gathered the whole *Roman* ²cohort to Him. 28 And they stripped Him and put a red cloak on Him. 29 And after twisting together a crown of thorns, they put it on His head, and *put* a ¹reed in His right hand; and they knelt down before Him and mocked Him, saying, "Hail, King of the Jews!" 30 And they spit on Him, and took the reed and beat Him on the head. 31 And after they had mocked Him, they took the cloak off Him and put His *own* garments back on Him, and led Him away to crucify *Him.*

32 As they were coming out, they found a man of Cyrene named Simon, whom they compelled to carry His ¹cross.

The Crucifixion

33 And when they came to a place called Golgotha, which means Place of a Skull, 34 they gave Him wine mixed with bile to drink; and after tasting *it,* He was unwilling to drink *it.*

35 And when they had crucified Him, they divided His garments among themselves by casting lots. 36 And sitting down, they *began* to keep watch over Him there. 37 And above His head they put up the charge against Him which read, "THIS IS JESUS THE KING OF THE JEWS."

38 At that time two ¹rebels *were being crucified with Him, one on the right and one on the left. 39 And those passing by were speaking abusively to Him, shaking their heads, 40 and saying, "You who *are going to* destroy the temple and rebuild *it* in three days, save Yourself! If You are the Son of God, come down from the cross." 41 In the same way the chief priests also, along with the scribes and elders, were mocking *Him* and saying, 42 "He saved others; He cannot save Himself! He is the King of Israel; let Him now come down from the cross, and we will believe in Him. 43 HE HAS TRUSTED IN GOD; LET GOD RESCUE

27:27 ¹I.e., the governor's official residence   27:27 ²Normally 600 men (the number varied)   27:29 ¹Or *staff;* i.e., to mimic a king's scepter   27:32 ¹I.e., the crossbeam for a cross   27:38 ¹Or *robbers*

Him now, IF HE TAKES PLEASURE IN HIM; for He said, 'I am the Son of God.' " **44** And the ¹rebels who had been crucified with Him were also insulting Him in the same *way.*

45 Now from the ¹sixth hour darkness fell upon all the land until the ²ninth hour. **46** And about the ninth hour Jesus cried out with a loud voice, saying, "ELI, ELI, LEMA SABAKTANEI?" that is, "MY GOD, MY GOD, WHY HAVE YOU FORSAKEN ME?" **47** And some of those who were standing there, when they heard it, said, "This man is calling for Elijah." **48** And immediately one of them ran, and taking a sponge, he filled it with sour wine and put it on a reed, and gave Him a drink. **49** But the rest *of them* said, "Let us see if Elijah comes to save Him¹." **50** And Jesus cried out again with a loud voice, and gave up His spirit. **51** And behold, the veil of the temple was torn in two from top to bottom; and the earth shook and the rocks were split. **52** Also the tombs were opened, and many bodies of the saints who had fallen asleep were raised; **53** and coming out of the tombs after His resurrection, they entered the holy city and appeared to many. **54** Now as for the centurion and those who were with him keeping guard over Jesus, when they saw the earthquake and the *other* things that were happening, they became extremely frightened and said, "Truly this was the Son of God!"

55 And many women were there watching from a distance, who had followed Jesus from Galilee while caring for Him. **56** Among them were Mary Magdalene, Mary the mother of James and Joseph, and the mother of the sons of Zebedee.

Jesus Is Buried

57 Now when it was evening, a rich man from Arimathea came, named Joseph, who himself had also become a disciple of Jesus. **58** This man went to Pilate and asked for the body of Jesus. Then Pilate ordered it to be given *to him.* **59** And Joseph took the body and wrapped it in a clean linen cloth, **60** and laid it in his own new tomb, which he had cut out in the rock; and he rolled a large stone against the entrance of the tomb and went away.

27:44 ¹Or *robbers*   27:45 ¹I.e., noon   27:45 ²I.e., 3 p.m.
27:49 ¹Some early mss *And another took a spear and pierced His side, and there came out water and blood* (cf. John 19:34)

61 And Mary Magdalene was there, and the other Mary, sitting opposite the tomb.

62 Now on the next day, *that is, the day* which is after the preparation, the chief priests and the Pharisees gathered together with Pilate, **63** and they said, "Sir, we remember that when that deceiver was still alive, He said, 'After three days I am rising.' **64** Therefore, give orders for the tomb to be made secure until the third day; otherwise, His disciples may come and steal Him, and say to the people, 'He has risen from the dead,' and the last deception will be worse than the first." **65** Pilate said to them, "You have a guard; go, make it *as* secure as you know how." **66** And they went and made the tomb secure with the guard, sealing the stone.

Jesus Is Risen!

28 Now after the Sabbath, as it began to dawn toward the first *day* of the week, Mary Magdalene and the other Mary came to look at the tomb. **2** And behold, a severe earthquake had occurred, for an angel of the Lord descended from heaven and came and rolled away the stone, and sat upon it. **3** And his appearance was like lightning, and his clothing as white as snow. **4** The guards shook from fear of him and became like dead men. **5** And the angel said to the women, "Do not be afraid; for I know that you are looking for Jesus who has been crucified. **6** He is not here, for He has risen, just as He said. Come, see the place where He was lying. **7** And go quickly and tell His disciples that He has risen from the dead; and behold, He is going ahead of you to Galilee. There you will see Him; behold, I have told you."

8 And they left the tomb quickly with fear and great joy, and ran to report to His disciples. **9** And behold, Jesus met them and said, "Rejoice!" And they came up and took hold of His feet, and worshiped Him. **10** Then Jesus *said to them, "Do not be afraid; go, bring word to My brothers to leave for Galilee, and there they will see Me."

11 Now while they were on their way, some of the *men from the* guard came into the city and reported to the chief priests all that had happened. **12** And when they had assembled with the elders and consulted together, they gave a large sum of money to the soldiers, **13** and said, "You are to say, 'His disciples came at night and stole

Him while we were asleep.' **14** And if this comes to the governor's ears, we will appease him and keep you out of trouble." **15** And they took the money and did as they had been instructed; and this story was widely spread among the Jews *and is* to this day.

The Great Commission

16 But the eleven disciples proceeded to Galilee, to the mountain which Jesus had designated to them. **17** And when they saw Him, they worshiped *Him;* but some were doubtful. **18** And Jesus came up and spoke to them, saying, "All authority in heaven and on earth has been given to Me. **19** Go, therefore, and make disciples of all the nations, baptizing them in the name of the Father and the Son and the Holy Spirit, **20** teaching them to follow all that I commanded you; and behold, I am with you always, to the end of the age."

The Gospel According to

MARK

Preaching of John the Baptist

1 The beginning of the gospel of Jesus Christ, the Son of God,

² just as it is written in Isaiah the prophet:

"BEHOLD, I AM SENDING MY MESSENGER BEFORE YOU,
WHO WILL PREPARE YOUR WAY;

³   THE VOICE OF ONE CALLING ¹OUT IN THE WILDERNESS,
'PREPARE THE WAY OF THE LORD,
MAKE HIS PATHS STRAIGHT!' "

⁴ John the Baptist appeared in the wilderness, preaching a baptism of repentance for the forgiveness of sins. ⁵ And all the country of Judea was going out to him, and all the people of Jerusalem; and they were being baptized by him in the Jordan River, confessing their sins. ⁶ John was clothed with camel's hair and *wore* a leather belt around his waist, and his diet was locusts and wild honey. ⁷ And he was preaching, saying, "After me One is coming who is mightier than I, and I am not fit to bend down and untie the straps of His sandals. ⁸ I baptized you ¹with water; but He will baptize you ²with the Holy Spirit."

The Baptism of Jesus

⁹ In those days Jesus came from Nazareth in Galilee and was baptized by John in the Jordan. ¹⁰ And immediately coming up out of the water, He saw the heavens opening, and the Spirit, like a dove, descending upon Him; ¹¹ and a voice came from the heavens: "You are My beloved Son; in You I am well pleased."

¹² And immediately the Spirit *brought Him out into the wilderness. ¹³ And He was in the wilderness for forty days, being tempted by Satan; and He was with the wild animals, and the angels were serving Him.

Jesus Preaches in Galilee

¹⁴ Now after John was taken into custody, Jesus came

1:3 ¹Or *out, Prepare in the wilderness the way*   1:8 ¹The Gr here can be translated *in, with,* or *by*   1:8 ²The Gr here can be translated *in, with,* or *by*

into Galilee, preaching the gospel of God, **15** and saying, "The time is fulfilled, and the kingdom of God is at hand; repent and believe in the gospel."

16 As He was going along the Sea of Galilee, He saw Simon and Andrew, the brother of Simon, casting a net in the sea; for they were fishermen. **17** And Jesus said to them, "Follow Me, and I will have you become fishers of people." **18** Immediately they left their nets and followed Him. **19** And going on a little farther, He saw James the son of Zebedee, and his brother John, who were also in the boat mending the nets. **20** Immediately He called them; and they left their father Zebedee in the boat with the hired men, and went away to follow Him.

21 They *went into Capernaum; and immediately on the Sabbath *Jesus* entered the synagogue and *began* to teach. **22** And they were amazed at His teaching; for He was teaching them as *one* having authority, and not as the scribes. **23** Just then there was a man in their synagogue with an unclean spirit; and he cried out, **24** saying, "What business do you have with us, Jesus ¹of Nazareth? Have You come to destroy us? I know who You are: the Holy One of God!" **25** And Jesus rebuked him, saying, "Be quiet, and come out of him!" **26** After throwing him into convulsions and crying out with a loud voice, the unclean spirit came out of him. **27** And they were all amazed, so they debated among themselves, saying, "What is this? A new teaching with authority! He commands even the unclean spirits, and they obey Him." **28** Immediately the news about Him spread everywhere into all the surrounding region of Galilee.

Crowds Healed

29 And immediately after they left the synagogue, they entered the house of Simon and Andrew, with James and John. **30** Now Simon's mother-in-law was lying sick with a fever; and they immediately *spoke to Jesus about her. **31** And He came to her and raised her up, taking *her by* the hand, and the fever left her, and she served them.

32 Now when evening came, after the sun had set, they *began* bringing to Him all who were ill and those who were demon-possessed. **33** And the whole city had gathered at the door. **34** And He healed many who were

---

ill with various diseases, and cast out many demons; and He would not permit the demons to speak, because they knew who He was.

35 And in the early morning, while it was still dark, Jesus got up, left *the house,* and went away to a secluded place, and prayed there *for a time.* **36** Simon and his companions eagerly searched for Him; **37** and they found Him and *said to Him, "Everyone is looking for You." **38** He *said to them, "Let's go somewhere else to the towns nearby, so that I may also preach there; for this is why I came." **39** And He went into their synagogues preaching throughout Galilee, and casting out the demons.

40 And a man with ¹leprosy *came to Jesus, imploring Him and kneeling down, and saying to Him, "If You are willing, You can make me clean." **41** Moved with compassion, *Jesus* reached out with His hand and touched him, and *said to him, "I am willing; be cleansed." **42** And immediately the leprosy left him, and he was cleansed. **43** And He sternly warned him and immediately sent him away, **44** and He *said to him, "See that you say nothing to anyone; but go, show yourself to the priest and offer for your cleansing what Moses commanded, as a testimony to them." **45** But he went out and began to proclaim it freely and to spread the news around, to such an extent that Jesus could no longer publicly enter a city, but stayed out in unpopulated areas; and they were coming to Him from everywhere.

The Paralyzed Man Healed

2 When *Jesus* came back to Capernaum a few days later, it was heard that He was at home. **2** And many were gathered together, so that there was no longer space, not even near the door; and He was speaking the word to them. **3** And *some people* *came, bringing to Him a man who was paralyzed, carried by four *men.* **4** And when they were unable to get to Him because of the crowd, they removed the roof above Him; and after digging an opening, they let down the pallet on which the paralyzed man was lying. **5** And Jesus, seeing their faith, *said to the paralyzed man, "Son, your sins are forgiven." **6** But some of the scribes were sitting there and

---

1:40 ¹I.e., leprosy or a serious, unspecified disease, and so throughout the ch; see Lev 13

thinking *it* over in their hearts, **7** "Why does this man speak that way? He is blaspheming! Who can forgive sins except God alone?" **8** Immediately Jesus, aware in His spirit that they were thinking that way within themselves, *said to them, "Why are you thinking about these things in your hearts? **9** Which is easier, to say to the paralyzed man, 'Your sins are forgiven'; or to say, 'Get up, and pick up your pallet and walk'? **10** But so that you may know that the Son of Man has authority on earth to forgive sins"—He *said to the paralyzed man, **11** "I say to you, get up, pick up your pallet, and go home." **12** And he got up and immediately picked up the pallet and went out in the sight of everyone, so that they were all amazed and were glorifying God, saying, "We have never seen *anything* like this!"

13 And He went out again by the seashore; and all the people were coming to Him, and He was teaching them.

Levi (Matthew) Called

14 As He passed by, He saw Levi the *son* of Alphaeus sitting in the tax office, and He *said to him, "Follow Me!" And he got up and followed Him.

15 And it *happened that He was reclining *at the table* in his house, and many tax collectors and sinners were dining with Jesus and His disciples; for there were many *of them,* and they were following Him. **16** When the scribes of the Pharisees saw that He was eating with the sinners and tax collectors, they said to His disciples, "Why is He eating with tax collectors and sinners?" **17** And hearing *this,* Jesus *said to them, "*It is* not those who are healthy who need a physician, but those who are sick; I did not come to call the righteous, but sinners."

18 John's disciples and the Pharisees were fasting; and they *came and *said to Him, "Why do John's disciples and the disciples of the Pharisees fast, but Your disciples do not fast?" **19** And Jesus said to them, "While the groom is with them, the attendants of the groom cannot fast, can they? As long as they have the groom with them, they cannot fast. **20** But the days will come when the groom is taken away from them, and then they will fast, on that day.

21 "No one sews a patch of unshrunk cloth on an old garment; otherwise, the patch pulls away from it, the

new from the old, and a worse tear results. ²² And no one
puts new wine into old wineskins; otherwise the wine
will burst the skins, and the wine is lost and the skins *as
well;* but *one puts* new wine into fresh wineskins."

Question of the Sabbath

²³ And it happened that He was passing through the
grainfields on the Sabbath, and His disciples began to
make their way *along* while picking the heads *of grain.*
²⁴ The Pharisees were saying to Him, "Look, why are
they doing what is not lawful on the Sabbath?" ²⁵ And He
*said to them, "Have you never read what David did
when he was in need and he and his companions
became hungry; ²⁶ how he entered the house of God in
the time of Abiathar *the* high priest, and ate the consecrated bread, which is not lawful for *anyone* to eat
except the priests, and he also gave it to those who were
with him?" ²⁷ Jesus said to them, "The Sabbath was made
for man, and not man for the Sabbath. ²⁸ So the Son of
Man is Lord, even of the Sabbath."

Jesus Heals on the Sabbath

3 He entered a synagogue again; and a man was there
whose hand was withered. ² And they were watching
Him closely *to see* if He would heal him on the Sabbath,
so that they might accuse Him. ³ He *said to the man
with the withered hand, "Get up and come forward!"
⁴ And He *said to them, "Is it lawful to do good on the
Sabbath or to do harm, to save a life or to kill?" But they
kept silent. ⁵ After looking around at them with anger,
grieved at their hardness of heart, He *said to the man,
"Stretch out your hand." And he stretched it out, and
his hand was restored. ⁶ The Pharisees went out and
immediately *began* conspiring with the Herodians
against Him, *as to* how they might put Him to death.

⁷ Jesus withdrew to the sea with His disciples; and a
large multitude from Galilee followed, and *also* from
Judea, ⁸ and from Jerusalem, and from Idumea, and beyond the Jordan, and the vicinity of Tyre and Sidon, a
great number of people heard about everything that He
was doing and came to Him. ⁹ And He told His disciples
to see that a boat would be ready for Him because of
the masses, so that they would not crowd Him; ¹⁰ for He
had healed many, with the result that all those who had

diseases pushed in around Him in order to touch Him. ¹¹ And whenever the unclean spirits saw Him, they would fall down before Him and shout, "You are the Son of God!" ¹² And He strongly warned them not to reveal who He was.

The Twelve Are Chosen

¹³ And He *went up on the mountain and *summoned those whom He Himself wanted, and they came to Him. ¹⁴ And He appointed twelve, so that they would be with Him and that He *could* send them out to preach, ¹⁵ and to have authority to cast out the demons. ¹⁶ And He appointed the twelve: Simon (to whom He gave the name Peter), ¹⁷ James the *son* of Zebedee and John the brother of James (to them He gave the name Boanerges, which means, "Sons of Thunder"); ¹⁸ and Andrew, Philip, Bartholomew, Matthew, Thomas, James the son of Alphaeus, Thaddaeus, and Simon the Zealot; ¹⁹ and Judas Iscariot, who also betrayed Him.

²⁰ And He *came home, and the crowd *gathered again, to such an extent that they could not even eat a meal. ²¹ And when His own people heard *about this,* they came out to take custody of Him; for they were saying, "He has lost His senses." ²² The scribes who came down from Jerusalem were saying, "He is possessed by Beelzebul," and "He casts out the demons by the ruler of the demons." ²³ And *so* He called them to Himself and *began* speaking to them in parables: "How can Satan cast out Satan? ²⁴ And if a kingdom is divided against itself, that kingdom cannot stand. ²⁵ If a house is divided against itself, that house will not be able to stand. ²⁶ And if Satan has risen up against himself and is divided, he cannot stand, but he is finished! ²⁷ But no one can enter the strong man's house and plunder his property unless he first ties up the strong man, and then he will plunder his house.

²⁸ "Truly I say to you, all sins will be forgiven the sons *and daughters* of men, and whatever blasphemies they commit; ²⁹ but whoever blasphemes against the Holy Spirit never has forgiveness, but is guilty of an eternal sin"— ³⁰ because they were saying, "He has an unclean spirit."

³¹ Then His mother and His brothers *came, and while standing outside they sent *word* to Him, calling *for* Him.

32 And a crowd was sitting around Him, and they *said to Him, "Behold, Your mother and Your brothers are outside looking for You." **33** Answering them, He *said, "Who are My mother and My brothers?" **34** And looking around at those who were sitting around Him, He *said, "Here are My mother and My brothers! **35** For whoever does the will of God, this is My brother, and sister, and mother."

Parable of the Sower and Soils

4 Again He began to teach by the sea. And such a very large crowd gathered to Him that He got into a boat on the sea and sat down; and the whole crowd was by the sea on the land. **2** And He was teaching them many things in parables, and was saying to them in His teaching, **3** "Listen *to this!* Behold, the sower went out to sow; **4** as he was sowing, some *seed* fell beside the road, and the birds came and ate it up. **5** Other *seed* fell on the rocky *ground* where it did not have much soil; and immediately it sprang up because it had no depth of soil. **6** And when the sun had risen, it was scorched; and because it had no root, it withered away. **7** Other *seed* fell among the thorns, and the thorns came up and choked it, and it yielded no crop. **8** Other *seeds* fell into the good soil, and as they grew up and increased, they yielded a crop and produced thirty, sixty, and a hundred *times as much.*" **9** And He was saying, "He who has ears to hear, let him hear."

10 As soon as He was alone, His followers, along with the twelve *disciples, began* asking Him *about* the parables. **11** And He was saying to them, "To you has been given the mystery of the kingdom of God, but for those who are outside, everything comes in parables, **12** so that WHILE SEEING THEY MAY SEE, AND NOT PERCEIVE, AND WHILE HEARING, THEY MAY HEAR, AND NOT UNDERSTAND, OTHERWISE THEY MIGHT RETURN AND IT WOULD BE FORGIVEN THEM."

Explanation of the Parable

13 And He *said to them, "Do you not understand this parable? How will you understand all the parables? **14** The sower sows the word. **15** These are the ones who are beside the road where the word is sown; and when they hear, immediately Satan comes and takes away the word which has been sown in them. **16** And in a similar way these are the ones sown *with seed* on the rocky *places*, who, when they hear the word, immediately receive it with joy; **17** and *yet* they have no *firm* root in themselves, but are *only* temporary; then, when affliction or persecution occurs because of the word, immediately they fall away. **18** And others are the ones sown *with seed* among the thorns; these are the ones who have heard the word, **19** but the worries of the world, and the deceitfulness of wealth, and the desires for other things enter and choke the word, and it becomes unfruitful. **20** And those are the ones sown *with seed* on the good soil; and they hear the word and accept *it* and bear fruit, thirty, sixty, and a hundred *times as much.*"

21 And He was saying to them, "A lamp is not brought to be put under a basket, or under a bed, is it? Is it not *brought* to be put on the lampstand? **22** For nothing is hidden, except to be revealed; nor has *anything* been secret, but that it would come to light. **23** If anyone has ears to hear, let him hear." **24** And He was saying to them, "Take care what you listen to. By your standard of measure it will be measured to you; and *more* will be given you besides. **25** For whoever has, to him *more* will be given; and whoever does not have, even what he has will be taken away from him."

Parable of the Seed

26 And He was saying, "The kingdom of God is like a man who casts seed upon the soil; **27** and he goes to bed at night and gets up daily, and the seed sprouts and grows—how, he himself does not know. **28** The soil produces crops by itself; first the stalk, then the head, then the mature grain in the head. **29** Now when the crop permits, he immediately puts in the sickle, because the harvest has come."

Parable of the Mustard Seed

30 And He was saying, "How shall we picture the kingdom of God, or by what parable shall we present it? **31** *It is* like a mustard seed, which, when sown upon the soil, though it is the smallest of all the seeds that are upon the soil, **32** yet when it is sown, it grows up and becomes larger than all the garden plants, and forms large branches, with the result that THE BIRDS OF THE SKY can NEST UNDER its shade."

33 And with many such parables He was speaking the word to them, so far as they were able to understand *it;* 34 and He did not speak to them without a parable; but He was explaining everything privately to His own disciples.

Jesus Stills the Sea

35 On that day, when evening came, He *said to them, "Let's go over to the other side." 36 After dismissing the crowd, they *took Him along with them in the boat, just as He was; and other boats were with Him. 37 And a fierce gale of wind *developed, and the waves were breaking over the boat so much that the boat was already filling *with water.* 38 And *yet Jesus* Himself was in the stern, asleep on the cushion; and they *woke Him and *said to Him, "Teacher, do You not care that we are perishing?" 39 And He got up and rebuked the wind and said to the sea, "Hush, be still." And the wind died down and it became perfectly calm. 40 And He said to them, "Why are you afraid? Do you still have no faith?" 41 They became very much afraid and said to one another, "Who, then, is this, that even the wind and the sea obey Him?"

The Demon-possessed Man Cured

5 They came to the other side of the sea, into the region of the Gerasenes. 2 When He got out of the boat, immediately a man from the tombs with an unclean spirit met Him. 3 He lived among the tombs; and no one was able to bind him anymore, not even with a chain, 4 because he had often been bound with shackles and chains, and the chains had been torn apart by him and the shackles broken in pieces; and no one was strong enough to subdue him. 5 Constantly, night and day, he was screaming among the tombs and in the mountains, and cutting himself with stones. 6 Seeing Jesus from a distance, he ran up and bowed down before Him; 7 and shouting with a loud voice, he *said, "What business do You have with me, Jesus, Son of the Most High God? I implore You by God, do not torment me!" 8 For He had *already* been saying to him, "Come out of the man, you unclean spirit!" 9 And He was asking him, "What is your name?" And he *said to Him, "My name is Legion, for we are many." 10 And he begged Him earnestly not to send them out of the region. 11 Now there was a large

herd of pigs feeding nearby on the mountain. 12 And *the demons* begged Him, saying, "Send us into the pigs so that we may enter them." 13 *Jesus* gave them permission. And coming out, the unclean spirits entered the pigs; and the herd rushed down the steep bank into the sea, about two thousand *of them;* and they were drowned in the sea.

14 Their herdsmen ran away and reported *it* in the city and in the countryside. And *the people* came to see what it was that had happened. 15 And *then* they *came to Jesus and *saw the man who had been demon-possessed sitting down, clothed and in his right mind, the *very* man who had *previously* had the "legion"; and they became frightened. 16 Those who had seen *it* described to them how it had happened to the demon-possessed man, and *all* about the pigs. 17 And they began to beg Him to leave their region. 18 And as He was getting into the boat, the man who had been demon-possessed was begging Him that he might accompany Him. 19 And He did not let him, but He *said to him, "Go home to your people and report to them what great things the Lord has done for you, and *how* He had mercy on you." 20 And he went away and began to proclaim in Decapolis what great things Jesus had done for him; and everyone was amazed.

Miracles and Healing

21 When Jesus had crossed over again in the boat to the other side, a large crowd gathered around Him; and He stayed by the seashore. 22 And one of the synagogue officials, named Jairus, *came, and upon seeing Him, *fell at His feet 23 and *pleaded with Him earnestly, saying, "My little daughter is at the point of death; *please* come and lay Your hands on her, so that she will get well and live." 24 And He went off with him; and a large crowd was following Him and pressing in on Him.

25 A woman who had had a hemorrhage for twelve years, 26 and had endured much at the hands of many physicians, and had spent all that she had and was not helped at all, but instead had become worse— 27 after hearing about Jesus, she came up in the crowd behind *Him* and touched His cloak. 28 For she had been saying *to herself,* "If I just touch His garments, I will get well." 29 And immediately the flow of her blood was dried up;

and she felt in her body that she was healed of her disease. 30 And immediately Jesus, perceiving in Himself that power from Him had gone out, turned around in the crowd and said, "Who touched My garments?" 31 And His disciples said to Him, "You see the crowd pressing in on You, and You say, 'Who touched Me?' " 32 And He looked around to see the woman who had done this. 33 But the woman, fearing and trembling, aware of what had happened to her, came and fell down before Him and told Him the whole truth. 34 And He said to her, "Daughter, your faith has made you well; go in peace and be cured of your disease."

35 While He was still speaking, *people* *came from *the house of* the synagogue official, saying, "Your daughter has died; why bother the Teacher further?" 36 But Jesus, overhearing what was being spoken, *said to the synagogue official, "Do not be afraid, only believe." 37 And He allowed no one to accompany Him except Peter, James, and John the brother of James. 38 They *came to the house of the synagogue official, and He *saw a commotion, and *people* loudly weeping and wailing. 39 And after entering, He *said to them, "Why are you making a commotion and weeping? The child has not died, but is asleep." 40 And they *began* laughing at Him. But putting them all outside, He *took along the child's father and mother and His own companions, and *entered *the room* where the child was *in bed.* 41 And taking the child by the hand, He *said to her, "Talitha, kum!" (which translated means, "Little girl, I say to you, get up!"). 42 And immediately the girl got up and *began* to walk, for she was twelve years old. And immediately they were completely astonished. 43 And He gave them strict orders that no one was to know about this, and He told *them* to have *something* given her to eat.

Teaching at Nazareth

6 Jesus went out from there and *came into His hometown; and His disciples *followed Him. 2 And when the Sabbath came, He began to teach in the synagogue; and the many listeners were astonished, saying, "Where did this man *learn* these things, and what is *this* wisdom that has been given to Him, and such miracles as these performed by His hands? 3 Is this not the carpenter, the son of Mary and brother of James, Joses, Judas, and

Simon? And are His sisters not here with us?" And they took offense at Him. **4** Jesus said to them, "A prophet is not dishonored except in his hometown and among his *own* relatives, and in his *own* household." **5** And He could not do any miracle there except that He laid His hands on a few sick people and healed *them.* **6** And He was amazed at their unbelief.

And He was going around the villages, teaching.

The Twelve Sent Out

7 And He *summoned the twelve and began to send them out in pairs, and gave them authority over the unclean spirits; **8** and He instructed them that they were to take nothing for *their* journey, except a mere staff—no bread, no bag, no money in their belt—**9** but *to* wear sandals; and *He added,* "Do not wear two [1]tunics." **10** And He said to them, "Wherever you enter a house, stay there until you leave town. **11** Any place that does not receive you or listen to you, as you go out from there, shake the dust off the soles of your feet as a testimony against them." **12** And they went out and preached that *people* are to repent. **13** And they were casting out many demons and were anointing with oil many sick people and healing them.

John's Fate Recalled

14 And King Herod heard *about it,* for His name had become well known; and *people* were saying, "John the Baptist has risen from the dead, and that is why these miraculous powers are at work in Him." **15** But others were saying, "He is Elijah." And others were saying, "*He is* a prophet, like one of the prophets *of old.*" **16** But when Herod heard *about it,* he kept saying, "John, whom I beheaded, has risen!"

17 For Herod himself had sent *men* and had John arrested and bound in prison on account of Herodias, the wife of his brother Philip, because he had married her. **18** For John had been saying to Herod, "It is not lawful for you to have your brother's wife." **19** And Herodias held a grudge against him and wanted to put him to death, and could not *do so;* **20** for Herod was afraid of John, knowing that he was a righteous and holy man, and he had been

---

6:9 [1] A long shirt worn next to the skin

protecting him. And when he heard him, he was very perplexed; and *yet* he used to enjoy listening to him.

21 An opportune day came when Herod, on his birthday, held a banquet for his nobles and military commanders, and the leading people of Galilee; 22 and when the daughter of Herodias herself came in and danced, she pleased Herod and his dinner guests; and the king said to the girl, "Ask me for whatever you want, and I will give it to you." 23 And he swore to her, "Whatever you ask of me, I will give *it* to you, up to half of my kingdom." 24 And she went out and said to her mother, "What shall I ask for?" And she said, "The head of John the Baptist." 25 Immediately she came in a hurry to the king and asked, saying, "I want you to give me at once the head of John the Baptist on a platter." 26 And although the king was very sorry, because of his oaths and his dinner guests, he was unwilling to refuse her. 27 Immediately the king sent an executioner and commanded *him* to bring *back* his head. And he went and beheaded him in the prison, 28 and brought his head on a platter, and gave it to the girl; and the girl gave it to her mother. 29 When his disciples heard *about this,* they came and carried away his body, and laid it in a tomb.

30 The apostles *gathered together with Jesus; and they reported to Him all that they had done and taught. 31 And He *said to them, "Come *away* by yourselves to a secluded place and rest a little while." (For there were many *people* coming and going, and they did not even have time to eat.) 32 And they went away in the boat to a secluded place by themselves.

Five Thousand Men Fed

33 *The people* saw them going, and many recognized *them* and ran there together on foot from all the cities, and got there ahead of them. 34 When Jesus went ashore, He saw a large crowd, and He felt compassion for them because they were like sheep without a shepherd; and He began to teach them many things. 35 And when it was already late, His disciples came up to Him and said, "This place is secluded and it is already late; 36 send them away so that they may go into the surrounding country-side and villages and buy themselves something to eat." 37 But He answered them, "You give them *something* to eat!" And they *said to Him, "Shall we go and spend two

hundred [1]denarii on bread, and give *it* to them to eat?"
38 But He *said to them, "How many loaves do you have?
Go look!" And when they found out, they *said, "Five,
and two fish." **39** And He ordered them all to recline by
groups on the green grass. **40** They reclined in groups of
hundreds and fifties. **41** And He took the five loaves and
the two fish, and looking up toward heaven, He blessed
the food and broke the loaves and He gave *them* to the
disciples *again and again* to set before them; and He
divided the two fish among them all. **42** And they all ate
and were satisfied; **43** and they picked up twelve full
baskets of the broken pieces *of bread,* and of the fish.
44 There were five thousand [1]men who ate the loaves.

Jesus Walks on the Water

45 And immediately Jesus had His disciples get into the
boat and go ahead of *Him* to the other side, to Bethsaida,
while He Himself *dismissed the crowd. **46** And after saying goodbye to them, He left for the mountain to pray.
47 When it was evening, the boat was in the middle of
the sea, and He was alone on the land. **48** Seeing them
straining at the oars—for the wind was against them—at
about the fourth watch of the night, He *came to them,
walking on the sea; and He intended to pass by them.
49 But when they saw Him walking on the sea, they
thought that it was a ghost, and they cried out; **50** for they
all saw Him and were terrified. But immediately He
spoke with them and *said to them, "Take courage; it is
I, do not be afraid." **51** Then He got into the boat with
them, and the wind stopped; and they were utterly
astonished, **52** for they had not gained any insight from
the incident of the loaves, but their hearts were
hardened.

Healing at Gennesaret

53 When they had crossed over they came to land at
Gennesaret, and moored at the shore. **54** And when they
got out of the boat, immediately *the people* recognized
Him, **55** and ran about that entire country and began
carrying here and there on their pallets those who were
sick, to wherever they heard He was. **56** And wherever

6:37 [1] The denarius was a day's wages for a laborer   6:44 [1] I.e., 5,000
men plus women and children, cf. Matt 14:21

He entered villages, or cities, or a countryside, they were laying the sick in the marketplaces and imploring Him that they might just touch the fringe of His cloak; and all who touched it were being healed.

Followers of Tradition

7 The Pharisees and some of the scribes *gathered to Him after they came from Jerusalem, 2 and saw that some of His disciples were eating their bread with unholy hands, that is, unwashed. 3 (For the Pharisees and all the *other* Jews do not eat unless they carefully wash their hands, *thereby* holding firmly to the tradition of the elders; 4 and *when they come* from the marketplace, they do not eat unless they completely cleanse themselves; and there are many other things which they have received *as traditions* to firmly hold, *such as* the washing of cups, pitchers, and copper pots.) 5 And the Pharisees and the scribes *asked Him, "Why do Your disciples not walk in accordance with the tradition of the elders, but eat their bread with unholy hands?" 6 But He said to them, "Rightly did Isaiah prophesy about you hypocrites, as it is written:

'THIS PEOPLE HONORS ME WITH THEIR LIPS,
   BUT THEIR HEART IS FAR AWAY FROM ME.
7   'AND IN VAIN DO THEY WORSHIP ME,
   TEACHING AS DOCTRINES THE COMMANDMENTS OF MEN.'

8 Neglecting the commandment of God, you hold to the tradition of men."

9 He was also saying to them, "You are experts at setting aside the commandment of God in order to keep your tradition. 10 For Moses said, 'HONOR YOUR FATHER AND YOUR MOTHER'; and, 'THE ONE WHO SPEAKS EVIL OF FATHER OR MOTHER, IS CERTAINLY TO BE PUT TO DEATH'; 11 but you say, 'If a person says to his father or his mother, whatever I have that would help you is Corban (that is, 'given *to God*),' 12 you no longer allow him to do anything for *his* father or *his* mother; 13 *thereby* invalidating the word of God by your tradition which you have handed down; and you do many things such as that."

The Heart of Man

14 After He called the crowd to Him again, He *began*

7:11 1 Lit a *gift;* i.e., an offering

saying to them, "Listen to Me, all of you, and understand: [15] there is nothing outside the person which can defile him if it goes into him; but the things which come out of the person are what defile the person[1]."

[17] And when He *later* entered a house, away from the crowd, His disciples asked Him about the parable. [18] And He *said to them, "Are you so lacking in understanding as well? Do you not understand that whatever goes into the person from outside cannot defile him, [19] because it does not go into his heart, but into his stomach, and [1] is eliminated?" (*Thereby* He declared all foods clean.) [20] And He was saying, "That which comes out of the person, that *is what* defiles the person. [21] For from within, out of the hearts of people, come the evil thoughts, *acts of* sexual immorality, thefts, murders, *acts of* adultery, [22] deeds of greed, wickedness, deceit, indecent behavior, envy, slander, pride, *and* foolishness. [23] All these evil things come from within and defile the person."

The Syrophoenician Woman

[24] Now Jesus got up and went from there to the region of Tyre[1]. And when He had entered a house, He wanted no one to know *about it;* and *yet* He could not escape notice. [25] But after hearing about Him, a woman whose little daughter had an unclean spirit immediately came and fell at His feet. [26] Now the woman was a [1] Gentile, of Syrophoenician descent. And she *repeatedly* asked Him to cast the demon out of her daughter. [27] And He was saying to her, "Let the children be satisfied first, for it is not good to take the children's bread and throw it to the dogs." [28] But she answered and *said to Him, "Yes, Lord, *but* even the dogs under the table feed on the children's crumbs." [29] And He said to her, "Because of this answer, go; the demon has gone out of your daughter." [30] And after going back to her home, she found the child lying on the bed, and the demon gone.

[31] Again He left the region of Tyre and came through Sidon to the Sea of Galilee, within the region of Decapolis. [32] And they *brought to Him one who was

---

7:15 [1] Late mss add, as v 16: *If anyone has ears to hear, let him hear.*
7:19 [1] Lit *goes out into the latrine*   7:24 [1] Two early mss add *and Sidon*   7:26 [1] Lit *Greek*

deaf and had difficulty speaking, and they *begged Him to lay His hand on him. 33 And *Jesus* took him aside from the crowd, by himself, and put His fingers in his ears, and after spitting, He touched his tongue *with the saliva;* 34 and looking up to heaven with a deep sigh, He *said to him, "Ephphatha!" that is, "Be opened!" 35 And his ears were opened, and the impediment of his tongue was removed, and he *began* speaking plainly. 36 And He gave them orders not to tell anyone; but the more He ordered them, the more widely they continued to proclaim *it.* 37 And they were utterly astonished, saying, "He has done all things well; He makes even those who are deaf hear, and those who are unable to talk, speak."

Four Thousand Men Fed

8 In those days, when there was again a large crowd and they had nothing to eat, *Jesus* summoned His disciples and *said to them, 2 "I feel compassion for the people because they have remained with Me for three days already and have nothing to eat. 3 And if I send them away hungry to their homes, they will faint on the way; and some of them have come from a great distance." 4 And His disciples replied to Him, "Where will anyone be able *to find enough* bread here in *this* desolate place to satisfy these people?" 5 And He was asking them, "How many loaves do you have?" And they said, "Seven." 6 And He *directed the people to recline on the ground; and taking the seven loaves, He gave thanks and broke them, and started giving them to His disciples to serve, and they served them to the people. 7 They also had a few small fish; and after He had blessed them, He told *the disciples* to serve these as well. 8 And they ate and were satisfied; and they picked up seven large baskets *full* of what was left over of the broken pieces. 9 About four thousand †men were *there;* and He dismissed them. 10 And immediately He got into the boat with His disciples and came to the region of Dalmanutha.

11 And the Pharisees came out and began to argue with Him, demanding from Him a sign from heaven, to test Him. 12 Sighing deeply in His spirit, He *said, "Why does this generation demand a sign? Truly I say to you, no sign will be given to this generation!" 13 And leaving

---

8:9 †I.e., 4,000 men plus women and children, cf. Matt 15:38

them, He again embarked and went away to the other side.

14 And *the disciples* had forgotten to take bread, and did not have more than one loaf in the boat with them. **15** And He was giving orders to them, saying, "Watch out! Beware of the leaven of the Pharisees, and the leaven of Herod." **16** And they *began* to discuss with one another *the fact* that they had no bread. **17** And Jesus, aware of this, *said to them, "Why are you discussing *the fact* that you have no bread? Do you not yet comprehend or understand? Do you *still* have your heart hardened? **18** HAVING EYES, DO YOU NOT SEE? AND HAVING EARS, DO YOU NOT HEAR? And do you not remember, **19** when I broke the five loaves for the five thousand, how many baskets full of broken pieces you picked up?" They *said to Him, "Twelve." **20** "When *I broke* the seven for the four thousand, how many large baskets full of broken pieces did you pick up?" And they *said to Him, "Seven." **21** And He was saying to them, "Do you not yet understand?"

22 And they *came to Bethsaida. And *some people* *brought a man who was blind to Jesus and *begged Him to touch him. **23** Taking the man who was blind by the hand, He brought him out of the village; and after spitting in his eyes and laying His hands on him, He asked him, "Do you see anything?" **24** And he looked up and said, "I see people, for I see *them* like trees, walking around." **25** Then again He laid His hands on his eyes; and he looked intently and was restored, and *began* to see everything clearly. **26** And He sent him to his home, saying, "Do not even enter the village."

Peter's Confession of Christ

27 Jesus went out, along with His disciples, to the villages of Caesarea Philippi; and on the way He questioned His disciples, saying to them, "Who do people say that I am?" **28** They told Him, saying, "John the Baptist; and others *say* Elijah; and others, one of the prophets." **29** And He *continued* questioning them: "But who do you say that I am?" Peter answered and *said to Him, "You are the Christ." **30** And He warned them to tell no one about Him.

31 And He began to teach them that the Son of Man must suffer many things and be rejected by the elders and the chief priests and the scribes, and be killed, and after three days rise *from the dead.* 32 And He was stating the matter plainly. And Peter took Him aside and began to rebuke Him. 33 But turning around and seeing His disciples, He rebuked Peter and *said, "Get behind Me, Satan; for you are not setting your mind on God's purposes, but on man's."

34 And He summoned the crowd together with His disciples, and said to them, "If anyone wants to come after Me, he must deny himself, take up his cross, and follow Me. 35 For whoever wants to save his life will lose it, but whoever loses his life for My sake and the gospel's will save it. 36 For what does it benefit a person to gain the whole world, and forfeit his soul? 37 For what could a person give in exchange for his soul? 38 For whoever is ashamed of Me and My words in this adulterous and sinful generation, the Son of Man will also be ashamed of him when He comes in the glory of His Father with the holy angels."

The Transfiguration

9 And Jesus was saying to them, "Truly I say to you, there are some of those who are standing here who will not taste death until they see the kingdom of God when it has come with power."

2 And six days later Jesus *took with Him Peter, James, and John, and *brought them up on a high mountain by themselves. And He was transfigured before them; 3 and His garments became radiant and exceedingly white, as no launderer on earth can whiten them. 4 And Elijah appeared to them along with Moses; and they were talking with Jesus. 5 Peter responded and *said to Jesus, "Rabbi, it is good that we are here; let's make three tabernacles, one for You, one for Moses, and one for Elijah." 6 For he did not know how to reply; for they became terrified. 7 Then a cloud formed, overshadowing them, and a voice came out of the cloud: "This is My beloved Son; listen to Him!" 8 And suddenly they looked around and saw no one with them anymore, except Jesus alone.

9 As they were coming down from the mountain, He gave them orders not to relate to anyone what they had seen, until the Son of Man rose from the dead. 10 They seized upon that statement, discussing with one another what rising from the dead meant. 11 And they asked Him,

saying, *"Why is it* that the scribes say that Elijah must come first?" **12** And He said to them, "Elijah does come first and he restores all things. And *yet* how is it written of the Son of Man that He will suffer many things and be treated with contempt? **13** But I say to you that Elijah has indeed come, and they did to him whatever they wanted, just as it is written of him."

All Things Possible

14 And when they came *back* to the *other* disciples, they saw a large crowd around them, and *some* scribes arguing with them. **15** Immediately, when the entire crowd saw Him, they were amazed and *began* running up to greet Him. **16** And He asked them, "What are you disputing with them?" **17** And one *person* from the crowd answered Him, "Teacher, I brought You my son, because he has a spirit *that makes him* unable to speak; **18** and whenever it seizes him, it slams him to the ground, and he foams *at the mouth* and grinds his teeth and becomes stiff. And I told Your disciples so that they would cast it out, but they could not *do it.*" **19** And He answered them and *said, "O unbelieving generation, how long shall I be with you? How long shall I put up with you? Bring him to Me!" **20** And they brought the boy to Him. When he saw Him, the spirit immediately threw him into convulsions, and falling to the ground, he *began* rolling around and foaming *at the mouth.* **21** And He asked his father, "How long has this been happening to him?" And he said, "From childhood. **22** It has often thrown him both into the fire and into the water to kill him. But if You can do anything, take pity on us and help us!" **23** But Jesus said to him, " 'If You can?' All things are possible for the one who believes." **24** Immediately the boy's father cried out and said, "I do believe; help my unbelief!" **25** When Jesus saw that a crowd was rapidly gathering, He rebuked the unclean spirit, saying to it, "You mute and deaf spirit, I command you, come out of him and do not enter him again!" **26** And after crying out and throwing him into terrible convulsions, it came out; and *the boy* became so much like a corpse that most *of them* said, "He is dead!" **27** But Jesus took him by the hand and raised him, and he got up. **28** When He came into *the* house, His disciples *began* asking Him privately, *"Why is it* that we could not cast it out?" **29** And He said to them, "This kind cannot come out by anything except prayer."

Death and Resurrection Foretold

30 And from there they went out and *began* to go through Galilee, and He did not want anyone to know *about it.* **31** For He was teaching His disciples and telling them, "The Son of Man is to be handed over to men, and they will kill Him; and when He has been killed, He will rise three days later." **32** But they did not understand *this* statement, and they were afraid to ask Him.

33 They came to Capernaum; and when He was in the house, He *began* to question them: "What were you discussing on the way?" **34** But they kept silent, for on the way they had discussed with one another which *of them was* the greatest. **35** And sitting down, He called the twelve and *said to them, "If anyone wants to be first, he shall be last of all and servant of all." **36** And He took a child and placed him among them, and taking him in His arms, He said to them, **37** "Whoever receives one child like this in My name receives Me; and whoever receives Me does not receive Me, but Him who sent Me."

Dire Warnings

38 John said to Him, "Teacher, we saw someone casting out demons in Your name, and we tried to prevent him because he was not following us." **39** But Jesus said, "Do not hinder him, for there is no one who will perform a miracle in My name, and be able soon *afterward* to speak evil of Me. **40** For the one who is not against us is ¹for us. **41** For whoever gives you a cup of water to drink because of your name as *followers* of Christ, truly I say to you, he shall by no means lose his reward.

42 "Whoever causes one of these little ones who believe in Me to sin, it is better for him if a heavy millstone is hung around his neck and he is thrown into the sea. **43** And if your hand causes you to sin, cut it off; it is better for you to enter life maimed, than, having your two hands, to go into ¹hell, into the unquenchable fire.² **45** And if your foot is causing you to sin, cut it off; it is

---

9:40 ¹Or *on our side*   9:43 ¹Gr *Gehenna*   9:43 ²Late mss repeat v 48 here as v 44

better for you to enter life without a foot, than, having your two feet, to be thrown into hell.[1] [47] And if your eye is causing you to sin, throw it away; it is better for you to enter the kingdom of God with one eye, than, having two eyes, to be thrown into hell, [48] where THEIR WORM DOES NOT DIE, AND THE FIRE IS NOT EXTINGUISHED. [49] For everyone will be salted with fire. [50] Salt is good; but if the salt becomes unsalty, with what will you make it salty *again?* Have salt in yourselves, and be at peace with one another."

Jesus' Teaching about Divorce

10 Setting out from there, *Jesus* *went to the region of Judea and beyond the Jordan; crowds *gathered to Him again, and, as He was accustomed, He once more *began* to teach them.

[2] And *some* Pharisees came up to Jesus, testing Him, and *began* questioning Him whether it was lawful for a man to divorce *his* wife. [3] And He answered and said to them, "What did Moses command you?" [4] They said, "Moses permitted *a man* to write a certificate of divorce and send *his wife* away." [5] But Jesus said to them, "Because of your hardness of heart he wrote you this commandment. [6] But from the beginning of creation, *God* CREATED THEM MALE AND FEMALE. [7] FOR THIS REASON A MAN SHALL LEAVE HIS FATHER AND MOTHER[1], [8] AND THE TWO SHALL BECOME ONE FLESH; so they are no longer two, but one flesh. [9] Therefore, what God has joined together, no person is to separate."

[10] And in the house the disciples again *began* questioning Him about this. [11] And He *said to them, "Whoever divorces his wife and marries another woman commits adultery against her; [12] and if she herself divorces her husband and marries another man, she is committing adultery."

Jesus Blesses Little Children

[13] And they were bringing children to Him so that He would touch them; but the disciples rebuked them. [14] But when Jesus saw *this,* He was indignant and said to them,

---

"Allow the children to come to Me; do not forbid them, for the kingdom of God belongs to such as these. **15** Truly I say to you, whoever does not receive the kingdom of God like a child will not enter it at all." **16** And He took them in His arms and *began* blessing them, laying His hands on them.

The Rich Young Ruler

17 As He was setting out on a journey, a man ran up to Him and knelt before Him, and asked Him, "Good Teacher, what shall I do so that I may inherit eternal life?" **18** But Jesus said to him, "Why do you call Me good? No one is good except God alone. **19** You know the commandments: 'DO NOT MURDER, DO NOT COMMIT ADULTERY, DO NOT STEAL, DO NOT GIVE FALSE TESTIMONY, Do not defraud, HONOR YOUR FATHER AND MOTHER.'" **20** And he said to Him, "Teacher, I have kept all these things from my youth." **21** Looking at him, Jesus showed love to him and said to him, "One thing you lack: go and sell all you possess and give to the poor, and you will have treasure in heaven; and come, follow Me." **22** But he was deeply dismayed by these words, and he went away grieving; for he was one who owned much property.

23 And Jesus, looking around, *said to His disciples, "How hard it will be for those who are wealthy to enter the kingdom of God!" **24** And the disciples were amazed at His words. But Jesus responded again and *said to them, "Children, how hard it is to enter the kingdom of God! **25** It is easier for a camel to go through the eye of a needle than for a rich person to enter the kingdom of God." **26** And they were even more astonished, and said to Him, "Then who can be saved?" **27** Looking at them, Jesus *said, "With people it is impossible, but not with God; for all things are possible with God."

28 Peter began to say to Him, "Behold, we have left everything and have followed You." **29** Jesus said, "Truly I say to you, there is no one who has left house or brothers or sisters or mother or father or children or farms, for My sake and for the gospel's sake, **30** but that he will receive a hundred times as much now in the present age, houses and brothers and sisters and mothers and children and farms, along with persecutions; and in the age to come, eternal life. **31** But many *who are* first will be last, and the last, first."

Jesus' Sufferings Foretold

32 Now they were on the road going up to Jerusalem, and Jesus was walking on ahead of them; and they were amazed, and those who followed were fearful. And again He took the twelve aside and began to tell them what was going to happen to Him, **33** *saying*, "Behold, we are going up to Jerusalem, and the Son of Man will be handed over to the chief priests and the scribes; and they will condemn Him to death and will hand Him over to the Gentiles. **34** And they will mock Him and spit on Him, and flog Him and kill *Him;* and three days later He will rise *from the dead.*"

35 James and John, the two sons of Zebedee, *came up to Jesus, saying to Him, "Teacher, we want You to do for us whatever we ask of You." **36** And He said to them, "What do you want Me to do for you?" **37** They said to Him, "Grant that we may sit, one on Your right and one on *Your* left, in Your glory." **38** But Jesus said to them, "You do not know what you are asking. Are you able to drink the cup that I drink, or to be baptized with the baptism with which I am baptized?" **39** They said to Him, "We are able." And Jesus said to them, "The cup that I drink you shall drink; and you shall be baptized with the baptism with which I am baptized. **40** But to sit on My right or on *My* left is not Mine to give; but *it is* for those for whom it has been prepared."

41 Hearing *this*, the *other* ten began to feel indignant with James and John. **42** Calling them to Himself, Jesus *said to them, "You know that those who are recognized as rulers of the Gentiles domineer over them; and their people in high position exercise authority over them. **43** But it is not this way among you; rather, whoever wants to become prominent among you shall be your servant; **44** and whoever wants to be first among you shall be slave of all. **45** For even the Son of Man did not come to be served, but to serve, and to give His life as a ransom for many."

Bartimaeus Receives His Sight

46 Then they *came to Jericho. And *later,* as He was leaving Jericho with His disciples and a large crowd, a beggar who was blind *named* Bartimaeus, the son of Timaeus, was sitting by the road. **47** And when he heard that it was Jesus the Nazarene, he began to cry out and

say, "Jesus, Son of David, have mercy on me!" **48** Many
were sternly telling him to be quiet, but he kept crying
out all the more, "Son of David, have mercy on me!"
49 And Jesus stopped and said, "Call him *here.*" So they
*called the man who was blind, saying to him, "Take
courage, stand up! He is calling for you." **50** And throwing
off his cloak, he jumped up and came to Jesus. **51** And
replying to him, Jesus said, "What do you want Me to do
for you?" And the man who was blind said to Him,
"*¹Rabboni, I want* to regain my sight!" **52** And Jesus said
to him, "Go; your faith has made you well." And
immediately he regained his sight and *began* following
Him on the road.

The Triumphal Entry

11 And as they *approached Jerusalem, at Bethphage
and Bethany, near the Mount of Olives, He *sent
two of His disciples, **2** and *said to them, "Go into the
village opposite you, and immediately as you enter it you
will find a colt tied *there,* on which no one has ever sat;
untie it and bring *it here.* **3** And if anyone says to you,
'Why are you doing this?' say, 'The Lord has need of it';
and immediately he will send it back here." **4** They went
away and found a colt tied at the door, outside in the
street; and they *untied it. **5** And some of the bystanders
were saying to them, "What are you doing, untying the
colt?" **6** And they told them just as Jesus had said, and
they gave them permission. **7** They *brought the colt to
Jesus and *put their cloaks on it; and He sat on it. **8** And
many people spread their cloaks on the road, and others
spread leafy branches which they had cut from the fields.
9 And those who went in front and those who followed
were shouting:

"Hosanna!
BLESSED IS HE WHO COMES IN THE NAME OF THE LORD;

10   Blessed *is* the coming kingdom of our father David;
Hosanna in the highest!"

11 And *Jesus* entered Jerusalem *and came* into the temple *area;* and after looking around at everything, He left
for Bethany with the twelve, since it was already late.

12 On the next day, when they had left Bethany,
He became hungry. **13** Seeing from a distance a fig tree in

---

leaf, He went *to see* if perhaps He would find anything on it; and when He came to it, He found nothing but leaves, for it was not the season for figs. **14** And He said to it, "May no one ever eat fruit from you again!" And His disciples were listening.

Jesus Drives Money Changers from the Temple

15 Then they *came to Jerusalem. And He entered the temple *area* and began to drive out those who were selling and buying on the temple *grounds,* and He overturned the tables of the money changers and the seats of those who were selling doves; **16** and He would not allow anyone to carry merchandise through the temple *grounds.* **17** And He *began* to teach and say to them, "Is it not written: 'MY HOUSE WILL BE CALLED A HOUSE OF PRAYER FOR ALL THE NATIONS'? But you have made it a DEN OF ROBBERS." **18** And the chief priests and the scribes heard *this,* and they *began* seeking how to put Him to death; for they were afraid of Him, because all the crowd was astonished at His teaching.

19 And whenever evening came, they would leave the city.

20 As they were passing by in the morning, they saw the fig tree withered from the roots *up.* **21** And being reminded, Peter *said to Him, "Rabbi, look, the fig tree that You cursed has withered." **22** And Jesus answered and *said to them, "Have faith in God. **23** Truly I say to you, whoever says to this mountain, 'Be taken up and thrown into the sea,' and does not doubt in his heart, but believes that what he says is going to happen, it will be *granted* to him. **24** Therefore, I say to you, all things for which you pray and ask, believe that you have received them, and they will be *granted* to you. **25** And whenever you stand praying, forgive, if you have anything against anyone, so that your Father who is in heaven will also forgive you for your offenses. **26** [¹But if you do not forgive, neither will your Father who is in heaven forgive your offenses."]

Jesus' Authority Questioned

27 And they *came again to Jerusalem. And as He was walking in the temple *area,* the chief priests, the scribes,

---

11:26 ¹Early mss do not contain this v

and the elders *came to Him, 28 and *began* saying to Him, "By what authority are You doing these things, or who gave You this authority to do these things?" 29 But Jesus said to them, "I will ask you one question, and you answer Me, and *then* I will tell you by what authority I do these things. 30 Was the baptism of John from heaven, or from men? Answer Me." 31 And they *began* considering *the implications* among themselves, saying, "If we say, 'From heaven,' He will say, 'Then why did you not believe him?' 32 But should we say, 'From men'?"—they were afraid of the people, for they all considered John to have been a real prophet. 33 Answering Jesus, they *said, "We do not know." And Jesus *said to them, "Neither am I telling you by what authority I do these things."

Parable of the Vine-growers

12 And He began to speak to them in parables: "A man planted a vineyard and put a fence around it, and dug a vat under the wine press and built a tower, and leased it to ¹vine-growers and went on a journey. 2 And at the *harvest* time he sent a slave to the vine-growers, in order to receive *his share* of the produce of the vineyard from the vine-growers. 3 And they took him, and beat him, and sent him away empty-handed. 4 And again he sent them another slave, and they wounded him in the head, and treated him shamefully. 5 And he sent another, and that one they killed; and *so with* many others, beating some and killing others. 6 He had one more *man to send,* a beloved son; he sent him to them last *of all,* saying, 'They will respect my son.' 7 But those vine-growers said to one another, 'This is the heir; come, let's kill him, and the inheritance will be ours!' 8 And they took him and killed him, and threw him out of the vineyard. 9 What will the owner of the vineyard do? He will come and put the vine-growers to death, and give the vineyard to others. 10 Have you not even read this Scripture:

¹A STONE WHICH THE BUILDERS REJECTED,
THIS HAS BECOME THE CHIEF CORNERSTONE;
11   THIS CAME ABOUT FROM THE LORD,

12:1 ¹Or *tenant farmers,* also vv 2, 7, 9

AND IT IS MARVELOUS IN OUR EYES'?"

12 And they were seeking to seize Him, and *yet* they feared the people, for they understood that He told the parable against them. And *so* they left Him and went away.

Jesus Answers the Pharisees, Sadducees, and Scribes

13 Then they *sent some of the Pharisees and Herodians to Him in order to trap Him in a statement. **14** They came and *said to Him, "Teacher, we know that You are truthful and do not care what anyone thinks; for You are not partial to anyone, but You teach the way of God in truth. Is it permissible to pay a ¹poll-tax to Caesar, or not? **15** Are we to pay, or not pay?" But He, knowing their hypocrisy, said to them, "Why are you testing Me? Bring Me a ¹denarius to look at." **16** And they brought *one.* And He *said to them, "Whose image and inscription is this?" And they said to Him, "Caesar's." **17** And Jesus said to them, "Pay to Caesar the things that are Caesar's, and to God the things that are God's." And they were utterly amazed at Him.

18 *Some* Sadducees (who say that there is no resurrection) *came to Jesus, and *began* questioning Him, saying, **19** "Teacher, Moses wrote for us that if a man's brother dies and leaves behind a wife and does not leave a child, his brother is to marry the wife and raise up children for his brother. **20** There were seven brothers; and the first took a wife, and died leaving no children. **21** The second one married her, and died leaving behind no children; and the third likewise; **22** and *so* the seven *together* left no children. Last of all the woman also died. **23** In the resurrection, which one's wife will she be? For *each of* the seven had her as *his* wife." **24** Jesus said to them, "Is this not the reason you are mistaken, that you do not understand the Scriptures nor the power of God? **25** For when they rise from the dead, they neither marry nor are given in marriage, but are like angels in heaven. **26** But regarding the fact that the dead rise, have you not read in the book of Moses, in *the passage about* the *burning* bush, how God spoke to him, saying, 'I AM THE

12:14 ¹I.e., a tax on each person in the census   12:15 ¹The denarius was a day's wages for a laborer

GOD OF ABRAHAM, THE GOD OF ISAAC, AND THE GOD OF JACOB'? 27 He is not the God of the dead, but of the living; you are greatly mistaken."

28 One of the scribes came up and heard them arguing, and recognizing that He had answered them well, asked Him, "What commandment is the foremost of all?" 29 Jesus answered, "The foremost is, 'HEAR, ISRAEL! THE LORD IS OUR GOD, THE LORD IS ONE; 30 AND YOU SHALL LOVE THE LORD YOUR GOD WITH ALL YOUR HEART, AND WITH ALL YOUR SOUL, AND WITH ALL YOUR MIND, AND WITH ALL YOUR STRENGTH.' 31 The second is this: 'YOU SHALL LOVE YOUR NEIGHBOR AS YOURSELF.' There is no other commandment greater than these." 32 And the scribe said to Him, "Well *said*, Teacher; You have truly stated that HE IS ONE, AND THERE IS NO OTHER BESIDES HIM; 33 and to love Him with all the heart, and with all the understanding, and with all the strength, and to love one's neighbor as oneself, is much more than all the burnt offerings and sacrifices." 34 When Jesus saw that he had answered intelligently, He said to him, "You are not far from the kingdom of God." And *then,* no one dared any longer to question Him.

35 And Jesus responded and *began* saying, as He taught in the temple *area,* "How *is it that* the scribes say that the Christ is the son of David? 36 David himself said in the Holy Spirit,

'THE LORD SAID TO MY LORD,

"SIT AT MY RIGHT HAND,

UNTIL I PUT YOUR ENEMIES UNDER YOUR FEET."'

37 David himself calls Him 'Lord'; so in what sense is He his son?" And the large crowd enjoyed listening to Him.

38 And in His teaching He was saying: "Beware of the scribes who like to walk around in long robes, and *like* personal greetings in the marketplaces, 39 and seats of honor in the synagogues, and places of honor at banquets, 40 who devour widows' houses, and for appearance's sake offer long prayers. These will receive all the more condemnation."

The Widow's Coins

41 And *Jesus* sat down opposite the treasury, and *began* watching how the people were putting money into the treasury; and many rich people were putting in large amounts. 42 And a poor widow came and put in

two ⁷lepta coins, which amount to a ²quadrans. **43** Calling
His disciples to Him, He said to them, "Truly I say to
you, this poor widow put in more than all the con-
tributors to the treasury; **44** for they all put in out of their
surplus, but she, out of her poverty, put in all she owned,
all she had to live on."

Things to Come

13 As He was going out of the temple, one of His disciples *said to Him, "Teacher, look! What
wonderful stones and what wonderful buildings!" **2** And
Jesus said to him, "Do you see these great buildings? Not
one stone will be left upon another, which will not be
torn down."

3 As He was sitting on the Mount of Olives opposite
the temple, Peter, James, John, and Andrew were
questioning Him privately, **4** "Tell us, when will these
things come about, and what *will be* the sign when all
these things are going to be fulfilled?" **5** And Jesus began
to say to them, "See to it that no one misleads you.
6 Many will come in My name, saying, 'I am *He!*' and
they will mislead many. **7** When you hear of wars and
rumors of wars, do not be alarmed; *those things* must
take place; but *that is* not yet the end. **8** For nation will
rise up against nation, and kingdom against kingdom;
there will be earthquakes in various places; there will
also be famines. These things are *only* the beginning of
birth pains.

9 "But be on your guard; for they will hand you over to
the courts, and you will be flogged in *the* synagogues,
and you will stand before governors and kings for My
sake, as a testimony to them. **10** And the gospel must first
be preached to all the nations. **11** And when they arrest
you and hand you over, do not worry beforehand about
what you are to say, but say whatever is given you at that
time; for you are not the ones speaking, but *it is* the
Holy Spirit. **12** And brother will betray brother to death,
and a father *his* child; and children will rise up
against parents and have them put to death. **13** And you
will be hated by everyone because of My name, but it is

12:42¹ The smallest Greek copper coin, about 1/128 of a laborer's
daily wage   12:42² A small Roman copper coin, worth about 1/64 of
a laborer's daily wage

the one who has endured to the end who will be saved.

14 "Now when you see the ABOMINATION OF DESOLATION standing where it should not be—let the [1]reader understand—then those who are in Judea must flee to the mountains. **15** Whoever is on the housetop must not go down, nor go in to get anything out of his house. **16** And whoever is in the field must not turn back to get his cloak. **17** But woe to those women who are pregnant, and to those who are nursing babies in those days! **18** Moreover, pray that it will not happen in winter. **19** For those days will be such a *time of* tribulation as has not occurred since the beginning of the creation which God created until now, and never will *again.* **20** And if the Lord had not shortened *those* days, no life would have been saved; but for the sake of the elect, whom He chose, He shortened the days. **21** And then if anyone says to you, 'Look, here is the Christ'; *or,* 'Look, there *He is*'; do not believe *it;* **22** for false christs and false prophets will arise, and will provide signs and wonders, in order to mislead, if possible, the elect. **23** But beware; I have told you everything in advance.

The Return of Christ

24 "But in those days, after that tribulation, THE SUN WILL BE DARKENED AND THE MOON WILL NOT GIVE ITS LIGHT, **25** AND THE STARS WILL BE FALLING from heaven, and the powers that are in the heavens will be shaken. **26** And then they will see THE SON OF MAN COMING IN CLOUDS with great power and glory. **27** And then He will send forth the angels, and will gather together His elect from the four winds, from the end of the earth to the end of heaven.

28 "Now learn the parable from the fig tree: as soon as its branch has become tender and sprouts its leaves, you know that summer is near. **29** So you too, when you see these things happening, recognize that He is near, *right* at the door. **30** Truly I say to you, this generation will not pass away until all these things take place. **31** Heaven and earth will pass away, but My words will not pass away. **32** But about that day or hour no one knows, not even the angels in heaven, nor the Son, but the Father *alone.*

13:14 [1] I.e., of the book of Daniel

33 "Watch out, stay alert; for you do not know when the *appointed* time is. **34** *It is* like a man away on a journey, *who* upon leaving his house and putting his slaves in charge, *assigning* to each one his task, also commanded the doorkeeper to stay alert. **35** Therefore, stay alert—for you do not know when the master of the house is coming, whether in the evening, at midnight, or when the rooster crows, or in the morning— **36** so that he does not come suddenly and find you asleep. **37** What I say to you I say to all: 'Stay alert!' "

Death Plot and Anointing

14 Now the Passover and *Festival of* Unleavened Bread were two days away; and the chief priests and the scribes were seeking how to arrest Him covertly and kill *Him;* **2** for they were saying, "Not during the festival, otherwise there will be a riot of the people."

3 While He was in Bethany at the home of Simon ¹the Leper, He was reclining *at the table,* and a woman came with an alabaster vial of very expensive perfume of pure ²nard. She broke the vial and poured *the perfume* over His head. **4** But there were some indignantly *remarking* to one another, "Why has this perfume been wasted? **5** For this perfume could have been sold for over three hundred ¹denarii, and *the money* given to the poor." And they were scolding her. **6** But Jesus said, "Leave her alone! Why are you bothering her? She has done a good deed for Me. **7** For you always have the poor with you, and whenever you want, you can do good to them; but you do not always have Me. **8** She has done what she could; she has anointed My body beforehand for the burial. **9** Truly I say to you, wherever the gospel is preached in the entire world, what this woman has done will also be told in memory of her."

10 Then Judas Iscariot, who was one of the twelve, went off to the chief priests in order to betray Him to them. **11** They were delighted when they heard *this,* and promised to give him money. And he *began* seeking how to betray Him at an opportune time.

14:3 ¹I.e., a nickname; the man no doubt was cured   14:3 ²An aromatic oil extracted from an East Indian plant   14:5 ¹The denarius was a day's wages for a laborer

The Last Passover

12 On the first day of ¹Unleavened Bread, when the Passover *lamb* was being sacrificed, His disciples *said to Him, "Where do You want us to go and prepare for You to eat the Passover?" **13** And He *sent two of His disciples and *said to them, "Go into the city, and a man carrying a pitcher of water will meet you; follow him; **14** and wherever he enters, say to the owner of the house, 'The Teacher says, "Where is My guest room in which I may eat the Passover with My disciples?" ' **15** And he himself will show you a large upstairs room furnished *and* ready; prepare for us there." **16** The disciples left and came to the city, and found *everything* just as He had told them; and they prepared the Passover.

17 When it was evening He *came with the twelve. **18** And as they were reclining *at the table* and eating, Jesus said, "Truly I say to you that one of you will betray Me—one who is eating with Me." **19** They began to be grieved and to say to Him one by one, "Surely not I?" **20** But He said to them, "*It is* one of the twelve, the one who dips *bread* with Me in the bowl. **21** For the Son of Man is going away just as it is written about Him; but woe to that man by whom the Son of Man is betrayed! *It would have been* good for that man if he had not been born."

The Lord's Supper

22 While they were eating, He took *some* bread, and after a blessing He broke *it,* and gave *it* to them, and said, "Take *it;* this is My body." **23** And when He had taken a cup *and* given thanks, He gave *it* to them, and they all drank from it. **24** And He said to them, "This is My blood of the covenant, which is being poured out for many. **25** Truly I say to you, I will not drink of the fruit of the vine again, until that day when I drink it, new, in the kingdom of God."

26 And after singing a hymn, they went out to the Mount of Olives.

27 And Jesus *said to them, "You will all ¹fall away, because it is written: 'I WILL STRIKE THE SHEPHERD, AND THE SHEEP WILL BE SCATTERED.' **28** But after I am raised, I will go ahead of you to Galilee." **29** But Peter said to Him, "Even

---

14:12 ¹I.e., Passover week   14:27 ¹I.e., have a lapse in faith

if they all fall away, yet I *will* not!" **30** And Jesus *said to him, "Truly I say to you, that this very night, before a rooster crows twice, you yourself will deny Me three times." **31** But Peter *repeatedly* said insistently, *"Even* if I have to die with You, I will not deny You!" And they all were saying the same thing as well.

Jesus in Gethsemane

32 They *came to a place named Gethsemane; and He *said to His disciples, "Sit here until I have prayed." **33** And He *took with Him Peter, James, and John, and began to be very distressed and troubled. **34** And He *said to them, "My soul is deeply grieved, to the point of death; remain here and keep watch." **35** And He went a little beyond *them,* and fell to the ground and *began* praying that if it were possible, the hour might pass Him by. **36** And He was saying, "Abba! Father! All things are possible for You; remove this cup from Me; yet not what I will, but what You *will."* **37** And He *came and *found them sleeping, and *said to Peter, "Simon, are you asleep? Could you not keep watch for one hour? **38** Keep watching and praying, so that you will not come into temptation; the spirit is willing, but the flesh is weak." **39** And again He went away and prayed, saying the same words. **40** And again He came and found them sleeping, for their eyes were heavy; and they did not know what to say in reply to Him. **41** And He *came the third time, and *said to them, "Are you still sleeping and resting? That is enough. The hour has come; behold, the Son of Man is being betrayed into the hands of sinners. **42** Get up, let's go; behold, the one who is betraying Me is near!"

Betrayal and Arrest

43 And immediately, while He was still speaking, Judas, one of the twelve, *came up, accompanied by a crowd with swords and clubs *who were* from the chief priests, the scribes, and the elders. **44** Now he who was betraying Him had given them a signal, saying, "Whomever I kiss, He is the one; arrest Him and lead Him away under guard." **45** And after coming, Judas immediately went to Him and *said, "Rabbi!" and kissed Him. **46** And they laid hands on Him and arrested Him. **47** But one of those who stood by drew his sword, and struck the slave of the high priest and cut off his ear. **48** And Jesus said to them, "Have you come out with swords and clubs to arrest Me, as *you would* against a man inciting a revolt? **49** Every day I was with you within the temple *grounds* teaching, and you did not arrest Me; but *this has taken place* so that the Scriptures will be fulfilled." **50** And His disciples all left Him and fled.

51 A young man was following Him, wearing *nothing but* a linen sheet over *his* naked *body;* and they *seized him. **52** But he pulled free of the linen sheet and escaped naked.

Jesus before His Accusers

53 They led Jesus away to the high priest; and all the chief priests, the elders, and the scribes *gathered together. **54** And Peter had followed Him at a distance, right into the courtyard of the high priest; and he was sitting with the officers and warming himself at the fire. **55** Now the chief priests and the entire ¹Council were trying to obtain testimony against Jesus to put Him to death, and they were not finding any. **56** For many people were giving false testimony against Him, and *so* their testimonies were not consistent. **57** And *then* some stood up and *began* giving false testimony against Him, saying, **58** "We heard Him say, 'I will destroy this temple that was made by hands, and in three days I will build another, made without hands.' " **59** And not even in this respect was their testimony consistent. **60** And *then* the high priest stood up *and came* forward and questioned Jesus, saying, "Do You not offer any answer for what these men are testifying against You?" **61** But He kept silent and did not offer any answer. Again the high priest was questioning Him, and *said to Him, "Are You the Christ, the Son of ¹the Blessed *One?*" **62** And Jesus said, "I am; and you shall see the Son of Man sitting at the right hand of power, and coming with the clouds of heaven." **63** Tearing his clothes, the high priest *said, "What further need do we have of witnesses? **64** You have heard the blasphemy; how does it seem to you?" And they all condemned Him as deserving of death. **65** And some began to spit on Him, and to blindfold Him, and to

---

14:55 ¹Or *Sanhedrin*   14:61 ¹A common way for the Jewish leaders to refer to God

beat Him with their fists and say to Him, "Prophesy!"
Then the officers took custody of Him and slapped Him
in the face.

Peter's Denials

66 And while Peter was below in the courtyard, one of
the slave women of the high priest *came, **67** and seeing
Peter warming himself, she looked at him and *said,
"You were with Jesus the Nazarene as well." **68** But he
denied *it,* saying, "I neither know nor understand what
you are talking about." And he went out onto the porch.[1]
69 The slave woman saw him, and began once more to
say to the bystanders, "This man is *one* of them!" **70** But
again he denied it. And after a little while the bystanders
were again saying to Peter, "You really are *one* of them,
for you are a Galilean as well." **71** But he began to curse
himself and to swear, "I do not know this man of whom
you speak!" **72** And immediately a rooster crowed a second time. And Peter remembered how Jesus had made
the remark to him, "Before a rooster crows twice, you
will deny Me three times." And he hurried on and *began
to* weep.

Jesus before Pilate

15 Early in the morning the chief priests with the elders, scribes, and the entire [1]Council immediately
held a consultation; and they bound Jesus and led Him
away, and turned Him over to Pilate. **2** Pilate questioned
Him: "*So* You are the King of the Jews?" And He
answered him, "*It is as* you say." **3** And the chief priests
started accusing Him of many things. **4** But Pilate
questioned Him again, saying, "Do You offer nothing in
answer? See how many charges they are bringing against
You!" **5** But Jesus said nothing further in answer, so Pilate
was amazed.

6 Now at *the Passover* Feast he used to release for
them *any* one prisoner whom they requested. **7** And the
one named Barabbas had been imprisoned with the
rebels who had committed murder in the revolt. **8** And
the crowd went up and began asking *Pilate to do* as he
had been accustomed to do for them. **9** Pilate answered
them, saying, "Do you want me to release for you the

14:68 [1]Later mss add *and a rooster crowed*   15:1 [1]Or *Sanhedrin*

King of the Jews?" **10** For he was aware that the chief priests had handed Him over because of envy. **11** But the chief priests stirred up the crowd *to ask him* to release Barabbas for them instead. **12** And responding again, Pilate said to them, "Then what shall I do with Him whom you call the King of the Jews?" **13** They shouted back, "Crucify Him!" **14** But Pilate said to them, "Why, what evil has He done?" But they shouted all the more, "Crucify Him!" **15** Intent on satisfying the crowd, Pilate released Barabbas for them, and after having Jesus flogged, he handed Him over to be crucified.

Jesus Is Mocked

16 Now the soldiers took Him away into the palace (that is, the Praetorium), and they *called together the whole *Roman* 'cohort. **17** And they *dressed Him in purple, and after twisting together a crown of thorns, they put it on Him; **18** and they began saluting Him: "Hail, King of the Jews!" **19** And they *repeatedly* beat His head with a reed and spit on Him, and kneeling, they bowed down before Him. **20** And after they had mocked Him, they took the purple *cloak* off Him and put His *own* garments on Him. And they *led Him out to crucify Him.

21 And they *compelled a passer-by coming from the country, Simon of Cyrene (the father of Alexander and Rufus), to carry His cross.

The Crucifixion

22 Then they *brought Him to the place Golgotha, which is translated, Place of a Skull. **23** And they tried to give Him wine mixed with myrrh; but He did not take *it*. **24** And they *crucified Him, and *divided up His garments among themselves, casting lots for them *to decide* what each man would take. **25** Now it was the 'third hour when they crucified Him. **26** The inscription of the charge against Him read, "THE KING OF THE JEWS."

27 And they *crucified two 'rebels with Him, one on His right and one on His left. **2 29** Those passing by were hurling abuse at Him, shaking their heads and saying,

---

15:16 **1** Normally 600 men (the number varied)
15:25 **1** I.e., 9 a.m.   15:27 **1** Or *robbers*   15:27 **2** Late mss add the following as v 28: *And the Scripture was fulfilled which says, "And He was counted with wrongdoers."*

"Ha! You who *are going to* destroy the temple and rebuild it in three days, 30 save Yourself by coming down from the cross!" 31 In the same way the chief priests also, along with the scribes, were mocking *Him* among themselves and saying, "He saved others; He cannot save Himself! 32 Let *this* Christ, the King of Israel, come down now from the cross, so that we may see and believe!" Those who were crucified with Him were also insulting Him.

33 When the ¹sixth hour came, darkness fell over the whole land until the ²ninth hour. 34 At the ¹ninth hour Jesus cried out with a loud voice, "ELOI, ELOI, LEMA SABAKTANEI?" which is translated, "MY GOD, MY GOD, WHY HAVE YOU FORSAKEN ME?" 35 And when some of the bystanders heard *Him,* they *began* saying, "Look! He is calling for Elijah!" 36 And someone ran and filled a sponge with sour wine, put it on a reed, and gave Him a drink, saying, "Let us see if Elijah comes to take Him down." 37 But Jesus let out a loud cry, and died. 38 And the veil of the temple was torn in two from top to bottom. 39 And when the centurion, who was standing right in front of Him, saw that He died in this way, he said, "Truly this man was the Son of God!"

40 Now there were also *some* women watching from a distance, among whom *were* Mary Magdalene, Mary the mother of James the Less and Joses, and Salome. 41 When He was in Galilee, they used to follow Him and serve Him; and *there were* many other women who came up with Him to Jerusalem.

Jesus Is Buried

42 When evening had already come, since it was the preparation day, that is, the day before the Sabbath, 43 Joseph of Arimathea came, a prominent member of the Council, who was himself also waiting for the kingdom of God; and he gathered up courage and went in before Pilate, and asked for the body of Jesus. 44 Now Pilate wondered if He was dead by this time, and summoning the centurion, he questioned him as to whether He was already dead. 45 And after learning this from the centurion, he granted the body to Joseph. 46 Joseph bought a linen cloth, took Him down, wrapped Him in

---

15:33 ¹I.e., noon   15:33 ²I.e., 3 p.m.   15:34 ¹I.e., 3 p.m.

the linen cloth, and laid Him in a tomb which had been cut out in the rock; and he rolled a stone against the entrance of the tomb. [47] Mary Magdalene and Mary the *mother* of Joses were watching *to see* where He was laid.

The Resurrection

16 When the Sabbath was over, Mary Magdalene, Mary the *mother* of James, and Salome bought spices so that they might come and anoint Him. [2] And very early on the first day of the week, they *came to the tomb when the sun had risen. [3] They were saying to one another, "Who will roll away the stone from the entrance of the tomb for us?" [4] And looking up, they *noticed that the stone had been rolled away; for it was extremely large. [5] And entering the tomb, they saw a young man sitting at the right, wearing a white robe; and they were amazed. [6] But he *said to them, "Do not be amazed; you are looking for Jesus the Nazarene, who has been crucified. He has risen; He is not here; see, *here is* the place where they laid Him. [7] But go, tell His disciples and Peter, 'He is going ahead of you to Galilee; there you will see Him, just as He told you.'" [8] And they went out and fled from the tomb, for trembling and astonishment had gripped them; and they said nothing to anyone, for they were afraid.

[9] [['Now after He had risen early on the first day of the week, He first appeared to Mary Magdalene, from whom He had cast out seven demons. [10] She went and reported to those who had been with Him, while they were mourning and weeping. [11] And when they heard that He was alive and had been seen by her, they refused to believe *it.*

[12] Now after that, He appeared in a different form to two of them while they were walking along on their way to the country. [13] And they went away and reported it to the rest, but they did not believe them, either.

The Disciples Commissioned

[14] Later He appeared to the eleven *disciples* themselves as they were reclining *at the table;* and He reprimanded them for their unbelief and hardness of heart, because they had not believed those who had seen

---

Him after He had risen *from the dead.* [15] And He said to them, "Go into all the world and preach the gospel to all creation. [16] The one who has believed and has been baptized will be saved; but the one who has not believed will be condemned. [17] These signs will accompany those who have believed: in My name they will cast out demons, they will speak with new tongues; [18] they will pick up serpents, and if they drink any deadly *poison,* it will not harm them; they will lay hands on the sick, and they will recover."

[19] So then, when the Lord Jesus had spoken to them, He was received up into heaven and sat down at the right hand of God. [20] And they went out and preached everywhere, while the Lord worked with *them,* and confirmed the word by the signs that followed.]]

[[[1]*And they promptly reported all these instructions to Peter and his companions. And after that, Jesus Himself also sent out through them from east to west the sacred and imperishable proclamation of eternal salvation.*]]

16:20 [1] A few late mss and ancient versions contain this paragraph, usually after v 8; a few have it at the end of the ch

The Gospel According to
LUKE

Introduction

1 Since many have undertaken to compile an account of the things accomplished among us, 2 just as they were handed down to us from the beginning were eyewitnesses and servants of the ¹word, 3 it seemed fitting to me as well, having investigated everything carefully from the beginning, to write *it out* for you in an orderly sequence, most excellent Theophilus; 4 so that you may know the exact truth about the things you have been taught.

John the Baptist's Birth Foretold

5 In the days of Herod, king of Judea, there was a priest named Zechariah, of the division of ¹Abijah; and he had a wife ²from the daughters of Aaron, and her name was Elizabeth. 6 They were both righteous in the sight of God, walking blamelessly in all the commandments and requirements of the Lord. 7 And *yet* they had no child, because Elizabeth was infertile, and they were both advanced in years.

8 Now it happened *that* while he was performing his priestly service before God in the appointed order of his division, 9 according to the custom of the priestly office, he was chosen by lot to enter the temple of the Lord and burn incense. 10 And the whole multitude of the people were in prayer outside at the hour of the incense offering. 11 Now an angel of the Lord appeared to him, standing to the right of the altar of incense. 12 Zechariah was troubled when he saw *the angel,* and fear gripped him. 13 But the angel said to him, "Do not be afraid, Zechariah, for your prayer has been heard, and your wife Elizabeth will bear you a son, and you shall name him John. 14 You will have joy and gladness, and many will rejoice over his birth. 15 For he will be great in the sight of the Lord; and he will drink no wine or liquor, and he will be filled with the Holy Spirit while still in his mother's womb. 16 And he will turn many of the sons of

---

1:2 ¹I.e., gospel   1:5 ¹Gr *Abia*   1:5 ²I.e., of priestly descent

Israel back to the Lord their God. **17** And *it is* he *who* will go *as a forerunner* before Him in the spirit and power of Elijah, TO TURN THE HEARTS OF FATHERS BACK TO *THEIR* CHILDREN, and the disobedient to the attitude of the righteous, to make ready a people prepared for the Lord."

18 Zechariah said to the angel, "How will I know this? For I am an old man, and my wife is advanced in her years." **19** The angel answered and said to him, "I am Gabriel, who stands in the presence of God, and I was sent to speak to you and to bring you this good news. **20** And behold, you will be silent and unable to speak until the day when these things take place, because you did not believe my words, which will be fulfilled at their proper time."

21 And *meanwhile* the people were waiting for Zechariah, and were wondering at his delay in the temple. **22** But when he came out, he was unable to speak to them; and they realized that he had seen a vision in the temple, and he *repeatedly* made signs to them, and remained speechless. **23** When the days of his priestly service were concluded, he went back home.

24 Now after these days his wife Elizabeth became pregnant, and she kept herself in seclusion for five months, saying, **25** "This is the way the Lord has dealt with me in the days when He looked *with favor* upon *me,* to take away my disgrace among people."

Jesus' Birth Foretold

26 Now in the sixth month the angel Gabriel was sent from God to a city in Galilee named Nazareth, **27** to a virgin ʹbetrothed to a man whose name was Joseph, of the descendants of David; and the virgin's name was Mary. **28** And coming in, he said to her, "Greetings, favored one! The Lord *is* with you." **29** But she was very perplexed at *this* statement, and was pondering what kind of greeting this was. **30** And the angel said to her, "Do not be afraid, Mary, for you have found favor with God. **31** And behold, you will conceive in your womb and give birth to a son, and you shall name Him Jesus. **32** He will be great and will be called the Son of the Most High; and the Lord God will give Him the throne of His father

---

1:27 ¹ Unlike engagement, a betrothed couple was considered married, but did not yet live together

David; 33 and He will reign over the house of Jacob forever, and His kingdom will have no end." 34 But Mary said to the angel, "How will this be, since I am a virgin?" 35 The angel answered and said to her, "The Holy Spirit will come upon you, and the power of the Most High will overshadow you; for that reason also the holy Child will be called the Son of God. 36 And behold, even your relative Elizabeth herself has conceived a son in her old age, and she who was called infertile is now in her sixth month. 37 For nothing will be impossible with God." 38 And Mary said, "Behold, the Lord's bond-servant; may it be done to me according to your word." And the angel departed from her.

Mary Visits Elizabeth

39 Now at this time Mary set out and went in a hurry to the hill country, to a city of Judah, 40 and she entered the house of Zechariah and greeted Elizabeth. 41 When Elizabeth heard Mary's greeting, the baby leaped in her womb, and Elizabeth was filled with the Holy Spirit. 42 And she cried out with a loud voice and said, "Blessed *are* you among women, and blessed *is* the fruit of your womb! 43 And how has it happened to me that the mother of my Lord would come to me? 44 For behold, when the sound of your greeting reached my ears, the baby leaped in my womb for joy. 45 And blessed *is* she who believed that there would be a fulfillment of what had been spoken to her by the Lord."

Mary's Song: The Magnificat

46 And Mary said:
"My soul exalts the Lord,
47 And my spirit has rejoiced in God my Savior.
48 "For He has had regard for the humble state of His
       bond-servant;
   For behold, from now *on* all generations will call me
       blessed.
49 "For the Mighty One has done great things for me;
   And holy is His name.
50 "And His mercy is to generation after generation
   Toward those who fear Him.
51 "He has done mighty deeds with His arm;
   He has scattered *those who were* proud in the
       thoughts of their hearts.

⁵² "He has brought down rulers from *their* thrones,
    And has exalted those who were humble.
⁵³ "He has filled the hungry with good things,
    And sent the rich away empty-handed.
⁵⁴ "He has given help to His servant Israel,
    In remembrance of His mercy,
⁵⁵ Just as He spoke to our fathers,
    To Abraham and his descendants forever."

⁵⁶ Mary stayed with her about three months, and *then* returned to her home.

John the Baptist Is Born

⁵⁷ Now the time had come for Elizabeth to give birth, and she gave birth to a son. ⁵⁸ Her neighbors and her relatives heard that the Lord had displayed His great mercy toward her; and they were rejoicing with her.

⁵⁹ And it happened that on the eighth day they came to circumcise the child, and they were going to call him Zechariah, after his father. ⁶⁰ And *yet* his mother responded and said, "No indeed; but he shall be called John." ⁶¹ And they said to her, "There is no one among your relatives who is called by this name." ⁶² And they ¹made signs to his father, as to what he wanted him called. ⁶³ And he asked for a tablet and wrote as follows, "His name is John." And they were all amazed. ⁶⁴ And at once his mouth was opened and his tongue *freed,* and he *began* speaking in praise of God. ⁶⁵ And fear came on all those who lived around them; and all these matters were being talked about in the entire hill country of Judea. ⁶⁶ All who heard *them* kept *them* in mind, saying, "What then will this child *turn out to* be?" For indeed the hand of the Lord was with him.

Zechariah's Prophecy

⁶⁷ And his father Zechariah was filled with the Holy Spirit and prophesied, saying:
⁶⁸ "Blessed *be* the Lord God of Israel,
    For He has visited *us* and accomplished redemption
      for His people,
⁶⁹ And has raised up a horn of salvation for us
    In the house of His servant David—

1:62 ¹I.e., gestured or nodded

70 Just as He spoke by the mouth of His holy prophets
    from ancient times—
71 Salvation from our enemies,
    And from the hand of all who hate us;
72 To show mercy to our fathers,
    And to remember His holy covenant,
73 *The* oath which He swore to our father Abraham,
74 To grant us that we, being rescued from the hand of
    our enemies,
    Would serve Him without fear,
75 In holiness and righteousness before Him all our
    days.
76 "And you, child, also will be called the prophet of the
    Most High;
    For you will go on before the Lord to prepare His
    ways;
77 To give His people *the* knowledge of salvation
    By the forgiveness of their sins,
78 Because of the tender mercy of our God,
    With which the Sunrise from on high will visit us,
79 To shine on those who sit in darkness and the
    shadow of death,
    To guide our feet into the way of peace."

80 Now the child grew and was becoming strong in
spirit, and he lived in the deserts until the day of his
public appearance to Israel.

Jesus' Birth in Bethlehem

2 Now in those days a decree went out from Caesar
Augustus, that a census be taken of all 'the inhabited
earth. 2 This was the first census taken while 'Quirinius
was governor of Syria. 3 And all *the people* were on their
way to register for the census, each to his own city.
4 Now Joseph also went up from Galilee, from the city of
Nazareth, to Judea, to the city of David which is called
Bethlehem, because he was of the house and family of
David, 5 in order to register along with Mary, who was
'betrothed to him, and was pregnant. 6 While they were
there, the time came for her to give birth. 7 And she
gave birth to her firstborn son; and she wrapped Him in

2:1 'I.e., the Roman Empire   2:2 'Gr *Kyrenios*   2:5 'Unlike
engagement, a betrothed couple was considered married, but did not
yet live together

cloths, and laid Him in a manger, because there was no room for them in the inn.

8 In the same region there were *some* shepherds staying out in the fields and keeping watch over their flock at night. **9** And an angel of the Lord *suddenly* stood near them, and the glory of the Lord shone around them; and they were terribly frightened. **10** And *so* the angel said to them, "Do not be afraid; for behold, I bring you good news of great joy which will be for all the people; **11** for today in the city of David there has been born for you a Savior, who is Christ the Lord. **12** And this *will be* a sign for you: you will find a baby wrapped in cloths and lying in a manger." **13** And suddenly there appeared with the angel a multitude of the heavenly army *of angels* praising God and saying,

14   "Glory to God in the highest,
           And on earth peace among people with whom He is
               pleased."

15 When the angels had departed from them into heaven, the shepherds *began* saying to one another, "Let's go straight to Bethlehem, then, and see this thing that has happened, which the Lord has made known to us." **16** And they came in a hurry and found their way to Mary and Joseph, and the baby as He lay in the manger. **17** When they had seen *Him,* they made known the statement which had been told them about this Child. **18** And all who heard it were amazed about the things which were told them by the shepherds. **19** But Mary treasured all these things, pondering them in her heart. **20** And the shepherds went back, glorifying and praising God for all that they had heard and seen, just as had been told them.

Jesus Presented at the Temple

21 And when eight days were completed so that it was time for His circumcision, He was also named Jesus, the *name* given by the angel before He was conceived in the womb.

22 And when the days for their purification according to the Law of Moses were completed, they brought Him up to Jerusalem to present Him to the Lord **23** (as it is written in the Law of the Lord: "EVERY FIRSTBORN MALE THAT OPENS THE WOMB SHALL BE CALLED HOLY TO THE LORD"), **24** and to offer a sacrifice according to what has been stated in the Law of the Lord: "A PAIR OF TURTLEDOVES OR TWO YOUNG DOVES."

25 And there was a man in Jerusalem whose name was Simeon; and this man was righteous and devout, looking forward to the consolation of Israel; and the Holy Spirit was upon him. **26** And it had been revealed to him by the Holy Spirit that he would not see death before he had seen the Lord's Christ. **27** And he came by the Spirit into the temple; and when the parents brought in the child Jesus, to carry out for Him the custom of the Law, **28** then he took Him in his arms, and blessed God, and said,

29   "Now, Lord, You are letting Your bond-servant depart in peace,
          According to Your word;
30   For my eyes have seen Your salvation,
31   Which You have prepared in the presence of all the peoples:
32   A light for revelation for the Gentiles,
          And the glory of Your people Israel."

33 And His father and mother were amazed at the things which were being said about Him. **34** And Simeon blessed them and said to His mother Mary, "Behold, this *Child* is appointed for the fall and rise of many in Israel, and as a sign to be opposed— **35** and a sword will pierce your own soul—to the end that thoughts from many hearts may be revealed."

36 And there was a prophetess, Anna, the daughter of Phanuel, of the tribe of Asher. She was advanced in years and had lived with *her* husband for seven years after her marriage, **37** and *then* as a widow to the age of eighty-four. She did not leave the temple *grounds,* serving night and day with fasts and prayers. **38** And at that very moment she came up and *began* giving thanks to God, and continued to speak about Him to all those who were looking forward to the redemption of Jerusalem.

Return to Nazareth

39 And when *His parents* had completed everything in accordance with the Law of the Lord, they returned to Galilee, to their own city of Nazareth. **40** Now the Child continued to grow and to become strong, increasing in wisdom; and the favor of God was upon Him.

Visit to Jerusalem

41 His parents went to Jerusalem every year at the
Feast of the Passover. **42** And when He was twelve years
old, they went up *there* according to the custom of the
feast; **43** and as they were returning, after spending the
full number of days *required,* the boy Jesus stayed behind
in Jerusalem, but His parents were unaware *of it.*
44 Instead, they thought that He was *somewhere* in the
caravan, and they went a day's journey; and *then* they
began looking for Him among their relatives and acquaintances. **45** And when they did not find Him, they returned
to Jerusalem, looking for Him. **46** Then, after three days
they found Him in the temple, sitting in the midst of the
teachers, both listening to them and asking them
questions. **47** And all who heard Him were amazed at His
understanding and His answers. **48** When *Joseph and
Mary* saw Him, they were bewildered; and His mother
said to Him, "Son, why have You treated us this way?
Behold, Your father and I have been anxiously looking for
You!" **49** And He said to them, "Why *is it* that you were
looking for Me? Did you not know that I had to be in My
Father's *house?*" **50** And *yet* they on their part did not
understand the statement which He had made to them.
51 And He went down with them and came to Nazareth,
and He continued to be subject to them; and His mother
treasured all *these* things in her heart.

52 And Jesus kept increasing in wisdom and stature,
and in favor with God and people.

John the Baptist Preaches

3 Now in the fifteenth year of the reign of Tiberius
Caesar, when Pontius Pilate was governor of Judea,
and Herod was tetrarch of Galilee and his brother Philip
was tetrarch of the region of Ituraea and Trachonitis, and
Lysanias was tetrarch of Abilene, **2** in the high priesthood
of Annas and Caiaphas, the word of God came to John,
the son of Zechariah, in the wilderness. **3** And he came
into all the region around the Jordan, preaching a
baptism of repentance for the forgiveness of sins; **4** as it is
written in the book of the words of Isaiah the prophet:

"THE VOICE OF ONE CALLING *¹*OUT IN THE WILDERNESS,
'PREPARE THE WAY OF THE LORD,

3:4 ¹ Or *out, Prepare in the wilderness the way*

MAKE HIS PATHS STRAIGHT!
5   'EVERY RAVINE WILL BE FILLED,
     AND EVERY MOUNTAIN AND HILL WILL BE LOWERED;
     THE CROOKED WILL BECOME STRAIGHT,
     AND THE ROUGH ROADS SMOOTH;
6   AND ALL FLESH WILL SEE THE SALVATION OF GOD!' "

7 So he was saying to the crowds who were going out to be baptized by him, "You offspring of vipers, who warned you to flee from the wrath to come? **8** Therefore produce fruits that are consistent with repentance, and do not start saying to yourselves, 'We have Abraham *as our* father,' for I say to you that from these stones God is able to raise up children for Abraham. **9** But indeed the axe is already being laid at the root of the trees; so every tree that does not bear good fruit is cut down and thrown into the fire."

10 And the crowds were questioning him, saying, "Then what are we to do?" **11** And he would answer and say to them, "The one who has two ¹tunics is to share with the one who has none; and the one who has food is to do likewise." **12** Now even tax collectors came to be baptized, and they said to him, "Teacher, what are we to do?" **13** And he said to them, "Collect no more than what you have been ordered to." **14** And soldiers also were questioning him, saying, "What are we to do, we as well?" And he said to them, "Do not extort money from anyone, nor harass *anyone,* and be content with your wages."

15 Now while the people were in a state of expectation and they all were thinking carefully in their hearts about John, whether he himself perhaps was the Christ, **16** John responded to them all, saying, "As for me, I baptize you with water; but He is coming who is mightier than I, and I am not fit to untie the straps of His sandals; He will baptize you with the Holy Spirit and fire. **17** His winnowing fork is in His hand to thoroughly clear His threshing floor, and to gather the wheat into His barn; but He will burn up the chaff with unquenchable fire."

18 So with many other exhortations he preached the gospel to the people. **19** But when Herod the tetrarch was reprimanded by him regarding Herodias, his brother's wife, and regarding all the evil things which Herod had

---

3:11 ¹A long shirt worn next to the skin

done, ²⁰ *Herod* also added this to them all: he locked John up in prison.

Jesus Is Baptized

²¹ Now when all the people were baptized, Jesus also was baptized, and while He was praying, heaven was opened, ²² and the Holy Spirit descended upon Him in bodily form like a dove, and a voice came from heaven: "You are My beloved Son, in You I am well pleased."

Genealogy of Jesus

²³ When He began *His ministry,* Jesus Himself was about thirty years old, being, as was commonly held, the son of Joseph, the son of Eli, ²⁴ the son of Matthat, the son of Levi, the son of Melchi, the son of Jannai, the son of Joseph, ²⁵ the son of Mattathias, the son of Amos, the son of Nahum, the son of Hesli, the son of Naggai, ²⁶ the son of Maath, the son of Mattathias, the son of Semein, the son of Josech, the son of Joda, ²⁷ the son of Joanan, the son of Rhesa, the son of Zerubbabel, the son of Shealtiel, the son of Neri, ²⁸ the son of Melchi, the son of Addi, the son of Cosam, the son of Elmadam, the son of Er, ²⁹ the son of Joshua, the son of Eliezer, the son of Jorim, the son of Matthat, the son of Levi, ³⁰ the son of Simeon, the son of Judah, the son of Joseph, the son of Jonam, the son of Eliakim, ³¹ the son of Melea, the son of Menna, the son of Mattatha, the son of Nathan, the son of David, ³² the son of Jesse, the son of Obed, the son of Boaz, the son of Salmon, the son of Nahshon, ³³ the son of Amminadab, the son of Admin, the son of Ram, the son of Hezron, the son of Perez, the son of Judah, ³⁴ the son of Jacob, the son of Isaac, the son of Abraham, the son of Terah, the son of Nahor, ³⁵ the son of Serug, the son of Reu, the son of Peleg, the son of Heber, the son of Shelah, ³⁶ the son of Cainan, the son of Arphaxad, the son of Shem, the son of Noah, the son of Lamech, ³⁷ the son of Methuselah, the son of Enoch, the son of Jared, the son of Mahalaleel, the son of Cainan, ³⁸ the son of Enosh, the son of Seth, the son of Adam, the son of God.

The Temptation of Jesus

4 Now Jesus, full of the Holy Spirit, returned from the Jordan and was led *around* by the Spirit in the wilderness ² for forty days, being tempted by the devil. And He

ate nothing during those days, and when they had ended, He was hungry. 3 And the devil said to Him, "If You are the Son of God, tell this stone to become bread." 4 And Jesus answered him, "It is written: 'MAN SHALL NOT LIVE ON BREAD ALONE.' "

5 And he led Him up and showed Him all the kingdoms of the world in a moment of time. 6 And the devil said to Him, "I will give You all this domain and its glory, for it has been handed over to me, and I give it to whomever I want. 7 Therefore if You worship before me, it shall all be Yours." 8 Jesus replied to him, "It is written: 'YOU SHALL WORSHIP THE LORD YOUR GOD AND SERVE HIM ONLY.' "

9 And he brought Him into Jerusalem and had Him stand on the pinnacle of the temple, and said to Him, "If You are the Son of God, throw Yourself down from here; 10 for it is written:

'HE WILL GIVE HIS ANGELS ORDERS CONCERNING YOU, TO PRO-
    TECT YOU,'
11 and,

'ON *THEIR* HANDS THEY WILL LIFT YOU UP,
  SO THAT YOU DO NOT STRIKE YOUR FOOT AGAINST A STONE.' "
12 And Jesus answered and said to him, "It has been stated, 'YOU SHALL NOT PUT THE LORD YOUR GOD TO THE TEST.' "

13 And *so* when the devil had finished every temptation, he left Him until an opportune time.

Jesus' Public Ministry

14 And Jesus returned to Galilee in the power of the Spirit, and news about Him spread through all the surrounding region. 15 And He *began* teaching in their synagogues and was praised by all.

16 And He came to Nazareth, where He had been brought up; and as was His custom, He entered the synagogue on the Sabbath, and stood up to read. 17 And the scroll of Isaiah the prophet was handed to Him. And He unrolled the scroll and found the place where it was written:

18 "THE SPIRIT OF THE LORD IS UPON ME,
    BECAUSE HE ANOINTED ME TO BRING GOOD NEWS TO THE
        POOR.
    HE HAS SENT ME TO PROCLAIM RELEASE TO CAPTIVES,
    AND RECOVERY OF SIGHT TO THE BLIND,
    TO SET FREE THOSE WHO ARE OPPRESSED,

19 TO PROCLAIM THE FAVORABLE YEAR OF THE LORD."
20 And He rolled up the scroll, gave it back to the attendant, and sat down; and the eyes of all *the people* in the synagogue were intently directed at Him. **21** Now He began to say to them, "Today this Scripture has been fulfilled in your hearing." **22** And all *the people* were speaking well of Him, and admiring the gracious words which were coming from His lips; and *yet* they were saying, "Is this not Joseph's son?" **23** And He said to them, "No doubt you will quote this proverb to Me: 'Physician, heal yourself! All *the miracles that* we heard were done in Capernaum, do here in your hometown as well.'"
24 But He said, "Truly I say to you, no prophet is welcome in his hometown. **25** But I say to you in truth, there were many widows in Israel in the days of Elijah, when the sky was shut up for three years and six months, when a severe famine came over all the land; **26** and *yet* Elijah was sent to none of them, but *only* to Zarephath, *in the land* of Sidon, to a woman who was a widow. **27** And there were many with leprosy in Israel in the time of Elisha the prophet; and none of them was cleansed, but *only* Naaman the Syrian." **28** And all *the people* in the synagogue were filled with rage as they heard these things; **29** and they got up and drove Him out of the city, and brought Him to the crest of the hill on which their city had been built, so that they could throw Him down from the cliff. **30** But He passed through their midst and went on His way.

31 And He came down to Capernaum, a city of Galilee; and He was teaching them on the Sabbath; **32** and they were amazed at His teaching, because His message was *delivered* with authority. **33** In the synagogue there was a man possessed by the spirit of an unclean demon, and he cried out with a loud voice, **34** "Leave us alone! What business do You have with us, Jesus of Nazareth? Have You come to destroy us? I know who You are—the Holy One of God!" **35** But Jesus rebuked him, saying, "Be quiet and come out of him!" And when the demon had thrown him down in the midst *of the people,* it came out of him without doing him any harm. **36** And amazement came upon them all, and they *began* talking with one another, saying, "What is this message? For with authority and power He commands the unclean spirits, and they come out!" **37** And the news about Him was spreading into every locality of the surrounding region.

Many Are Healed

38 Then He got up and *left* the synagogue, and entered Simon's home. Now Simon's mother-in-law was suffering from a high fever, and they asked Him to help her. **39** And standing over her, He rebuked the fever, and it left her; and she immediately got up and served them.

40 Now while the sun was setting, all those who had *any who were* sick with various diseases brought them to Him; and He was laying His hands on each one of them and healing them. **41** Demons also were coming out of many, shouting, "You are the Son of God!" And *yet* He was rebuking them and would not allow them to speak, because they knew that He was the Christ.

42 Now when day came, Jesus left and went to a secluded place; and the crowds were searching for Him, and they came to Him and tried to keep Him from leaving them. **43** But He said to them, "I must also preach the kingdom of God to the other cities, because I was sent for this *purpose.*"

44 So He kept on preaching in the synagogues of [1]Judea.

The First Disciples

5 Now it happened that while the crowd was pressing around Him and listening to the word of God, He was standing by the lake of Gennesaret; **2** and He saw two boats lying at the edge of the lake; but the fishermen had gotten out of them and were washing their nets. **3** And He got into one of the boats, which was Simon's, and asked him to put out a little *distance* from the land. And He sat down and *continued* teaching the crowds from the boat. **4** Now when He had finished speaking, He said to Simon, "Put out into the deep water and let down your nets for a catch." **5** Simon responded and said, "Master, we worked hard all night and caught nothing, but I will do as You say *and* let down the nets." **6** And when they had done this, they caught a great quantity of fish, and their nets *began* to tear; **7** so they signaled to their partners in the other boat to come and help them.

4:44 [1] I.e., the country of the Jews (including Galilee)

And they came and filled both of the boats, to the point that they were sinking. **8** But when Simon Peter saw *this,* he fell down at Jesus' knees, saying, "Go away from me, Lord, for I am a sinful man!" **9** For amazement had seized him and all his companions because of the catch of fish which they had taken; **10** and likewise also *were* James and John, sons of Zebedee, who were partners with Simon. And Jesus said to Simon, "Do not fear; from now on you will be catching people." **11** When they had brought their boats to land, they left everything and followed Him.

A Man with Leprosy Healed

12 While He was in one of the cities, behold, *there was* a man covered with leprosy; and when he saw Jesus, he fell on his face and begged Him, saying, "Lord, if You are willing, You can make me clean." **13** And He reached out with His hand and touched him, saying, "I am willing; be cleansed." And immediately the leprosy left him. **14** And He ordered him to tell no one, *saying,* "But go and show yourself to the priest, and make an offering for your cleansing, just as Moses commanded, as a testimony to them." **15** But the news about Him was spreading *even* farther, and large crowds were gathering to hear *Him* and to be healed of their sicknesses. **16** But *Jesus* Himself would *often* slip away to the wilderness and pray.

A Man Lowered Through a Roof

17 One day He was teaching, and there were *some* Pharisees and teachers of the Law sitting *there* who had come from every village of Galilee and Judea, and *from* Jerusalem; and the power of the Lord was *present* for Him to perform healing. **18** And *some* men *were* carrying a man on a stretcher who was paralyzed; and they were trying to bring him in and to set him down in front of Him. **19** But when they did not find any *way* to bring him in because of the crowd, they went up on the roof and let him down through the tiles with his stretcher, into the middle *of the crowd,* in front of Jesus. **20** And seeing their faith, He said, "Friend, your sins are forgiven you." **21** The scribes and the Pharisees began thinking of the implications, saying, "Who is this *man* who speaks blasphemies? Who can forgive sins, except God alone?"

22 But Jesus, aware of their thoughts, responded and said to them, "Why are you thinking this way in your hearts? **23** Which is easier, to say: 'Your sins are forgiven you,' or to say, 'Get up and walk'? **24** But so that you may know that the Son of Man has authority on earth to forgive sins," He said to the man who was paralyzed, "I say to you, get up, and pick up your stretcher, and go home." **25** And immediately he got up before them, and picked up what he had been lying on, and went home glorifying God. **26** And they were all struck with astonishment, and *began* glorifying God. They were also filled with fear, saying, "We have seen remarkable things today!"

Call of Levi (Matthew)

27 After that He went out and looked at a tax collector named Levi sitting in the tax office, and He said to him, "Follow Me." **28** And he left everything behind, and got up and *began* following Him.

29 And Levi gave a big reception for Him in his house; and there was a large crowd of tax collectors and other *people* who were reclining *at the table* with them. **30** The Pharisees and their scribes *began* grumbling to His disciples, saying, "Why do you eat and drink with the tax collectors and sinners?" **31** And Jesus answered and said to them, "*It is* not those who are healthy who need a physician, but those who are sick. **32** I have not come to call the righteous to repentance, but sinners."

33 And they said to Him, "The disciples of John often fast and offer prayers, the *disciples* of the Pharisees also do the same, but Yours eat and drink." **34** And Jesus said to them, "You cannot make the attendants of the groom fast while the groom is with them, can you? **35** But *the* days will come; and when the groom is taken away from them, then they will fast in those days." **36** And He was also telling them a parable: "No one tears a piece of cloth from a new garment and puts it on an old garment; otherwise he will both tear the new, and the patch from the new *garment* will not match the old. **37** And no one pours new wine into old wineskins; otherwise the new wine will burst the skins and it will be spilled out, and the skins will be ruined. **38** But new wine must be put into fresh wineskins. **39** And no one, after drinking old *wine* wants new; for he says, 'The old is fine.'"

Jesus Is Lord of the Sabbath

6 Now it happened that Jesus was passing through *some* grainfields on a Sabbath, and His disciples were picking the heads of grain, rubbing them in their hands, and eating *them.* **2** But some of the Pharisees said, "Why are you doing what is not lawful on the Sabbath?" **3** And Jesus, answering them, said, "Have you not even read what David did when he was hungry, he and those who were with him, **4** how he entered the house of God, and took and ate the ¹consecrated bread, which is not lawful *for anyone* to eat except the priests alone, and gave it to his companions?" **5** And He was saying to them, "The Son of Man is Lord of the Sabbath."

6 On another Sabbath He entered the synagogue and taught; and a man was there whose right hand was withered. **7** Now the scribes and the Pharisees were watching Him closely *to see* if He healed on the Sabbath, so that they might find *a reason* to accuse Him. **8** But He knew what they were thinking, and He said to the man with the withered hand, "Get up and come forward!" And he got up and came forward. **9** And Jesus said to them, "I ask you whether it is lawful to do good on the Sabbath or to do harm, to save a life or to destroy *it?*" **10** And after looking around at them all, He said to him, "Stretch out your hand!" And he did *so;* and his hand was restored. **11** But they themselves were filled with senseless rage, and *began* discussing together what they might do to Jesus.

Choosing the Twelve

12 Now it was at this time that He went off to the mountain to pray, and He spent the whole night in prayer with God. **13** And when day came, He called His disciples to Him and chose twelve of them, whom He also named as apostles: **14** Simon, whom He also named Peter, and his brother Andrew; and James and John; and Philip and Bartholomew; **15** and Matthew and Thomas; James *the son* of Alphaeus, and Simon who was called the Zealot; **16** Judas *the son* of James, and Judas Iscariot, who became a traitor.

17 And *then* Jesus came down with them and stood on a level place; and *there was* a large crowd of His

---

disciples, and a great multitude of the people from all
Judea and Jerusalem, and the coastal region of Tyre and
Sidon, **18** who had come to hear Him and to be healed of
their diseases; and those who were troubled by unclean
spirits were being cured. **19** And all the people were
trying to touch Him, because power was coming from
Him and healing *them* all.

The Beatitudes

20 And He raised His eyes toward His disciples and
began saying, "Blessed *are* you who are poor, for yours is
the kingdom of God. **21** Blessed *are* you who are hungry
now, for you will be satisfied. Blessed *are* you who weep
now, for you will laugh. **22** Blessed are you when the
people hate you, and when they exclude you, and insult
you, and scorn your name as evil, on account of the Son
of Man. **23** Rejoice on that day and jump *for joy,* for
behold, your reward is great in heaven. For their fathers
used to treat the prophets the same way. **24** But woe to
you who are rich, for you are receiving your comfort in
full. **25** Woe to you who are well-fed now, for you will be
hungry. Woe *to you* who laugh now, for you will mourn
and weep. **26** Woe *to you* when all the people speak well
of you; for their fathers used to treat the false prophets
the same way.

27 "But I say to you who hear, love your enemies, do
good to those who hate you, **28** bless those who curse
you, pray for those who are abusive to you. **29** Whoever
hits you on the cheek, offer him the other also; and
whoever takes away your cloak, do not withhold
your ¹tunic from him either. **30** Give to everyone who asks
of you, and whoever takes away what is yours, do not
demand *it* back. **31** Treat people the same way you want
them to treat you. **32** If you love those who love you, what
credit is *that* to you? For even sinners love those who
love them. **33** And if you do good to those who do good to
you, what credit is *that* to you? For even sinners do the
same. **34** And if you lend to those from whom you expect
to receive, what credit is *that* to you? Even sinners lend
to sinners in order to receive back the same *amount.*
35 But love your enemies and do good, and lend,
expecting nothing in return; and your reward will be

6:29 ¹ A long shirt worn next to the skin

great, and you will be sons of the Most High; for He Himself is kind to ungrateful and evil *people.* 36 Be merciful, just as your Father is merciful.

37 "Do not judge, and you will not be judged; and do not condemn, and you will not be condemned; pardon, and you will be pardoned. 38 Give, and it will be given to you. They will pour into your lap a good measure— pressed down, shaken together, *and* running over. For by your standard of measure it will be measured to you in return."

39 Now He also spoke a parable to them: "A person who is blind cannot guide *another* who is blind, can he? Will they not both fall into a pit? 40 A student is not above the teacher; but everyone, when he has been fully trained, will be like his teacher. 41 Why do you look at the speck that is in your brother's eye, but do not notice the log that is in your own eye? 42 How can you say to your brother, 'Brother, let me take out the speck that is in your eye,' when you yourself do not see the log that is in your own eye? You hypocrite, first take the log out of your own eye, and then you will see clearly to take out the speck that is in your brother's eye. 43 For there is no good tree that bears bad fruit, nor, on the other hand, a bad tree that bears good fruit. 44 For each tree is known by its own fruit. For *people* do not gather figs from thorns, nor do they pick grapes from a briar bush. 45 The good person out of the good treasure of his heart brings forth what is good; and the evil *person* out of the evil *treasure* brings forth what is evil; for his mouth speaks from that which fills *his* heart.

The Parable of the Builders

46 "Now why do you call Me, 'Lord, Lord,' and do not do what I say? 47 Everyone who comes to Me and hears My words and acts on them, I will show you whom he is like: 48 he is like a man building a house, who dug deep and laid a foundation on the rock; and when there was a flood, the river burst against that house and *yet* it could not shake it, because it had been well built. 49 But the one who has heard and has not acted *accordingly* is like a man who built a house on the ground without a foundation; and the river burst against it and it immediately collapsed, and the ruin of that house was great."

Jesus Heals a Centurion's Slave

7 When He had completed all His teaching in the hearing of the people, He went to Capernaum.

2 Now a centurion's slave, who was highly regarded by him, was sick and about to die. 3 When he heard about Jesus, he sent some Jewish elders to Him, asking Him to come and save the life of his slave. 4 When they came to Jesus, they strongly urged Him, saying, "He is worthy for You to grant this to him; 5 for he loves our nation, and it was he who built us our synagogue." 6 Now Jesus *started* on His way with them; but already, when He was not *yet* far from the house, the centurion sent friends, saying to Him, "Lord, do not trouble Yourself *further,* for I am not worthy for You to enter under my roof; 7 for that reason I did not even consider myself worthy to come to You; but *just* say the word, and my servant shall be healed. 8 For I also am a man placed under authority, with soldiers under myself; and I say to this one, 'Go!' and he goes, and to another, 'Come!' and he comes, and to my slave, 'Do this!' and he does *it.*" 9 Now when Jesus heard this, He was amazed at him, and turned and said to the crowd that was following Him, "I say to you, not even in Israel have I found such great faith." 10 And when those who had been sent returned to the house, they found the slave in good health.

11 Soon afterward *Jesus* went to a city called Nain; and His disciples were going along with Him, accompanied by a large crowd. 12 Now as He approached the gate of the city, a dead man was being carried out, the only son of his mother, and she was a widow; and a sizeable crowd from the city was with her. 13 When the Lord saw her, He felt compassion for her and said to her, "Do not go on weeping." 14 And He came up and touched the coffin; and the bearers came to a halt. And He said, "Young man, I say to you, arise!" 15 And the dead man sat up and began to speak. And *Jesus* gave him *back* to his mother. 16 Fear gripped them all, and they *began* glorifying God, saying, "A great prophet has appeared among us!" and, "God has visited His people!" 17 And this report about Him spread throughout Judea and in all the surrounding region.

The Messengers from John

18 The disciples of John also reported to him about all

these things. **19** And after summoning two of his disciples, John sent them to the Lord, saying, "Are You the Coming One, or are we to look for another?" **20** When the men came to Him, they said, "John the Baptist has sent us to You, to ask, 'Are You the Coming One, or are we to look for another?' " **21** At that *very* time He cured many *people* of diseases and afflictions and evil spirits; and He gave sight to many *who were* blind. **22** And He answered and said to them, "Go and report to John what you have seen and heard: people who were blind receive sight, people who limped walk, people with leprosy are cleansed and people who were deaf hear, dead people are raised up, *and* people who are poor have the gospel preached to them. **23** And blessed is anyone who does not take offense at Me."

24 When the messengers of John had left, He began to speak to the crowds about John: "What did you go out into the wilderness to see? A reed shaken by the wind? **25** But what did you go out to see? A man dressed in soft clothing? Those who are splendidly clothed and live in luxury are *found* in royal palaces! **26** But what did you go out to see? A prophet? Yes, I tell you, and one who is more than a prophet. **27** This is the one about whom it is written:

'Behold, I am sending My messenger ahead of You,
    Who will prepare Your way before You.'

28 I say to you, among those born of women there is no one greater than John; yet the one who is least in the kingdom of God is greater than he." **29** When all the people and the tax collectors heard *this,* they acknowledged God's justice, having been baptized with the baptism of John. **30** But the Pharisees and the ¹lawyers rejected God's purpose for themselves, not having been baptized by John.

31 "To what then shall I compare the people of this generation, and what are they like? **32** They are like children who sit in the marketplace and call to one another, and say, 'We played the flute for you, and you did not dance; we sang a song of mourning, and you did not weep.' **33** For John the Baptist has come neither eating bread nor drinking wine, and you say, 'He has a demon!' **34** The Son of Man has come eating and drinking, and

---

7:30 ¹I.e., experts in the Mosaic Law

you say, 'Behold, a gluttonous man and a heavy drinker, a friend of tax collectors and sinners!' 35 And *yet* wisdom is vindicated by all her children."

The Anointing in Galilee

36 Now one of the Pharisees was requesting Him to eat with him, and He entered the Pharisee's house and reclined *at the table.* 37 And there was a woman in the city who was a sinner; and when she learned that He was reclining *at the table* in the Pharisee's house, she brought an alabaster vial of perfume, 38 and standing behind *Him* at His feet, weeping, she began to wet His feet with her tears, and she wiped them with the hair of her head, and *began* kissing His feet and anointing them with the perfume. 39 Now when the Pharisee who had invited Him saw *this,* he said to himself, "If this man were a prophet He would know who and what sort of person this woman *is* who is touching Him, that she is a sinner!"

Parable of Two Debtors

40 And Jesus responded and said to him, "Simon, I have something to say to you." And he replied, "Say it, Teacher." 41 "A moneylender had two debtors: the one owed five hundred 'denarii, and the other, fifty. 42 When they were unable to repay, he canceled the debts of both. So which of them will love him more?" 43 Simon answered and said, "I assume the one for whom he canceled the greater debt." And He said to him, "You have judged correctly." 44 And turning toward the woman, He said to Simon, "Do you see this woman? I entered your house; you gave Me no water for My feet, but she has wet My feet with her tears and wiped them with her hair. 45 You gave Me no kiss; but she has not stopped kissing My feet since the time I came in. 46 You did not anoint My head with oil, but she anointed My feet with perfume. 47 For this reason I say to you, her sins, which are many, have been forgiven, for she loved much; but the one who is forgiven little, loves little." 48 And He said to her, "Your sins have been forgiven." 49 And *then* those who were reclining *at the table* with Him began saying to themselves, "Who is this *man* who

---

7:41 ¹ The denarius was a day's wages for a laborer

even forgives sins?" **50** And He said to the woman, "Your faith has saved you; go in peace."

Women Support Jesus

8 Soon afterward, Jesus *began* going around from one city and village to another, proclaiming and preaching the kingdom of God. The twelve were with Him, **2** and *also* some women who had been healed of evil spirits and sicknesses: Mary who was called Magdalene, from whom seven demons had gone out, **3** and Joanna the wife of Chuza, Herod's steward, and Susanna, and many others who were contributing to their support out of their private means.

Parable of the Sower

4 Now when a large crowd was coming together, and those from the various cities were journeying to Him, He spoke by way of a parable: **5** "The sower went out to sow his seed; and as he sowed, some fell beside the road, and it was trampled underfoot, and the birds of the sky ate it up. **6** Other *seed* fell on rocky *soil,* and when it came up, it withered away because it had no moisture. **7** Other *seed* fell among the thorns; and the thorns grew up with it and choked it out. **8** And *yet* other *seed* fell into the good soil, and grew up, and produced a crop a hundred times as much." As He said these things, He would call out, "The one who has ears to hear, let him hear."

9 Now His disciples *began* asking Him what this parable meant. **10** And He said, "To you it has been granted to know the mysteries of the kingdom of God, but to the rest *they are told* in parables, so that while seeing they may not see, and while hearing they may not understand.

11 "Now this is the parable: the seed is the word of God. **12** And those beside the road are the ones who have heard, then the devil comes and takes away the word from their heart, so that they will not believe and be saved. **13** Those on the rocky *soil are* the ones who, when they hear, receive the word with joy; and *yet* these do not have a *firm* root; they believe for a while, and in a time of temptation they fall away. **14** And the *seed* which fell among the thorns, these are the ones who have heard, and as they go on their way they are choked by worries, riches, and pleasures of *this* life, and they bring no fruit to maturity. 15 But the *seed* in the good soil, these are the ones who have heard the word with a good and virtuous heart, and hold it firmly, and produce fruit with perseverance.

Parable of the Lamp

16 "Now no one lights a lamp and covers it over with a container, or puts it under a bed; but he puts it on a lampstand so that those who come in may see the light. 17 For nothing is concealed that will not become evident, nor *anything* hidden that will not be known and come to light. 18 So take care how you listen; for whoever has, to him *more* will be given; and whoever does not have, even what he thinks he has will be taken away from him."

19 Now His mother and brothers came to Him, and they were unable to get to Him because of the crowd. 20 And it was reported to Him, "Your mother and Your brothers are standing outside, wishing to see You." 21 But He answered and said to them, "My mother and My brothers are these who hear the word of God and do *it.*"

Jesus Stills the Sea

22 Now on one of *those* days Jesus and His disciples got into a boat, and He said to them, "Let's cross over to the other side of the lake." So they launched out. 23 But as they were sailing along He fell asleep; and a fierce gale of wind descended on the lake, and they *began* to be swamped and to be in danger. 24 They came up to *Jesus* and woke Him, saying, "Master, Master, we are perishing!" And He got up and rebuked the wind and the surging waves, and they stopped, and it became calm. 25 And He said to them, "Where is your faith?" But they were fearful and amazed, saying to one another, "Who then is this, that He commands even the winds and the water, and they obey Him?"

The Demon-possessed Man Cured

26 Then they sailed to the country of the Gerasenes, which is opposite Galilee. 27 And when He stepped out onto the land, a man from the city met Him who was possessed with demons; and he had not put on clothing for a long time and was not living in a house, but among the tombs. 28 And seeing Jesus, he cried out and fell

down before Him, and said with a loud voice, "What business do You have with me, Jesus, Son of the Most High God? I beg You, do not torment me!" 29 For He *had already* commanded the unclean spirit to come out of the man. For it had seized him many times; and he was bound with chains and shackles and kept under guard, and *yet* he would break the restraints and be driven by the demon into the desert. 30 And Jesus asked him, "What is your name?" And he said, "Legion"; because many demons had entered him. 31 And they were begging Him not to command them to go away into the abyss.

32 Now there was a herd of many pigs feeding there on the mountain; and *the demons* begged Him to permit them to enter the pigs. And He gave them permission. 33 And the demons came out of the man and entered the pigs; and the herd rushed down the steep bank into the lake and was drowned.

34 Now when the herdsmen saw what had happened, they ran away and reported *everything* in the city, and in the country. 35 And *the people* came out to see what had happened; and they came to Jesus and found the man from whom the demons had gone out, sitting down at the feet of Jesus, clothed and in his right mind; and they became frightened. 36 Those who had seen *everything* reported to them how the man who had been demon-possessed had been made well. 37 And all the people of the territory of the Gerasenes and the surrounding region asked Him to leave them, because they were overwhelmed by great fear; and He got into a boat and returned. 38 But the man from whom the demons had gone out was begging Him that he might accompany Him; but *Jesus* sent him away, saying, 39 "Return to your home and describe what great things God has done for you." So he went away, proclaiming throughout the city what great things Jesus had done for him.

Miracles of Healing

40 And as Jesus was returning, the people welcomed Him, for they had all been waiting for Him. 41 And a man named Jairus came, and he was an official of the synagogue; and he fell at Jesus' feet, and *began* urging Him to come to his house; 42 for he had an only daughter, about twelve years old, and she was dying. But as He went, the crowds were pressing against Him.

43 And a woman who had suffered a *chronic* flow of blood for twelve years, and could not be healed by anyone, **44** came up behind Him and touched the fringe of His cloak, and immediately her bleeding stopped. **45** And Jesus said, "Who is the one who touched Me?" And while they were all denying it, Peter said, "Master, the people are crowding and pressing in on You." **46** But Jesus said, "Someone did touch Me, for I was aware that power had left Me." **47** Now when the woman saw that she had not escaped notice, she came trembling and fell down before Him, and admitted in the presence of all the people the reason why she had touched Him, and how she had been immediately healed. **48** And He said to her, "Daughter, your faith has made you well; go in peace."

49 While He was still speaking, someone *came from *the house of* the synagogue official, saying, "Your daughter has died; do not trouble the Teacher anymore." **50** But when Jesus heard *this,* He responded to him, "Do not be afraid *any longer;* only believe, and she will be made well." **51** When He came to the house, He did not allow anyone to enter with Him except Peter, John, and James, and the girl's father and mother. **52** Now they were all weeping and mourning for her; but He said, "Stop weeping, for she has not died, but is asleep." **53** And they *began* laughing at Him, knowing that she had died. **54** He, however, took her by the hand and spoke forcefully, saying, "Child, arise!" **55** And her spirit returned, and she got up immediately; and He ordered that *something* be given her to eat. **56** Her parents were amazed; but He instructed them to tell no one what had happened.

Ministry of the Twelve

9 Now He called the twelve together and gave them power and authority over all the demons, and *the power* to heal diseases. **2** And He sent them out to proclaim the kingdom of God and to perform healing. **3** And He said to them, "Take nothing for *your* journey, neither a staff, nor a bag, nor bread, nor money; and do not *even* have two ¹tunics. **4** And whatever house you enter, stay there until you leave that city. **5** And as for all who do not receive you, when you leave that city, shake

---

9:3 ¹A long shirt worn next to the skin

the dust off your feet as a testimony against them." 6 And as they were leaving, they *began* going throughout the villages, preaching the gospel and healing everywhere.

7 Now Herod the tetrarch heard *about* all that was happening; and he was greatly perplexed, because it was said by some that John had risen from the dead, 8 and by some that Elijah had appeared, and by others that one of the prophets of old had risen. 9 Herod said, "I myself had John beheaded; but who is this man about whom I hear such things?" And he kept trying to see Him.

10 When the apostles returned, they gave an account to Him of all that they had done. And taking them with Him, He withdrew privately to a city called Bethsaida. 11 But the crowds were aware *of this* and followed Him; and He welcomed them and *began* speaking to them about the kingdom of God, and curing those who had need of healing.

Five Thousand Men Fed

12 Now the day was ending, and the twelve came up and said to Him, "Dismiss the crowd, so that they may go into the surrounding villages and countryside and find lodging and get something to eat; because here, we are in a secluded place." 13 But He said to them, "You give them *something* to eat!" But they said, "We have no more than five loaves and two fish, unless perhaps we go and buy food for all these people." 14 (For there were about five thousand men.) But He said to His disciples, "Have them recline *to eat* in groups of about fifty each." 15 They did so, and had them all recline. 16 And He took the five loaves and the two fish, and, looking up to heaven, He blessed them and broke *them,* and gave *them* to the disciples *again and again,* to serve the crowd. 17 And they all ate and were satisfied; and the broken pieces which they had left over were picked up, twelve baskets *full.*

Peter Says Jesus is The Christ

18 And it happened that while He was praying alone, the disciples were with Him, and He questioned them, saying, "Who do the people say that I am?" 19 They answered and said, "John the Baptist, and others *say* Elijah; but others, that one of the prophets of old has risen." 20 And He said to them, "But who do you say that

I am?" And Peter answered and said, "The Christ of God." 21 But He warned them and instructed *them* not to tell this to anyone, 22 saying, "The Son of Man must suffer many things and be rejected by the elders and chief priests and scribes, and be killed and be raised on the third day."

23 And He was saying to *them* all, "If anyone wants to come after Me, he must deny himself, take up his cross daily, and follow Me. 24 For whoever wants to save his life will lose it, but whoever loses his life for My sake, this is the one who will save it. 25 For what good does it do a person if he gains the whole world, but loses or forfeits himself? 26 For whoever is ashamed of Me and My words, the Son of Man will be ashamed of him when He comes in His glory and *the glory* of the Father and the holy angels. 27 But I say to you truthfully, there are some of those standing here who will not taste death until they see the kingdom of God."

The Transfiguration

28 About eight days after these sayings, He took along Peter, John, and James, and went up on the mountain to pray. 29 And while He was praying, the appearance of His face became different, and His clothing *became* white *and* gleaming. 30 And behold, two men were talking with Him; and they were Moses and Elijah, 31 who, appearing in glory, were speaking of His departure, which He was about to accomplish at Jerusalem. 32 Now Peter and his companions had been overcome with sleep; but when they were fully awake, they saw His glory and the two men who were standing with Him. 33 And as these *two men* were leaving Him, Peter said to Jesus, "Master, it is good that we are here; and let's make three tabernacles: one for You, one for Moses, and one for Elijah"—not realizing what he was saying. 34 But while he was saying this, a cloud formed and *began* to overshadow them; and they were afraid as they entered the cloud. 35 And *then* a voice came from the cloud, saying, "This is My Son, *My* Chosen One; listen to Him!" 36 And when the voice had spoken, Jesus was found alone. And they kept silent, and reported to no one in those days any of the things which they had seen.

37 On the next day, when they came down from the mountain, a large crowd met Him. 38 And a man from the

crowd shouted, saying, "Teacher, I beg You to look at my son, because he is my only *son,* 39 and a spirit seizes him and he suddenly screams, and it throws him into a convulsion with foaming *at the mouth;* and only with difficulty does it leave him, mauling him *as it leaves.* 40 And I begged Your disciples to cast it out, and they could not." 41 And Jesus answered and said, "You unbelieving and perverse generation, how long shall I be with you and put up with you? Bring your son here." 42 Now while he was still approaching, the demon slammed him to the ground and threw him into a convulsion. But Jesus rebuked the unclean spirit, and healed the boy and gave him back to his father. 43 And they were all amazed at the greatness of God.

But while everyone was astonished at all that He was doing, He said to His disciples, 44 "As for you, let these words sink into your ears: for the Son of Man is going to be handed over to men." 45 But they did not understand this statement, and it was concealed from them so that they would not comprehend it; and they were afraid to ask Him about this statement.

The Test of Greatness

46 Now an argument started among them as to which of them might be the greatest. 47 But Jesus, knowing what they were thinking in their hearts, took a child and had him stand by His side, 48 and He said to them, "Whoever receives this child in My name receives Me, and whoever receives Me receives Him who sent Me; for the one who is least among all of you, this is the one who is great."

49 John answered and said, "Master, we saw someone casting out demons in Your name; and we *tried to* prevent him, because he does not follow along with us." 50 But Jesus said to him, "Do not hinder *him;* for the one who is not against you is for you."

51 When the days were approaching for His ascension, He was determined to go to Jerusalem; 52 and He sent messengers on ahead of Him, and they went and entered a village of the Samaritans to make arrangements for Him. 53 And they did not receive Him, because He was traveling toward Jerusalem. 54 When His disciples James and John saw *this,* they said, "Lord, do You want us to command fire to come down from heaven and consume

them?" 55 But He turned and rebuked them.[1] 56 And they went on to another village.

Exacting Discipleship

57 As they were going on the road, someone said to Him, "I will follow You wherever You go." 58 And Jesus said to him, "The foxes have holes and the birds of the sky *have* nests, but the Son of Man has nowhere to lay His head." 59 And He said to another, "Follow Me." But he said, "Lord, permit me first to go and bury my father." 60 But He said to him, "Allow the dead to bury their own dead; but as for you, go and proclaim everywhere the kingdom of God." 61 Another also said, "I will follow You, Lord; but first permit me to say goodbye to those at my home." 62 But Jesus said to him, "No one, after putting his hand to the plow and looking back, is fit for the kingdom of God."

The Seventy-two Sent Out

10 Now after this the Lord appointed seventy-two others, and sent them in pairs ahead of Him to every city and place where He Himself was going to come. 2 And He was saying to them, "The harvest is plentiful, but the laborers are few; therefore plead with the Lord of the harvest to send out laborers into His harvest. 3 Go; behold, I am sending you out like lambs in the midst of wolves. 4 Carry no money belt, no bag, no sandals, and greet no one along the way. 5 And whatever house you enter, first say, 'Peace *be* to this house.' 6 And if a man of peace is there, your peace will rest upon him; but if not, it will return to you. 7 Stay in that house, eating and drinking what they provide; for the laborer is deserving of his wages. Do not move from house to house. 8 Whatever city you enter and they receive you, eat what is served to you; 9 and heal those in it who are sick, and say to them, 'The kingdom of God has come near to you.' 10 But whatever city you enter and they do not receive you, go out into its streets and say, 11 'Even the dust of your city which clings to our feet we wipe off *in protest* against you; yet be sure of this, that the

---

9:55 [1] Some late mss add: *and said, "You do not know of what kind of spirit you are; for the Son of Man did not come to destroy people's lives, but to save them."*

kingdom of God has come near.' [12] I say to you, it will be more tolerable on that day for Sodom than for that city.

[13] "Woe to you, Chorazin! Woe to you, Bethsaida! For if the miracles that occurred in you had occurred in Tyre and Sidon, they would have repented long ago, sitting in [1]sackcloth and ashes. [14] But it will be more tolerable for Tyre and Sidon in the judgment than for you. [15] And you, Capernaum, will not be exalted to heaven, will you? You will be brought down to Hades!

[16] "The one who listens to you listens to Me, and the one who rejects you rejects Me; but the one who rejects Me rejects the One who sent Me."

The Joyful Results

[17] Now the seventy-two returned with joy, saying, "Lord, even the demons are subject to us in Your name!" [18] And He said to them, "I watched Satan fall from heaven like lightning. [19] Behold, I have given you authority to walk on snakes and scorpions, and *authority* over all the power of the enemy, and nothing will injure you. [20] Nevertheless, do not rejoice in this, that the spirits are subject to you, but rejoice that your names are recorded in heaven."

[21] At that very time He rejoiced greatly in the Holy Spirit, and said, "I praise You, Father, Lord of heaven and earth, that You have hidden these things from *the* wise and intelligent and have revealed them to infants. Yes, Father, for *doing* so was well pleasing in Your sight. [22] All things have been handed over to Me by My Father, and no one knows who the Son is except the Father, and who the Father is except the Son, and anyone to whom the Son determines to reveal *Him.*"

[23] Turning to the disciples, He said privately, "Blessed *are* the eyes that see the things you see; [24] for I tell you that many prophets and kings wanted to see the things that you see, and did not see *them,* and to hear the things that you hear, and did not hear *them.*"

[25] And behold, a lawyer stood up and put Him to the test, saying, "Teacher, what shall I do to inherit eternal life?" [26] And He said to him, "What is written in the Law? How does it read to you?" [27] And he answered, "YOU SHALL LOVE THE LORD YOUR GOD WITH ALL YOUR HEART,

---

10:13 [1] I.e., symbols of mourning

AND WITH ALL YOUR SOUL, AND WITH ALL YOUR STRENGTH, AND
WITH ALL YOUR MIND; AND YOUR NEIGHBOR AS YOURSELF." **28** And
He said to him, "You have answered correctly; do this
and you will live." **29** But wanting to justify himself, he
said to Jesus, "And who is my neighbor?"

The Good Samaritan

30 Jesus replied and said, "A man was going down from
Jerusalem to Jericho, and he encountered robbers, and
they stripped him and beat him, and went away leaving
him half dead. **31** And by coincidence a priest was going
down on that road, and when he saw him, he passed by
on the other side. **32** Likewise a Levite also, when he
came to the place and saw him, passed by on the other
side. **33** But a Samaritan who was on a journey came
upon him; and when he saw him, he felt compassion,
34 and came to him and bandaged up his wounds,
pouring oil and wine on *them;* and he put him on his
own animal, and brought him to an inn and took care of
him. **35** On the next day he took out two ¹denarii and
gave them to the innkeeper and said, 'Take care of him;
and whatever more you spend, when I return, I will
repay you.' **36** Which of these three do you think proved
to be a neighbor to the man who fell into the robbers'
hands?" **37** And he said, "The one who showed compassion to him." Then Jesus said to him, "Go and do the
same."

Martha and Mary

38 Now as they were traveling along, He entered a
village; and a woman named Martha welcomed Him into
her home. **39** And she had a sister called Mary, who was
also seated at the Lord's feet, and was listening to His
word. **40** But Martha was distracted with all her
preparations; and she came up *to Him* and said, "Lord,
do You not care that my sister has left me to do the
serving by myself? Then tell her to help me." **41** But the
Lord answered and said to her, "Martha, Martha, you are
worried and distracted by many things; **42** but *only* one
thing is necessary; for Mary has chosen the good part,
which shall not be taken away from her."

10:35 ¹ The denarius was a day's wages for a laborer

Instruction about Prayer

11 It happened that while Jesus was praying in a certain place, when He had finished, one of His disciples said to Him, "Lord, teach us to pray, just as John also taught his disciples." **2** And He said to them, "When you pray, say:

'Father, hallowed be Your name.
Your kingdom come.
3 'Give us each day our daily bread.
4 'And forgive us our sins,
For we ourselves also forgive everyone who is indebted to us.
And do not lead us into temptation.'"

5 And He said to them, "Suppose one of you has a friend, and goes to him at midnight and says to him, 'Friend, lend me three loaves, **6** because a friend of mine has come to me from a journey and I have nothing to serve him'; **7** and from inside he answers and says, 'Do not bother me; the door has already been shut and my children and I are in bed; I cannot get up and give you *anything.*' **8** I tell you, even if he will not get up and give him *anything just* because he is his friend, yet because of his shamelessness he will get up and give him as much as he needs.

9 "So I say to you, ask, and it will be given to you; seek, and you will find; knock, and it will be opened to you. **10** For everyone who asks receives, and the one who seeks finds, and to the one who knocks, it will be opened. **11** Now which one of you fathers will his son ask for a fish, and instead of a fish, he will give him a snake? **12** Or he will even ask for an egg, *and his father* will give him a scorpion? **13** So if you, *despite* being evil, know how to give good gifts to your children, how much more will your heavenly Father give the Holy Spirit to those who ask Him?"

Pharisees' Blasphemy

14 And He was casting out a mute demon; when the demon had gone out, the man who was *previously* unable to speak talked, and the crowds were amazed. **15** But some of them said, "He casts out the demons by

---

11:2 ¹Later mss add phrases from Matt 6:9-13 to make the two passages closely similar

Beelzebul, the ruler of the demons." 16 Others, to test *Him,* were demanding of Him a sign from heaven. 17 But He knew their thoughts and said to them, "Every kingdom divided against itself is laid waste; and a house *divided* against itself falls. 18 And if Satan also has been divided against himself, how will his kingdom stand? For you claim that I cast out the demons by Beelzebul. 19 Yet if by Beelzebul I cast out the demons, by whom do your sons cast *them* out? Therefore, they will be your judges. 20 But if I cast out the demons by the finger of God, then the kingdom of God has come upon you. 21 When a strong *man,* fully armed, guards his own house, his possessions are secure. 22 But when *someone* stronger than he attacks him and overpowers him, *that man* takes away his armor on which he had relied and distributes his plunder. 23 The one who is not with Me is against Me; and the one who does not gather with Me scatters.

24 "When the unclean spirit comes out of a person, it passes through waterless places seeking rest, and not finding *any,* it then says, 'I will return to my house from which I came.' 25 And when it comes, it finds it swept and put in order. 26 Then it goes and brings along seven other spirits more evil than itself, and they come in and live there; and the last *condition* of that person becomes worse than the first."

27 While Jesus was saying these things, one of the women in the crowd raised her voice and said to Him, "Blessed is the womb that carried You, and the breasts at which You nursed!" 28 But He said, "On the contrary, blessed are those who hear the word of God and follow it."

The Sign of Jonah

29 Now as the crowds were increasing, He began to say, "This generation is a wicked generation; it demands a sign, and *so* no sign will be given to it except the sign of Jonah. 30 For just as Jonah became a sign to the Ninevites, so will the Son of Man be to this generation. 31 The Queen of the South will rise up with the men of this generation at the judgment and condemn them, because she came from the ends of the earth to listen to the wisdom of Solomon; and behold, *something* greater than Solomon is here. 32 The men of Nineveh will stand up with this generation at the judgment and condemn it,

because they repented at the preaching of Jonah; and behold, *something* greater than Jonah is here.

33 "No one lights a lamp and puts *it away* in a cellar nor under a basket, but on the lampstand, so that those who enter may see the light. 34 Your eye is the lamp of your body; when your eye is clear, your whole body also is full of light; but when it is bad, your body also is full of darkness. 35 So watch out that the light in you is not darkness. 36 Therefore if your whole body is full of light, without any dark part, it will be wholly illuminated, as when the lamp illuminates you with its light."

Woes upon the Pharisees

37 Now when He had spoken, a Pharisee *asked Him to have lunch with him; and He went in and reclined *at the table.* 38 When the Pharisee saw *this,* he was surprised that *Jesus* had not first ceremonially washed before the meal. 39 But the Lord said to him, "Now you Pharisees clean the outside of the cup and of the dish; but your inside is full of greed and wickedness. 40 You foolish ones, did He who made the outside not make the inside also? 41 But give that which is within as a charitable gift, and then all things are clean for you.

42 "But woe to you Pharisees! For you pay tithes of mint, rue, and every *kind of* garden herb, and *yet* you ignore justice and the love of God; but these are the things you should have done without neglecting the others. 43 Woe to you Pharisees! For you love the seat of honor in the synagogues and personal greetings in the marketplaces. 44 Woe to you! For you are like unseen tombs, and the people who walk over *them* are unaware *of it.*"

45 One of the ¹lawyers *said to Him in reply, "Teacher, when You say these things, You insult us too." 46 But He said, "Woe to you lawyers as well! For you load people with burdens that are hard to bear, while you yourselves will not even touch the burdens with one of your fingers. 47 Woe to you! For you build the tombs of the prophets, and *it was* your fathers *who* killed them. 48 So you are witnesses and you approve of the deeds of your fathers; because *it was* they *who* killed them, and you build *their* tombs. 49 For this reason also, the wisdom of God said, 'I

11:45 ¹I.e., experts in the Mosaic Law

will send them prophets and apostles, and *some* of them they will kill, and *some* they will persecute, [50] so that the blood of all the prophets, shed since the foundation of the world, may be charged against this generation, [51] from the blood of Abel to the blood of Zechariah, who was killed between the altar and the house *of God;* yes, I tell you, it shall be charged against this generation.'

[52] Woe to you lawyers! For you have taken away the key of knowledge; you yourselves did not enter, and you hindered those who were entering."

[53] When He left that place, the scribes and the Pharisees began to be very hostile and to interrogate Him about many *subjects,* [54] plotting against Him to catch Him in something He might say.

God Knows and Cares

12 Under these circumstances, after so many thousands of people had gathered together that they were stepping on one another, He began saying to His disciples first *of all,* "Beware of the leaven of the Pharisees, which is hypocrisy. [2] But there is nothing covered up that will not be revealed, and hidden that will not be known. [3] Accordingly, whatever you have said in the dark will be heard in the light, and what you have whispered in the inner rooms will be proclaimed on the housetops.

[4] "Now I say to you, My friends, do not be afraid of those who kill the body, and after that have nothing more that they can do. [5] But I will warn you whom to fear: fear the One who, after He has killed *someone,* has *the* power to throw *that person* into [1]hell; yes, I tell you, fear Him! [6] Are five sparrows not sold for two [1]assaria? And *yet* not one of them has gone unnoticed in the sight of God. [7] But even the hairs of your head are all counted. Do not fear; you are more valuable than a great number of sparrows.

[8] "Now I say to you, everyone who confesses Me before people, the Son of Man will also confess him before the angels of God; [9] but the one who denies Me before people will be denied before the angels of God. [10] And everyone who speaks a word against the Son of

---

12:5 [1]Gr *Gehenna*   12:6 [1]A Roman copper coin (singular *assarion*), about 1/16 of a laborer's daily wage

Man, it will be forgiven him; but the one who blasphemes against the Holy Spirit, it will not be forgiven him. 11 Now when they bring you before the synagogues and the officials and the authorities, do not worry about how or what you are to speak in your defense, or what you are to say; 12 for the Holy Spirit will teach you in that very hour what you ought to say."

Greed Denounced

13 Now someone in the crowd said to Him, "Teacher, tell my brother to divide the *family* inheritance with me." 14 But He said to him, "You there—who appointed Me a judge or arbitrator over *the two of* you?" 15 But He said to them, "Beware, and be on your guard against every form of greed; for not *even* when one is affluent does his life consist of his possessions." 16 And He told them a parable, saying, "The land of a rich man was very productive. 17 And he began thinking to himself, saying, 'What shall I do, since I have no place to store my crops?' 18 And he said, 'This *is what* I will do: I will tear down my barns and build larger ones, and I will store all my grain and my goods there. 19 And I will say to myself, "You have many goods stored up for many years *to come;* relax, eat, drink, *and* enjoy yourself!" ' 20 But God said to him, 'You fool! This *very* night your soul is demanded of you; and *as for all* that you have prepared, who will own *it now?*' 21 Such is the one who stores up treasure for himself, and is not rich in relation to God."

22 And He said to His disciples, "For this reason I tell you, do not worry about *your* life, *as to* what you are to eat; nor for your body, *as to* what you are to wear. 23 For life is more than food, and the body *is more* than clothing. 24 Consider the ravens, that they neither sow nor reap; they have no storeroom nor barn, and *yet* God feeds them; how much more valuable you are than the birds! 25 And which of you by worrying can add a 1day to his 2life's span? 26 Therefore if you cannot do even a very little thing, why do you worry about the other things? 27 Consider the lilies, how they grow: they neither labor nor spin; but I tell you, not even Solomon in all his glory clothed himself like one of these. 28 Now if God so clothes the grass in the field, which is *alive* today and

---

12:25 1 Lit *cubit* (about 18 in. or 45 cm)   12:25 2 Or *height*

tomorrow is thrown into the furnace, how much more *will He clothe* you? You of little faith! **29** And do not seek what you are to eat and what you are to drink, and do not keep worrying. **30** For all these things *are what* the nations of the world eagerly seek; and your Father knows that you need these things. **31** But seek His kingdom, and these things will be provided to you. **32** Do not be afraid, little flock, because your Father has chosen to give you the kingdom.

33 "Sell your possessions and give to charity; make yourselves money belts that do not wear out, an inexhaustible treasure in heaven, where no thief comes near nor does a moth destroy. **34** For where your treasure is, there your heart will be also.

Be in Readiness

35 "Be prepared, and *keep* your lamps lit. **36** You are also *to be* like people who are waiting for their master when he returns from the wedding feast, so that they may immediately open *the door* for him when he comes and knocks. **37** Blessed are those slaves whom the master will find on the alert when he comes; truly I say to you, that he will prepare himself *to serve,* and have them recline *at the table,* and he will come up and serve them. **38** Whether he comes in the *¹second watch, or even in the ²third, and finds *them* so, blessed are those *slaves.*

39 "But be sure of this, that if the head of the house had known at what hour the thief was coming, he would not have allowed his house to be broken into. **40** You too, be ready; because the Son of Man is coming at an hour that you do not think *He will.*"

41 Peter said, "Lord, are You telling this parable to us, or to everyone *else* as well?" **42** And the Lord said, "Who then is the faithful and sensible steward, whom his master will put in charge of his servants, to give them their rations at the proper time? **43** Blessed is that slave whom his master finds so doing when he comes. **44** Truly I say to you that he will put him in charge of all his possessions. **45** But if that slave says in his heart, 'My master will take a long time to come,' and he begins to beat the *other* slaves, *both* men and women, and to

---

12:38 ¹I.e., 9 p.m. to midnight   12:38 ²I.e., midnight to 3 a.m.

eat and drink and get drunk; **46** *then* the master of that slave will come on a day that he does not expect, and at an hour that he does not know, and will cut him in two, and assign him a place with the unbelievers. **47** And that slave who knew his master's will and did not get ready or act in accordance with his will, will receive many blows, **48** but the one who did not know *it,* and committed acts deserving of a beating, will receive *only* a few blows. From everyone who has been given much, much will be demanded; and to whom they entrusted much, of him they will ask all the more.

Christ Divides People

49 "I have come to cast fire upon the earth; and how I wish it were already kindled! **50** But I have a baptism to undergo, and how distressed I am until it is accomplished! **51** Do you think that I came to provide peace on earth? No, I tell you, but rather division; **52** for from now on five *members* in one household will be divided, three against two and two against three. **53** They will be divided, father against son and son against father, mother against daughter and daughter against mother, mother-in-law against daughter-in-law and daughter-in-law against mother-in-law."

54 And He was also saying to the crowds, "Whenever you see a cloud rising in the west, you immediately say, 'A shower is coming,' and so it turns out. **55** And whenever *you feel* a south wind blowing, you say, 'It will be a hot *day,*' and it turns out *that way.* **56** You hypocrites! You know how to analyze the appearance of the earth and the sky, but how *is it that* you do not know how to analyze this *present* time?

57 "And why do you not even judge by yourselves what is right? **58** For when you are going with your accuser *to appear* before the magistrate, on the way, make an effort to settle with him, so that he does not drag you before the judge, and the judge hand you over to the officer, and the officer throw you into prison. **59** I tell you, you will not get out of there until you have paid up the very last [1]lepton."

12:59 [1] The smallest Greek copper coin, about 1/128 of a laborer's daily wage

Call to Repent

13 Now on that very occasion there were some present who reported to Him about the Galileans whose blood Pilate had mixed with their sacrifices. ² And Jesus responded and said to them, "Do you think that these Galileans were *worse* sinners than all the *other* Galileans *just* because they have suffered this *fate?* ³ No, I tell you, but unless you repent, you will all likewise perish. ⁴ Or do you think that those eighteen on whom the tower in Siloam fell and killed them were *worse* offenders than all the *other* people who live in Jerusalem? ⁵ No, I tell you, but unless you repent, you will all likewise perish."

⁶ And He *began* telling this parable: "A man had a fig tree which had been planted in his vineyard; and he came looking for fruit on it and did not find *any.* ⁷ And he said to the vineyard-keeper, 'Look! For three years I have come looking for fruit on this fig tree without finding any. Cut it down! Why does it even use up the ground?' ⁸ But he answered and said to him, 'Sir, leave it alone for this year too, until I dig around it and put in fertilizer; ⁹ and if it bears fruit next *year, fine;* but if not, cut it down.' "

Healing on the Sabbath

¹⁰ Now *Jesus* was teaching in one of the synagogues on the Sabbath. ¹¹ And there was a woman who for eighteen years had had a sickness caused by a spirit; and she was bent over double, and could not straighten up at all. ¹² When Jesus saw her, He called her over and said to her, "Woman, you are freed from your sickness." ¹³ And He laid His hands on her; and immediately she stood up straight again, and *began* glorifying God. ¹⁴ But the synagogue leader, indignant because Jesus had healed on the Sabbath, *began* saying to the crowd in response, "There are six days during which work should be done; so come during them and get healed, and not on the Sabbath day." ¹⁵ But the Lord answered him and said, "You hypocrites, does each of you on the Sabbath not untie his ox or donkey from the stall and lead it away to water *it?* ¹⁶ And this woman, a daughter of Abraham as she is, whom Satan has bound for eighteen long years, should she not have been released from this restraint on the Sabbath day?" ¹⁷ And as He said this, all His opponents

were being humiliated; and the entire crowd was rejoicing over all the glorious things being done by Him.

Parables of Mustard Seed and Leaven

18 So He was saying, "What is the kingdom of God like, and to what shall I compare it? 19 It is like a mustard seed, which a man took and threw into his own garden; and it grew and became a tree, and the birds of the sky nested in its branches."

20 And again He said, "To what shall I compare the kingdom of God? 21 It is like leaven, which a woman took and hid in three sata of flour until it was all leavened."

Teaching in the Villages

22 And He was passing through one city and village after another, teaching, and proceeding on His way to Jerusalem. 23 And someone said to Him, "Lord, are there *just* a few who are being saved?" And He said to them, 24 "Strive to enter through the narrow door; for many, I tell you, will seek to enter and will not be able. 25 Once the head of the house gets up and shuts the door, and you begin standing outside and knocking on the door, saying, 'Lord, open up to us!' and He *then* will answer and say to you, 'I do not know where you are from.' 26 Then you will begin saying, 'We ate and drank in Your presence, and You taught in our streets!' 27 And *yet* He will say, 'I do not know where you are from; LEAVE ME, ALL YOU EVILDOERS.' 28 In that place there will be weeping and gnashing of teeth when you see Abraham, Isaac, Jacob, and all the prophets in the kingdom of God, but yourselves being thrown out. 29 And they will come from east and west, and from north and south, and will recline *at the table* in the kingdom of God. 30 And behold, *some* are last who will be first, and *some* are first who will be last."

31 At that very time some Pharisees approached, saying to Him, "Go away and leave this place, because Herod wants to kill You." 32 And He said to them, "Go and tell that fox, 'Behold, I am casting out demons and performing healings today and tomorrow, and on the third *day* I reach My goal.' 33 Nevertheless I must go on My journey today and tomorrow and the next *day;* for it cannot be that a prophet would perish outside Jerusalem. 34 Jerusalem, Jerusalem, the *city* that kills the prophets

and stones those who have been sent to her! How often I wanted to gather your children together, just as a hen *gathers* her young under her wings, and you were unwilling! **35** Behold, your house is left to you *desolate;* and I say to you, you will not see Me until you say, 'BLESSED IS THE ONE WHO COMES IN THE NAME OF THE LORD!' "

Jesus Heals on the Sabbath

14 It happened that when He went into the house of one of the leaders of the Pharisees on *the* Sabbath to eat bread, they were watching Him closely. **2** And there in front of Him was a man suffering from ¹edema. **3** And Jesus responded and said to the lawyers and Pharisees, "Is it lawful to heal on the Sabbath, or not?" **4** But they kept silent. And He took hold of him and healed him, and sent him away. **5** And He said to them, "Which one of you will have a son or an ox fall into a well, and will not immediately pull him out on a Sabbath day?" **6** And they could offer no reply to this.

Parable of the Guests

7 Now He *began* telling a parable to the invited guests when He noticed how they had been picking out the places of honor *at the table,* saying to them, **8** "Whenever you are invited by someone to a wedding feast, do not take the place of honor, for someone more distinguished than you may have been invited by him, **9** and the one who invited you both will come and say to you, 'Give *your* place to this person,' and then in disgrace you will proceed to occupy the last place. **10** But whenever you are invited, go and take the last place, so that when the one who has invited you comes, he will say to you, 'Friend, move up higher'; then you will have honor in the sight of all who are dining at the table with you. **11** For everyone who exalts himself will be humbled, and the one who humbles himself will be exalted."

12 Now He also went on to say to the one who had invited Him, "Whenever you give a luncheon or a dinner, do not invite your friends, your brothers, your relatives, nor wealthy neighbors, otherwise they may also invite you *to a meal* in return, and *that* will be your repayment. **13** But whenever you give a banquet, invite

---

14:2 ¹I.e., extreme swelling

people who are poor, who have disabilities, who are limping, *and* people who are blind; **14** and you will be blessed, since they do not have *the means* to repay you; for you will be repaid at the resurrection of the righteous."

15 Now when one of those who were reclining *at the table* with Him heard this, he said to Him, "Blessed is everyone who will eat bread in the kingdom of God!"

Parable of the Dinner

16 But He said to him, "A man was giving a big dinner, and he invited many; **17** and at the dinner hour he sent his slave to tell those who had been invited, 'Come, because everything is ready now.' **18** And *yet* they all alike began to make excuses. The first one said to him, 'I purchased a field and I need to go out to look at it; please consider me excused.' **19** And another one said, 'I bought five yoke of oxen, and I am going to try them out; please consider me excused.' **20** And another one said, 'I took a woman as my wife, and for that reason I cannot come.' **21** And the slave came *back* and reported this to his master. Then the head of the household became angry and said to his slave, 'Go out at once into the streets and lanes of the city and bring in here those who are poor, those with disabilities, those who are blind, and those who are limping.' **22** And *later* the slave said, 'Master, what you commanded has been done, and still there is room.' **23** And the master said to the slave, 'Go out into the roads and the hedges and press upon *them* to come in, so that my house will be filled. **24** For I tell you, none of those men who were invited shall taste my dinner.'"

Discipleship Tested

25 Now large crowds were going along with Him, and He turned and said to them, **26** "If anyone comes to Me and does not ¹hate his own father, mother, wife, children, brothers, sisters, yes, and even his own life, he cannot be My disciple. **27** Whoever does not carry his own cross and come after Me cannot be My disciple. **28** For which one of you, when he wants to build a tower, does not first sit down and calculate the cost, *to see* if he has *enough* to complete *it*? **29** Otherwise, when he has

---

14:26 ¹I.e., in comparison to his love for Me

laid a foundation and is not able to finish, all who are watching *it* will begin to ridicule him, **30** saying, 'This person began to build, and was not able to finish!' **31** Or what king, when he sets out to meet another king in battle, will not first sit down and consider whether he is strong *enough* with ten thousand *men* to face the one coming against him with twenty thousand? **32** Otherwise, while the other is still far away, he sends a delegation and requests terms of peace. **33** So then, none of you can be My disciple who does not give up all his own possessions.

34 "Therefore, salt is good; but if even salt has become tasteless, with what will it be seasoned? **35** It is useless either for the soil or the manure pile, *so* it is thrown out. The one who has ears to hear, let him hear."

The Lost Sheep

15 Now all the tax collectors and sinners were coming near Jesus to listen to Him. **2** And both the Pharisees and the scribes *began* to complain, saying, "This man receives sinners and eats with them."

3 And *so* He told them this parable, saying, **4** "What man among you, if he has a hundred sheep and has lost one of them, does not leave the *other* ninety-nine in the open pasture and go after the one that is lost, until he finds it? **5** And when he has found it, he puts it on his shoulders, rejoicing. **6** And when he comes home, he calls together his friends and his neighbors, saying to them, 'Rejoice with me, because I have found my sheep that was lost!' **7** I tell you that in the same way, there will be *more* joy in heaven over one sinner who repents than over ninety-nine righteous people who have no need of repentance.

The Lost Coin

8 "Or what woman, if she has ten silver coins and loses one coin, does not light a lamp and sweep the house and search carefully until she finds *it?* **9** And when she has found *it,* she calls together her friends and neighbors, saying, 'Rejoice with me, because I have found the coin which I had lost!' **10** In the same way, I tell you, there is joy in the presence of the angels of God over one sinner who repents."

The Prodigal Son

11 And He said, "A man had two sons. 12 The younger of them said to his father, 'Father, give me the share of the estate that is coming to me.' And *so* he divided his wealth between them. 13 And not many days later, the younger son gathered everything together and went on a journey to a distant country, and there he squandered his estate in wild living. 14 Now when he had spent everything, a severe famine occurred in that country, and he began doing without. 15 So he went and hired himself out to one of the citizens of that country, and he sent him into his fields to feed pigs. 16 And he longed to have his fill of the carob pods that the pigs were eating, and no one was giving him *anything.* 17 But when he came to his senses, he said, 'How many of my father's hired laborers have more than enough bread, but I am dying here from hunger! 18 I will set out and go to my father, and will say to him, "Father, I have sinned against heaven, and in your sight; 19 I am no longer worthy to be called your son; treat me as one of your hired laborers." ' 20 So he set out and came to his father. But when he was still a long way off, his father saw him and felt compassion *for him,* and ran and embraced him and kissed him. 21 And the son said to him, 'Father, I have sinned against heaven and in your sight; I am no longer worthy to be called your son.' 22 But the father said to his slaves, 'Quickly bring out the best robe and put it on him, and put a ring on his finger and sandals on his feet; 23 and bring the fattened calf, slaughter it, and let's eat and celebrate; 24 for this son of mine was dead and has come to life again; he was lost and has been found.' And they began to celebrate.

25 "Now his older son was in the field, and when he came and approached the house, he heard music and dancing. 26 And he summoned one of the servants and *began* inquiring what these things could be. 27 And he said to him, 'Your brother has come, and your father has slaughtered the fattened calf because he has received him back safe and sound.' 28 But he became angry and was not willing to go in; and his father came out and *began* pleading with him. 29 But he answered and said to his father, 'Look! For so many years I have been serving you and I have never neglected a command of yours; and *yet* you never gave me a young goat, so that I might

celebrate with my friends; **30** but when this son of yours came, who has devoured your wealth with prostitutes, you slaughtered the fattened calf for him.' **31** And he said to him, 'Son, you have always been with me, and all that is mine is yours. **32** But we had to celebrate and rejoice, because this brother of yours was dead and *has begun* to live, and *was* lost and has been found.' "

The Unrighteous Manager

16 Now He was also saying to the disciples, "There was a rich man who had a manager, and this *manager* was reported to him as squandering his possessions. **2** And he summoned him and said to him, 'What is this I hear about you? Give an accounting of your management, for you can no longer be manager.' **3** And the manager said to himself, 'What am I to do, since my master is taking the management away from me? I am not strong enough to dig; I am ashamed to beg. **4** I know what I will do, so that when I am removed from the management *people* will welcome me into their homes.' **5** And he summoned each one of his master's debtors, and he *began* saying to the first, 'How much do you owe my master?' **6** And he said, 'A hundred jugs of oil.' And he said to him, 'Take your bill, and sit down quickly and write fifty.' **7** Then he said to another, 'And how much do you owe?' And he said, 'A hundred kors of wheat.' He *said to him, 'Take your bill, and write eighty.' **8** And his master complimented the unrighteous manager because he had acted shrewdly; for the sons of this age are more shrewd in relation to their own kind than the sons of light. **9** And I say to you, make friends for yourselves by means of the ¹wealth of unrighteousness, so that when it is all gone, they will receive you into the eternal dwellings.

10 "The one who is faithful in a very little thing is also faithful in much; and the one who is unrighteous in a very little thing is also unrighteous in much. **11** Therefore if you have not been faithful in the *use of* unrighteous wealth, who will entrust the true *wealth* to you? **12** And if you have not been faithful in *the use of* that which is another's, who will give you that which is your own?

16:9 ¹Gr *mamonas,* for Aramaic *mamon* (mammon); i.e., wealth, or money

13 No servant can serve two masters; for either he will hate the one and love the other, or he will be devoted to one and despise the other. You cannot serve God and wealth."

14 Now the Pharisees, who were lovers of money, were listening to all these things and were ridiculing Him. 15 And He said to them, "You are the ones who justify yourselves in the sight of people, but God knows your hearts; because that which is highly esteemed among people is detestable in the sight of God.

16 "The Law and the Prophets *were proclaimed* until John *came;* since that time the gospel of the kingdom of God has been preached, and everyone is forcing his way into it. 17 But it is easier for heaven and earth to pass away than for one stroke of a letter of the Law to fail.

18 "Everyone who divorces his wife and marries another commits adultery, and he who marries one who is divorced from a husband commits adultery.

The Rich Man and Lazarus

19 "Now there was a rich man, and he habitually dressed in purple and fine linen, enjoying himself in splendor every day. 20 And a poor man named Lazarus was laid at his gate, covered with sores, 21 and longing to be fed from the *scraps* which fell from the rich man's table; not only *that,* the dogs also were coming and licking his sores. 22 Now it happened that the poor man died and was carried away by the angels to [1]Abraham's arms; and the rich man also died and was buried. 23 And in Hades he raised his eyes, being in torment, and *saw Abraham far away and Lazarus in his [1]arms. 24 And he cried out and said, 'Father Abraham, have mercy on me and send Lazarus, so that he may dip the tip of his finger in water and cool off my tongue, for I am in agony in this flame.' 25 But Abraham said, 'Child, remember that during your life you received your good things, and likewise Lazarus bad things; but now he is being comforted here, and you are in agony. 26 And besides all this, between us and you a great chasm has been set, so that those who want to go over from here to you will not be able, nor will *any people* cross over from there to us.'

16:22 [1] Lit *Abraham's bosom;* or *lap;* ancient Jewish terminology for the place of the righteous dead   16:23 [1] See note v 22

27 And he said, 'Then I request of you, father, that you send him to my father's house— **28** for I have five brothers—in order that he may warn them, so that they will not come to this place of torment as well.' **29** But Abraham *said, 'They have Moses and the Prophets; let them hear them.' **30** But he said, 'No, father Abraham, but if someone goes to them from the dead, they will repent!' **31** But he said to him, 'If they do not listen to Moses and the Prophets, they will not be persuaded even if someone rises from the dead.' "

Instructions

17 Now He said to His disciples, "It is inevitable that stumbling blocks come, but woe to one through whom they come! **2** It is better for him if a millstone is hung around his neck and he is thrown into the sea, than that he may cause one of these little ones to sin. **3** Be on your guard! If your brother sins, rebuke him; and if he repents, forgive him. **4** And if he sins against you seven times a day, and returns to you seven times, saying, 'I repent,' you shall forgive him."

5 The apostles said to the Lord, "Increase our faith!" **6** But the Lord said, "If you had faith the size of a mustard seed, you could say to this mulberry tree, 'Be uprooted and be planted in the sea'; and it would obey you.

7 "Now which of you, having a slave plowing or tending sheep, will say to him after he comes in from the field, 'Come immediately and recline *at the table* to eat'? **8** On the contrary, will he not say to him, 'Prepare something for me to eat, and *properly* clothe yourself and serve me while I eat and drink; and afterward you may eat and drink'? **9** He does not thank the slave because he did the things which were commanded, does he? **10** So you too, when you do all the things which were commanded you, say, 'We are unworthy slaves; we have done *only* that which we ought to have done.' "

Ten Men with Leprosy Healed

11 While He was on the way to Jerusalem, He was passing between Samaria and Galilee. **12** And as He entered a village, ten men with leprosy who stood at a distance met Him; **13** and they raised their voices, saying, "Jesus, Master, have mercy on us!" **14** When He saw *them,* He said to them, "Go and show yourselves to the priests."

And as they were going, they were cleansed. 15 Now one of them, when he saw that he had been healed, turned back, glorifying God with a loud voice, 16 and he fell on his face at His feet, giving thanks to Him. And he was a Samaritan. 17 But Jesus responded and said, "Were there not ten cleansed? But the nine—where *are they?* 18 Was no one found who returned to give glory to God, except this foreigner?" 19 And He said to him, "Stand up and go; your faith has made you well."

Second Coming Foretold

20 Now He was questioned by the Pharisees as to when the kingdom of God was coming, and He answered them and said, "The kingdom of God is not coming with signs that can be observed; 21 nor will they say, 'Look, here *it is!*' or, 'There *it is!*' For behold, the kingdom of God is in your midst."

22 And He said to the disciples, "The days will come when you will long to see one of the days of the Son of Man, and you will not see *it.* 23 And they will say to you, 'Look there,' or, 'Look here!' Do not leave, and do not run after *them.* 24 For just like the lightning, when it flashes out of one part of the sky, shines to the other part of the sky, so will the Son of Man be in His day. 25 But first He must suffer many things and be rejected by this generation. 26 And just as it happened in the days of Noah, so will it also be in the days of the Son of Man: 27 *people* were eating, they were drinking, they were marrying, *and* they were being given in marriage, until the day that Noah entered the ark, and the flood came and destroyed them all. 28 It was the same as happened in the days of Lot: they were eating, they were drinking, they were buying, they were selling, they were planting, *and* they were building; 29 but on the day that Lot left Sodom, it rained fire and brimstone from heaven and destroyed them all. 30 It will be just the same on the day that the Son of Man is revealed. 31 On that day, the one who will be on the housetop, with his goods in the house, must not go down to take them out; and likewise the one in the field must not turn back. 32 Remember Lot's wife. 33 Whoever strives to save his life will lose it, and whoever loses *his life* will keep it. 34 I tell you, on that night there will be two in one bed; one will be taken and the other will be left. 35 There will be two

women grinding at the same *place;* one will be taken and the other will be left. **36** ['Two men will be in the field; one will be taken and the other will be left."] **37** And responding, they *said to Him, "Where, Lord?" And He said to them, "Where the body *is,* there also the vultures will be gathered."

Parables on Prayer

18 Now He was telling them a parable to show that at all times they ought to pray and not become discouraged, **2** saying, "In a certain city there was a judge who did not fear God and did not respect *any* person. **3** Now there was a widow in that city, and she kept coming to him, saying, 'Give me justice against my opponent.' **4** For a while he was unwilling; but later he said to himself, 'Even though I do not fear God nor respect *any* person, **5** yet because this widow is bothering me, I will give her justice; otherwise by continually coming she will wear me out.'" **6** And the Lord said, "Listen to what the unrighteous judge *said; **7** now, will God not bring about justice for His elect who cry out to Him day and night, and will He delay long for them? **8** I tell you that He will bring about justice for them quickly. However, when the Son of Man comes, will He find faith on the earth?"

The Pharisee and the Tax Collector

9 Now He also told this parable to some people who trusted in themselves that they were righteous, and viewed others with contempt: **10** "Two men went up into the temple to pray, one a Pharisee and the other a tax collector. **11** The Pharisee stood and *began* praying this in regard to himself: 'God, I thank You that I am not like other people: swindlers, crooked, adulterers, or even like this tax collector. **12** I fast twice a week; I pay tithes of all that I get.' **13** But the tax collector, standing some distance away, was even unwilling to raise his eyes toward heaven, but was beating his chest, saying, 'God, be merciful to me, the sinner!' **14** I tell you, this man went to his house justified rather than the other one; for everyone who exalts himself will be humbled, but the one who humbles himself will be exalted."

17:36 **1** Early mss do not contain this v

15 Now they were bringing even their babies to Him so that He would touch them; but when the disciples saw *it,* they *began* rebuking them. **16** But Jesus called for the little ones, saying, "Allow the children to come to Me, and do not forbid them, for the kingdom of God belongs to such as these. **17** Truly I say to you, whoever does not receive the kingdom of God like a child will not enter it at all."

The Rich Young Ruler

18 A ruler questioned Him, saying, "Good Teacher, what shall I do to inherit eternal life?" **19** But Jesus said to him, "Why do you call Me good? No one is good except God alone. **20** You know the commandments, 'DO NOT COMMIT ADULTERY, DO NOT MURDER, DO NOT STEAL, DO NOT GIVE FALSE TESTIMONY, HONOR YOUR FATHER AND MOTHER.' " **21** And he said, "All these things I have kept since *my* youth." **22** Now when Jesus heard *this,* He said to him, "One thing you still lack; sell all that you possess and distribute *the money* to the poor, and you will have treasure in heaven; and come, follow Me." **23** But when he had heard these things, he became very sad, for he was extremely wealthy. **24** And Jesus looked at him and said, "How hard it is for those who are wealthy to enter the kingdom of God! **25** For it is easier for a camel to go through the eye of a needle, than for a rich person to enter the kingdom of God!" **26** Those who heard *Him* said, "And *so* who can be saved?" **27** But He said, "The things that are impossible with people are possible with God."

28 Peter said, "Behold, we have left our own homes and followed You." **29** And He said to them, "Truly I say to you, there is no one who has left house, or wife, or brothers, or parents, or children for the sake of the kingdom of God, **30** who will not receive many times as much at this time, and in the age to come, eternal life."

31 Now He took the twelve aside and said to them, "Behold, we are going up to Jerusalem, and all the things that have been written through the prophets about the Son of Man will be accomplished. **32** For He will be handed over to the Gentiles, and will be ridiculed, and abused, and spit upon, **33** and after they have flogged Him, they will kill Him; and on the third day He will rise." **34** The disciples understood none of these things, and *the meaning of* this statement was hidden from them, and they did not comprehend the things that were said.

Bartimaeus Receives Sight

35 Now as Jesus was approaching Jericho, a man who was blind was sitting by the road, begging. 36 But when he heard a crowd going by, he *began* inquiring what this was. 37 They told him that Jesus of Nazareth was passing by. 38 And he called out, saying, "Jesus, Son of David, have mercy on me!" 39 Those who led the way were sternly telling him to be quiet; but he kept crying out all the more, "Son of David, have mercy on me!" 40 And Jesus stopped and commanded that he be brought to Him; and when he came near, He asked him, 41 "What do you want Me to do for you?" And he said, "Lord, *I want* to regain my sight!" 42 And Jesus said to him, "Regain your sight; your faith has made you well." 43 And immediately he regained his sight and *began* following Him, glorifying God; and when all the people saw *it,* they gave praise to God.

Zaccheus Converted

19 *Jesus* entered Jericho and was passing through. 2 And there was a man called by the name of Zaccheus; he was a chief tax collector and he was rich. 3 *Zaccheus* was trying to see who Jesus was, and he was unable due to the crowd, because he was short in stature. 4 So he ran on ahead and climbed up a sycamore tree in order to see Him, because He was about to pass through that *way.* 5 And when Jesus came to the place, He looked up and said to him, "Zaccheus, hurry and come down, for today I must stay at your house." 6 And he hurried and came down, and received Him joyfully. 7 When *the people* saw *this,* they all *began* to complain, saying, "He has gone in to be the guest of a man who is a sinner!" 8 But Zaccheus stopped and said to the Lord, "Behold, Lord, half of my possessions I am giving to the poor, and if I have extorted anything from anyone, I am giving back four times as much." 9 And Jesus said to him, "Today salvation has come to this house, because he, too, is a son of Abraham. 10 For the Son of Man has come to seek and to save that which was lost."

Parable of the Ten Minas

11 Now while they were listening to these things, *Jesus* went on to tell a parable, because He was near Jerusalem and they thought that the kingdom of God was going to appear immediately. **12** So He said, "A nobleman went to a distant country to receive a kingdom for himself, and *then* to return. **13** And he called ten of his own slaves and gave them ten ¹minas, and said to them, 'Do business *with this money* until I come *back.*' **14** But his citizens hated him and sent a delegation after him, saying, 'We do not want this man to reign over us.' **15** When he returned after receiving the kingdom, he ordered that these slaves, to whom he had given the money, be summoned to him so that he would learn how much they had made by the business they had done. **16** The first *slave* appeared, saying, 'Master, your mina has made ten minas more.' **17** And he said to him, 'Well done, good slave; since you have been faithful in a very little thing, you are to have authority over ten cities.' **18** The second one came, saying, 'Your mina, master, has made five minas.' **19** And he said to him also, 'And you are to be over five cities.' **20** And *then* another came, saying, 'Master, here is your mina, which I kept tucked away in a handkerchief; **21** for I was afraid of you, because you are a demanding man; you take up what you did not lay down, and reap what you did not sow.' **22** He *said to him, 'From your own lips I will judge you, you worthless slave. Did you know that I am a demanding man, taking up what I did not lay down, and reaping what I did not sow? **23** And *so* why did you not put my money in the bank, and when I came *back,* I would have collected it with interest?' **24** And *then* he said to the *other slaves* who were present, 'Take the mina away from him and give it to the one who has the ten minas.' **25** And they said to him, 'Master, he *already* has ten minas.' **26** 'I tell you that to everyone who has, *more* shall be given, but from the one who does not have, even what he does have shall be taken away. **27** But as for these enemies of mine who did not want me to reign over them, bring *them* here and slaughter them in my presence.'"

19:13 ¹A mina was equal to about 100 days' wages for a laborer

Triumphal Entry

28 After *Jesus* said these things, He was going on ahead, going up to Jerusalem.

29 When He approached Bethphage and Bethany, near the mountain that is called Olivet, He sent two of the disciples, **30** saying, "Go into the village ahead of *you;* there, as you enter, you will find a colt tied, on which no one yet has ever sat; untie it and bring it *here.* **31** And if anyone asks you, 'Why are you untying *it?*' you shall say this: 'The Lord has need of it.' " **32** So those who were sent left and found *it* just as He had told them. **33** And as they were untying the colt, its owners said to them, "Why are you untying the colt?" **34** They said, "The Lord has need of it." **35** And they brought it to Jesus, and they threw their cloaks on the colt and put Jesus *on it.* **36** Now as He was going, they were spreading their cloaks on the road. **37** And as soon as He was approaching, near the descent of the Mount of Olives, the whole crowd of the disciples began to praise God joyfully with a loud voice for all the miracles which they had seen, **38** shouting:

"BLESSED IS the King, THE ONE WHO COMES IN THE NAME OF THE LORD;

Peace in heaven and glory in the highest!"

39 And *yet* some of the Pharisees in the crowd said to Him, "Teacher, rebuke Your disciples!" **40** Jesus replied, "I tell you, if these stop speaking, the stones will cry out!"

41 When He approached *Jerusalem,* He saw the city and wept over it, **42** saying, "If you had known on this day, even you, the *conditions* for peace! But now they have been hidden from your eyes. **43** For the days will come upon you when your enemies will put up a barricade against you, and surround you and hem you in on every side, **44** and they will level you to the ground, and *throw down* your children within you, and they will not leave in you one stone upon another, because you did not recognize the time of your visitation."

Traders Driven from the Temple

45 And Jesus entered the temple *grounds* and began to drive out those who were selling, **46** saying to them, "It is written: 'AND MY HOUSE WILL BE A HOUSE OF PRAYER,' but you have made it a DEN OF ROBBERS."

47 And He was teaching daily in the temple; but the chief priests and the scribes and the leading men among the people were trying to put Him to death, **48** and *yet* they could not find anything that they might do, for all the people were hanging on to every word He said.

Jesus' Authority Questioned

20 On one of the days while He was teaching the people in the temple and preaching the gospel, the chief priests and the scribes with the elders confronted *Him,* **2** and they declared, saying to Him, "Tell us by what authority You are doing these things, or who is the one who gave You this authority?" **3** But He replied to them, "I will also ask you a question, and you tell Me: **4** Was the baptism of John from heaven or from men?" **5** They discussed among themselves, saying, "If we say, 'From heaven,' He will say, 'Why did you not believe him?' **6** But if we say, 'From men,' all the people will stone us to death, since they are convinced that John was a prophet." **7** And *so* they answered that they did not know where *it came* from. **8** And Jesus said to them, "Neither am I telling you by what authority I do these things."

Parable of the Vine-growers

9 But He began to tell the people this parable: "A man planted a vineyard and leased it to vine-growers, and went on a journey for a long time. **10** At *the harvest* time he sent a slave to the vine-growers, so that they would give him *his share* of the produce of the vineyard; but the vine-growers beat him and sent him away empty-handed. **11** And he proceeded to send another slave; but they beat him also and treated him shamefully, and sent him away empty-handed. **12** And he proceeded to send a third; but this one too they wounded and threw out. **13** Now the owner of the vineyard said, 'What am I to do? I will send my beloved son; perhaps they will respect him.' **14** But when the vine-growers saw him, they discussed with one another, saying, 'This is the heir; let's kill him so that the inheritance will be ours.' **15** And *so* they threw him out of the vineyard and killed him. What, then, will the owner of the vineyard do to them? **16** He will come and put these vine-growers to death, and will give the vineyard to others." However, when they heard *this,* they said, "May it never happen!" **17** But Jesus looked at them and said, "Then what is this *statement* that has been written:

'A STONE WHICH THE BUILDERS REJECTED,
THIS HAS BECOME THE CHIEF CORNERSTONE'?
18 Everyone who falls on that stone will be broken to pieces; but on whomever it falls, it will crush him."

Paying Taxes to Caesar

19 The scribes and the chief priests tried to lay hands on Him that very hour, and *yet* they feared the people; for they were aware that He had spoken this parable against them. 20 And *so* they watched Him closely, and sent spies who pretended to be righteous, in order that they might catch Him in *some* statement, so that they *could* hand Him over to the jurisdiction and authority of the governor. 21 And *the spies* questioned Him, saying, "Teacher, we know that You speak and teach correctly, and You are not partial to anyone, but You teach the way of God on the basis of truth. 22 Is it permissible for us to pay taxes to Caesar, or not?" 23 But He saw through their trickery and said to them, 24 "Show Me a ¹denarius. Whose image and inscription does it have?" They said, "Caesar's." 25 And He said to them, "Then pay to Caesar the things that are Caesar's, and to God the things that are God's." 26 And they were unable to catch Him in a statement in the presence of the people; and they were amazed at His answer, and said nothing.

Is There a Resurrection?

27 Now some of the Sadducees (who maintain that there is no resurrection) came to Him, 28 and they questioned Him, saying, "Teacher, Moses wrote for us that if a man's brother dies, leaving a wife, and he is childless, that his brother is to marry the wife and raise up children for his brother. 29 So then, there were seven brothers; and the first took a wife and died childless; 30 and the second 31 and the third married her; and in the same way all seven died, leaving no children. 32 Finally the woman also died. 33 Therefore, in the resurrection, which one's wife does the woman become? For all seven married her."

34 Jesus said to them, "The sons of this age marry and *the women* are given in marriage, 35 but those who are considered worthy to attain to that age and the

---

20:24 ¹ The denarius was a day's wages for a laborer

resurrection from the dead, neither marry nor are given in marriage; 36 for they cannot even die anymore, for they are like angels, and are sons of God, being sons of the resurrection. 37 But *as for* the fact that the dead are raised, even Moses revealed *this* in the *passage about the burning* bush, where he calls the Lord THE GOD OF ABRAHAM, THE GOD OF ISAAC, AND THE GOD OF JACOB. 38 Now He is not the God of the dead, but of the living; for all live to Him." 39 Some of the scribes answered and said, "Teacher, You have spoken well." 40 For they did not have the courage to question Him any longer about anything.

41 But He said to them, "How *is it that* they say the Christ is David's son? 42 For David himself says in the book of Psalms,

'THE LORD SAID TO MY LORD,
    "SIT AT MY RIGHT HAND,
43   UNTIL I MAKE YOUR ENEMIES A FOOTSTOOL FOR YOUR FEET." '
44 Therefore David calls Him 'Lord,' and *so* how is He his son?"

45 And while all the people were listening, He said to the disciples, 46 "Beware of the scribes, who like to walk around in long robes, and love personal greetings in the marketplaces, and chief seats in the synagogues and places of honor at banquets, 47 who devour widows' houses, and for appearance's sake offer long prayers. These will receive all the more condemnation."

The Widow's Gift

21 Now He looked up and saw the wealthy putting their gifts into the *temple* treasury. 2 And He saw a poor widow putting in two ¹lepta coins. 3 And He said, "Truly I say to you, this poor widow put in more than all *of them;* 4 for they all contributed to the offering from their surplus; but she, from her poverty, put in all that she had to live on."

5 And while some were talking about the temple, that it was decorated with beautiful stones and ¹vowed gifts, He said, 6 "*As for* these things which you are observing, the days will come when there will not be left *one* stone upon another, which will not be torn down."

21:2 ¹The smallest Greek copper coin, about 1/128 of a laborer's daily wage   21:5 ¹I.e., gifts promised by vows

⁷ They asked Him questions, saying, "Teacher, when therefore will these things happen? And what *will be* the sign when these things are about to take place?" ⁸ And He said, "See to it that you are not misled; for many will come in My name, saying, 'I am *He*,' and, 'The time is near.' Do not go after them. ⁹ And when you hear of wars and revolts, do not be alarmed; for these things must take place first, but the end *will* not *follow* immediately."

Things to Come

¹⁰ Then He *continued by* saying to them, "Nation will rise against nation, and kingdom against kingdom, ¹¹ and there will be massive earthquakes, and in various places plagues and famines; and there will be terrible sights and great signs from heaven.

¹² "But before all these things, they will lay their hands on you and persecute you, turning you over to the synagogues and prisons, bringing you before kings and governors on account of My name. ¹³ It will lead to an opportunity for your testimony. ¹⁴ So make up your minds not to prepare beforehand to defend yourselves; ¹⁵ for I will provide you eloquence and wisdom which none of your adversaries will be able to oppose or refute. ¹⁶ But you will be betrayed even by parents, brothers *and sisters, other* relatives, and friends, and they will put *some* of you to death, ¹⁷ and you will be hated by all people because of My name. ¹⁸ And *yet* not a hair of your head will perish. ¹⁹ By your endurance you will gain your lives.

²⁰ "But when you see Jerusalem surrounded by armies, then recognize that her desolation is near. ²¹ Then those who are in Judea must flee to the mountains, and those who are inside the city must leave, and those who are in the country must not enter the city; ²² because these are days of punishment, so that all things which have been written will be fulfilled. ²³ Woe to those women who are pregnant, and to those who are nursing babies in those days; for there will be great distress upon the land, and wrath to this people; ²⁴ and they will fall by the edge of the sword, and will be led captive into all the nations; and Jerusalem will be trampled underfoot by the Gentiles until *the* times of the Gentiles are fulfilled.

The Return of Christ

25 "There will be signs in *the* sun and moon and stars, and on the earth distress among nations, in perplexity at the roaring of the sea and the waves, **26** people fainting from fear and the expectation of the things that are coming upon the world; for the powers of the heavens will be shaken. **27** And then they will see the Son of Man coming in a cloud with power and great glory. **28** But when these things begin to take place, straighten up and lift up your heads, because your redemption is drawing near."

29 And He told them a parable: "Look at the fig tree and all the trees: **30** as soon as they put forth *leaves,* you see for yourselves and know that summer is now near. **31** So you too, when you see these things happening, recognize that the kingdom of God is near. **32** Truly I say to you, this generation will not pass away until all things take place. **33** Heaven and earth will pass away, but My words will not pass away.

34 "But be on your guard, so that your hearts will not be weighed down with dissipation and drunkenness and the worries of life, and that this day will not come on you suddenly, like a trap; **35** for it will come upon all those who live on the face of all the earth. **36** But stay alert at all times, praying that you will have strength to escape all these things that are going to take place, and to stand before the Son of Man."

37 Now during the day He was teaching in the temple, but at evening He would go out and spend the night on the mountain that is called Olivet. **38** And all the people would get up very early in the morning *to come* to Him in the temple to listen to Him.

Preparing the Passover

22 Now the Feast of Unleavened Bread, which is called the Passover, was approaching. **2** And the chief priests and the scribes were trying to find a way to put Him to death, since they were afraid of the people.

3 And Satan entered Judas, the one called Iscariot, who belonged to the number of the twelve. **4** And he left and discussed with the chief priests and officers how he was to betray Him to them. **5** And they were delighted, and agreed to give him money. **6** And *so* he consented, and *began* looking for a good opportunity to betray Him to them away from the crowd.

7 Now the *first* day of Unleavened Bread came, on which the Passover *lamb* had to be sacrificed. **8** And *so Jesus* sent Peter and John, saying, "Go and prepare the Passover for us, so that we may eat *it.*" **9** They said to Him, "Where do You want us to prepare *it?*" **10** And He said to them, "When you have entered the city, a man carrying a pitcher of water will meet you; follow him into the house that he enters. **11** And you shall say to the owner of the house, 'The Teacher says to you, "Where is the guest room in which I may eat the Passover with My disciples?"' **12** And he will show you a large, furnished upstairs room; prepare *it* there." **13** And they left and found *everything* just as He had told them; and they prepared the Passover.

The Lord's Supper

14 When the hour came, He reclined *at the table,* and the apostles with Him. **15** And He said to them, "I have eagerly desired to eat this Passover with you before I suffer; **16** for I say to you, I shall not eat it *again* until it is fulfilled in the kingdom of God." **17** And when He had taken a cup *and* given thanks, He said, "Take this and share it among yourselves; **18** for I say to you, I will not drink of the fruit of the vine from now on until the kingdom of God comes." **19** And when He had taken *some* bread *and* given thanks, He broke it and gave it to them, saying, "This is My body, which is being given for you; do this in remembrance of Me." **20** And in the same way *He took* the cup after they had eaten, saying, "This cup, which is poured out for you, is the new covenant in My blood. **21** But behold, the hand of the one betraying Me is with Mine on the table. **22** For indeed, the Son of Man is going as it has been determined; but woe to that man by whom He is betrayed!" **23** And they began to debate among themselves which one of them it was who was going to do this.

Who Is Greatest

24 And a dispute also developed among them *as to* which one of them was regarded as being the greatest. **25** And He said to them, "The kings of the Gentiles domineer over them; and those who have authority over them are called 'Benefactors.' **26** But *it is* not this way for you; rather, the one who is the greatest among you must become like the youngest, and the leader like the servant. **27** For who is greater, the one who reclines *at the table* or the one who serves? Is it not the one who reclines *at the table?* But I am among you as the one who serves.

28 "You are the ones who have stood by Me in My trials; **29** and just as My Father has granted Me a kingdom, I grant you **30** that you may eat and drink at My table in My kingdom, and you will sit on thrones judging the twelve tribes of Israel.

31 "Simon, Simon, behold, Satan has demanded to sift you *men* like wheat; **32** but I have prayed for ¹you, that ²your faith will not fail; and ³you, when you have turned back, strengthen your brothers." **33** But he said to Him, "Lord, I am ready to go with You both to prison and to death!" **34** But He said, "I tell you, Peter, the rooster will not crow today until you have denied three times that you know Me."

35 And He said to them, "When I sent you out without money belt and bag and sandals, you did not lack anything, did you?" They said, "*No, nothing.*" **36** And He said to them, "But now, whoever has a money belt is to take it along, likewise also a bag, and whoever has no sword is to sell his cloak and buy *one.* **37** For I tell you that this which is written must be fulfilled in Me: 'AND HE WAS COUNTED WITH WRONGDOERS'; for that which refers to Me has *its* fulfillment." **38** They said, "Lord, look, here are two swords." And He said to them, "It is enough."

The Garden of Gethsemane

39 And He came out and went, as was His habit, to the Mount of Olives; and the disciples also followed Him. **40** Now when He arrived at the place, He said to them, "Pray that you do not come into temptation." **41** And He withdrew from them about a stone's throw, and He knelt down and *began* to pray, **42** saying, "Father, if You are willing, remove this cup from Me; yet not My will, but Yours be done." **43** [¹Now an angel from heaven appeared

---

22:32 ¹Gr singular, referring only to Peter   22:32 ²Gr singular, referring only to Peter   22:32 ³Gr singular, referring only to Peter
22:43 ¹Most early mss do not contain vv 43 and 44

to Him, strengthening Him. 44 And being in agony, He was praying very fervently; and His sweat became like drops of blood, falling down upon the ground]. 45 When He rose from prayer, He came to the disciples and found them sleeping from sorrow, 46 and He said to them, "Why are you sleeping? Get up and pray that you do not come into temptation."

Jesus Betrayed by Judas

47 While He was still speaking, behold, a crowd *came,* and the one called Judas, one of the twelve, was leading the way for them; and he approached Jesus to kiss Him. 48 But Jesus said to him, "Judas, are you betraying the Son of Man with a kiss?" 49 When those who were around Him saw what was going to happen, they said, "Lord, shall we strike with the sword?" 50 And one of them struck the slave of the high priest and cut off his right ear. 51 But Jesus responded and said, "Stop! No more of this." And He touched his ear and healed him. 52 And Jesus said to the chief priests and officers of the temple and elders who had come against Him, "Have you come out with swords and clubs as *you would* against a man inciting a revolt? 53 While I was with you daily in the temple, you did not lay hands on Me; but this hour and the power of darkness are yours."

Jesus' Arrest

54 Now they arrested Him and led *Him away,* and brought *Him* to the house of the high priest; but Peter was following at a distance. 55 After they kindled a fire in the middle of the courtyard and sat down together, Peter was sitting among them. 56 And a slave woman, seeing him as he sat in the firelight, and staring at him, said, "This man was with Him as well." 57 But he denied *it,* saying, "I do not know Him, woman!" 58 And a little later, another person saw him and said, "You are *one* of them too!" But Peter said, "Man, I am not!" 59 And after about an hour had passed, some other man *began* to insist, saying, "Certainly this man also was with Him, for he, too, is a Galilean." 60 But Peter said, "Man, I do not know what you are talking about!" And immediately, while he was still speaking, a rooster crowed. 61 And *then* the Lord turned and looked at Peter. And Peter remembered the word of the Lord, how He had told him, "Before a

rooster crows today, you will deny Me three times." 62 And he went out and wept bitterly.

63 The men who were holding Jesus in custody *began* mocking Him and beating Him, 64 and they blindfolded Him and *repeatedly* asked Him, saying, "Prophesy, who is the one who hit You?" 65 And they were saying many other things against Him, blaspheming.

Jesus before the Sanhedrin

66 When it was day, the 1Council of elders of the people assembled, both chief priests and scribes, and they led Him away to their council chamber, saying, 67 "If You are the Christ, tell us." But He said to them, "If I tell you, you will not believe; 68 and if I ask a question, you will not answer. 69 But from now on the Son of Man will be seated at the right hand of the power of God." 70 And they all said, "So You are the Son of God?" And He said to them, "You say *correctly* that I am." 71 And *then* they said, "What further need do we have of testimony? For we have heard *it* ourselves from His *own* mouth!"

Jesus before Pilate

23 Then the entire assembly of them set out and brought Him before Pilate. 2 And they began to bring charges against Him, saying, "We found this man misleading our nation and forbidding *us* to pay taxes to Caesar, and saying that He Himself is Christ, a King." 3 Now Pilate asked Him, saying, "*So* You are the King of the Jews?" And He answered him and said, "*It is as* you say." 4 But Pilate said to the chief priests and the crowds, "I find no grounds for charges in *the case of* this man." 5 But they kept on insisting, saying, "He is stirring up the people, teaching all over Judea, starting from Galilee, as far as this place!"

6 Now when Pilate heard *this*, he asked whether the man was a Galilean. 7 And when he learned that He belonged to Herod's jurisdiction, he sent Him to Herod, since he also was in Jerusalem at this time.

Jesus before Herod

8 Now Herod was overjoyed when he saw Jesus; for he

22:66 1Or *Sanhedrin*

had wanted to see Him for a long time, because he had been hearing about Him and was hoping to see some sign performed by Him. [9] And he questioned Him at some length; but He offered him no answer at all. [10] Now the chief priests and the scribes stood *there,* vehemently charging Him. [11] And Herod, together with his soldiers, treated Him with contempt and mocked Him, dressing Him in a brightly shining robe, and sent Him back to Pilate. [12] And *so* Herod and Pilate became friends with one another that very day; for previously, they had been enemies toward each other.

Pilate Seeks Jesus' Release

[13] Now Pilate summoned to himself the chief priests, the [1]rulers, and the people, [14] and he said to them, "You brought this man to me on the ground that he is inciting the people to revolt; and behold, after examining *Him* before you, I have found no basis at all in *the case of* this man for the charges which you are bringing against Him. [15] No, nor has Herod, for he sent Him back to us; and behold, nothing deserving death has been done by Him. [16] Therefore I will punish Him and release Him." [17] [[1]Now he was obligated to release to them at the feast one *prisoner.*]

[18] But they cried out all together, saying, "Away with this man, and release to us Barabbas!" [19] (*He was* one who had been thrown into prison for a revolt that took place in the city, and for murder.) [20] But Pilate, wanting to release Jesus, addressed them again, [21] but they kept on crying out, saying, "Crucify, crucify Him!" [22] And he said to them a third time, "Why, what has this man done wrong? I have found in His case no grounds for *a sentence of* death; therefore I will punish Him and release Him." [23] But they were insistent, with loud voices, demanding that He be crucified. And their voices *began* to prevail. [24] And *so* Pilate decided to have their demand carried out. [25] And he released the man for whom they were asking, who had been thrown into prison for a revolt and murder; but he handed Jesus over to their will.

23:13 [1]I.e., other Jewish leaders   23:17 [1]Most early mss do not contain this v

Simon Carries the Cross

26 And when they led Him away, they seized a man, Simon of Cyrene, as he was coming in from the country, and placed on him the cross to carry behind Jesus.

27 Now following Him was a large crowd of the people, and of women who were mourning and grieving for Him. **28** But Jesus turned to them and said, "Daughters of Jerusalem, stop weeping for Me, but weep for yourselves and for your children. **29** For behold, days are coming when they will say, 'Blessed are those who cannot bear, and the wombs that have not given birth, and the breasts that have not nursed.' **30** Then they will begin TO SAY TO THE MOUNTAINS, 'FALL ON US,' AND TO THE HILLS, 'COVER US.' **31** For if they do these things when the tree is green, what will happen when it is dry?"

32 Now two others, who were criminals, were also being led away to be put to death with Him.

The Crucifixion

33 And when they came to the place called The Skull, there they crucified Him and the criminals, one on the right and the other on the left. **34** ['But Jesus was saying, "Father, forgive them; for they do not know what they are doing."] And they cast lots, dividing His garments among themselves. **35** And the people stood by, watching. And even the rulers were sneering at Him, saying, "He saved others; let Him save Himself if this is the Christ of God, His Chosen One." **36** The soldiers also ridiculed Him, coming up to Him, offering Him sour wine, **37** and saying, "If You are the King of the Jews, save Yourself!" **38** Now there was also an inscription above Him, "THIS IS THE KING OF THE JEWS."

39 One of the criminals who were hanged *there* was hurling abuse at Him, saying, "Are You not the Christ? Save Yourself and us!" **40** But the other responded, and rebuking him, said, "Do you not even fear God, since you are under the same sentence of condemnation? **41** And we indeed *are suffering* justly, for we are receiving what we deserve for our crimes; but this man has done nothing wrong." **42** And he was saying, "Jesus, remember me when You come into Your kingdom!"

23:34 [1] Most early mss do not contain *But Jesus was saying...doing*

43 And He said to him, "Truly I say to you, today you will be with Me in Paradise."

44 It was now about ¹the sixth hour, and darkness came over the entire land until ²the ninth hour, 45 because the sun stopped shining; and the veil of the temple was torn in two. 46 And Jesus, crying out with a loud voice, said, "Father, INTO YOUR HANDS I ENTRUST MY SPIRIT." And having said this, He died. 47 Now when the centurion saw what had happened, he *began* praising God, saying, "This man was in fact innocent." 48 And all the crowds who came together for this spectacle, after watching what had happened, *began* to return *home,* ¹beating their chests. 49 And all His acquaintances and the women who accompanied Him from Galilee were standing at a distance, seeing these things.

Jesus Is Buried

50 And a man named Joseph, who was a member of the Council, a good and righteous man 51 (he had not consented to their plan and action), *a man* from Arimathea, a city of the Jews, who was waiting for the kingdom of God— 52 this man went to Pilate and asked for the body of Jesus. 53 And he took it down and wrapped it in a linen cloth, and laid Him in a tomb cut into the rock, where no one had ever lain. 54 It was a preparation day, and a Sabbath was about to begin. 55 Now the women who had come with Him from Galilee followed, and they saw the tomb and how His body was laid. 56 And *then* they returned and prepared spices and perfumes.

And on the Sabbath they rested according to the commandment.

The Resurrection

24 But on the first day of the week, at early dawn, they came to the tomb bringing the spices which they had prepared. 2 And they found the stone rolled away from the tomb, 3 but when they entered, they did not find the body of the Lord Jesus. 4 While they were perplexed about this, behold, two men *suddenly* stood near them in gleaming clothing; 5 and as the women were terrified and bowed their faces to the ground, *the*

23:44 ¹I.e., noon   23:44 ²I.e., 3 p.m.   23:48 ¹I.e., as a traditional sign of mourning or contrition

men said to them, "Why are you seeking the living One among the dead? [6] He is not here, but He has risen. Remember how He spoke to you while He was still in Galilee, [7] saying that the Son of Man must be handed over to sinful men, and be crucified, and on the third day rise *from the dead.*" [8] And they remembered His words, [9] and returned from the tomb and reported all these things to the eleven, and to all the rest. [10] Now *these women* were Mary Magdalene, Joanna, and Mary the *mother* of James; also the other women with them were telling these things to the apostles. [11] But these words appeared to them as nonsense, and they would not believe the women. [12] Nevertheless, Peter got up and ran to the tomb; and when he stooped and looked in, he *saw the linen wrappings only; and he went away to his home, marveling at what had happened.

The Road to Emmaus

[13] And behold, on that very day two of them were going to a village named Emmaus, which was [1]sixty stadia from Jerusalem. [14] And they were talking with each other about all these things which had taken place. [15] While they were talking and discussing, Jesus Himself approached and *began* traveling with them. [16] But their eyes were kept from recognizing Him. [17] And He said to them, "What are these words that you are exchanging with one another as you are walking?" And they came to a stop, looking sad. [18] One *of them,* named Cleopas, answered and said to Him, "Are You *possibly* the only one living near Jerusalem who does not know about the things that happened here in these days?" [19] And He said to them, "What sort of things?" And they said to Him, "Those about Jesus the Nazarene, who proved to be a prophet mighty in deed and word in the sight of God and all the people, [20] and how the chief priests and our rulers handed Him over to be sentenced to death, and crucified Him. [21] But we were hoping that it was He who was going to redeem Israel. Indeed, besides all this, it is *now* the third day since these things happened. [22] But also some women among us left us bewildered. When they were at the tomb early in the morning, [23] and did not

---

24:13 [1] Possibly about 7 miles or 11.3 km; a Roman stadion perhaps averaged 607 ft. or 185 m

find His body, they came, saying that they had also seen
a vision of angels who said that He was alive. **24** And *so*
some of those who were with us went to the tomb, and
found it just exactly as the women also had said; but Him
they did not see." **25** And *then* He said to them, "You
foolish men and slow of heart to believe in all that the
prophets have spoken! **26** Was it not necessary for the
Christ to suffer these things and to come into His glory?"
27 Then beginning with Moses and with all the Prophets,
He explained to them the things *written* about Himself
in all the Scriptures.

  28 And they approached the village where they were
going, and He gave the impression that He was going
farther. **29** And *so* they strongly urged Him, saying, "Stay
with us, for it is *getting* toward evening, and the day is
now nearly over." So He went in to stay with them.
30 And it came about, when He had reclined *at the table*
with them, that He took the bread and blessed *it,* and He
broke *it* and *began* giving *it* to them. **31** And *then* their
eyes were opened and they recognized Him; and He
vanished from their sight. **32** They said to one another,
"Were our hearts not burning within us when He was
speaking to us on the road, while He was explaining the
Scriptures to us?" **33** And they got up that very hour and
returned to Jerusalem, and found the eleven gathered
together and those who were with them, **34** saying,
"The Lord has really risen and has appeared to Simon!"
35 They *began* to relate their experiences on the road,
and how He was recognized by them at the breaking of
the bread.

Other Appearances

  36 Now while they were telling these things, *Jesus*
Himself *suddenly* stood in their midst and *said to them,
"Peace *be* to you." **37** But they were startled and
frightened, and thought that they were looking at a
spirit. **38** And He said to them, "Why are you frightened,
and why are doubts arising in your hearts? **39** See My
hands and My feet, that it is I Myself; touch Me and see,
because a spirit does not have flesh and bones as you
plainly see that I have." **40** And when He had said this,
He showed them His hands and His feet. **41** While they
still could not believe *it* because of their joy and astonishment, He said to them, "Have you anything here to

eat?" **42** They served Him a piece of broiled fish; **43** and He took it and ate *it* in front of them.

44 Now He said to them, "These are My words which I spoke to you while I was still with you, that all the things that are written about Me in the Law of Moses and the Prophets and the Psalms must be fulfilled." **45** Then He opened their minds to understand the Scriptures, **46** and He said to them, "So it is written, that the Christ would suffer and rise from the dead on the third day, **47** and that repentance for forgiveness of sins would be proclaimed in His name to all the nations, beginning from Jerusalem. **48** You are witnesses of these things. **49** And behold, I am sending the promise of My Father upon you; but you are to stay in the city until you are clothed with power from on high."

The Ascension

50 And He led them out as far as Bethany, and He lifted up His hands and blessed them. **51** While He was blessing them, He parted from them and was carried up into heaven. **52** And they, after worshiping Him, returned to Jerusalem with great joy, **53** and were continually in the temple praising God.

The Gospel According to
JOHN

The Deity of Jesus Christ

1 In the beginning was the Word, and the Word was
with God, and the Word was God. 2 He was in the
beginning with God. 3 All things came into being
through Him, and apart from Him not even one thing
came into being that has come into being. 4 In Him was
life, and the life was the Light of mankind. 5 And the
Light shines in the darkness, and the darkness did not
grasp it.

The Witness John the Baptist

6 A man [1]came, *one* sent from God, *and* his name was
John. 7 He came as a witness, to testify about the Light,
so that all might believe through him. 8 [1]He was not the
Light, but *he came* to testify about the Light.

9 [1]*This* was the true Light [2]that, coming into the world,
enlightens every person. 10 He was in the world, and the
world came into being through Him, and *yet* the world
did not know Him. 11 He came to His own, and His own
people did not accept Him. 12 But as many as received
Him, to them He gave the right to become children of
God, to those who believe in His name, 13 who were
born, not of blood, nor of the will of the flesh, nor of the
will of a man, but of God.

The Word Made Flesh

14 And the Word became flesh, and dwelt among us;
and we saw His glory, glory as of the only *Son* from the
Father, full of grace and truth. 15 John *testified about
Him and called out, saying, "This was He of whom I said,
'He who is coming after me has proved to be my superior, because He existed before me.' " 16 For of His fullness
we have all received, and grace upon grace. 17 For the
Law was given through Moses; grace and truth were
realized through Jesus Christ. 18 No one has seen God at

1:6 [1]Or *came into being*   1:8 [1]Lit *That one;* i.e., John   1:9 [1]I.e., the
Word, Christ   1:9 [2]Or *that enlightens every person coming
into the world*

any time; God the only *Son*, who is in the arms of the Father, He has explained *Him*.

The Testimony of John the Baptist

19 This is the testimony of John, when the Jews sent priests and Levites to him from Jerusalem to ask him, "Who are you?" **20** And he confessed and did not deny; and *this is what* he confessed: "I am not the Christ." **21** And *so* they asked him, "What then? Are you Elijah?" And he *said, "I am not." "Are you the Prophet?" And he answered, "No." **22** Then they said to him, "Who are you? *Tell us,* so that we may give an answer to those who sent us. What do you say about yourself?" **23** He said, "I am THE VOICE OF ONE CALLING ¹OUT IN THE WILDERNESS, 'MAKE THE WAY OF THE LORD STRAIGHT,' as Isaiah the prophet said."

24 And *the messengers* had been sent from the Pharisees. **25** They asked him, and said to him, "Why then are you baptizing, if you are not the Christ, nor Elijah, nor the Prophet?" **26** John answered them, saying, "I baptize ¹in water, *but* among you stands One whom you do not know. **27** *It is* He who comes after me, of whom I am not worthy *even* to untie the strap of His sandal." **28** These things took place in Bethany beyond the Jordan, where John was baptizing *people*.

29 The next day he *saw Jesus coming to him, and *said, "Behold, the Lamb of God who takes away the sin of the world! **30** This is He in behalf of whom I said, 'After me is coming a Man who has proved to be my superior, because He existed before me.' **31** And I did not recognize Him, but so that He would be revealed to Israel, I came baptizing ¹in water." **32** And John testified, saying, "I have seen the Spirit descending as a dove out of heaven, and He remained upon Him. **33** And I did not recognize Him, but He who sent me to baptize ¹in water said to me, 'He upon whom you see the Spirit descending and remaining upon Him, this is the One who baptizes in the Holy Spirit.' **34** And I myself have seen, and have testified that this is the Son of God."

1:23 ¹Or *out, In the wilderness make the way*   1:26 ¹The Gr here can be translated *in, with,* or *by*   1:31 ¹The Gr here can be translated *in, with,* or *by*   1:33 ¹The Gr here can be translated *in, with,* or *by*

Jesus' Public Ministry; First Converts

35 Again the next day John was standing with two of his disciples, **36** and he looked at Jesus as He walked, and *said, "Behold, the Lamb of God!" **37** And the two disciples heard him speak, and they followed Jesus. **38** And Jesus turned and saw them following, and *said to them, "What are you seeking?" They said to Him, "Rabbi (which translated means Teacher), where are You staying?" **39** He *said to them, "Come, and you will see." So they came and saw where He was staying, and they stayed with Him that day; it was about the [1]tenth hour. **40** One of the two who heard John *speak,* and followed Him, was Andrew, Simon Peter's brother. **41** He first *found his own brother Simon and *said to him, "We have found the Messiah" (which translated means [1]Christ). **42** He brought him to Jesus. Jesus looked at him and said, "You are Simon the son of John; you shall be called Cephas" (which is translated Peter).

43 The next day He decided to go to Galilee, and He *found Philip. And Jesus *said to him, "Follow Me." **44** Now Philip was from Bethsaida, the city of Andrew and Peter. **45** Philip *found Nathanael and *said to him, "We have found Him of whom Moses wrote in the Law, and the prophets *also wrote:* Jesus the son of Joseph, from Nazareth!" **46** Nathanael said to him, "Can anything good be from Nazareth?" Philip *said to him, "Come and see." **47** Jesus saw Nathanael coming to Him, and *said of him, "Here is truly an Israelite, in whom there is no deceit!" **48** Nathanael *said to Him, "How do You know me?" Jesus answered and said to him, "Before Philip called you, when you were under the fig tree, I saw you." **49** Nathanael answered Him, "Rabbi, You are the Son of God; You are the King of Israel!" **50** Jesus answered and said to him, "Because I said to you that I saw you under the fig tree, do you believe? You will see greater things than these." **51** And He *said to him, "Truly, truly, I say to you, you will see heaven opened and the angels of God ascending and descending on the Son of Man."

Miracle at Cana

2 On the third day there was a wedding in Cana of Galilee, and the mother of Jesus was there; **2** and both

---

1:39 [1] I.e., about 4 p.m.   1:41 [1] Gr *Anointed One*

Jesus and His disciples were invited to the wedding. [3] When the wine ran out, the mother of Jesus *said to Him, "They have no wine." [4] And Jesus *said to her, "What *business* do you have with Me, woman? My hour has not yet come." [5] His mother *said to the servants, "Whatever He tells you, do it." [6] Now there were six stone waterpots standing there for the Jewish custom of purification, containing [†]two or three measures each. [7] Jesus *said to them, "Fill the waterpots with water." So they filled them up to the brim. [8] And He *said to them, "Draw *some* out now and take *it* to the [†]headwaiter." And they took *it to him.* [9] Now when the headwaiter tasted the water which had become wine, and did not know where it came from (but the servants who had drawn the water knew), the headwaiter *called the groom, [10] and *said to him, "Every man serves the good wine first, and when *the guests* are drunk, *then he serves* the poorer *wine; but* you have kept the good wine until now." [11] This beginning of *His* signs Jesus did in Cana of Galilee, and revealed His glory; and His disciples believed in Him.

[12] After this He went down to Capernaum, He and His mother, and *His* brothers and His disciples; and they stayed there a few days.

First Passover—Cleansing the Temple

[13] The Passover of the Jews was near, and Jesus went up to Jerusalem. [14] And within the temple *grounds* He found those who were selling oxen, sheep, and doves, and the money changers seated *at their tables.* [15] And He made a whip of cords, and drove *them* all out of the temple *area,* with the sheep and the oxen; and He poured out the coins of the money changers and overturned their tables; [16] and to those who were selling the doves He said, "Take these things away from here; stop making My Father's house a place of business!" [17] His disciples remembered that it was written: "ZEAL FOR YOUR HOUSE WILL CONSUME ME." [18] The Jews then said to Him, "What sign do You show us as your authority for doing these things?" [19] Jesus answered them, "Destroy this temple, and in three days I will raise it up." [20] The Jews then

---

2:6 [1]About 18 or 27 gallons each; or 68 or 102 liters   2:8 [1]I.e., manager of the banquet

said, "It took forty-six years to build this temple, and *yet* You will raise it up in three days?" **21** But He was speaking about the temple of His body. **22** So when He was raised from the dead, His disciples remembered that He said this; and they believed the Scripture and the word which Jesus had spoken.

23 Now when He was in Jerusalem at the Passover, during the feast, many believed in His name as they observed His signs which He was doing. **24** But Jesus, on His part, was not entrusting Himself to them, because He knew all people, **25** and because He did not need anyone to testify about mankind, for He Himself knew what was in mankind.

The New Birth

3 Now there was a man of the Pharisees, named Nicodemus, a ruler of the Jews; **2** this man came to Jesus at night and said to Him, "Rabbi, we know that You have come from God *as* a teacher; for no one can do these signs that You do unless God is with him." **3** Jesus responded and said to him, "Truly, truly, I say to you, unless someone is born again he cannot see the kingdom of God."

4 Nicodemus *said to Him, "How can a person be born when he is old? He cannot enter his mother's womb a second time and be born, can he?" **5** Jesus answered, "Truly, truly, I say to you, unless someone is born of water and *the* Spirit, he cannot enter the kingdom of God. **6** That which has been born of the flesh is flesh, and that which has been born of the Spirit is spirit. **7** Do not be amazed that I said to you, 'You must be born again.' **8** The wind blows where it wishes, and you hear the sound of it, but you do not know where it is coming from and where it is going; so is everyone who has been born of the Spirit."

9 Nicodemus responded and said to Him, "How can these things be?" **10** Jesus answered and said to him, "You are the teacher of Israel, and *yet* you do not understand these things? **11** Truly, truly, I say to you, we speak of what we know and testify of what we have seen, and you *people* do not accept our testimony. **12** If I told you earthly things and you do not believe, how will you believe if I tell you heavenly things? **13** No one has ascended into heaven, except He who descended from heaven: the Son of Man. [14] And just as Moses lifted up the serpent in the wilderness, so must the Son of Man be lifted up, [15] so that everyone who [r]believes will have eternal life in Him.

[16] "For God so loved the world, that He gave His only Son, so that everyone who believes in Him will not perish, but have eternal life. [17] For God did not send the Son into the world to judge the world, but so that the world might be saved through Him. [18] The one who believes in Him is not judged; the one who does not believe has been judged already, because he has not believed in the name of the only Son of God. [19] And this is the judgment, that the Light has come into the world, and people loved the darkness rather than the Light; for their deeds were evil. [20] For everyone who does evil hates the Light, and does not come to the Light, so that his deeds will not be exposed. [21] But the one who practices the truth comes to the Light, so that his deeds will be revealed as having been performed in God."

John the Baptist's Last Testimony

[22] After these things Jesus and His disciples came into the land of Judea; and there He was spending time with them and baptizing. [23] Now John also was baptizing in Aenon, near Salim, because there was an abundance of water there; and *people* were coming and being baptized— [24] for John had not yet been thrown into prison.

[25] Then a matter of dispute developed on the part of John's disciples with a Jew about purification. [26] And they came to John and said to him, "Rabbi, He who was with you beyond the Jordan, to whom you have testified— behold, He is baptizing and all *the people* are coming to Him." [27] John replied, "A person can receive not even one thing unless it has been given to him from heaven. [28] You yourselves are my witnesses that I said, 'I am not the Christ,' but, 'I have been sent ahead of Him.' [29] He who has the bride is the groom; but the friend of the groom, who stands and listens to him, rejoices greatly because of the groom's voice. So this joy of mine has been made full. [30] He must increase, but I must decrease.

[31] "He who comes from above is above all; the one

3:15 [1] Or *believes in Him will have eternal life*

who is *only* from the earth is of the earth and speaks of the earth. He who comes from heaven is above all. ³²What He has seen and heard, of this He testifies; and no one accepts His testimony. ³³The one who has accepted His testimony has certified that God is true. ³⁴For He whom God sent speaks the words of God; for He does not give the Spirit sparingly. ³⁵The Father loves the Son and has entrusted all things to His hand. ³⁶The one who believes in the Son has eternal life; but the one who does not obey the Son will not see life, but the wrath of God remains on him."

Jesus Goes to Galilee

4 So then, when the Lord knew that the Pharisees had heard that He was making and baptizing more disciples than John ²(although Jesus Himself was not baptizing; rather, His disciples *were*), ³He left Judea and went away again to Galilee. ⁴And He had to pass through Samaria. ⁵So He *came to a city of Samaria called Sychar, near the parcel of land that Jacob gave to his son Joseph; ⁶and Jacob's well was there. So Jesus, tired from His journey, was just sitting by the well. It was about ¹the sixth hour.

The Woman of Samaria

⁷A woman of Samaria *came to draw water. Jesus *said to her, "Give Me a drink." ⁸For His disciples had gone away to the city to buy food. ⁹So the Samaritan woman *said to Him, "How *is it that* You, *though* You are a Jew, are asking me for a drink, *though* I am a Samaritan woman?" (For Jews do not associate with Samaritans.) ¹⁰Jesus replied to her, "If you knew the gift of God, and who it is who is saying to you, 'Give Me a drink,' you would have asked Him, and He would have given you living water." ¹¹She *said to Him, "Sir, You have no bucket and the well is deep; where then do You get *this* living water? ¹²You are not greater than our father Jacob, are You, who gave us the well and drank of it himself, and his sons and his cattle?" ¹³Jesus answered and said to her, "Everyone who drinks of this water will be thirsty again; ¹⁴but whoever drinks of the water that I will give him shall never be thirsty; but the water that I

will give him will become in him a fountain of water springing up to eternal life."

15 The woman *said to Him, "Sir, give me this water so that I will not be thirsty, nor come *all the way* here to draw *water.*" 16 He *said to her, "Go, call your husband and come here." 17 The woman answered and said to Him, "I have no husband." Jesus *said to her, "You have correctly said, 'I have no husband'; 18 for you have had five husbands, and the one whom you now have is not your husband; this *which* you have said *is* true." 19 The woman *said to Him, "Sir, I perceive that You are a prophet. 20 Our fathers worshiped on this mountain, and *yet* you *Jews* say that in Jerusalem is the place where one must worship." 21 Jesus *said to her, "Believe Me, woman, that a time is coming when you will worship the Father neither on this mountain nor in Jerusalem. 22 You *Samaritans* worship what you do not know; we worship what we do know, because salvation is from the Jews. 23 But a time is coming, and even now has arrived, when the true worshipers will worship the Father in spirit and truth; for such people the Father seeks *to be* His worshipers. 24 God is spirit, and those who worship Him must worship in spirit and truth." 25 The woman *said to Him, "I know that Messiah is coming (He who is called Christ); when that One comes, He will declare all things to us." 26 Jesus *said to her, "I am *He,* the One speaking to you."

27 And at this point His disciples came, and they were amazed that He had been speaking with a woman, yet no one said, "What are You seeking?" or, "Why are You speaking with her?" 28 So the woman left her waterpot and went into the city, and *said to the people, 29 "Come, see a man who told me all the things that I have done; this is not the Christ, is He?" 30 They left the city and were coming to Him.

31 Meanwhile the disciples were urging Him, saying, "Rabbi, eat *something.*" 32 But He said to them, "I have food to eat that you do not know about." 33 So the disciples were saying to one another, "No one brought Him *anything* to eat, did he?" 34 Jesus *said to them, "My food is to do the will of Him who sent Me, and to accomplish His work. 35 Do you not say, 'There are still four months, and *then* comes the harvest'? Behold, I tell you, raise your eyes and observe the fields, that they are white for

harvest. **36** Already the one who reaps is receiving wages and is gathering fruit for eternal life, so that the one who sows and the one who reaps may rejoice together. **37** For in this *case* the saying is true: 'One sows and another reaps.' **38** I sent you to reap that for which you have not labored; others have labored, and you have ¹come into their labor."

The Samaritans

39 Now from that city many of the Samaritans believed in Him because of the word of the woman who testified, "He told me all the things that I have done." **40** So when the Samaritans came to Jesus, they were asking Him to stay with them; and He stayed there two days. **41** Many more believed because of His word; **42** and they were saying to the woman, "*It is* no longer because of what you said *that* we believe, for we have heard for ourselves and know that this One truly is the Savior of the world."

43 And after the two days, He departed from there for Galilee. **44** For Jesus Himself testified that a prophet has no honor in his own country. **45** So when He came to Galilee, the Galileans received Him, *only because* they had seen all the things that He did in Jerusalem at the feast; for they themselves also went to the feast.

Healing an Official's Son

46 Therefore He came again to Cana of Galilee, where He had made the water *into* wine. And there was a royal official whose son was sick at Capernaum. **47** When he heard that Jesus had come from Judea into Galilee, he went to Him and *began* asking *Him* to come down and heal his son; for he was at the point of death. **48** Then Jesus said to him, "Unless you *people* see signs and wonders, you *simply* will not believe." **49** The royal official *said to Him, "Sir, come down before my child dies." **50** Jesus *said to him, "Go; your son is alive." The man believed the word that Jesus spoke to him and went *home.* **51** And as he was now going down, his slaves met him, saying that his son was alive. **52** So he inquired of them the hour when he began to get better. Then they said to him, "Yesterday at the ¹seventh hour the fever left

---

4:38 ¹I.e., enjoyed the fruit of their labor   4:52 ¹I.e., 1 p.m.

him." 53 So the father knew that *it was* at that hour in which Jesus said to him, "Your son is alive"; and he himself believed, and his entire household. 54 This is again a second sign that Jesus performed when He had come from Judea into Galilee.

The Healing at Bethesda

5 After these things there was a feast of the Jews, and Jesus went up to Jerusalem.

2 Now in Jerusalem, by the Sheep *Gate,* there is a pool which in Hebrew is called Bethesda, having five porticoes. 3 In these *porticoes* lay a multitude of those who were sick, blind, limping, *or* paralyzed.¹ 5 Now a man was there who had been ill for thirty-eight years. 6 Jesus, upon seeing this man lying *there* and knowing that he had already been *in that condition* for a long time, *said to him, "Do you want to get well?" 7 The sick man answered Him, "Sir, I have no man to put me into the pool when the water is stirred up, but while I am coming, another steps down before me." 8 Jesus *said to him, "Get up, pick up your pallet and walk."
9 Immediately the man became well, and picked up his pallet and *began* to walk.

Now it was a Sabbath on that day. 10 So the Jews were saying to the man who was cured, "It is a Sabbath, and it is not permissible for you to carry your pallet." 11 But he answered them, "He who made me well was the one who said to me, 'Pick up your pallet and walk.'" 12 They asked him, "Who is the man who said to you, 'Pick *it* up and walk'?" 13 But the man who was healed did not know who it was, for Jesus had slipped away while there was a crowd in *that* place. 14 Afterward, Jesus *found him in the temple and said to him, "Behold, you have become well; do not sin anymore, so that nothing worse happens to you." 15 The man went away, and informed the Jews that it was Jesus who had made him well. 16 For this reason the Jews were persecuting Jesus, because He was

---

5:3 ¹ Late mss add the following as the remainder of v 3, and v 4: *paralyzed, waiting for the moving of the waters; for an angel of the Lord went down at certain seasons into the pool and stirred up the water; whoever then first stepped in after the stirring up of the water was made well from whatever disease with which he was afflicted*

doing these things on a Sabbath. [17] But He answered them, "My Father is working until now, and I Myself am working."

Jesus' Equality with God

[18] For this reason therefore the Jews were seeking all the more to kill Him, because He not only was breaking the Sabbath, but also was calling God His own Father, making Himself equal with God.

[19] Therefore Jesus answered and was saying to them, "Truly, truly, I say to you, the Son can do nothing of Himself, unless *it is* something He sees the Father doing; for whatever the Father does, these things the Son also does in the same way. [20] For the Father loves the Son and shows Him all things that He Himself is doing; and *the Father* will show Him greater works than these, so that you will be amazed. [21] For just as the Father raises the dead and gives them life, so the Son also gives life to whom He wishes. [22] For not even the Father judges anyone, but He has given all judgment to the Son, [23] so that all will honor the Son just as they honor the Father. The one who does not honor the Son does not honor the Father who sent Him.

[24] "Truly, truly, I say to you, the one who hears My word, and believes Him who sent Me, has eternal life, and does not come into judgment, but has passed out of death into life.

Two Resurrections

[25] Truly, truly, I say to you, a time is coming and even now has arrived, when the dead will hear the voice of the Son of God, and those who hear will live. [26] For just as the Father has life in Himself, so He gave to the Son also to have life in Himself; [27] and He gave Him authority to execute judgment, because He is *the* Son of Man. [28] Do not be amazed at this; for a time is coming when all who are in the tombs will hear His voice, [29] and will come out: those who did the good *deeds* to a resurrection of life, those who committed the bad *deeds* to a resurrection of judgment.

[30] "I can do nothing on My own. As I hear, I judge; and My judgment is righteous, because I do not seek My own will but the will of Him who sent Me.

31 "If I *alone* testify about Myself, My testimony is not true. **32** There is another who testifies about Me, and I know that the testimony which He gives about Me is true.

Testimony of John the Baptist

33 You have sent *messengers* to John, and he has testified to the truth. **34** But the testimony I receive is not from man, but I say these things so that you may be saved. **35** He was the lamp that was burning and shining, and you were willing to rejoice for a while in his light.

Testimony of Works

36 But the testimony I have is greater than *the testimony of* John; for the works which the Father has given Me to accomplish—the very works that I do—testify about Me, that the Father has sent Me.

Testimony of the Father

37 And the Father who sent Me, He has testified about Me. You have neither heard His voice at any time, nor seen His form. **38** Also you do not have His word remaining in you, because you do not believe Him whom He sent.

Testimony of the Scripture

39 ¹You examine the Scriptures because you think that in them you have eternal life; and it is those *very Scriptures* that testify about Me; **40** and *yet* you are unwilling to come to Me so that you may have life. **41** I do not receive glory from people; **42** but I know you, that you do not have the love of God in yourselves. **43** I have come in My Father's name, and you do not receive Me; if another comes in his own name, you will receive him. **44** How can you believe, when you accept glory from one another and you do not seek the glory that is from the *one and only* God? **45** Do not think that I will accuse you before the Father; the one who accuses you is Moses, in whom you have put your hope. **46** For if you believed Moses, you would believe Me; for he wrote about Me. **47** But if you do not believe his writings, how will you believe My words?"

5:39 ¹Or (a command) *Examine the Scriptures*

Five Thousand Men Fed

6 After these things Jesus went away to the other side of the Sea of Galilee (*or* Tiberias). **2** A large crowd was following Him, because they were watching the signs which He was performing on those who were sick. **3** But Jesus went up on the mountain, and there He sat with His disciples. **4** Now the Passover, the feast of the Jews, was near. **5** So Jesus, after raising His eyes and seeing that a large crowd was coming to Him, *said to Philip, "Where are we to buy bread so that these *people* may eat?" **6** But He was saying this *only* to test him, for He Himself knew what He intended to do. **7** Philip answered Him, "Two hundred 'denarii worth of bread is not enough for them, for each to receive *just* a little!" **8** One of His disciples, Andrew, Simon Peter's brother, *said to Him, **9** "There is a boy here who has five barley loaves and two fish; but what are these for so many *people?*" **10** Jesus said, "Have the people recline *to eat.*" Now there was plenty of grass in the place. So the men reclined, about 'five thousand in number. **11** Jesus then took the loaves, and after giving thanks He distributed *them* to those who were reclining; likewise also of the fish, as much as they wanted. **12** And when they had eaten their fill, He *said to His disciples, "Gather up the leftover pieces so that nothing will be lost." **13** So they gathered them up, and filled twelve baskets with pieces from the five barley loaves which were left over by those who had eaten. **14** Therefore when the people saw the sign which He had performed, they said, "This is truly the Prophet who is to come into the world."

Jesus Walks on the Water

15 So Jesus, aware that they intended to come and take Him by force to make Him king, withdrew again to the mountain by Himself, alone.

16 Now when evening came, His disciples went down to the sea, **17** and after getting into a boat, they *started to* cross the sea to Capernaum. It had already become dark, and Jesus had not yet come to them. **18** In addition, the sea *began* getting rough, because a strong wind was

---

6:7 1 The denarius was a day's wages for a laborer   6:10 1 I.e., 5,000 men plus women and children, cf. Matt 14:21

blowing. [19] Then, when they had rowed about ¹twenty-five or thirty stadia, they *saw Jesus walking on the sea and coming near the boat; and they were frightened. [20] But He *said to them, "It is I; do not be afraid." [21] So they were willing to take Him into the boat, and immediately the boat was at the land to which they were going.

[22] The next day the crowd that stood on the other side of the sea saw that there was no other small boat there except one, and that Jesus had not gotten into the boat with His disciples, but *that* His disciples had departed alone. [23] Other small boats came from Tiberias near to the place where they ate the bread after the Lord had given thanks. [24] So when the crowd saw that Jesus was not there, nor His disciples, they themselves got into the small boats and came to Capernaum, looking for Jesus. [25] And when they found Him on the other side of the sea, they said to Him, "Rabbi, when did You get here?"

Words to the People

[26] Jesus answered them and said, "Truly, truly, I say to you, you seek Me, not because you saw ¹signs, but because you ate some of the loaves and were filled. [27] Do not work for the food that perishes, but for the food that lasts for eternal life, which the Son of Man will give you, for on Him the Father, God, has set His seal." [28] Therefore they said to Him, "What are we to do, so that we may accomplish the works of God?" [29] Jesus answered and said to them, "This is the work of God, that you believe in Him whom He has sent." [30] So they said to Him, "What then are You doing as a sign, so that we may see, and believe You? What work are You performing? [31] Our fathers ate the manna in the wilderness; as it is written: 'HE GAVE THEM BREAD OUT OF HEAVEN TO EAT.'"

[32] Jesus then said to them, "Truly, truly, I say to you, it is not Moses who has given you the bread out of heaven, but it is My Father who gives you the true bread out of heaven. [33] For the bread of God is that which comes down out of heaven and gives life to the world." [34] Then they said to Him, "Lord, always give us this bread."

[35] Jesus said to them, "I am the bread of life; the one

6:19 ¹ Possibly 3-4 miles or 4.8-6.4 km; a Roman stadion perhaps averaged 607 ft. or 185 m   6:26 ¹ I.e., confirming miracles

who comes to Me will not be hungry, and the one who believes in Me will never be thirsty. ³⁶ But I said to you that you have indeed seen Me, and *yet* you do not believe. ³⁷ Everything that the Father gives Me will come to Me, and the one who comes to Me I certainly will not cast out. ³⁸ For I have come down from heaven, not to do My own will, but the will of Him who sent Me. ³⁹ And this is the will of Him who sent Me, that of everything that He has given Me I will lose nothing, but will raise it up on the last day. ⁴⁰ For this is the will of My Father, that everyone who sees the Son and believes in Him will have eternal life, and I Myself will raise him up on the last day."

Words to the Jews

⁴¹ So then the Jews were complaining about Him because He said, "I am the bread that came down out of heaven." ⁴² And they were saying, "Is this not Jesus, the son of Joseph, whose father and mother we know? How does He now say, 'I have come down out of heaven'?" ⁴³ Jesus answered and said to them, "Stop complaining among yourselves. ⁴⁴ No one can come to Me unless the Father who sent Me draws him; and I will raise him up on the last day. ⁴⁵ It is written in the Prophets: 'AND THEY SHALL ALL BE TAUGHT OF GOD.' Everyone who has heard and learned from the Father, comes to Me. ⁴⁶ Not that anyone has seen the Father, except the One who is from God; He has seen the Father. ⁴⁷ Truly, truly, I say to you, the one who believes has eternal life. ⁴⁸ I am the bread of life. ⁴⁹ Your fathers ate the manna in the wilderness, and they died. ⁵⁰ This is the bread that comes down out of heaven, so that anyone may eat from it and not die. ⁵¹ I am the living bread that came down out of heaven; if anyone eats from this bread, he will live forever; and the bread which I will give for the life of the world also is My flesh."

⁵² Then the Jews *began* to argue with one another, saying, "How can this man give us His flesh to eat?" ⁵³ So Jesus said to them, "Truly, truly, I say to you, unless you eat the flesh of the Son of Man and drink His blood, you have no life in yourselves. ⁵⁴ The one who eats My flesh and drinks My blood has eternal life, and I will raise him up on the last day. ⁵⁵ For My flesh is true food, and My blood is true drink. ⁵⁶ The one who eats My flesh and

drinks My blood remains in Me, and I in him. **57** Just as the living Father sent Me, and I live because of the Father, the one who eats Me, he also will live because of Me. **58** This is the bread that came down out of heaven, not as the fathers ate and died; the one who eats this bread will live forever."

Words to the Disciples

59 These things He said in the synagogue as He taught in Capernaum.

60 So then many of His disciples, when they heard *this,* said, "This statement is *very* unpleasant; who can listen to it?" **61** But Jesus, aware that His disciples were complaining about this, said to them, "Is this offensive to you? **62** *What* then if you see the Son of Man ascending to where He was before? **63** It is the Spirit who gives life; the flesh provides no benefit; the words that I have spoken to you are spirit, and are life. **64** But there are some of you who do not believe." For Jesus knew from the beginning who they were who did not believe, and who it was who would betray Him. **65** And He was saying, "For this reason I have told you that no one can come to Me unless it has been granted him from the Father."

Peter's Confession of Faith

66 As a result of this many of His disciples left, and would no longer walk with Him. **67** So Jesus said to the twelve, "You do not want to leave also, do you?" **68** Simon Peter answered Him, "Lord, to whom shall we go? You have words of eternal life. **69** And we have *already* believed and have come to know that You are the Holy One of God." **70** Jesus answered them, "Did I Myself not choose you, the twelve? And *yet* one of you is a devil." **71** Now He meant Judas *the son* of Simon Iscariot; for he, one of the twelve, was going to betray Him.

Jesus Teaches at the Feast

7 After these things Jesus was walking in Galilee, for He was unwilling to walk in Judea because the Jews were seeking to kill Him. **2** Now the feast of the Jews, the Feast of Booths, was near. **3** So His brothers said to Him, "Move on from here and go into Judea, so that Your disciples also may see Your works which You are doing. **4** For no one does anything in secret when he himself is striving to be *known* publicly. If You are doing these things, show Yourself to the world." ⁵ For not even His brothers believed in Him. ⁶ So Jesus *said to them, "My time is not yet here, but your time is always ready. ⁷ The world cannot hate you, but it hates Me because I testify about it, that its deeds are evil. ⁸ Go up to the feast yourselves; I am not going up to this feast, because My time has not yet fully arrived." ⁹ Now having said these things to them, He stayed in Galilee.

¹⁰ But when His brothers had gone up to the feast, then He Himself also went up, not publicly, but as *though* in secret. ¹¹ So the Jews were looking for Him at the feast and saying, "Where is He?" ¹² And there was a great deal of talk about Him in secret among the crowds: some were saying, "He is a good man"; others were saying, "No, on the contrary, He is misleading the people." ¹³ However, no one was speaking openly about Him, for fear of ¹the Jews.

¹⁴ But when it was now the middle of the feast, Jesus went up into the temple *area,* and *began to* teach. ¹⁵ The Jews then were astonished, saying, "How has this man become learned, not having been educated?" ¹⁶ So Jesus answered them and said, "My teaching is not My own, but His who sent Me. ¹⁷ If anyone is willing to do His will, he will know about the teaching, whether it is of God, or I am speaking from Myself. ¹⁸ The one who speaks from himself seeks his own glory; but He who is seeking the glory of the One who sent Him, He is true, and there is no unrighteousness in Him.

¹⁹ "Did Moses not give you the Law, and *yet* none of you carries out the Law? Why are you seeking to kill Me?" ²⁰ The crowd answered, "You have a demon! Who is seeking to kill You?" ²¹ Jesus answered them, "I did one deed, and you all are astonished. ²² For this reason Moses has given you circumcision (not that it is from Moses, but from the fathers), and *even* on a Sabbath you circumcise a man. ²³ If a man receives circumcision on a Sabbath so that the Law of Moses will not be broken, are you angry at Me because I made an entire man well on a Sabbath? ²⁴ Do not judge by the outward appearance, but judge with righteous judgment."

²⁵ So some of the people of Jerusalem were saying, "Is

7:13 ¹I.e., the Jewish leaders

this man not the one whom they are seeking to kill?
²⁶ And *yet* look, He is speaking publicly, and they are saying nothing to Him. The rulers do not really know that
this is the Christ, do they? ²⁷ However, we know where
this man is from; but when the Christ comes, no one
knows where He is from." ²⁸ Then Jesus cried out in the
temple, teaching and saying, "You both know Me and
you know where I am from; and I have not come of
Myself, but He who sent Me is true, whom you do not
know. ²⁹ I do know Him, because I am from Him, and He
sent Me." ³⁰ So they were seeking to arrest Him; and *yet*
no one laid a hand on Him, because His hour had not yet
come. ³¹ But many of the crowd believed in Him; and
they were saying, "When the Christ comes, He will not
perform more signs than those which this man has done,
will He?"

³² The Pharisees heard the crowd whispering these
things about Him, and the chief priests and the Pharisees
sent officers to arrest Him. ³³ Therefore Jesus said, "For a
little while longer I am *going to be* with you, and *then* I
am going to Him who sent Me. ³⁴ You will seek Me, and
will not find Me; and where I am, you cannot come."
³⁵ The Jews then said to one another, "Where does this
man intend to go that we will not find Him? He does not
intend to go to the Dispersion among the Greeks, and
teach the Greeks, does He? ³⁶ What is this statement that
He said, 'You will seek Me, and will not find Me; and
where I am, you cannot come'?"

³⁷ Now on the last day, the great *day* of the feast, Jesus
stood and cried out, saying, "If anyone is thirsty, let him
come to Me and drink. ³⁸ The one who believes in Me, as
the Scripture said, 'From his innermost being will flow
rivers of living water.'" ³⁹ But this He said in reference to
the Spirit, whom those who believed in Him were to
receive; for the Spirit was not yet *given,* because Jesus
was not yet glorified.

People's Division over Jesus

⁴⁰ *Some* of the people therefore, after they heard these
words, were saying, "This truly is the Prophet." ⁴¹ Others
were saying, "This is the Christ." But others were saying,
"Surely the Christ is not coming from Galilee, is
He? ⁴² Has the Scripture not said that the Christ comes
from the descendants of David, and from Bethlehem, the

village where David was?" 43 So a dissension occurred in the crowd because of Him. 44 And some of them wanted to arrest Him, but no one laid hands on Him.

45 The officers then came to the chief priests and Pharisees, and they said to them, "Why did you not bring Him?" 46 The officers answered, "Never has a man spoken in this way!" 47 The Pharisees then replied to them, "You have not been led astray too, have you? 48 Not one of the rulers or Pharisees has believed in Him, has he? 49 But this crowd that does not know the Law is accursed!" 50 Nicodemus (the one who came to Him before, being one of them) *said to them, 51 "Our Law does not judge the person unless it first hears from him and knows what he is doing, does it?" 52 They answered and said to him, "You are not from Galilee as well, are you? Examine *the Scriptures,* and see that no prophet arises out of Galilee." 53 [[¹And everyone went to his home.

The Adulterous Woman

8 But Jesus went to the Mount of Olives. 2 And early in the morning He came again into the temple *area,* and all the people were coming to Him; and He sat down and *began* teaching them. 3 Now the scribes and the Pharisees *brought a woman caught in the act of adultery, and after placing her in the center *of the courtyard,* 4 they *said to Him, "Teacher, this woman has been caught in the very act of committing adultery. 5 Now in the Law, Moses commanded us to stone such women; what then do You say?" 6 Now they were saying this to test Him, so that they might have *grounds for* accusing Him. But Jesus stooped down and with His finger wrote on the ground. 7 When they persisted in asking Him, He straightened up and said to them, "He who is without sin among you, let him *be the* first to throw a stone at her." 8 And again He stooped down and wrote on the ground. 9 Now when they heard *this,* they *began* leaving, one by one, beginning with the older ones, and He was left alone, and the woman *where she* was, in the center *of the courtyard.* 10 And straightening up, Jesus said to her, "Woman, where are they? Did no one condemn

---

7:53 ¹Later mss add the story of the adulterous woman; numbering it as John 7:53-8:11

you?" **11** She said, "No one, Lord." And Jesus said, "I do not condemn you, either. Go. From now on do not sin any longer."]]

Jesus Is the Light of the World

12 Then Jesus again spoke to them, saying, "I am the Light of the world; the one who follows Me will not walk in the darkness, but will have the Light of life." **13** So the Pharisees said to Him, "You are testifying about Yourself; Your testimony is not true." **14** Jesus answered and said to them, "Even if I am testifying about Myself, My testimony is true, because I know where I came from and where I am going; but you do not know where I come from or where I am going. **15** You judge according to the flesh; I am not judging anyone. **16** But even if I do judge, My judgment is true; for I am not alone *in it,* but I and the Father who sent Me. **17** Even in your Law it has been written that the testimony of two people is true. **18** I am He who testifies about Myself, and the Father who sent Me testifies about Me." **19** So they were saying to Him, "Where is Your Father?" Jesus answered, "You know neither Me nor My Father; if you knew Me, you would know My Father also." **20** These words He spoke in the treasury, as He taught in the temple *area;* and no one arrested Him, because His hour had not yet come.

21 Then He said again to them, "I am going away, and you will look for Me, and will die in your sin; where I am going, you cannot come." **22** So the Jews were saying, "Surely He will not kill Himself, will He, since He says, 'Where I am going, you cannot come'?" **23** And He was saying to them, "You are from below, I am from above; you are of this world, I am not of this world. **24** Therefore I said to you that you will die in your sins; for unless you believe that I am, you will die in your sins." **25** Then they were saying to Him, "Who are You?" Jesus said to them, "What have I even been saying to you *from* the beginning? **26** I have many things to say and to judge regarding you, but He who sent Me is true; and the things which I heard from Him, these I say to the world." **27** They did not realize that He was speaking to them *about* the Father. **28** So Jesus said, "When you lift up the Son of Man, then you will know that I am, and I do nothing on My own, but I say these things as the Father instructed Me. **29** And He who sent Me is with Me; He has not left

Me alone, for I always do the things that are pleasing to Him." ³⁰ As He said these things, many came to believe in Him.

The Truth Will Set You Free

³¹ So Jesus was saying to those Jews who had believed Him, "If you continue in My word, *then* you are truly My disciples; ³² and you will know the truth, and the truth will set you free." ³³ They answered Him, "We are Abraham's descendants and have never been enslaved to anyone; how *is it that* You say, 'You will become free'?"

³⁴ Jesus answered them, "Truly, truly I say to you, everyone who commits sin is a slave of sin. ³⁵ Now the slave does not remain in the house forever; the son does remain forever. ³⁶ So if the Son sets you free, you really will be free. ³⁷ I know that you are Abraham's descendants; yet you are seeking to kill Me, because My word has no place in you. ³⁸ I speak of the things which I have seen with *My* Father; therefore you also do the things which you heard from *your* father."

³⁹ They answered and said to Him, "Abraham is our father." Jesus *said to them, "If you are Abraham's children, do the deeds of Abraham. ⁴⁰ But as it is, you are seeking to kill Me, a man who has told you the truth, which I heard from God; this Abraham did not do. ⁴¹ You are doing the deeds of your father." They said to Him, "We were not born as a result of sexual immorality; we have one Father: God." ⁴² Jesus said to them, "If God were your Father, you would love Me, for I came forth from God and am here; for I have not even come on My own, but He sent Me. ⁴³ Why do you not understand what I am saying? *It is* because you cannot listen to My word. ⁴⁴ You are of *your* father the devil, and you want to do the desires of your father. He was a murderer from the beginning, and does not stand in the truth because there is no truth in him. Whenever he tells a lie, he speaks from his own *nature,* because he is a liar and the father of lies. ⁴⁵ But because I say the truth, you do not believe Me. ⁴⁶ Which one of you convicts Me of sin? If I speak truth, why do you not believe Me? ⁴⁷ The one who is of God hears the words of God; for this reason you do not hear *them,* because you are not of God."

⁴⁸ The Jews answered and said to Him, "Do we not

rightly say that You are a Samaritan, and You have a demon?" **49** Jesus answered, "I do not have a demon; on the contrary, I honor My Father, and you dishonor Me. **50** But I am not seeking My glory; there is One who seeks *it,* and judges. **51** Truly, truly I say to you, if anyone follows My word, he will never see death." **52** The Jews said to Him, "Now we know that You have a demon. Abraham died, and the prophets *as well;* and *yet* You say, 'If anyone follows My word, he will never taste of death.' **53** You are not greater than our father Abraham, who died, are You? The prophets died too. Whom do You make Yourself *out to be?*" **54** Jesus answered, "If I glorify Myself, My glory is nothing; it is My Father who glorifies Me, of whom you say, 'He is our God'; **55** and you have not come to know Him, but I know Him. And if I say that I do not know Him, I will be a liar like you; but I do know Him, and I follow His word. **56** Your father Abraham was overjoyed that he would see My day, and he saw *it* and rejoiced." **57** So the Jews said to Him, "You are not yet fifty years old, and You have seen Abraham?" **58** Jesus said to them, "Truly, truly I say to you, before Abraham was born, 'I am." **59** Therefore they picked up stones to throw at Him, but Jesus hid Himself and left the temple *grounds.*

Healing the Man Born Blind

9 As *Jesus* passed by, He saw a man *who had been* blind from birth. **2** And His disciples asked Him, "Rabbi, who sinned, this man or his parents, that he would be born blind?" **3** Jesus answered, "*It was* neither *that* this man sinned, nor his parents; but *it was* so that the works of God might be displayed in him. **4** We must carry out the works of Him who sent Me as long as it is day; night is coming, when no one can work. **5** While I am in the world, I am the Light of the world." **6** When He had said this, He spit on the ground, and made mud from the saliva, and applied the mud to his eyes, **7** and said to him, "Go, wash in the pool of Siloam" (which is translated, Sent). So he left and washed, and came *back* seeing. **8** So the neighbors, and those who previously saw him as a beggar, were saying, "Is this not the one who used to sit and beg?" **9** Others were saying, "This is he," *still* others

---

8:58 **1** Or *I AM;* Jesus may be referring to Ex 3:14, *I AM WHO I AM*

were saying, "No, but he is like him." The man himself
kept saying, "I am *the one.*" [10] So they were saying to
him, "How then were your eyes opened?" [11] He
answered, "The man who is called Jesus made mud, and
spread *it* on my eyes, and said to me, 'Go to Siloam and
wash'; so I went away and washed, and I received sight."
[12] And they said to him, "Where is He?" He *said, "I do
not know."

Controversy over the Man

[13] They *brought the man who was previously blind to
the Pharisees. [14] Now it was a Sabbath on the day that
Jesus made the mud and opened his eyes. [15] Then the
Pharisees also were asking him again how he received
his sight. And he said to them, "He applied mud to my
eyes, and I washed, and I see." [16] Therefore some of the
Pharisees were saying, "This man is not from God,
because He does not keep the Sabbath." But others were
saying, "How can a man who is a sinner perform such
signs?" And there was dissension among them. [17] So they
*said again to the man who was blind, "What do you say
about Him, since He opened your eyes?" And he said,
"He is a prophet."

[18] The Jews then did not believe *it* about him, that he
had been blind and had received sight, until they called
the parents of the very one who had received his sight,
[19] and they questioned them, saying, "Is this your son,
who you say was born blind? Then how does he now
see?" [20] His parents then answered and said, "We know
that this is our son, and that he was born blind; [21] but
how he now sees, we do not know; or who opened his
eyes, we do not know. Ask him; he is of age, he will
speak for himself." [22] His parents said this because
they were afraid of the [1]Jews; for the Jews had already
reached the decision that if anyone confessed Him to
be Christ, he was to be excommunicated from the synagogue. [23] *It was* for this reason *that* his parents said, "He
is of age; ask him."

[24] So for a second time they summoned the man who
had been blind, and said to him, "Give glory to God; we
know that this man is a sinner." [25] He then answered,
"Whether He is a sinner, I do not know; one thing I do

9:22 [1] I.e., the Jewish leaders

know, that though I was blind, now I see." **26** So they said to him, "What did He do to you? How did He open your eyes?" **27** He answered them, "I told you already and you did not listen; why do you want to hear *it* again? You do not want to become His disciples too, do you?" **28** They spoke abusively to him and said, "You are His disciple, but we are disciples of Moses. **29** We know that God has spoken to Moses, but as for this man, we do not know where He is from." **30** The man answered and said to them, "Well, here is the amazing thing, that you do not know where He is from, and *yet* He opened my eyes! **31** We know that God does not listen to sinners; but if someone is God-fearing and does His will, He listens to him. **32** Since the beginning of time it has never been heard that anyone opened the eyes of a person born blind. **33** If this man were not from God, He could do nothing." **34** They answered him, "You were born entirely in sins, and *yet* you are teaching us?" So they put him out.

Jesus Affirms His Deity

35 Jesus heard that they had put him out, and upon finding him, He said, "Do you believe in the Son of Man?" **36** He answered by saying, "And who is He, Sir, that I may believe in Him?" **37** Jesus said to him, "You have both seen Him, and He is the one who is talking with you." **38** And he said, "I believe, Lord." And he worshiped Him. **39** And Jesus said, "For judgment I came into this world, so that those who do not see may see, and those who see may become blind." **40** Those who were with Him from the Pharisees heard these things and said to Him, "We are not blind too, are we?" **41** Jesus said to them, "If you were blind, you would have no sin; but now *that* you maintain, 'We see,' your sin remains.

Parable of the Good Shepherd

10 "Truly, truly I say to you, the one who does not enter by the door into the fold of the sheep, but climbs up some other way, he is a thief and a robber. **2** But the one who enters by the door is a shepherd of the sheep. **3** To him the doorkeeper opens, and the sheep listen to his voice, and he calls his own sheep by name and leads them out. **4** When he puts all his own *sheep* outside, he goes ahead of them, and the sheep follow

him because they know his voice. [5] However, a stranger
they simply will not follow, but will flee from him,
because they do not know the voice of strangers." [6] Jesus
told them this figure of speech, but they did not understand what the things which He was saying to them
meant.

[7] So Jesus said to them again, "Truly, truly I say to you,
I am the door of the sheep. [8] All those who came before
Me are thieves and robbers, but the sheep did not listen
to them. [9] I am the door; if anyone enters through Me, he
will be saved, and will go in and out and find pasture.
[10] The thief comes only to steal and kill and destroy; I
came so that they would have life, and have *it*
abundantly.

[11] "I am the good shepherd; the good shepherd lays
down His life for the sheep. [12] He who is a hired hand,
and not a shepherd, who is not the owner of the sheep,
sees the wolf coming, and leaves the sheep and flees;
and the wolf snatches them and scatters *the flock.* [13] *He
flees* because he is a hired hand and does not care about
the sheep. [14] I am the good shepherd, and I know My
own, and My own know Me, [15] just as the Father knows
Me and I know the Father; and I lay down My life for the
sheep. [16] And I have other sheep that are not of this fold;
I must bring them also, and they will listen to My voice;
and they will become one flock, *with* one shepherd.
[17] For this reason the Father loves Me, because I lay
down My life so that I may take it back. [18] No one has
taken it away from Me, but I lay it down on My own. I
have authority to lay it down, and I have authority to
take it back. This commandment I received from My
Father."

[19] Dissension occurred again among the Jews because
of these words. [20] Many of them were saying, "He has a
demon and is insane. Why do you listen to Him?"
[21] Others were saying, "These are not the words of one
who is demon-possessed. A demon cannot open the eyes
of those who are blind, can it?"

Jesus Asserts His Deity

[22] At that time the [1] Feast of the Dedication took place
in Jerusalem; [23] it was winter, and Jesus was walking in

10:22 [1] Now known as Hanukkah, also the Feast of Lights

the temple *area,* in the portico of Solomon. **24** The Jews then surrounded Him and *began* saying to Him, "How long will You keep us in suspense? If You are the Christ, tell us plainly." **25** Jesus answered them, "I told you, and you do not believe; the works that I do in My Father's name, these testify of Me. **26** But you do not believe, because you are not of My sheep. **27** My sheep listen to My voice, and I know them, and they follow Me; **28** and I give them eternal life, and they will never perish; and no one will snatch them out of My hand. **29** ¹My Father, who has given *them* to Me, is greater than all; and no one is able to snatch *them* out of the Father's hand. **30** I and the Father are one."

31 The Jews picked up stones again to stone Him. **32** Jesus replied to them, "I showed you many good works from the Father; for which of them are you stoning Me?" **33** The Jews answered Him, "We are not stoning You for a good work, but for blasphemy; and because You, being a man, make Yourself *out to be* God." **34** Jesus answered them, "Has it not been written in your Law: 'I SAID, YOU ARE GODS'? **35** If he called them gods, to whom the word of God came (and the Scripture cannot be nullified), **36** are you saying of Him whom the Father sanctified and sent into the world, 'You are blaspheming,' because I said, 'I am the Son of God'? **37** If I do not do the works of My Father, do not believe Me; **38** but if I do *them,* even though you do not believe Me, believe the works, so that you may know and understand that the Father is in Me, and I in the Father." **39** Therefore they were seeking again to arrest Him, and He eluded their grasp.

40 And He went away again beyond the Jordan to the place where John was first baptizing, and He stayed there. **41** Many came to Him and were saying, "While John performed no sign, yet everything John said about this man was true." **42** And many believed in Him there.

The Death and Resurrection of Lazarus

11 Now a certain man was sick: Lazarus of Bethany, the village of Mary and her sister Martha. **2** And it was the Mary who anointed the Lord with ointment, and wiped His feet with her hair, whose brother Lazarus was sick. **3** So the sisters sent *word* to Him, saying, "Lord,

---

10:29 ¹ One early ms *What My Father has given Me is greater than all*

behold, he whom You love is sick." **4** But when Jesus heard *this,* He said, "This sickness is not meant for death, but *is* for the glory of God, so that the Son of God may be glorified by it." **5** (Now Jesus loved Martha and her sister, and Lazarus.) **6** So when He heard that he was sick, He then stayed two days *longer* in the place where He was. **7** Then after this He *said to the disciples, "Let's go to Judea again." **8** The disciples *said to Him, "Rabbi, the Jews were just now seeking to stone You, and *yet* You are going there again?" **9** Jesus replied, "Are there not twelve hours in the day? If anyone walks during the day, he does not stumble, because he sees the light of this world. **10** But if anyone walks during the night, he stumbles, because the light is not in him." **11** This He said, and after this He *said to them, "Our friend Lazarus has fallen asleep; but I am going so that I may awaken him from sleep." **12** The disciples then said to Him, "Lord, if he has fallen asleep, he will come out of it." **13** Now Jesus had spoken of his death, but they thought that He was speaking about actual sleep. **14** So Jesus then said to them plainly, "Lazarus died, **15** and I am glad for your sakes that I was not there, so that you may believe; but let's go to him." **16** Therefore Thomas, who was called Didymus, said to *his* fellow disciples, "Let's also go, so that we may die with Him!"

17 So when Jesus came, He found that he had already been in the tomb four days. **18** Now Bethany was near Jerusalem, about ¹fifteen stadia away; **19** and many of the Jews had come to Martha and Mary, to console them about *their* brother. **20** So then Martha, when she heard that Jesus was coming, went to meet Him, but Mary stayed in the house. **21** Martha then said to Jesus, "Lord, if You had been here, my brother would not have died. **22** Even now I know that whatever You ask of God, God will give You." **23** Jesus *said to her, "Your brother will rise *from the dead.*" **24** Martha *said to Him, "I know that he will rise in the resurrection on the last day." **25** Jesus said to her, "I am the resurrection and the life; the one who believes in Me will live, even if he dies, **26** and everyone who lives and believes in Me will never die. Do you believe this?" **27** She *said to Him, "Yes, Lord; I

11:18 ¹ Possibly 2 miles or 3 km; a Roman stadion perhaps averaged 607 ft. or 185 m have come to believe that You are the Christ, the Son of God, *and* He who comes into the world."

28 When she had said this, she left and called Mary her sister, saying secretly, "The Teacher is here and is calling for you." **29** And when she heard *this,* she *got up quickly and came to Him.

30 Now Jesus had not yet come into the village, but was still at the place where Martha met Him. **31** Then the Jews who were with her in the house and were consoling her, when they saw that Mary had gotten up quickly and left, they followed her, thinking that she was going to the tomb to weep there. **32** So when Mary came *to the place* where Jesus was, she saw Him and fell at His feet, saying to Him, "Lord, if You had been here, my brother would not have died." **33** Therefore when Jesus saw her weeping, and the Jews who came with her *also* weeping, He was deeply moved in spirit and was troubled, **34** and He said, "Where have you laid him?" They *said to Him, "Lord, come and see." **35** Jesus wept. **36** So the Jews were saying, "See how He loved him!" **37** But some of them said, "Could this man, who opened the eyes of the man who was blind, not have also kept this man from dying?"

38 So Jesus, again being deeply moved within, *came to the tomb. Now it was a cave, and a stone was lying against it. **39** Jesus *said, "Remove the stone." Martha, the sister of the deceased, *said to Him, "Lord, by this time there will be a stench, for he has been *dead* four days." **40** Jesus *said to her, "Did I not say to you that if you believe, you will see the glory of God?" **41** So they removed the stone. And Jesus raised His eyes, and said, "Father, I thank You that You have heard Me. **42** But I knew that You always hear Me; nevertheless, because of the people standing around I said *it,* so that they may believe that You sent Me." **43** And when He had said these things, He cried out with a loud voice, "Lazarus, come out!" **44** Out came the man who had died, bound hand and foot with wrappings, and his face was wrapped around with a cloth. Jesus *said to them, "Unbind him, and let him go."

45 Therefore many of the Jews who came to Mary, and saw what He had done, believed in Him. **46** But some of them went to the Pharisees and told them the things which Jesus had done.

Conspiracy to Kill Jesus

47 Therefore the chief priests and the Pharisees convened a council meeting, and they were saying, "What are we doing in regard to the fact that this man is performing many signs? **48** If we let Him *go on* like this, all *the people* will believe in Him, and the Romans will come and take over both our place and our nation." **49** But one of them, Caiaphas, who was high priest that year, said to them, "You know nothing at all, **50** nor are you taking into account that it is in your best interest that one man die for the people, and that the whole nation not perish *instead*." **51** Now he did not say this on his own, but as he was high priest that year, he prophesied that Jesus was going to die for the nation; **52** and not for the nation only, but in order that He might also gather together into one the children of God who are scattered abroad. **53** So from that day on they planned together to kill Him.

54 Therefore Jesus no longer *continued to* walk publicly among the Jews, but went away from there to the region near the wilderness, into a city called Ephraim; and there He stayed with the disciples.

55 Now the Passover of the Jews was near, and many went up to Jerusalem from the country prior to the Passover, in order to purify themselves. **56** So they were looking for Jesus, and saying to one another as they stood in the temple *area,* "What do you think; that He will not come to the feast at all?" **57** Now the chief priests and the Pharisees had given orders that if anyone knew where He was, he was to report it, so that they might arrest Him.

Mary Anoints Jesus

12 Therefore, six days before the Passover, Jesus came to Bethany where Lazarus was, whom Jesus had raised from the dead. **2** So they made Him a dinner there, and Martha was serving; and Lazarus was one of those reclining *at the table* with Him. **3** Mary then took a pound of very expensive perfume of pure nard, and anointed the feet of Jesus and wiped His feet with her hair; and the house was filled with the fragrance of the perfume. **4** But Judas Iscariot, one of His disciples, the one who intended to betray Him, *said, **5** "Why was this perfume not sold for three hundred

¹denarii and *the proceeds* given to poor *people?*" ⁶ Now he said this, not because he cared about the poor, but because he was a thief, and as he kept the money box, he used to steal from what was put into it. ⁷ Therefore Jesus said, "Leave her alone, so that she may keep it ¹for the day of My burial. ⁸ For you always have the poor with you, but you do not always have Me."

⁹ The large crowd of the Jews then learned that He was there; and they came, not on account of Jesus only, but so that they might also see Lazarus, whom He raised from the dead. ¹⁰ But the chief priests planned to put Lazarus to death also, ¹¹ because on account of him many of the Jews were going away and were believing in Jesus.

The Triumphal Entry

¹² On the next day, when the large crowd that had come to the feast heard that Jesus was coming to Jerusalem, ¹³ they took the branches of the palm trees and went out to meet Him, and *began* shouting, "Hosanna! Blessed is He who comes in the name of the Lord, indeed, the King of Israel!" ¹⁴ Jesus, finding a young donkey, sat on it; as it is written: ¹⁵ "Do not fear, daughter of Zion; behold, your King is coming, seated on a donkey's colt." ¹⁶ These things His disciples did not understand at the first; but when Jesus was glorified, then they remembered that these things were written of Him, and that they had done these things for Him. ¹⁷ So the people, who were with Him when He called Lazarus out of the tomb and raised him from the dead, continued to testify *about Him.* ¹⁸ For this reason also the people went to meet Him, because they heard that He had performed this sign. ¹⁹ So the Pharisees said to one another, "You see that you are not accomplishing anything; look, the world has gone after Him!"

Greeks Seek Jesus

²⁰ Now there were some Greeks among those who were going up to worship at the feast; ²¹ these *people* then came to Philip, who was from Bethsaida of Galilee, and were making a request of him, saying, "Sir, we wish to see Jesus." ²² Philip *came and *told Andrew; *then*

12:5 ¹ The denarius was a day's wages for a laborer
12:7 ¹ Or *in view of*

Andrew and Philip *came and *told Jesus. 23 But Jesus *answered them by saying, "The hour has come for the Son of Man to be glorified. 24 Truly, truly I say to you, unless a grain of wheat falls into the earth and dies, it remains alone; but if it dies, it bears much fruit. 25 The one who loves his life loses it, and the one who hates his life in this world will keep it to eternal life. 26 If anyone serves Me, he must follow Me; and where I am, there My servant will be also; if anyone serves Me, the Father will honor him.

Jesus Foretells His Death

27 "Now My soul has become troubled; and what am I to say? 'Father, save Me from this hour'? But for this purpose I came to this hour. 28 Father, glorify Your name." Then a voice came out of heaven: "I have both glorified *it,* and will glorify *it* again." 29 So the crowd who stood by and heard *it* were saying that it had thundered; others were saying, "An angel has spoken to Him!" 30 Jesus responded and said, "This voice has not come for My sake, but for yours. 31 Now judgment is *upon* this world; now the ruler of this world will be cast out. 32 And I, if I am lifted up from the earth, will draw all *people* to Myself." 33 Now He was saying this to indicate what kind of death He was going to die. 34 The crowd then answered Him, "We have heard from the Law that the Christ is to remain forever; and how *is it that* You say, 'The Son of Man must be lifted up'? Who is this Son of Man?" 35 So Jesus said to them, "For a little while longer the Light is among you. Walk while you have the Light, so that darkness will not overtake you; also, the one who walks in the darkness does not know where he is going. 36 While you have the Light, believe in the Light, so that you may become sons of Light."

These things Jesus proclaimed, and He went away and hid Himself from them. 37 But though He had performed so many signs in their sight, they *still* were not believing in Him. 38 *This happened* so that the word of Isaiah the prophet which he spoke would be fulfilled: "LORD, WHO HAS BELIEVED OUR REPORT? AND TO WHOM HAS THE ARM OF THE LORD BEEN REVEALED?" 39 For this reason they could not believe, for Isaiah said again, 40 "HE HAS BLINDED THEIR EYES AND HE HARDENED THEIR HEART, SO THAT THEY WILL NOT SEE WITH THEIR EYES AND UNDERSTAND WITH THEIR HEART, AND BE

CONVERTED, AND *SO* I WILL *NOT* HEAL THEM." **41** These things Isaiah said because he saw His glory, and he spoke about Him. **42** Nevertheless many, even of the rulers, believed in Him, but because of the Pharisees they were not confessing *Him,* so that they would not be excommunicated from the synagogue; **43** for they loved the approval of people rather than the approval of God.

44 Now Jesus cried out and said, "The one who believes in Me, does not believe *only* in Me, but *also* in Him who sent Me. **45** And the one who sees Me sees Him who sent Me. **46** I have come *as* Light into the world, so that no one who believes in Me will remain in darkness. **47** If anyone hears My teachings and does not keep them, I do not judge him; for I did not come to judge the world, but to save the world. **48** The one who rejects Me and does not accept My teachings has one who judges him: the word which I spoke. That will judge him on the last day. **49** For I did not speak on My own, but the Father Himself who sent Me has given Me a commandment *as to* what to say and what to speak. **50** And I know that His commandment is eternal life; therefore the things I speak, I speak just as the Father has told Me."

The Lord's Supper

13 Now before the Feast of the Passover, Jesus, knowing that His hour had come that He would depart from this world to the Father, having loved His own who were in the world, He loved them to the end. **2** And during supper, the devil having already put into the heart of Judas Iscariot, *the son* of Simon, to betray Him, **3** *Jesus,* knowing that the Father had handed all things over to Him, and that He had come forth from God and was going *back* to God, **4** *got up from supper and *laid His outer garments *aside;* and He took a towel and tied it around Himself.

Jesus Washes the Disciples' Feet

5 Then He *poured water into the basin, and began washing the disciples' feet and wiping them with the towel which He had tied around Himself. **6** So He *came to Simon Peter. He *said to Him, "Lord, You are washing my feet?" **7** Jesus answered and said to him, "What I am doing, you do not realize right now, but you will understand later." **8** Peter *said to Him, "Never shall

You wash my feet!" Jesus answered him, "If I do not wash you, you have no place with Me." **9** Simon Peter *said to Him, "Lord, *then wash* not only my feet, but also my hands and my head!" **10** Jesus *said to him, "He who has bathed needs only to wash his feet; otherwise he is completely clean. And you are clean—but not all *of you.*" **11** For He knew the one who was betraying Him; *it was* for this reason *that* He said, "Not all *of you* are clean."

12 Then, when He had washed their feet, and taken His garments and reclined *at the table* again, He said to them, "Do you know what I have done for you? **13** You call Me 'Teacher' and 'Lord'; and you are correct, for *so* I am. **14** So if I, the Lord and the Teacher, washed your feet, you also ought to wash one another's feet. **15** For I gave you an example, so that you also would do just as I did for you. **16** Truly, truly I say to you, a slave is not greater than his master, nor *is* one who is sent greater than the one who sent him. **17** If you know these things, you are blessed if you do them. **18** I am not speaking about all of you. I know *the ones* whom I have chosen; but *this is happening* so that the Scripture may be fulfilled, 'HE WHO EATS MY BREAD HAS LIFTED UP HIS HEEL AGAINST ME.' **19** From now on I am telling you before *it* happens, so that when it does happen, you may believe that I am *He.* **20** Truly, truly I say to you, the one who receives anyone I send, receives Me; and the one who receives Me receives Him who sent Me."

Jesus Predicts His Betrayal

21 When Jesus had said these things, He became troubled in spirit, and testified and said, "Truly, truly I say to you that one of you will betray Me." **22** The disciples *began* looking at one another, at a loss *to know* of which one He was speaking. **23** Lying back on Jesus' chest was one of His disciples, whom Jesus loved. **24** So Simon Peter *nodded to this *disciple* and *said to him, "Tell *us* who it is of whom He is speaking." **25** He then simply leaned back on Jesus' chest and *said to Him, "Lord, who is it?" **26** Jesus then *answered, "That man is the one for whom I shall dip the piece *of bread* and give it to him." So when He had dipped the piece *of bread,* He *took and *gave *it* to Judas, *the son* of Simon Iscariot. **27** After this, Satan then entered him. Therefore Jesus

*said to him, "What you are doing, do *it* quickly."
28 Now none of those reclining *at the table* knew for
what purpose He had said this to him. **29** For some were
assuming, since Judas kept the money box, that Jesus
was saying to him, "Buy the things we need for the
feast"; or else, that he was to give something to the
poor. **30** So after receiving the piece *of bread,* he left
immediately; and it was night.

31 Therefore when he had left, Jesus *said, "Now is
the Son of Man glorified, and God is glorified in Him; **32** if
God is glorified in Him, God will also glorify Him in
Himself, and will glorify Him immediately. **33** Little children, I am *still* with you a little longer. You will look for
Me; and just as I said to the Jews, now I also say to you:
'Where I am going, you cannot come.' **34** I am giving you
a new commandment, that you love one another; just as
I have loved you, that you also love one another. **35** By
this all *people* will know that you are My disciples: if you
have love for one another."

36 Simon Peter *said to Him, "Lord, where are You
going?" Jesus answered, "Where I am going, you cannot
follow Me now; but you will follow later." **37** Peter *said
to Him, "Lord, why can I not follow You right now? I will
lay down my life for You." **38** Jesus *replied, "Will you lay
down your life for Me? Truly, truly I say to you, a rooster
will not crow until you deny Me three times.

Jesus Comforts His Disciples

14 "Do not let your heart be troubled; [1]believe in
God, believe also in Me. **2** In My Father's house are
many rooms; if *that* were not *so,* I would have told you,
because I am going *there* to prepare a place for you. **3** And
if I go and prepare a place for you, I am coming again and
will take you to Myself, so that where I am, *there* you
also will be. **4** And you know the way where I am going."
5 Thomas *said to Him, "Lord, we do not know where
You are going; how do we know the way?" **6** Jesus *said
to him, "I am the way, and the truth, and the life; no one
comes to the Father except through Me.

Oneness with the Father

7 If you had known Me, you would have known My

14:1 [1] Or *you believe in God, believe also*

Father also; from now on you know Him, and have seen Him."

8 Philip *said to Him, "Lord, show us the Father, and it is enough for us." 9 Jesus *said to him, "Have I been with you for so long a time, and *yet* you have not come to know Me, Philip? The one who has seen Me has seen the Father; how *can* you say, 'Show us the Father'? 10 Do you not believe that I am in the Father, and the Father is in Me? The words that I say to you I do not speak on My own, but the Father, as He remains in Me, does His works. 11 Believe Me that I am in the Father and the Father is in Me; otherwise believe because of the works themselves. 12 Truly, truly I say to you, the one who believes in Me, the works that I do, he will do also; and greater *works* than these he will do; because I am going to the Father. 13 And whatever you ask in My name, this I will do, so that the Father may be glorified in the Son. 14 If you ask Me anything in My name, I will do *it*.

15 "If you love Me, you will keep My commandments.

The Holy Spirit

16 I will ask the Father, and He will give you another Helper, so that He may be with you forever; 17 *the Helper is* the Spirit of truth, whom the world cannot receive, because it does not see Him or know *Him; but* you know Him because He remains with you and will be in you.

18 "I will not leave you as orphans; I am coming to you. 19 After a little while, the world no longer *is going to* see Me, but you *are going to* see Me; because I live, you also will live. 20 On that day you will know that I *am* in My Father, and you *are* in Me, and I in you. 21 The one who has My commandments and keeps them is the one who loves Me; and the one who loves Me will be loved by My Father, and I will love him and will reveal Myself to him." 22 Judas (not Iscariot) *said to Him, "Lord, what has happened that You are going to reveal Yourself to us and not to the world?" 23 Jesus answered and said to him, "If anyone loves Me, he will follow My word; and My Father will love him, and We will come to him and make *Our* dwelling with him. 24 The one who does not love Me does not follow My words; and the word which you hear is not Mine, but the Father's who sent Me.

25 "These things I have spoken to you while remaining with you. 26 But the Helper, the Holy Spirit whom the

Father will send in My name, He will teach you all things, and remind you of all that I said to you. 27 Peace I leave you, My peace I give you; not as the world gives, do I give to you. Do not let your hearts be troubled, nor fearful. 28 You heard that I said to you, 'I am going away, and I am coming to you.' If you loved Me, you would have rejoiced because I am going to the Father, for the Father is greater than I. 29 And now I have told you before it happens, so that when it happens, you may believe. 30 I will not speak much more with you, for the ruler of the world is coming, and he has [1]nothing in *regard to* Me, 31 but so that the world may know that I love the Father, I do exactly as the Father commanded Me. Get up, let's go from here.

Jesus Is the Vine—Followers Are Branches

15 "I am the true vine, and My Father is the vinedresser. 2 Every branch in Me that does not bear fruit, He takes away; and every *branch* that bears fruit, He prunes it so that it may bear more fruit. 3 You are already clean because of the word which I have spoken to you. 4 Remain in Me, and I in you. Just as the branch cannot bear fruit of itself but must remain in the vine, so neither *can* you unless you remain in Me. 5 I am the vine, you are the branches; the one who remains in Me, and I in him bears much fruit, for apart from Me you can do nothing. 6 If anyone does not remain in Me, he is thrown away like a branch and dries up; and they gather them and throw them into the fire, and they are burned. 7 If you remain in Me, and My words remain in you, ask whatever you wish, and it will be done for you. 8 My Father is glorified by this, that you bear much fruit, and *so* prove to be My disciples. 9 Just as the Father has loved Me, I also have loved you; remain in My love. 10 If you keep My commandments, you will remain in My love; just as I have kept My Father's commandments and remain in His love. 11 These things I have spoken to you so that My joy may be in you, and *that* your joy may be made full.

Disciples' Relation to Each Other

12 "This is My commandment, that you love one

14:30 [1] I.e., no grounds for any accusation

another, just as I have loved you. ¹³ Greater love has no one than this, that a person will lay down his life for his friends. ¹⁴ You are My friends if you do what I command you. ¹⁵ No longer do I call you slaves, for the slave does not know what his master is doing; but I have called you friends, because all things that I have heard from My Father I have made known to you. ¹⁶ You did not choose Me but I chose you, and appointed you that you would go and bear fruit, and *that* your fruit would remain, so that whatever you ask of the Father in My name He may give to you. ¹⁷ This I command you, that you love one another.

Disciples' Relation to the World

¹⁸ "If the world hates you, you know that it has hated Me before *it hated* you. ¹⁹ If you were of the world, the world would love *you as* its own; but because you are not of the world, but I chose you out of the world, because of this the world hates you. ²⁰ Remember the word that I said to you, 'A slave is not greater than his master.' If they persecuted Me, they will persecute you as well; if they followed My word, they will follow yours also. ²¹ But all these things they will do to you on account of My name, because they do not know the One who sent Me. ²² If I had not come and spoken to them, they would not have sin; but now they have no excuse for their sin. ²³ The one who hates Me hates My Father also. ²⁴ If I had not done among them the works which no one else did, they would not have sin; but now they have both seen and hated Me and My Father as well. ²⁵ But *this has happened* so that the word that is written in their Law will be fulfilled: 'THEY HATED ME FOR NO REASON.'

²⁶ "When the Helper comes, whom I will send to you from the Father, *namely,* the Spirit of truth who comes from the Father, He will testify about Me, ²⁷ and you are testifying as well, because you have been with Me from the beginning.

Jesus' Warning

16 "These things I have spoken to you so that you will not be led into sin. ² They will ban you from the synagogue, yet an hour is coming for everyone who kills you to think that he is offering a service to God.

³These things they will do because they have not known the Father nor Me. ⁴But these things I have spoken to you, so that when their hour comes, you may remember that I told you of them. However, I did not say these things to you at the beginning, because I was with you.

The Holy Spirit Promised

⁵"But now I am going to Him who sent Me; and none of you asks Me, 'Where are You going?' ⁶But because I have said these things to you, grief has filled your heart. ⁷But I tell you the truth: it is to your advantage that I am leaving; for if I do not leave, the Helper will not come to you; but if I go, I will send Him to you. ⁸And He, when He comes, will convict the world regarding sin, and righteousness, and judgment: ⁹regarding sin, because they do not believe in Me; ¹⁰and regarding righteousness, because I am going to the Father and you no longer *are going to* see Me; ¹¹and regarding judgment, because the ruler of this world has been judged.

¹²"I have many more things to say to you, but you cannot bear *them* at the present time. ¹³But when He, the Spirit of truth, comes, He will guide you into all the truth; for He will not speak on His own, but whatever He hears, He will speak; and He will disclose to you what is to come. ¹⁴He will glorify Me, for He will take from Mine and will disclose *it* to you. ¹⁵All things that the Father has are Mine; this is why I said that He takes from Mine and will disclose *it* to you.

Jesus' Death and Resurrection Foretold

¹⁶"A little while, and you no longer *are going to* see Me; and again a little while, and you will see Me." ¹⁷So some of His disciples said to one another, "What is this that He is telling us, 'A little while, and you are not *going to* see Me; and again a little while, and you will see Me'; and, 'because I am going to the Father'?" ¹⁸So they were saying, "What is this that He says, 'A little while'? We do not know what He is talking *about.*"
¹⁹Jesus knew that they wanted to question Him, and He said to them, "Are you deliberating together about this, that I said, 'A little while, and you are not *going to* see Me, and again a little while, and you will see Me'? ²⁰Truly, truly I say to you that you will weep and mourn, but the world will rejoice; you will grieve, but your grief

will be turned into joy! **21** Whenever a woman is in labor she has pain, because her hour has come; but when she gives birth to the child, she no longer remembers the anguish because of the joy that a child has been born into the world. **22** Therefore you too have grief now; but I will see you again, and your heart will rejoice, and no one *is going to* take your joy away from you.

Prayer Promises

23 And on that day you will not question Me about anything. Truly, truly I say to you, if you ask the Father for anything in My name, He will give it to you. **24** Until now you have asked for nothing in My name; ask and you will receive, so that your joy may be made full.

25 "These things I have spoken to you in figures of speech; an hour is coming when I will no longer speak to you in figures of speech, but will tell you plainly about the Father. **26** On that day you will ask in My name, and I am not saying to you that I will request of the Father on your behalf; **27** for the Father Himself loves you, because you have loved Me and have believed that I came forth from the Father. **28** I came forth from the Father and have come into the world; again, I am leaving the world and going to the Father."

29 His disciples *said, "See, now You are speaking plainly and are not using any figure of speech. **30** Now we know that You know all things, and *that* You have no need for anyone to question You; this is why we believe that You came forth from God." **31** Jesus replied to them, "Do you now believe? **32** Behold, an hour is coming, and has *already* come, for you to be scattered, each to his own *home,* and to leave Me alone; and *yet* I am not alone, because the Father is with Me. **33** These things I have spoken to you so that in Me you may have peace. In the world you have tribulation, but take courage; I have overcome the world."

The High Priestly Prayer

17 Jesus spoke these things; and raising His eyes to heaven, He said, "Father, the hour has come; glorify Your Son, so that the Son may glorify You, **2** just as You gave Him authority over all mankind, so that to all whom You have given Him, He may give eternal life. **3** And this is eternal life, that they may know You, the only true God, and Jesus Christ whom You have sent. **4** I glorified You on the earth by accomplishing the work which You have given Me to do. **5** And now You, Father, glorify Me together with Yourself, with the glory which I had with You before the world existed.

6 "I have revealed Your name to the men whom You gave Me out of the world; they were Yours and You gave them to Me, and they have followed Your word. **7** Now they have come to know that everything which You have given Me is from You; **8** for the words which You gave Me I have given to them; and they received *them* and truly understood that I came forth from You, and they believed that You sent Me. **9** I ask on their behalf; I do not ask on behalf of the world, but on the behalf of those whom You have given Me, because they are Yours; **10** and all things that are Mine are Yours, and Yours are Mine; and I have been glorified in them. **11** I am no longer *going to be* in the world; and *yet* they themselves are in the world, and I am coming to You. Holy Father, keep them in Your name, *the name* which You have given Me, so that they may be one just as We *are.* **12** While I was with them, I was keeping them in Your name, which You have given Me; and I guarded them, and not one of them perished except the son of destruction, so that the Scripture would be fulfilled.

The Disciples in the World

13 But now I am coming to You; and these things I speak in the world so that they may have My joy made full in themselves. **14** I have given them Your word; and the world has hated them because they are not of the world, just as I am not of the world. **15** I am not asking You to take them out of the world, but to keep them away from the evil one. **16** They are not of the world, just as I am not of the world. **17** Sanctify them in the truth; Your word is truth. **18** Just as You sent Me into the world, I also sent them into the world. **19** And for their sakes I sanctify Myself, so that they themselves also may be sanctified in truth.

20 "I am not asking on behalf of these alone, but also for those who believe in Me through their word, **21** that they may all be one; just as You, Father, *are* in Me and I in You, that they also may be in Us, so that the world may believe that You sent Me.

Disciples' Future Glory

22 The glory which You have given Me I also have given to them, so that they may be one, just as We are one; 23 I in them and You in Me, that they may be perfected in unity, so that the world may know that You sent Me, and You loved them, just as You loved Me. 24 Father, I desire that they also, whom You have given Me, be with Me where I am, so that they may see My glory which You have given Me, for You loved Me before the foundation of the world.

25 "Righteous Father, although the world has not known You, yet I have known You; and these have known that You sent Me; 26 and I have made Your name known to them, and will make it known, so that the love with which You loved Me may be in them, and I in them."

Judas Betrays Jesus

18 When Jesus had spoken these words, He went away with His disciples across the ravine of the Kidron, where there was a garden which He entered with His disciples. 2 Now Judas, who was betraying Him, also knew the place, because Jesus had often met there with His disciples. 3 So Judas, having obtained the *Roman* [1]cohort and officers from the chief priests and the Pharisees, *came there with lanterns, torches, and weapons. 4 Jesus therefore, knowing all the things that were coming upon Him, came out *into the open* and *said to them, "Whom are you seeking?" 5 They answered Him, "Jesus the Nazarene." He *said to them, "I am *He.*" And Judas also, who was betraying Him, was standing with them. 6 Now then, when He said to them, "I am *He,*" they drew back and fell to the ground. 7 He then asked them again, "Whom are you seeking?" And they said, "Jesus the Nazarene." 8 Jesus answered, "I told you that I am *He;* so if you are seeking Me, let these *men* go on their way." 9 *This took place* so that the word which He spoke would be fulfilled: "Of those whom You have given Me I lost not one." 10 Then Simon Peter, since he had a sword, drew it and struck the high priest's slave, and cut off his right ear; and the slave's name was Malchus. 11 So Jesus said to Peter, "Put the sword into the

---

18:3 [1]Normally 600 men (the number varied)

sheath; the cup which the Father has given Me, am I not
to drink it?"

Jesus before the Priests

12 So the *Roman* [1]cohort, the commander, and the
officers of the Jews arrested Jesus and bound Him, **13** and
brought Him to Annas first; for he was the father-in-law
of Caiaphas, who was high priest that year. **14** Now Caiaphas was the one who had advised the Jews that it was
in their best interest for one man to die in behalf of the
people.

15 Simon Peter was following Jesus, and *so was*
another disciple. Now that disciple was known to the
high priest, and he entered with Jesus into the courtyard
of the high priest, **16** but Peter was standing at the door
outside. So the other disciple, who was known to the
high priest, went out and spoke to the doorkeeper, and
brought Peter in. **17** Then the slave woman who was the
doorkeeper *said to Peter, "You are not also *one* of this
Man's disciples, are you?" He *said, "I am not." **18** Now
the slaves and the officers were standing *there,* having
made a charcoal fire, for it was cold and they were
warming themselves; and Peter was also with them,
standing and warming himself.

19 The high priest then questioned Jesus about His disciples, and about His teaching. **20** Jesus answered him, "I
have spoken openly to the world; I always taught in synagogues and in the temple *area,* where all the Jews con-
gregate; and I said nothing in secret. **21** Why are you
asking Me? Ask those who have heard what I spoke to
them. Look: these people know what I said." **22** But when
He said this, one of the officers, who was standing
nearby, struck Jesus, saying, "Is that the way You answer
the high priest?" **23** Jesus answered him, "If I have
spoken wrongly, testify of the wrong; but if rightly, why
do you strike Me?" **24** So Annas sent Him bound to Caiaphas the high priest.

Peter's Denial of Jesus

25 Now Simon Peter was *still* standing and warming
himself. So they said to him, "You are not *one* of His
disciples as well, are you?" He denied *it,* and said, "I am

18:12 [1] Normally 600 men (the number varied)

not." **26** One of the slaves of the high priest, who was related to the one whose ear Peter cut off, *said, "Did I not see you in the garden with Him?" **27** Peter then denied *it* again, and immediately a rooster crowed.

Jesus before Pilate

28 Then they *brought Jesus from Caiaphas into the ʹPraetorium, and it was early; and they themselves did not enter the Praetorium, so that they would not be defiled, but might eat the Passover. **29** Therefore Pilate came out to them and *said, "What accusation are you bringing against this Man?" **30** They answered and said to him, "If this Man were not a criminal, we would not have handed Him over to you." **31** So Pilate said to them, "Take Him yourselves, and judge Him according to your law." The Jews said to him, "We are not ʹpermitted to put anyone to death." **32** *This happened* so that the word of Jesus which He said, indicating what kind of death He was going to die, would be fulfilled.

33 Therefore Pilate entered the Praetorium again, and summoned Jesus and said to Him, "You are the King of the Jews?" **34** Jesus answered, "Are you saying this on your own, or did others tell you about Me?" **35** Pilate answered, "I am not a Jew, am I? Your own nation and the chief priests handed You over to me; what have You done?" **36** Jesus answered, "My kingdom is not of this world. If My kingdom were of this world, My servants would be fighting so that I would not be handed over to the Jews; but as it is, My kingdom is not of this realm." **37** Therefore Pilate said to Him, "So You are a king?" Jesus answered, "You say *correctly* that I am a king. For this *purpose* I have been born, and for this I have come into the world: to testify to the truth. Everyone who is of the truth listens to My voice." **38** Pilate *said to Him, "What is truth?"

And after saying this, he came out again to the Jews and *said to them, "I find no grounds at all for charges in His case. **39** However, you have a custom that I release one *prisoner* for you at the Passover; therefore do you wish that I release for you the King of the Jews?" **40** So

---

18:28 ʹI.e., governor's official residence
18:31 ʹI.e., under Roman law

they shouted again, saying, "Not this Man, but Barabbas." Now Barabbas was a rebel.

The Crown of Thorns

19 So Pilate then took Jesus and had Him flogged. ² And the soldiers twisted together a crown of thorns and placed it on His head, and put a purple cloak on Him; ³ and they *repeatedly* came up to Him and said, "Hail, King of the Jews!" and slapped Him in the face *again and again.* ⁴ And *then* Pilate came out again and *said to them, "See, I am bringing Him out to you so that you will know that I find no grounds at all for charges in His case." ⁵ Jesus then came out, wearing the crown of thorns and the purple robe. And *Pilate* *said to them, "Behold, the Man!" ⁶ So when the chief priests and the officers saw Him, they shouted, saying, "Crucify, crucify!" Pilate *said to them, "Take Him yourselves and crucify *Him;* for I find no grounds for charges in His case!" ⁷ The Jews answered him, "We have a law, and by that law He ought to die, because He made Himself *out to be* the Son of God!"

⁸ Therefore when Pilate heard this statement, he was *even* more afraid; ⁹ and he entered the ¹Praetorium again and *said to Jesus, "Where are You from?" But Jesus gave him no answer. ¹⁰ So Pilate *said to Him, "Are you not speaking to me? Do You not know that I have authority to release You, and I have authority to crucify You?" ¹¹ Jesus answered him, "You would have no authority over Me at all, if it had not been given to you from above; for this reason the one who handed Me over to you has *the* greater sin." ¹² As a result of this, Pilate made efforts to release Him; but the Jews shouted, saying, "If you release this Man, you are not a friend of Caesar; everyone who makes himself *out to be* a king opposes Caesar!"

¹³ Therefore when Pilate heard these words, he brought Jesus out, and sat down on the judgment seat at a place called The Pavement—but in Hebrew, Gabbatha. ¹⁴ Now it was the day of preparation for the Passover; it was about the ¹sixth hour. And he *said to the Jews, "Look, your King!" ¹⁵ So they shouted, "Away with *Him,* away with *Him,* crucify Him!" Pilate *said to them,

---

19:9 ¹I.e., governor's official residence   19:14 ¹I.e., about noon

"Shall I crucify your King?" The chief priests answered, "We have no king except Caesar."

The Crucifixion

16 So he then handed Him over to them to be crucified.

17 They took Jesus, therefore, and He went out, carrying His own cross, to the *place* called the Place of a Skull, which in Hebrew is called, Golgotha. 18 There they crucified Him, and with Him two other men, one on either side, and Jesus in between. 19 Now Pilate also wrote an inscription and put it on the cross. It was written: "JESUS THE NAZARENE, THE KING OF THE JEWS." 20 Therefore many of the Jews read this inscription, because the place where Jesus was crucified was near the city; and it was written in Hebrew, Latin, *and* in Greek. 21 So the chief priests of the Jews were saying to Pilate, "Do not write, 'The King of the Jews'; rather, *write* that He said, 'I am King of the Jews.'" 22 Pilate answered, "What I have written, I have written."

23 Then the soldiers, when they had crucified Jesus, took His outer garments and made four parts: a part to each soldier, and the ʹtunic *also;* but the tunic was seamless, woven in one piece. 24 So they said to one another, "Let's not tear it, but cast lots for it, *to decide* whose it shall be." *This happened* so that the Scripture would be fulfilled: "THEY DIVIDED MY GARMENTS AMONG THEMSELVES, AND THEY CAST LOTS FOR MY CLOTHING." Therefore the soldiers did these things.

25 Now beside the cross of Jesus stood His mother, His mother's sister, Mary the *wife* of Clopas, and Mary Magdalene. 26 So when Jesus saw His mother, and the disciple whom He loved standing nearby, He *said to His mother, "Woman, behold, your son!" 27 Then He *said to the disciple, "Behold, your mother!" And from that hour the disciple took her into his own *household.*

28 After this, Jesus, knowing that all things had already been accomplished, in order that the Scripture would be fulfilled, *said, "I am thirsty." 29 A jar full of sour wine was standing *there;* so they put a sponge full of the sour wine on *a branch of* hyssop and brought it *up* to His

---

19:23 ¹ A long shirt worn next to the skin

mouth. **30** Therefore when Jesus had received the sour wine, He said, "It is finished!" And He bowed His head and gave up His spirit.

Care of the Body of Jesus

31 Now then, since it was the day of preparation, to prevent the bodies from remaining on the cross on the Sabbath (for that Sabbath was a high day), the Jews requested of Pilate that their legs be broken, and *the bodies* be taken away. **32** So the soldiers came and broke the legs of the first man, and of the other who was crucified with Him; **33** but after they came to Jesus, when they saw that He was already dead, they did not break His legs. **34** Yet one of the soldiers pierced His side with a spear, and immediately blood and water came out. **35** And he who has seen has testified, and his testimony is true; and he knows that he is telling the truth, so that you also may believe. **36** For these things took place so that the Scripture would be fulfilled: "NOT A BONE OF HIM SHALL BE BROKEN." **37** And again another Scripture says, "THEY WILL LOOK AT HIM WHOM THEY PIERCED."

38 Now after these things Joseph of Arimathea, being a disciple of Jesus, but a secret *one* for fear of the ¹Jews, requested of Pilate that he might take away the body of Jesus; and Pilate granted permission. So he came and took away His body. **39** Nicodemus, who had first come to Him by night, also came, bringing a mixture of myrrh and aloes, about a ¹hundred litras *weight.* **40** So they took the body of Jesus and bound it in linen wrappings with the spices, as is the burial custom of the Jews. **41** Now in the place where He was crucified there was a garden, and in the garden *was* a new tomb in which no one had yet been laid. **42** Therefore because of the Jewish day of preparation, since the tomb was nearby, they laid Jesus there.

The Empty Tomb

20 Now on the first *day* of the week Mary Magdalene *came early to the tomb, while it was still dark, and *saw the stone *already* removed from the tomb. **2** So she *ran and *came to Simon Peter and to the other

---

disciple whom Jesus loved, and *said to them, "They have taken the Lord from the tomb, and we do not know where they have put Him." [3] So Peter and the other disciple left, and they were going to the tomb. [4] The two were running together; and the other disciple ran ahead, faster than Peter, and came to the tomb first; [5] and he stooped to look *in,* and *saw the linen wrappings lying *there;* however he did not go in. [6] So Simon Peter also *came, following him, and he entered the tomb; and he *looked at the linen wrappings lying *there,* [7] and the face-cloth which had been on His head, not lying with the linen wrappings but folded up in a place by itself. [8] So the other disciple who had first come to the tomb also entered then, and he saw and believed. [9] For they did not yet understand the Scripture, that He must rise from the dead. [10] So the disciples went away again to their own *homes.*

[11] But Mary was standing outside the tomb, weeping; so as she wept, she stooped to look into the tomb; [12] and she *saw two angels in white sitting, one at the head and one at the feet, where the body of Jesus had been lying. [13] And they *said to her, "Woman, why are you weeping?" She *said to them, "Because they have taken away my Lord, and I do not know where they put Him." [14] When she had said this, she turned around and *saw Jesus standing *there,* and *yet* she did not know that it was Jesus. [15] Jesus *said to her, "Woman, why are you weeping? Whom are you seeking?" Thinking that He was the gardener, she *said to Him, "Sir, if you have carried Him away, tell me where you put Him, and I will take Him away." [16] Jesus *said to her, "Mary!" She turned and *said to Him in Hebrew, "Rabboni!" (which means, Teacher). [17] Jesus *said to her, "Stop clinging to Me, for I have not yet ascended to the Father; but go to My brothers and say to them, 'I am ascending to My Father and your Father, and My God and your God.' " [18] Mary Magdalene *came and announced to the disciples, "I have seen the Lord," and *that* He had said these things to her.

Jesus among His Disciples

[19] Now when it was evening on that day, the first *day* of the week, and when the doors were shut where the disciples were *together* due to fear of the

[1]Jews, Jesus came and stood in their midst, and *said to them, "Peace be to you." 20 And when He had said this, He showed them both His hands and His side. The disciples then rejoiced when they saw the Lord. 21 So Jesus said to them again, "Peace be to you; just as the Father has sent Me, I also send you." 22 And when He had said this, He breathed on them and *said to them, "Receive the Holy Spirit. 23 If you forgive the sins of any, their sins have been forgiven them; if you retain the sins of any, they have been retained."

24 But Thomas, one of the twelve, who was called Didymus, was not with them when Jesus came. 25 So the other disciples were saying to him, "We have seen the Lord!" But he said to them, "Unless I see in His hands the imprint of the nails, and put my finger into the place of the nails, and put my hand into His side, I will not believe."

26 Eight days later His disciples were again inside, and Thomas was with them. Jesus *came, the doors having been shut, and stood in their midst and said, "Peace be to you." 27 Then He *said to Thomas, "Place your finger here, and see My hands; and take your hand and put it into My side; and do not continue in disbelief, but be a believer." 28 Thomas answered and said to Him, "My Lord and my God!" 29 Jesus *said to him, "Because you have seen Me, have you now believed? Blessed are they who did not see, and yet believed."

Why This Gospel Was Written

30 So then, many other signs Jesus also performed in the presence of the disciples, which are not written in this book; 31 but these have been written so that you may believe that Jesus is the Christ, the Son of God; and that by believing you may have life in His name.

Jesus Appears at the Sea of Galilee

21 After these things Jesus revealed Himself again to the disciples at the Sea of Tiberias, and He revealed Himself in this way: 2 Simon Peter, Thomas who was called Didymus, Nathanael of Cana in Galilee, the sons of Zebedee, and two others of His disciples were together. 3 Simon Peter *said to them, "I am going

---

20:19 [1] I.e., the Jewish leaders

fishing." They *said to him, "We are also coming with you." They went out and got into the boat; and that night they caught nothing.

4 But when the day was now breaking, Jesus stood on the beach; yet the disciples did not know that it was Jesus. **5** So Jesus *said to them, "Children, you do not have any fish to eat, do you?" They answered Him, "No." **6** And He said to them, "Cast the net on the right-hand side of the boat, and you will find *the fish.*" So they cast *it,* and then they were not able to haul it in because of the great quantity of fish. **7** Therefore that disciple whom Jesus loved *said to Peter, "It is the Lord!" So when Simon Peter heard that it was the Lord, he put on his outer garment (for he was stripped *for work),* and threw himself into the sea. **8** But the other disciples came in the little boat, for they were not far from the land, but about [1] two hundred cubits away, dragging the net *full* of fish.

9 So when they got out on the land, they *saw a charcoal fire *already* made and fish placed on it, and bread. **10** Jesus *said to them, "Bring some of the fish which you have now caught." **11** So Simon Peter went up and hauled the net to land, full of large fish, 153; and although there were so many, the net was not torn.

Jesus Provides

12 Jesus *said to them, "Come *and* have breakfast." None of the disciples ventured to inquire of Him, "Who are You?" knowing that it was the Lord. **13** Jesus *came and *took the bread and *gave *it* to them, and the fish likewise. **14** This was now the third time that Jesus revealed Himself to the disciples, after He was raised from the dead.

The Love Question

15 Now when they had finished breakfast, Jesus *said to Simon Peter, "Simon, *son* of John, do you love Me more than these?" He *said to Him, "Yes, Lord; You know that I love You." He *said to him, "Tend My lambs." **16** He *said to him again, a second time, "Simon, *son* of John, do you love Me?" He *said to Him, "Yes, Lord; You know that I love You." He *said to him,

---

"Shepherd My sheep." **17** He *said to him the third time, "Simon, *son* of John, do you love Me?" Peter was hurt because He said to him the third time, "Do you love Me?" And he said to Him, "Lord, You know all things; You know that I love You." Jesus *said to him, "Tend My sheep.

Our Times Are in His Hand

18 Truly, truly I tell you, when you were younger, you used to put on your belt and walk wherever you wanted; but when you grow old, you will stretch out your hands and someone else will put your belt on you, and bring *you* where you do not want *to go.*" **19** Now He said this, indicating by what kind of death he would glorify God. And when He had said this, He *said to him, "Follow Me!"

20 Peter turned around and *saw the disciple whom Jesus loved following *them*—the one who also had leaned back on His chest at the supper and said, "Lord, who is the one who is betraying You?" **21** So Peter, upon seeing him, *said to Jesus, "Lord, and what *about* this man?" **22** Jesus *said to him, "If I want him to remain until I come, what *is that* to you? You follow Me!" **23** Therefore this account went out among the brothers, that that disciple would not die; yet Jesus did not say to him that he would not die, but *only,* "If I want him to remain until I come, what *is that* to you?"

24 This is the disciple who is testifying about these things and wrote these things, and we know that his testimony is true.

25 But there are also many other things which Jesus did, which, if they were written in detail, I expect that even the world itself would not contain the books that would be written.

THE ACTS
of the Apostles

Introduction

1 The first account I composed, Theophilus, about all that Jesus began to do and teach, 2 until the day when He was taken up *to heaven,* after He had given orders by the Holy Spirit to the apostles whom He had chosen. 3 To these He also presented Himself alive after His suffering, by many convincing proofs, appearing to them over *a period of* forty days and speaking of things regarding the kingdom of God. 4 Gathering them together, He commanded them not to leave Jerusalem, but to wait for what the Father had promised, "Which," *He said,* "you heard of from Me; 5 for John baptized with water, but you will be baptized with the Holy Spirit not many days from now."

6 So, when they had come together, they *began* asking Him, saying, "Lord, is it at this time that You are restoring the kingdom to Israel?" 7 But He said to them, "It is not for you to know periods of time or appointed times which the Father has set by His own authority; 8 but you will receive power when the Holy Spirit has come upon you; and you shall be My witnesses both in Jerusalem and in all Judea, and Samaria, and as far as the remotest part of the earth."

The Ascension

9 And after He had said these things, He was lifted up while they were watching, and a cloud took Him up, out of their sight. 10 And as they were gazing intently into the sky while He was going, then behold, two men in white clothing stood beside them, 11 and they said, "Men of Galilee, why do you stand looking into the sky? This Jesus, who has been taken up from you into heaven, will come in the same way as you have watched Him go into heaven."

The Upper Room

12 Then they returned to Jerusalem from the mountain

called Olivet, which is near Jerusalem, a ¹Sabbath day's journey away. ¹³ When they had entered *the city,* they went up to the upstairs room where they were staying, that is, Peter, John, James, and Andrew, Philip and Thomas, Bartholomew and Matthew, James *the son* of Alphaeus, Simon the Zealot, and Judas *the son* of James. ¹⁴ All these were continually devoting themselves with one mind to prayer, along with *the* women, and Mary the mother of Jesus, and with His brothers.

¹⁵ At this time Peter stood up among the brothers *and sisters* (a group of about 120 people was there together), and said, ¹⁶ "Brothers, the Scripture had to be fulfilled, which the Holy Spirit foretold by the mouth of David concerning Judas, who became a guide to those who arrested Jesus. ¹⁷ For he was counted among us and received his share in this ministry." ¹⁸ (Now this man acquired a field with the price of his wickedness, and falling headlong, he burst open in the middle and all his intestines gushed out. ¹⁹ And it became known to all the residents of Jerusalem; as a result that field was called Hakeldama in their own language, that is, Field of Blood.) ²⁰ "For it is written in the book of Psalms:

　'MAY HIS RESIDENCE BE MADE DESOLATE,
　AND MAY THERE BE NONE LIVING IN IT';
and,
　'MAY ANOTHER TAKE HIS OFFICE.'

²¹ Therefore it is necessary that of the men who have accompanied us all the time that the Lord Jesus went in and out among us—²² beginning with the baptism of John until the day that He was taken up from us—one of these *must* become a witness with us of His resurrection." ²³ So they put forward two men, Joseph called Barsabbas (who was also called Justus), and Matthias. ²⁴ And they prayed and said, "You, Lord, who know the hearts of all *people,* show which one of these two You have chosen ²⁵ to occupy this ministry and apostleship from which Judas turned aside to go to his own place." ²⁶ And they drew lots for them, and the lot fell to Matthias; and he was added to the eleven apostles.

1:12 ¹ 2,000 cubits, or about 0.6 miles or 1 km

The Day of Pentecost

2 When the day of Pentecost had come, they were all together in one place. 2 And suddenly a noise like a violent rushing wind came from heaven, and it filled the whole house where they were sitting. 3 And tongues *that looked* like fire appeared to them, distributing themselves, and *a tongue* rested on each one of them. 4 And they were all filled with the Holy Spirit and began to speak with different tongues, as the Spirit was giving them *the ability* to speak out.

5 Now there were Jews residing in Jerusalem, devout men from every nation under heaven. 6 And when this sound occurred, the crowd came together and they were bewildered, because each one of them was hearing them speak in his own language. 7 They were amazed and astonished, saying, "Why, are not all these who are speaking Galileans? 8 And how *is it that* we each hear *them* in our own language to which we were born? 9 Parthians, Medes, and Elamites, and residents of Mesopotamia, Judea, and Cappadocia, Pontus and Asia, 10 Phrygia and Pamphylia, Egypt and the parts of Libya around Cyrene, and visitors from Rome, both Jews and ¹proselytes, 11 Cretans and Arabs—we hear them speaking in our *own* tongues of the mighty deeds of God." 12 And they all continued in amazement and great perplexity, saying to one another, "What does this mean?" 13 But others were jeering and saying, "They are full of sweet wine!"

Peter's Sermon

14 But Peter, taking his stand with the *other* eleven, raised his voice and declared to them: "Men of Judea and all you who live in Jerusalem, know this, and pay attention to my words. 15 For these people are not drunk, as you assume, since it is *only* the ¹third hour of the day; 16 but this is what has been spoken through the prophet Joel:

17 'AND IT SHALL BE IN THE LAST DAYS,' God says,
  'THAT I WILL POUR OUT MY SPIRIT ON ALL MANKIND;
   AND YOUR SONS AND YOUR DAUGHTERS WILL PROPHESY,
   AND YOUR YOUNG MEN WILL SEE VISIONS,
   AND YOUR OLD MEN WILL HAVE DREAMS;

2:10 ¹I.e., Gentile converts to Judaism   2:15 ¹I.e., 9 a.m.

18   AND EVEN ON MY MALE AND FEMALE SERVANTS
      I WILL POUR OUT MY SPIRIT IN THOSE DAYS,
      And they will prophesy.

19   'AND I WILL DISPLAY WONDERS IN THE SKY ABOVE
      AND SIGNS ON THE EARTH BELOW,
      BLOOD, FIRE, AND VAPOR OF SMOKE.

20   'THE SUN WILL BE TURNED INTO DARKNESS
      AND THE MOON INTO BLOOD,
      BEFORE THE GREAT AND GLORIOUS DAY OF THE LORD COMES.

21   'AND IT SHALL BE *THAT* EVERYONE WHO CALLS ON THE NAME OF
         THE LORD WILL BE SAVED.'

22 "Men of Israel, listen to these words: Jesus the
Nazarene, a Man attested to you by God with miracles
and wonders and signs which God performed through
Him in your midst, just as you yourselves know— 23 this
Man, delivered over by the predetermined plan and foreknowledge of God, you nailed to a cross by the hands of
godless men and put *Him* to death. 24 But God raised Him
from the dead, putting an end to the agony of death,
since it was impossible for Him to be held in its power.
25 For David says of Him,
      'I SAW THE LORD CONTINUALLY BEFORE ME,
      BECAUSE HE IS AT MY RIGHT HAND, SO THAT I WILL NOT BE
         SHAKEN.

26   'THEREFORE MY HEART WAS GLAD AND MY TONGUE WAS OVER-
         JOYED;
      MOREOVER MY FLESH ALSO WILL LIVE IN HOPE;

27   FOR YOU WILL NOT ABANDON MY SOUL TO HADES,
      NOR WILL YOU ALLOW YOUR HOLY ONE TO UNDERGO DECAY.

28   'YOU HAVE MADE KNOWN TO ME THE WAYS OF LIFE;
      YOU WILL MAKE ME FULL OF GLADNESS WITH YOUR
         PRESENCE.'

29 "Brothers, I may confidently say to you regarding
the patriarch David that he both died and was buried,
and his tomb is with us to this day. 30 So because he was
a prophet and knew that God had sworn to him with an
oath to seat *one* of his descendants on his throne, 31 he
looked ahead and spoke of the resurrection of the Christ,
that He was neither abandoned to Hades, nor did His
flesh suffer decay. 32 *It is* this Jesus *whom* God raised up,
a fact to which we are all witnesses. 33 Therefore, since
He has been exalted at the right hand of God, and has
received the promise of the Holy Spirit from the Father,
He has poured out this which you both see and hear.

34 For it was not David who ascended into heaven, but he himself says:

'THE LORD SAID TO MY LORD,
"SIT AT MY RIGHT HAND,
35 UNTIL I MAKE YOUR ENEMIES A FOOTSTOOL FOR YOUR FEET." '

36 Therefore let all the house of Israel know for certain that God has made Him both Lord and Christ—this Jesus whom you crucified."

37 Now when they heard *this,* they were pierced to the heart, and said to Peter and the rest of the apostles, "Brothers, what are we to do?" **38** Peter *said* to them, "Repent, and each of you be baptized in the name of Jesus Christ for the forgiveness of your sins; and you will receive the gift of the Holy Spirit. **39** For the promise is for you and your children and for all who are far away, as many as the Lord our God will call to Himself." **40** And with many other words he solemnly testified and kept on urging them, saying, "Be saved from this perverse generation!" **41** So then, those who had received his word were baptized; and that day there were added about three thousand ʼsouls. **42** They were continually devoting themselves to the apostles' teaching and to fellowship, to the breaking of bread and to ʼprayer.

43 Everyone kept feeling a sense of awe; and many wonders and signs were taking place through the apostles. **44** And all the believers ʼwere together and had all things in common; **45** and they would sell their property and possessions and share them with all, to the extent that anyone had need. **46** Day by day continuing with one mind in the temple, and breaking bread from house to house, they were taking their meals together with gladness and sincerity of heart, **47** praising God and having favor with all the people. And the Lord was adding to their number day by day those who were being saved.

Healing the Beggar Who Was Unable to Walk

3 Now Peter and John were going up to the temple at the ʼninth *hour,* the hour of prayer. **2** And a man who had been unable to walk from birth was being carried, whom they used to set down every day at the gate of the temple which is called Beautiful, in order *for him* to beg

---

2:41 ¹I.e., persons   2:42 ¹Lit *the prayers*   2:44 ¹One early ms does not contain *were* and *and*   3:1 ¹I.e., 3 p.m.

for charitable gifts from those entering the temple
grounds. **3** When he saw Peter and John about to go into
the temple *grounds,* he *began* asking to receive a
charitable gift. **4** But Peter, along with John, looked at him
intently and said, "Look at us!" **5** And he gave them his
attention, expecting to receive something from them.
6 But Peter said, "I do not have silver and gold, but what
I do have I give to you: In the name of Jesus Christ the
Nazarene, walk!" **7** And grasping him by the right hand,
he raised him up; and immediately his feet and his
ankles were strengthened. **8** And leaping up, he stood and
began to walk; and he entered the temple with them,
walking and leaping and praising God. **9** And all the
people saw him walking and praising God; **10** and they
recognized him as being the very one who used to sit at
the Beautiful Gate of the temple *to beg* for charitable
gifts, and they were filled with wonder and amazement
at what had happened to him.

Peter's Second Sermon

11 While he was clinging to Peter and John, all the
people ran together to them at the portico named
Solomon's, completely astonished. **12** But when Peter saw
this, he replied to the people, "Men of Israel, why are
you amazed at this, or why are you staring at us, as
though by our own power or godliness we had made him
walk? **13** The God of Abraham, Isaac, and Jacob, the God
of our fathers, has glorified His servant Jesus, *the one*
whom you handed over and disowned in the presence of
Pilate, when he had decided to release *Him.* **14** But you
disowned the Holy and Righteous One, and asked for a
murderer to be granted to you, **15** but put to death the
Prince of life, whom God raised from the dead, *a fact* to
which we are witnesses. **16** And on the basis of faith in
His name, *it is* the name of Jesus which has strengthened
this man whom you see and know; and the faith which
comes through Him has given him this perfect health in
the presence of you all.

17 "And now, brothers, I know that you acted in
ignorance, just as your rulers also did. **18** But the things
which God previously announced by the mouths of all
the prophets, that His Christ would suffer, He has
fulfilled in this way. **19** Therefore repent and return, so
that your sins may be wiped away, in order that times of

refreshing may come from the presence of the Lord; **20** and that He may send Jesus, the Christ appointed for you, **21** whom heaven must receive until *the* period of restoration of all things, about which God spoke by the mouths of His holy prophets from ancient times. **22** Moses said, 'THE LORD GOD WILL RAISE UP FOR YOU A PROPHET LIKE ME FROM YOUR COUNTRYMEN; TO HIM YOU SHALL LISTEN regarding everything He says to you. **23** And it shall be that every soul that does not listen to that prophet shall be utterly destroyed from among the people.' **24** And likewise, all the prophets who have spoken from Samuel and *his* successors *onward,* have also announced these days. **25** It is you who are the sons of the prophets and of the covenant which God ordained with your fathers, saying to Abraham, 'AND IN YOUR SEED ALL THE FAMILIES OF THE EARTH SHALL BE BLESSED.' **26** God raised up His Servant for you first, and sent Him to bless you by turning every one *of you* from your wicked ways."

Peter and John Arrested

4 As they were speaking to the people, the priests and the captain of the temple *guard* and the Sadducees came up to them, **2** being greatly disturbed because they were teaching the people and proclaiming in Jesus the resurrection from the dead. **3** And they laid hands on them and put *them* in prison until the next day, for it was already evening. **4** But many of those who had heard the message believed; and the number of the men came to be about five thousand.

5 On the next day, their rulers and elders and scribes were gathered together in Jerusalem; **6** and Annas the high priest *was there,* and Caiaphas, John, and Alexander, and all who were of high-priestly descent. **7** When they had placed them in the center, they *began to* inquire, "By what power, or in what name, have you done this?" **8** Then Peter, filled with the Holy Spirit, said to them, "Rulers and elders of the people, **9** if we are on trial today for a benefit done to a sick man, as to how this man has been made well, **10** let it be known to all of you and to all the people of Israel, that by the name of Jesus Christ the Nazarene, whom you crucified, whom God raised from the dead—by this *name* this man stands here before you in good health. **11** He is the STONE WHICH WAS REJECTED by you, THE BUILDERS, *but* WHICH BECAME THE

CHIEF CORNERSTONE. **12** And there is salvation in no one else; for there is no other name under heaven that has been given among mankind by which we must be saved."

Threat and Release

13 Now as they observed the confidence of Peter and John and understood that they were uneducated and untrained men, they were amazed, and *began* to recognize them as having been with Jesus. **14** And seeing the man who had been healed standing with them, they had nothing to say in reply. **15** But when they had ordered them to leave the Council, they *began* to confer with one another, **16** saying, "What are we to do with these men? For the fact that a noteworthy miracle has taken place through them is apparent to all who live in Jerusalem, and we cannot deny it. **17** But so that it will not spread any further among the people, let's warn them not to speak any longer to any person in this name." **18** And when they had summoned them, they commanded them not to speak or teach at all in the name of Jesus. **19** But Peter and John answered and said to them, "Whether it is right in the sight of God to listen to you rather than to God, make your *own* judgment; **20** for we cannot stop speaking about what we have seen and heard." **21** When they had threatened them further, they let them go (finding no basis on which to punish them) on account of the people, because they were all glorifying God for what had happened; **22** for the man on whom this miracle of healing had been performed was more than forty years old.

23 When they had been released, they went to their own *companions* and reported everything that the chief priests and the elders had said to them. **24** And when they heard *this,* they raised their voices to God with one mind and said, "Lord, it is You who MADE THE HEAVEN AND THE EARTH AND THE SEA, AND EVERYTHING THAT IS IN THEM, **25** who by the Holy Spirit, *through* the mouth of our father David Your servant, said,

'WHY WERE THE ¹NATIONS INSOLENT,
    AND THE PEOPLES PLOTTING IN VAIN?
26 'THE KINGS OF THE EARTH TOOK THEIR STAND,

4:25 ¹Or *Gentiles*

AND THE RULERS WERE GATHERED TOGETHER
AGAINST THE LORD AND AGAINST HIS CHRIST.'

27 For truly in this city there were gathered together against Your holy servant Jesus, whom You anointed, both Herod and Pontius Pilate, along with the Gentiles and the peoples of Israel, **28** to do whatever Your hand and purpose predestined to occur. **29** And now, Lord, look at their threats, and grant *it* to Your bond-servants to speak Your word with all confidence, **30** while You extend Your hand to heal, and signs and wonders take place through the name of Your holy servant Jesus." **31** And when they had prayed, the place where they had gathered together was shaken, and they were all filled with the Holy Spirit and *began* to speak the word of God with boldness.

Sharing among Believers

32 And the congregation of those who believed were of one heart and soul; and not one *of them* claimed that anything belonging to him was his own, but all things were common property to them. **33** And with great power the apostles were giving testimony to the resurrection of the Lord Jesus, and abundant grace was upon them all. **34** For there was not a needy person among them, for all who were owners of land or houses would sell them and bring the proceeds of the sales **35** and lay *them* at the apostles' feet, and they would be distributed to each to the extent that any had need.

36 Now Joseph, a Levite of Cyprian birth, who was also called Barnabas by the apostles (which translated means Son of Encouragement), **37** owned a tract of land. So he sold it, and brought the money and laid it at the apostles' feet.

Fate of Ananias and Sapphira

5 But a man named Ananias, with his wife Sapphira, sold a piece of property, **2** and kept back *some* of the proceeds for himself, with his wife's full knowledge, and bringing a portion of it, he laid it at the apostles' feet. **3** But Peter said, "Ananias, why has Satan filled your heart to lie to the Holy Spirit and to keep back *some* of the proceeds of the land? **4** While it remained *unsold,* did it not remain your own? And after it was sold, was it not under your control? Why *is it* that you have conceived this deed in your heart? You have not lied to men, but to God." **5** And as he heard these words, Ananias collapsed and died; and great fear came over all who heard *about it.* **6** The young men got up and covered him up, and after carrying him out, they buried him.

7 Now an interval of about three hours elapsed, and his wife came in, not knowing what had happened. **8** And Peter responded to her, "Tell me whether you sold the land for this price?" And she said, "Yes, for that price." **9** Then Peter *said* to her, "Why *is it* that you have agreed together to put the Spirit of the Lord to the test? Behold, the feet of those who have buried your husband are at the door, and they will carry you out *as well.*" **10** And immediately she collapsed at his feet and died; and the young men came in and found her dead, and they carried her out and buried her beside her husband. **11** And great fear came over the whole church, and over all who heard *about* these things.

12 At the hands of the apostles many signs and wonders were taking place among the people; and they were all together in Solomon's portico. **13** But none of the rest dared to associate with them; however, the people held them in high esteem. **14** And increasingly believers in the Lord, large numbers of men and women, were being added to *their number,* **15** to such an extent that they even carried the sick out into the streets and laid them on cots and pallets, so that when Peter came by at least his shadow might fall on any of them. **16** The people from the cities in the vicinity of Jerusalem were coming together as well, bringing people who were sick [1] or tormented with unclean spirits, and they were all being healed.

Imprisonment and Release

17 But the high priest stood up, along with all his associates (that is the sect of the Sadducees), and they were filled with jealousy. **18** They laid hands on the apostles and put them in a public prison. **19** But during the night an angel of the Lord opened the gates of the prison, and leading them out, he said, **20** "Go, stand and speak to the people in the temple *area* the whole message of this Life." **21** Upon hearing *this,* they entered

---

5:16 [1] Lit *and*

into the temple *area* about daybreak and *began* to teach.

Now when the high priest and his associates came, they called the Council together, that is, all the Senate of the sons of Israel, and sent *orders* to the prison for them to be brought. 22 But the officers who came did not find them in the prison; and they returned and reported, 23 saying, "We found the prison locked quite securely and the guards standing at the doors; but when we opened *them,* we found no one inside." 24 Now when the captain of the temple *guard* and the chief priests heard these words, they were greatly perplexed about them as to what would come of this. 25 But someone came and reported to them, "The men whom you put in prison are standing in the temple *area* and teaching the people!" 26 Then the captain went along with the officers and *proceeded* to bring them *back* without violence (for they were afraid of the people, that they might be stoned).

27 When they had brought them, they had them stand before the Council. The high priest interrogated them, 28 saying, "We gave you strict orders not to continue teaching in this name, and yet, you have filled Jerusalem with your teaching and intend to bring this Man's blood upon us." 29 But Peter and the apostles answered, "We must obey God rather than men. 30 The God of our fathers raised up Jesus, whom you put to death by hanging Him on ¹a cross. 31 He is the one whom God exalted to His right hand as a Prince and a Savior, to grant repentance to Israel, and forgiveness of sins. 32 And we are witnesses ¹of these things; and *so is* the Holy Spirit, whom God has given to those who obey Him."

Gamaliel's Counsel

33 But when they heard *this,* they became infuriated and *nearly* decided to execute them. 34 But a Pharisee named Gamaliel, a teacher of the Law, respected by all the people, stood up in the Council and gave orders to put the men outside for a short time. 35 And he said to them, "Men of Israel, be careful as to what you are about to do with these men. 36 For, some time ago Theudas appeared, claiming to be somebody, and a group of about four hundred men joined him. But he was killed, and all

---

5:30 ¹Lit *wood;* see Deut 21:23   5:32 ¹One early ms adds *in Him*

who followed him were dispersed and came to nothing.
[37] After this man, Judas of Galilee appeared in the days of
the census and drew away *some* people after him; he
also perished, and all those who followed him were
scattered. [38] And *so* in the present case, I say to you, stay
away from these men and leave them alone, for if the
source of this plan or movement is men, it will be over-
thrown; [39] but if the source is God, you will not be able
to overthrow them; or else you may even be found
fighting against God."

[40] They followed his advice; and after calling the apostles in, they flogged them and ordered them not to speak
in the name of Jesus, and *then* released them. [41] So they
went on their way from the presence of the Council,
rejoicing that they had been considered worthy to suffer
shame for *His* name. [42] And every day, in the temple and
from house to house, they did not stop teaching and
preaching the good news of Jesus *as* the Christ.

Choosing of the Seven

6 Now at this time, as the disciples were increasing *in
number,* a complaint developed *on the part of* the
[1]Hellenistic *Jews* against the *native* Hebrews, because
their widows were being overlooked in the daily serving
of food. [2] So the twelve summoned the congregation of
the disciples and said, "It is not desirable for us to neglect the word of God in order to serve tables. [3] Instead,
brothers *and sisters,* select from among you seven men
of good reputation, full of the Spirit and of wisdom,
whom we may put in charge of this task. [4] But we will
devote ourselves to prayer and to the ministry of the
word." [5] The announcement found approval with the
whole congregation; and they chose Stephen, a man full
of faith and of the Holy Spirit, and Philip, Prochorus,
Nicanor, Timon, Parmenas, and Nicolas, a [1]proselyte from
Antioch. [6] And they brought these men before the apostles; and after praying, they laid their hands on them.

[7] The word of God kept spreading; and the number of
the disciples continued to increase greatly in Jerusalem,
and a great many of the priests were becoming obedient
to the faith.

6:1 [1] Jews who adopted the Gr language and much of Gr culture
through acculturation   6:5 [1] I.e., a Gentile convert to Judaism

8 And Stephen, full of grace and power, was performing great wonders and signs among the people. 9 But some men from what was called the Synagogue of the Freedmen, *including* both Cyrenians and Alexandrians, and some from Cilicia and Asia, rose up and argued with Stephen. 10 But they were unable to cope with his wisdom and the Spirit by whom he was speaking. 11 Then they secretly induced men to say, "We have heard him speak blasphemous words against Moses and God." 12 And they stirred up the people, the elders, and the scribes, and they came up to him and dragged him away, and brought him before the Council. 13 They put forward false witnesses who said, "This man does not stop speaking against this holy place and the Law; 14 for we have heard him say that this Nazarene, Jesus, will destroy this place and change the customs which Moses handed down to us." 15 And all who were sitting in the Council stared at him, and they saw his face, *which was* like the face of an angel.

Stephen's Defense

7 Now the high priest said, "Are these things so?" 2 And Stephen said, "Listen to me, brothers and fathers! The God of glory appeared to our father Abraham when he was in Mesopotamia, before he lived in Haran, 3 and He said to him, 'GO FROM YOUR COUNTRY AND YOUR RELATIVES, AND COME TO THE LAND WHICH I WILL SHOW YOU.' 4 Then he left the land of the Chaldeans and settled in Haran. And from there, after his father died, *God* had him move to this country in which you are now living. 5 But He gave him no inheritance in it, not even a foot of ground, and *yet,* He promised that He would give it to him as a possession, and to his descendants after him, *even* though he had no child. 6 But God spoke to this effect, that his DESCENDANTS WOULD BE STRANGERS IN A LAND THAT WAS NOT THEIRS, AND THEY WOULD ENSLAVE AND MISTREAT *THEM* FOR FOUR HUNDRED YEARS. 7 'AND WHATEVER NATION TO WHICH THEY ARE ENSLAVED I MYSELF WILL JUDGE,' said God, 'AND AFTER THAT THEY WILL COME OUT AND SERVE ME IN THIS PLACE.' 8 And He gave him the covenant of circumcision; and so *Abraham* fathered Isaac, and circumcised him on the eighth day; and Isaac *fathered* Jacob, and Jacob, the twelve patriarchs.

9 "The patriarchs became jealous of Joseph and sold

him into Egypt. *Yet* God was with him, **10** and rescued him from all his afflictions, and granted him favor and wisdom in the sight of Pharaoh, king of Egypt, and he made him governor over Egypt and his entire household.

11 "Now a famine came over all Egypt and Canaan, and great affliction *with it,* and our fathers could find no food. **12** But when Jacob heard that there was grain in Egypt, he sent our fathers *there* the first time. **13** And on the second *visit,* Joseph made himself known to his brothers, and Joseph's family was revealed to Pharaoh. **14** Then Joseph sent *word* and invited his father Jacob and all his relatives to come to him, seventy-five people *in all.* **15** And Jacob went down to Egypt, and he and our fathers died *there.* **16** And they were brought back *from there* to Shechem and laid in the tomb which Abraham had purchased for a sum of money from the sons of Hamor in Shechem.

17 "But as the time of the promise which God had assured to Abraham was approaching, the people increased and multiplied in Egypt, **18** until ANOTHER KING AROSE OVER EGYPT WHO DID NOT KNOW JOSEPH. **19** It was he who shrewdly took advantage of our nation and mistreated our fathers in order that they would abandon their infants *in the Nile,* so that they would not survive. **20** At this time Moses was born; and he was beautiful to God. He was nurtured for three months in his father's home. **21** And after he had been put outside, Pharaoh's daughter took him away and nurtured him as her own son. **22** Moses was educated in all the wisdom of the Egyptians, and he was proficient in speaking and action. **23** But when he was approaching the age of forty, it entered his mind to visit his countrymen, the sons of Israel. **24** And when he saw one *of them* being treated unjustly, he defended and took vengeance for the oppressed man by *fatally* striking the Egyptian. **25** And he thought that his brothers understood that God was granting them deliverance through him; but they did not understand. **26** And on the following day he appeared to them as they were fighting each other, and he tried to reconcile them to peace, by saying, 'Men, you are brothers, why are you injuring each other?' **27** But the one who was injuring his neighbor pushed him away, saying, 'WHO MADE YOU A RULER AND JUDGE OVER US? **28** YOU DO

NOT INTEND TO KILL ME AS YOU KILLED THE EGYPTIAN YESTERDAY, DO YOU?' **29** At this remark, MOSES FLED AND BECAME A STRANGER IN THE LAND OF MIDIAN, where he fathered two sons.

30 "After forty years had passed, an angel appeared to him in the wilderness of Mount Sinai, in the flame of a burning thorn bush. **31** When Moses saw *it,* he was astonished at the sight; and as he approached to look *more* closely, the voice of the Lord came: **32** 'I AM THE GOD OF YOUR FATHERS, THE GOD OF ABRAHAM, AND ISAAC, AND JACOB.' Moses shook with fear and did not dare to look closely. **33** But the Lord said to him, 'REMOVE YOUR SANDALS FROM YOUR FEET, FOR THE PLACE ON WHICH YOU ARE STANDING IS HOLY GROUND. **34** I HAVE CERTAINLY SEEN THE OPPRESSION OF MY PEOPLE WHO ARE IN EGYPT, AND HAVE HEARD THEIR GROANING, AND I HAVE COME DOWN TO RESCUE THEM; AND NOW COME, I WILL SEND YOU TO EGYPT.'

35 "This Moses whom they disowned, saying, 'WHO MADE YOU A RULER AND A JUDGE?' is the one whom God sent *to be* both a ruler and a deliverer with the help of the angel who appeared to him in the thorn bush. **36** This man led them out, performing wonders and signs in the land of Egypt and in the Red Sea, and in the wilderness for forty years. **37** This is the Moses who said to the sons of Israel, 'GOD WILL RAISE UP FOR YOU A PROPHET LIKE ME FROM YOUR COUNTRYMEN.' **38** This is the one who was in the assembly in the wilderness together with the angel who spoke to him *at length* on Mount Sinai, and *who was with* our fathers; and he received living words to pass on to you. **39** Our fathers were unwilling to be obedient to him; on the contrary they rejected him and turned back to Egypt in their hearts, **40** saying to Aaron, 'MAKE US A GOD WHO WILL GO BEFORE US; FOR THIS MOSES WHO LED US OUT OF THE LAND OF EGYPT—WE DO NOT KNOW WHAT HAPPENED TO HIM.' **41** At that time they made a calf and brought a sacrifice to the idol, and were rejoicing in the works of their hands. **42** But God turned away and gave them over to serve the heavenly lights; as it is written in the book of the prophets: 'YOU DID NOT OFFER ME VICTIMS AND SACRIFICES FOR FORTY YEARS IN THE WILDERNESS, DID YOU, HOUSE OF ISRAEL? **43** YOU ALSO TOOK ALONG THE TABERNACLE OF MOLOCH AND THE STAR OF YOUR GOD ROMPHA, THE IMAGES WHICH YOU MADE TO WORSHIP. I ALSO WILL DEPORT YOU BEYOND BABYLON.'

44 "Our fathers had the tabernacle of testimony in the

wilderness, just as He who spoke to Moses directed *him* to make it according to the pattern which he had seen. **45** Our fathers in turn received it, and they also brought it in with Joshua upon dispossessing the nations that God drove out from our fathers, until the time of David. **46** David found favor in God's sight, and asked that he might find a dwelling place for the ¹house of Jacob. **47** But it was Solomon who built a house for Him. **48** However, the Most High does not dwell in *houses* made by *human* hands; as the prophet says:

49   'HEAVEN IS MY THRONE,
      AND THE EARTH IS THE FOOTSTOOL OF MY FEET;
      WHAT KIND OF HOUSE WILL YOU BUILD FOR ME?' says the
         Lord,
      'OR WHAT PLACE IS THERE FOR MY REST?
50   'WAS IT NOT MY HAND THAT MADE ALL THESE THINGS?'

51 "You men who are stiff-necked and uncircumcised in heart and ears are always resisting the Holy Spirit; you are doing just as your fathers did. **52** Which one of the prophets did your fathers not persecute? They killed those who had previously announced the coming of the Righteous One, and you have now become betrayers and murderers of Him; **53** you who received the Law as ordained by angels, and *yet* did not keep it."

Stephen Put to Death

54 Now when they heard this, they were infuriated, and they *began* gnashing their teeth at him. **55** But he, being full of the Holy Spirit, looked intently into heaven and saw the glory of God, and Jesus standing at the right hand of God; **56** and he said, "Behold, I see the heavens opened and the Son of Man standing at the right hand of God." **57** But they shouted with loud voices, and covered their ears and rushed at him with one mind. **58** When they had driven him out of the city, they *began* stoning *him;* and the witnesses laid aside their cloaks at the feet of a young man named Saul. **59** They *went on* stoning Stephen as he called on *the Lord* and said, "Lord Jesus, receive my spirit!" **60** Then he fell on his knees and cried out with a loud voice, "Lord, do not hold this sin against them!" Having said this, he fell asleep.

7:46 ¹I.e., the people of Israel

Saul Persecutes the Church

8 Now Saul approved of putting Stephen to
death.

And on that day a great persecution began against the
church in Jerusalem, and they were all scattered
throughout the regions of Judea and Samaria, except for
the apostles. ²*Some* devout men buried Stephen, and
mourned loudly for him. ³But Saul *began* ravaging the
church, entering house after house; and he would drag
away men and women and put them in prison.

Philip in Samaria

⁴Therefore, those who had been scattered went
through *places* preaching the word. ⁵Philip went down
to the city of Samaria and *began* proclaiming the Christ
to them. ⁶The crowds were paying attention with one
mind to what was being said by Philip, as they heard and
saw the signs which he was performing. ⁷For *in the case
of* many who had unclean spirits, they were coming out
of them shouting with a loud voice; and many who had
been paralyzed or limped *on crutches* were healed. ⁸So
there was much rejoicing in that city.

⁹Now a man named Simon had previously been
practicing magic in the city and astonishing the people of
Samaria, claiming to be someone great; ¹⁰and all *the
people,* from small to great, were paying attention to
him, saying, "This man is the Power of God that is called
Great." ¹¹And they were paying attention to him because
for a long time he had astounded them with his magic
arts. ¹²But when they believed Philip as he was
preaching the good news about the kingdom of God and
the name of Jesus Christ, both men and women were
being baptized. ¹³Now even Simon himself believed; and
after being baptized, he continued on with Philip, and as
he observed signs and great miracles taking place, he
was *repeatedly* amazed.

¹⁴Now when the apostles in Jerusalem heard that
Samaria had received the word of God, they sent them
Peter and John, ¹⁵who came down and prayed for them
that they would receive the Holy Spirit. ¹⁶(For He had
not yet fallen upon any of them; they had simply been
baptized in the name of the Lord Jesus.) ¹⁷Then they
began laying their hands on them, and they were
receiving the Holy Spirit. ¹⁸Now when Simon saw that

the Spirit was given through the laying on of the apostles' hands, he offered them money, **19** saying, "Give this authority to me as well, so that everyone on whom I lay my hands may receive the Holy Spirit." **20** But Peter said to him, "May your silver perish with you, because you thought you could acquire the gift of God with money! **21** You have no part or share in this matter, for your heart is not right before God. **22** Therefore, repent of this wickedness of yours, and pray to the Lord *that,* if possible, the intention of your heart will be forgiven you. **23** For I see that you are in the gall of bitterness and in the bondage of unrighteousness." **24** But Simon answered and said, "Pray to the Lord for me yourselves, so that nothing of what you have said may come upon me."

An Ethiopian Receives Christ

25 So, when they had solemnly testified and spoken the word of the Lord, they started back to Jerusalem, and were preaching the gospel to many villages of the Samaritans.

26 But an angel of the Lord spoke to Philip, saying, "Get ready and go south to the road that descends from Jerusalem to Gaza." (This is a desert *road.*) **27** So he got ready and went; and there was an Ethiopian eunuch, a court official of Candace, queen of the Ethiopians, who was in charge of all her treasure; and he had come to Jerusalem to worship, **28** and he was returning and sitting in his chariot, and was reading Isaiah the prophet. **29** Then the Spirit said to Philip, "Go up and join this chariot." **30** Philip ran up and heard him reading Isaiah the prophet, and said, "Do you understand what you are reading?" **31** And he said, "Well, how could I, unless someone guides me?" And he invited Philip to come up and sit with him. **32** Now the passage of Scripture which he was reading was this:

"HE WAS LED LIKE A SHEEP TO SLAUGHTER;
 AND LIKE A LAMB THAT IS SILENT BEFORE ITS SHEARER,
 SO HE DOES NOT OPEN HIS MOUTH.
33 "IN HUMILIATION HIS JUSTICE WAS TAKEN AWAY;
 WHO WILL DESCRIBE HIS GENERATION?
 FOR HIS LIFE IS TAKEN AWAY FROM THE EARTH."

34 The eunuch answered Philip and said, "Please *tell me,* of whom does the prophet say this? Of himself, or of someone else?" **35** Then Philip opened his mouth, and

beginning from this Scripture he preached Jesus to him.
36 As they went along the road they came to some water;
and the eunuch *said, "Look! Water! What prevents me
from being baptized?"¹ **38** And he ordered that the chariot
stop; and they both went down into the water, Philip as
well as the eunuch, and he baptized him. **39** When they
came up out of the water, the Spirit of the Lord snatched
Philip away; and the eunuch no longer saw him, but
went on his way rejoicing. **40** But Philip found himself at
Azotus, and as he passed through he kept preaching the
gospel to all the cities, until he came to Caesarea.

The Conversion of Saul

9 Now Saul, still breathing threats and murder against
the disciples of the Lord, went to the high priest, **2** and
asked for letters from him to the synagogues in
Damascus, so that if he found any belonging to ¹the Way,
whether men or women, he might bring them in shackles to Jerusalem. **3** Now as he was traveling, it happened
that he was approaching Damascus, and suddenly a light
from heaven flashed around him; **4** and he fell to the
ground and heard a voice saying to him, "Saul, Saul, why
are you persecuting Me?" **5** And he said, "Who are You,
Lord?" And He *said,* "I am Jesus whom you are
persecuting, **6** but get up and enter the city, and it will be
told to you what you must do." **7** The men who traveled
with him stood speechless, hearing the voice but seeing
no one. **8** Saul got up from the ground, and though his
eyes were open, he could see nothing; and leading him
by the hand, they brought him into Damascus. **9** And for
three days he was without sight, and neither ate nor
drank.

10 Now there was a disciple in Damascus named
Ananias; and the Lord said to him in a vision, "Ananias."
And he said, "Here I am, Lord." **11** And the Lord *said* to
him, "Get up and go to the street called Straight, and
inquire at the house of Judas for a man from Tarsus
named Saul, for he is praying, **12** and he has seen ¹in a
vision a man named Ananias come in and lay his hands

8:36 ¹Late mss add as v 37: *And Philip said, "If you believe with all
your heart, you may." And he answered and said, "I believe that
Jesus Christ is the Son of God."* 9:2 ¹See John 14:6
9:12 ¹A few early mss do not contain *in a vision*

on him, so that he might regain his sight." **13** But Ananias answered, "Lord, I have heard from many people about this man, how much harm he did to Your saints in Jerusalem; **14** and here he has authority from the chief priests to arrest all who call on Your name." **15** But the Lord said to him, "Go, for he is a chosen instrument of Mine, to bear My name before the Gentiles and kings and the sons of Israel; **16** for I will show him how much he must suffer in behalf of My name." **17** So Ananias departed and entered the house, and after laying his hands on him said, "Brother Saul, the Lord Jesus, who appeared to you on the road by which you were coming, has sent me so that you may regain your sight and be filled with the Holy Spirit." **18** And immediately *something* like *fish* scales fell from his eyes, and he regained his sight, and he got up and was baptized; **19** and he took food and was strengthened.

Saul Begins to Preach Christ

Now for several days he was with the disciples who were in Damascus, **20** and immediately he *began* to proclaim Jesus in the synagogues, saying, "He is the Son of God." **21** All those hearing *him* continued to be amazed, and were saying, "Is this not the one who in Jerusalem destroyed those who called on this name, and had come here for the purpose of bringing them bound before the chief priests?" **22** But Saul kept increasing in strength and confounding Jews who lived in Damascus by proving that this *Jesus* is the Christ.

23 When many days had elapsed, the Jews plotted together to do away with him, **24** but their plot became known to Saul. They were also closely watching the gates day and night so that they might put him to death; **25** but his disciples took him at night and let him down through *an opening in* the wall, lowering him in a large basket.

26 When he came to Jerusalem, he tried *repeatedly* to associate with the disciples; and *yet* they were all afraid of him, as they did not believe that he was a disciple. **27** But Barnabas took hold of him and brought him to the apostles and described to them how he had seen the Lord on the road, and that He had talked to him, and how he had spoken out boldly in the name of Jesus at Damascus. **28** And he was with them, moving about freely in Jerusalem, speaking out boldly in the name of the Lord. **29** And he was talking and arguing with the Hellenistic *Jews;* but they were attempting to put him to death. **30** Now when the brothers learned *of it,* they brought him down to Caesarea and sent him away to Tarsus.

31 So the church throughout Judea, Galilee, and Samaria enjoyed peace, as it was being built up; and as it continued in the fear of the Lord and in the comfort of the Holy Spirit, it kept increasing.

Peter's Ministry

32 Now as Peter was traveling through all *those regions,* he also came down to the saints who lived at Lydda. **33** There he found a man named Aeneas who had been bedridden for eight years, because he was paralyzed. **34** Peter said to him, "Aeneas, Jesus Christ heals you; get up and make your own bed." Immediately he got up. **35** And all who lived at Lydda and Sharon saw him, and they turned to the Lord.

36 Now in Joppa there was a disciple named Tabitha (which when translated means [1]Dorcas); this woman was excelling in acts of kindness and charity which she did *habitually.* **37** But it happened at that time that she became sick and died; and when they had washed *her body,* they laid *it* in an upstairs room. **38** Since Lydda was near Joppa, the disciples, having heard that Peter was there, sent two men to him, urging him, "Do not delay in coming to us." **39** So Peter got ready and went with them. When he arrived, they brought him into the room upstairs; and all the widows stood beside him, weeping and showing all the [1]tunics and garments that Dorcas used to make while she was with them. **40** But Peter sent them all out and knelt down and prayed, and turning to the body, he said, "Tabitha, arise." And she opened her eyes, and when she saw Peter, she sat up. **41** And he gave her his hand and raised her up; and calling the saints and widows, he presented her alive. **42** It became known all over Joppa, and many believed in the Lord. **43** And *Peter* stayed in Joppa many days with a tanner *named* Simon.

9:36 [1] I.e., Gr for Gazelle
9:39 [1] A long shirt worn next to the skin

Cornelius' Vision

10 Now *there was* a man in Caesarea named Cornelius, a centurion of what was called the Italian [1]cohort, [2] a devout man and one who feared God with all his household, and made many charitable contributions to the *Jewish* people and prayed to God continually. [3] About the [1]ninth hour of the day he clearly saw in a vision an angel of God who had *just* come in and said to him, "Cornelius!" [4] And he looked at him intently and became terrified, and said, "What is it, lord?" And he said to him, "Your prayers and charitable gifts have ascended as a memorial offering before God. [5] Now dispatch *some* men to Joppa and send for a man *named* Simon, who is also called Peter; [6] he is staying with a tanner *named* Simon, whose house is by the sea." [7] When the angel who *spoke to him left, he summoned two of his servants and a devout soldier from his personal attendants, [8] and after he had explained everything to them, he sent them to Joppa.

[9] On the next day, as they were on their way and approaching the city, Peter went up on the housetop about [1]the sixth hour to pray. [10] But he became hungry and wanted to eat; but while they were making preparations, he fell into a trance; [11] and he *saw the sky opened up, and an object like a great sheet coming down, lowered by four corners to the ground, [12] and on it were all *kinds of* four-footed animals and crawling creatures of the earth and birds of the sky. [13] A voice came to him, "Get up, Peter, kill and eat!" [14] But Peter said, "By no means, Lord, for I have never eaten anything unholy and unclean." [15] Again a voice *came* to him a second time, "What God has cleansed, no *longer* consider unholy." [16] This happened three times, and immediately the object was taken up into the sky.

[17] Now while Peter was greatly perplexed in mind as to what the vision which he had seen might mean, behold, the men who had been sent by Cornelius had asked directions to Simon's house, and they appeared at the gate; [18] and calling out, they were asking whether Simon, who was also called Peter, was staying there.

10:1 [1] Normally 600 men (the number varied)
10:3 [1] I.e., 3 p.m.   10:9 [1] I.e., noon

19 While Peter was reflecting on the vision, the Spirit
said to him, "Behold, three men are looking for you.
20 But get up, go downstairs and accompany them without misgivings, for I have sent them Myself." **21** Peter
went down to the men and said, "Behold, I am the one
you are looking for; what is the reason for which you
have come?" **22** They said, "Cornelius, a centurion, a
righteous and God-fearing man well spoken of by the
entire nation of the Jews, was *divinely* directed by a holy
angel to send for you *to come* to his house and hear a
message from you." **23** So he invited them in and gave
them lodging.

Peter in Caesarea

Now on the next day he got ready and went away
with them, and some of the brothers from Joppa
accompanied him. **24** On the following day he entered
Caesarea. Now Cornelius was expecting them and had
called together his relatives and close friends. **25** When
Peter entered, Cornelius met him, and fell at his feet and
worshiped *him.* **26** But Peter helped him up, saying,
"Stand up; I, too, am just a man." **27** As he talked with
him, he entered and *found many people assembled.
28 And he said to them, "You yourselves know that it
is forbidden for a Jewish man to associate with or visit
a foreigner; and *yet* God has shown me that I am not
to call any person unholy or unclean. **29** That is why I
came without even raising any objection when I
was sent for. So I ask, for what reason did you send
for me?"

30 Cornelius said, "Four days ago to this hour, I was
praying in my house during the ⸨ninth hour; and behold,
a man stood before me in shining clothing, **31** and he
*said, 'Cornelius, your prayer has been heard and your
charitable gifts have been remembered before God.
32 Therefore send *some men* to Joppa and invite Simon,
who is also called Peter, to come to you; he is staying at
the house of Simon *the* tanner, by the sea.' **33** So I sent
men to you immediately, and you have been kind enough
to come. Now then, we are all here present before God
to hear everything that you have been commanded by
the Lord."

10:30 ⸨ I.e., 3 to 4 p.m.

Gentiles Hear Good News

34 Opening his mouth, Peter said:

"I most certainly understand *now* that God is not one to show partiality, 35 but in every nation the one who fears Him and does what is right is acceptable to Him. 36 The word which He sent to the sons of Israel, preaching peace through Jesus Christ (He is Lord of all)— 37 you yourselves know the thing that happened throughout Judea, starting from Galilee, after the baptism which John proclaimed. 38 *You know of* Jesus of Nazareth, how God anointed Him with the Holy Spirit and with power, and *how* He went about doing good and healing all who were oppressed by the devil, for God was with Him. 39 We are witnesses of all the things that He did both in the country of the Jews and in Jerusalem. They also put Him to death by hanging Him on ¹a cross. 40 God raised Him up on the third day and granted that He be revealed, 41 not to all the people, but to witnesses who had been chosen beforehand by God, *that is,* to us who ate and drank with Him after He arose from the dead. 42 And He ordered us to preach to the people, and to testify solemnly that this is the One who has been appointed by God as Judge of the living and the dead. 43 All the prophets testify of Him, that through His name everyone who believes in Him receives forgiveness of sins."

44 While Peter was still speaking these words, the Holy Spirit fell upon all those who were listening to the message. 45 All the ¹Jewish believers who came with Peter were amazed, because the gift of the Holy Spirit had also been poured out on the Gentiles. 46 For they were hearing them speaking with tongues and exalting God. Then Peter responded, 47 "Surely no one can refuse the water for these to be baptized, who have received the Holy Spirit just as we *did,* can he?" 48 And he ordered them to be baptized in the name of Jesus Christ. Then they asked him to stay on for a few days.

Peter Reports in Jerusalem

11 Now the apostles and the brothers *and sisters* who were throughout Judea heard that the Gentiles also

---

10:39 ¹ Lit *wood;* see Deut 21:23
10:45 ¹ Lit *believers from the circumcision*

had received the word of God. ² And when Peter came up to Jerusalem, ¹the Jewish *believers* took issue with him, ³ saying, "You went to ¹uncircumcised men and ate with them." ⁴ But Peter began and explained *at length* to them in an orderly sequence, saying, ⁵ "I was in the city of Joppa praying; and in a trance I saw a vision, an object coming down like a great sheet lowered by four corners from the sky; and it came to where I *was*, ⁶ and I stared at it and was thinking about it, and I saw the four-footed animals of the earth, the wild animals, the crawling creatures, and the birds of the sky. ⁷ I also heard a voice saying to me, 'Get up, Peter; kill and eat.' ⁸ But I said, 'By no means, Lord, for nothing unholy or unclean has ever entered my mouth.' ⁹ But a voice from heaven answered a second time, 'What God has cleansed, no longer consider unholy.' ¹⁰ This happened three times, and everything was drawn back up into the sky. ¹¹ And behold, at that moment three men who had been sent to me from Caesarea came up to the house where we were *staying*. ¹² And the Spirit told me to go with them without misgivings. These six brothers also went with me, and we entered the man's house. ¹³ And he reported to us how he had seen the angel standing in his house, and saying, 'Send *some men* to Joppa and have Simon, who is also called Peter, brought here; ¹⁴ and he will speak words to you by which you will be saved, you and all your household.' ¹⁵ And as I began to speak, the Holy Spirit fell upon them just as *He did* upon us at the beginning. ¹⁶ And I remembered the word of the Lord, how He used to say, 'John baptized with water, but you will be baptized with the Holy Spirit.' ¹⁷ Therefore, if God gave them the same gift as *He* also *gave* to us after believing in the Lord Jesus Christ, who was I that I could stand in God's way?" ¹⁸ When they heard this, they quieted down and glorified God, saying, "Well then, God has also granted to the Gentiles the repentance *that leads* to life."

The Church in Antioch

¹⁹ So then those who were scattered because of the persecution that occurred in connection with Stephen made their way to Phoenicia, Cyprus, and Antioch, speaking the word to no one except to Jews alone. ²⁰ But

---

11:2 ¹ Lit *those from the circumcision*   11:3 ¹ I.e., Gentiles there were some of them, men of Cyprus and Cyrene, who came to Antioch and *began* speaking to the ¹Greeks as well, preaching the good news of the Lord Jesus. ²¹And the hand of the Lord was with them, and a large number who believed turned to the Lord. ²²The news about them reached the ears of the church in Jerusalem, and they sent Barnabas off to Antioch. ²³Then when he arrived and witnessed the grace of God, he rejoiced and *began* to encourage them all with resolute heart to remain *true* to the Lord; ²⁴for he was a good man, and full of the Holy Spirit and faith. And considerable numbers were added to the Lord. ²⁵And he left for Tarsus to look for Saul; ²⁶and when he had found him, he brought him to Antioch. And for an entire year they met with the church and taught considerable numbers of people; and the disciples were first called Christians in Antioch.

²⁷Now at this time *some* prophets came down from Jerusalem to Antioch. ²⁸One of them, named Agabus, stood up and indicated by the Spirit that there would definitely be a severe famine all over the world. And this took place in the *reign* of Claudius. ²⁹And to the extent that any of the disciples had means, each of them determined to send *a contribution* for the relief of the brothers *and sisters* living in Judea. ³⁰And they did this, sending it with Barnabas and Saul to the elders.

Peter's Arrest and Deliverance

12 Now about that time Herod the king laid hands on some who belonged to the church, to do them harm. ²And he had James the brother of John executed with a sword. ³When he saw that it pleased the Jews, he proceeded to arrest Peter as well. (Now *these* were ¹the days of Unleavened Bread.) ⁴When he had arrested him, he put him in prison, turning him over to four squads of soldiers to guard him, intending *only* after the Passover to bring him before the people. ⁵So Peter was kept in the prison, but prayer for him was being made to God intensely by the church.

⁶On the very night when Herod was about to bring him forward, Peter was sleeping between two soldiers,

---

11:20 ¹Lit *Hellenists;* people who lived by Greek customs and culture
12:3 ¹I.e., Passover week

bound with two chains, and guards in front of the door were watching over the prison. **7** And behold, an angel of the Lord suddenly stood near *Peter,* and a light shone in the cell; and he struck Peter's side and woke him, saying, "Get up quickly." And his chains fell off his hands. **8** And the angel said to him, "Put on your belt and strap on your sandals." And he did so. And he *said to him, "Wrap your cloak around you and follow me." **9** And he went out and continued to follow, and *yet* he did not know that what was being done by the angel was real, but thought he was seeing a vision. **10** Now when they had passed the first and second guard, they came to the iron gate that leads into the city, which opened for them by itself; and they went out and went along one street, and immediately the angel departed from him. **11** When Peter came to himself, he said, "Now I know for sure that the Lord has sent forth His angel and rescued me from the hand of Herod and from all that the Jewish people were expecting." **12** And when he realized *this,* he went to the house of Mary, the mother of John, who was also called Mark, where many were gathered together and were praying. **13** When he knocked at the door of the gate, a slave woman named Rhoda came to answer. **14** When she recognized Peter's voice, because of her joy she did not open the gate, but ran in and announced that Peter was standing in front of the gate. **15** They said to her, "You are out of your mind!" But she kept insisting that it was so. They said, "It is his angel." **16** But Peter continued knocking; and when they had opened *the door,* they saw him and were amazed. **17** But motioning to them with his hand to be silent, he described to them how the Lord had led him out of the prison. And he said, "Report these things to James and the brothers." Then he left and went to another place.

18 Now when day came, there was no small disturbance among the soldiers *as to* what could have become of Peter. **19** When Herod had searched for him and had not found him, he examined the guards and ordered that they be led away *to execution.* Then he went down from Judea to Caesarea and was spending time there.

Death of Herod

20 Now he was very angry with the people of Tyre and Sidon; and with one mind they came to him, and having won over Blastus the king's chamberlain, they were asking for peace, because their country was supported *with grain* from the king's country. **21** On an appointed day, after putting on his royal apparel, Herod took his seat on the rostrum and *began* delivering an address to them. **22** The people *repeatedly* cried out, "The voice of a god and not of a man!" **23** And immediately an angel of the Lord struck him because he did not give God the glory, and he was eaten by worms and died.

24 But the word of the Lord continued to grow and to be multiplied.

25 And Barnabas and Saul returned when they had fulfilled their mission to Jerusalem, taking along with *them* John, who was also called Mark.

First Missionary Journey

13 Now there were prophets and teachers at Antioch, in the church that was *there:* Barnabas, Simeon who was called Niger, Lucius of Cyrene, Manaen who had been brought up with Herod the tetrarch, and Saul. **2** While they were serving the Lord and fasting, the Holy Spirit said, "Set Barnabas and Saul apart for Me for the work to which I have called them." **3** Then, when they had fasted, prayed, and laid their hands on them, they sent them away.

4 So, being sent out by the Holy Spirit, they went down to Seleucia and from there they sailed to Cyprus. **5** When they reached Salamis, they *began* to proclaim the word of God in the synagogues of the Jews; and they also had John as their helper. **6** When they had gone through the whole island as far as Paphos, they found a magician, a Jewish false prophet whose name was Bar-Jesus, **7** who was with the proconsul, Sergius Paulus, a man of intelligence. This man summoned Barnabas and Saul and sought to hear the word of God. **8** But Elymas the magician (for so his name is translated) was opposing them, seeking to turn the proconsul away from the faith. **9** But Saul, who was also *known as* Paul, filled with the Holy Spirit, stared at him, **10** and said, "You who are full of all deceit and fraud, you son of the devil, you enemy of all righteousness, will you not stop making crooked the straight ways of the Lord? **11** Now, behold, the hand of the Lord is upon you, and you will be blind and not see the sun for a time." And immediately a mist and a darkness fell upon him, and he went about seeking those who would lead him by the hand. 12 Then the proconsul believed when he saw what had happened, being amazed at the teaching of the Lord.

13 Now Paul and his companions put out to sea from Paphos and came to Perga in Pamphylia; but John left them and returned to Jerusalem. 14 But going on from Perga, they arrived at Pisidian Antioch, and on the Sabbath day they went into the synagogue and sat down. 15 After the reading of the Law and the Prophets, the synagogue officials sent *word* to them, saying, "Brothers, if you have any word of exhortation for the people, say it." 16 Paul stood up, and motioning with his hand said,

"Men of Israel, and you who fear God, listen: 17 The God of this people Israel chose our fathers and made the people great during their stay in the land of Egypt, and with an uplifted arm He led them out from it. 18 For a period of about forty years He put up with them in the wilderness. 19 When He had destroyed seven nations in the land of Canaan, He distributed their land as an inheritance—*all of which took* about 450 years. 20 After these things He gave *them* judges until Samuel the prophet. 21 Then they asked for a king, and God gave them Saul the son of Kish, a man of the tribe of Benjamin, for forty years. 22 After He had removed him, He raised up David to be their king, concerning whom He also testified and said, 'I have found David, the son of Jesse, a man after My heart, who will do all My will.' 23 From the descendants of this man, according to promise, God has brought to Israel a Savior, Jesus, 24 after John had proclaimed, before His coming, a baptism of repentance to all the people of Israel. 25 And while John was completing his course, he kept saying, 'What do you suppose that I am? I am not *He.* But behold, one is coming after me, the sandals of whose feet I am not worthy to untie.'

26 "Brothers, sons of Abraham's family, and those among you who fear God, to us the message of this salvation has been sent. 27 For those who live in Jerusalem, and their rulers, recognizing neither Him nor the declarations of the prophets which are read every Sabbath, fulfilled *these* by condemning *Him.* 28 And though they found no grounds for *putting Him to* death, they asked Pilate that He be executed. 29 When they had carried out everything that was written concerning Him,

they took Him down from the 'cross and laid Him in a tomb. **30** But God raised Him from the dead; **31** and for many days He appeared to those who came up with Him from Galilee to Jerusalem, the very ones who are now His witnesses to the people. **32** And we preach to you the good news of the promise made to the fathers, **33** that God has fulfilled this *promise* to those of us *who are the* descendants by raising Jesus, as it is also written in the second Psalm: 'YOU ARE MY SON; TODAY I HAVE FATHERED YOU.' **34** *As for the fact* that He raised Him from the dead, never again to return to decay, He has spoken in this way: 'I WILL GIVE YOU THE HOLY *AND* FAITHFUL *MERCIES* OF DAVID.' **35** Therefore, He also says in another *Psalm:* 'YOU WILL NOT ALLOW YOUR HOLY ONE TO UNDERGO DECAY.' **36** For David, after he had served God's purpose in his own generation, fell asleep, and was buried among his fathers and underwent decay; **37** but He whom God raised did not undergo decay. **38** Therefore let it be known to you, brothers, that through Him forgiveness of sins is proclaimed to you, **39** and through Him everyone who believes is freed from all things, from which you could not be freed through the Law of Moses. **40** Therefore, see that the thing spoken of in the Prophets does not come upon *you:*

41 'LOOK, YOU SCOFFERS, AND BE ASTONISHED, AND PERISH;
FOR I AM ACCOMPLISHING A WORK IN YOUR DAYS,
A WORK WHICH YOU WILL NEVER BELIEVE, THOUGH SOMEONE
  SHOULD DESCRIBE IT TO YOU.' "

42 As Paul and Barnabas were going out, *the people repeatedly* begged to have these things spoken to them the next Sabbath. **43** Now when *the meeting of* the synagogue had broken up, many of the Jews and the God-fearing proselytes followed Paul and Barnabas, who were speaking to them and urging them to continue in the grace of God.

Paul Turns to the Gentiles

44 The next Sabbath nearly all the city assembled to hear the word of the Lord. **45** But when the Jews saw the crowds, they were filled with jealousy and *began* contradicting the things spoken by Paul, and were blaspheming. **46** Paul and Barnabas spoke out boldly and said,

---

13:29 1Lit *wood;* see Deut 21:23

"It was necessary that the word of God be spoken to you
first. Since you repudiate it and consider yourselves
unworthy of eternal life, behold, we are turning to the
Gentiles. 47 For so the Lord has commanded us,

> 'I HAVE APPOINTED YOU AS A LIGHT TO THE GENTILES,
> THAT YOU MAY BRING SALVATION TO THE END OF THE
> EARTH.' "

48 When the Gentiles heard this, they *began* rejoicing
and glorifying the word of the Lord; and all who had
been appointed to eternal life believed. 49 And the word
of the Lord was being spread through the whole region.
50 But the Jews incited the devout women of prominence
and the leading men of the city, and instigated a
persecution against Paul and Barnabas, and drove them
out of their region. 51 But they shook off the dust *from*
their feet *in protest* against them and went to Iconium.
52 And the disciples were continually filled with joy and
with the Holy Spirit.

Acceptance and Opposition

14 In Iconium they entered the synagogue of the Jews
together, and spoke in such a way that a large
number of people believed, both of Jews and of Greeks.
2 But the unbelieving Jews stirred up the minds of the
Gentiles and embittered them against the brothers.
3 Therefore they spent a long time *there* speaking boldly
with reliance upon the Lord, who was testifying to the
word of His grace, granting that signs and wonders be
performed by their hands. 4 But the people of the city
were divided; and some sided with the Jews, while
others, with the apostles. 5 And when an attempt was
made by both the Gentiles and the Jews with their
rulers, to treat them abusively and to stone them, 6 they
became aware of it and fled to the cities of Lycaonia, Lystra and Derbe, and the surrounding region; 7 and there
they continued to preach the gospel.

8 In Lystra a man was sitting whose feet were
incapacitated. *He had been* disabled from his mother's
womb, and had never walked. 9 This man was listening to
Paul as he spoke. *Paul* looked at him intently and saw
that he had faith to be made well, 10 and he said with a
loud voice, "Stand upright on your feet!" And *the man*
leaped up and *began* to walk. 11 When the crowds saw
what Paul had done, they raised their voice, saying in

the Lycaonian language, "The gods have become like men and have come down to us!" [12] And they *began* calling Barnabas, Zeus, and Paul, Hermes, since he was the chief speaker. [13] Moreover, the priest of Zeus, whose *temple* was just outside the city, brought oxen and garlands to the gates, and wanted to offer sacrifice with the crowds. [14] But when the apostles Barnabas and Paul heard *about it,* they tore their robes and rushed out into the crowd, crying out [15] and saying, "Men, why are you doing these things? We are also men, of the same nature as you, preaching the gospel to you, to turn from these [1]useless things to a living God, who MADE THE HEAVEN AND THE EARTH AND THE SEA, AND EVERYTHING THAT IS IN THEM. [16] In past generations He permitted all the nations to go their own ways; [17] yet He did not leave Himself without witness, in that He did good and gave you rains from heaven and fruitful seasons, satisfying your hearts with food and gladness." [18] And *even by* saying these things, *only with* difficulty did they restrain the crowds from offering sacrifices to them.

[19] But Jews came from Antioch and Iconium, and having won over the crowds, they stoned Paul and dragged him out of the city, thinking that he was dead. [20] But while the disciples stood around him, he got up and entered the city. The next day he left with Barnabas for Derbe. [21] And after they had preached the gospel to that city and had made a good number of disciples, they returned to Lystra, to Iconium, and to Antioch, [22] strengthening the souls of the disciples, encouraging them to continue in the faith, and *saying,* "*It is* through many tribulations *that* we must enter the kingdom of God." [23] When they had appointed elders for them in every church, having prayed with fasting, they entrusted them to the Lord in whom they had believed.

[24] They passed through Pisidia and came into Pamphylia. [25] When they had spoken the word in Perga, they went down to Attalia. [26] From there they sailed to Antioch, where they had been entrusted to the grace of God for the work that they had accomplished. [27] When they had arrived and gathered the church together, they *began* to report all the things that God had done with them and how He had opened a door of faith to

---

14:15[1]I.e., idols

the Gentiles. 28 And they spent a long time with the disciples.

The Council in Jerusalem

15 Some men came down from Judea and *began* teaching the brothers, "Unless you are circumcised according to the custom of Moses, you cannot be saved." 2 And after Paul and Barnabas had a heated argument and debate with them, *the brothers* determined that Paul and Barnabas and some others of them should go up to Jerusalem to the apostles and elders concerning this issue. 3 Therefore, after being sent on their way by the church, they were passing through both Phoenicia and Samaria, describing in detail the conversion of the Gentiles, and they were bringing great joy to all the brothers *and sisters.* 4 When they arrived in Jerusalem, they were received by the church, the apostles, and the elders, and they reported all that God had done with them. 5 But some of the sect of the Pharisees who had believed stood up, saying, "It is necessary to circumcise 'them and to direct them to keep the Law of Moses."

6 The apostles and the elders came together to look into this matter. 7 After there had been much debate, Peter stood up and said to them, "Brothers, you know that in the early days God made a choice among you, that by my mouth the Gentiles would hear the word of the gospel and believe. 8 And God, who knows the heart, testified to them giving them the Holy Spirit, just as He also did to us; 9 and He made no distinction between us and them, cleansing their hearts by faith. 10 Since this *is the* case, why are you putting God to the test by placing upon the neck of the disciples a yoke which neither our forefathers nor we have been able to bear? 11 But we believe that we are saved through the grace of the Lord Jesus, in the same way as they also are."

12 All the people kept silent, and they were listening to Barnabas and Paul as they were relating all the signs and wonders that God had done through them among the Gentiles.

James' Judgment

13 After they stopped speaking, James responded, saying,

15:5 1 I.e., Gentile believers

"Brothers, listen to me. 14 Simeon has described how God first concerned Himself about taking a people for His name from among the Gentiles. 15 The words of the Prophets agree with this, just as it is written:

16   'AFTER THESE THINGS I will return,
     AND I WILL REBUILD THE FALLEN TABERNACLE OF DAVID,
     AND I WILL REBUILD ITS RUINS,
     AND I WILL RESTORE IT,
17   SO THAT THE REST OF MANKIND MAY SEEK THE LORD,
     AND ALL THE GENTILES WHO ARE CALLED BY MY NAME,'
18   SAYS THE LORD, WHO MAKES THESE THINGS known from
        long ago.

19 Therefore, it is my judgment that we do not cause trouble for those from the Gentiles who are turning to God, 20 but that we write to them that they abstain from things contaminated by idols, from *acts of* sexual immorality, from what has been strangled, and from blood. 21 For from ancient generations Moses has those who preach him in every city, since he is read in the synagogues every Sabbath."

22 Then it seemed good to the apostles and the elders, with the whole church, to choose men from among them to send to Antioch with Paul and Barnabas: Judas who was called Barsabbas, and Silas, leading men among the brothers, 23 and they sent this letter with them:

"The apostles and the brothers who are elders, to the brothers *and sisters* in Antioch, Syria, and Cilicia who are from the Gentiles: Greetings. 24 Since we have heard that some of our number to whom we gave no instruction have confused you by *their* teaching, upsetting your souls, 25 it seemed good to us, having become of one mind, to select men to send to you with our beloved Barnabas and Paul, 26 men who have risked their lives for the name of our Lord Jesus Christ. 27 Therefore, we have sent Judas and Silas, who themselves will also report the same things by word *of mouth.* 28 For it seemed good to the Holy Spirit and to us to lay upon you no greater burden than these essentials: 29 that you abstain from things sacrificed to idols, from blood, from things strangled, and from *acts of* sexual immorality; if you keep yourselves free from such things, you will do well. Farewell."

30 So when they were sent away, they went down to Antioch; and after gathering the congregation together,

they delivered the letter. **31** When they had read it, they rejoiced because of its encouragement. **32** Judas and Silas, also being prophets themselves, encouraged and strengthened the brothers *and sisters* with a lengthy message. **33** After they had spent time *there,* they were sent away from the brothers *and sisters* in peace to those who had sent them out.¹ **35** But Paul and Barnabas stayed in Antioch, teaching and preaching the word of the Lord, with many others also.

Second Missionary Journey

36 After some days Paul said to Barnabas, "Let's return and visit the brothers *and sisters* in every city in which we proclaimed the word of the Lord, *and see* how they are." **37** Barnabas wanted to take John, called Mark, along with them also. **38** But Paul was of the opinion that they should not take along with them this man who had deserted them in Pamphylia and had not gone with them to the work. **39** Now it turned into such a sharp disagreement that they separated from one another, and Barnabas took Mark with him and sailed away to Cyprus. **40** But Paul chose Silas, and left after being entrusted by the brothers to the grace of the Lord. **41** And he was traveling through Syria and Cilicia, strengthening the churches.

The Macedonian Vision

16 Now *Paul* also came to Derbe and to Lystra. And a disciple was there, named Timothy, the son of a Jewish woman who was a believer, but his father was a Greek, **2** and he was well spoken of by the brothers *and sisters* who were in Lystra and Iconium. **3** Paul wanted this man to leave with him; and he took him and circumcised him because of the Jews who were in those parts, for they all knew that his father was a Greek. **4** Now while they were passing through the cities, they were delivering the ordinances for them to follow which had been determined by the apostles and elders in Jerusalem. **5** So the churches were being strengthened in the faith, and were increasing in number daily.

6 They passed through the Phrygian and Galatian region, after being forbidden by the Holy Spirit to speak

---

15:33 ¹ Late mss add as v 34: *But it seemed good to Silas to remain there.*

the word in Asia; 7 and after they came to Mysia, they were trying to go into Bithynia, and the Spirit of Jesus did not allow them; 8 and passing by Mysia, they went down to Troas. 9 And a vision appeared to Paul in the night: a man of Macedonia was standing and pleading with him, and saying, "Come over to Macedonia and help us." 10 When he had seen the vision, we immediately sought to leave for Macedonia, concluding that God had called us to preach the gospel to them.

11 So after setting sail from Troas, we ran a straight course to Samothrace, and on the following *day* to Neapolis; 12 and from there to Philippi, which *is* a leading city of the district of Macedonia, a *Roman* colony; and we were spending some days in this city. 13 And on the Sabbath day we went outside the gate to a riverside, where we were thinking that there was a place of prayer; and we sat down and began speaking to the women who had assembled.

First Convert in Europe

14 A woman named Lydia was listening; *she was* a seller of purple fabrics from the city of Thyatira, *and* a worshiper of God. The Lord opened her heart to respond to the things spoken by Paul. 15 Now when she and her household had been baptized, she urged *us,* saying, "If you have judged me to be faithful to the Lord, come into my house and stay." And she prevailed upon us.

16 It happened that as we were going to the place of prayer, a slave woman who had a spirit of divination met us, who was bringing great profit to her masters by fortune-telling. 17 She followed Paul and us and cried out *repeatedly,* saying, "These men are bond-servants of the Most High God, who are proclaiming to you a way of salvation." 18 Now she continued doing this for many days. But Paul was greatly annoyed, and he turned and said to the spirit, "I command you in the name of Jesus Christ to come out of her!" And it came out at that very moment.

19 But when her masters saw that their hope of profit was *suddenly* gone, they seized Paul and Silas and dragged them into the marketplace before the authorities, 20 and when they had brought them to the chief magistrates, they said, "These men, Jews as they are, are causing our city trouble, 21 and they are

proclaiming customs that are not lawful for us to accept or to practice, *since* we are Romans."

Paul and Silas Imprisoned

22 The crowd joined in an attack against them, and the chief magistrates tore their robes off them and proceeded to order *them* to be beaten with rods. 23 When they had struck them with many blows, they threw them into prison, commanding the jailer to guard them securely; 24 and he, having received such a command, threw them into the inner prison and fastened their feet in the stocks.

25 Now about midnight Paul and Silas were praying and singing hymns of praise to God, and the prisoners were listening to them; 26 and suddenly there was a great earthquake, so that the foundations of the prison were shaken; and immediately all the doors were opened, and everyone's chains were unfastened. 27 When the jailer awoke and saw the prison doors opened, he drew *his* sword and was about to kill himself, thinking that the prisoners had escaped. 28 But Paul called out with a loud voice, saying, "Do not harm yourself, for we are all here!" 29 And *the jailer* asked for lights and rushed in, and trembling with fear, he fell down before Paul and Silas; 30 and after he brought them out, he said, "Sirs, what must I do to be saved?"

The Jailer Converted

31 They said, "Believe in the Lord Jesus, and you will be saved, you and your household." 32 And they spoke the word of God to him together with all who were in his house. 33 And he took them that *very* hour of the night and washed their wounds, and immediately he was baptized, he and all his *household*. 34 And he brought them into his house and set food before them, and was overjoyed, since he had become a believer in God together with his whole household.

35 Now when day came, the chief magistrates sent their officers, saying, "Release those men." 36 And the jailer reported these words to Paul, *saying,* "The chief magistrates have sent *word* that you be released. So come out now and go in peace." 37 But Paul said to them, "After beating us in public without due process—men *who* are Romans—they threw us into prison; and now

they are releasing us secretly? No indeed! On the contrary, let them come in person and lead us out." **38** The officers reported these words to the chief magistrates. And they became fearful when they heard that they were Romans, **39** and they came and pleaded with them, and when they had led them out, they *repeatedly* asked them to leave the city. **40** They left the prison and entered *the house of* Lydia, and when they saw the brothers *and sisters,* they encouraged *them* and departed.

Paul in Thessalonica

17 Now when they had traveled through Amphipolis and Apollonia, they came to Thessalonica, where there was a synagogue of the Jews. **2** And according to Paul's custom, he visited them, and for three Sabbaths reasoned with them from the Scriptures, **3** explaining and giving evidence that the Christ had to suffer and rise from the dead, and *saying,* "This Jesus whom I am proclaiming to you is the Christ." **4** And some of them were persuaded and joined Paul and Silas, along with a large number of the God-fearing Greeks and a significant number of the leading women. **5** But the Jews, becoming jealous and taking along some wicked men from the marketplace, formed a mob and set the city in an uproar; and they attacked the house of Jason and were seeking to bring them out to the people. **6** When they did not find them, they *began* dragging Jason and some brothers before the city authorities, shouting, "These men who have upset the world have come here also; **7** and Jason has welcomed them, and they all act contrary to the decrees of Caesar, saying that there is another king, Jesus." **8** They stirred up the crowd and the city authorities who heard these things. **9** And when they had received a pledge from Jason and the others, they released them.

Paul in Berea

10 The brothers immediately sent Paul and Silas away by night to Berea, and when they arrived, they went into the synagogue of the Jews. **11** Now these people were more noble-minded than those in Thessalonica, for they received the word with great eagerness, examining the Scriptures daily *to see* whether these things were so. **12** Therefore, many of them believed, along with a significant number of prominent Greek women and men. [13] But when the Jews of Thessalonica found out that the word of God had been proclaimed by Paul in Berea also, they came there as well, agitating and stirring up the crowds. [14] Then immediately the brothers sent Paul out to go as far as the sea; and Silas and Timothy remained there. [15] Now those who escorted Paul brought him as far as Athens; and receiving a command for Silas and Timothy to come to him as soon as possible, they left.

Paul in Athens

[16] Now while Paul was waiting for them in Athens, his spirit was being provoked within him as he observed that the city was full of idols. [17] So he was reasoning in the synagogue with the Jews and the God-fearing *Gentiles,* and in the marketplace every day with those who happened to be present. [18] And some of the Epicurean and Stoic philosophers as well were conversing with him. Some were saying, "What could this scavenger of tidbits want to say?" Others, "He seems to be a proclaimer of strange deities,"—because he was preaching Jesus and the resurrection. [19] And they took him and brought him to the [1]Areopagus, saying, "May we know what this new teaching is which you are proclaiming? [20] For you are bringing some strange things to our ears; so we want to know what these things mean." [21] (Now all the Athenians and the strangers visiting there used to spend their time in nothing other than telling or hearing something new.)

Sermon on Mars Hill

[22] So Paul stood in the midst of the Areopagus and said, "Men of Athens, I see that you are very religious in all respects. [23] For while I was passing through and examining the objects of your worship, I also found an altar with this inscription, 'TO AN UNKNOWN GOD.' Therefore, what you worship in ignorance, this I proclaim to you. [24] The God who made the world and everything that is in it, since He is Lord of heaven and earth, does not dwell in temples made by hands; [25] nor is He served by human hands, as though He needed anything, since He Himself gives to all *people* life and

---

17:19 [1] Or *Hill of Ares;* Greek god of war

breath and all things; **26** and He made from one *man* every nation of mankind to live on all the face of the earth, having determined *their* appointed times and the boundaries of their habitation, **27** that they would seek God, if perhaps they might feel around for Him and find *Him,* though He is not far from each one of us; **28** for in Him we live and move and exist, as even some of your own poets have said, 'For we also are His descendants.' **29** Therefore, since we are the descendants of God, we ought not to think that the Divine *Nature* is like gold or silver or stone, an image formed by human skill and thought. **30** So having overlooked the times of ignorance, God is now proclaiming to mankind that all people everywhere are to repent, **31** because He has set a day on which He will judge the world in righteousness through a Man whom He has appointed, having furnished proof to all people by raising Him from the dead."

32 Now when they heard of the resurrection of the dead, some *began* to scoff, but others said, "We shall hear from you again concerning this." **33** So Paul went out from among them. **34** But some men joined him and believed, among whom also were Dionysius the Areopagite and a woman named Damaris, and others with them.

Paul in Corinth

18 After these *events Paul* left Athens and went to Corinth. **2** And he found a Jew named Aquila, a native of Pontus having recently come from Italy with his wife Priscilla, because Claudius had commanded all the Jews to leave Rome. He came to them, **3** and because he was of the same trade he stayed with them, and they worked *together,* for they were tent-makers by trade. **4** And *Paul* was reasoning in the synagogue every Sabbath and trying to persuade Jews and Greeks.

5 But when Silas and Timothy came down from Macedonia, Paul *began* devoting himself completely to the word, testifying to the Jews that Jesus was the Christ. **6** But when they resisted and blasphemed, he shook out his garments and said to them, "Your blood *is* on your own heads! I am clean. From now on I will go to the Gentiles." **7** Then he left the synagogue and went to the house of a man named Titius Justus, a worshiper of God, whose house was next door to the synagogue. **8** Crispus, the leader of the synagogue, believed in the Lord together with his entire household; and many of the Corinthians, as they listened *to Paul,* were believing and being baptized. 9 And the Lord said to Paul by a vision at night, "Do not be afraid *any longer,* but go on speaking and do not be silent; 10 for I am with you, and no one will attack you to harm you, for I have many people in this city." 11 And he settled *there* for a year and six months, teaching the word of God among them.

12 But while Gallio was proconsul of Achaia, the Jews rose up together against Paul and brought him before the judgment seat, 13 saying, "This man is inciting the people to worship God contrary to the [1] law." 14 But when Paul was about to open his mouth, Gallio said to the Jews, "If it were *a matter of* some crime or vicious, unscrupulous act, O Jews, it would be reasonable for me to put up with you; 15 but if there are questions about teaching and persons and your own law, see to it yourselves; I am unwilling to be a judge of these matters." 16 And he drove them away from the judgment seat. 17 But they all took hold of Sosthenes, the leader of the synagogue, and *began* beating him in front of the judgment seat. And *yet* Gallio was not concerned about any of these things.

18 Now Paul, when he had remained many days longer, took leave of the brothers *and sisters* and sailed away to Syria, and Priscilla and Aquila were with him. Paul *first* had his hair cut at Cenchrea, for he was keeping a vow. 19 They came to Ephesus, and he left them there. Now he himself entered the synagogue and reasoned with the Jews. 20 When they asked him to stay for a longer time, he did not consent, 21 but took leave of them and said, "I will return to you again if God wills," and he set sail from Ephesus.

22 When he had landed in Caesarea, he went up *to Jerusalem* and greeted the church, and went down to Antioch.

Third Missionary Journey
23 And after spending some time *there,* he left and passed successively through the Galatian region and Phrygia, strengthening all the disciples.

18:13 [1] Or *Law*

24 Now a Jew named Apollos, an Alexandrian by birth, an eloquent man, came to Ephesus; and he was proficient in the Scriptures. **25** This man had been instructed in the way of the Lord; and being fervent in spirit, he was accurately speaking and teaching things about Jesus, being acquainted only with the baptism of John; **26** and he began speaking boldly in the synagogue. But when Priscilla and Aquila heard him, they took him aside and explained the way of God more accurately to him. **27** And when he wanted to go across to Achaia, the brothers encouraged him and wrote to the disciples to welcome him; and when he had arrived, he greatly helped those who had believed through grace, **28** for he powerfully refuted the Jews in public, demonstrating by the Scriptures that Jesus was the Christ.

Paul in Ephesus

19 Now it happened that while Apollos was in Corinth, Paul passed through the upper country and came to Ephesus, and found some disciples. **2** He said to them, "Did you receive the Holy Spirit when you believed?" And they *said* to him, "On the contrary, we have not even heard if there is a Holy Spirit." **3** And he said, "Into what then were you baptized?" And they said, "Into John's baptism." **4** Paul said, "John baptized with a baptism of repentance, telling the people to believe in Him who was coming after him, that is, in Jesus." **5** When they heard this, they were baptized in the name of the Lord Jesus. **6** And when Paul had laid hands upon them, the Holy Spirit came on them and they *began* speaking with tongues and prophesying. **7** There were about twelve men in all.

8 And he entered the synagogue and continued speaking out boldly for three months, having discussions and persuading *them* about the kingdom of God. **9** But when some were becoming hardened and disobedient, speaking evil of ¹the Way before the people, he withdrew from them and took the disciples away *with him,* and had discussions daily in the school of Tyrannus. **10** This took place for two years, so that all who lived in Asia heard the word of the Lord, both Jews and Greeks.

19:9 ¹See John 14:6

Miracles at Ephesus

11 God was performing extraordinary miracles by the hands of Paul, **12** so that handkerchiefs or aprons were even carried from his body to the sick, and the diseases left them and the evil spirits went out. **13** But also some of the Jewish exorcists, who went from place to place, attempted to use the name of the Lord Jesus over those who had the evil spirits, saying, "I order you in the name of Jesus whom Paul preaches!" **14** Now there were seven sons of Sceva, a Jewish chief priest, doing this. **15** But the evil spirit responded and said to them, "I recognize Jesus, and I know of Paul, but who are you?" **16** And the man in whom was the evil spirit, pounced on them and subdued all of them and overpowered them, so that they fled out of that house naked and wounded. **17** This became known to all who lived in Ephesus, both Jews and Greeks; and fear fell upon them all and the name of the Lord Jesus was being magnified. **18** Also many of those who had believed kept coming, confessing and disclosing their practices. **19** And many of those who practiced magic brought their books together and *began* burning *them* in the sight of everyone; and they added up the prices of the books and found *it to be* fifty thousand *pieces* of silver. **20** So the word of the Lord was growing and prevailing mightily.

21 Now after these things were finished, Paul resolved in the Spirit to go to Jerusalem after he had passed through Macedonia and Achaia, saying, "After I have been there, I must also see Rome." **22** And after he sent into Macedonia two of those who assisted him, Timothy and Erastus, he himself stayed in Asia for a while.

23 About that time 'a major disturbance occurred in regard to the Way. **24** For a man named Demetrius, a silversmith who made silver shrines of Artemis, was bringing considerable business to the craftsmen; **25** he gathered these men together with the workmen of similar *trades,* and said, "Men, you know that our prosperity depends upon this business. **26** You see and hear that not only in Ephesus, but in almost all of Asia, this Paul has persuaded and turned away a considerable number of people, saying that gods made by hands are not gods *at all.* **27** Not only is there danger that this trade

---

19:23 1 Lit *no small*

of ours will fall into disrepute, but also that the temple of the great goddess Artemis will be regarded as worthless, and that she whom all of Asia and the world worship will even be dethroned from her magnificence."

28 When they heard *this* and were filled with rage, they *began* shouting, saying, "Great is Artemis of the Ephesians!" 29 The city was filled with the confusion, and they rushed together into the theater, dragging along Gaius and Aristarchus, Paul's Macedonian traveling companions. 30 And when Paul wanted to go into the assembly, the disciples would not let him. 31 Also some of the ¹Asiarchs who were friends of his sent *word* to him and *repeatedly* urged him not to venture into the theater. 32 So then, some were shouting one thing and some another, for the assembly was in confusion, and the majority did not know for what reason they had come together. 33 Some of the crowd concluded *it was* Alexander, since the Jews had put him forward; and having motioned with his hand, Alexander was intending to make a defense to the assembly. 34 But when they recognized that he was a Jew, a single outcry arose from them all as they shouted for about two hours, "Great is Artemis of the Ephesians!"

35 After quieting the crowd, the town clerk *said, "Men of Ephesus, what person is there after all who does not know that the city of the Ephesians is guardian of the temple of the great Artemis and of the *image* which fell down from the sky? 36 So, since these are undeniable *facts,* you ought to keep calm and to do nothing rash. 37 For you have brought these men *here who are* neither temple robbers nor blasphemers of our goddess. 38 So then, if Demetrius and the craftsmen who are with him have a complaint against anyone, the courts are in session and proconsuls are *available;* have them bring charges against one another. 39 But if you want anything beyond this, it shall be settled in the lawful assembly. 40 For indeed, we are in danger of being accused of a riot in connection with today's *events,* since there is no *real* reason *for it,* and in this connection we will be unable to account for this disorderly gathering." 41 After saying this he dismissed the assembly.

19:31 ¹ I.e., political or religious officials of the province of Asia

Paul in Macedonia and Greece

20 After the uproar had ceased, Paul sent for the disciples, and when he had encouraged them and taken his leave of them, he left to go to Macedonia. ² When he had gone through those regions and had given them much encouragement, he came to Greece. ³ And *there* he spent three months, and when a plot was formed against him by the Jews as he was about to set sail for Syria, he decided to return through Macedonia. ⁴ And he was accompanied by Sopater of Berea, *the son* of Pyrrhus, and by Aristarchus and Secundus of the Thessalonians, and Gaius of Derbe, and Timothy, and Tychicus and Trophimus of Asia. ⁵ Now these had gone on ahead and were waiting for us at Troas. ⁶ We sailed from Philippi after ¹the days of Unleavened Bread, and reached them at Troas within five days; and we stayed there for seven days.

⁷ On the first day of the week, when we were gathered together to break bread, Paul *began* talking to them, intending to leave the next day, and he prolonged his message until midnight. ⁸ There were many lamps in the upstairs room where we were gathered together. ⁹ And there was a young man named Eutychus sitting on the window sill, sinking into a deep sleep; and as Paul kept on talking, *Eutychus* was overcome by sleep and fell down from the third floor, and was picked up dead. ¹⁰ But Paul went down and fell upon him, and after embracing him, he said, "Do not be troubled, for he is still alive." ¹¹ When *Paul* had gone *back* up and had broken the bread and eaten, he talked with them a long while until daybreak, and then left. ¹² They took away the boy alive, and were greatly comforted.

Troas to Miletus

¹³ But we went ahead to the ship and set sail for Assos, intending from there to take Paul on board; for that was what he had arranged, intending himself to go by land. ¹⁴ And when he met us at Assos, we took him on board and came to Mitylene. ¹⁵ Sailing from there, we arrived the following day opposite Chios; and the next day we crossed over to Samos, and on the following day we came to Miletus. ¹⁶ For Paul had decided to sail past

Ephesus so that he would not have to lose time in Asia;
for he was hurrying, if it might be possible for him to be
in Jerusalem the day of Pentecost.

Farewell to Ephesus

17 From Miletus he sent *word* to Ephesus and called to
himself the elders of the church. **18** And when they came
to him, he said to them,

"**Y**ou yourselves know, from the first day that I set foot
in Asia, how I was with you the whole time, **19** serving
the Lord with all humility and with tears and trials
which came upon me through the plots of the Jews;
20 how I did not shrink from declaring to you anything
that was beneficial, and teaching you publicly and from
house to house, **21** solemnly testifying to both Jews and
Greeks of repentance toward God and faith in our Lord
Jesus Christ. **22** And now, behold, bound by the Spirit, I
am on my way to Jerusalem, not knowing what will
happen to me there, **23** except that the Holy Spirit
solemnly testifies to me in every city, saying that chains
and afflictions await me. **24** But I do not consider my life
of any account as dear to myself, so that I may finish my
course and the ministry which I received from the Lord
Jesus, to testify solemnly of the gospel of God's grace.

25 "And now behold, I know that all of you, among
whom I went about preaching the kingdom, will no
longer see my face. **26** Therefore, I testify to you this day
that I am innocent of the blood of all people. **27** For I did
not shrink from declaring to you the whole purpose of
God. **28** Be on guard for yourselves and for all the flock,
among which the Holy Spirit has made you overseers, to
shepherd the church of God which He purchased with
His own blood. **29** I know that after my departure savage
wolves will come in among you, not sparing the flock;
30 and from among your own selves men will arise,
speaking perverse things to draw away the disciples after
them. **31** Therefore, be on the alert, remembering that
night and day for a period of three years I did not cease
to admonish each one with tears. **32** And now I entrust
you to God and to the word of His grace, which is able to
build *you* up and to give *you* the inheritance among all
those who are sanctified. **33** I have coveted no one's silver
or gold or clothes. **34** You yourselves know that these
hands served my *own* needs and the men who were

with me. 35 In everything I showed you that by working hard in this way you must help the weak and remember the words of the Lord Jesus, that He Himself said, 'It is more blessed to give than to receive.'"

36 When he had said these things, he knelt down and prayed with them all. 37 And they all *began* to weep aloud and embraced Paul, and *repeatedly* kissed him, 38 grieving especially over the word which he had spoken, that they would not see his face again. And they were accompanying him to the ship.

Paul Sails from Miletus

21 Now when we had parted from them and had set sail, we ran a straight course to Cos, and on the next day to Rhodes, and from there to Patara; 2 and having found a ship crossing over to Phoenicia, we went aboard and set sail. 3 When we came in sight of Cyprus, leaving it on the left, we kept sailing to Syria and landed at Tyre; for the ship was to unload its cargo there. 4 After looking up the disciples, we stayed there for seven days; and they kept telling Paul, through the Spirit, not to set foot in Jerusalem. 5 When our days there were ended, we left and started on our journey, while they all, with wives and children, escorted us until *we were* out of the city. After kneeling down on the beach and praying, we said farewell to one another. 6 Then we boarded the ship, and they returned home.

7 When we had finished the voyage from Tyre, we arrived at Ptolemais, and after greeting the brothers *and sisters,* we stayed with them for a day. 8 On the next day we left and came to Caesarea, and we entered the house of Philip the evangelist, who was one of the seven, and stayed with him. 9 Now this man had four virgin daughters who were prophetesses. 10 As we were staying there for some days, a prophet named Agabus came down from Judea. 11 And he came to us and took Paul's belt and bound his own feet and hands, and said, "This is what the Holy Spirit says: 'In this way the Jews in Jerusalem will bind the man who owns this belt and hand him over to the Gentiles.'" 12 When we had heard this, we as well as the local residents *began* begging him not to go up to Jerusalem. 13 Then Paul replied, "What are you doing, weeping and breaking my heart? For I am ready not only to be bound, but even to die in Jerusalem

for the name of the Lord Jesus." **14** And since he would not be persuaded, we became quiet, remarking, "The will of the Lord be done!"

Paul in Jerusalem

15 After these days we got ready and started on our way up to Jerusalem. **16** *Some* of the disciples from Caesarea also came with us, taking us to Mnason of Cyprus, a disciple of long standing with whom we were to stay.

17 After we arrived in Jerusalem, the brothers *and sisters* received us gladly. **18** And the following day Paul went in with us to James, and all the elders were present. **19** After he had greeted them, he *began* to relate one by one the things which God had done among the Gentiles through his ministry. **20** And when they heard *about them,* they *began* glorifying God; and they said to him, "You see, brother, how many thousands there are among the Jews of those who have believed, and they are all zealous for the Law; **21** and they have been told about you, that you are teaching all the Jews who are among the Gentiles to abandon Moses, telling them not to circumcise their children nor to walk according to the customs. **22** So what is *to be done?* They will certainly hear that you have come. **23** Therefore, do as we tell you: we have four men who have a vow upon themselves; **24** take them along and purify yourself together with them, and pay their expenses so that they may shave their heads; and *then* everyone will know that there is nothing to what they have been told about you, but that you yourself also conform, keeping the Law. **25** But regarding the Gentiles who have believed, we sent a letter, having decided that they should abstain from meat sacrificed to idols and from blood and what is strangled, and from sexual immorality." **26** Then Paul took along the men, and the next day, after purifying himself together with them, he went into the temple giving notice of the completion of the days of purification, until the sacrifice was offered for each one of them.

Paul Seized in the Temple

27 When the seven days were almost over, the Jews from Asia, upon seeing him in the temple, *began* to stir up all the crowd and laid hands on him, **28** crying out,

"Men of Israel, help! This is the man who instructs everyone everywhere against our people and the Law and this place; and besides, he has even brought Greeks into the temple and has defiled this holy place!" **29** For they had previously seen Trophimus the Ephesian in the city with him, and they thought that Paul had brought him into the temple. **30** Then the whole city was provoked and the people rushed together, and taking hold of Paul they dragged him out of the temple, and immediately the doors were shut. **31** While they were intent on killing him, a report came up to the commander of the *Roman* ¹cohort that all Jerusalem was in confusion. **32** He immediately took along *some* soldiers and centurions and ran down to the crowd; and when they saw the commander and the soldiers, they stopped beating Paul. **33** Then the commander came up and took hold of him, and ordered that he be bound with two chains; and he *began* asking who he was and what he had done. **34** But among the crowd, some were shouting one thing *and* some another, and when he could not find out the facts because of the uproar, he ordered that Paul be brought into the barracks. **35** When *Paul* got to the stairs, it came about that he was carried by the soldiers because of the violence of the mob; **36** for the multitude of people kept following *them,* shouting, "Away with him!"

37 As Paul was about to be brought into the barracks, he *said to the commander, "May I say something to you?" And he said, "Do you know Greek? **38** Then you are not the Egyptian who some time ago stirred up a revolt and led the four thousand men of the Assassins out into the wilderness?" **39** But Paul said, "I am a Jew of Tarsus in Cilicia, a citizen of no insignificant city; and I beg you, allow me to speak to the people." **40** When he had given him permission, Paul, standing on the stairs, motioned to the people with his hand; and when there was a great silence, he spoke to them in the Hebrew dialect, saying,

Paul's Defense before the Jews

22 "Brothers and fathers, hear my defense *which I* now *offer* to you."

21:31 ¹ Normally 600 men (the number varied)

²And when they heard that he was addressing them in the Hebrew dialect, they became *even* more quiet; and he *said,

³"I am a Jew, born in Tarsus of Cilicia, but brought up in this city, educated under Gamaliel, strictly according to the Law of our fathers, being zealous for God just as you all are today. ⁴I persecuted this Way to the death, binding and putting both men and women into prisons, ⁵as also the high priest and all the Council of the elders can testify. From them I also received letters to the brothers, and started off for Damascus in order to bring even those who were there to Jerusalem as prisoners to be punished.

⁶"But it happened that as I was on my way, approaching Damascus at about noon, a very bright light suddenly flashed from heaven all around me, ⁷and I fell to the ground and heard a voice saying to me, 'Saul, Saul, why are you persecuting Me?' ⁸And I answered, 'Who are You, Lord?' And He said to me, 'I am Jesus the Nazarene, whom you are persecuting.' ⁹And those who were with me saw the light, but did not understand the voice of the One who was speaking to me. ¹⁰And I said, 'What shall I do, Lord?' And the Lord said to me, 'Get up and go on into Damascus, and there you will be told about everything that has been appointed for you to do.' ¹¹But since I could not see because of the brightness of that light, I came into Damascus being led by the hand by those who were with me.

¹²"Now a certain Ananias, a man who was devout by the standard of the Law *and* well spoken of by all the Jews who lived *there,* ¹³came to me, and standing nearby he said to me, 'Brother Saul, receive your sight!' And at that very moment I looked up at him. ¹⁴And he said, 'The God of our fathers has appointed you to know His will and to see the Righteous One and to hear a message from His mouth. ¹⁵For you will be a witness for Him to all people of what you have seen and heard. ¹⁶Now why do you delay? Get up and be baptized, and wash away your sins by calling on His name.'

¹⁷"It happened when I returned to Jerusalem and was praying in the temple, that I fell into a trance, ¹⁸and I saw Him saying to me, 'Hurry and get out of Jerusalem quickly, because they will not accept your testimony about Me.' ¹⁹And I said, 'Lord, they themselves

understand that in one synagogue after another I used to imprison and beat those who believed in You. 20 And when the blood of Your witness Stephen was being shed, I also was standing nearby and approving, and watching over the cloaks of those who were killing him.' 21 And He said to me, 'Go! For I will send you far away to the Gentiles.'"

22 They listened to him up to this statement, and *then* they raised their voices and said, "Away with such a man from the earth, for he should not be allowed to live!" 23 And as they were shouting and throwing off their cloaks and tossing dust into the air, 24 the commander ordered that he be brought into the barracks, saying that he was to be interrogated by flogging so that he would find out the reason why they were shouting against him that way. 25 But when they stretched him out with straps, Paul said to the centurion who was standing by, "Is it lawful for you to flog a man who is a Roman and uncondemned?" 26 When the centurion heard *this,* he went to the commander and told *him,* saying, "What are you about to do? For this man is a Roman." 27 The commander came and said to Paul, "Tell me, are you a Roman?" And he said, "Yes." 28 The commander answered, "I acquired this citizenship for a large sum of money." And Paul said, "But I was actually born *a citizen.*" 29 Therefore, those who were about to interrogate him immediately backed away from him; and the commander also was afraid when he found out that he was a Roman, and because he had put him in chains.

30 Now on the next day, wanting to know for certain why *Paul* had been accused by the Jews, he released him and ordered the chief priests and all the Council to assemble, and he brought Paul down and placed him before them.

Paul before the Council

23 Now looking intently at the Council, Paul said, "Brothers, I have lived my life with an entirely good conscience before God up to this day." 2 But the high priest Ananias commanded those standing beside him to strike him on the mouth. 3 Then Paul said to him, "God is going to strike you, you whitewashed wall! Do you sit to try me according to the Law, and in violation of the Law, order me to be struck?" 4 But those present said,

"Are you insulting God's high priest?" 5 And Paul said, "I was not aware, brothers, that he is high priest; for it is written: 'YOU SHALL NOT SPEAK EVIL OF A RULER OF YOUR PEOPLE.'"

6 But Paul, perceiving that one group were Sadducees and the other Pharisees, *began* crying out in the Council, "Brothers, I am a Pharisee, a son of Pharisees; I am on trial for the hope and resurrection of the dead!" 7 When he said this, a dissension occurred between the Pharisees and Sadducees, and the assembly was divided. 8 For the Sadducees say that there is no resurrection, nor an angel, nor a spirit, but the Pharisees acknowledge them all. 9 And a great uproar occurred; and some of the scribes of the Pharisaic party stood up and *started* arguing heatedly, saying, "We find nothing wrong with this man; suppose a spirit or an angel has spoken to him?" 10 And when a great dissension occurred, the commander was afraid that Paul would be torn to pieces by them, and he ordered the troops to go down and take him away from them by force, and bring him into the barracks.

11 But on the following night, the Lord stood near him and said, "Be courageous! For as you have testified to the *truth* about Me in Jerusalem, so you must testify in Rome also."

A Conspiracy to Kill Paul

12 When it was day, the Jews formed a conspiracy and put themselves under an oath, saying that they would neither eat nor drink until they had killed Paul. 13 There were more than forty who formed this plot. 14 They came to the chief priests and the elders and said, "We have put ourselves under an oath to taste nothing until we have killed Paul. 15 Now therefore, you and the Council notify the commander to bring him down to you, as though you were going to investigate his case more thoroughly; and as for us, we are ready to kill him before he comes near *the place.*"

16 But the son of Paul's sister heard about their ambush, and he came and entered the barracks and told Paul. 17 Paul called one of the centurions to himself and said, "Take this young man to the commander, for he has something to report to him." 18 So he took him and led him to the commander and *said, "Paul the prisoner

called me over to him and asked me to bring this young man to you because he has something to tell you." **19** The commander took him by the hand, and stepping aside, *began* to inquire of him privately, "What is it that you have to report to me?" **20** And he said, "The Jews have agreed to ask you to bring Paul down tomorrow to the Council, as though they were going to inquire somewhat more thoroughly about him. **21** So do not listen to them, for more than forty of them are in hiding to ambush him, and these men have put themselves under an oath not to eat or drink until they kill him; and now they are ready and waiting for assurance from you." **22** Then the commander let the young man go, instructing him, "Tell no one that you have notified me of these things."

Paul Moved to Caesarea

23 And he called to him two of the centurions and said, "Get two hundred soldiers ready by ¹the third hour of the night to proceed to Caesarea, with seventy horsemen and two hundred spearmen." **24** *They were* also to provide mounts to put Paul on and bring him safely to Felix the governor. **25** And he wrote a letter with the following content:

26 "Claudius Lysias, to the most excellent governor Felix: Greetings.

27 When this man was seized by the Jews and was about to be killed by them, I came up to them with the troops and rescued him, after learning that he was a Roman. **28** And wanting to ascertain the basis for the charges they were bringing against him, I brought him down to their Council; **29** and I found that he was being accused regarding questions in their Law, but was not charged with anything deserving death or imprisonment.

30 When I was informed that there would be a plot against the man, I sent him to you at once, also instructing his accusers to bring charges against him before you."

31 So the soldiers, in accordance with their orders, took Paul and brought him by night to Antipatris. **32** But on the next day they let the horsemen go on with him, and they returned to the barracks. **33** When these

---

23:23 ¹I.e., 9 p.m.

horsemen had come to Caesarea and delivered the letter
to the governor, they also presented Paul to him. **34** Now
when he had read *it,* he also asked from what province
Paul was, and when he learned that he was from Cilicia,
35 he said, "I will give you a hearing when your accusers
arrive as well," giving orders for Paul to be kept in
Herod's ʼPraetorium.

Paul before Felix

24 Now after five days the high priest Ananias came
down with some elders and an attorney *named*
Tertullus, and they brought charges against Paul to the
governor. **2** After Paul had been summoned, Tertullus
began accusing him, saying *to the governor,*

"Since we have attained great peace through you, and
since reforms are being carried out for this nation by
your foresight, **3** we acknowledge *this* in every way and
everywhere, most excellent Felix, with all thankfulness.
4 But, that I may not weary you further, I beg you to grant
us a brief hearing, by your kindness. **5** For we have found
this man a public menace and one who stirs up dissensions among all the Jews throughout the world, and a
ringleader of the sect of the Nazarenes. **6** And he even
tried to desecrate the temple, so indeed we arrested
him.ʼ **8** By interrogating him yourself concerning all these
matters, you will be able to ascertain the things of which
we are accusing him." **9** The Jews also joined in the
attack, asserting that these things were so.

10 And when the governor had nodded for him to
speak, Paul responded:

"Knowing that for many years you have been a judge
to this nation, I cheerfully make my defense, **11** since you
can take note of the fact that no more than twelve days
ago I went up to Jerusalem to worship. **12** And neither in
the temple did they find me carrying on a discussion
with anyone or causing a riot, nor in the synagogues,
nor in the city *itself.* **13** Nor can they prove to you *the
things* of which they now accuse me. **14** But I confess this

---

23:35 ¹I.e., governor's official residence   24:6 ¹Late mss add as the
remainder of v 6: *We wanted to judge him according to our own Law.*
v 7: *But Lysias the commander came along and took him out of our
hands with much violence,* and the first part of v 8: *ordering his
accusers to come before you.*

to you, that in accordance with [1]the Way, which they call a sect, I do serve the God of our fathers, believing everything that is in accordance with the Law and is written in the Prophets; 15having a hope in God, which these men cherish themselves, that there shall certainly be a resurrection of both the righteous and the wicked. 16In view of this I also do my best to maintain a blameless conscience *both* before God and before *other* people, always. 17Now after several years I came to bring charitable gifts to my nation and to present offerings, 18in which they found me *occupied* in the temple, having been purified, without *any* crowd or uproar. But *there were* some Jews from Asia— 19who ought to have been present before you and to have been bringing charges, if they should have anything against me. 20Or *else* have these men themselves declare what violation they discovered when I stood before the Council, 21other than in regard to this one declaration which I shouted while standing among them, 'For the resurrection of the dead I am on trial before you today!' "

22But Felix, having quite accurate knowledge about [1]the Way, adjourned them, saying, "When Lysias the commander comes down, I will decide your case." 23He gave orders to the centurion for Paul to be kept in custody and *yet* have *some* freedom, and not to prevent any of his friends from providing for his needs.

24Now some days later Felix arrived with Drusilla his wife, who was Jewish, and he sent for Paul and heard him *speak* about faith in Christ Jesus. 25But as he was discussing righteousness, self-control, and the judgment to come, Felix became frightened and responded, "Go away for now, and when I have an opportunity, I will summon you." 26At the same time he was also hoping that money would be given to him by Paul; therefore he also used to send for him quite often and talk with him. 27But after two years had passed, Felix was succeeded by Porcius Festus; and Felix, wanting to do the Jews a favor, left Paul imprisoned.

Paul before Festus

25 Festus, then, after arriving in the province, went up to Jerusalem from Caesarea three days later.

24:14 [1]See John 14:6   24:22 [1]See John 14:6

2 And the chief priests and the leading men of the Jews brought charges against Paul, and they were pleading with Festus, 3 requesting a concession against Paul, that he might have him brought to Jerusalem (*at the same time,* setting an ambush to kill him on the way). 4 Festus then answered that Paul was being kept in custody in Caesarea, and that he himself was about to leave shortly. 5 "Therefore," he *said, "have the influential men among you go there with me, and if there is anything wrong about the man, have them bring charges against him."

6 After *Festus* had spent no more than eight or ten days among them, he went down to Caesarea, and on the next day he took his seat on the tribunal and ordered that Paul be brought. 7 After Paul arrived, the Jews who had come down from Jerusalem stood around him, bringing many, and serious, charges against him which they could not prove, 8 while Paul said in his own defense, "I have not done anything wrong either against the Law of the Jews, or against the temple, or against Caesar." 9 But Festus, wanting to do the Jews a favor, replied to Paul and said, "Are you willing to go up to Jerusalem and stand trial before me on these *charges?*" 10 But Paul said, "I am standing before Caesar's tribunal, where I ought to be tried. I have done nothing wrong to *the* Jews, as you also very well know. 11 If, therefore, I am in the wrong and have committed something deserving death, I am not trying to avoid execution; but if there is nothing to the accusations which these men are bringing against me, no one can hand me over to them. I appeal to Caesar." 12 Then when Festus had conferred with his council, he answered, "You have appealed to Caesar; to Caesar you shall go."

13 Now when several days had passed, King Agrippa and Bernice arrived in Caesarea, paying their respects to Festus. 14 And while they were spending many days there, Festus presented Paul's case to the king, saying, "There is a man who was left as a prisoner by Felix; 15 and when I was in Jerusalem, the chief priests and the elders of the Jews brought charges against him, asking for a sentence of condemnation against him. 16 I replied to them that it is not the custom of the Romans to hand over any person before the accused meets his accusers face to face, and has an opportunity to make his defense against the charges. 17 So after they had assembled here, I

did not delay, but on the next day took my seat on the tribunal and ordered that the man be brought. 18 When the accusers stood up, they did not *begin* bringing any charges against him of crimes that I suspected, 19 but they *simply* had some points of disagreement with him about their own religion and about a dead man, Jesus, whom Paul asserted to be alive. 20 And being at a loss how to investigate such matters, I asked whether he was willing to go to Jerusalem and stand trial there on these matters. 21 But when Paul appealed to be held in custody for 'the Emperor's decision, I ordered that he be kept in custody until I send him to Caesar." 22 Then Agrippa *said* to Festus, "I also would like to hear the man myself." "Tomorrow," he *said, "you shall hear him."

Paul before Agrippa

23 So, on the next day when Agrippa and Bernice came amid great pomp and entered the auditorium, accompanied by the commanders and the prominent men of the city, at the command of Festus, Paul was brought *before them*. 24 And Festus *said, "King Agrippa, and all you gentlemen present with us, you see this man about whom all the people of the Jews appealed to me, both in Jerusalem and here, shouting that he ought not to live any longer. 25 But I found that he had committed nothing deserving death; and since he himself appealed to the Emperor, I decided to send him. 26 Yet, I have nothing definite about him to write to my lord. Therefore, I have brought him before you *all* and especially before you, King Agrippa, so that after the investigation has taken place, I may have something to write. 27 For it seems absurd to me in sending a prisoner, not to indicate the charges against him as well."

Paul's Defense before Agrippa

26 Now Agrippa said to Paul, "You are permitted to speak for yourself." Then Paul extended his hand and *proceeded* to make his defense:

2 "Regarding all the things of which I am accused by the Jews, King Agrippa, I consider myself fortunate that I am about to make my defense before you today,

---

25:21 1 Lit *the Augustus'* (in this case Nero)

ally because you are an expert in all customs and
ns among *the* Jews; therefore I beg you to listen
atiently.

then, all Jews know my way of life since *my*
which from the beginning was spent among my
tion and in Jerusalem, 5 since they have known
me for a long time, if they are willing to testify,
that I lived *as* a Pharisee according to the strictest sect of
our religion. 6 And now I am standing trial for the hope of
the promise made by God to our fathers; 7 *the promise* to
which our twelve tribes hope to attain, as they earnestly
serve *God* night and day. For this hope, O king, I am
being accused by Jews. 8 Why is it considered incredible
among you *people* if God raises the dead?

9 "So I thought to myself that I had to act in strong
opposition to the name of Jesus of Nazareth. 10 And this is
just what I did in Jerusalem; not only did I lock up many
of the saints in prisons, after receiving authority from the
chief priests, but I also cast my vote against them when
they were being put to death. 11 And as I punished them
often in all the synagogues, I tried to force them to blaspheme; and since I was extremely enraged at them, I
kept pursuing them even to foreign cities.

12 "While so engaged, as I was journeying to Damascus
with the authority and commission of the chief priests,
13 at midday, O king, I saw on the way a light from
heaven, brighter than the sun, shining around me and
those who were journeying with me. 14 And when we
had all fallen to the ground, I heard a voice saying to me
in the Hebrew dialect, 'Saul, Saul, why are you
persecuting Me? 1 It is hard for you to kick against the
goads.' 15 And I said, 'Who are You, Lord?' And the Lord
said, 'I am Jesus whom you are persecuting. 16 But get up
and stand on your feet; for this *purpose* I have appeared
to you, to appoint you as a servant and a witness not only
to the things in which you have seen Me, but also to the
things in which I will appear to you, 17 rescuing you
from the *Jewish* people and from the Gentiles, to whom I
am sending you, 18 to open their eyes so that they may
turn from darkness to light, and from the power of Satan
to God, that they may receive forgiveness of sins and an

26:14 1 An idiom referring to an animal's futile resistance to being
prodded with a spiked stick

inheritance among those who have been sanctified by faith in Me.'

19 "For that reason, King Agrippa, I did not prove disobedient to the heavenly vision, 20 but *continually* proclaimed to those in Damascus first, and in Jerusalem, and *then* all the region of Judea, and *even* to the Gentiles, that they are to repent and turn to God, performing deeds consistent with repentance. 21 For these reasons *some* Jews seized me in the temple and tried to murder me. 22 So, having obtained help from God, I stand to this day testifying both to small and great, stating nothing but what the Prophets and Moses said was going to take place, 23 *as to* whether the Christ was to suffer, *and* whether, as first from the resurrection of the dead, He would proclaim light both to the *Jewish* people and to the Gentiles."

24 While Paul was stating these things in his defense, Festus *said in a loud voice, "Paul, you are out of your mind! *Your* great learning is driving you insane." 25 But Paul *said, "I am not insane, most excellent Festus; on the contrary, I am speaking out *with* truthful and rational words. 26 For the king knows about these matters, and I also speak to him with confidence, since I am persuaded that none of these things escape his notice; for this has not been done in a corner. 27 King Agrippa, do you believe the Prophets? I know that you believe."

28 Agrippa *replied* to Paul, "In a short *time* you *are going to* persuade me to make a Christian *of myself.*" 29 And Paul *said,* "I would wish to God that even in a short or long *time* not only you, but also all who hear me this day would become such as I myself am, except for these chains."

30 The king stood up and the governor and Bernice, and those who were sitting with them, 31 and when they had gone out, they *began* talking to one another, saying, "This man is not doing anything deserving death or imprisonment." 32 And Agrippa said to Festus, "This man could have been set free if he had not appealed to Caesar."

Paul Is Sent to Rome

27 Now when it was decided that we would sail for Italy, they proceeded to turn Paul and some other prisoners over to a centurion of the Augustan

¹cohort, named Julius. ² And we boarded an Adramyttian ship that was about to sail to the regions along *the coast of* Asia, and put out to sea accompanied by Aristarchus, a Macedonian of Thessalonica. ³ The next day we put in at Sidon; and Julius treated Paul with consideration and allowed him to go to his friends and receive care. ⁴ From there we put out to sea and sailed under the shelter of Cyprus, because the winds were contrary. ⁵ When we had sailed through the sea along the coast of Cilicia and Pamphylia, we landed at Myra in Lycia. ⁶ There the centurion found an Alexandrian ship sailing for Italy, and he put us aboard it. ⁷ When we had sailed slowly for a good many days, and with difficulty had arrived off Cnidus, since the wind did not permit us *to go* farther, we sailed under the shelter of Crete, off Salmone; ⁸ and with difficulty sailing past it, we came to a place called Fair Havens, near which was the city of Lasea.

⁹ When considerable time had passed and the voyage was now dangerous, since even the ᶠfast was already over, Paul *started* admonishing *them*, ¹⁰ saying to them, "Men, I perceive that the voyage will certainly be with damage and great loss, not only of the cargo and the ship, but also of our lives." ¹¹ But the centurion was more persuaded by the pilot and the captain of the ship than by what was being said by Paul. ¹² The harbor was not suitable for wintering, so the majority reached a decision to put out to sea from there, if somehow they could reach Phoenix, a harbor of Crete facing southwest and northwest, and spend the winter *there*.

¹³ When a moderate south wind came up, thinking that they had attained their purpose, they weighed anchor and *began* sailing along Crete, closer *to shore*.

Shipwreck

¹⁴ But before very long a violent wind, called ᶠEuraquilo, rushed down from the land; ¹⁵ and when the ship was caught *in it* and could not head up into the wind, we gave up and let ourselves be driven *by the wind*. ¹⁶ Running under the shelter of a small island called Cauda, we were able to get the *ship's* boat under control *only* with

---

27:1 ¹ Normally 600 men (the number varied)   27:9 ¹ I.e., Day of Atonement in September or October, which was a dangerous time of year for navigation   27:14 ¹ I.e., a northeaster

difficulty. **17** After they had hoisted it up, they used supporting cables in undergirding the ship; and fearing that they might run aground on *the shallows* of Syrtis, they let down the sea anchor and let themselves be driven along in this way. **18** The next day as we were being violently tossed by the storm, they began to jettison the cargo; **19** and on the third day they threw the ship's tackle *overboard* with their own hands. **20** Since neither sun nor stars appeared for many days, and no small storm was assailing *us,* from then on all hope of our being saved was *slowly* abandoned.

21 When many had lost their appetites, Paul then stood among them and said, "Men, you should have followed my advice and not have set sail from Crete, and *thereby* spared yourselves this damage and loss. **22** And *yet* now I urge you to keep up your courage, for there will be no loss of life among you, but *only* of the ship. **23** For this *very* night an angel of the God to whom I belong, whom I also serve, came to me, **24** saying, 'Do not be afraid, Paul; you must stand before Caesar; and behold, God has graciously granted you all those who are sailing with you.' **25** Therefore, keep up your courage, men, for I believe God that it will turn out exactly as I have been told. **26** But we must run aground on a certain island."

27 But when the fourteenth night came, as we were being driven about in the Adriatic Sea, about midnight the sailors *began* to suspect that they were approaching some land. **28** And they took soundings and found *it to be* twenty fathoms; and a little farther on they took another sounding and found *it to be* fifteen fathoms. **29** Fearing that we might run aground somewhere on the rocks, they cast four anchors from the stern and prayed for daybreak. **30** But as the sailors were trying to escape from the ship and had let down the *ship's* boat into the sea, on the pretense that they were going to lay out anchors from the bow, **31** Paul said to the centurion and the soldiers, "Unless these men remain on the ship, you yourselves cannot be saved." **32** Then the soldiers cut away the ropes of the *ship's* boat and let it fall away.

33 Until the day was about to dawn, Paul kept encouraging them all to take some food, saying, "Today is the fourteenth day that you have been constantly watching and going without eating, having taken in nothing. **34** Therefore, I encourage you to take some food, for this is for your survival, for not a hair from the head of any of you will perish." [35] Having said this, he took bread and gave thanks to God in the presence of them all, and he broke it and began to eat. [36] All of them were encouraged and they themselves also took food. [37] We were 276 people on the ship in all. [38] When they had eaten enough, they *began* lightening the ship by throwing the wheat out into the sea.

[39] Now when day came, they could not recognize the land; but they did notice a bay with a beach, and they resolved to run the ship onto it if they could. [40] And casting off the anchors, they left them in the sea while at the same time they were loosening the ropes of the rudders; and they hoisted the foresail to the wind and were heading for the beach. [41] But they struck a reef where two seas met and ran the ship aground; and the prow stuck firmly and remained immovable, while the stern *started to* break up due to the force *of the waves*. [42] The soldiers' plan was to kill the prisoners, so that none *of them* would swim away and escape; [43] but the centurion, wanting to bring Paul safely through, kept them from *accomplishing* their intention, and commanded that those who could swim were to jump overboard first and get to land, [44] and the rest *were to follow,* some on planks, and others on various things from the ship. And so it happened that they all were brought safely to land.

Safe at Malta

28 When they had been brought safely through, then we found out that the island was called Malta. [2] The natives showed us extraordinary kindness, for they kindled a fire and took us all in because of the rain that had started and because of the cold. [3] But when Paul had gathered a bundle of sticks and laid them on the fire, a viper came out because of the heat and fastened itself on his hand. [4] When the natives saw the creature hanging from his hand, they *began* saying to one another, "Undoubtedly this man is a murderer, and though he has been saved from the sea, justice has not allowed him to live." [5] However, Paul shook the creature off into the fire and suffered no harm. [6] Now they were expecting that he was going to swell up or suddenly fall down dead. But after they had waited a long time and had seen nothing

unusual happen to him, they changed their minds and
began to say that he was a god.

⁷ Now in the neighboring parts of that place were
lands belonging to the leading man of the island, named
Publius, who welcomed us and entertained us warmly
for three days. ⁸ And it happened that the father of Publius was lying *in bed* afflicted with a *recurring* fever and
dysentery. Paul went in *to see* him, and after he prayed,
he laid his hands on him and healed him. ⁹ After this
happened, the rest of the people on the island who had
diseases were coming to him and being cured. ¹⁰ They
also showed us many honors, and when we were *about
to* set sail, they supplied *us* with everything we needed.

Paul Arrives in Rome

¹¹ After three months we set sail on an Alexandrian
ship which had wintered at the island, and which had
the Twin Brothers for its figurehead. ¹² After we put in at
Syracuse, we stayed there for three days. ¹³ From there
we sailed around and arrived at Rhegium, and a day later
a south wind came up, and on the second day we came
to Puteoli. ¹⁴ There we found *some* brothers *and sisters,*
and were invited to stay with them for seven days; and
that is how we came to Rome. ¹⁵ And from there the
brothers *and sisters,* when they heard about us, came as
far as the Market of Appius and the Three Inns to meet
us; and when Paul saw them, he thanked God and took
courage.

¹⁶ When we entered Rome, Paul was allowed to stay
by himself, with the soldier who was guarding him.

¹⁷ After three days Paul called together those who
were the leading men of the Jews, and when they came
together, he *began* saying to them, "Brothers, though I
had done nothing against our people or the customs of
our fathers, *yet* I was handed over to the Romans as a
prisoner from Jerusalem. ¹⁸ And when they had examined
me, they were willing to release me because there were
no grounds for putting me to death. ¹⁹ But when the Jews
objected, I was forced to appeal to Caesar, not that I
had any accusation against my nation. ²⁰ For this reason,
therefore, I requested to see you and to speak with
you, since I am wearing this chain for the sake of the
hope of Israel." ²¹ They said to him, "We have neither
received letters from Judea concerning you, nor has any

of the brothers come here and reported or spoken anything bad about you. **22** But we desire to hear from you what your views are; for regarding this sect, it is known to us that it is spoken against everywhere."

23 When they had set a day for Paul, *people* came to him at his lodging in large numbers; and he was explaining to them by solemnly testifying about the kingdom of God and trying to persuade them concerning Jesus, from both the Law of Moses and from the Prophets, from morning until evening. **24** Some were being persuaded by the things said *by Paul,* but others would not believe. **25** And when they disagreed with one another, they *began* leaving after Paul said one *parting* statement: "The Holy Spirit rightly spoke through Isaiah the prophet to your fathers, **26** saying,

'Go to this people and say,
"You will keep on hearing, and will not understand;
And you will keep on seeing, and will not perceive;
27   For the hearts of this people have become insensitive,
And with their ears they hardly hear,
And they have closed their eyes;
Otherwise they might see with their eyes,
And hear with their ears,
And understand with their heart and return,
And I would heal them."'

28 Therefore, let it be known to you that this salvation of God has been sent to the Gentiles; they will also listen."[1]

30 Now Paul stayed two full years in his own rented lodging and welcomed all who came to him, **31** preaching the kingdom of God and teaching things about the Lord Jesus Christ with all openness, unhindered.

28:28[1] Late mss add as v 29: *When he had spoken these words, the Jews departed, having a great dispute among themselves.*

The Letter of Paul to the

ROMANS

The Gospel Exalted

1 Paul, a bond-servant of Christ Jesus, called *as* an apostle, set apart for the gospel of God, 2 which He promised beforehand through His prophets in the holy Scriptures, 3 concerning His Son, who was born of a descendant of David according to the flesh, 4 who was declared the Son of God with power according to the Spirit of holiness by the resurrection from the dead, Jesus Christ our Lord, 5 through whom we have received grace and apostleship to bring about *the* obedience of faith among all the Gentiles in behalf of His name, 6 among whom you also are *the* called of Jesus Christ;

7 to all who are beloved of God in Rome, called *as* saints: Grace to you and peace from God our Father and the Lord Jesus Christ.

8 First, I thank my God through Jesus Christ for you all, because your faith is being proclaimed throughout the world. 9 For God, whom I serve in my spirit in the *preaching of the* gospel of His Son, is my witness *as to* how unceasingly I make mention of you, 10 always in my prayers requesting if perhaps now, at last by the will of God, I will succeed in coming to you. 11 For I long to see you so that I may impart some spiritual gift to you, that you may be established; 12 that is, that I may be encouraged together with you *while* among you, each of us by the other's faith, both yours and mine. 13 I do not want you to be unaware, brothers *and sisters,* that often I have planned to come to you (and have been prevented so far) so that I may obtain some fruit among you also just as among the rest of the Gentiles. 14 I am under obligation both to Greeks and to the ¹uncultured, both to the wise and to the foolish. 15 So, for my part, I am eager to preach the gospel to you also who are in Rome.

16 For I am not ashamed of the gospel, for it is the power of God for salvation to everyone who believes, to

---

1:14 ¹ I.e., non-Hellenes

the Jew first and also to the Greek. **17** For in it *the* righteousness of God is revealed from faith to faith; as it is written: "BUT THE RIGHTEOUS *ONE* WILL LIVE BY FAITH."

Unbelief and Its Consequences

18 For the wrath of God is revealed from heaven against all ungodliness and unrighteousness of people who suppress the truth in unrighteousness, **19** because that which is known about God is evident within them; for God made it evident to them. **20** For since the creation of the world His invisible *attributes, that is,* His eternal power and divine nature, have been clearly perceived, being understood by what has been made, so that they are without excuse. **21** For even though they knew God, they did not honor Him as God or give thanks, but they became futile in their reasonings, and their senseless hearts were darkened. **22** Claiming to be wise, they became fools, **23** and they exchanged the glory of the incorruptible God for an image in the form of corruptible mankind, of birds, four-footed animals, and crawling creatures.

24 Therefore God gave them up to vile impurity in the lusts of their hearts, so that their bodies would be dishonored among them. **25** For they exchanged the truth of God for falsehood, and worshiped and served the creature rather than the Creator, who is blessed forever. Amen.

26 For this reason God gave them over to degrading passions; for their women exchanged natural relations for that which is contrary to nature, **27** and likewise the men, too, abandoned natural relations with women and burned in their desire toward one another, males with males committing shameful acts and receiving in their own persons the due penalty of their error.

28 And just as they did not see fit to acknowledge God, God gave them up to a depraved mind, to do those things that are not proper, **29** *people* having been filled with all unrighteousness, wickedness, greed, *and* evil; full of envy, murder, strife, deceit, *and* malice; *they are* gossips, **30** slanderers, haters of God, insolent, arrogant, boastful, inventors of evil, disobedient to parents, **31** without understanding, untrustworthy, unfeeling, *and* unmerciful; **32** and although they know the ordinance of

God, that those who practice such things are worthy of death, they not only do the same, but also approve of those who practice them.

The Impartiality of God

2 Therefore you have no excuse, you *foolish* person, everyone *of you* who passes judgment; for in that *matter in* which you judge someone else, you condemn yourself; for you who judge practice the same things. ² And we know that the judgment of God rightly falls upon those who practice such things. ³ But do you suppose this, you *foolish* person who passes judgment on those who practice such things, and *yet* does them *as well,* that you will escape the judgment of God? ⁴ Or do you think lightly of the riches of His kindness and restraint and patience, not knowing that the kindness of God leads you to repentance? ⁵ But because of your stubbornness and unrepentant heart you are storing up wrath for yourself on the day of wrath and revelation of the righteous judgment of God, ⁶ who WILL REPAY EACH PERSON ACCORDING TO HIS DEEDS: ⁷ to those who by perseverance in doing good seek glory, honor, and immortality, *He will give* eternal life; ⁸ but to those who are self-serving and do not obey the truth, but obey unrighteousness, *He will give* wrath and indignation. ⁹ *There will be* tribulation and distress for every soul of mankind who does evil, for the Jew first and also for the Greek, ¹⁰ but glory, honor, and peace to everyone who does what is good, to the Jew first and also to the Greek. ¹¹ For there is no partiality with God.

¹² For all who have sinned without the Law will also perish without the Law, and all who have sinned under the Law will be judged by the Law; ¹³ for *it is* not the hearers of the Law *who* are righteous before God, but the doers of the Law *who* will be justified. ¹⁴ For when Gentiles who do not have the Law instinctively perform the *requirements* of the Law, these, though not having the Law, are a law to themselves, ¹⁵ in that they show the work of the Law written in their hearts, their conscience testifying and their thoughts alternately accusing or else defending them, ¹⁶ on the day when, according to my gospel, God will judge the secrets of mankind through Christ Jesus.

The Jews under the Law

17 But if you call yourself a Jew and rely upon the Law and boast in God, **18** and know *His* will and distinguish the things that matter, being instructed from the Law, **19** and are confident that you yourself are a guide to people who are blind, a light to those in darkness, **20** a corrector of the foolish, a teacher of the immature, possessing in the Law the embodiment of knowledge and of the truth— **21** *you,* therefore, who teach someone else, do you not teach yourself? *You* who preach that one is not to steal, do you steal? **22** *You* who say that one is not to commit adultery, do you commit adultery? *You* who loathe idols, do you rob temples? **23** You who boast in the Law, through your breaking the Law, do you dishonor God? **24** For "THE NAME OF GOD IS BLASPHEMED AMONG THE GENTILES BECAUSE OF YOU," just as it is written.

25 For indeed circumcision is of value if you practice the Law; but if you are a violator of the Law, your circumcision has turned into uncircumcision. **26** So if the uncircumcised man keeps the requirements of the Law, will his uncircumcision not be regarded as circumcision? **27** And he who is physically uncircumcised, if he keeps the Law, will he not judge you who though having the letter *of the Law* and circumcision are a violator of the Law? **28** For he is not a Jew who is one outwardly, nor is circumcision that which is outward in the flesh. **29** But he is a Jew who is one inwardly; and circumcision is of the heart, by the Spirit, not by the letter; and his praise is not from people, but from God.

All the World Guilty

3 Then what advantage does the Jew have? Or what is the benefit of circumcision? **2** Great in every respect. First, that they were entrusted with the actual words of God. **3** What then? If some did not believe, their unbelief will not nullify the faithfulness of God, will it? **4** ¹Far from it! Rather, God must prove to be true, though every person *be found* a liar, as it is written:

"SO THAT YOU ARE JUSTIFIED IN YOUR WORDS,
AND PREVAIL WHEN YOU ARE JUDGED."

5 But if our unrighteousness demonstrates the righteousness of God, what shall we say? The God who inflicts

---

3:4 ¹ Lit *May it never happen!* And so throughout the ch

wrath is not unrighteous, is He? (I am speaking from a human viewpoint.) **6** Far from it! For *otherwise,* how will God judge the world? **7** But if through my lie the truth of God abounded to His glory, why am I also still being judged as a sinner? **8** And *why* not *say* (just as we are slanderously reported and as some claim that we say), "Let's do evil that good may come *of it*"? Their condemnation is deserved.

9 What then? Are we better *than they*? Not at all; for we have already charged that both Jews and Greeks are all under sin; **10** as it is written:

"THERE IS NO RIGHTEOUS PERSON, NOT EVEN ONE;

11   THERE IS NO ONE WHO UNDERSTANDS,
   THERE IS NO ONE WHO SEEKS OUT GOD;

12   THEY HAVE ALL TURNED ASIDE, TOGETHER THEY HAVE BECOME
         CORRUPT;
   THERE IS NO ONE WHO DOES GOOD,
   THERE IS NOT EVEN ONE."

13   "THEIR THROAT IS AN OPEN GRAVE,
   WITH THEIR TONGUES THEY KEEP DECEIVING,"
   "THE VENOM OF [1]ASPS IS UNDER THEIR LIPS";

14   "THEIR MOUTH IS FULL OF CURSING AND BITTERNESS";

15   "THEIR FEET ARE SWIFT TO SHED BLOOD,

16   DESTRUCTION AND MISERY ARE IN THEIR PATHS,

17   AND THEY HAVE NOT KNOWN THE WAY OF PEACE."

18   "THERE IS NO FEAR OF GOD BEFORE THEIR EYES."

19 Now we know that whatever the Law says, it speaks to those who are under the Law, so that every mouth may be closed and all the world may become accountable to God; **20** because by the works of the Law none of mankind will be justified in His sight; for through the Law *comes* knowledge of sin.

Justification by Faith

21 But now apart from the Law *the* righteousness of God has been revealed, being witnessed by the Law and the Prophets, **22** but *it is the* righteousness of God through faith in Jesus Christ for all those who believe; for there is no distinction, **23** for all have sinned and fall short of the glory of God, **24** being justified as a gift by His grace through the redemption which is in Christ Jesus, **25** whom God displayed publicly as a

---

3:13 [1] I.e., venomous snakes

[1]propitiation in His blood through faith. *This was* to demonstrate His righteousness, because in God's *merciful* restraint He let the sins previously committed go unpunished; 26 for the demonstration, *that is,* of His righteousness at the present time, so that He would be just and the justifier of the one who has faith in Jesus.

27 Where then is boasting? It has been excluded. By what kind of law? Of works? No, but by a law of faith. 28 For we maintain that a person is justified by faith apart from works of the Law. 29 Or is God *the God* of Jews only? Is He not *the God* of Gentiles also? Yes, of Gentiles also, 30 since indeed God who will justify the circumcised by faith and the uncircumcised through faith is one.

31 Do we then nullify the Law through faith? Far from it! On the contrary, we establish the Law.

Abraham's Justification by Faith

4 What then shall we say that Abraham, our forefather according to the flesh, has found? 2 For if Abraham was justified by works, he has something to boast about; but not before God. 3 For what does the Scripture say? "ABRAHAM BELIEVED GOD, AND IT WAS CREDITED TO HIM AS RIGHTEOUSNESS." 4 Now to the one who works, the wages are not credited as a favor, but as what is due. 5 But to the one who does not work, but believes in Him who justifies the ungodly, his faith is credited as righteousness, 6 just as David also speaks of the blessing of the person to whom God credits righteousness apart from works:

7   "BLESSED ARE THOSE WHOSE LAWLESS DEEDS HAVE BEEN FOR-
          GIVEN,
       AND WHOSE SINS HAVE BEEN COVERED.
8   "BLESSED IS THE MAN WHOSE SIN THE LORD WILL NOT TAKE
          INTO ACCOUNT."

9 Is this blessing then on the circumcised, or on the uncircumcised also? For we say, "FAITH WAS CREDITED TO ABRAHAM AS RIGHTEOUSNESS." 10 How then was it credited? While he was circumcised, or uncircumcised? Not while circumcised, but while uncircumcised; 11 and he received the sign of circumcision, a seal of the righteousness of the faith which he had while uncircumcised, so that he

---

3:25 [1] I.e., a means of reconciliation between God and mankind by paying the penalty for sin

might be the father of all who believe without being circumcised, that righteousness might be credited to them, 12 and the father of circumcision to those who not only are of the circumcision, but who also follow in the steps of the faith of our father Abraham which he had while uncircumcised.

13 For the promise to Abraham or to his descendants that he would be heir of the world was not through the Law, but through the righteousness of faith. 14 For if those who are of the Law are heirs, then faith is made void and the promise is nullified; 15 for the Law brings about wrath, but where there is no law, there also is no violation.

16 For this reason *it is* by faith, in order that *it may be* in accordance with grace, so that the promise will be guaranteed to all the descendants, not only to those who are of the Law, but also to those who are of the faith of Abraham, who is the father of us all, 17 (as it is written: "I HAVE MADE YOU A FATHER OF MANY NATIONS") in the presence of Him whom he believed, *that is,* God, who gives life to the dead and calls into being things that do not exist. 18 In hope against hope he believed, so that he might become a father of many nations according to that which had been spoken, "SO SHALL YOUR DESCENDANTS BE." 19 Without becoming weak in faith he contemplated his own body, now *as good as* dead since he was about a hundred years old, and the deadness of Sarah's womb; 20 yet, with respect to the promise of God, he did not waver in unbelief but grew strong in faith, giving glory to God, 21 and being fully assured that what *God* had promised, He was able also to perform. 22 Therefore IT WAS ALSO CREDITED TO HIM AS RIGHTEOUSNESS. 23 Now not for his sake only was it written that it was credited to him, 24 but for our sake also, to whom it will be credited, to *us* who believe in Him who raised Jesus our Lord from the dead, 25 *He* who was delivered over because of our wrongdoings, and was raised because of our justification.

Results of Justification

5 Therefore, having been justified by faith, we have peace with God through our Lord Jesus Christ, 2 through whom we also have obtained our introduction by faith into this grace in which we stand; and we celebrate in hope of the glory of God. 3 And not only *this,*

but we also celebrate in our tribulations, knowing that tribulation brings about perseverance; 4 and perseverance, proven character; and proven character, hope; 5 and hope does not disappoint, because the love of God has been poured out within our hearts through the Holy Spirit who was given to us.

6 For while we were still helpless, at *the* right time Christ died for the ungodly. 7 For one will hardly die for a righteous person; though perhaps for the good person someone would even dare to die. 8 But God demonstrates His own love toward us, in that while we were still sinners, Christ died for us. 9 Much more then, having now been justified by His blood, we shall be saved from the wrath *of God* through Him. 10 For if while we were enemies we were reconciled to God through the death of His Son, much more, having been reconciled, we shall be saved by His life. 11 And not only *this,* but we also celebrate in God through our Lord Jesus Christ, through whom we have now received the reconciliation.

12 Therefore, just as through one man sin entered into the world, and death through sin, and so death spread to all mankind, because all sinned— 13 for until the Law sin was in the world, but sin is not counted against *anyone* when there is no law. 14 Nevertheless death reigned from Adam until Moses, even over those who had not sinned in the likeness of the ¹violation *committed* by Adam, who is a ²type of Him who was to come.

15 But the gracious gift is not like the offense. For if by the offense of the one the many died, much more did the grace of God and the gift by the grace of the one Man, Jesus Christ, overflow to the many. 16 The gift is not like *that which came* through the one who sinned; for on the one hand the judgment *arose* from one *offense,* resulting in condemnation, but on the other hand the gracious gift *arose* from many offenses, resulting in justification. 17 For if by the offense of the one, death reigned through the one, much more will those who receive the abundance of grace and of the gift of righteousness reign in life through the One, Jesus Christ.

18 So then, as through one offense the result was condemnation to all mankind, so also through one act of righteousness the result was justification of life to all

5:14 ¹I.e., of God's command   5:14 ²Or *foreshadowing*

mankind. ¹⁹ For as through the one man's disobedience the many were made sinners, so also through the obedience of the One the many will be made righteous. ²⁰ The Law came in so that the offense would increase; but where sin increased, grace abounded all the more, ²¹ so that, as sin reigned in death, so also grace would reign through righteousness to eternal life through Jesus Christ our Lord.

Believers Are Dead to Sin, Alive to God

6 What shall we say then? Are we to continue in sin so that grace may increase? ² ¹Far from it! How shall we who died to sin still live in it? ³ Or do you not know that all of us who have been baptized into Christ Jesus have been baptized into His death? ⁴ Therefore we have been buried with Him through baptism into death, so that, just as Christ was raised from the dead through the glory of the Father, so we too may walk in newness of life. ⁵ For if we have become united with *Him* in the likeness of His death, certainly we shall also be *in the likeness* of His resurrection, ⁶ knowing this, that our old self was crucified with *Him,* in order that our body of sin might be done away with, so that we would no longer be slaves to sin; ⁷ for the one who has died is freed from sin.

⁸ Now if we have died with Christ, we believe that we shall also live with Him, ⁹ knowing that Christ, having been raised from the dead, is never to die again; death no longer is master over Him. ¹⁰ For the death that He died, He died to sin once for all *time;* but the life that He lives, He lives to God. ¹¹ So you too, consider yourselves to be dead to sin, but alive to God in Christ Jesus.

¹² Therefore sin is not to reign in your mortal body so that you obey its lusts, ¹³ and do not go on presenting the parts of your body to sin *as* ¹instruments of unrighteousness; but present yourselves to God as those who are alive from the dead, and your body's parts *as* instruments of righteousness for God. ¹⁴ For sin shall not be master over you, for you are not under ¹the Law but under grace.

¹⁵ What then? Are we to sin because we are not under ¹the Law but under grace? ²Far from it! ¹⁶ Do you

---

6:2 ¹Lit *May it never happen!*   6:13 ¹Or *weapons*   6:14 ¹Or *law*
6:15 ¹Or *law*   6:15 ²Lit *May it never happen!*

not know that *the one* to whom you present yourselves *as* slaves for obedience, you are slaves of *that same one* whom you obey, either of sin resulting in death, or of obedience resulting in righteousness? **17** But thanks be to God that though you were slaves of sin, you became obedient from the heart to *that* form of teaching to which you were entrusted, **18** and after being freed from sin, you became slaves to righteousness. **19** I am speaking in human terms because of the weakness of your flesh. For just as you presented the parts of your body as slaves to impurity and to lawlessness, resulting in *further* lawlessness, so now present your body's parts as slaves to righteousness, resulting in sanctification.

20 For when you were slaves of sin, you were free in relation to righteousness. **21** Therefore what benefit were you then deriving from the things of which you are now ashamed? For the outcome of those things is death. **22** But now having been freed from sin and enslaved to God, you derive your benefit, resulting in sanctification, and the outcome, eternal life. **23** For the wages of sin is death, but the gracious gift of God is eternal life in Christ Jesus our Lord.

Believers United to Christ

7 Or do you not know, brothers *and sisters* (for I am speaking to those who know the Law), that the Law has jurisdiction over a person as long as he lives? **2** For the married woman is bound by law to her husband as long as he is alive; but if her husband dies, she is released from the law concerning the husband. **3** So then, if while her husband is alive she gives herself to another man, she will be called an adulteress; but if her husband dies, she is free from the law, so that she is not an adulteress if she ¹gives herself to another man.

4 Therefore, my brothers *and sisters,* you also were put to death in regard to the Law through the body of Christ, so that you might belong to another, to Him who was raised from the dead, in order that we might bear fruit for God. **5** For while we were in the flesh, the sinful passions, which were *brought to light* by the Law, were at work in the parts of our body to bear fruit for death. **6** But now we have been released from the Law, having died to

---

7:3 ¹I.e., in marriage; lit *becomes another man's*

that by which we were bound, so that we serve in newness of the ʳSpirit and not in oldness of the letter.

⁷ What shall we say then? Is the Law sin? ʳFar from it!
On the contrary, I would not have come to know sin
except through the Law; for I would not have known
about coveting if the Law had not said, "YOU SHALL NOT
COVET." ⁸ But sin, taking an opportunity through the
commandment, produced in me coveting of every kind;
for apart from the Law sin *is* dead. ⁹ I was once alive
apart from the Law; but when the commandment came,
sin came to life, and I died; ¹⁰ and this commandment,
which was to result in life, proved to result in death for
me; ¹¹ for sin, taking an opportunity through the
commandment, deceived me, and through it, killed *me*.
¹² So then, the Law is holy, and the commandment is
holy and righteous and good.

¹³ Therefore did that which is good become *a cause of*
death for me? Far from it! Rather *it was* sin, in order that
it might be shown to be sin by bringing about my death
through that which is good, so that through the
commandment sin would become utterly sinful.

The Conflict of Serving Two Masters

¹⁴ For we know that the Law is spiritual, but I am
fleshly, sold into bondage to sin. ¹⁵ For I do not understand what I am doing; for I am not practicing what I
want *to do,* but I do the very thing I hate. ¹⁶ However, if I
do the very thing I do not want *to do,* I agree with the
Law, that *the Law is* good. ¹⁷ But now, no longer am I *the
one* doing it, but sin that dwells in me. ¹⁸ For I know that
good does not dwell in me, that is, in my flesh; for the
willing is present in me, but the doing of the good *is* not.
¹⁹ For the good that I want, I do not do, but I practice the
very evil that I do not want. ²⁰ But if I do the very thing I
do not want, I am no longer *the one* doing it, but sin that
dwells in me.

²¹ I find then the principle that evil is present in me,
the one who wants to do good. ²² For I joyfully agree with
the law of God in the inner person, ²³ but I see a different
law in the parts of my body waging war against the law
of my mind, and making me a prisoner of the law of
sin, *the law* which is in my body's parts. ²⁴ Wretched man

7:6 ¹Or *spirit*   7:7 ¹Lit *May it never happen!*

that I am! Who will set me free from the body of this death? **25** Thanks be to God through Jesus Christ our Lord! So then, on the one hand I myself with my mind am serving the law of God, but on the other, with my flesh the law of sin.

Deliverance from Bondage

8 Therefore there is now no condemnation at all for those who are in Christ Jesus. **2** For the law of the Spirit of life in Christ Jesus has set you free from the law of sin and of death. **3** For what the Law could not do, weak as it was through the flesh, God *did:* sending His own Son in the likeness of sinful flesh and *as an offering* for sin, He condemned sin in the flesh, **4** so that the requirement of the Law might be fulfilled in us who do not walk according to the flesh but according to the Spirit. **5** For those who are in accord with the flesh set their minds on the things of the flesh, but those who are in accord with the Spirit, the things of the Spirit. **6** For the mind set on the flesh is death, but the mind set on the Spirit is life and peace, **7** because the mind set on the flesh is hostile toward God; for it does not subject itself to the law of God, for it is not even able *to do so,* **8** and those who are in the flesh cannot please God.

9 However, you are not in the flesh but in the Spirit, if indeed the Spirit of God dwells in you. But if anyone does not have the Spirit of Christ, he does not belong to Him. **10** If Christ is in you, though the body is dead because of sin, yet the spirit is alive because of righteousness. **11** But if the Spirit of Him who raised Jesus from the dead dwells in you, He who raised Christ Jesus from the dead will also give life to your mortal bodies ¹through His Spirit who dwells in you.

12 So then, brothers *and sisters,* we are under obligation, not to the flesh, to live according to the flesh— **13** for if you are living in accord with the flesh, you are going to die; but if by the Spirit you are putting to death the deeds of the body, you will live. **14** For all who are being led by the Spirit of God, these are sons *and daughters* of God. **15** For you have not received a spirit of slavery leading to fear again, but you have received a spirit of adoption as sons *and daughters* by which we cry

---

8:11 ¹One early ms *because of*

out, "Abba! Father!" 16 The Spirit Himself testifies with
our spirit that we are children of God, 17 and if children,
heirs also, heirs of God and fellow heirs with Christ, if
indeed we suffer with *Him* so that we may also be
glorified with *Him.*

18 For I consider that the sufferings of this present time
are not worthy *to be* compared with the glory that is to
be revealed to us. 19 For the eagerly awaiting creation
waits for the revealing of the sons *and daughters* of God.
20 For the creation was subjected to futility, not willingly,
but because of Him who subjected *it,* in hope 21 that the
creation itself also will be set free from its slavery to corruption into the freedom of the glory of the children of
God. 22 For we know that the whole creation groans and
suffers the pains of childbirth together until now. 23 And
not only *that,* but also we ourselves, having the first
fruits of the Spirit, even we ourselves groan within
ourselves, waiting eagerly for *our* adoption as sons *and
daughters,* the redemption of our body. 24 For in hope we
have been saved, but hope that is seen is not hope; for
who hopes for what he *already* sees? 25 But if we hope for
what we do not see, through perseverance we wait
eagerly *for it.*

Our Victory in Christ

26 Now in the same way the Spirit also helps our weakness; for we do not know what to pray for as we should,
but the Spirit Himself intercedes for *us* with groanings
too deep for words; 27 and He who searches the hearts
knows what the mind of the Spirit is, because He intercedes for the saints according to *the will of* God.
28 And we know that 1God causes all things to work
together for good to those who love God, to those who
are called according to *His* purpose. 29 For those whom
He foreknew, He also predestined *to become* conformed
to the image of His Son, so that He would be the firstborn among many brothers *and sisters;* 30 and these
whom He predestined, He also called; and these whom
He called, He also justified; and these whom He justified,
He also glorified.

31 What then shall we say to these things? If God *is* for
us, who *is* against us? 32 He who did not spare His own

8:28 1One early ms *He;* i.e., God

Son, but delivered Him over for us all, how will He not also with Him freely give us all things? **33** Who will bring charges against God's elect? God is the one who justifies; **34** who is the one who condemns? Christ Jesus is He who died, but rather, was ¹raised, who is at the right hand of God, who also intercedes for us. **35** Who will separate us from the love of ¹Christ? *Will* tribulation, or trouble, or persecution, or famine, or nakedness, or danger, or sword? **36** Just as it is written:

"FOR YOUR SAKE WE ARE KILLED ALL DAY LONG;
WE WERE REGARDED AS SHEEP TO BE SLAUGHTERED."

37 But in all these things we overwhelmingly conquer through Him who loved us. **38** For I am convinced that neither death, nor life, nor angels, nor principalities, nor things present, nor things to come, nor powers, **39** nor height, nor depth, nor any other created thing will be able to separate us from the love of God that is in Christ Jesus our Lord.

Deep Concern for Israel

9 I am telling the truth in Christ, I am not lying; my conscience testifies with me in the Holy Spirit, **2** that I have great sorrow and unceasing grief in my heart. **3** For I could wish that I myself were accursed, *separated* from Christ for the sake of my countrymen, my kinsmen according to the flesh, **4** who are Israelites, to whom belongs the adoption as sons *and daughters,* the glory, the covenants, the giving of the Law, the *temple* service, and the promises; **5** whose are the fathers, and from whom is the Christ according to the flesh, who is over all, God blessed forever. Amen.

6 But *it is* not as though the word of God has failed. For they are not all Israel who are *descended* from Israel; **7** nor are they all children because they are Abraham's descendants, but: "THROUGH ISAAC YOUR DESCENDANTS SHALL BE NAMED." **8** That is, it is not the children of the flesh who are children of God, but the children of the promise are regarded as descendants. **9** For this is the word of promise: "AT THIS TIME I WILL COME, AND SARAH WILL HAVE A SON." **10** And not only *that,* but there was also Rebekah, when she had conceived *twins* by one man, our father Isaac; **11** for though *the twins* were not yet born and had not

---

8:34 ¹One early ms *raised from the dead*   8:35 ¹Two early mss *God*

done anything good or bad, so that God's purpose according to *His* choice would stand, not because of works but because of Him who calls, **12** it was said to her, "THE OLDER WILL SERVE THE YOUNGER." **13** Just as it is written: "JACOB I HAVE LOVED, BUT ESAU I HAVE HATED."

14 What shall we say then? There is no injustice with God, is there? ¹Far from it! **15** For He says to Moses, "I WILL HAVE MERCY ON WHOMEVER I HAVE MERCY, AND I WILL SHOW COMPASSION TO WHOMEVER I SHOW COMPASSION." **16** So then, *it does* not *depend* on the *person* who wants *it* nor the one who ¹runs, but on God who has mercy. **17** For the Scripture says to Pharaoh, "FOR THIS VERY REASON I RAISED YOU UP, IN ORDER TO DEMONSTRATE MY POWER IN YOU, AND THAT MY NAME MIGHT BE PROCLAIMED THROUGHOUT THE EARTH." **18** So then He has mercy on whom He desires, and He hardens whom He desires.

19 You will say to me then, "Why does He still find fault? For who has resisted His will?" **20** On the contrary, who are you, you *foolish* person, who answers back to God? The thing molded will not say to the molder, "Why did you make me like this," will it? **21** Or does the potter not have a right over the clay, to make from the same lump one object for honorable use, and another for common use? **22** What if God, although willing to demonstrate His wrath and to make His power known, endured with great patience objects of wrath prepared for destruction? **23** And *He did so* to make known the riches of His glory upon objects of mercy, which He prepared beforehand for glory, **24** *namely* us, whom He also called, not only from among Jews, but also from among Gentiles, **25** as He also says in Hosea:

"I WILL CALL THOSE WHO WERE NOT MY PEOPLE, 'MY PEOPLE,'
AND HER WHO WAS NOT BELOVED, 'BELOVED.'"
26 "AND IT SHALL BE THAT IN THE PLACE WHERE IT WAS SAID TO
THEM, 'YOU ARE NOT MY PEOPLE,'
THERE THEY SHALL BE CALLED SONS OF THE LIVING GOD."

27 Isaiah cries out concerning Israel, "THOUGH THE NUMBER OF THE SONS OF ISRAEL MAY BE LIKE THE SAND OF THE SEA, *ONLY* THE REMNANT WILL BE SAVED; **28** FOR THE LORD WILL EXECUTE HIS WORD ON THE EARTH, THOROUGHLY AND QUICKLY." **29** And just as Isaiah foretold:

"IF THE LORD OF ARMIES HAD NOT LEFT US DESCENDANTS,

9:14 ¹Lit *May it never happen!*   9:16 ¹I.e., to win mercy or favor

WE WOULD HAVE BECOME LIKE SODOM, AND WOULD HAVE
  BEEN LIKE GOMORRAH."

30 What shall we say then? That Gentiles, who did not
pursue righteousness, attained righteousness, but the
righteousness that is by faith; **31** however, Israel, pursuing
a law of righteousness, did not arrive at *that* law. **32** Why?
Because *they did* not *pursue it* by faith, but as though
they could by works. They stumbled over the stumbling
stone, **33** just as it is written:
  "BEHOLD, I AM LAYING IN ZION A STONE OF STUMBLING AND A
    ROCK OF OFFENSE,
  AND THE ONE WHO BELIEVES IN HIM WILL NOT BE PUT TO
    SHAME."

The Word of Faith Brings Salvation

10 Brothers *and sisters,* my heart's desire and my
prayer to God for them is for *their* salvation. **2** For I
testify about them that they have a zeal for God, but not
in accordance with knowledge. **3** For not knowing about
God's righteousness and seeking to establish their own,
they did not subject themselves to the righteousness of
God. **4** For Christ is the end of the Law for righteousness
to everyone who believes.

5 For Moses writes of the righteousness that is based
on the Law, that the person who performs them will live
by them. **6** But the righteousness based on faith speaks as
follows: "DO NOT SAY IN YOUR HEART, 'WHO WILL GO UP INTO
HEAVEN?' (that is, to bring Christ down), **7** or 'WHO WILL
DESCEND INTO THE ABYSS?' (that is, to bring Christ up from
the dead)." **8** But what does it say? "THE WORD IS NEAR YOU,
IN YOUR MOUTH AND IN YOUR HEART"—that is, the word of
faith which we are preaching, **9** that if you confess with
your mouth Jesus *as* Lord, and believe in your heart that
God raised Him from the dead, you will be saved; **10** for
with the heart *a person* believes, resulting in righteousness, and with the mouth he confesses, resulting in
salvation. **11** For the Scripture says, "WHOEVER BELIEVES IN
HIM WILL NOT BE PUT TO SHAME." **12** For there is no distinction between Jew and Greek; for the same *Lord* is
Lord of all, abounding in riches for all who call on Him;
13 for "EVERYONE WHO CALLS ON THE NAME OF THE LORD WILL BE
SAVED."

14 How then are they to call on Him in whom
they have not believed? How are they to believe in Him

whom they have not heard? And how are they to hear without a preacher? **15** But how are they to preach unless they are sent? Just as it is written: "HOW BEAUTIFUL ARE THE FEET OF THOSE WHO BRING GOOD NEWS OF GOOD THINGS!"

16 However, they did not all heed the good news; for Isaiah says, "LORD, WHO HAS BELIEVED OUR REPORT?" **17** So faith *comes* from hearing, and hearing by the word of Christ.

18 But I say, surely they have never heard, have they? On the contrary:

"THEIR VOICE HAS GONE OUT INTO ALL THE EARTH,
AND THEIR WORDS TO THE ENDS OF THE WORLD."

19 But I say, surely Israel did not know, did they? First Moses says,

"I WILL MAKE YOU JEALOUS WITH *THOSE WHO ARE* NOT A
NATION,
WITH A FOOLISH NATION I WILL ANGER YOU."

20 And Isaiah is very bold and says,

"I WAS FOUND BY THOSE WHO DID NOT SEEK ME,
I REVEALED MYSELF TO THOSE WHO DID NOT ASK FOR ME."

21 But as for Israel, He says, "I HAVE SPREAD OUT MY HANDS ALL DAY LONG TO A DISOBEDIENT AND OBSTINATE PEOPLE."

Israel Has Not Been Rejected

11 I say then, God has not rejected His people, has He? 'Far from it! For I too am an Israelite, a descendant of Abraham, of the tribe of Benjamin. **2** God has not rejected His people whom He foreknew. Or do you not know what the Scripture says in *the passage about* Elijah, how he pleads with God against Israel? **3** "Lord, THEY HAVE KILLED YOUR PROPHETS, THEY HAVE TORN DOWN YOUR ALTARS, AND I ALONE AM LEFT, AND THEY ARE SEEKING MY LIFE." **4** But what is the divine response to him? "I HAVE KEPT for Myself SEVEN THOUSAND MEN WHO HAVE NOT BOWED THE KNEE TO BAAL." **5** In the same way then, there has also come to be at the present time a remnant according to *God's* gracious choice. **6** But if *it is* by grace, *it is* no longer on the basis of works, since *otherwise* grace is no longer grace.

7 What then? What Israel is seeking, it has not obtained, but those who were chosen obtained it, and the rest were hardened; **8** just as it is written:

11:1 ¹Lit *May it never happen!*

"GOD GAVE THEM A SPIRIT OF STUPOR,
    EYES TO SEE NOT AND EARS TO HEAR NOT,
    DOWN TO THIS VERY DAY."
9 And David says,
    "MAY THEIR TABLE BECOME A SNARE AND A TRAP,
        AND A STUMBLING BLOCK AND A RETRIBUTION TO THEM.
10 "MAY THEIR EYES BE DARKENED TO SEE NOT,
        AND BEND THEIR BACKS CONTINUALLY."

11 I say then, they did not stumble so as to fall, did they? Far from it! But by their wrongdoing salvation *has come* to the Gentiles, to make them jealous. **12** Now if their wrongdoing *proves to be* riches for the world, and their failure, riches for the Gentiles, how much more *will* their fulfillment *be!* **13** But I am speaking to you who are Gentiles. Therefore insofar as I am an apostle of Gentiles, I magnify my ministry **14** if somehow I may move my own people to jealousy and save some of them. **15** For if their rejection *proves to be* the reconciliation of the world, what *will their* acceptance *be* but life from the dead? **16** If the first piece *of dough* is holy, the lump is also; and if the root is holy, the branches are as well.

17 But if some of the branches were broken off, and you, being a wild olive, were grafted in among them and became partaker with them of the rich root of the olive tree, **18** do not be arrogant toward the branches; but if you are arrogant, *remember that* it is not you who supports the root, but the root *supports* you. **19** You will say then, "Branches were broken off so that I might be grafted in." **20** Quite right, they were broken off for their unbelief, but you stand by your faith. Do not be conceited, but fear; **21** for if God did not spare the natural branches, He will not spare you, either. **22** See then the kindness and severity of God: to those who fell, severity, but to you, God's kindness, if you continue in His kindness; for otherwise you too will be cut off. **23** And they also, if they do not continue in their unbelief, will be grafted in; for God is able to graft them in again. **24** For if you were cut off from what is by nature a wild olive tree, and contrary to nature were grafted into a cultivated olive tree, how much more will these who are the natural *branches* be grafted into their own olive tree?

25 For I do not want you, brothers *and sisters,* to be uninformed of this mystery—so that you will not be wise in your own estimation—that a partial hardening has happened to Israel until the fullness of the Gentiles has come in; 26 and so all Israel will be saved; just as it is written:

"The Deliverer will come from Zion,
  He will remove ungodliness from Jacob."
27 "This is My covenant with them,
  When I take away their sins."

28 In relation to the gospel *they are* enemies on your account, but in relation to *God's* choice *they are* beloved on account of the fathers; 29 for the gifts and the calling of God are irrevocable. 30 For just as you once were disobedient to God, but now have been shown mercy because of their disobedience, 31 so these also now have been disobedient, that because of the mercy shown to you they also may now be shown mercy. 32 For God has shut up all in disobedience, so that He may show mercy to all.

33 Oh, the depth of the riches, both of the wisdom and knowledge of God! How unsearchable are His judgments and unfathomable His ways! 34 For who has known the mind of the Lord, or who became His counselor? 35 Or who has first given to Him, that it would be paid back to him? 36 For from Him, and through Him, and to Him are all things. To Him *be* the glory forever. Amen.

Dedicated Service

12 Therefore I urge you, brothers *and sisters,* by the mercies of God, to present your bodies as a living and holy sacrifice, acceptable to God, *which is* your ¹spiritual service of worship. 2 And do not be conformed to this world, but be transformed by the renewing of your mind, so that you may prove what the will of God is, that which is good and acceptable and perfect.

3 For through the grace given to me I say to everyone among you not to think more highly of himself than he ought to think; but to think so as to have sound judgment, as God has allotted to each a measure of faith. 4 For just as we have many parts in one body and all the body's parts do not have the same function, 5 so we, who are many, are one body in Christ, and individually parts of one another. 6 However, since we have gifts that differ according to the grace given to us, *each of us is to use them properly:* if prophecy, in proportion to *one's* faith;

12:1 ¹ I.e., in contrast to offering a literal sacrifice

7 if service, in the *act of* serving; or the one who teaches, in the *act of* teaching; **8** or the one who ¹exhorts, in the *work of* ²exhortation; the one who gives, with generosity; the one who is in leadership, with diligence; the one who shows mercy, with cheerfulness.

9 Love *must be* free of hypocrisy. Detest what is evil; cling to what is good. **10** *Be* devoted to one another in brotherly love; give preference to one another in honor, **11** not lagging behind in diligence, fervent in spirit, serving the Lord; **12** rejoicing in hope, persevering in tribulation, devoted to prayer, **13** contributing to the needs of the saints, practicing hospitality.

14 Bless those who persecute ¹you; bless and do not curse. **15** Rejoice with those who rejoice, and weep with those who weep. **16** Be of the same mind toward one another; do not be haughty in mind, but associate with the lowly. Do not be wise in your own estimation. **17** Never repay evil for evil to anyone. Respect what is right in the sight of all people. **18** If possible, so far as it depends on you, be at peace with all people. **19** Never take your own revenge, beloved, but leave room for the wrath *of God,* for it is written: "VENGEANCE IS MINE, I WILL REPAY," says the Lord. **20** "BUT IF YOUR ENEMY IS HUNGRY, FEED HIM; IF HE IS THIRSTY, GIVE HIM A DRINK; FOR IN SO DOING YOU WILL HEAP BURNING COALS ON HIS HEAD." **21** Do not be overcome by evil, but overcome evil with good.

Be Subject to Government

13 Every person is to be subject to the governing authorities. For there is no authority except from God, and those which exist are established by God. **2** Therefore whoever resists authority has opposed the ordinance of God; and they who have opposed will receive condemnation upon themselves. **3** For rulers are not a cause of fear for good behavior, but for evil. Do you want to have no fear of authority? Do what is good and you will have praise from the same; **4** for it is a servant of God to you for good. But if you do what is evil, be afraid; for it does not bear the sword for nothing; for it is a servant of God, an avenger who brings wrath on the one who practices evil. **5** Therefore it is necessary to be in

---

subjection, not only because of wrath, but also for the sake of conscience. **6** For because of this you also pay taxes, for *rulers* are servants of God, devoting themselves to this very thing. **7** Pay to all what is due them: tax to whom tax *is due*; custom to whom custom; respect to whom respect; honor to whom honor.

8 Owe nothing to anyone except to love one another; for the one who loves his neighbor has fulfilled *the* Law. **9** For this, "YOU SHALL NOT COMMIT ADULTERY, YOU SHALL NOT MURDER, YOU SHALL NOT STEAL, YOU SHALL NOT COVET," and if there is any other commandment, it is summed up in this saying, "YOU SHALL LOVE YOUR NEIGHBOR AS YOURSELF." **10** Love does no wrong to a neighbor; therefore love is the fulfillment of *the* Law.

11 *Do* this, knowing the time, that it is already the hour for you to awaken from sleep; for now salvation is nearer to us than when we *first* believed. **12** The night is almost gone, and the day is near. Therefore let's rid ourselves of the deeds of darkness and put on the armor of light. **13** Let's behave properly as in the day, not in carousing and drunkenness, not in sexual promiscuity and debauchery, not in strife and jealousy. **14** But put on the Lord Jesus Christ, and make no provision for the flesh in regard to *its* lusts.

Principles of Conscience

14 Now accept the one who is weak in faith, *but* not to have quarrels over opinions. **2** One person has faith that he may eat all things, but the one who is weak eats *only* vegetables. **3** The one who eats is not to regard with contempt the one who does not eat, and the one who does not eat is not to judge the one who eats, for God has accepted him. **4** Who are you to judge the servant of another? To his own master he stands or falls; and he will stand, for the Lord is able to make him stand.

5 One *person* values one day over another, another values every day *the same*. Each person must be fully convinced in his own mind. **6** The one who observes the day, observes it for the Lord, and the one who eats, does so with regard to the Lord, for he gives thanks to God; and the one who does not eat, *it is* for the Lord *that* he does not eat, and he gives thanks to God. **7** For not one of us lives for himself, and not one dies for himself; **8** for if we live, we live for the Lord, or if we die, we die for the

Lord; therefore whether we live or die, we are the Lord's. ⁹For to this *end* Christ died and lived *again,* that He might be Lord both of the dead and of the living.

¹⁰But *as for* you, why do you judge your brother *or sister?* Or you as well, why do you regard your brother *or sister* with contempt? For we will all appear before the judgment seat of God. ¹¹For it is written:

"AS I LIVE, SAYS THE LORD, TO ME every knee will bow,
    AND EVERY TONGUE WILL GIVE PRAISE TO GOD."

¹²So then each one of us will give an account of himself to God.

¹³Therefore let's not judge one another anymore, but rather determine this: not to put an obstacle or a stumbling block in a brother's *or sister's* way. ¹⁴I know and am convinced in the Lord Jesus that nothing is unclean in itself; but to the one who thinks something is unclean, to that *person it is* unclean. ¹⁵For if because of food your brother *or sister* is hurt, you are no longer walking in accordance with love. Do not destroy with your *choice* of food that *person* for whom Christ died. ¹⁶Therefore do not let what is for you a good thing be spoken of as evil; ¹⁷for the kingdom of God is not eating and drinking, but righteousness and peace and joy in the Holy Spirit. ¹⁸For the one who serves Christ in this *way* is acceptable to God and approved by *other* people. ¹⁹So then we pursue the things which make for peace and the building up of one another. ²⁰Do not tear down the work of God for the sake of food. All things indeed are clean, but they are evil for the person who eats and causes offense. ²¹It is good not to eat meat or to drink wine, or *to do anything* by which your brother *or sister* stumbles. ²²The faith which you have, have as your own conviction before God. Happy is the one who does not condemn himself in what he approves. ²³But the one who doubts is condemned if he eats, because *his eating is* not from faith; and whatever is not from faith is sin.

Self-denial in behalf of Others

15 Now we who are strong ought to bear the weaknesses of those without strength, and not *just* please ourselves. ²Each of us is to please his neighbor for his good, to *his* edification. ³For even Christ did not please Himself, but as it is written: "THE TAUNTS OF THOSE WHO TAUNT YOU HAVE FALLEN ON ME." ⁴For whatever was written in earlier times was written for our instruction, so that through perseverance and the encouragement of the Scriptures we might have hope. 5 Now may the God who gives perseverance and encouragement grant you to be of the same mind with one another, according to Christ Jesus, 6 so that with one purpose *and* one voice you may glorify the God and Father of our Lord Jesus Christ.

7 Therefore, accept one another, just as Christ also accepted us, for the glory of God. 8 For I say that Christ has become a servant to the circumcision in behalf of the truth of God, to confirm the promises *given* to the fathers, 9 and for the Gentiles to glorify God for His mercy; as it is written:

"Therefore I will give praise to You among the
Gentiles,
And I will sing praises to Your name."

10 Again he says,

"Rejoice, you Gentiles, with His people."

11 And again,

"Praise the Lord all you Gentiles,
And let all the peoples praise Him."

12 Again Isaiah says,

"There shall come the root of Jesse,
And He who arises to rule over the Gentiles,
In Him will the Gentiles hope."

13 Now may the God of hope fill you with all joy and peace in believing, so that you will abound in hope by the power of the Holy Spirit.

14 And concerning you, my brothers *and sisters,* I myself also am convinced that you yourselves are full of goodness, filled with all knowledge and able also to admonish one another. 15 But I have written very boldly to you on some points so as to remind you again, because of the grace that was given to me from God, 16 to be a minister of Christ Jesus to the Gentiles, ministering as a priest the gospel of God, so that *my* offering of the Gentiles may become acceptable, sanctified by the Holy Spirit. 17 Therefore in Christ Jesus I have found reason for boasting in things pertaining to God. 18 For I will not presume to speak of anything except what Christ has accomplished through me, resulting in the obedience of the Gentiles by word and deed, 19 in the power of signs and wonders, in the power of the Spirit; so that from

Jerusalem and all around as far as Illyricum I have fully
preached the gospel of Christ. 20 And in this way I
aspired to preach the gospel, not where Christ was
already known by name, so that I would not build on
another person's foundation; 21 but just as it is written:

"THEY WHO HAVE NOT BEEN TOLD ABOUT HIM WILL SEE,
AND THEY WHO HAVE NOT HEARD WILL UNDERSTAND."

22 For this reason I have often been prevented from
coming to you; 23 but now, with no further place for me
in these regions, and since I have had for many years a
longing to come to you 24 whenever I go to Spain—for I
hope to see you in passing, and to be helped on my way
there by you, when I have first enjoyed your company for
a while— 25 but now, I am going to Jerusalem, serving
the saints. 26 For Macedonia and Achaia have been
pleased to make a contribution for the poor among the
saints in Jerusalem. 27 For they were pleased *to do so,*
and they are indebted to them. For if the Gentiles have
shared in their spiritual things, they are indebted to do
them a service also in material things. 28 Therefore, when
I have finished this, and have put my seal on this fruit of
theirs, I will go on by way of you to Spain. 29 I know that
when I come to you, I will come in the fullness of the
blessing of Christ.

30 Now I urge you, brothers *and sisters,* by our Lord
Jesus Christ and by the love of the Spirit, to strive
together with me in your prayers to God for me, 31 that I
may be rescued from those who are disobedient in Judea,
and *that* my service for Jerusalem may prove acceptable
to the saints; 32 so that I may come to you in joy by the
will of God and relax in your company. 33 Now the God of
peace *be* with you all. Amen.

Greetings and Love Expressed

16 I recommend to you our sister Phoebe, who is a
servant of the church which is at Cenchrea, 2 that
you receive her in the Lord in a manner worthy of the
saints, and that you help her in whatever matter she may
have need of you; for she herself has also been a helper
of many, and of myself as well.

3 Greet Prisca and Aquila, my fellow workers in Christ
Jesus, 4 who risked their own necks for my life, to whom
not only do I give thanks, but also all the churches of the
Gentiles; 5 also *greet* the church that is in their house.

Greet Epaenetus, my beloved, who is the first convert to Christ from Asia. 6 Greet Mary, who has worked hard for you. 7 Greet Andronicus and Junia, my kinsfolk and my fellow prisoners, who are outstanding in the view of the apostles, who also were in Christ before me. 8 Greet Ampliatus, my beloved in the Lord. 9 Greet Urbanus, our fellow worker in Christ, and Stachys my beloved. 10 Greet Apelles, the approved in Christ. Greet those who are of the *household* of Aristobulus. 11 Greet Herodion, my kinsman. Greet those of the *household* of Narcissus, who are in the Lord. 12 Greet Tryphaena and Tryphosa, workers in the Lord. Greet Persis the beloved, who has worked hard in the Lord. 13 Greet Rufus, a choice man in the Lord, also his mother and mine. 14 Greet Asyncritus, Phlegon, Hermes, Patrobas, Hermas, and the brothers *and sisters* with them. 15 Greet Philologus and Julia, Nereus and his sister, and Olympas, and all the saints who are with them. 16 Greet one another with a holy kiss. All the churches of Christ greet you.

17 Now I urge you, brothers *and sisters,* keep your eye on those who cause dissensions and hindrances contrary to the teaching which you learned, and turn away from them. 18 For such people are slaves, not of our Lord Christ but of their own appetites; and by their smooth and flattering speech they deceive the hearts of the unsuspecting. 19 For the report of your obedience has reached everyone; therefore I am rejoicing over you, but I want you to be wise in what is good, and innocent in what is evil. 20 The God of peace will soon crush Satan under your feet.

The grace of our Lord Jesus be with you.

21 Timothy, my fellow worker, greets you, and *so do* Lucius, Jason, and Sosipater, my kinsmen.

22 I, Tertius, who have written this letter, greet you in the Lord.

23 Gaius, host to me and to the whole church, greets you. Erastus, the city treasurer, greets you, and Quartus, the brother.[1]

25 Now to Him who is able to establish you according to my gospel and the preaching of Jesus Christ, according to the revelation of the mystery which has been kept

---

16:23 [1] Late mss add as v 24: *The grace of our Lord Jesus Christ be with you all. Amen.*

secret for long ages past, **26** but now has been disclosed, and through the Scriptures of the prophets, in accordance with the commandment of the eternal God, has been made known to all the nations, *leading* to obedience of faith; **27** to the only wise God, through Jesus Christ, be the glory forever. Amen.

The First Letter of Paul to the
CORINTHIANS

Appeal to Unity

1 Paul, called *as* an apostle of Jesus Christ by the will of God, and our brother Sosthenes,

2 To the church of God which is in Corinth, to those who have been sanctified in Christ Jesus, saints by calling, with all who in every place call on the name of our Lord Jesus Christ, their *Lord* and ours:

3 Grace to you and peace from God our Father and the Lord Jesus Christ.

4 I thank ¹my God always concerning you for the grace of God which was given you in Christ Jesus, **5** that in everything you were enriched in Him, in all speech and all knowledge, **6** just as the testimony concerning Christ was confirmed in you, **7** so that you are not lacking in any gift, as you eagerly await the revelation of our Lord Jesus Christ, **8** who will also confirm you to the end, blameless on the day of our Lord Jesus Christ. **9** God is faithful, through whom you were called into fellowship with His Son, Jesus Christ our Lord.

10 Now I urge you, brothers *and sisters,* by the name of our Lord Jesus Christ, that you all agree and that there be no divisions among you, but that you be made complete in the same mind and in the same judgment. **11** For I have been informed concerning you, my brothers *and sisters,* by Chloe's *people,* that there are quarrels among you. **12** Now I mean this, that each one of you is saying, "I am with Paul," or "I *am* with Apollos," or "I *am* with Cephas," or "I *am* with Christ." **13** Has Christ been divided? Paul was not crucified for you, was he? Or were you baptized in the name of Paul? **14** I am thankful that I baptized none of you except Crispus and Gaius, **15** so that no one would say you were baptized in my name! **16** But I did baptize the household of Stephanas also; beyond that, I do not know if I baptized anyone else. **17** For Christ did not send me to baptize, but to preach the gospel, not with cleverness of speech, so that the cross of Christ would not be made of no effect.

1:4 ¹ Two early mss do not contain *my*

The Wisdom of God

18 For the word of the cross is foolishness to those who are perishing, but to us who are being saved it is the power of God. **19** For it is written:

"I WILL DESTROY THE WISDOM OF THE WISE,
   AND THE UNDERSTANDING OF THOSE WHO HAVE UNDERSTAND-
      ING, I WILL CONFOUND."

20 Where is the wise person? Where is the scribe? Where is the debater of this age? Has God not made foolish the wisdom of the world? **21** For since in the wisdom of God the world through its wisdom did not *come to* know God, God was pleased through the foolishness of the message preached to save those who believe. **22** For indeed Jews ask for signs and Greeks search for wisdom; **23** but we preach Christ crucified, to Jews a stumbling block, and to Gentiles foolishness, **24** but to those who are the called, both Jews and Greeks, Christ the power of God and the wisdom of God. **25** For the foolishness of God is wiser than mankind, and the weakness of God is stronger than mankind.

26 For consider your calling, brothers *and sisters,* that there were not many wise according to the flesh, not many mighty, not many noble; **27** but God has chosen the foolish things of the world to shame the wise, and God has chosen the weak things of the world to shame the things which are strong, **28** and the insignificant things of the world and the despised God has chosen, the things that are not, so that He may nullify the things that are, **29** so that no human may boast before God. **30** But *it is* due to Him *that* you are in Christ Jesus, who became to us wisdom from God, and righteousness and sanctification, and redemption, **31** so that, just as it is written: "LET THE ONE WHO BOASTS, BOAST IN THE LORD."

Paul's Reliance upon the Spirit

2 And when I came to you, brothers *and sisters,* I did not come as *someone* superior in speaking ability or wisdom, as I proclaimed to you the ʹtestimony of God. **2** For I determined to know nothing among you except Jesus Christ, and Him crucified. **3** I also was with you in weakness and fear, and in great trembling, **4** and my message and my preaching were not in persuasive words

---

2:1 ¹One early ms *mystery*

of wisdom, but in demonstration of the Spirit and of power, [5] so that your faith would not rest on the wisdom of mankind, but on the power of God.

[6] Yet we do speak wisdom among those who are mature; a wisdom, however, not of this age nor of the rulers of this age, who are passing away; [7] but we speak God's wisdom in a mystery, the hidden *wisdom* which God predestined before the ages to our glory; [8] *the wisdom* which none of the rulers of this age has understood; for if they had understood it, they would not have crucified the Lord of glory; [9] but just as it is written:

"THINGS WHICH EYE HAS NOT SEEN AND EAR HAS NOT HEARD,

AND *WHICH* HAVE NOT ENTERED THE HUMAN HEART,

ALL THAT GOD HAS PREPARED FOR THOSE WHO LOVE HIM."

[10] [1]For to us God revealed *them* through the Spirit; for the Spirit searches all things, even the depths of God. [11] For who among people knows the *thoughts* of a person except the spirit of the person that is in him? So also the *thoughts* of God no one knows, except the Spirit of God. [12] Now we have not received the spirit of the world, but the Spirit who is from God, so that we may know the things freely given to us by God. [13] We also speak these things, not in words taught by human wisdom, but in those taught by the Spirit, combining spiritual *thoughts* with spiritual *words.*

[14] But a natural person does not accept the things of the Spirit of God, for they are foolishness to him; and he cannot understand them, because they are spiritually discerned. [15] But the one who is spiritual discerns all things, yet he himself is discerned by no one. [16] For WHO HAS KNOWN THE MIND OF THE LORD, THAT HE WILL INSTRUCT HIM? But we have the mind of Christ.

Foundations for Living

3 And I, brothers *and sisters,* could not speak to you as spiritual people, but *only* as fleshly, as to infants in Christ. [2] I gave you milk to drink, not solid food; for you were not yet able *to consume it.* But even now you are not yet able, [3] for you are still fleshly. For since there is jealousy and strife among you, are you not fleshly, and

---

2:10 [1] One early ms *But*

are you not walking like *ordinary* people? 4 For when one person says, "I am with Paul," and another, "I *am* with Apollos," are you not *ordinary* people?

5 What then is Apollos? And what is Paul? Servants through whom you believed, even as the Lord gave *opportunity* to each one. 6 I planted, Apollos watered, but God was causing the growth. 7 So then neither the one who plants nor the one who waters is anything, but God who causes the growth. 8 Now the one who plants and the one who waters are one; but each will receive his own reward according to his own labor. 9 For we are God's fellow workers; you are God's field, God's building.

10 According to the grace of God which was given to me, like a wise master builder I laid a foundation, and another is building on it. But each person must be careful how he builds on it. 11 For no one can lay a foundation other than the one which is laid, which is Jesus Christ. 12 Now if anyone builds on the foundation with gold, silver, precious stones, wood, hay, *or* straw, 13 each one's work will become evident; for the day will show it because it is *to be* revealed with fire, and the fire itself will test the quality of each one's work. 14 If anyone's work which he has built on it remains, he will receive a reward. 15 If anyone's work is burned up, he will suffer loss; but he himself will be saved, yet *only* so as through fire.

16 Do you not know that you are a temple of God and *that* the Spirit of God dwells in you? 17 If anyone destroys the temple of God, God will destroy that person; for the temple of God is holy, and that is what you are.

18 *Take care that* no one deceives himself. If anyone among you thinks that he is wise in this age, he must become foolish, so that he may become wise. 19 For the wisdom of this world is foolishness in the sight of God. For it is written: "*He is* THE ONE WHO CATCHES THE WISE BY THEIR CRAFTINESS"; 20 and again, "THE LORD KNOWS THE THOUGHTS of the wise, THAT THEY ARE useless." 21 So then, no one is to be boasting in people. For all things belong to you, 22 whether Paul or Apollos or Cephas, or the world or life or death, or things present or things to come; all things belong to you, 23 and you belong to Christ, and Christ belongs to God.

Servants of Christ

4 This is the way *any* person is to regard us: as servants of Christ and stewards of the mysteries of God. ² In this case, moreover, it is required of stewards that one be found trustworthy. ³ But to me it is an insignificant matter that I would be examined by you, or by *any* human court; in fact, I do not even examine myself. ⁴ For I am not aware of anything against myself; however I am not vindicated by this, but the one who examines me is the Lord. ⁵ Therefore do not go on passing judgment before ¹*the* time, *but wait* until the Lord comes, who will both bring to light the things hidden in the darkness and disclose the motives of *human* hearts; and then praise will come to each person from God.

⁶ Now these things, brothers *and sisters,* I have figuratively applied to myself and Apollos on your account, so that in us you may learn not to exceed what is written, so that no one of you will become arrogant in behalf of one against the other. ⁷ For who considers you as superior? What do you have that you did not receive? And if you did receive it, why do you boast as if you had not received it?

⁸ You are already filled, you have already become rich, you have become kings without us; and indeed, *I* wish that you had become kings so that we also might reign with you! ⁹ For I think, God has exhibited us, the apostles, last of all as men condemned to death, because we have become a spectacle to the world, both to angels and to mankind. ¹⁰ We are fools on account of Christ, but you are prudent in Christ! We are weak, but you are strong! You are distinguished, but we are without honor! ¹¹ Up to this present hour we are both hungry and thirsty, and are poorly clothed and roughly treated and homeless; ¹² and we labor, working with our own hands; when we are verbally abused, we bless; when we are persecuted, we endure *it;* ¹³ when we are slandered, we reply as friends; we have become as the scum of the world, the dregs of all things, *even* until now.

¹⁴ I do not write these things to shame you, but to admonish you as my beloved children. ¹⁵ For if you were to have countless tutors in Christ, yet *you would* not *have* many fathers, for in Christ Jesus I became your

---

4:5 ¹I.e., the appointed time of judgment

father through the gospel. [16] Therefore I urge you, be imitators of me. [17] For this reason I have sent to you Timothy, who is my beloved and faithful child in the Lord, and he will remind you of my ways which are in Christ, just as I teach everywhere in every church. [18] Now some have become arrogant, as though I were not coming to you. [19] But I will come to you soon, if the Lord wills, and I shall find out, not the words of those who are arrogant, but their power. [20] For the kingdom of God is not in words, but in power. [21] What do you desire? That I come to you with a rod, or with love and a spirit of gentleness?

Sexual Immorality Rebuked

5 It is actually reported that there is sexual immorality among you, and sexual immorality of such a kind as does not exist even among the Gentiles, *namely,* that someone has his father's wife. [2] You have become arrogant and have not mourned instead, so that the one who had done this deed would be removed from your midst.

[3] For I, on my part, though absent in body but present in spirit, have already judged him who has so committed this, as though I were present. [4] In the name of our Lord Jesus, when you are assembled, and I with you in spirit, with the power of our Lord Jesus, [5] *I have decided* to turn such a person over to Satan for the destruction of his body, so that his spirit may be saved on the day of the [1]Lord.

[6] Your boasting is not good. Do you not know that a little leaven leavens the whole lump *of dough?* [7] Clean out the old leaven so that you may be a new lump, just as you are *in fact* unleavened. For Christ our Passover also has been sacrificed. [8] Therefore let's celebrate the feast, not with old leaven, nor with the leaven of malice and wickedness, but with the unleavened bread of sincerity and truth.

[9] I wrote to you in my letter not to associate with sexually immoral people; [10] I *did* not at all *mean* with the sexually immoral people of this world, or with the greedy and swindlers, or with idolaters, for then you would have to leave the world. [11] But actually, I wrote to

---

5:5 [1] One early ms *Lord Jesus*

you not to associate with any so-called brother if he is a sexually immoral person, or a greedy person, or an idolater, or is verbally abusive, or habitually drunk, or a swindler—not even to eat with such a person. **12** For what *business* of mine *is it* to judge outsiders? Do you not judge those who are within *the church?* **13** But those who are outside, God judges. REMOVE THE EVIL PERSON FROM AMONG YOURSELVES.

Lawsuits Discouraged

6 Does any one of you, when he has a case against his neighbor, dare to go to law before the unrighteous and not before the saints? **2** Or do you not know that the saints will judge the world? If the world is judged by you, are you not competent *to form* the smallest law courts? **3** Do you not know that we will judge angels? How much more matters of this life? **4** So if you have law courts dealing with matters of this life, do you appoint them *as judges* who are of no account in the church? **5** I say *this* to your shame. *Is it* so, *that* there is not among you anyone wise who will be able to decide between his brothers *and sisters,* **6** but brother goes to law with brother, and that before unbelievers?

7 Actually, then, it is already a defeat for you, that you have lawsuits with one another. Why not rather suffer the wrong? Why not rather be defrauded? **8** On the contrary, you yourselves do wrong and defraud. And this to *your* brothers *and sisters!*

9 Or do you not know that the unrighteous will not inherit the kingdom of God? Do not be deceived; neither the sexually immoral, nor idolaters, nor adulterers, nor ¹homosexuals, **10** nor thieves, nor *the* greedy, nor those habitually drunk, nor verbal abusers, nor swindlers, will inherit the kingdom of God. **11** Such were some of you; but you were washed, but you were sanctified, but you were justified in the name of the Lord Jesus Christ and in the Spirit of our God.

The Body Is the Lord's

12 All things are permitted for me, but not all things are of benefit. All things are permitted for me, but I will

---

6:9 ¹ Two Gr words in the text, prob. submissive and dominant male homosexuals

not be mastered by anything. **13** Food is for the stomach and the stomach is for food, however God will do away with both of them. But the body is not for sexual immorality, but for the Lord, and the Lord is for the body. **14** Now God has not only raised the Lord, but will also raise us up through His power. **15** Do you not know that your bodies are parts of Christ? Shall I then take away the parts of Christ and make them parts of a prostitute? *1* Far from it! **16** Or do you not know that the one who joins himself to a prostitute is one body *with her?* For He says, "THE TWO SHALL BECOME ONE FLESH." **17** But the one who joins himself to the Lord is one spirit *with Him.* **18** Flee sexual immorality. Every other sin that a person commits is outside the body, but the sexually immoral person sins against his own body. **19** Or do you not know that your body is a temple of the Holy Spirit within you, whom you have from God, and *that* you are not your own? **20** For you have been bought for a price: therefore glorify God in your body.

Teaching on Marriage

7 Now concerning the things about which you wrote, it is good for a man *1* not to touch a woman. **2** But because of sexual immoralities, each man is to have his own wife, and each woman is to have her own husband. **3** The husband must fulfill his duty to his wife, and likewise the wife also to her husband. **4** The wife does not have authority over her own body, but the husband *does;* and likewise the husband also does not have authority over his own body, but the wife *does.* **5** Stop depriving one another, except by agreement for a time so that you may devote yourselves to prayer, and come together again so that Satan will not tempt you because of your lack of self-control. **6** But this I say by way of concession, not of command. **7** *1* Yet I wish that all men were even as I myself am. However, each has his own gift from God, one in this way, and another in that.

8 But I say to the unmarried and to widows that it is good for them if they remain even as I. **9** But if they do not have self-control, let them marry; for it is better to marry than to burn *with passion.*

6:15 *1* Lit *May it never happen!*   7:1 *1* Prob. referring to abstinence
7:7 *1* One early ms *For*

10 But to the married I give instructions, not I, but the Lord, that the wife is not to leave her husband **11** (but if she does leave, she must remain unmarried, or else be reconciled to her husband), and that the husband is not to divorce his wife.

12 But to the rest I say, not the Lord, that if any brother has an unbelieving wife, and she consents to live with him, he must not divorce her. **13** And if any woman has an unbelieving husband, and he consents to live with her, she must not divorce her husband. **14** For the unbelieving husband is sanctified through his wife, and the unbelieving wife is sanctified through her believing husband; for otherwise your children are unclean, but now they are holy. **15** Yet if the unbelieving one is leaving, let him leave; the brother or the sister is not under bondage in such *cases,* but God has called 'us in peace. **16** For how do you know, wife, whether you will save your husband? Or how do you know, husband, whether you will save your wife?

17 Only, as the Lord has assigned to each one, as God has called each, in this way let him walk. And so I direct in all the churches. **18** Was any man called *when he was already* circumcised? He is not to become uncircumcised. Has anyone been called in uncircumcision? He is not to be circumcised. **19** Circumcision is nothing, and uncircumcision is nothing, but *what matters is* the keeping of the commandments of God. **20** Each *person* is to remain in that state in which he was called.

21 Were you called as a slave? Do not let it concern you. But if you are also able to become free, take advantage of *that.* **22** For the one who was called in the Lord as a slave, is the Lord's freed person; likewise the one who was called as free, is Christ's slave. **23** You were bought for a price; do not become slaves of people. **24** Brothers *and sisters,* each one is to remain with God in that *condition* in which he was called.

25 Now concerning virgins, I have no command of the Lord, but I am offering direction as one who by the mercy of the Lord is trustworthy. **26** I think, then, that this is good in view of the present distress, that it is good for a man to remain as he is. **27** Are you bound to a

---

7:15 ¹One early ms *you*

wife? Do not seek to be released. Are you released from a wife? Do not seek a wife. **28** But if you marry, you have not sinned; and if a virgin marries, she has not sinned. Yet such people *as yourselves* will have trouble in this life, and I *am trying to* spare you. **29** But this I say, brothers, the time has been shortened, so that from now on those who have wives should be as though they had none; **30** and those who weep, as though they did not weep; and those who rejoice, as though they did not rejoice; and those who buy, as though they did not possess; **31** and those who use the world, as though they did not make full use of it; for the *present* form of this world is passing away.

32 But I want you to be free from concern. One who is unmarried is concerned about the things of the Lord, how he may please the Lord; **33** but one who is married is concerned about the things of the world, how he may please his wife, **34** and *his interests* are divided. The woman who is unmarried, and the virgin, is concerned about the things of the Lord, that she may be holy both in body and spirit; but one who is married is concerned about the things of the world, how she may please her husband. **35** I say this for your own benefit, not to put a restraint on you, but to promote what is appropriate and *to secure* undistracted devotion to the Lord.

36 But if anyone thinks that he is acting dishonorably toward his virgin, if she is ¹past her youth and it ought to be so, let him do what he wishes, he is not sinning; let ²them marry. **37** But the one who stands firm in his heart, if he is not under constraint, but has authority over his own will, and has decided this in his own heart, to keep his own virgin, he will do well. **38** So then, both the one who gives his own virgin in marriage does well, and the one who does not give *her* in marriage will do better.

39 A wife is bound as long as her husband lives; but if her husband dies, she is free to be married to whom she wishes, only in the Lord. **40** But in my opinion she is happier if she remains as she is; and I think that I also have the Spirit of God.

7:36 ¹ Or *past puberty*   7:36 ² I.e., the woman and her betrothed or fiancé

Take Care with Your Liberty

8 Now concerning food sacrificed to idols, we know that we all have knowledge. Knowledge makes *one* conceited, but love edifies *people*. **2** If anyone thinks that he knows anything, he has not yet known as he ought to know; **3** but if anyone loves God, he is known by Him.

4 Therefore, concerning the eating of food sacrificed to idols, we know that an idol is *nothing at all in the world, and that there is no God but one. **5** For even if there are so-called gods whether in heaven or on earth, as indeed there are many gods and many lords, **6** yet for us there is *only* one God, the Father, from whom are all things, and we *exist* for Him; and one Lord, Jesus Christ, by whom are all things, and we *exist* through Him.

7 However, not all people have this knowledge; but some, being accustomed to the idol until now, eat *food* as if it were sacrificed to an idol; and their conscience, being weak, is defiled. **8** Now food will not bring us close to God; we are neither the worse if we do not eat, nor the better if we do eat. **9** But take care that this freedom of yours does not somehow become a stumbling block to the weak. **10** For if someone sees you, the one who has knowledge, dining in an idol's temple, will his conscience, if he is weak, not be strengthened to eat things sacrificed to idols? **11** For through your knowledge the one who is weak is ruined, the brother *or sister* for whose sake Christ died. **12** And so, by sinning against the brothers *and sisters* and wounding their conscience when it is weak, you sin against Christ. **13** Therefore, if food causes my brother to sin, I will never eat meat again, so that I will not cause my brother to sin.

Paul's Use of Freedom

9 Am I not free? Am I not an apostle? Have I not seen Jesus our Lord? Are you not my work in the Lord? **2** If I am not an apostle to others, at least I am to you; for you are the seal of my apostleship in the Lord.

3 My defense to those who examine me is this: **4** Do we not have a right to eat and drink? **5** Do we not have a right to take along a believing wife, even as the rest of the apostles and the brothers of the Lord, and Cephas? **6** Or do only Barnabas and I have no right to refrain from

---

8:4 [1] I.e., what it represents does not exist

working? **7** Who at any time serves as a soldier at his own expense? Who plants a vineyard and does not eat its fruit? Or who tends a flock and does not consume some of the milk of the flock?

8 I am not *just* asserting these things according to human judgment, am I? Or does the Law not say these things as well? **9** For it is written in the Law of Moses: "YOU SHALL NOT MUZZLE THE OX WHILE IT IS THRESHING." God is not concerned about oxen, is He? **10** Or is He speaking entirely for our sake? Yes, it was written for our sake, because the plowman ought to plow in hope, and the thresher *to thresh* in hope of sharing *in the crops.* **11** If we sowed spiritual things in you, is it too much if we reap material things from you? **12** If others share the right over you, do we not more? Nevertheless, we did not use this right, but we endure all things so that we will cause no hindrance to the gospel of Christ. **13** Do you not know that those who perform sacred services eat *the food* of the temple, *and* those who attend regularly to the altar have their share from the altar? **14** So also the Lord directed those who proclaim the gospel to get their living from the gospel.

15 But I have used none of these things. And I have not written these things so that it will be done so in my case; for it would be better for me to die than *that.* No one shall make my boast an empty one! **16** For if I preach the gospel, I have nothing to boast *about,* for I am under compulsion; for woe to me if I do not preach the gospel. **17** For if I do this voluntarily, I have a reward; but if against my will, I have been entrusted with a commission *nonetheless.* **18** What, then, is my reward? That, when I preach the gospel, I may offer the gospel without charge, so as not to make full use of my right in the gospel.

19 For though I am free from all people, I have made myself a slave to all, so that I may gain more. **20** To the Jews I became as a Jew, so that I might gain Jews; to those who are under the Law, *I became* as *one* under the Law, though not being under the Law myself, so that I might gain those who are under the Law; **21** to those who are without the Law, *I became* as one without the Law, though not being without the law of God but under the law of Christ, so that I might gain those who are without the Law. **22** To the weak I became weak, that I might gain the weak; I have become all things to all people, so that I may by all means save some. 23 I do all things for the sake of the gospel, so that I may become a fellow partaker of it.

24 Do you not know that those who run in a race all run, but *only* one receives the prize? Run in such a way that you may win. 25 Everyone who competes in the games exercises self-control in all things. So they *do it* to obtain a perishable wreath, but we an imperishable. 26 Therefore I run in such a way as not *to run* aimlessly; I box in such a way, as to avoid hitting air; 27 but I strictly discipline my body and make it my slave, so that, after I have preached to others, I myself will not be disqualified.

Avoid Israel's Mistakes

10 For I do not want you to be unaware, brothers *and sisters,* that our fathers were all under the cloud and they all passed through the sea; 2 and they all were baptized into Moses in the cloud and in the sea; 3 and they all ate the same spiritual food, 4 and all drank the same spiritual drink, for they were drinking from a spiritual rock which followed them; and the rock was Christ. 5 Nevertheless, with most of them God was not pleased; for *their dead bodies* were spread out in the wilderness.

6 Now these things happened as examples for us, so that we would not crave evil things as they indeed craved *them.* 7 Do not be idolaters, as some of them were; as it is written: "THE PEOPLE SAT DOWN TO EAT AND TO DRINK, AND ROSE UP TO PLAY." 8 Nor are we to commit sexual immorality, as some of them did, and twenty-three thousand fell in one day. 9 Nor are we to put the Lord to the test, as some of them did, and were killed by the snakes. 10 Nor grumble, as some of them did, and were killed by the destroyer. 11 Now these things happened to them as an example, and they were written for our instruction, upon whom the ends of the ages have come. 12 Therefore let the one who thinks he stands watch out that he does not fall. 13 No temptation has overtaken you except *something* common to mankind; and God is faithful, so He will not allow you to be tempted beyond what you are able, but with the temptation will provide the way of escape also, so that you will be able to endure it.

14 Therefore, my beloved, flee from idolatry. **15** I speak as to wise people; you *then,* judge what I say. **16** Is the cup of blessing which we bless not a sharing in the blood of Christ? Is the bread which we break not a sharing in the body of Christ? **17** Since there is one loaf, we who are many are one body; for we all partake of the one loaf. **18** Look at the people of Israel; are those who eat the sacrifices not partners in the altar? **19** What do I mean then? That food sacrificed to idols is anything, or that an idol is anything? **20** *No,* but *I say* that things which *the Gentiles* sacrifice, they sacrifice to demons and not to God; and I do not want you to become partners with demons. **21** You cannot drink the cup of the Lord and the cup of demons; you cannot partake of the table of the Lord and the table of demons. **22** Or do we provoke the Lord to jealousy? We are not stronger than He, are we?

23 All things are permitted, but not all things are of benefit. All things are permitted, but not all things build *people* up. **24** No one is to seek his own *advantage,* but rather that of his neighbor. **25** Eat anything that is sold in the meat market without asking questions, for the sake of conscience; **26** FOR THE EARTH IS THE LORD'S, AND ALL IT CONTAINS. **27** If one of the unbelievers invites you and you want to go, eat anything that is set before you without asking questions, for the sake of conscience. **28** But if anyone says to you, "This is meat sacrificed to idols," do not eat *it,* for the sake of that one who informed *you* and for the sake of conscience; **29** Now *by* "conscience" I do not mean your own, but the other person's; for why is my freedom judged by another's conscience? **30** If I partake with thankfulness, why am I slandered about that for which I give thanks?

31 Therefore, whether you eat or drink, or whatever you do, do all things for the glory of God. **32** Do not offend Jews or Greeks, or the church of God; **33** just as I also please everyone in all things, not seeking my own benefit but the *benefit* of the many, so that they may be saved.

Christian Order

11 Be imitators of me, just as I also am of Christ. **2** Now I praise you because you remember me in everything and hold firmly to the traditions, just as I handed them down to you. **3** But I want you to understand that Christ is the head of every man, and the man is the head of a woman, and God is the head of Christ. **4** Every man who has *something* on his head while praying or prophesying disgraces his head. **5** But every woman who has her head uncovered while praying or prophesying disgraces her head, for it is one and the same as the woman whose head is shaved. **6** For if a woman does not cover her head, have her also cut her hair off; however, if it is disgraceful for a woman to have her hair cut off or her head shaved, have her cover her head. **7** For a man should not have his head covered, since he is the image and glory of God; but the woman is the glory of man. **8** For man does not originate from woman, but woman from man; **9** for indeed man was not created for the woman's sake, but woman for the man's sake. **10** Therefore the woman should have *a symbol of* authority on her head, because of the angels. **11** However, in the Lord, neither is woman independent of man, nor is man independent of woman. **12** For as the woman *originated* from the man, so also the man *has his birth* through the woman; and all things *originate* from God. **13** Judge for yourselves: is it proper for a woman to pray to God *with her head* uncovered? **14** Does even nature itself not teach you that if a man has long hair, it is a dishonor to him, **15** but if a woman has long hair, it is a glory to her? For her hair is given to her as a covering. **16** But if anyone is inclined to be contentious, we have no such practice, nor have the churches of God.

17 Now in giving this *next* instruction I do not praise you, because you come together not for the better, but for the worse. **18** For, in the first place, when you come together as a church, I hear that divisions exist among you; and in part I believe it. **19** For there also have to be factions among you, so that those who are approved may become evident among you. **20** Therefore when you come together it is not to eat the Lord's Supper, **21** for when you eat, each one takes his own supper first; and one goes hungry while another gets drunk. **22** What! Do you not have houses in which to eat and drink? Or do you despise the church of God and shame those who have nothing? What am I to say to you? Shall I praise you? In this I do not praise you.

The Lord's Supper

23 For I received from the Lord that which I also delivered to you, that the Lord Jesus, on the night when He was betrayed, took bread; **24** and when He had given thanks, He broke it and said, "This is My body, which is for you; do this in remembrance of Me." **25** In the same way *He* also *took* the cup after supper, saying, "This cup is the new covenant in My blood; do this, as often as you drink *it,* in remembrance of Me." **26** For as often as you eat this bread and drink the cup, you proclaim the Lord's death until He comes.

27 Therefore whoever eats the bread or drinks the cup of the Lord in an unworthy way, shall be guilty of the body and the blood of the Lord. **28** But a person must examine himself, and in so doing he is to eat of the bread and drink of the cup. **29** For the one who eats and drinks, eats and drinks judgment to himself if he does not *properly* recognize the body. **30** For this reason many among you are weak and sick, and a number are asleep. **31** But if we judged ourselves rightly, we would not be judged. **32** But when we are judged, we are disciplined by the Lord so that we will not be condemned along with the world.

33 So then, my brothers *and sisters,* when you come together to eat, wait for one another. **34** If anyone is hungry, have him eat at home, so that you do not come together for judgment. As to the remaining matters, I will give instructions when I come.

The Use of Spiritual Gifts

12 Now concerning spiritual *gifts,* brothers *and sisters,* I do not want you to be unaware. **2** You know that when you were pagans, *you were* led astray to the mute idols, however you were led. **3** Therefore I make known to you that no one speaking by the Spirit of God says, "Jesus is accursed"; and no one can say, "Jesus is Lord," except by the Holy Spirit.

4 Now there are varieties of gifts, but the same Spirit. **5** And there are varieties of ministries, and the same Lord. **6** There are varieties of effects, but the same God who works all things in all *persons.* **7** But to each one is given the manifestation of the Spirit for the common good. **8** For to one is given the word of wisdom through the Spirit, and to another the word of knowledge according to the same Spirit; **9** to another faith by the same Spirit, and to another gifts of healing by the one Spirit, **10** and to another the effecting of miracles, and to another prophecy, and to another the distinguishing of spirits, to another *various* kinds of tongues, and to another the interpretation of tongues. **11** But one and the same Spirit works all these things, distributing to each one individually just as He wills.

12 For just as the body is one and *yet* has many parts, and all the parts of the body, though they are many, are one body, so also is Christ. **13** For by one Spirit we were all baptized into one body, whether Jews or Greeks, whether slaves or free, and we were all made to drink of one Spirit.

14 For the body is not one part, but many. **15** If the foot says, "Because I am not a hand, I am not *a part* of the body," it is not for this reason any less *a part* of the body. **16** And if the ear says, "Because I am not an eye, I am not *a part* of the body," it is not for this reason any less *a part* of the body. **17** If the whole body were an eye, where would the hearing be? If the whole *body* were hearing, where would the sense of smell be? **18** But now God has arranged the parts, each one of them in the body, just as He desired. **19** If they were all one part, where would the body be? **20** But now there are many parts, but one body. **21** And the eye cannot say to the hand, "I have no need of you"; or again, the head to the feet, "I have no need of you." **22** On the contrary, it is much truer that the parts of the body which seem to be weaker are necessary; **23** and those *parts* of the body which we consider less honorable, on these we bestow greater honor, and our less presentable parts become much more presentable, **24** whereas our more presentable parts have no need *of it.* But God has *so* composed the body, giving more abundant honor to that *part* which lacked, **25** so that there may be no division in the body, but *that* the parts may have the same care for one another. **26** And if one part *of the body* suffers, all the parts suffer with it; if a part is honored, all the parts rejoice with it.

27 Now you are Christ's body, and individually parts of it. **28** And God has appointed in the church, first apostles, second prophets, third teachers, then miracles, then gifts of healings, helps, administrations, *and various* kinds of tongues. **29** All are not apostles, are they? All are not prophets, are they? All are not teachers, are they? All are not *workers of* miracles, are they? **30** All do not have gifts of healings, do they? All do not speak with tongues, do they? All do not interpret, do they? **31** But earnestly desire the greater gifts.

And yet, I *am going to* show you a far better way.

The Excellence of Love

13 If I speak with the tongues of mankind and of angels, but do not have love, I have become a noisy gong or a clanging cymbal. **2** If I have *the gift of* prophecy and know all mysteries and all knowledge, and if I have all faith so as to remove mountains, but do not have love, I am nothing. **3** And if I give away all my possessions *to charity,* and if I surrender my body so that I may *glory,* but do not have love, it does me no good.

4 Love is patient, love is kind, it is not jealous; love does not brag, it is not arrogant. **5** It does not act disgracefully, it does not seek its own *benefit;* it is not provoked, does not keep an account of a wrong *suffered,* **6** it does not rejoice in unrighteousness, but rejoices with the truth; **7** it keeps every confidence, it believes all things, hopes all things, endures all things.

8 Love never fails; but if *there are gifts of* prophecy, they will be done away with; if *there are* tongues, they will cease; if *there is* knowledge, it will be done away with. **9** For we know in part and prophesy in part; **10** but when the perfect comes, the partial will be done away with. **11** When I was a child, I used to speak like a child, think like a child, reason like a child; when I became a man, I did away with childish things. **12** For now we see in a mirror dimly, but then face to face; now I know in part, but then I will know fully, just as I also have been fully known. **13** But now faith, hope, *and* love remain, these three; but the greatest of these is love.

Prophecy a Superior Gift

14 Pursue love, yet earnestly desire spiritual *gifts,* but especially that you may prophesy. **2** For the one who speaks in a tongue does not speak to people, but to God; for no one understands, but in *his* spirit he speaks mysteries. **3** But the one who prophesies speaks to people

---

13:3 ¹ I.e., in martyrdom

for edification, exhortation, and consolation. **4** The one who speaks in a tongue edifies himself; but the one who prophesies edifies the church. **5** Now I wish that you all spoke in tongues, but rather that you would prophesy; and greater is the one who prophesies than the one who speaks in tongues, unless he interprets, so that the church may receive edification.

6 But now, brothers *and sisters,* if I come to you speaking in tongues, how will I benefit you unless I speak to you either by way of revelation, or of knowledge, or of prophecy, or of teaching? **7** Yet *even* lifeless *instruments,* whether flute or harp, in producing a sound, if they do not produce a distinction in the tones, how will it be known what is played on the flute or on the harp? **8** For if the trumpet produces an indistinct sound, who will prepare himself for battle? **9** So you too, unless you produce intelligible speech by the tongue, how will it be known what is spoken? For you will *just* be talking to the air. **10** There are, perhaps, a great many kinds of languages in the world, and none is incapable of meaning. **11** So if I do not know the meaning of the language, I will be unintelligible to the one who speaks, and the one who speaks will be unintelligible to me. **12** So you too, since you are eager to possess spiritual *gifts,* strive to excel for the edification of the church.

13 Therefore, one who speaks in a tongue is to pray that he may interpret. **14** For if I pray in a tongue, my spirit prays, but my mind is unproductive. **15** What is *the outcome* then? I will pray with the spirit, but I will pray with the mind also; I will sing with the spirit, but I will sing with the mind also. **16** For otherwise, if you bless *God* in the spirit *only,* how will the one who occupies the place of the outsider *know to* say the "Amen" at your giving of thanks, since he does not understand what you are saying? **17** For you are giving thanks well *enough,* but the other person is not edified. **18** I thank God, I speak in tongues more than you all; **19** nevertheless, in church I prefer to speak five words with my mind so that I may instruct others also, rather than ten thousand words in a tongue.

Instruction for the Church

20 Brothers *and sisters,* do not be children in your thinking; yet in evil be infants, but in your thinking be mature. **21** In the Law it is written: "BY MEN OF STRANGE TONGUES AND BY THE LIPS OF STRANGERS I WILL SPEAK TO THIS PEOPLE, AND EVEN SO THEY WILL NOT LISTEN TO ME," says the Lord. **22** So then, tongues are for a sign, not to those who believe but to unbelievers; but prophecy is not for unbelievers, but for those who believe. **23** Therefore if the whole church gathers together and all *the people* speak in tongues, and outsiders or unbelievers enter, will they not say that you are insane? **24** But if all prophesy, and an unbeliever or an outsider enters, he is convicted by all, he is called to account by all; **25** the secrets of his heart are disclosed; and so he will fall on his face and worship God, declaring that God is certainly among you.

26 What is *the outcome* then, brothers *and sisters?* When you assemble, each one has a psalm, has a teaching, has a revelation, has a tongue, has an interpretation. All things are to be done for edification. **27** If anyone speaks in a tongue, *it must be* by two or at the most three, and *each one* in turn, and one is to interpret; **28** but if there is no interpreter, he is to keep silent in church; and have him speak to himself and to God. **29** Have two or three prophets speak, and have the others pass judgment. **30** But if a revelation is made to another who is seated, then the first one is to keep silent. **31** For you can all prophesy one by one, so that all may learn and all may be exhorted; **32** and the spirits of prophets are subject to prophets; **33** for God is not *a God* of confusion, but of peace.

As in all the churches of the saints, **34** the women are to keep silent in the churches; for they are not permitted to speak, but are to subject themselves, just as the Law also says. **35** If they desire to learn anything, let them ask their own husbands at home; for it is improper for a woman to speak in church. **36** Or was it from you that the word of God *first* went out? Or has it come to you only?

37 If anyone thinks that he is a prophet or spiritual, let him recognize that the things which I write to you are the Lord's commandment. **38** But if anyone does not recognize *this,* [1]he is not recognized.

39 Therefore, my brothers *and sisters,* earnestly desire to prophesy, and do not forbid speaking in tongues. **40** But all things must be done properly and in an orderly way.

14:38 [1] Two early mss *let him continue not to recognize* it

The Fact of Christ's Resurrection

15 Now I make known to you, brothers *and sisters,* the gospel which I preached to you, which you also received, in which you also stand, **2** by which you also are saved, if you hold firmly to the word which I preached to you, unless you believed in vain.

3 For I handed down to you as of first importance what I also received, that Christ died for our sins according to the Scriptures, **4** and that He was buried, and that He was raised on the third day according to the Scriptures, **5** and that He appeared to Cephas, then to the twelve. **6** After that He appeared to more than five hundred brothers *and sisters* at one time, most of whom remain until now, but some have fallen asleep; **7** then He appeared to James, then to all the apostles; **8** and last of all, as to one untimely born, He appeared to me also. **9** For I am the least of the apostles, and not fit to be called an apostle, because I persecuted the church of God. **10** But by the grace of God I am what I am, and His grace toward me did not prove vain; but I labored even more than all of them, yet not I, but the grace of God with me. **11** Whether then *it was* I or they, so we preach and so you believed.

12 Now if Christ is preached, that He has been raised from the dead, how do some among you say that there is no resurrection of the dead? **13** But if there is no resurrection of the dead, then not even Christ has been raised; **14** and if Christ has not been raised, then our preaching is in vain, your faith also is in vain. **15** Moreover, we are even found *to be* false witnesses of God, because we testified against God that He raised 'Christ, whom He did not raise, if in fact the dead are not raised. **16** For if the dead are not raised, then not even Christ has been raised; **17** and if Christ has not been raised, your faith is worthless; you are still in your sins. **18** Then also those who have fallen asleep in Christ have perished. **19** If we have hoped in Christ only in this life, we are of all people most to be pitied.

The Order of Resurrection

20 But the fact is, Christ has been raised from the dead, the first fruits of those who are asleep. **21** For since by a

---

15:15 ¹I.e., the Messiah

man death *came,* by a man also *came* the resurrection of the dead. 22 For as in Adam all die, so also in Christ all will be made alive. 23 But each in his own order: Christ the first fruits, after that those who are Christ's at His coming, 24 then *comes* the end, when He hands over the kingdom to *our* God and Father, when He has abolished all rule and all authority and power. 25 For He must reign until He has put all His enemies under His feet. 26 The last enemy that will be abolished is death. 27 For HE HAS PUT ALL THINGS IN SUBJECTION UNDER HIS FEET. But when He says, "All things are put in subjection," it is clear that this excludes the *Father* who put all things in subjection to Him. 28 When all things are subjected to Him, then the Son Himself will also be subjected to the One who subjected all things to Him, so that God may be all in all.

29 For otherwise, what will those do who are baptized for the dead? If the dead are not raised at all, why then are they baptized for them? 30 Why are we also in danger every hour? 31 I affirm, brothers *and sisters,* by the boasting in you which I have in Christ Jesus our Lord, that I die daily. 32 If from human motives I fought with wild beasts at Ephesus, what good is it to me? If the dead are not raised, LET'S EAT AND DRINK, FOR TOMORROW WE DIE. 33 Do not be deceived: "Bad company corrupts good morals." 34 Sober up morally and stop sinning, for some have no knowledge of God. I say *this* to your shame.

35 But someone will say, "How are the dead raised? And with what kind of body do they come?" 36 You fool! That which you sow does not come to life unless it dies; 37 and that which you sow, you do not sow the body which is to be, but a bare grain, perhaps of wheat or of something else. 38 But God gives it a body just as He wished, and to each of the seeds a body of its own. 39 All flesh is not the same flesh, but there is one *flesh* of mankind, another flesh of animals, another flesh of birds, and another of fish. 40 There are also heavenly bodies and earthly bodies, but the glory of the heavenly is one, and the *glory* of the earthly is another. 41 There is one glory of the sun, another glory of the moon, and another glory of the stars; for star differs from star in glory.

42 So also is the resurrection of the dead. It is sown a perishable *body,* it is raised an imperishable *body;* 43 it is sown in dishonor, it is raised in glory; it is sown in weakness, it is raised in power; 44 it is sown a natural body, it

is raised a spiritual body. If there is a natural body, there is also a spiritual *body*. [45] So also it is written: "The first MAN, Adam, BECAME A LIVING PERSON." The last Adam *was* a life-giving spirit. [46] However, the spiritual is not first, but the natural; then the spiritual. [47] The first man is from the earth, earthy; the second man is from heaven. [48] As is the earthy one, so also are those who are earthy; and as is the heavenly one, so also are those who are heavenly. [49] Just as we have borne the image of the earthy, 'we will also bear the image of the heavenly.

The Mystery of Resurrection

[50] Now I say this, brothers *and sisters,* that flesh and blood cannot inherit the kingdom of God; nor does the perishable inherit the imperishable. [51] Behold, I am telling you a mystery; we will not all sleep, but we will all be changed, [52] in a moment, in the twinkling of an eye, at the last trumpet; for the trumpet will sound, and the dead will be raised imperishable, and we will be changed. [53] For this perishable must put on the imperishable, and this mortal *must* put on immortality. [54] But when this perishable puts on the imperishable, and this mortal puts on immortality, then will come about the saying that is written: "DEATH HAS BEEN SWALLOWED UP in victory. [55] WHERE, O DEATH, IS YOUR VICTORY? WHERE, O DEATH, IS YOUR STING?" [56] The sting of death is sin, and the power of sin is the Law; [57] but thanks be to God, who gives us the victory through our Lord Jesus Christ.

[58] Therefore, my beloved brothers *and sisters,* be firm, immovable, always excelling in the work of the Lord, knowing that your labor is not *in* vain in the Lord.

Instructions and Greetings

16 Now concerning the collection for the saints, as I directed the churches of Galatia, so you are to do as well. [2] On the first day of every week, each of you is to put aside and save as he may prosper, so that no collections *need to* be made when I come. [3] When I arrive, whomever you approve, I will send them with letters to take your gift to Jerusalem; [4] and if it is appropriate for me to go also, they will go with me.

15:49 1 Two early mss *let's also*

5 But I will come to you after I go through Macedonia; for I am going through Macedonia, **6** and perhaps I will stay with you or even spend the winter, so that you may send me on my way wherever I go. **7** For I do not want to see you now *just* in passing; for I hope to remain with you for some time, if the Lord permits. **8** But I will remain in Ephesus until Pentecost; **9** for a wide door for effective *service* has opened to me, and there are many adversaries.

10 Now if Timothy comes, see that he has no reason to be afraid *while* among you, for he is doing the Lord's work, as I also am. **11** So do not look down on him, anyone. But send him on his way in peace, so that he may come to me; for I expect him with the brothers.

12 Now concerning our brother Apollos, I strongly encouraged him to come to you with the brothers; and it was not at all *his* desire to come now, but he will come when he has the opportunity.

13 Be on the alert, stand firm in the faith, act like men, be strong. **14** All that you do must be done in love.

15 Now I urge you, brothers *and sisters:* you know the household of Stephanas, that they are the first fruits of Achaia, and that they have devoted themselves to ministry to the saints; **16** *I urge* that you also be subject to such as these and to everyone who helps in the work and labors. **17** I rejoice over the coming of Stephanas, Fortunatus, and Achaicus, because they have supplied what was lacking on your part. **18** For they have refreshed my spirit and yours. Therefore acknowledge such men.

19 The churches of Asia greet you. Aquila and Prisca greet you heartily in the Lord, with the church that is in their house. **20** All the brothers *and sisters* greet you. Greet one another with a holy kiss.

21 The greeting is in my own hand—*that* of Paul. **22** If anyone does not love the Lord, he is to be accursed. *¹*Maranatha! **23** The grace of the Lord Jesus be with you. **24** My love be with you all in Christ Jesus. Amen.

16:22 ¹Aramaic *[Our] Lord, come!*

The Second Letter of Paul to the
CORINTHIANS

Introduction

1 Paul, an apostle of Christ Jesus by the will of God, and *our* brother Timothy,

To the church of God which is at Corinth with all the saints who are throughout Achaia:

2 Grace to you and peace from God our Father and the Lord Jesus Christ.

3 Blessed *be* the God and Father of our Lord Jesus Christ, the Father of mercies and God of all comfort, **4** who comforts us in all our affliction so that we will be able to comfort those who are in any affliction with the comfort with which we ourselves are comforted by God. **5** For just as the sufferings of Christ are ours in abundance, so also our comfort is abundant through Christ. **6** But if we are afflicted, it is for your comfort and salvation; or if we are comforted, it is for your comfort, which is effective in the patient enduring of the same sufferings which we also suffer; **7** and our hope for you is firmly grounded, knowing that as you are partners in our sufferings, so also you are in our comfort.

8 For we do not want you to be unaware, brothers *and sisters,* of our affliction which occurred in Asia, that we were burdened excessively, beyond our strength, so that we despaired even of life. **9** Indeed, we had the sentence of death within ourselves so that we would not trust in ourselves, but in God who raises the dead, **10** who rescued us from so great a *danger of* death, and will rescue *us,* He on whom we have set our hope. And He will yet deliver us, **11** *if* you also join in helping us through your prayers, so that thanks may be given by many persons in our behalf for the favor *granted* to us through *the prayers of* many.

Paul's Integrity

12 For our proud confidence is this: the testimony of our conscience, that in holiness and godly sincerity, not in fleshly wisdom but in the grace of God, we have conducted ourselves in the world, and especially toward you. **13** For we write nothing else to you than what you read and understand, and I hope you will understand until the end; **14** just as you also partially did understand us, that we are your reason to be proud as you also are ours, on the day of our Lord Jesus.

15 In this confidence I intended at first to come to you, so that you might twice receive a blessing; **16** that is, to pass your way into Macedonia, and again from Macedonia to come to you, and by you to be helped on my journey to Judea. **17** Therefore, I was not vacillating when I intended to do this, was I? Or what I decide, do I decide according to the flesh, so that with me there will be yes, yes and no, no *at the same time?* **18** But *as* God is faithful, our word to you is not yes and no. **19** For the Son of God, Christ Jesus, who was preached among you by us—by me and Silvanus and Timothy—was not yes and no, but has been yes in Him. **20** For as many as the promises of God are, in Him they are yes; therefore through Him also is our Amen to the glory of God through us. **21** Now He who establishes us with you in Christ and anointed us is God, **22** who also sealed us and gave *us* the Spirit in our hearts as a ¹pledge.

23 But I call God as witness to my soul, that *it was* to spare you *that* I did not come again to Corinth. **24** Not that we domineer over your faith, but we are workers with you for your joy; for in your faith you are standing firm.

Reaffirm Your Love

2 But I decided this for my own sake, that I would not come to you in sorrow again. **2** For if I cause you sorrow, who then *will be* the one making me glad but the one who is made sorrowful by me? **3** This is the very thing I wrote you, so that when I came, I would not have sorrow from those who ought to make me rejoice; having confidence in you all that my joy was *the joy* of you all. **4** For out of much affliction and anguish of heart I wrote to you with many tears; not so that you would be made sorrowful, but that you might know the love which I have especially for you.

5 But if anyone has caused sorrow, he has caused sorrow not for me, but in some degree—not to say too much—for all of you. **6** Sufficient for such a person is this

---

1:22 ¹Or *first installment*

punishment which *was imposed* by the majority, **7** so that on the other hand, you should rather forgive and comfort *him,* otherwise such a person might be overwhelmed by excessive sorrow. **8** Therefore I urge you to reaffirm *your* love for him. **9** For to this end I also wrote, so that I might put you to the test, whether you are obedient in all things. **10** But one whom you forgive anything, I also *forgive;* for indeed what I have forgiven, if I have forgiven anything, *I did so* for your sakes in the presence of Christ, **11** so that no advantage would be taken of us by Satan, for we are not ignorant of his schemes.

12 Now when I came to Troas for the gospel of Christ and when a door was opened for me in the Lord, **13** I had no rest for my spirit, not finding Titus my brother; but saying goodbye to them, I went on to Macedonia.

14 But thanks be to God, who always leads us in triumph in Christ, and through us reveals the fragrance of the knowledge of Him in every place. **15** For we are a fragrance of Christ to God among those who are being saved and among those who are perishing: **16** to the one an aroma from death to death, to the other an aroma from life to life. And who is adequate for these things? **17** For we are not like the many, ¹peddling the word of God, but as from sincerity, but as from God, we speak in Christ in the sight of God.

Ministers of a New Covenant

3 Are we beginning to commend ourselves again? Or do we need, as some, letters of commendation to you or from you? **2** You are our letter, written in our hearts, known and read by all people, **3** revealing yourselves, that you are a letter of Christ, delivered by us, written not with ink but with the Spirit of the living God, not on tablets of stone but on tablets of human hearts.

4 Such *is the* confidence we have toward God through Christ. **5** Not that we are adequate in ourselves *so as* to consider anything as *having come* from ourselves, but our adequacy is from God, **6** who also made us adequate *as* servants of a new covenant, not of the letter but of the Spirit; for the letter kills, but the Spirit gives life.

7 But if the ministry of death, engraved in letters on stones, came with glory so that the sons of Israel could

---

2:17 ¹ Or *diluting*

not look intently at the face of Moses because of the glory of his face, fading *as* it was, [8] how will the ministry of the Spirit fail to be *even* more with glory? [9] For if the ministry of condemnation has glory, much more does the ministry of righteousness excel in glory. [10] For indeed what had glory in this case has no glory, because of the glory that surpasses *it*. [11] For if that which fades away *was* with glory, much more that which remains *is* in glory.

[12] Therefore, having such a hope, we use great boldness in *our* speech, [13] and *we are* not like Moses, *who* used to put a veil over his face so that the sons of Israel would not stare at the end of what was fading away. [14] But their minds were hardened; for until this very day at the reading of the old covenant the same veil remains unlifted, because it is removed in Christ. [15] But to this day whenever Moses is read, a veil lies over their hearts; [16] but whenever *someone* turns to the Lord, the veil is taken away. [17] Now the Lord is the Spirit, and where the Spirit of the Lord is, *there* is freedom. [18] But we all, with unveiled faces, looking as in a mirror at the glory of the Lord, are being transformed into the same image from glory to glory, just as from the Lord, the Spirit.

Paul's Apostolic Ministry

4 Therefore, since we have this ministry, as we received mercy, we do not lose heart, [2] but we have renounced the things hidden because of shame, not walking in trickery nor distorting the word of God, but by the open proclamation of the truth commending ourselves to every person's conscience in the sight of God. [3] And even if our gospel is veiled, it is veiled to those who are perishing, [4] in whose case the god of this world has blinded the minds of the unbelieving so that they will not see the light of the gospel of the glory of Christ, who is the image of God. [5] For we do not preach ourselves, but Christ Jesus as Lord, and ourselves as your bond-servants on account of Jesus. [6] For God, who said, "Light shall shine out of darkness," is the One who has shone in our hearts to give the Light of the knowledge of the glory of God in the face of Christ.

[7] But we have this treasure in earthen containers, so that the extraordinary *greatness* of the power will be of God and not from ourselves; [8] *we are* afflicted in every

way, but not crushed; perplexed, but not despairing; [9]persecuted, but not abandoned; struck down, but not destroyed; [10]always carrying around in the body the dying of Jesus, so that the life of Jesus may also be revealed in our body. [11]For we who live are constantly being handed over to death because of Jesus, so that the life of Jesus may also be revealed in our mortal flesh. [12]So death works in us, but life in you.

[13]But having the same spirit of faith, according to what is written: "I BELIEVED, THEREFORE I SPOKE," we also believe, therefore we also speak, [14]knowing that He who raised the Lord Jesus will also raise us with Jesus, and will present *us* with you. [15]For all things *are* for your sakes, so that grace, having spread to more and more people, will cause thanksgiving to overflow to the glory of God.

[16]Therefore we do not lose heart, but though our outer person is decaying, yet our inner *person* is being renewed day by day. [17]For our momentary, light affliction is producing for us an eternal weight of glory far beyond all comparison, [18]while we look not at the things which are seen, but at the things which are not seen; for the things which are seen are temporal, but the things which are not seen are eternal.

The Temporal and Eternal

5 For we know that if our earthly tent which is our house is torn down, we have a building from God, a house not made by hands, eternal in the heavens. [2]For indeed, in this *tent* we groan, longing to be clothed with our [1]dwelling from heaven, [3]since in fact after putting it on, we will not be found naked. [4]For indeed, we who are in this tent groan, being burdened, because we do not want to be unclothed but to be clothed, so that what is mortal will be swallowed up by life. [5]Now He who prepared us for this very *purpose is* God, who gave us the Spirit as a [1]pledge.

[6]Therefore, being always of good courage, and knowing that while we are at home in the body we are absent from the Lord—[7]for we walk by faith, not by sight—[8]but we are of good courage and prefer rather to be absent from the body and to be at home with the

---

5:2 [1] I.e., the resurrected body   5:5 [1] Or *first installment*

Lord. **9** Therefore we also have as our ambition, whether at home or absent, to be pleasing to Him. **10** For we must all appear before the judgment seat of Christ, so that each one may receive compensation for his deeds *done* through the body, in accordance with what he has done, whether good or bad.

11 Therefore, knowing the fear of the Lord, we persuade people, but we are well known to God; and I hope that we are also well known in your consciences. **12** We are not commending ourselves to you again, but *are* giving you an opportunity to be proud of us, so that you will have *an answer* for those who take pride in appearance and not in heart. **13** For if we have lost our minds, *it is* for God; if we are of sound mind, *it is* for you. **14** For the love of Christ controls us, having concluded this, that one died for all, therefore all died; **15** and He died for all, so that those who live would no longer live for themselves, but for Him who died and rose on their behalf.

16 Therefore from now on we recognize no one by the flesh; even though we have known Christ by the flesh, yet now we know *Him in this way* no longer. **17** Therefore if anyone is in Christ, *this person is* a new creation; the old things passed away; behold, new things have come. **18** Now all *these* things are from God, who reconciled us to Himself through Christ and gave us the ministry of reconciliation, **19** namely, that God was in Christ reconciling the world to Himself, not counting their wrongdoings against them, and He has committed to us the word of reconciliation.

20 Therefore, we are ambassadors for Christ, as though God were making an appeal through us; we beg you on behalf of Christ, be reconciled to God. **21** He made Him who knew no sin *to be* ¹sin in our behalf, so that we might become the righteousness of God in Him.

Their Ministry Commended

6 And working together *with Him,* we also urge you not to receive the grace of God in vain— **2** for He says,

"AT A FAVORABLE TIME I LISTENED TO YOU,
  AND ON A DAY OF SALVATION I HELPED YOU."
Behold, now is "A FAVORABLE TIME," behold, now is "A DAY

5:21 ¹Or *a sin offering*

OF SALVATION"—³giving no reason for *taking* offense in anything, so that the ministry will not be discredited, ⁴but in everything commending ourselves as servants of God, in much endurance, in afflictions, in hardships, in difficulties, ⁵in beatings, in imprisonments, in mob attacks, in labors, in sleeplessness, in hunger, ⁶in purity, in knowledge, in patience, in kindness, in the Holy Spirit, in genuine love, ⁷in the word of truth, *and* in the power of God; by the weapons of righteousness for the right hand and the left, ⁸by glory and dishonor, by evil report and good report; *regarded* as deceivers and yet true; ⁹as unknown and *yet* well known, as dying and *yet* behold, we are alive; as punished and *yet* not put to death, ¹⁰as sorrowful yet always rejoicing, as poor yet making many rich, as having nothing and *yet* possessing all things.

¹¹Our mouth has spoken freely to you, you Corinthians, our heart is opened wide. ¹²You are not restrained by us, but you are restrained in your own affections. ¹³Now in the same way in exchange—I am speaking as to children—open wide *your hearts to us,* you as well.

¹⁴Do not be mismatched with unbelievers; for what do righteousness and lawlessness share together, or what does light have in common with darkness? ¹⁵Or what harmony does Christ have with Belial, or what does a believer share with an unbeliever? ¹⁶Or what agreement does the temple of God have with idols? For we are the temple of the living God; just as God said,

"I WILL DWELL AMONG THEM AND WALK AMONG THEM;
    AND I WILL BE THEIR GOD, AND THEY SHALL BE MY PEOPLE.

¹⁷ "Therefore, COME OUT FROM THEIR MIDST AND BE SEPARATE,"
        says the Lord.
    "AND DO NOT TOUCH WHAT IS UNCLEAN;
    And I will welcome you.

¹⁸ "And I will be a father to you,
    And you shall be sons and daughters to Me,"
        Says the Lord Almighty.

Paul Reveals His Heart

7 Therefore, having these promises, beloved, let's cleanse ourselves from all defilement of flesh and spirit, perfecting holiness in the fear of God.

2 Make room for us *in your hearts;* we have wronged no one, we corrupted no one, we have taken advantage of no one. **3** I do not speak to condemn *you,* for I have said before that you are in our hearts, to die together and to live together. **4** My confidence in you is great; my boasting in your behalf is great. I am filled with comfort; I am overflowing with joy in all our affliction.

5 For even when we came into Macedonia our flesh had no rest, but we were afflicted on every side: conflicts on the outside, fears inside. **6** But God, who comforts the discouraged, comforted us by the arrival of Titus; **7** and not only by his arrival, but also by the comfort with which he was comforted among you, as he reported to us your longing, your mourning, your zeal for me; so that I rejoiced even more. **8** For though I caused you sorrow by my letter, I do not regret it; though I did regret it—*for* I see that that letter caused you sorrow, though only for a while— **9** I now rejoice, not that you were made sorrowful, but that you were made sorrowful to *the point of* repentance; for you were made sorrowful according to *the will of* God, so that you might not suffer loss in anything through us. **10** For the sorrow that is according to *the will of* God produces a repentance without regret, *leading* to salvation, but the sorrow of the world produces death. **11** For behold what earnestness this very thing, this godly sorrow, has produced in you: what vindication *of yourselves,* what indignation, what fear, what longing, what zeal, what punishment of wrong! In everything you demonstrated yourselves to be innocent in the matter. **12** So although I wrote to you, *it was* not for the sake of the offender nor for the sake of the one offended, but that your earnestness in our behalf might be made known to you in the sight of God. **13** Because of this, we have been comforted.

And besides our comfort, we rejoiced even much more for the joy of Titus, because his spirit has been refreshed by you all. **14** For if I have boasted to him about you regarding anything, I was not put to shame. But as we spoke all things to you in truth, so also our boasting before Titus proved to be *the* truth. **15** His affection abounds all the more toward you, as he remembers the obedience of you all, how you received him with fear and trembling. **16** I rejoice that in everything I have confidence in you.

Great Generosity

8 Now, brothers *and sisters,* we make known to you the grace of God which has been given in the churches of Macedonia, **2** that in a great ordeal of affliction their abundance of joy and their deep poverty overflowed in the wealth of their liberality. **3** For I testify that according to their ability, and beyond their ability, *they gave* voluntarily, **4** begging us with much urging for the favor of participation in the support of the saints, **5** and *this,* not as we had expected, but they first gave themselves to the Lord and to us by the will of God. **6** So we urged Titus that as he had previously made a beginning, so he would also complete in you this gracious work as well.

7 But just as you excel in everything, in faith, speaking, knowledge, and in all earnestness and in the love we inspired in you, *see* that you also excel in this gracious work. **8** I am not saying *this* as a command, but as proving, through the earnestness of others, the sincerity of your love as well. **9** For you know the grace of our Lord Jesus Christ, that though He was rich, yet for your sake He became poor, so that you through His poverty might become rich. **10** I give *my* opinion in this matter, for this is to your advantage, who were the first to begin a year ago not only to do *this,* but also to desire *to do it.* **11** But now finish doing it also, so that just as *there was* the willingness to desire it, so *there may be* also the completion of it by your ability. **12** For if the willingness is present, it is acceptable according to what *a person* has, not according to what he does not have. **13** For *this* is not for the relief of others *and* for your hardship, but by way of equality— **14** at this present time your abundance *will serve as assistance* for their need, so that their abundance also may serve as *assistance* for your need, so that there may be equality; **15** as it is written: "THE ONE WHO *HAD GATHERED* MUCH DID NOT HAVE TOO MUCH, AND THE ONE WHO *HAD GATHERED* LITTLE DID NOT HAVE TOO LITTLE."

16 But thanks be to God who puts the same earnestness in your behalf in the heart of Titus. **17** For he not only accepted our appeal, but being himself very earnest, he has gone to you of his own accord. **18** We have sent along with him the brother whose fame in *the things of* the gospel *has spread* through all the churches; **19** and not only *that,* but he has also been appointed by the churches to travel with us in this gracious work, which is being administered by us for the glory of the Lord Himself, and *to show* our readiness, [20] taking precaution so that no one will discredit us in our administration of this generous gift; [21] for we have regard for what is honorable, not only in the sight of the Lord, but also in the sight of *other* people. [22] We have sent with them our brother, whom we have often tested and found diligent in many things, but now even more diligent because of *his* great confidence in you. [23] As for Titus, *he is* my partner and fellow worker among you; as for our brothers, *they are* messengers of the churches, a glory to Christ. [24] Therefore, openly before the churches, show them the proof of your love and of our reason for boasting about you.

God Gives Most

9 For it is superfluous for me to write to you about this ministry to the saints; [2] for I know your willingness, of which I boast about you to the Macedonians, *namely,* that Achaia has been prepared since last year, and your zeal has stirred up most of them. [3] But I have sent the brothers, in order that our boasting about you may not prove empty in this case, so that, as I was saying, you will be prepared; [4] otherwise, if *any* Macedonians come with me and find you unprepared, we—not to mention you—would be put to shame by this confidence. [5] So I considered it necessary to urge the brothers that they go on ahead to you and arrange in advance your previously promised generous gift, that the same would be ready as a generous gift, and not as *one grudgingly given due to greediness.*

[6] Now *I say* this: the one who sows sparingly will also reap sparingly, and the one who sows generously will also reap generously. [7] Each one *must do* just as he has decided in his heart, not reluctantly or under compulsion, for God loves a cheerful giver. [8] And God is able to make all grace overflow to you, so that, always having all sufficiency in everything, you may have an abundance for every good deed; [9] as it is written:

> "He scattered abroad, he gave to the poor,
> His righteousness endures forever."

[10] Now He who supplies seed to the sower and bread for food will supply and multiply your seed for sowing and increase the harvest of your righteousness; [11] you will be

enriched in everything for all liberality, which through us is producing thanksgiving to God. **12** For the ministry of this service is not only fully supplying the needs of the saints, but is also overflowing through many thanksgivings to God. **13** Because of the proof given by this ministry, they will glorify God for *your* obedience to your confession of the gospel of Christ and for the liberality of your contribution to them and to all, **14** while they also, by prayer on your behalf, yearn for you because of the surpassing grace of God in you. **15** Thanks be to God for His indescribable gift!

Paul Confronts the Corinthians

10 Now I, Paul, myself urge you by the meekness and gentleness of Christ—I who am meek when face to face with you, but bold toward you when absent! **2** I ask that when I am present I *need* not be bold with the confidence with which I intend to be courageous against some, who regard us as if we walked according to the flesh. **3** For though we walk in the flesh, we do not wage battle according to the flesh, **4** for the weapons of our warfare are not of the flesh, but divinely powerful for the destruction of fortresses. **5** *We are* destroying arguments and all arrogance raised against the knowledge of God, and *we are* taking every thought captive to the obedience of Christ, **6** and we are ready to punish all disobedience, whenever your obedience is complete.

7 You are looking at things as they are outwardly. If anyone is confident in himself that he is Christ's, have him consider this again within himself, that just as he is Christ's, so too are we. **8** For if I boast somewhat more about our authority, which the Lord gave for building you up and not for destroying you, I will not be put to shame, **9** for I do not want to seem as if I would terrify you by my letters. **10** For they say, "His letters are weighty and strong, but his personal presence is unimpressive and his speech contemptible." **11** Have such a person consider this, that what we are in word by letters when absent, such persons *we are* also in deed when present.

12 For we do not presume to rank or compare ourselves with some of those who commend themselves; but when they measure themselves by themselves and compare themselves with themselves, they have no understanding. **13** But we will not boast beyond *our* measure, but within the measure of the domain which God assigned to us as a measure, to reach even as far as you. **14** For we are not overextending ourselves, as if we did not reach to you, for we were the first to come even as far as you in the gospel of Christ; **15** not boasting beyond *our* measure, *that is,* in other people's labors, but with the hope that as your faith grows, we will be, within our domain, enlarged even more by you, **16** so as to preach the gospel even to the regions beyond you, *and* not to boast in what has been accomplished in the domain of another. **17** But THE ONE WHO BOASTS IS TO BOAST IN THE LORD. **18** For *it is* not the one who commends himself that is approved, but the one whom the Lord commends.

Paul Defends His Apostleship

11 I wish that you would bear with me in a little foolishness; but indeed you are bearing with me. **2** For I am jealous for you with a godly jealousy; for I betrothed you to one husband, to present you *as* a pure virgin to Christ. **3** But I am afraid that, as the serpent deceived Eve by his trickery, your minds will be led astray from sincere and pure devotion to Christ. **4** For if one comes and preaches another Jesus whom we have not preached, or you receive a different spirit which you have not received, or a different gospel which you have not accepted, *this* you tolerate *very* well! **5** For I consider myself not in the least inferior to the most eminent apostles. **6** But even if I am unskilled in speech, yet I am not *so* in knowledge; in fact, in every way we have made *this* evident to you in all things.

7 Or did I commit a sin by humbling myself so that you might be exalted, because I preached the gospel of God to you without charge? **8** I robbed other churches by taking wages *from them* to serve you; **9** and when I was present with you and was in need, I was not a burden to anyone; for when the brothers came from Macedonia they fully supplied my need, and in everything I kept myself from being a burden to you, and will continue to do so. **10** As the truth of Christ is in me, this boasting of mine will not be stopped in the regions of Achaia. **11** Why? Because I do not love you? God knows *that I do!*

12 But what I am doing I will also *continue to* do, so that I may eliminate the opportunity from those who want an opportunity to be regarded just as we are in the matter about which they are boasting. 13 For such men are false apostles, deceitful workers, disguising themselves as apostles of Christ. 14 No wonder, for even Satan disguises himself as an angel of light. 15 Therefore it is not surprising if his servants also disguise themselves as servants of righteousness, whose end will be according to their deeds.

16 Again I say, let no one think me foolish; but if *you do,* receive me even as foolish, so that I also may boast a little. 17 What I am saying, I am not saying as the Lord would, but as in foolishness, in this confidence of boasting. 18 Since many boast according to the flesh, I will boast also. 19 For you, being *so* wise, tolerate the foolish gladly. 20 For you tolerate it if anyone enslaves you, if anyone devours you, if anyone takes *advantage of* you, if anyone exalts himself, if anyone hits you in the face. 21 To *my* shame I *must* say that we have been weak *by comparison.*

But in whatever respect anyone *else* is bold—I am speaking in foolishness—I too am bold. 22 Are they Hebrews? So am I. Are they Israelites? So am I. Are they descendants of Abraham? So am I. 23 Are they servants of Christ?—I am speaking as if insane—I more so; in far more labors, in far more imprisonments, beaten times without number, often in *danger of* death. 24 Five times I received from the Jews thirty-nine *lashes.* 25 Three times I was beaten with rods, once I was stoned, three times I was shipwrecked, a night and a day I have spent *adrift* at sea. 26 *I have been* on frequent journeys, in dangers from rivers, dangers from robbers, dangers from *my* countrymen, dangers from the Gentiles, dangers in the city, dangers in the wilderness, dangers at sea, dangers among false brothers; 27 *I have been* in labor and hardship, through many sleepless nights, in hunger and thirst, often without food, in cold and exposure. 28 Apart from *such* external things, there is the daily pressure on me *of* concern for all the churches. 29 Who is weak without my being weak? Who is led into sin without my intense concern?

30 If I have to boast, I will boast of what pertains to my weakness. 31 The God and Father of the Lord Jesus, He who is blessed forever, knows that I am not lying. 32 In Damascus the ethnarch under Aretas the king was guarding the city of the Damascenes in order to seize

me, **33** and I was let down in a basket through a window in the wall, and *so* escaped his hands.

Paul's Vision

12 Boasting is necessary, though it is not beneficial; but I will go on to visions and revelations of the Lord. **2** I know a man in Christ, who fourteen years ago— whether in the body I do not know, or out of the body I do not know, God knows—such a man was caught up to the third heaven. **3** And I know how such a man— whether in the body or apart from the body I do not know, God knows—**4** was caught up into Paradise and heard inexpressible words, which a man is not permitted to speak. **5** In behalf of such a man I will boast; but in my own behalf I will not boast, except regarding *my* weaknesses. **6** For if I do wish to boast I will not be foolish, for I will be speaking the truth; but I refrain *from this,* so that no one will credit me with more than he sees *in* me or hears from me.

A Thorn in the Flesh

7 Because of the extraordinary *greatness* of the revelations, for this reason, to keep me from exalting myself, there was given to me a thorn in the flesh, a messenger of Satan to torment me—to keep me from exalting myself! **8** Concerning this I pleaded with the Lord three times that it might leave me. **9** And He has said to me, "My grace is sufficient for you, for power is perfected in weakness." Most gladly, therefore, I will rather boast about my weaknesses, so that the power of Christ may dwell in me. **10** Therefore I delight in weaknesses, in insults, in distresses, in persecutions, in difficulties, in behalf of Christ; for when I am weak, then I am strong.

11 I have become foolish; you yourselves compelled me. Actually I should have been commended by you, since I was in no respect inferior to the most eminent apostles, even though I am a nobody. **12** The distinguishing marks of a true apostle were performed among you with all perseverance, by signs, wonders, and miracles. **13** For in what respect were you treated as inferior to the rest of the churches, except that I myself did not become a burden to you? Forgive me this wrong!

14 Here for this third time I am ready to come to you,

and I will not be a burden to you; for I do not seek what is yours, but you; for children are not responsible to save up for *their* parents, but parents for *their* children. **15** I will most gladly spend and be expended for your souls. If I love you more, am I to be loved less? **16** But be that as it may, I did not burden you myself; nevertheless, devious person that I am, I took you in by deceit. **17** *Certainly* I have not taken advantage of you through any of those whom I have sent to you, have I? **18** I urged Titus *to go,* and I sent the brother with him. Titus did not take any advantage of you, did he? Did we not conduct ourselves in the same spirit *and walk* in the same steps?

19 All this time you have been thinking that we are defending ourselves to you. *Actually,* it is in the sight of God that we have been speaking in Christ; and all for building you up, beloved. **20** For I am afraid that perhaps when I come I may find you to be not what I wish, and may be found by you to be not what you wish; that perhaps *there will be* strife, jealousy, angry tempers, self-ishness, slanders, gossip, arrogance, disturbances; **21** *I am afraid* that when I come again my God may humiliate me before you, and I may mourn over many of those who have sinned in the past and not repented of the impurity, sexual immorality, and indecent behavior which they have practiced.

Examine Yourselves

13 This is the third time that I am coming to you. ON THE TESTIMONY OF TWO OR THREE WITNESSES EVERY MATTER SHALL BE CONFIRMED. **2** I have previously said when I was present the second time, and though now absent I say in advance to those who have sinned in the past and to all the rest *as well,* that if I come again I will not spare *anyone,* **3** since you are seeking proof of the Christ who speaks in me, who is not weak toward you, but mighty in you. **4** For indeed He was crucified because of weakness, yet He lives because of the power of God. For we too are weak [1] in Him, yet we will live with Him because of the power of God *directed* toward you.

5 Test yourselves *to see* if you are in the faith; examine yourselves! Or do you not recognize *this about* yourselves, that Jesus Christ is in you—unless indeed

---

13:4 [1] One early ms *with Him*

you fail the test? **6** But I expect that you will realize that we ourselves do not fail the test. **7** Now we pray to God that you do nothing wrong; not so that we ourselves may appear approved, but that you may do what is right, though we may appear unapproved. **8** For we cannot do anything against the truth, but *only* for the truth. **9** For we rejoice when we ourselves are weak, but you are strong; this we also pray for, that you become mature. **10** For this reason I am writing these things while absent, so that when present I *need* not use severity, in accordance with the authority which the Lord gave me for building up and not for tearing down.

11 Finally, brothers *and sisters,* rejoice, mend your ways, be comforted, be like-minded, live in peace; and the God of love and peace will be with you. **12** Greet one another with a holy kiss. **13** All the saints greet you.

14 The grace of the Lord Jesus Christ, and the love of God, and the fellowship of the Holy Spirit, be with you all.

The Letter of Paul to the
GALATIANS

Introduction

1 Paul, an apostle (not *sent* from men nor through human agency, but through Jesus Christ and God the Father, who raised Him from the dead), 2 and all the brothers who are with me,

To the churches of Galatia:

3 Grace to you and peace from God the Father and our Lord Jesus Christ, 4 who gave Himself for our sins so that He might rescue us from this present evil age, according to the will of our God and Father, 5 to whom *be* the glory forevermore. Amen.

Distortion of the Gospel

6 I am amazed that you are so quickly deserting Him who called you by the grace of Christ, for a different gospel, 7 which is not *just* another *account;* but there are some who are disturbing you and want to distort the gospel of Christ. 8 But even if we, or an angel from heaven, should preach to you a gospel contrary to what we have preached to you, he is to be accursed! 9 As we have said before, even now I say again: if anyone is preaching to you a gospel contrary to what you received, he is to be accursed!

10 For am I now seeking the favor of people, or of God? Or am I striving to please people? If I were still trying to please people, I would not be a bond-servant of Christ.

Paul Defends His Ministry

11 For I would have you know, brothers *and sisters,* that the gospel which was preached by me is not of human invention. 12 For I neither received it from man, nor was I taught it, but *I received it* through a revelation of Jesus Christ.

13 For you have heard of my former way of life in Judaism, how I used to persecute the church of God beyond measure and tried to destroy it; 14 and I was advancing in Judaism beyond many of my contemporaries among my countrymen, being more extremely zealous for my ancestral traditions. 15 But

when He who had set me apart *even* from my mother's womb and called *me* through His grace was pleased [16]to reveal His Son in me so that I might preach Him among the Gentiles, I did not immediately consult with flesh and blood, [17]nor did I go up to Jerusalem to those *who were* apostles before me; but I went away to Arabia, and returned once more to Damascus.

[18]Then three years later I went up to Jerusalem to become acquainted with Cephas, and stayed with him for fifteen days. [19]But I did not see another one of the apostles except James, the Lord's brother. [20](Now in what I am writing to you, I assure you before God that I am not lying.) [21]Then I went into the regions of Syria and Cilicia. [22]I was *still* unknown by sight to the churches of Judea which are in Christ; [23]but they only kept hearing, "The man who once persecuted us is now preaching the faith which he once tried to destroy." [24]And they were glorifying God because of me.

The Council at Jerusalem

2 Then after an interval of fourteen years I went up again to Jerusalem with Barnabas, taking Titus along also. [2]It was because of a revelation that I went up; and I submitted to them the gospel which I preach among the Gentiles, but *I did so* in private to those who were of reputation, for fear that somehow I might be running, or had run, in vain. [3]But not even Titus, who was with me, though he was a Greek, was compelled to be circumcised. [4]Yet *it was a concern* because of the false brothers secretly brought in, who had sneaked in to spy on our freedom which we have in Christ Jesus, in order to enslave us. [5]But we did not yield in subjection to them, even for an hour, so that the truth of the gospel would remain with you. [6]But from those who were of considerable repute (what they were makes no difference to me; God shows no favoritism)—well, those who were of repute contributed nothing to me. [7]But on the contrary, seeing that I had been entrusted with the gospel [1]to the uncircumcised, just as Peter *had been* [2]to the circumcised [8](for He who was at work for Peter in *his* apostleship to the circumcised was at work for me

---

2:7 [1] Lit *of the uncircumcision;* i.e., to Gentiles   2:7 [2] Lit *of the circumcision;* i.e., to Jews also to the Gentiles), 9 and recognizing the grace that had been given to me, James and Cephas and John, who were reputed to be pillars, gave to me and Barnabas the right hand of fellowship, so that we *might go* to the Gentiles, and they to the circumcised. 10 *They* only *asked* us to remember the poor—the very thing I also was eager to do.

Peter (Cephas) Opposed by Paul

11 But when Cephas came to Antioch, I opposed him to his face, because he stood condemned. 12 For prior to the coming of some men from James, he used to eat with the Gentiles; but when they came, he *began* to withdraw and separate himself, fearing those from the circumcision. 13 The rest of the Jews joined him in hypocrisy, with the result that even Barnabas was carried away by their hypocrisy. 14 But when I saw that they were not straightforward about the truth of the gospel, I said to Cephas in the presence of all, "If you, being a Jew, live like the Gentiles and not like the Jews, how *is it that* you compel the Gentiles to live like Jews?

15 "We *are* Jews by nature and not sinners from the Gentiles; 16 nevertheless, knowing that a person is not justified by works of the Law but through faith in Christ Jesus, even we have believed in Christ Jesus, so that we may be justified by faith in Christ and not by works of the Law; since by works of the Law no flesh will be justified. 17 But if, while seeking to be justified in Christ, we ourselves have also been found sinners, is Christ then a servant of sin? 1Far from it! 18 For if I rebuild what I have *once* destroyed, I prove myself to be a wrongdoer. 19 For through the Law I died to the Law, so that I might live for God. 20 I have been crucified with Christ; and it is no longer I who live, but Christ lives in me; and the *life* which I now live in the flesh I live by faith in the Son of God, who loved me and gave Himself up for me. 21 I do not nullify the grace of God, for if righteousness *comes* through the Law, then Christ died needlessly."

Faith Brings Righteousness

3 You foolish Galatians, who has bewitched you, before whose eyes Jesus Christ was publicly portrayed *as*

2:17 1 Lit *May it never happen!*

crucified? **2** This is the only thing I want to find out from you: did you receive the Spirit by works of the Law, or by hearing with faith? **3** Are you so foolish? Having begun by the Spirit, are you now being perfected by the flesh? **4** Did you suffer so many things in vain—if indeed it was in vain? **5** So then, does He who provides you with the Spirit and works miracles among you, do it by works of the Law, or by hearing with faith?

6 Just as Abraham BELIEVED GOD, AND IT WAS CREDITED TO HIM AS RIGHTEOUSNESS. **7** Therefore, recognize that it is those who are of faith who are sons of Abraham. **8** The Scripture, foreseeing that God would justify the Gentiles by faith, preached the gospel beforehand to Abraham, *saying,* "ALL THE NATIONS WILL BE BLESSED IN YOU." **9** So then, those who are of faith are blessed with Abraham, the believer.

10 For all who are of works of the Law are under a curse; for it is written: "CURSED IS EVERYONE WHO DOES NOT ABIDE BY ALL THE THINGS WRITTEN IN THE BOOK OF THE LAW, TO DO THEM." **11** Now, that no one is justified by the Law before God is evident; for, "THE RIGHTEOUS ONE WILL LIVE BY FAITH." **12** However, the Law is not of faith; on the contrary, "THE PERSON WHO PERFORMS THEM WILL LIVE BY THEM." **13** Christ redeemed us from the curse of the Law, having become a curse for us—for it is written: "CURSED IS EVERYONE WHO HANGS ON A ¹TREE"—**14** in order that in Christ Jesus the blessing of Abraham would come to the Gentiles, so that we would receive the promise of the Spirit through faith.

Intent of the Law

15 Brothers *and sisters,* I speak in terms of human relations: even though it is *only* a man's covenant, yet when it has been ratified, no one sets it aside or adds conditions to it. **16** Now the promises were spoken to Abraham and to his seed. He does not say, "And to seeds," as *one would in referring* to many, but *rather* as *in referring* to one, "And to your seed," that is, Christ. **17** What I am saying is this: the Law, which came 430 years later, does not invalidate a covenant previously ratified by God, so as to nullify the promise. **18** For if the inheritance is based on law, it is no longer based on a

---

3:13 ¹Or *cross;* lit *wood;* see Deut 21:23

promise; but God has granted it to Abraham by means of a promise.

19 Why the Law then? It was added on account of the ᵗviolations, having been ordered through angels at the hand of a mediator, until the Seed would come to whom the promise had been made. **20** Now a mediator is not for one *party only;* but God is *only* one. **21** Is the Law then contrary to the promises of God? Far from it! For if a law had been given that was able to impart life, then righteousness would indeed have been based on law. **22** But the Scripture has confined everyone under sin, so that the promise by faith in Jesus Christ might be given to those who believe.

23 But before faith came, we were kept in custody under the Law, being confined for the faith that was destined to be revealed. **24** Therefore the Law has become our guardian *to lead us* to Christ, so that we may be justified by faith. **25** But now that faith has come, we are no longer under a guardian. **26** For you are all sons *and daughters* of God through faith in Christ Jesus. **27** For all of you who were baptized into Christ have clothed yourselves with Christ. **28** There is neither Jew nor Greek, there is neither slave nor free, there is neither male nor female; for you are all one in Christ Jesus. **29** And if you belong to Christ, then you are Abraham's descendants, heirs according to promise.

Sonship in Christ

4 Now I say, as long as the heir is a child, he does not differ at all from a slave, although he is owner of everything, **2** but he is under guardians and managers until the date set by the father. **3** So we too, when we were children, were held in bondage under the elementary principles of the world. **4** But when the fullness of the time came, God sent His Son, born of a woman, born under the Law, **5** so that He might redeem those who were under the Law, that we might receive the adoption as sons *and daughters*. **6** Because you are sons, God has sent the Spirit of His Son into our hearts, crying out, "Abba! Father!" **7** Therefore you are no longer a slave, but a son; and if a son, then an heir through God.

3:19 ᵗI.e., of God's commands

8 However at that time, when you did not know God, you were slaves to those which by nature are not gods. 9 But now that you have come to know God, or rather to be known by God, how is it that you turn back again to the weak and worthless elementary principles, to which you want to be enslaved all over again? 10 You meticulously observe days and months and seasons and years. 11 I fear for you, that perhaps I have labored over you in vain.

12 I beg of you, brothers *and sisters,* become as I *am,* for I also *have become* as you *are.* You have done me no wrong; 13 but you know that it was because of a bodily illness that I preached the gospel to you the first time; 14 and you did not despise that which was a trial to you in my bodily condition, nor express contempt, but you received me as an angel of God, as Christ Jesus *Himself.* 15 Where then is that sense of blessing you had? For I testify about you that, if possible, you would have torn out your eyes and given them to me. 16 So have I become your enemy by telling you the truth? 17 They eagerly seek you, not in a commendable way, but they want to shut you out so that you will seek them. 18 But it is good always to be eagerly sought in a commendable way, and not only when I am present with you. 19 My children, with whom I am again in labor until Christ is formed in you— 20 but I could wish to be present with you now and to change my *tone of* voice, for I am at a loss about you!

Slave and Free

21 Tell me, you who want to be under law, do you not listen to the Law? 22 For it is written that Abraham had two sons, one by the slave woman and one by the free woman. 23 But the son by the slave woman was born according to the flesh, and the son by the free woman through the promise. 24 This is speaking allegorically, for these *women* are two covenants: one *coming* from Mount Sinai giving birth to children who are to be slaves; she is Hagar. 25 Now this Hagar is Mount Sinai in Arabia and corresponds to the present Jerusalem, for she is enslaved with her children. 26 But the Jerusalem above is free; she is our mother. 27 For it is written:

"REJOICE, INFERTILE ONE, YOU WHO DO NOT GIVE BIRTH;
 BREAK FORTH AND SHOUT, YOU WHO ARE NOT IN LABOR;

> For the children of the desolate one *are* more
>   numerous
> Than *those* of the one who has a husband."

28 And you, brothers *and sisters,* like Isaac, are children of promise. **29** But as at that time the *son* who was born according to the flesh persecuted the one *who was born* according to the Spirit, so it is even now. **30** But what does the Scripture say?

> "Drive out the slave woman and her son,
> For the son of the slave woman shall not be an heir
>   with the son of the free woman."

31 So then, brothers *and sisters,* we are not children of a slave woman, but of the free woman.

Follow the Spirit

5 It was for freedom that Christ set us free; therefore keep standing firm and do not be subject again to a yoke of slavery.

2 Look! I, Paul, tell you that if you have yourselves circumcised, Christ will be of no benefit to you. **3** And I testify again to every man who has himself circumcised, that he is obligated to keep the whole Law. **4** You have been severed from Christ, you who are seeking to be justified by the [1]Law; you have fallen from grace. **5** For we, through the Spirit, by faith, are waiting for the hope of righteousness. **6** For in Christ Jesus neither circumcision nor uncircumcision means anything, but faith working through love.

7 You were running well; who hindered you from obeying the truth? **8** This persuasion *did* not *come* from Him who calls you. **9** A little leaven leavens the whole lump *of dough.* **10** I have confidence in you in the Lord, that you will adopt no other view; but the one who is disturbing you will bear the punishment, whoever he is. **11** But as for me, brothers *and sisters,* if I still preach circumcision, why am I still persecuted? Then the stumbling block of the cross has been eliminated. **12** I wish that those who are troubling you would even emasculate themselves.

13 For you were called to freedom, brothers *and sisters; only do* not *turn* your freedom into an opportunity for the flesh, but serve one another through

---

love. **14** For the whole Law is fulfilled in one word, in the *statement,* "YOU SHALL LOVE YOUR NEIGHBOR AS YOURSELF." **15** But if you bite and devour one another, take care that you are not consumed by one another.

16 But I say, walk by the Spirit, and you will not carry out the desire of the flesh. **17** For the desire of the flesh is against the Spirit, and the Spirit against the flesh; for these are in opposition to one another, in order to keep you from doing whatever you want. **18** But if you are led by the Spirit, you are not under the Law. **19** Now the deeds of the flesh are evident, which are: sexual immorality, impurity, indecent behavior, **20** idolatry, witchcraft, hostilities, strife, jealousy, outbursts of anger, selfish ambition, dissensions, factions, **21** envy, drunkenness, carousing, and things like these, of which I forewarn you, just as I have forewarned you, that those who practice such things will not inherit the kingdom of God. **22** But the fruit of the Spirit is love, joy, peace, patience, kindness, goodness, faithfulness, **23** gentleness, self-control; against such things there is no law. **24** Now those who belong to Christ Jesus crucified the flesh with its passions and desires.

25 If we live by the Spirit, let's follow the Spirit as well. **26** Let's not become boastful, challenging one another, envying one another.

Bear One Another's Burdens

6 Brothers *and sisters,* even if a person is caught in any wrongdoing, you who are spiritual are to restore such a person in a spirit of gentleness; *each one* looking to yourself, so that you are not tempted as well. **2** Bear one another's burdens, and thereby fulfill the law of Christ. **3** For if anyone thinks that he is something when he is nothing, he deceives himself. **4** But each one must examine his own work, and then he will have *reason for* boasting, *but* to himself alone, and not to another. **5** For each one will bear his own load.

6 The one who is taught the word is to share all good things with the one who teaches *him.* **7** Do not be deceived, God is not mocked; for whatever a person sows, this he will also reap. **8** For the one who sows to his own flesh will reap destruction from the flesh, but the one who sows to the Spirit will reap eternal life from the Spirit. **9** Let's not become discouraged in doing good, for in due time we will reap, if we do not become weary. [10] So then, while we have opportunity, let's do good to all people, and especially to those who are of the household of the faith.

[11] See with what large letters I have written to you with my own hand! [12] All who want to make a good showing in the flesh try to compel you to be circumcised, simply so that they will not be persecuted for the cross of Christ. [13] For those who ʸare circumcised do not even keep the Law themselves, but they want to have you circumcised so that they may boast in your flesh. [14] But far be it from me to boast, except in the cross of our Lord Jesus Christ, through which the world has been crucified to me, and I to the world. [15] For neither is circumcision anything, nor uncircumcision, but a new creation. [16] And all who will follow this rule, peace and mercy *be* upon them, and upon the Israel of God.

[17] From now on let no one cause trouble for me, for I bear on my body the marks of Jesus.

[18] The grace of our Lord Jesus Christ be with your spirit, brothers *and sisters.* Amen.

6:13 [1] Two early mss *have been*

The Letter of Paul to the

EPHESIANS

The Blessings of Redemption

1 Paul, an apostle of Christ Jesus by the will of God,
To the saints who are [1]at Ephesus and *are* faithful in
Christ Jesus: **2** Grace to you and peace from God our
Father and the Lord Jesus Christ.

3 Blessed *be* the God and Father of our Lord Jesus
Christ, who has blessed us with every spiritual blessing
in the heavenly *places* in Christ, **4** just as He chose us in
Him before the foundation of the world, that we would
be holy and blameless before [1]Him. In love **5** He
predestined us to adoption as sons *and daughters*
through Jesus Christ to Himself, according to the good
pleasure of His will, **6** to the praise of the glory of His
grace, with which He favored us in the Beloved.
7 In Him we have redemption through His blood, the forgiveness of our wrongdoings, according to the riches of
His grace **8** which He lavished on us. In all wisdom and
insight **9** He made known to us the mystery of His will,
according to His good pleasure which He set forth in
Him, **10** regarding *His* plan of the fullness of the times,
to bring all things together in Christ, things in the
heavens and things on the earth. **11** In Him we also have
obtained an inheritance, having been predestined
according to the purpose of Him who works all things
in accordance with the plan of His will, **12** to the end
that we who were the first to hope in the Christ would
be to the praise of His glory. **13** In Him, you also, after
listening to the message of truth, the gospel of your
salvation—having also believed, you were sealed in Him
with the Holy Spirit of the promise, **14** who is a first
installment of our inheritance, in regard to the
redemption of *God's own* possession, to the praise of His
glory.

15 For this reason I too, having heard of the faith in the
Lord Jesus which *exists* among you and [1]your love for
all the saints, **16** do not cease giving thanks for you, while

---

1:1 [1] Three early mss do not contain *at Ephesus*   1:4 [1] Or *Him, in love. He*   1:15 [1] Three early mss do not contain *your love* making mention *of you* in my prayers; 17 that the God of our Lord Jesus Christ, the Father of glory, may give you a spirit of wisdom and of revelation in the knowledge of Him. 18 *I pray that* the eyes of your heart may be enlightened, so that you will know what is the hope of His calling, what are the riches of the glory of His inheritance in the saints, 19 and what is the boundless greatness of His power toward us who believe. *These are* in accordance with the working of the strength of His might 20 which He brought about in Christ, when He raised Him from the dead and seated Him at His right hand in the heavenly *places,* 21 far above all rule and authority and power and dominion, and every name that is named, not only in this age but also in the one to come. 22 And He put all things in subjection under His feet, and made Him head over all things to the church, 23 which is His body, the fullness of Him who fills all in all.

Made Alive in Christ

2 And you were dead in your offenses and sins, 2 in which you previously walked according to the course of this world, according to the prince of the power of the air, of the spirit that is now working in the 1sons of disobedience. 3 Among them we too all previously lived in the lusts of our flesh, indulging the desires of the flesh and of the mind, and were by nature children of wrath, just as the rest. 4 But God, being rich in mercy, because of His great love with which He loved us, 5 even when we were dead in our wrongdoings, made us alive together 1with Christ (by grace you have been saved), 6 and raised us up with Him, and seated us with Him in the heavenly *places* in Christ Jesus, 7 so that in the ages to come He might show the boundless riches of His grace in kindness toward us in Christ Jesus. 8 For by grace you have been saved through faith; and 1this *is* not of yourselves, *it is* the gift of God; 9 not a result of works, so that no one may boast. 10 For we are His workmanship, created in Christ Jesus for good works, which God prepared beforehand so that we would walk in them.

11 Therefore remember that previously you, the Gentiles in the flesh, who are called "Uncircumcision"

2:2 1I.e., people opposed to God   2:5 1Two early mss *in Christ*
2:8 1I.e., this salvation

by the so-called "Circumcision" *which is* performed in the flesh by human hands— **12** *remember* that you were at that time separate from Christ, excluded from the people of Israel, and strangers to the covenants of the promise, having no hope and without God in the world. **13** But now in Christ Jesus you who previously were far away have been brought near by the blood of Christ. **14** For He Himself is our peace, who made both *groups into* one and broke down the barrier of the dividing wall, **15** by abolishing in His flesh the hostility, *which is* the Law *composed* of commandments *expressed* in ordinances, so that in Himself He might make the two one new person, *in this way* establishing peace; **16** and that He might reconcile them both in one body to God through the cross, by it having put to death the hostility. **17** And He came and preached peace to you who were far away, and peace to those who were near; **18** for through Him we both have our access in one Spirit to the Father. **19** So then you are no longer strangers and foreigners, but you are fellow citizens with the saints, and are of God's household, **20** having been built on the foundation of the apostles and prophets, Christ Jesus Himself being the cornerstone, **21** in whom the whole building, being fitted together, is growing into a holy temple in the Lord, **22** in whom you also are being built together into a dwelling of God in the Spirit.

Paul's Stewardship

3 For this reason I, Paul, the prisoner of Christ Jesus for the sake of you Gentiles— **2** if indeed you have heard of the administration of God's grace which was given to me for you; **3** that by revelation there was made known to me the mystery, as I wrote before briefly. **4** By referring to this, when you read you can understand my insight into the mystery of Christ, **5** which in other generations was not made known to mankind, as it has now been revealed to His holy apostles and prophets in the Spirit; **6** *to be specific,* that the Gentiles are fellow heirs and fellow members of the body, and fellow partakers of the promise in Christ Jesus through the gospel, **7** of which I was made a minister, according to the gift of God's grace which was given to me according to the working of His power. **8** To me, the very least of all saints, this grace was given, to preach to the Gentiles the unfathomable riches of Christ, 9 and to enlighten all people as to what the plan of the mystery is which for ages has been hidden in God, who created all things; 10 so that the multifaceted wisdom of God might now be made known through the church to the rulers and the authorities in the heavenly *places.* 11 *This was* in accordance with the eternal purpose which He carried out in Christ Jesus our Lord, 12 in whom we have boldness and confident access through faith in Him. 13 Therefore I ask you not to become discouraged about my tribulations in your behalf, since they are your glory.

14 For this reason I bend my knees before the Father, 15 from whom every family in heaven and on earth derives its name, 16 that He would grant you, according to the riches of His glory, to be strengthened with power through His Spirit in the inner self, 17 so that Christ may dwell in your hearts through faith; *and* that you, being rooted and grounded in love, 18 may be able to comprehend with all the saints what is the width and length and height and depth, 19 and to know the love of Christ which surpasses knowledge, that you may be filled to all the fullness of God.

20 Now to Him who is able to do far more abundantly beyond all that we ask or think, according to the power that works within us, 21 to Him *be* the glory in the church and in Christ Jesus to all generations forever and ever. Amen.

Unity of the Spirit

4 Therefore I, the prisoner of the Lord, urge you to walk in a manner worthy of the calling with which you have been called, 2 with all humility and gentleness, with patience, bearing with one another in love, 3 being diligent to keep the unity of the Spirit in the bond of peace. 4 *There is* one body and one Spirit, just as you also were called in one hope of your calling; 5 one Lord, one faith, one baptism, 6 one God and Father of all who is over all and through all and in all.

7 But to each one of us grace was given according to the measure of Christ's gift. 8 Therefore it says,

"WHEN HE ASCENDED ON HIGH,
HE LED CAPTIVE *THE* CAPTIVES,
AND HE GAVE GIFTS TO PEOPLE."

9 (Now this *expression,* "He ascended," what does it

mean except that He also had descended into the lower parts of the earth? 10 He who descended is Himself also He who ascended far above all the heavens, so that He might fill all things.) 11 And He gave some *as* apostles, some *as* prophets, some *as* evangelists, some *as* ¹pastors and teachers, 12 for the equipping of the saints for the work of ministry, for the building up of the body of Christ; 13 until we all attain to the unity of the faith, and of the knowledge of the Son of God, to a mature man, to the measure of the stature which belongs to the fullness of Christ. 14 As a result, we are no longer to be children, tossed here and there by waves and carried about by every wind of doctrine, by the trickery of people, by craftiness in deceitful scheming; 15 but speaking the truth in love, we are to grow up in all *aspects* into Him who is the head, *that is,* Christ, 16 from whom the whole body, being fitted and held together by what every joint supplies, according to the proper working of each individual part, causes the growth of the body for the building up of itself in love.

The Christian's Walk

17 So I say this, and affirm in the Lord, that you are to no longer walk just as the Gentiles also walk, in the futility of their minds, 18 being darkened in their understanding, excluded from the life of God because of the ignorance that is in them, because of the hardness of their heart; 19 and they, having become callous, have given themselves up to indecent behavior for the practice of every kind of impurity with greediness. 20 But you did not learn Christ in this way, 21 if indeed you have heard Him and have been taught in Him, just as truth is in Jesus, 22 that, in reference to your former way of life, you are to rid yourselves of the old self, which is being corrupted in accordance with the lusts of deceit, 23 and that you are to be renewed in the spirit of your minds, 24 and to put on the new self, which in *the likeness of* God has been created in righteousness and holiness of the truth.

25 Therefore, ridding yourselves of falsehood, SPEAK TRUTH EACH ONE *OF YOU* WITH HIS NEIGHBOR, because we are parts of one another. 26 BE ANGRY, AND *YET* DO NOT SIN;

4:11 ¹From Gr for *shepherds*

do not let the sun go down on your anger, [27] and do not give the devil an opportunity. [28] The one who steals must no longer steal; but rather he must labor, producing with his own hands what is good, so that he will have *something* to share with the one who has need. [29] Let no unwholesome word come out of your mouth, but if *there is* any good *word* for edification according to the need *of the moment, say that,* so that it will give grace to those who hear. [30] Do not grieve the Holy Spirit of God, by whom you were sealed for the day of redemption. [31] All bitterness, wrath, anger, clamor, and slander must be removed from you, along with all malice. [32] Be kind to one another, compassionate, forgiving each other, just as God in Christ also has forgiven [1]you.

Be Imitators of God

5 Therefore be imitators of God, as beloved children; [2] and walk in love, just as Christ also loved [1]you and gave Himself up for us, an offering and a sacrifice to God as a fragrant aroma.

[3] But sexual immorality or any impurity or greed must not even be mentioned among you, as is proper among saints; [4] and *there must be no* filthiness or foolish talk, or vulgar joking, which are not fitting, but rather giving of thanks. [5] For this you know with certainty, that no sexually immoral or impure or greedy person, which amounts to an idolater, has an inheritance in the kingdom of Christ and God.

[6]*See that* no one deceives you with empty words, for because of these things the wrath of God comes upon the [1]sons of disobedience. [7] Therefore do not become partners with them; [8] for you were once darkness, but now you are light in the Lord; walk as children of light [9] (for the fruit of the light *consists* in all goodness, righteousness, and truth), [10] as you try to learn what is pleasing to the Lord. [11] Do not participate in the useless deeds of darkness, but instead even expose them; [12] for it is disgraceful even to speak of the things which are done by them in secret. [13] But all things become visible when they are exposed by the light, for everything that becomes visible is light. [14] For this reason it says,

---

4:32 [1]Two early mss *us*   5:2 [1]One early ms *us*   5:6 [1]I.e., people opposed to God

> "Awake, sleeper,
>   And arise from the dead,
>   And Christ will shine on you."

15 So then, be careful how you walk, not as unwise people but as wise, **16** making the most of your time, because the days are evil. **17** Therefore do not be foolish, but understand what the will of the Lord *is*. **18** And do not get drunk with wine, in which there is debauchery, but be filled with the Spirit, **19** speaking to one another in psalms and hymns and spiritual songs, singing and making melody with your hearts to the Lord; **20** always giving thanks for all things in the name of our Lord Jesus Christ to *our* God and Father; **21** and subject yourselves to one another in the fear of Christ.

Marriage like Christ and the Church

22 Wives, *subject yourselves* to your own husbands, as to the Lord. **23** For the husband is the head of the wife, as Christ also is the head of the church, He Himself *being* the Savior of the body. **24** But as the church is subject to Christ, so also the wives *ought to be* to their husbands in everything.

25 Husbands, love your wives, just as Christ also loved the church and gave Himself up for her, **26** so that He might sanctify her, having cleansed her by the washing of water with the word, **27** that He might present to Himself the church in all her glory, having no spot or wrinkle or any such thing; but that she would be holy and blameless. **28** So husbands also ought to love their own wives as their own bodies. He who loves his own wife loves himself; **29** for no one ever hated his own flesh, but nourishes and cherishes it, just as Christ also *does* the church, **30** because we are parts of His body. **31** FOR THIS REASON A MAN SHALL LEAVE HIS FATHER AND HIS MOTHER AND BE JOINED TO HIS WIFE, AND THE TWO SHALL BECOME ONE FLESH. **32** This mystery is great; but I am speaking with reference to Christ and the church. **33** Nevertheless, as for you individually, each *husband* is to love his own wife the same as himself, and the wife *must see to it* that she respects her husband.

Children and Parents

6 Children, obey your parents in the Lord, for this is right. **2** HONOR YOUR FATHER AND MOTHER (which is the first commandment with a promise), ³ SO THAT IT MAY TURN OUT WELL FOR YOU, AND THAT YOU MAY LIVE LONG ON THE EARTH.

⁴ Fathers, do not provoke your children to anger, but bring them up in the discipline and instruction of the Lord.

Slaves and Masters

⁵ Slaves, be obedient to those who are your masters according to the flesh, with fear and trembling, in the sincerity of your heart, as to Christ; ⁶ not by way of eye-service, as people-pleasers, but as slaves of Christ, doing the will of God from the heart. ⁷ With goodwill render service, as to the Lord, and not to people, ⁸ knowing that whatever good thing each one does, he will receive this back from the Lord, whether slave or free.

⁹ And masters, do the same things to them, and give up threatening, knowing that both their Master and yours is in heaven, and there is no partiality with Him.

The Armor of God

¹⁰ Finally, be strong in the Lord and in the strength of His might. ¹¹ Put on the full armor of God, so that you will be able to stand firm against the schemes of the devil. ¹² For our struggle is not against flesh and blood, but against the rulers, against the powers, against the world forces of this darkness, against the spiritual *forces* of wickedness in the heavenly *places.* ¹³ Therefore, take up the full armor of God, so that you will be able to resist on the evil day, and having done everything, to stand firm. ¹⁴ Stand firm therefore, having belted your waist with truth, and having put on the breastplate of righteousness, ¹⁵ and having strapped on your feet the preparation of the gospel of peace; ¹⁶ in addition to all, taking up the shield of faith with which you will be able to extinguish all the flaming arrows of the evil *one.* ¹⁷ And take the helmet of salvation and the sword of the Spirit, which is the word of God.

¹⁸ With every prayer and request, pray at all times in the Spirit, and with this in view, be alert with all perseverance and *every* request for all the saints, ¹⁹ and *pray* in my behalf, that speech may be given to me in the opening of my mouth, to make known with boldness the mystery of the gospel, ²⁰ for which I am an ambassador in

chains; that [1]in *proclaiming* it I may speak boldly, as I
ought to speak.

21 Now, so that you also may know about my circumstances *as to* what I am doing, Tychicus, the beloved
brother and faithful servant in the Lord, will make
everything known to you. **22** I have sent him to you for
this very purpose, so that you may know about us, and
that he may comfort your hearts.

23 Peace be to the brothers *and sisters,* and love with
faith, from God the Father and the Lord Jesus Christ.
24 Grace be with all those who love our Lord Jesus Christ
with incorruptible *love.*

6:20 [1] Two early mss *I may speak it boldly*

The Letter of Paul to the
PHILIPPIANS

Thanksgiving

1 Paul and Timothy, bond-servants of Christ
Jesus,
To all the saints in Christ Jesus who are in Philippi,
including the overseers and deacons: 2 Grace to you and
peace from God our Father and the Lord Jesus Christ.

3 I thank my God in all my remembrance of you,
4 always offering prayer with joy in my every prayer for
you all, 5 in view of your participation in the gospel from
the first day until now. 6 *For I am* confident of this very
thing, that He who began a good work among you will
complete it by the day of Christ Jesus. 7 For it is only right
for me to feel this way about you all, because I have you
in my heart, since both in my imprisonment and in the
defense and confirmation of the gospel, you all are partakers of grace with me. 8 For God is my witness, how I
long for you all with the affection of Christ Jesus. 9 And
this I pray, that your love may overflow still more and
more in real knowledge and all discernment, 10 so that
you may discover the things that are excellent, that you
may be sincere and blameless for the day of Christ;
11 having been filled with the fruit of righteousness
which *comes* through Jesus Christ, for the glory and
praise of God.

The Gospel Is Preached

12 Now I want you to know, brothers *and sisters,* that
my circumstances have turned out for the greater
progress of the gospel, 13 so that my imprisonment in *the
cause of* Christ has become well known throughout
the ¹praetorian guard and to everyone else, 14 and that
most of the brothers *and sisters,* trusting in the Lord
because of my imprisonment, have far more courage to
speak the word of God without fear. 15 Some, to be sure,
are preaching Christ even from envy and strife, but some
also from goodwill; 16 the latter *do it* out of love, knowing
that I am appointed for the defense of the gospel; 17 the

1:13 ¹Or *governor's palace*

former proclaim Christ out of selfish ambition rather than from pure motives, thinking that they are causing me distress in my imprisonment. **18** What then? Only that in every way, whether in pretense or in truth, Christ is proclaimed, and in this I rejoice.

But *not only that,* I also will rejoice, **19** for I know that this will turn out for my deliverance through your prayers and the provision of the Spirit of Jesus Christ, **20** according to my eager expectation and hope, that I will not be put to shame in anything, but *that* with all boldness, Christ will even now, as always, be exalted in my body, whether by life or by death.

To Live Is Christ

21 For to me, to live is Christ, and to die is gain. **22** But if *I am* to live *on* in the flesh, this *will mean* fruitful labor for me; and I do not know which to choose. **23** But I am hard-pressed from both *directions,* having the desire to depart and be with Christ, for *that* is very much better; **24** yet to remain on in the flesh is more necessary for your sakes. **25** Convinced of this, I know that I will remain and continue with you all for your progress and joy in the faith, **26** so that your pride in Christ Jesus may be abundant because of me by my coming to you again.

27 Only conduct yourselves in a manner worthy of the gospel of Christ, so that whether I come and see you or remain absent, I will hear about you that you are standing firm in one spirit, with one mind striving together for the faith of the gospel; **28** and in no way alarmed by *your* opponents—which is a sign of destruction for them, but of salvation for you, and this *too,* from God. **29** For to you it has been granted for Christ's sake, not only to believe in Him, but also to suffer on His behalf, **30** experiencing the same conflict which you saw in me, and now hear *to be* in me.

Be like Christ

2 Therefore if there is any encouragement in Christ, if any consolation of love, if any fellowship of the Spirit, if any affection and compassion, **2** make my joy complete by being of the same mind, maintaining the same love, united in spirit, intent on one purpose. **3** Do nothing from selfishness or empty conceit, but with humility consider one another as more important than yourselves; **4** do not *merely* look out for your own personal *interests,* but also for the *interests* of others. 5 Have this attitude in yourselves which was also in Christ Jesus, 6 who, as He *already* existed in the form of God, did not consider equality with God something to be grasped, 7 but 'emptied Himself *by* taking the form of a bond-servant *and* being born in the likeness of men. 8 And being found in appearance as a man, He humbled Himself by becoming obedient to the point of death: death on a cross. 9 For this reason also God highly exalted Him, and bestowed on Him the name which is above every name, 10 so that at the name of Jesus EVERY KNEE WILL BOW, of those who are in heaven and on earth and under the earth, 11 and *that* every tongue will confess that Jesus Christ is Lord, to the glory of God the Father.

12 So then, my beloved, just as you have always obeyed, not as in my presence only, but now much more in my absence, work out your own salvation with fear and trembling; 13 for it is God who is at work in you, both to desire and to work for *His* good pleasure.

14 Do all things without complaining or arguments; 15 so that you will prove yourselves to be blameless and innocent, children of God above reproach in the midst of a crooked and perverse generation, among whom you appear as lights in the world, 16 holding firmly the word of life, so that on the day of Christ I can take pride because I did not run in vain nor labor in vain. 17 But even if I am being poured out as a drink offering upon the sacrifice and service of your faith, I rejoice and share my joy with you all. 18 You too, *I urge you,* rejoice in the same way and share your joy with me.

Timothy and Epaphroditus

19 But I hope, in the Lord Jesus, to send Timothy to you shortly, so that I also may be encouraged when I learn of your condition. 20 For I have no one *else* of kindred spirit who will genuinely be concerned for your welfare. 21 For they all seek after their own *interests,* not those of Christ Jesus. 22 But you know of his proven character, that he served with me in the furtherance of the gospel like a child *serving* his father. 23 Therefore I hope to send him immediately, as soon as I see how

---

2:7 1 I.e., set aside His divine rights

things *go* with me; **24** and I trust in the Lord that I myself will also be coming shortly. **25** But I thought it necessary to send to you Epaphroditus, my brother and fellow worker and fellow soldier, who is also your messenger and minister to my need, **26** because he was longing ¹for you all and was distressed because you had heard that he was sick. **27** For indeed he was sick to the point of death, but God had mercy on him, and not only on him but also on me, so that I would not have sorrow upon sorrow. **28** Therefore I have sent him all the more eagerly, so that when you see him again you may rejoice and I may be less concerned *about you.* **29** Receive him then in the Lord with all joy, and hold people like him in high regard, **30** because he came close to death for the work of Christ, risking his life to compensate for your absence in your service to me.

The Goal of Life

3 Finally, my brothers *and sisters,* rejoice in the Lord. To write the same things *again* is no trouble for me, and it is a safeguard for you.

2 Beware of the dogs, beware of the evil workers, beware of the false circumcision; **3** for we are the *true* circumcision, who worship in the Spirit of God and take pride in Christ Jesus, and put no confidence in the flesh, **4** although I myself *could boast as* having confidence even in the flesh. If anyone else thinks he is confident in the flesh, I *have* more *reason:* **5** circumcised the eighth day, of the nation of Israel, of the tribe of Benjamin, a Hebrew of Hebrews; as to the Law, a Pharisee; **6** as to zeal, a persecutor of the church; as to the righteousness which is in the Law, found blameless.

7 But whatever things were gain to me, these things I have counted as loss because of Christ. **8** More than that, I count all things to be loss in view of the surpassing value of knowing Christ Jesus my Lord, for whom I have suffered the loss of all things, and count them *mere* rubbish, so that I may gain Christ, **9** and may be found in Him, not having a righteousness of my own derived from *the* Law, but that which is through faith in Christ, the righteousness which *comes* from God on the basis of faith, **10** that I may know Him and the power of His

---

2:26 ¹One early ms *to see you all*

resurrection and the fellowship of His sufferings, being conformed to His death; 11 if somehow I may attain to the resurrection from the dead.

12 Not that I have already grasped *it all* or have already become perfect, but I press on if I may also take hold of that for which I was even taken hold of by Christ Jesus. 13 Brothers *and sisters,* I do not regard myself as having taken hold of *it yet;* but one thing *I do:* forgetting what *lies* behind and reaching forward to what *lies* ahead, 14 I press on toward the goal for the prize of the upward call of God in Christ Jesus. 15 Therefore, all who are mature, let's have this attitude; and if in anything you have a different attitude, God will reveal that to you as well; 16 however, let's keep living by that same *standard* to which we have attained.

17 Brothers *and sisters,* join in following my example, and observe those who walk according to the pattern you have in us. 18 For many walk, of whom I often told you, and now tell you even as I weep, *that they are* the enemies of the cross of Christ, 19 whose end is destruction, whose god is *their* appetite, and *whose* glory is in their shame, who have their minds on earthly things. 20 For our citizenship is in heaven, from which we also eagerly wait for a Savior, the Lord Jesus Christ; 21 who will transform the body of our lowly condition into conformity with His glorious body, by the exertion of the power that He has even to subject all things to Himself.

Think of Excellence

4 Therefore, my beloved brothers *and sisters,* whom I long *to see,* my joy and crown, stand firm in the Lord in this way, my beloved.

2 I urge Euodia and I urge Syntyche to live in harmony in the Lord. 3 Indeed, true companion, I ask you also, help these women who have shared my struggle in *the cause of* the gospel, together with Clement as well as the rest of my fellow workers, whose names are in the book of life.

4 Rejoice in the Lord always; again I will say, rejoice! 5 Let your gentle *spirit* be known to all people. The Lord is near. 6 Do not be anxious about anything, but in everything by prayer and pleading with thanksgiving let your requests be made known to God. 7 And the peace of

God, which surpasses all comprehension, will guard your hearts and minds in Christ Jesus.

8 Finally, brothers *and sisters,* whatever is true, whatever is honorable, whatever is right, whatever is pure, whatever is lovely, whatever is commendable, if there is any excellence and if anything worthy of praise, think about these things. 9 As for the things you have learned and received and heard and seen in me, practice these things, and the God of peace will be with you.

God's Provisions

10 But I rejoiced in the Lord greatly, that now at last you have revived your concern for me; indeed, you were concerned *before,* but you lacked an opportunity *to act.* 11 Not that I speak from need, for I have learned to be content in whatever *circumstances* I am. 12 I know how to get along with little, and I also know how to live in prosperity; in any and every *circumstance* I have learned the secret of being filled and going hungry, both of having abundance and suffering need. 13 I can do all things through Him who strengthens me. 14 Nevertheless, you have done well to share *with me* in my difficulty.

15 You yourselves also know, Philippians, that at the first *preaching* of the gospel, after I left Macedonia, no church shared with me in the matter of giving and receiving except you alone; 16 for even in Thessalonica you sent *a gift* more than once for my needs. 17 Not that I seek the gift *itself,* but I seek the profit which increases to your account. 18 But I have received everything in full and have an abundance; I am amply supplied, having received from Epaphroditus what you have sent, a fragrant aroma, an acceptable sacrifice, pleasing to God. 19 And my God will supply all your needs according to His riches in glory in Christ Jesus. 20 Now to our God and Father *be* the glory forever and ever. Amen.

21 Greet every saint in Christ Jesus. The brothers who are with me greet you. 22 All the saints greet you, especially those of Caesar's household.

23 The grace of the Lord Jesus Christ be with your spirit.

The Letter of Paul to the
COLOSSIANS

Thankfulness for Spiritual Attainments

1 Paul, an apostle of Christ Jesus by the will of God, and Timothy our brother,

2 To the saints and faithful brothers *and sisters* in Christ *who are* at Colossae: Grace to you and peace from God our Father.

3 We give thanks to God, the Father of our Lord Jesus Christ, praying always for you, 4 since we heard of your faith in Christ Jesus and the love which you have for all the saints; 5 because of the hope reserved for you in heaven, of which you previously heard in the word of truth, the gospel 6 which has come to you, just as in all the world also it is bearing fruit and increasing, even as *it has been doing* in you also since the day you heard *it* and understood the grace of God in truth; 7 just as you learned *it* from Epaphras, our beloved fellow bond-servant, who is a faithful servant of Christ on our behalf, 8 and he also informed us of your love in the Spirit.

9 For this reason we also, since the day we heard *about it,* have not ceased praying for you and asking that you may be filled with the knowledge of His will in all spiritual wisdom and understanding, 10 so that you will walk in a manner worthy of the Lord, to please *Him* in all respects, bearing fruit in every good work and increasing in the knowledge of God; 11 strengthened with all power, according to His glorious might, for the attaining of all perseverance and patience; joyously 12 giving thanks to the Father, who has qualified us to share in the inheritance of the saints in light.

The Incomparable Christ

13 For He rescued us from the domain of darkness, and transferred us to the kingdom of His beloved Son, 14 in whom we have redemption, the forgiveness of sins.

15 He is the image of the invisible God, the firstborn of all creation: 16 for by Him all things were created, *both* in the heavens and on earth, visible and invisible, whether thrones, or dominions, or rulers, or authorities—all things have been created through Him and for Him. 17 He

is before all things, and in Him all things hold together.
18 He is also the head of the body, the church; and He is
the beginning, the firstborn from the dead, so that He
Himself will come to have first place in everything. **19** For
it was the *Father's* good pleasure for all the fullness to
dwell in Him, **20** and through Him to reconcile all things
to Himself, whether things on earth or things in heaven,
having made peace through the blood of His cross.

21 And although you were previously alienated and
hostile in attitude, *engaged* in evil deeds, **22** yet He has
now reconciled you in His body of flesh through death,
in order to present you before Him holy and blameless
and beyond reproach— **23** if indeed you continue in the
faith firmly established and steadfast, and not shifting
from the hope of the gospel that you have heard, which
was proclaimed in all creation under heaven, and of
which I, Paul, was made a minister.

24 Now I rejoice in my sufferings for your sake, and in
my flesh I am supplementing what is lacking in Christ's
afflictions in behalf of His body, which is the church. **25** I
was made a minister of this *church* according to the
commission from God granted to me for your benefit, so
that I might fully carry out *the preaching of* the word of
God, **26** *that is,* the mystery which had been hidden from
the *past* ages and generations, but now has been
revealed to His saints, **27** to whom God willed to make
known what the wealth of the glory of this mystery
among the Gentiles is, *the mystery* that is Christ in you,
the hope of glory. **28** We proclaim Him, admonishing
every person and teaching every person with all wisdom,
so that we may present every person complete in Christ.
29 For this purpose I also labor, striving according to His
power which works mightily within me.

You Are Built Up in Christ

2 For I want you to know how great a struggle I have in
your behalf and for those who are at Laodicea, and for
all those who have not personally seen my face, **2** that
their hearts may be encouraged, having been knit
together in love, and *that they would attain* to all the
wealth that comes from the full assurance of understanding, *resulting* in a true knowledge of God's mystery, *that
is,* Christ *Himself,* **3** in whom are hidden all the treasures
of wisdom and knowledge. **4** I say this so that no one will

deceive you with persuasive arguments. 5 For even though I am absent in body, I am nevertheless with you in spirit, rejoicing to see your orderly manner and the stability of your faith in Christ.

6 Therefore, as you have received Christ Jesus the Lord, *so* walk in Him, 7 having been firmly rooted and *now* being built up in Him and established 'in your faith, just as you were instructed, *and* overflowing with gratitude.

8 See to it that there is no one who takes you captive through philosophy and empty deception in accordance with human tradition, in accordance with the elementary principles of the world, rather than in accordance with Christ. 9 For in Him all the fullness of Deity dwells in bodily form, 10 and in Him you have been made complete, and He is the head over every ruler and authority; 11 and in Him you were also circumcised with a circumcision performed without hands, in the removal of the body of the flesh by the circumcision of Christ, 12 having been buried with Him in baptism, in which you were also raised with Him through faith in the working of God, who raised Him from the dead. 13 And when you were dead in your wrongdoings and the uncircumcision of your flesh, He made you alive together with Him, having forgiven us all our wrongdoings, 14 having canceled the certificate of debt consisting of decrees against us, which was hostile to us; and He has taken it out of the way, having nailed it to the cross. 15 When He had disarmed the rulers and authorities, He made a public display *of them,* having triumphed over them through 'Him.

16 Therefore, no one is to act as your judge in regard to food and drink, or in respect to a festival or a new moon, or a Sabbath day— 17 things which are *only* a shadow of what is to come; but the substance belongs to Christ. 18 *Take care that* no one keeps defrauding you of your prize by delighting in humility and the worship of the angels, taking his stand on *visions* he has seen, inflated without cause by his fleshly mind, 19 and not holding firmly to the head, from whom the entire body, being supplied and held together by the joints and ligaments, grows with a growth which is from God.

2:7 1 Or *by*   2:15 1 Or *it;* i.e., the cross

20 If you have died with Christ to the elementary principles of the world, why, as if you were living in the world, do you submit yourself to decrees, *such as,* **21** "Do not handle, do not taste, do not touch!" **22** (which all *refer to* things destined to perish with use)—in accordance with the commandments and teachings of man? **23** These are matters which do have the appearance of wisdom in self-made religion and humility and severe treatment of the body, *but are* of no value against fleshly indulgence.

Put On the New Self

3 Therefore, if you have been raised with Christ, keep seeking the things *that are* above, where Christ is, seated at the right hand of God. **2** Set your minds on the things *that are* above, not on the things that are on earth. **3** For you have died, and your life is hidden with Christ in God. **4** When Christ, who is our life, is revealed, then you also will be revealed with Him in glory.

5 Therefore, treat the parts of your earthly body as dead *to* sexual immorality, impurity, passion, evil desire, and greed, which amounts to idolatry. **6** *For it is* because of these things *that* the wrath of God is coming [1]upon the [2]sons of disobedience, **7** and in them you also once walked, when you were living in them. **8** But now you also, rid yourselves of all of them: anger, wrath, malice, slander, *and* obscene speech from your mouth. **9** Do not lie to one another, since you stripped off the old self with its *evil* practices, **10** and have put on the new *self,* which is being renewed to a true knowledge according to the image of the One who created it— **11** *a renewal* in which there is no *distinction between* Greek and Jew, circumcised and uncircumcised, [1]barbarian, [2]Scythian, slave, *and* free, but Christ is all, and in all.

12 So, as those who have been chosen of God, holy and beloved, put on a heart of compassion, kindness, humility, gentleness, *and* patience; **13** bearing with one another, and forgiving each other, whoever has a complaint against anyone; just as the Lord forgave you, so *must* you *do* also. **14** In addition to all these things *put on*

3:6 [1] Two early mss do not contain *upon the sons of disobedience*
3:6 [2] I.e., people opposed to God   3:11 [1] I.e., uncultured
3:11 [2] I.e., a member of an ancient people near the Black Sea, often considered unrefined

love, which is the perfect bond of unity. **15** Let the peace of Christ, to which you were indeed called in one body, rule in your hearts; and be thankful. **16** Let the word of ¹Christ richly dwell within you, with all wisdom teaching and admonishing one another with psalms, hymns, *and* spiritual songs, singing with thankfulness in your hearts to God. **17** Whatever you do in word or deed, *do* everything in the name of the Lord Jesus, giving thanks through Him to God the Father.

Family Relations

18 Wives, be subject to your husbands, as is fitting in the Lord. **19** Husbands, love your wives and do not become bitter against them. **20** Children, obey your parents in everything, for this is pleasing to the Lord. **21** Fathers, do not antagonize your children, so that they will not become discouraged.

22 Slaves, obey those who are your human masters in everything, not with eye-service, as people-pleasers, but with sincerity of heart, fearing the Lord. **23** Whatever you do, do your work heartily, as for the Lord and not for people, **24** knowing that *it is* from the Lord *that* you will receive the reward of the inheritance. *It is* the Lord Christ *whom* you serve. **25** For the one who does wrong will receive the consequences of the wrong which he has done, and that without partiality.

4 Masters, grant your slaves justice and fairness, knowing that you also have a Master in heaven.

2 Devote yourselves to prayer, keeping alert in it with *an attitude of* thanksgiving; **3** praying at the same time for us as well, that God will open up to us a door for the word, so that we may proclaim the mystery of Christ, for which I have also been imprisoned; **4** that I may make it clear in the way that I ought to proclaim *it.*

5 Conduct yourselves with wisdom toward outsiders, making the most of the opportunity. **6** Your speech *must* always *be* with grace, *as though* seasoned with salt, so that you will know how you should respond to each person.

7 As to all my affairs, Tychicus, *our* beloved brother and faithful servant and fellow bond-servant in the Lord, will bring you information. **8** *For* I have sent him to you

---

3:16 ¹One early ms *the Lord*

for this very purpose, that you may know about our circumstances and that he may encourage your hearts; **9** and with him is Onesimus, *our* faithful and beloved brother, who is one of your *own*. They will inform you about the whole situation here.

10 Aristarchus, my fellow prisoner, sends you his greetings; and *also* Barnabas' cousin Mark (about whom you received instructions; if he comes to you, welcome him); **11** and *also* Jesus who is called Justus; these are the only fellow workers for the kingdom of God who are from the circumcision, and they have proved to be an encouragement to me. **12** Epaphras, who is one of your *own,* a bond-servant of Christ Jesus, sends you his greetings, always striving earnestly for you in his prayers, that you may stand mature and fully assured in all the will of God. **13** For I testify for him that he has a deep concern for you and for those who are in Laodicea and Hierapolis. **14** Luke, the beloved physician, sends you his greetings, and Demas *does also.* **15** Greet the brothers *and sisters* who are in Laodicea and also ¹Nympha and the church that is in her house. **16** When this letter is read among you, have it also read in the church of the Laodiceans; and you, for your part, read my letter *that is coming* from Laodicea. **17** Tell Archippus, "See to the ministry which you have received in the Lord, so that you may fulfill it."

18 I, Paul, write this greeting with my own hand. Remember my imprisonment. Grace be with you.

4:15 ¹ Or *Nymphas* (masc)

The First Letter of Paul to the
THESSALONIANS

Giving Thanks for These Believers

1 Paul, Silvanus, and Timothy,

To the church of the Thessalonians in God the Father and the Lord Jesus Christ: Grace to you and peace.

2 We always give thanks to God for all of you, making mention *of you* in our prayers; **3** constantly keeping in mind your work of faith and labor of love and perseverance of hope in our Lord Jesus Christ in the presence of our God and Father, **4** knowing, brothers *and sisters,* beloved by God, *His* choice of you; **5** for our gospel did not come to you in word only, but also in power and in the Holy Spirit and with full conviction; just as you know what kind of men we proved to be among you for your sakes. **6** You also became imitators of us and of the Lord, having received the word during great affliction with the joy of the Holy Spirit, **7** so that you became an example to all the believers in Macedonia and Achaia. **8** For the word of the Lord has sounded forth from you, not only in Macedonia and Achaia, but in every place *the news of* your faith toward God has gone out, so that we have no need to say anything. **9** For they themselves report about us as to the kind of reception we had with you, and how you turned to God from idols to serve a living and true God, **10** and to wait for His Son from heaven, whom He raised from the dead, *that is,* Jesus who rescues us from the wrath to come.

Paul's Ministry

2 For you yourselves know, brothers *and sisters,* that our reception among you was not in vain, **2** but after we had already suffered and been treated abusively in Philippi, as you know, we had the boldness in our God to speak to you the gospel of God amid much opposition. **3** For our exhortation does not *come* from error or impurity or by way of deceit; **4** but just as we have been approved by God to be entrusted with the gospel, so we speak, not intending to please people, but *to please* God, who examines our hearts. **5** For we never came with flattering speech, as you know, nor with a pretext for greed—God is *our* witness—⁶nor did we seek honor from people, either from you or from others, though we could have asserted our authority as apostles of Christ. ⁷But we proved to be ¹gentle among you. As a nursing *mother* tenderly cares for her own children, ⁸in the same way we had a fond affection for you and were delighted to share with you not only the gospel of God, but also our own lives, because you had become very dear to us.

⁹For you recall, brothers *and sisters,* our labor and hardship: *it was by* working night and day so as not to be a burden to any of you, *that* we proclaimed to you the gospel of God. ¹⁰You are witnesses, and *so is* God, *of* how devoutly and rightly and blamelessly we behaved toward you believers; ¹¹just as you know how *we were* exhorting and encouraging and imploring each one of you as a father *would* his own children, ¹²so that you would walk in a manner worthy of the God who calls you into His own kingdom and glory.

¹³For this reason we also constantly thank God that when you received the word of God which you heard from us, you accepted *it* not *as* the word of *mere* men, but as what it really is, the word of God, which also is at work in you who believe. ¹⁴For you, brothers *and sisters,* became imitators of the churches of God in Christ Jesus that are in Judea, for you also endured the same sufferings at the hands of your own countrymen, even as they *did* from the Jews, ¹⁵who both killed the Lord Jesus and the prophets, and drove us out. They are not pleasing to God, but hostile to all people, ¹⁶hindering us from speaking to the Gentiles so that they may be saved; with the result that they always reach the limit of their sins. But wrath has come upon them fully.

¹⁷But we, brothers *and sisters,* having been orphaned from you *by absence* for a short while—in person, not in spirit—were all the more eager with great desire to see your face. ¹⁸For we wanted to come to you—I, Paul, more than once—and Satan hindered us. ¹⁹For who *is* our hope, or joy or crown of pride, in the presence of our Lord Jesus at His coming? Or *is it* not indeed you? ²⁰For you are our glory and joy.

2:7 ¹Three early mss *infants*

Encouragement of Timothy's Visit

3 Therefore, when we could no longer endure *it,* we thought it best to be left behind, alone at Athens, **2** and we sent Timothy, our brother and God's fellow worker in the gospel of Christ, to strengthen and encourage you for the benefit of your faith, **3** so that no one would be disturbed by these afflictions. For you yourselves know that we have been destined for this. **4** For even when we were with you, we *kept* telling you in advance that we were going to suffer affliction; and so it happened, as you know. **5** For this reason, when I could no longer endure *it,* I also sent to find out about your faith, for fear that the tempter might have tempted you, and our labor would be for nothing.

6 But now that Timothy has come to us from you, and has brought us good news of your faith and love, and that you always think kindly of us, longing to see us just as we also *long to see* you, **7** for this reason, brothers *and sisters,* in all our distress and affliction we were comforted about you through your faith; **8** for now we *really* live, if you stand firm in the Lord. **9** For what thanks can we give to God for you in return for all the joy with which we rejoice because of you before our God, **10** as we keep praying most earnestly night and day that we may see your faces, and may complete what is lacking in your faith?

11 Now may our God and Father Himself, and our Lord Jesus, direct our way to you; **12** and may the Lord cause you to increase and overflow in love for one another, and for all people, just as we also *do* for you; **13** so that He may establish your hearts blameless in holiness before our God and Father at the coming of our Lord Jesus with all His saints.

Sanctification and Love

4 Finally then, brothers *and sisters,* we request and urge you in the Lord Jesus, that as you received *instruction* from us as to how you ought to walk and please God (just as you actually do walk), that you excel *even* more. **2** For you know what instructions we gave you by *the authority of* the Lord Jesus. **3** For this is the will of God, your sanctification; *that is,* that you abstain from sexual immorality; **4** that each of you know how to

possess his own ¹vessel in sanctification and honor, **5** not
in lustful passion, like the Gentiles who do not know
God; **6** *and* that no one violate the rights and take
advantage of his brother *or sister* in the matter, because
the Lord is *the* avenger in all these things, just as we also
told you previously and solemnly warned *you*. **7** For God
has not called us for impurity, but in sanctification.
8 Therefore, the one who rejects *this* is not rejecting
man, but the God who gives His Holy Spirit to you.

9 Now as to the love of the brothers *and* sisters, you
have no need for *anyone* to write to you, for you
yourselves are taught by God to love one another; **10** for
indeed you practice it toward all the brothers *and sisters*
who are in all Macedonia. But we urge you, brothers *and
sisters,* to excel *even* more, **11** and to make it your
ambition to lead a quiet life and attend to your own
business and work with your hands, just as we
instructed you, **12** so that you will behave properly toward
outsiders and not be in any need.

Those Who Died in Christ

13 But we do not want you to be uninformed, brothers
and sisters, about those who ¹are asleep, so that you will
not grieve as indeed the rest *of mankind do,* who have
no hope. **14** For if we believe that Jesus died and rose
from the dead, so also God will bring with Him those
who have fallen asleep ¹through Jesus. **15** For we say this
to you by the word of the Lord, that we who are alive
and remain until the coming of the Lord will not precede
those who have fallen asleep. **16** For the Lord Himself will
descend from heaven with a shout, with the voice of *the*
archangel and with the trumpet of God, and the dead in
Christ will rise first. **17** Then we who are alive, who
remain, will be caught up together with them in the
clouds to meet the Lord in the air, and so we will always
be with the Lord. **18** Therefore, comfort one another with
these words.

The Day of the Lord

5 Now as to the periods and times, brothers *and sisters,*
you have no need *of anything* to be written to you.
2 For you yourselves know full well that the day of the

4:4 ¹I.e., body; or wife   4:13 ¹I.e., have died   4:14 ¹I.e., as believers

Lord is coming just like a thief in the night. 3 While they are saying, "Peace and safety!" then sudden destruction will come upon them like labor pains upon a pregnant woman, and they will not escape. 4 But you, brothers *and sisters,* are not in darkness, so that the day would overtake you like a thief; 5 for you are all sons of light and sons of day. We are not of night nor of darkness; 6 so then, let's not sleep as others do, but let's be alert and *1sober.* 7 For those who sleep, sleep at night, and those who are drunk, get drunk at night. 8 But since we are of *the* day, let's be *1sober,* having put on the breastplate of faith and love, and as a helmet, the hope of salvation. 9 For God has not destined us for wrath, but for obtaining salvation through our Lord Jesus Christ, 10 who died for us, so that whether we are awake or asleep, we will live together with Him. 11 Therefore, encourage one another and build one another up, just as you also are doing.

Christian Conduct

12 But we ask you, brothers *and sisters,* to recognize those who diligently labor among you and are in leadership over you in the Lord, and give you instruction, 13 and that you regard them very highly in love because of their work. Live in peace with one another. 14 We urge you, brothers *and sisters,* admonish the unruly, encourage the fainthearted, help the weak, be patient with everyone. 15 See that no one repays another with evil for evil, but always seek what is good for one another and for all people. 16 Rejoice always, 17 pray without ceasing, 18 in everything give thanks; for this is the will of God for you in Christ Jesus. 19 Do not quench the Spirit, 20 do not utterly reject *1prophecies,* 21 but examine everything; hold firmly to that which is good, 22 abstain from every form of evil.

23 Now may the God of peace Himself sanctify you entirely; and may your spirit and soul and body be kept complete, without blame at the coming of our Lord Jesus Christ. 24 Faithful is He who calls you, and He also will do it.

25 Brothers *and sisters,* pray for us*1.*

5:6 1Or *self-controlled*　　5:8 1Or *self-controlled*　　5:20 1Or *prophetic gifts*　　5:25 1Two early mss add *also*

26 Greet all the brothers *and sisters* with a holy kiss.
27 I put you under oath by the Lord to have this letter read to all the brothers *and sisters.*
28 *May* the grace of our Lord Jesus Christ *be* with you.

The Second Letter of Paul to the
THESSALONIANS

Giving Thanks for Faith and Perseverance

1 Paul, Silvanus, and Timothy,
To the church of the Thessalonians in God our Father and the Lord Jesus Christ: **2** Grace to you and peace from God our Father and the Lord Jesus Christ.

3 We ought always to give thanks to God for you, brothers *and sisters,* as is *only* fitting, because your faith is increasing abundantly, and the love of each and every one of you toward one another grows *ever* greater. **4** As a result, we ourselves speak proudly of you among the churches of God for your perseverance and faith in the midst of all your persecutions and afflictions which you endure. **5** *This is* a plain indication of God's righteous judgment so that you will be considered worthy of the kingdom of God, for which you indeed are suffering. **6** For after all it is *only* right for God to repay with affliction those who afflict you, **7** and *to give* relief to you who are afflicted, *along* with us, when the Lord Jesus will be revealed from heaven with His mighty angels **8** in flaming fire, dealing out retribution to those who do not know God, and to those who do not obey the gospel of our Lord Jesus. **9** These people will pay the penalty of eternal destruction, away from the presence of the Lord and from the glory of His power, **10** when He comes to be glorified among His saints on that day, and to be marveled at among all who have believed—because our testimony to you was believed. **11** To this end also we pray for you always, that our God will consider you worthy of your calling, and fulfill every desire for goodness and the work of faith with power, **12** so that the name of our Lord Jesus will be glorified in you, and you in Him, in accordance with the grace of our God and *the* Lord Jesus Christ.

Man of Lawlessness

2 Now we ask you, brothers *and sisters,* regarding the coming of our Lord Jesus Christ and our gathering together to Him, **2** that you not be quickly shaken from your composure or be disturbed either by a spirit, or a message, or a letter as if from us, to the effect that the day of the Lord has come. ³No one is to deceive you in any way! For *it will not come* unless the ¹apostasy comes first, and the man of lawlessness is revealed, the son of destruction, ⁴who opposes and exalts himself above every so-called god or object of worship, so that he takes his seat in the temple of God, displaying himself as being God. ⁵Do you not remember that while I was still with you, I was telling you these things? ⁶And you know what restrains *him* now, so that he will be revealed in his time. ⁷For the mystery of lawlessness is already at work; only ¹He who now restrains *will do so* until ²He is removed. ⁸Then that lawless one will be revealed, whom the Lord will eliminate with the breath of His mouth and bring to an end by the appearance of His coming; ⁹*that is,* the one whose coming is in accord with the activity of Satan, with all power and false signs and wonders, ¹⁰and with all the deception of wickedness for those who perish, because they did not accept the love of the truth so as to be saved. ¹¹For this reason God will send upon them a deluding influence so that they will believe what is false, ¹²in order that they all may be judged who did not believe the truth, but took pleasure in wickedness.

Stand Firm

¹³But we should always give thanks to God for you, brothers *and sisters* beloved by the Lord, because God has chosen you ¹from the beginning for salvation through sanctification by the Spirit and faith in the truth. ¹⁴It was for this He called you through our gospel, that you may obtain the glory of our Lord Jesus Christ. ¹⁵So then, brothers *and sisters,* stand firm and hold on to the traditions which you were taught, whether by word *of mouth* or by letter from us.

¹⁶Now may our Lord Jesus Christ Himself and God our Father, who has loved us and given us eternal comfort and good hope by grace, ¹⁷comfort and strengthen your hearts in every good work and word.

2:3 ¹Or *falling away* from the faith   2:7 ¹Or *he*   2:7 ²Or *he*
2:13 ¹One early ms *first fruits*

Request for Prayer

3 Finally, brothers *and sisters,* pray for us that the word of the Lord will spread rapidly and be glorified, just as *it was* also with you; 2 and that we will be rescued from troublesome and evil people; for not all have the faith. 3 But the Lord is faithful, and He will strengthen and protect you from the evil one. 4 We have confidence in the Lord concerning you, that you are doing, and will do, what we command. 5 May the Lord direct your hearts to the love of God and to the perseverance of Christ.

6 Now we command you, brothers *and sisters,* in the name of our Lord Jesus Christ, that you keep away from every brother *or sister* who leads a disorderly life and not *one* in accordance with the tradition which you received from us. 7 For you yourselves know how you ought to follow our example, because we did not act in an undisciplined way among you, 8 nor did we eat anyone's bread without paying for it, but with labor and hardship we *kept* working night and day so that we would not be a burden to any of you; 9 not because we do not have the right *to this,* but in order to offer ourselves as a role model for you, so that you would follow our example. 10 For even when we were with you, we used to give you this order: if anyone is not willing to work, then he is not to eat, either. 11 For we hear that some among you are leading an undisciplined life, doing no work at all, but acting like busybodies. 12 Now we command and exhort such persons in the Lord Jesus Christ to work peacefully and eat their own bread. 13 But as for you, brothers *and sisters,* do not grow weary of doing good.

14 If anyone does not obey our instruction in this letter, take special note of that person *so as* not to associate with him, so that he will be put to shame. 15 And *yet* do not regard *that person* as an enemy, but admonish *that one* as a brother *or sister.*

16 Now may the Lord of peace Himself continually grant you peace in every circumstance. The Lord be with you all!

17 I, Paul, write this greeting with my own hand, and this is a distinguishing mark in every letter; this is the way I write. 18 The grace of our Lord Jesus Christ be with you all.

The First Letter of Paul to
TIMOTHY

Correcting False Teaching

1 Paul, an apostle of Christ Jesus according to the commandment of God our Savior, and of Christ Jesus, *who is* our hope,

2 To Timothy, *my* true son in *the* faith: Grace, mercy, *and* peace from God the Father and Christ Jesus our Lord.

3 Just as I urged you upon my departure for Macedonia, to remain on at Ephesus so that you would instruct certain people not to teach strange doctrines, 4 nor to pay attention to myths and endless genealogies, which give rise to useless speculation rather than *advance* the plan of God, which is by faith, *so I urge you now.* 5 But the goal of our instruction is love from a pure heart, *from* a good conscience, and *from* a sincere faith. 6 Some people have strayed from these things and have turned aside to fruitless discussion, 7 wanting to be teachers of the Law, even though they do not understand either what they are saying or the matters about which they make confident assertions.

8 But we know that the Law is good, if one uses it lawfully, 9 realizing the fact that law is not made for a righteous person but for those who are lawless and rebellious, for the ungodly and sinners, for the unholy and worldly, for those who kill their fathers or mothers, for murderers, 10 for the sexually immoral, homosexuals, slave traders, liars, perjurers, and whatever else is contrary to sound teaching, 11 according to the glorious gospel of the blessed God, with which I have been entrusted.

Paul's Testimony

12 I thank Christ Jesus our Lord, who has strengthened me, because He considered me faithful, putting me into service, 13 even though I was previously a blasphemer and a persecutor and a violent aggressor. Yet I was shown mercy because I acted ignorantly in unbelief; 14 and the grace of our Lord was more than abundant, with the faith and love which are *found* in Christ Jesus. 15 It is a

trustworthy statement, deserving full acceptance, that Christ Jesus came into the world to save sinners, among whom I am foremost. 16 Yet for this reason I found mercy, so that in me as the foremost *sinner* Jesus Christ might demonstrate His perfect patience as an example for those who would believe in Him for eternal life. 17 Now to the King eternal, immortal, invisible, the only God, *be* honor and glory forever and ever. Amen.

18 This command I entrust to you, Timothy, *my* son, in accordance with the prophecies previously made concerning you, that by them you fight the good fight, 19 keeping faith and a good conscience, which some have rejected and suffered shipwreck in regard to their faith. 20 Among these are Hymenaeus and Alexander, whom I have handed over to Satan, so that they will be taught not to blaspheme.

A Call to Prayer

2 First of all, then, I urge that requests, prayers, intercession, *and* thanksgiving be made in behalf of all people, 2 for kings and all who are in authority, so that we may lead a tranquil and quiet life in all godliness and dignity. 3 This is good and acceptable in the sight of God our Savior, 4 who wants all people to be saved and to come to the knowledge of the truth. 5 For there is one God, *and* one mediator also between God and mankind, *the* man Christ Jesus, 6 who gave Himself as a ransom for all, the testimony *given* at the proper time. 7 For this I was appointed as a preacher and an apostle (I am telling the truth, I am not lying), as a teacher of the Gentiles in faith and truth.

Instructions for Believers

8 Therefore I want the men in every place to pray, lifting up holy hands, without anger and dispute. 9 Likewise, *I want* women to adorn themselves with proper clothing, modestly and discreetly, not with braided hair and gold or pearls or expensive apparel, 10 but rather by means of good works, as is proper for women making a claim to godliness. 11 A woman must quietly receive instruction with entire submissiveness. 12 But I do not allow a woman to teach or to exercise authority over a man, but to remain quiet. 13 For *it was* Adam *who* was first created, *and* then Eve. 14 And *it was*

not Adam *who* was deceived, but the woman was deceived and became a wrongdoer. **15** But women will be preserved through childbirth—if they continue in faith, love, and sanctity, with moderation.

Overseers and Deacons

3 It is a trustworthy statement: if any man aspires to the office of overseer, *it is* a fine work he desires *to do.* **2** An overseer, then, must be above reproach, the husband of one wife, [1]temperate, self-controlled, respectable, hospitable, skillful in teaching, **3** not over-indulging in wine, not a bully, but gentle, not contentious, free from the love of money. **4** *He must be* one who manages his own household well, keeping his children under control with all dignity **5** (but if a man does not know how to manage his own household, how will he take care of the church of God?), **6** *and* not a new convert, so that he will not become conceited and fall into condemnation incurred by the devil. **7** And he must have a good reputation with those outside *the church,* so that he will not fall into disgrace and the snare of the devil.

8 Deacons likewise *must be* men of dignity, not insincere, not prone to *drink* much wine, not greedy for money, **9** *but* holding to the mystery of the faith with a clear conscience. **10** These men must also first be tested; then have them serve as deacons if they are beyond reproach. **11** [1]Women *must* likewise *be* dignified, not malicious gossips, but [2]temperate, faithful in all things. **12** Deacons must be husbands of one wife, *and* good managers of *their* children and their own households. **13** For those who have served well as deacons obtain for themselves a high standing and great confidence in the faith that is in Christ Jesus.

14 I am writing these things to you, hoping to come to you before long; **15** but in case I am delayed, *I write* so that you will know how one should act in the household of God, which is the church of the living God, the pillar and support of the truth. **16** Beyond question, great is the mystery of godliness:

He who was revealed in the flesh,

3:2 [1] Or *level-headed*   3:11 [1] I.e., either deacons' wives or deaconesses   3:11 [2] Or *level-headed*

> Was vindicated in the Spirit,
> Seen by angels,
> Proclaimed among the nations,
> Believed on in the world,
> Taken up in glory.

Abandonment of Faith

4 But the Spirit explicitly says that in later times some will fall away from the faith, paying attention to deceitful spirits and teachings of demons, 2 by means of the hypocrisy of liars seared in their own conscience as with a branding iron, 3 who forbid marriage *and advocate* abstaining from foods which God has created to be gratefully shared in by those who believe and know the truth. 4 For everything created by God is good, and nothing is to be rejected if it is received with gratitude; 5 for it is sanctified by means of the word of God and prayer.

A Good Minister's Discipline

6 In pointing out these things to the brothers *and sisters,* you will be a good servant of Christ Jesus, *constantly* nourished on the words of the faith and of the good doctrine which you have been following. 7 But stay away from worthless stories that are typical of old women. Rather, discipline yourself for the purpose of godliness; 8 for bodily training is *just* slightly beneficial, but godliness is beneficial for all things, since it holds promise for the present life and *also* for the *life* to come. 9 It is a trustworthy statement deserving full acceptance. 10 For it is for this we labor and strive, because we have set our hope on the living God, who is the Savior of all mankind, especially of believers.

11 Prescribe and teach these things. 12 Let no one look down on your youthfulness, but *rather* in speech, conduct, love, faith, *and* purity, show yourself an example of those who believe. 13 Until I come, give your attention to the *public* ¹reading, to exhortation, *and* teaching. 14 Do not neglect the spiritual gift within you, which was granted to you through *words of* prophecy with the laying on of hands by the council of elders. 15 Take pains with these things; be *absorbed* in them, so that your

---

4:13 ¹I.e., of Scripture in the church service

progress will be evident to all. 16 Pay close attention to yourself and to the teaching; persevere in these things, for as you do this you will save both yourself and those who hear you.

Honor Widows

5 Do not sharply rebuke an older man, but *rather* appeal to *him* as a father, *and to* the younger men as brothers, 2 to the older women as mothers, *and* to the younger women as sisters, in all purity.

3 Honor widows who are actually widows; 4 but if any widow has children or grandchildren, they must first learn to show proper respect for their own family and to give back compensation to their parents; for this is acceptable in the sight of God. 5 Now she who is actually a widow and has been left alone has set her hope on God, and she continues in requests and prayers night and day. 6 But she who indulges herself in luxury is dead, *even* while she lives. 7 Give these instructions as well, so that they may be above reproach. 8 But if anyone does not provide for his own, and especially for those of his household, he has denied the faith and is worse than an unbeliever.

9 A widow is to be put on the list only if she is not less than sixty years old, *having been* the wife of one man, 10 having a reputation for good works; *and* if she has brought up children, if she has shown hospitality to strangers, if she has washed the saints' feet, if she has assisted those in distress, *and* if she has devoted herself to every good work. 11 But refuse *to register* younger widows, for when they feel physical desires alienating them from Christ, they want to get married, 12 *thereby* incurring condemnation, because they have ignored their previous pledge. 13 At the same time they also learn *to be* idle, as they go around from house to house; and not merely idle, but also *they become* gossips and busybodies, talking about things not proper *to mention.* 14 Therefore, I want younger *widows* to get married, have children, manage their households, *and* give the enemy no opportunity for reproach; 15 for some have already turned away to follow Satan. 16 If any woman who is a believer has *dependent* widows, she must assist them and the church must not be burdened, so that it may assist those who are actually widows.

Concerning Elders

17 The elders who lead well are to be considered worthy of double honor, especially those who work hard at preaching and teaching. **18** For the Scripture says, "YOU SHALL NOT MUZZLE THE OX WHILE IT IS THRESHING," and "The laborer is worthy of his wages." **19** Do not accept an accusation against an elder except on the basis of two or three witnesses. **20** Those who continue in sin, rebuke in the presence of all, so that the rest also will be fearful *of sinning.* **21** I solemnly exhort you in the presence of God and of Christ Jesus and of *His* chosen angels, to maintain these *principles* without bias, doing nothing in a *spirit of* partiality. **22** Do not lay hands upon anyone too quickly and thereby share *responsibility for* the sins of others; keep yourself free from sin.

23 Do not go on drinking only water, but use a little wine for the sake of your stomach and your frequent ailments.

24 The sins of some people are quite evident, going before them to judgment; for others, their *sins* follow after. **25** Likewise also, deeds that are good are quite evident, and those which are otherwise cannot be concealed.

Instructions to Those Who Minister

6 All who are under the yoke as slaves are to regard their own masters as worthy of all honor so that the name of God and *our* doctrine will not be spoken against. **2** Those who have believers as their masters must not be disrespectful to them because they are brothers *or sisters,* but must serve them all the more, because those who partake of the benefit are believers and beloved. Teach and preach these *principles.*

3 If anyone advocates a different doctrine and does not agree with sound words, those of our Lord Jesus Christ, and with the doctrine conforming to godliness, **4** he is conceited *and* understands nothing; but he has a sick craving for controversial questions and disputes about words, from which come envy, strife, abusive language, evil suspicions, **5** and constant friction between people of depraved mind and deprived of the truth, who suppose that godliness is a means of gain. **6** But godliness *actually* is a means of great gain *when* accompanied by contentment. **7** For we have brought nothing into the world, so we cannot take anything out of it, either. **8** If we have food and covering, with these we shall be content. **9** But those who want to get rich fall into temptation and a trap, and many foolish and harmful desires which plunge people into ruin and destruction. **10** For the love of money is a root of all sorts of evil, and some by longing for it have wandered away from the faith and pierced themselves with many griefs.

11 But flee from these things, you man of God, and pursue righteousness, godliness, faith, love, perseverance, *and* gentleness. **12** Fight the good fight of faith; take hold of the eternal life to which you were called, and *for which* you made the good confession in the presence of many witnesses. **13** I direct you in the presence of God, who gives life to all things, and of Christ Jesus, who testified the good confession before Pontius Pilate, **14** that you keep the commandment without fault *or* reproach until the appearing of our Lord Jesus Christ, **15** which He will bring about at *the* proper time—He who is the blessed and only Sovereign, the King of kings and Lord of lords, **16** who alone possesses immortality and dwells in unapproachable light, whom no one has seen or can see. To Him *be* honor and eternal dominion! Amen.

17 Instruct those who are rich in this present world not to be conceited or to set their hope on the uncertainty of riches, but on God, who richly supplies us with all things to enjoy. **18** *Instruct them* to do good, to be rich in good works, to be generous and ready to share, **19** storing up for themselves the treasure of a good foundation for the future, so that they may take hold of that which is truly life.

20 Timothy, protect what has been entrusted to you, avoiding worldly, empty chatter and the opposing arguments of what is falsely called "knowledge"—**21** which some have professed and *thereby* have gone astray from the faith.

Grace be with you.

The Second Letter of Paul to
TIMOTHY

Timothy Charged to Guard His Trust

1 Paul, an apostle of Christ Jesus by the will of God, according to the promise of life in Christ Jesus,

2 To Timothy, my beloved son: Grace, mercy, *and* peace from God the Father and Christ Jesus our Lord.

3 I thank God, whom I serve with a clear conscience the way my forefathers did, as I constantly remember you in my prayers night and day, 4 longing to see you, even as I recall your tears, so that I may be filled with joy. 5 For I am mindful of the sincere faith within you, which first dwelled in your grandmother Lois and your mother Eunice, and I am sure that *it is* in you as well. 6 For this reason I remind you to kindle afresh the gift of God which is in you through the laying on of my hands. 7 For God has not given us a spirit of timidity, but of power and love and discipline.

8 Therefore do not be ashamed of the testimony of our Lord or of me His prisoner, but join with *me* in suffering for the gospel according to the power of God, 9 who saved us and called us with a holy calling, not according to our works, but according to His own purpose and grace, which was granted to us in Christ Jesus from all eternity, 10 but has now been revealed by the appearing of our Savior Christ Jesus, who abolished death and brought life and immortality to light through the gospel, 11 for which I was appointed a preacher, an apostle, and a teacher. 12 For this reason I also suffer these things; but I am not ashamed, for I know whom I have believed, and I am convinced that He is able to protect what I have entrusted to Him until that day. 13 Hold on to the example of sound words which you have heard from me, in *the* faith and love which are in Christ Jesus. 14 Protect, through the Holy Spirit who dwells in us, the treasure which has been entrusted to *you.*

15 You are aware of the fact that all who are in Asia turned away from me, among whom are Phygelus and Hermogenes. 16 The Lord grant mercy to the household of Onesiphorus, for he often refreshed me and was not ashamed of my chains; 17 but when he was in Rome, he

eagerly searched for me and found me—**18** the Lord grant to him to find mercy from the Lord on that day—and you know very well what services he rendered at Ephesus.

Be Strong

2 You therefore, my son, be strong in the grace that is in Christ Jesus. **2** The things which you have heard from me in the presence of many witnesses, entrust these to faithful ¹people who will be able to teach others also. **3** Suffer hardship with *me,* as a good soldier of Christ Jesus. **4** No soldier in active service entangles himself in the affairs of everyday life, so that he may please the one who enlisted *him.* **5** And if someone likewise competes as an athlete, he is not crowned *as victor* unless he competes according to the rules. **6** The hard-working farmer ought to be the first to receive his share of the crops. **7** Consider what I say, for the Lord will give you understanding in everything.

8 Remember Jesus Christ, risen from the dead, descendant of David, according to my gospel, **9** for which I suffer hardship even to imprisonment as a criminal; but the word of God is not imprisoned. **10** For this reason I endure all things for the sake of those who are chosen, so that they also may obtain the salvation which is in Christ Jesus *and* with *it* eternal glory. **11** The statement is trustworthy:

For if we died with Him, we will also live with Him;
12 If we endure, we will also reign with Him;
If we deny Him, He will also deny us;
13 If we are faithless, He remains faithful, for He cannot deny Himself.

An Unashamed Worker

14 Remind *them* of these things, and solemnly exhort *them* in the presence of God not to dispute about words, which is useless *and leads* to the ruin of the listeners. **15** Be diligent to present yourself approved to God as a worker who does not need to be ashamed, accurately handling the word of truth. **16** But avoid worldly *and* empty chatter, for it will lead to further ungodliness, **17** and their talk will spread like ¹gangrene. Among them are Hymenaeus and Philetus, **18** *men* who have

---

2:2 ¹Or men   2:17 ¹Or cancer

gone astray from the truth, claiming that the resurrection has already taken place; and they are jeopardizing the faith of some. ¹⁹ Nevertheless, the firm foundation of God stands, having this seal: "The Lord knows those who are His;" and, "Everyone who names the name of the Lord is to keep away from wickedness."

²⁰ Now in a large house there are not only gold and silver implements, but also *implements* of wood and of earthenware, and some *are* for honor while others *are* for dishonor. ²¹ Therefore, if anyone cleanses himself from these *things,* he will be an implement for honor, sanctified, useful to the Master, prepared for every good work. ²² Now flee from youthful lusts and pursue righteousness, faith, love, *and* peace with those who call on the Lord from a pure heart. ²³ But refuse foolish and ignorant speculations, knowing that they produce quarrels. ²⁴ The Lord's bond-servant must not be quarrelsome, but be kind to all, skillful in teaching, patient when wronged, ²⁵ with gentleness correcting those who are in opposition, if perhaps God may grant them repentance leading to the knowledge of the truth, ²⁶ and they may come to their senses *and escape* from the snare of the devil, having been held captive by him to do his will.

Difficult Times Will Come

3 But realize this, that in the last days difficult times will come. ² For people will be lovers of self, lovers of money, boastful, arrogant, slanderers, disobedient to parents, ungrateful, unholy, ³ unloving, irreconcilable, malicious gossips, without self-control, brutal, haters of good, ⁴ treacherous, reckless, conceited, lovers of pleasure rather than lovers of God, ⁵ holding to a form of godliness although they have denied its power; avoid *such people as* these. ⁶ For among them are those who slip into households and captivate weak women weighed down with sins, led on by various impulses, ⁷ always learning and never able to come to the knowledge of the truth. ⁸ Just as Jannes and Jambres opposed Moses, so these men also oppose the truth, men of depraved mind, worthless in regard to the faith. ⁹ But they will not make further progress; for their foolishness will be obvious to all, just as was that also of Jannes and Jambres.

¹⁰ Now you followed my teaching, conduct, purpose,

faith, patience, love, perseverance, [11] persecutions, *and* sufferings, such as happened to me at Antioch, at Iconium, *and* at Lystra; what persecutions I endured, and out of them all the Lord rescued me! [12] Indeed, all who want to live in a godly way in Christ Jesus will be persecuted. [13] But evil people and impostors will proceed *from bad* to worse, deceiving and being deceived. [14] You, however, continue in the things you have learned and become convinced of, knowing from whom you have learned *them,* [15] and that from childhood you have known the sacred writings which are able to give you the wisdom that leads to salvation through faith which is in Christ Jesus. [16] All Scripture is [1] inspired by God and beneficial for teaching, for rebuke, for correction, for training in righteousness; [17] so that the man *or woman* of God may be fully capable, equipped for every good work.

Preach the Word

4 I solemnly exhort *you* in the presence of God and of Christ Jesus, who is to judge the living and the dead, and by His appearing and His kingdom: [2] preach the word; be ready in season *and* out of season; correct, rebuke, *and* [1] exhort, with great patience and instruction. [3] For *the* time will come when they will not tolerate sound doctrine; but *wanting* to have their ears tickled, they will accumulate for themselves teachers in accordance with their own desires, [4] and they will turn their ears away from the truth and will turn aside to myths. [5] But *as for* you, use self-restraint in all things, endure hardship, do the work of an evangelist, fulfill your ministry.

[6] For I am already being poured out as a drink offering, and the time of my departure has come. [7] I have fought the good fight, I have finished the course, I have kept the faith; [8] in the future there is reserved for me the crown of righteousness, which the Lord, the righteous Judge, will award to me on that day; and not only to me, but also to all who have loved His appearing.

Personal Concerns

[9] Make every effort to come to me soon; [10] for Demas, having loved this present world, has deserted me and

---

3:16 [1] Lit *God-breathed*   4:2 [1] Or *encourage*

gone to Thessalonica; Crescens *has gone* to Galatia, Titus to Dalmatia. [11] Only Luke is with me. Take along Mark and bring him with you, for he is useful to me for service. [12] But I have sent Tychicus to Ephesus. [13] When you come, bring the overcoat which I left at Troas with Carpus, and the books, especially the parchments.
[14] Alexander the coppersmith did me great harm; the Lord will repay him according to his deeds. [15] Be on guard against him yourself too, for he vigorously opposed our teaching.

[16] At my first defense no one supported me, but all deserted me; may it not be counted against them. [17] But the Lord stood with me and strengthened me, so that through me the proclamation might be fully accomplished, and that all the Gentiles might hear; and I was rescued out of the lion's mouth. [18] The Lord will rescue me from every evil deed, and will bring me safely to His heavenly kingdom; to Him *be* the glory forever and ever. Amen.

[19] Greet Prisca and Aquila, and the household of Onesiphorus. [20] Erastus remained at Corinth, but I left Trophimus sick at Miletus. [21] Make every effort to come before winter. Eubulus greets you, also Pudens, Linus, Claudia, and all the brothers *and sisters.*

[22] The Lord be with your spirit. Grace be with you.

The Letter of Paul to

TITUS

Salutation

1 Paul, a bond-servant of God and an apostle of Jesus Christ, for the faith of those chosen of God and the knowledge of the truth which is according to godliness, 2 in the hope of eternal life, which God, who cannot lie, promised long ages ago, 3 but at the proper time revealed His word in the proclamation with which I was entrusted according to the commandment of God our Savior;

4 To Titus, my true son in a common faith: Grace and peace from God the Father and Christ Jesus our Savior.

Qualifications of Elders

5 For this reason I left you in Crete, that you would set in order what remains and appoint elders in every city as I directed you, 6 *namely,* if any man is beyond reproach, the husband of one wife, having children who believe, not accused of indecent behavior or rebellion. 7 For the overseer must be beyond reproach as God's steward, not self-willed, not quick-tempered, not overindulging in wine, not a bully, not greedy for money, 8 but hospitable, loving what is good, self-controlled, righteous, holy, disciplined, 9 holding firmly the faithful word which is in accordance with the teaching, so that he will be able both to 'exhort in sound doctrine and to refute those who contradict *it.*

10 For there are many rebellious people, empty talkers and deceivers, especially those of the circumcision, 11 who must be silenced because they are upsetting whole families, teaching things they should not *teach* for the sake of dishonest gain. 12 One of them, a prophet of their own, said, "Cretans are always liars, evil beasts, lazy gluttons." 13 This testimony is true. For this reason reprimand them severely so that they may be sound in the faith, 14 not paying attention to Jewish myths and commandments of men who turn away from the truth. 15 To the pure, all things are pure; but to those who are

---

defiled and unbelieving, nothing is pure, but both their mind and their conscience are defiled. [16] They profess to know God, but by *their* deeds they deny *Him,* being detestable and disobedient and worthless for any good deed.

Proclaim Sound Doctrine

2 But *as for* you, proclaim the things which are fitting for sound doctrine. [2] Older men are to be [1]temperate, dignified, self-controlled, sound in faith, in love, in perseverance.

[3] Older women likewise *are to be* reverent in their behavior, not malicious gossips nor enslaved to much wine, teaching what is good, [4] so that they may encourage the young women to love their husbands, to love their children, [5] *to be* sensible, pure, workers at home, kind, being subject to their own husbands, so that the word of God will not be dishonored.

[6] Likewise urge the young men to be sensible; [7] in all things show yourself *to be* an example of good deeds, *with* purity in doctrine, dignified, [8] sound *in* speech which is beyond reproach, so that the opponent will be put to shame, having nothing bad to say about us.

[9] *Urge* slaves to be subject to their own masters in everything, to be pleasing, not argumentative, [10] not stealing, but showing all good faith so that they will adorn the doctrine of God our Savior in every respect.

[11] For the grace of God has appeared, bringing salvation to all people, [12] instructing us to deny ungodliness and worldly desires and to live sensibly, righteously, and in a godly manner in the present age, [13] looking for the blessed hope and the appearing of the glory of our great God and Savior, Christ Jesus, [14] who gave Himself for us to redeem us from every lawless deed, and to purify for Himself a people for His own possession, eager for good deeds.

[15] These things speak and [1]exhort, and rebuke with all authority. No one is to disregard you.

Godly Living

3 Remind them to be subject to rulers, to authorities, to be obedient, to be ready for every good deed, [2] to

---

2:2 [1]Or *level-headed*   2:15 [1]Or *encourage*

slander no one, not to be contentious, *to be* gentle, showing every consideration for all people. **3** For we too were once foolish, disobedient, deceived, enslaved to various lusts and pleasures, spending our life in malice and envy, hateful, hating one another. **4** But when the kindness of God our Savior and *His* love for mankind appeared, **5** He saved us, not on the basis of deeds which we did in righteousness, but in accordance with His mercy, by the washing of regeneration and renewing by the Holy Spirit, **6** whom He richly poured out upon us through Jesus Christ our Savior, **7** so that being justified by His grace we would be made heirs according to *the* hope of eternal life. **8** This statement is trustworthy; and concerning these things I want you to speak confidently, so that those who have believed God will be careful to engage in good deeds. These things are good and beneficial for people. **9** But avoid foolish controversies and genealogies and strife and disputes about the Law, for they are useless and worthless. **10** Reject a divisive person after a first and second warning, **11** knowing that such a person has deviated from what is right and is sinning, being self-condemned.

Personal Concerns

12 When I send Artemas or Tychicus to you, make every effort to come to me at Nicopolis, for I have decided to spend the winter there. **13** Diligently help Zenas the lawyer and Apollos on their way so that nothing is lacking for them. **14** Our people must also learn to engage in good deeds to meet pressing needs, so that they will not be unproductive.

15 All who are with me greet you. Greet those who love us in *the* faith.

Grace be with you all.

The Letter of Paul to
PHILEMON

Salutation

1 Paul, a prisoner of Christ Jesus, and Timothy our brother,

To Philemon our beloved *brother* and fellow worker, **2** and to Apphia our sister, and to Archippus our fellow soldier, and to the church in your house: **3** Grace to you and peace from God our Father and the Lord Jesus Christ.

Philemon's Love and Faith

4 I thank my God always, making mention of you in my prayers, **5** because I hear of your love and of the faith which you have toward the Lord Jesus and toward all the saints; **6** *and I pray* that the fellowship of your faith may become effective ¹through the knowledge of every good thing which is in you for the sake of Christ. **7** For I have had great joy and comfort in your love, because the hearts of the saints have been refreshed through you, brother.

8 Therefore, though I have enough confidence in Christ to order you *to do* what is proper, **9** *yet* for love's sake I rather appeal *to you*—since I am such a person as Paul, an old man, and now also a prisoner of Christ Jesus—

Plea for Onesimus, a Free Man

10 I appeal to you for my son ¹Onesimus, whom I ²fathered in my imprisonment, **11** who previously was useless to you, but now is useful both to you and to me. **12** I have sent him back to you in person, that is, *sending my very heart*, **13** whom I wanted to keep with me, so that in your behalf he might be at my service in my imprisonment for the gospel; **14** but I did not want to do anything without your consent, so that your goodness would not be, in effect, by compulsion, but of your own free will. **15** For perhaps *it was* for this reason *that* he was separated *from you* for a while, that you would have him

---

1:6 ¹Or *in*   1:10 ¹I.e., useful   1:10 ²I.e., led to the Lord

back forever, **16** no longer as a slave, but more than a slave, a beloved brother, especially to me, but how much more to you, both in the flesh and in the Lord.

17 If then you regard me *as* a partner, accept him as *you would* me. **18** But if he has wronged you in any way or owes *you anything,* charge that to my account; **19** I, Paul, have written *this* with my own hand, I will repay *it* (not to mention to you that you owe to me even your own self as well). **20** Yes, brother, let me benefit from you in the Lord; refresh my heart in Christ.

21 Having confidence in your obedience, I write to you, since I know that you will do even more than what I say.

22 At the same time also prepare me a guest room, for I hope that through your prayers I will be given to you.

23 Epaphras, my fellow prisoner in Christ Jesus, greets you, **24** *as do* Mark, Aristarchus, Demas, *and* Luke, my fellow workers.

25 The grace of the Lord Jesus Christ be with your spirit.[1]

1:25 [1] One early ms adds *Amen*

The Letter to the

HEBREWS

God's Final Word in His Son

1 God, after He spoke long ago to the fathers in the prophets in many portions and in many ways, 2 in these last days has spoken to us in *His* Son, whom He appointed heir of all things, through whom He also made the world. 3 And He is the radiance of His glory and the exact representation of His nature, and upholds all things by the word of His power. When He had made purification of sins, He sat down at the right hand of the Majesty on high, 4 having become so much better than the angels, to the extent that He has inherited a more excellent name than they.

5 For to which of the angels did He ever say,

"YOU ARE MY SON,
TODAY I HAVE FATHERED YOU"?

And again,

"I WILL BE A FATHER TO HIM
AND HE WILL BE A SON TO ME"?

6 And when He again brings the firstborn into the world, He says,

"AND LET ALL THE ANGELS OF GOD WORSHIP HIM."

7 And regarding the angels He says,

"HE MAKES HIS ANGELS WINDS,
AND HIS MINISTERS A FLAME OF FIRE."

8 But regarding the Son *He says,*

"YOUR THRONE, GOD, IS FOREVER AND EVER,
AND THE SCEPTER OF RIGHTEOUSNESS IS THE SCEPTER OF [1]HIS
KINGDOM.

9   "YOU HAVE LOVED RIGHTEOUSNESS AND HATED LAWLESSNESS;
THEREFORE GOD, YOUR GOD, HAS ANOINTED YOU
WITH THE OIL OF JOY ABOVE YOUR COMPANIONS."

10 And,

"YOU, LORD, IN THE BEGINNING LAID THE FOUNDATION OF THE
EARTH,
AND THE HEAVENS ARE THE WORKS OF YOUR HANDS;

11   THEY WILL PERISH, BUT YOU REMAIN;
AND THEY ALL WILL WEAR OUT LIKE A GARMENT,.

---

12   AND LIKE A ROBE YOU WILL ROLL THEM UP;
      LIKE A GARMENT THEY WILL ALSO BE CHANGED.
      BUT YOU ARE THE SAME,
      AND YOUR YEARS WILL NOT COME TO AN END."

13 But to which of the angels has He ever said,
      "SIT AT MY RIGHT HAND,
      UNTIL I MAKE YOUR ENEMIES
      A FOOTSTOOL FOR YOUR FEET"?

14 Are they not all ministering spirits, sent out to *provide* service for the sake of those who will inherit salvation?

Pay Attention

2 For this reason we must pay much closer attention to what we have heard, so that we do not drift away *from it.* 2 For if the word spoken through angels proved unalterable, and every violation and act of disobedience received a just punishment, 3 how will we escape if we neglect so great a salvation? After it was at first spoken through the Lord, it was confirmed to us by those who heard, 4 God also testifying with them, both by signs and wonders, and by various miracles and by gifts of the Holy Spirit according to His own will.

Earth Subject to Man

5 For He did not subject to angels the world to come, about which we are speaking. 6 But someone has testified somewhere, saying,
      "WHAT IS MAN, THAT YOU THINK OF HIM?
      OR A SON OF MAN, THAT YOU ARE CONCERNED ABOUT HIM?
7   "YOU HAVE MADE HIM FOR A LITTLE WHILE LOWER THAN
         ANGELS;
      YOU HAVE CROWNED HIM WITH GLORY AND HONOR[1];
8   YOU HAVE PUT EVERYTHING IN SUBJECTION UNDER HIS FEET."
For in subjecting all things to him, He left nothing that is not subject to him. But now we do not yet see all things subjected to him.

Jesus Briefly Humbled

9 But we do see Him who was made for a little while lower than the angels, *namely,* Jesus, because of His

---

2:7 [1] One early ms continues, *and have appointed him over the works of Your hands*

suffering death crowned with glory and honor, so that by the grace of God He might taste death for everyone.
10 For it was fitting for Him, for whom are all things, and through whom are all things, in bringing many sons to glory, to perfect the originator of their salvation through sufferings. **11** For both He who sanctifies and those who are sanctified are all from one *Father;* for this reason He is not ashamed to call them brothers *and sisters,* **12** saying,

"I WILL PROCLAIM YOUR NAME TO MY BROTHERS,
    IN THE MIDST OF THE ASSEMBLY I WILL SING YOUR PRAISE."
13 And again,

"I WILL PUT MY TRUST IN HIM."
And again,

"BEHOLD, I AND THE CHILDREN WHOM GOD HAS GIVEN ME."

14 Therefore, since the children share in flesh and blood, He Himself likewise also partook of the same, so that through death He might destroy the one who has the power of death, that is, the devil, **15** and free those who through fear of death were subject to slavery all their lives. **16** For clearly He does not give help to angels, but He gives help to the descendants of Abraham. **17** Therefore, in all things He had to be made like His brothers so that He might become a merciful and faithful high priest in things pertaining to God, to make *propitiation for the sins of the people. **18** For since He Himself was tempted in that which He has suffered, He is able to come to the aid of those who are tempted.

Jesus Our High Priest

3 Therefore, holy brothers *and sisters,* partakers of a heavenly calling, consider the Apostle and High Priest of our confession: Jesus; **2** He was faithful to Him who appointed Him, as Moses also was in all His house. **3** For He has been counted worthy of more glory than Moses, by just so much as the builder of the house has more honor than the house. **4** For every house is built by someone, but the builder of all things is God. **5** Now Moses was faithful in all God's house as a servant, for a testimony of those things which were to be spoken *later;* **6** but Christ *was faithful* as a Son over His house—whose

---

2:17 ¹ I.e., reconciliation with God by atoning for the sins

house we are, if we hold firmly to our confidence and
the boast of our hope.

7 Therefore, just as the Holy Spirit says,

"TODAY IF YOU HEAR HIS VOICE,

8   DO NOT HARDEN YOUR HEARTS AS WHEN THEY PROVOKED ME,
       AS ON THE DAY OF TRIAL IN THE WILDERNESS,

9   WHERE YOUR FATHERS PUT ME TO THE TEST,
       AND SAW MY WORKS FOR FORTY YEARS.

10   "THEREFORE I WAS ANGRY WITH THIS GENERATION,
       AND SAID, 'THEY ALWAYS GO ASTRAY IN THEIR HEART,
       AND THEY DID NOT KNOW MY WAYS';

11   AS I SWORE IN MY ANGER,
       'THEY CERTAINLY SHALL NOT ENTER MY REST.' "

The Danger of Unbelief

12 Take care, brothers *and sisters,* that there will not be
in any one of you an evil, unbelieving heart that falls
away from the living God. **13** But encourage one another
every day, as long as it is *still* called "today," so that none
of you will be hardened by the deceitfulness of sin. **14** For
we have become partakers of Christ if we keep the
beginning of our commitment firm until the end, **15** while
it is said,

"TODAY IF YOU HEAR HIS VOICE,

DO NOT HARDEN YOUR HEARTS, AS WHEN THEY PROVOKED
       ME."

16 For who provoked *Him* when they had heard? Indeed,
did not all those who came out of Egypt *led* by Moses?
17 And with whom was He angry for forty years? Was it
not with those who sinned, whose dead bodies fell in the
wilderness? **18** And to whom did He swear that they
would not enter His rest, but to those who were disobedient? **19** And *so* we see that they were not able to enter
because of unbelief.

The Believer's Rest

4 Therefore, we must fear if, while a promise remains
of entering His rest, any one of you may seem to have
come short *of it.* **2** For indeed we have had good news
preached to us, just as they also *did;* but the word
they heard did not benefit them, because ¹they were not

4:2 ¹One early ms *it was not united with faith
in those who heard*

united with those who listened with faith. ³ For we who have believed enter *that* rest, just as He has said,

"As I swore in My anger,
    They certainly shall not enter My rest,"

although His works were finished from the foundation of the world. ⁴ For He has said somewhere concerning the seventh *day:* "And God rested on the seventh day from all His works"; ⁵ and again in this *passage,* "They certainly shall not enter My rest." ⁶ Therefore, since it remains for some to enter it, and those who previously had good news preached to them failed to enter because of disobedience, ⁷ He again sets a certain day, "Today," saying through David after so long a time just as has been said before,

"Today if you hear His voice,
    Do not harden your hearts."

⁸ For if Joshua had given them rest, He would not have spoken of another day after that. ⁹ Consequently, there remains a Sabbath rest for the people of God. ¹⁰ For the one who has entered His rest has himself also rested from his works, as God did from His. ¹¹ Therefore let's make every effort to enter that rest, so that no one will fall by *following* the same example of disobedience. ¹² For the word of God is living and active, and sharper than any two-edged sword, even penetrating as far as the division of soul and spirit, of both joints and marrow, and able to judge the thoughts and intentions of the heart. ¹³ And there is no creature hidden from His sight, but all things are open and laid bare to the eyes of Him to whom we must answer.

¹⁴ Therefore, since we have a great high priest who has passed through the heavens, Jesus the Son of God, let's hold firmly to our confession. ¹⁵ For we do not have a high priest who cannot sympathize with our weaknesses, but One who has been tempted in all things just as *we are, yet* without sin. ¹⁶ Therefore let's approach the throne of grace with confidence, so that we may receive mercy and find grace for help at the time of *our* need.

The Perfect High Priest

5 For every high priest taken from among men is appointed on behalf of people in things pertaining to God, in order to offer both gifts and sacrifices for sins; ² he can deal gently with the ignorant and misguided,

since he himself also is clothed in weakness; ³and
because of it he is obligated to offer *sacrifices* for sins for
himself, as well as for the people. ⁴And no one takes the
honor for himself, but *receives it* when he is called by
God, just as Aaron also was.

⁵So too Christ did not glorify Himself *in* becoming a
high priest, but *it was* He who said to Him,

"YOU ARE MY SON,
   TODAY I HAVE FATHERED YOU";

⁶just as He also says in another *passage,*

"YOU ARE A PRIEST FOREVER
   ACCORDING TO THE ORDER OF MELCHIZEDEK."

⁷In the days of His humanity, He offered up both
prayers and pleas with loud crying and tears to the One
able to save Him from death, and He was heard because
of His devout behavior. ⁸Although He was a Son, He
learned obedience from the things which He suffered.
⁹And having been perfected, He became the source of
eternal salvation for all those who obey Him, ¹⁰being
designated by God as High Priest according to the order
of Melchizedek.

¹¹Concerning him we have much to say, and *it is*
difficult to explain, since you have become poor
listeners. ¹²For though by this time you ought to be
teachers, you have need again for someone to teach you
the elementary principles of the actual words of God,
and you have come to need milk and not solid food.
¹³For everyone who partakes *only* of milk is
unacquainted with the word of righteousness, for he is
an infant. ¹⁴But solid food is for the mature, who because
of practice have their senses trained to distinguish
between good and evil.

The Danger of Falling Away

6 Therefore leaving the elementary teaching about the
Christ, let us press on to maturity, not laying again a
foundation of repentance from dead works and of faith
toward God, ²of instruction about washings and laying
on of hands, and about the resurrection of the dead and
eternal judgment. ³And this we will do, if God permits.
⁴For it is impossible, in the case of those who have once
been enlightened and have tasted of the heavenly gift
and have been made partakers of the Holy Spirit, ⁵and
have tasted the good word of God and the powers of the

age to come, 6 and *then* have [1]fallen away, to restore them again to repentance, since they again crucify to themselves the Son of God and put Him to open shame. 7 For ground that drinks the rain which often falls on it and produces vegetation useful to those for whose sake it is also tilled, receives a blessing from God; 8 but if it yields thorns and thistles, it is worthless and close to being cursed, and it ends up being burned.

Better Things for You

9 But, beloved, we are convinced of better things regarding you, and things that accompany salvation, even though we are speaking in this way. 10 For God is not unjust so as to forget your work and the love which you have shown toward His name, by having served and by *still* serving the saints. 11 And we desire that each one of you demonstrate the same diligence so as to realize the full assurance of hope until the end, 12 so that you will not be sluggish, but imitators of those who through faith and endurance inherit the promises.

13 For when God made the promise to Abraham, since He could swear an oath by no one greater, He swore by Himself, 14 saying, "INDEED I WILL GREATLY BLESS YOU AND I WILL GREATLY MULTIPLY YOU." 15 And so, having patiently waited, he obtained the promise. 16 For people swear an oath by one greater *than themselves,* and with them an oath *serving* as confirmation is an end of every dispute. 17 In the same way God, desiring even more to demonstrate to the heirs of the promise the fact that His purpose is unchangeable, confirmed it with an oath, 18 so that by two unchangeable things in which it is impossible for God to lie, we who have taken refuge would have strong encouragement to hold firmly to the hope set before us. 19 This hope we have as an anchor of the soul, a *hope* both sure and reliable and one which enters within the veil, 20 where Jesus has entered as a forerunner for us, having become a high priest forever according to the order of Melchizedek.

Melchizedek's Priesthood like Christ's

7 For this Melchizedek, king of Salem, priest of the Most High God, who met Abraham as he was

---

6:6 [1]Or *committed apostasy;* i.e., renounced the faith

returning from the slaughter of the kings and blessed him, [2] to whom also Abraham apportioned a tenth of all *the spoils,* was first of all, by the translation *of his name,* king of righteousness, and then also king of Salem, which is king of peace. [3] Without father, without mother, without genealogy, having neither beginning of days nor end of life, but made like the Son of God, he remains a priest perpetually.

[4] Now observe how great this man was to whom Abraham, the patriarch, gave a tenth of the choicest spoils. [5] And those indeed of the sons of Levi who receive the priest's office have a commandment in the Law to collect a tenth from the people, that is, from their countrymen, although they are descended from Abraham. [6] But the one whose genealogy is not traced from them collected a tenth from Abraham and blessed the one who had the promises. [7] But without any dispute the lesser *person* is blessed by the greater. [8] In this case mortal men receive tithes, but in that case one *receives them,* of whom it is witnessed that he lives *on.* [9] And, so to speak, through Abraham even Levi, who received tithes, has paid tithes, [10] for he was still in the loins of his forefather when Melchizedek met him.

[11] So if perfection was through the Levitical priesthood (for on the basis of it the people received the Law), what further need *was there* for another priest to arise according to the order of Melchizedek, and not be designated according to the order of Aaron? [12] For when the priesthood is changed, of necessity there takes place a change of law also. [13] For the one about whom these things are said belongs to another tribe, from which no one has officiated at the altar. [14] For it is evident that our Lord was descended from Judah, a tribe with reference to which Moses said nothing concerning priests. [15] And this is clearer still, if another priest arises according to the likeness of Melchizedek, [16] who has become *a priest* not on the basis of a law of physical requirement, but according to the power of an indestructible life. [17] For it is attested *of Him,*

> "YOU ARE A PRIEST FOREVER
>   ACCORDING TO THE ORDER OF MELCHIZEDEK."

[18] For, on the one hand, there is *the* nullification of a former commandment because of its weakness and uselessness [19] (for the Law made nothing perfect); on the

other hand, *there is the* introduction of a better hope,
through which we come near to God. 20 And to the
extent that *it was* not without an oath 21 (for they indeed
became priests without an oath, but He with an oath
through the One who said to Him,

"THE LORD HAS SWORN
  AND WILL NOT CHANGE HIS MIND,
'YOU ARE A PRIEST FOREVER'");
22 by the same extent Jesus also has become the
guarantee of a better covenant.

23 The *former* priests, on the one hand, existed in
greater numbers because they were prevented by death
from continuing; 24 Jesus, on the other hand, because He
continues forever, holds His priesthood permanently.
25 Therefore He is also able to save forever those who
come to God through Him, since He always lives to make
intercession for them.

26 For it was fitting for us to have such a high priest,
holy, innocent, undefiled, separated from sinners, and
exalted above the heavens; 27 who has no daily need,
like those high priests, to offer up sacrifices, first for His
own sins and then for the *sins* of the people, because
He did this once for all *time* when He offered up
Himself. 28 For the Law appoints men as high priests
who are weak, but the word of the oath, which came
after the Law, *appoints* a Son, who has been made
perfect forever.

A Better Ministry

8 Now the main point in what has been said *is this:* we
have such a high priest, who has taken His seat at the
right hand of the throne of the Majesty in the heavens,
2 a minister in the sanctuary and in the true tabernacle,
which the Lord set up, not man. 3 For every high priest is
appointed to offer both gifts and sacrifices; so it is necessary that this *high priest* also have something to offer.
4 Now if He were on earth, He would not be a priest at
all, since there are those who offer the gifts according to
the Law; 5 who serve a copy and shadow of the heavenly
things, just as Moses was warned *by God* when he
was about to erect the tabernacle; for, "SEE," He says,
"THAT YOU MAKE all things BY THE PATTERN WHICH WAS SHOWN
TO YOU ON THE MOUNTAIN." 6 But now He has obtained a
more excellent ministry, to the extent that He is also the

mediator of a better covenant, which has been enacted on better promises.

A New Covenant

7 For if that first *covenant* had been free of fault, no circumstances would have been sought for a second. **8** For in finding fault with the people, He says,

"BEHOLD, DAYS ARE COMING, SAYS THE LORD,
WHEN I WILL BRING ABOUT A NEW COVENANT
WITH THE HOUSE OF ISRAEL AND THE HOUSE OF JUDAH,
9   NOT LIKE THE COVENANT WHICH I MADE WITH THEIR
       FATHERS
ON THE DAY I TOOK THEM BY THE HAND
TO BRING THEM OUT OF THE LAND OF EGYPT;
FOR THEY DID NOT CONTINUE IN MY COVENANT,
AND I DID NOT CARE ABOUT THEM, SAYS THE LORD.
10 "FOR THIS IS THE COVENANT WHICH I WILL MAKE WITH THE
       HOUSE OF ISRAEL
AFTER THOSE DAYS, DECLARES THE LORD:
I WILL PUT MY LAWS INTO THEIR MINDS,
AND WRITE THEM ON THEIR HEARTS.
AND I WILL BE THEIR GOD,
AND THEY SHALL BE MY PEOPLE.
11 "AND THEY WILL NOT TEACH, EACH ONE HIS FELLOW CITIZEN,
AND EACH ONE HIS BROTHER, SAYING, 'KNOW THE LORD,'
FOR THEY WILL ALL KNOW ME,
FROM THE LEAST TO THE GREATEST OF THEM.
12 "FOR I WILL BE MERCIFUL TOWARD THEIR WRONGDOINGS,
AND THEIR SINS I WILL NO LONGER REMEMBER."

13 When He said, "A new *covenant,*" He has made the first obsolete. But whatever is becoming obsolete and growing old is about to disappear.

The Old and the New

9 Now even the first *covenant* had regulations for divine worship and the earthly sanctuary. **2** For a tabernacle was equipped, the outer *sanctuary,* in which *were* the lampstand, the table, and the sacred bread; this is called the Holy Place. **3** Behind the second veil there was a tabernacle which is called the Most Holy Place, **4** having a golden altar of incense and the ark of the covenant covered on all sides with gold, in which was a golden jar holding the manna, Aaron's staff which budded, and the tablets of the covenant; **5** and above it *were* the cherubim of glory overshadowing the ʹatoning cover; but about these things we cannot now speak in detail.

6 Now when these things have been so prepared, the priests are continually entering the outer tabernacle, performing the divine worship, 7 but into the second, only the high priest *enters* once a year, not without *taking* blood which he offers for himself and for the sins of the people committed in ignorance. 8 The Holy Spirit *is* signifying this, that the way into the holy place has not yet been disclosed while the outer tabernacle is still standing, 9 which *is* a symbol for the present time. Accordingly both gifts and sacrifices are offered which cannot make the worshiper perfect in conscience, 10 since they *relate* only to food, drink, and various washings, regulations for the body imposed until a time of reformation.

11 But when Christ appeared *as* a high priest of the good things ʹhaving come, *He entered* through the greater and more perfect tabernacle, not made by hands, that is, not of this creation; 12 and not through the blood of goats and calves, but through His own blood, He entered the holy place once for all *time,* having obtained eternal redemption. 13 For if the blood of goats and bulls, and the ʹashes of a heifer sprinkling those who have been defiled, sanctify for the cleansing of the flesh, 14 how much more will the blood of Christ, who through the eternal Spirit offered Himself without blemish to God, cleanse your conscience from dead works to serve the living God?

15 For this reason He is the mediator of a new covenant, so that, since a death has taken place for the redemption of the violations that were *committed* under the first covenant, those who have been called may receive the promise of the eternal inheritance. 16 For where there is a covenant, there must of necessity be the death of the one who made it. 17 For a covenant is valid *only* when *people are* dead, ʹfor it is never in force while the one who made it lives. 18 Therefore even the first *covenant* was not inaugurated without blood. 19 For when

---

9:5 1 Also called *mercy seat;* i.e., where blood was sprinkled on the Day of Atonement   9:11 1 One early ms *to come*
9:13 1 I.e., ashes mixed in water   9:17 1 One early ms *for is it then...lives?*

every commandment had been spoken by Moses to all the people according to the Law, he took the blood of the calves and the goats, with water and scarlet wool and hyssop, and sprinkled both the book itself and all the people, **20** saying, "THIS IS THE BLOOD OF THE COVENANT WHICH GOD COMMANDED YOU." **21** And in the same way he sprinkled both the tabernacle and all the vessels of the ministry with the blood. **22** And almost all things are cleansed with blood, according to the Law, and without the shedding of blood there is no forgiveness.

23 Therefore it was necessary for the copies of the things in the heavens to be cleansed with these things, but the heavenly things themselves with better sacrifices than these. **24** For Christ did not enter a holy place made by hands, a *mere* copy of the true one, but into heaven itself, now to appear in the presence of God for us; **25** nor was it that He would offer Himself often, as the high priest enters the Holy Place year by year with blood that is not his own. **26** Otherwise, He would have needed to suffer often since the foundation of the world; but now once at the consummation of the ages He has been revealed to put away sin by the sacrifice of Himself. **27** And just as it is destined for people to die once, and after this *comes* judgment, **28** so Christ also, having been offered once to bear the sins of many, will appear a second time for salvation without *reference to* sin, to those who eagerly await Him.

One Sacrifice of Christ Is Sufficient

10 For the Law, since it has *only* a shadow of the good things to come *and* not the form of those things itself, [1]can never, by the same sacrifices which they offer continually every year, make those who approach perfect. **2** Otherwise, would they not have ceased to be offered, because the worshipers, having once been cleansed, would no longer have had consciousness of sins? **3** But in those *sacrifices* there is a reminder of sins every year. **4** For it is impossible for the blood of bulls and goats to take away sins. **5** Therefore, when He comes into the world, He says,

"YOU HAVE NOT DESIRED SACRIFICE AND OFFERING,
    BUT YOU HAVE PREPARED A BODY FOR ME;

10:1 [1]One early ms *they can*

6   YOU HAVE NOT TAKEN PLEASURE IN WHOLE BURNT OFFERINGS
        AND *OFFERINGS* FOR SIN.
7   "THEN I SAID, 'BEHOLD, I HAVE COME
        (IT IS WRITTEN OF ME IN THE SCROLL OF THE BOOK)
        TO DO YOUR WILL, O GOD.' "

8 After saying above, "SACRIFICES AND OFFERINGS AND WHOLE
BURNT OFFERINGS AND *OFFERINGS* FOR SIN YOU HAVE NOT DESIRED,
NOR HAVE YOU TAKEN PLEASURE *IN THEM*" (which are offered
according to the Law), 9 then He said, "BEHOLD, I HAVE
COME TO DO YOUR WILL." He takes away the first in order to
establish the second. 10 By this will, we have been
sanctified through the offering of the body of Jesus Christ
once for all *time.*

11 Every priest stands daily ministering and offering
time after time the same sacrifices, which can never take
away sins; 12 but He, having offered one sacrifice for sins
for all time, SAT DOWN AT THE RIGHT HAND OF GOD, 13 waiting
from that time onward UNTIL HIS ENEMIES ARE MADE A FOOT-
STOOL FOR HIS FEET. 14 For by one offering He has perfected
for all time those who are sanctified. 15 And the Holy
Spirit also testifies to us; for after saying,

16   "THIS IS THE COVENANT WHICH I WILL MAKE WITH THEM
        AFTER THOSE DAYS, DECLARES THE LORD:
        I WILL PUT MY LAWS UPON THEIR HEARTS,
        AND WRITE THEM ON THEIR MIND,"

He then says,
17   "AND THEIR SINS AND THEIR LAWLESS DEEDS
        I WILL NO LONGER REMEMBER."

18 Now where there is forgiveness of these things, an
offering for sin is no longer *required.*

A New and Living Way

19 Therefore, brothers *and sisters,* since we have confidence to enter the holy place by the blood of Jesus, 20 by
a new and living way which He inaugurated for us
through the veil, that is, *through* His flesh, 21 and since
we have a great priest over the house of God, 22 let's
approach *God* with a sincere heart in full assurance of
faith, having our hearts sprinkled *clean* from an evil conscience and our bodies washed with pure water. 23 Let's
hold firmly to the confession of our hope without
wavering, for He who promised is faithful; 24 and let's
consider how to encourage one another in love and good
deeds, 25 not abandoning our own meeting together, as is

the habit of some people, but encouraging *one another;* and all the more as you see the day drawing near.

Christ or Judgment

26 For if we go on sinning willfully after receiving the knowledge of the truth, there no longer remains a sacrifice for sins, 27 but a terrifying expectation of judgment and THE FURY OF A FIRE WHICH WILL CONSUME THE ADVERSARIES. 28 Anyone who has ignored the Law of Moses is put to death without mercy on *the testimony of* two or three witnesses. 29 How much more severe punishment do you think he will deserve who has trampled underfoot the Son of God, and has regarded as unclean the blood of the covenant by which he was sanctified, and has insulted the Spirit of grace? 30 For we know Him who said, "VENGEANCE IS MINE, I WILL REPAY." And again, "THE LORD WILL JUDGE HIS PEOPLE." 31 It is a terrifying thing to fall into the hands of the living God.

32 But remember the former days, when, after being enlightened, you endured a great conflict of sufferings, 33 partly by being made a public spectacle through insults and distress, and partly by becoming companions with those who were so treated. 34 For you showed sympathy to the prisoners and accepted joyfully the seizure of your property, knowing that you have for yourselves a better and lasting possession. 35 Therefore, do not throw away your confidence, which has a great reward. 36 For you have need of endurance, so that when you have done the will of God, you may receive what was promised.

37   FOR YET IN A VERY LITTLE WHILE,
         HE WHO IS COMING WILL COME, AND WILL NOT DELAY.
38   BUT MY RIGHTEOUS ONE WILL LIVE BY FAITH;
         AND IF HE SHRINKS BACK, MY SOUL HAS NO PLEASURE IN HIM.
39 But we are not among those who shrink back to destruction, but of those who have faith for the safekeeping of the soul.

The Triumphs of Faith

11 Now faith is *the* certainty of *things* hoped for, a proof of things not seen. 2 For by it the people of old gained approval.

3 By faith we understand that the world has been created by the word of God so that what is seen has not

been made out of things that are visible. 4 By faith Abel offered to God a better sacrifice than Cain, through which he was attested to be righteous, God testifying about his gifts, and through faith, though he is dead, he still speaks. 5 By faith Enoch was taken up so that he would not see death; AND HE WAS NOT FOUND BECAUSE GOD TOOK HIM UP; for before he was taken up, he was attested to have been pleasing to God. 6 And without faith it is impossible to please *Him,* for the one who comes to God must believe that He exists, and *that* He proves to be One who rewards those who seek Him. 7 By faith Noah, being warned *by God* about things not yet seen, in reverence prepared an ark for the salvation of his household, by which he condemned the world, and became an heir of the righteousness which is according to faith.

8 By faith Abraham, when he was called, obeyed by going out to a place which he was to receive for an inheritance; and he left, not knowing where he was going. 9 By faith he lived as a stranger in the land of promise, as *in* a foreign *land,* living in tents with Isaac and Jacob, fellow heirs of the same promise; 10 for he was looking for the city which has foundations, whose architect and builder is God. 11 By faith even Sarah herself received ability to conceive, even beyond *the* proper time of life, since she considered Him faithful who had promised. 12 Therefore even from one man, and one who was *as good as* dead at that, there were born *descendants who were* just as the stars of heaven in number, and as the innumerable *grains of* sand along the seashore.

13 All these died in faith, without receiving the promises, but having seen and welcomed them from a distance, and having confessed that they were strangers and exiles on the earth. 14 For those who say such things make it clear that they are seeking a country of their own. 15 And indeed if they had been thinking of that *country* which they left, they would have had opportunity to return. 16 But as it is, they desire a better *country,* that is, a heavenly one. Therefore God is not ashamed to be called their God; for He has prepared a city for them.

17 By faith Abraham, when he was tested, offered up Isaac, and the one who had received the promises was

offering up his ¹only *son;* ¹⁸ *it was he* to whom it was said, "THROUGH ISAAC YOUR DESCENDANTS SHALL BE NAMED." ¹⁹ He considered that God is able to raise *people* even from the dead, from which he also received him back as a type. ²⁰ By faith Isaac blessed Jacob and Esau, even regarding things to come. ²¹ By faith Jacob, as he was dying, blessed each of the sons of Joseph, and worshiped, *leaning* on the top of his staff. ²² By faith Joseph, when he was dying, made mention of the exodus of the sons of Israel, and gave orders concerning his bones.

²³ By faith Moses, when he was born, was hidden for three months by his parents, because they saw he was a beautiful child; and they were not afraid of the king's edict. ²⁴ By faith Moses, when he had grown up, refused to be called the son of Pharaoh's daughter, ²⁵ choosing rather to endure ill-treatment with the people of God than to enjoy the temporary pleasures of sin, ²⁶ considering the reproach of Christ greater riches than the treasures of Egypt; for he was looking to the reward. ²⁷ By faith he left Egypt, not fearing the wrath of the king; for he persevered, as though seeing Him who is unseen. ²⁸ By faith he kept the Passover and the sprinkling of the blood, so that the destroyer of the firstborn would not touch them. ²⁹ By faith they passed through the Red Sea as through dry land; and the Egyptians, when they attempted it, were drowned.

³⁰ By faith the walls of Jericho fell down after *the Israelites* had marched around them for seven days. ³¹ By faith the prostitute Rahab did not perish along with those who were disobedient, after she had welcomed the spies in peace.

³² And what more shall I say? For time will fail me if I tell of Gideon, Barak, Samson, Jephthah, of David and Samuel and the prophets, ³³ who by faith conquered kingdoms, performed *acts of* righteousness, obtained promises, shut the mouths of lions, ³⁴ quenched the power of fire, escaped the edge of the sword, from weakness were made strong, became mighty in war, put foreign armies to flight. ³⁵ Women received *back* their dead by resurrection; and others were tortured, not accepting their release, so that they might obtain a better resurrection; ³⁶ and others experienced mocking

---

11:17 ¹I.e., only son with Sarah

and flogging, and further, chains and imprisonment. **37** They were stoned, they were sawn in two, [1] they were tempted, they were put to death with the sword; they went about in sheepskins, in goatskins, being destitute, afflicted, tormented **38** (*people* of whom the world was not worthy), wandering in deserts, *on* mountains, and *sheltering in* caves and holes in the ground.

39 And all these, having gained approval through their faith, did not receive what was promised, **40** because God had provided something better for us, so that apart from us they would not be made perfect.

Jesus, the Example

12 Therefore, since we also have such a great cloud of witnesses surrounding us, let's rid ourselves of every obstacle and the sin which so easily entangles us, and let's run with endurance the race that is set before us, **2** looking only at Jesus, the originator and perfecter of the faith, who for the joy set before Him endured the cross, despising the shame, and has sat down at the right hand of the throne of God.

3 For consider Him who has endured such hostility by sinners against Himself, so that you will not grow weary and lose heart.

A Father's Discipline

4 You have not yet resisted to the point of shedding blood in your striving against sin; **5** and you have forgotten the exhortation which is addressed to you as sons,

"MY SON, DO NOT REGARD LIGHTLY THE DISCIPLINE OF THE
    LORD,
NOR FAINT WHEN YOU ARE PUNISHED BY HIM;
6 FOR WHOM THE LORD LOVES HE DISCIPLINES,
AND HE PUNISHES EVERY SON WHOM HE ACCEPTS."

7 It is for discipline that you endure; God deals with you as with sons; for what son is there whom *his* father does not discipline? **8** But if you are without discipline, of which all have become partakers, then you are illegitimate children and not sons. **9** Furthermore, we had earthly fathers to discipline us, and we respected *them;* shall we not much more be subject to the Father of spirits, and live? **10** For they disciplined *us* for a short

---

11:37 [1] One early ms does not contain *they were tempted*

time, as seemed best to them, but He *disciplines us* for *our* good, so that we may share His holiness. **11** For the moment, all discipline seems not to be pleasant, but painful; yet to those who have been trained by it, afterward it yields the peaceful fruit of righteousness.

12 Therefore, strengthen the hands that are weak and the knees that are feeble, **13** and make straight paths for your feet, so that *the limb* which is impaired may not be dislocated, but rather be healed.

14 Pursue peace with all people, and the holiness without which no one will see the Lord. **15** See to it that no one comes short of the grace of God; that no root of bitterness springing up causes trouble, and by it many become defiled; **16** that *there be* no sexually immoral or godless person like Esau, who sold his own birthright for a *single* meal. **17** For you know that even afterward, when he wanted to inherit the blessing, he was rejected, for he found no place for repentance, though he sought for it with tears.

Contrast of Sinai and Zion

18 For you have not come to *a mountain* that can be touched and to a blazing fire, and to darkness and gloom and whirlwind, **19** and to the blast of a trumpet and the sound of words, which *sound was such that* those who heard begged that no further word be spoken to them. **20** For they could not cope with the command, "If even an animal touches the mountain, it shall be stoned." **21** And so terrible was the sight, *that* Moses said, "I am terrified and trembling." **22** But you have come to Mount Zion and to the city of the living God, the heavenly Jerusalem, and to myriads of angels, **23** to the general assembly and church of the firstborn who are enrolled in heaven, and to God, the Judge of all, and to the spirits of *the* righteous made perfect, **24** and to Jesus, the mediator of a new covenant, and to the sprinkled blood, which speaks better than *the blood* of Abel.

The Unshaken Kingdom

25 See to it that you do not refuse Him who is speaking. For if those did not escape when they refused him who warned *them* on earth, much less *will* we *escape* who turn away from Him who *warns us* from heaven. **26** And His voice shook the earth then, but now

He has promised, saying, "YET ONCE MORE I WILL SHAKE NOT ONLY THE EARTH, BUT ALSO THE HEAVEN." **27** This *expression,* "Yet once more," denotes the removing of those things which can be shaken, as of created things, so that those things which cannot be shaken may remain. **28** Therefore, since we receive a kingdom which cannot be shaken, let's show gratitude, by which we may offer to God an acceptable service with reverence and awe; **29** for our God is a consuming fire.

The Changeless Christ

13 Let love of the brothers *and* sisters continue. **2** Do not neglect hospitality to strangers, for by this some have entertained angels without knowing it. **3** Remember the prisoners, as though in prison with them, *and* those who are badly treated, since you yourselves also are in the body. **4** Marriage *is to be held* in honor among all, and the *marriage* bed *is to be* undefiled; for God will judge the sexually immoral and adulterers. **5** *Make sure that* your character is free from the love of money, being content with what you have; for He Himself has said, "I WILL NEVER DESERT YOU, NOR WILL I EVER ABANDON YOU," **6** so that we confidently say,

"THE LORD IS MY HELPER, I WILL NOT BE AFRAID.
   WHAT WILL MAN DO TO ME?"

7 Remember those who led you, who spoke the word of God to you; and considering the result of their way of life, imitate their faith. **8** Jesus Christ *is* the same yesterday and today, and forever. **9** Do not be misled by varied and strange teachings; for it is good for the heart to be strengthened by grace, not by foods, through which those who were so occupied were not benefited. **10** We have an altar from which those who serve the tabernacle have no right to eat. **11** For the bodies of those animals whose blood is brought into the Holy Place by the high priest *as an offering* for sin are burned outside the camp. **12** Therefore Jesus also suffered outside the gate, that He might sanctify the people through His own blood. **13** So then, let us go out to Him outside the camp, bearing His reproach. **14** For here we do not have a lasting city, but we are seeking *the city* which is to come.

God-pleasing Sacrifices

15 Through Him then, let's continually offer up a sacrifice of praise to God, that is, the fruit of lips praising His name. 16 And do not neglect doing good and sharing, for with such sacrifices God is pleased.

17 Obey your leaders and submit *to them*—for they keep watch over your souls as those who will give an account—so that they may do this with joy, not groaning; for this *would be* unhelpful for you.

18 Pray for us, for we are sure that we have a good conscience, desiring to conduct ourselves honorably in all things. 19 And I urge *you* all the more to do this, so that I may be restored to you more quickly.

Benediction

20 Now may the God of peace, who brought up from the dead the great Shepherd of the sheep through the blood of the eternal covenant, *that is,* Jesus our Lord, 21 equip you in every good thing to do His will, working in us that which is pleasing in His sight, through Jesus Christ, to whom *be* the glory forever and ever. Amen.

22 But I urge you, brothers *and sisters,* listen patiently to this word of exhortation, for I have written to you briefly. 23 Know that our brother Timothy has been released, with whom, if he comes soon, I will see you. 24 Greet all of your leaders and all the saints. Those from Italy greet you.

25 Grace be with you all.

The Letter of

JAMES

The Testing of Your Faith

1 James, a bond-servant of God and of the Lord Jesus Christ,

To the twelve tribes who are dispersed abroad: Greetings.

2 Consider it all joy, my brothers *and sisters,* when you encounter various trials, 3 knowing that the testing of your faith produces endurance. 4 And let endurance have *its* perfect result, so that you may be perfect and complete, lacking in nothing.

5 But if any of you lacks wisdom, let him ask of God, who gives to all generously and without reproach, and it will be given to him. 6 But he must ask in faith without any doubting, for the one who doubts is like the surf of the sea, driven and tossed by the wind. 7 For that person ought not to expect that he will receive anything from the Lord, 8 *being* a double-minded man, unstable in all his ways.

9 Now the brother *or sister* of humble *circumstances* is to glory in his high position; 10 but the rich person *is to glory* in his humiliation, because like flowering grass he will pass away. 11 For the sun rises with its scorching heat and withers the grass; and its flower falls off and the beauty of its appearance is destroyed; so also the rich person, in the midst of his pursuits, will die out.

12 Blessed is a man who perseveres under trial; for once he has been approved, he will receive the crown of life which *the Lord* has promised to those who love Him. 13 No one is to say when he is tempted, "I am being tempted by God"; for God cannot be tempted by evil, and He Himself does not tempt anyone. 14 But each one is tempted when he is carried away and enticed by his own lust. 15 Then when lust has conceived, it gives birth to sin; and sin, when it has run its course, brings forth death. 16 Do not be deceived, my beloved brothers *and sisters.* 17 Every good thing given and every perfect gift is from above, coming down from the Father of lights, with whom there is no variation or shifting shadow. 18 In the exercise of His will He gave us birth by the word of

truth, so that we would be a kind of first fruits among His creatures.

19 You know *this,* my beloved brothers *and sisters.* Now everyone must be quick to hear, slow to speak, *and* slow to anger; **20** for a man's anger does not bring about the righteousness of God. **21** Therefore, ridding *yourselves* of all filthiness and *all* that remains of wickedness, in humility receive the word implanted, which is able to save your souls. **22** But prove yourselves doers of the word, and not just hearers who deceive themselves. **23** For if anyone is a hearer of the word and not a doer, he is like a man who looks at his natural face in a mirror; **24** for *once* he has looked at himself and gone away, he has immediately forgotten what kind of person he was. **25** But one who has looked intently at the perfect law, the *law* of freedom, and has continued *in it,* not having become a forgetful hearer but an active doer, this person will be blessed in what he does.

26 If anyone thinks himself to be religious, yet does not bridle his tongue but deceives his *own* heart, this person's religion is worthless. **27** Pure and undefiled religion in the sight of *our* God and Father is this: to visit orphans and widows in their distress, *and* to keep oneself unstained by the world.

The Sin of Partiality

2 My brothers *and sisters,* do not hold your faith in our glorious Lord Jesus Christ with *an attitude of* personal favoritism. **2** For if a man comes into your assembly with a gold ring *and is dressed* in bright clothes, and a poor man in dirty clothes also comes in, **3** and you pay special attention to the one who is wearing the bright clothes, and say, "You sit here in a good *place,*" and you say to the poor man, "You stand over there, or sit down by my footstool," **4** have you not made distinctions among yourselves, and become judges with evil motives? **5** Listen, my beloved brothers *and sisters:* did God not choose the poor of this world *to be* rich in faith and heirs of the kingdom which He promised to those who love Him? **6** But you have dishonored the poor man. Is it not the rich who oppress you and personally drag you into court? **7** Do they not blaspheme the good name by which you have been called?

⁸If, however, you are fulfilling the royal law according to the Scripture, "You shall love your neighbor as yourself," you are doing well. ⁹But if you show partiality, you are committing sin *and* are convicted by the Law as violators. ¹⁰For whoever keeps the whole Law, yet stumbles in one *point,* has become guilty of all. ¹¹For He who said, "Do not commit adultery," also said, "Do not murder." Now if you do not commit adultery, but do murder, you have become a violator of the Law. ¹²So speak, and so act, as those who are to be judged by *the* law of freedom. ¹³For judgment *will be* merciless to one who has shown no mercy; mercy triumphs over judgment.

Faith and Works

¹⁴What use is it, my brothers *and sisters,* if someone says he has faith, but he has no works? Can that faith save him? ¹⁵If a brother or sister is without clothing and in need of daily food, ¹⁶and one of you says to them, "Go in peace, be warmed and be filled," yet you do not give them what is necessary for *their* body, what use is that? ¹⁷In the same way, faith also, if it has no works, is dead, *being* by itself.

¹⁸But someone may *well* say, "You have faith and I have works; show me your faith without the works, and I will show you my faith by my works." ¹⁹You believe that ¹God is one. You do well; the demons also believe, and shudder. ²⁰But are you willing to acknowledge, you foolish person, that faith without works is useless? ²¹Was our father Abraham not justified by works when he offered up his son Isaac on the altar? ²²You see that faith was working with his works, and as a result of the works, faith was perfected; ²³and the Scripture was fulfilled which says, "And Abraham believed God, and it was credited to him as righteousness," and he was called a friend of God. ²⁴You see that a person is justified by works and not by faith alone. ²⁵In the same way, was Rahab the prostitute not justified by works also when she received the messengers and sent them out by another way? ²⁶For just as the body without *the* spirit is dead, so also faith without works is dead.

2:19 ¹One early ms *there is one God*

The Tongue Is a Fire

3 Do not become teachers in large numbers, my brothers, since you know that we *who are teachers* will incur a stricter judgment. 2 For we all stumble in many *ways.* If anyone does not stumble in what he says, he is a perfect man, able to rein in the whole body as well. 3 Now if we put the bits into the horses' mouths so that they will obey us, we direct their whole body as well. 4 Look at the ships too: though they are so large and are driven by strong winds, they are *nevertheless* directed by a very small rudder wherever the inclination of the pilot determines. 5 So also the tongue is a small part *of the body,* and *yet* it boasts of great things.

See how great a forest is set aflame by such a small fire! 6 And the tongue is a fire, the *very* world of unrighteousness; the tongue is set among our body's parts as that which defiles the whole body and sets on fire the course of *our* life, and is set on fire by [1]hell. 7 For every species of beasts and birds, of reptiles and creatures of the sea, is tamed and has been tamed by the human race. 8 But no one *among* mankind can tame the tongue; *it is* a restless evil, full of deadly poison. 9 With it we bless *our* Lord and Father, and with it we curse people, who have been made in the likeness of God; 10 from the same mouth come *both* blessing and cursing. My brothers *and sisters,* these things should not be this way. 11 Does a spring send out from the same opening *both* fresh and bitter *water?* 12 Can a fig tree, my brothers *and sisters,* bear olives, or a vine *bear* figs? Nor *can* salt water produce fresh.

Wisdom from Above

13 Who among you is wise and understanding? Let him show by his good behavior his deeds in the gentleness of wisdom. 14 But if you have bitter jealousy and selfish ambition in your heart, do not be arrogant and *so* lie against the truth. 15 This wisdom is not that which comes down from above, but is earthly, natural, demonic. 16 For where jealousy and selfish ambition exist, there is disorder and every evil thing. 17 But the wisdom from above is first pure, then peace-loving, gentle, reasonable, full of mercy and good fruits, impartial, free of hypocrisy.

3:6 [1] Gr *Gehenna*

18 And the fruit of righteousness is sown in peace by those who make peace.

Things to Avoid

4 What is the source of quarrels and conflicts among you? Is the source not your pleasures that wage war in your body's parts? 2 You lust and do not have, *so* you commit murder. And you are envious and cannot obtain, *so* you fight and quarrel. You do not have because you do not ask. 3 You ask and do not receive, because you ask with the wrong motives, so that you may spend *what you request* on your pleasures. 4 You adulteresses, do you not know that friendship with the world is hostility toward God? Therefore whoever wants to be a friend of the world makes himself an enemy of God. 5 Or do you think that the Scripture says to no purpose, "'He jealously desires the Spirit whom He has made to dwell in us"? 6 But He gives a greater grace. Therefore *it* says, "GOD IS OPPOSED TO THE PROUD, BUT GIVES GRACE TO THE HUMBLE." 7 Submit therefore to God. But resist the devil, and he will flee from you. 8 Come close to God and He will come close to you. Cleanse *your* hands, you sinners; and purify *your* hearts, you double-minded. 9 Be miserable, and mourn, and weep; let your laughter be turned into mourning, and your joy into gloom. 10 Humble yourselves in the presence of the Lord, and He will exalt you.

11 Do not speak against one another, brothers *and sisters.* The one who speaks against a brother *or sister,* or judges his brother *or sister,* speaks against the law and judges the law; but if you judge the law, you are not a doer of the law but a judge *of it.* 12 There is *only* one Lawgiver and Judge, the One who is able to save and to destroy; but who are you, judging your neighbor?

13 Come now, you who say, "Today or tomorrow we will go to such and such a city, and spend a year there and engage in business and make a profit." 14 Yet you do not know what your life will be like tomorrow. For you are *just* a vapor that appears for a little while, and then vanishes away. 15 Instead, *you ought* to say, "If the Lord wills, we will live and also do this or that." 16 But as it is,

---

4:5 1 Or *The spirit which He has made to dwell in us lusts with envy*

you boast in your arrogance; all such boasting is evil.
17 So for one who knows *the* right thing to do and does
not do it, for him it is sin.

Misuse of Riches

5 Come now, you rich people, weep and howl for your
miseries which are coming upon you. **2** Your riches
have rotted and your garments have become moth-eaten.
3 Your gold and your silver have corroded, and their
corrosion will serve as a testimony against you and will
consume your flesh like fire. It is in the last days that you
have stored up your treasure! **4** Behold, the pay of the
laborers who mowed your fields, *and* which has been
withheld by you, cries out *against you;* and the outcry of
those who did the harvesting has reached the ears of the
Lord of armies. **5** You have lived for pleasure on the earth
and lived luxuriously; you have fattened your hearts in a
day of slaughter. **6** You have condemned and put to death
the righteous person; he offers you no resistance.

Exhortation

7 Therefore be patient, brothers *and sisters,* until the
coming of the Lord. The farmer waits for the precious
produce of the soil, being patient about it, until it gets
the early and late rains. **8** You too be patient; strengthen
your hearts, for the coming of the Lord is near. **9** Do not
complain, brothers *and sisters,* against one another,
so that you may not be judged; behold, the Judge is
standing right at the door. **10** As an example, brothers
and sisters, of suffering and patience, take the prophets
who spoke in the name of the Lord. **11** We count
those blessed who endured. You have heard of the
endurance of Job and have seen the outcome of the
Lord's dealings, that the Lord is full of compassion and *is*
merciful.

12 But above all, my brothers *and sisters,* do not swear,
either by heaven or by earth or with any other oath; but
your yes is to be yes, and your no, no, so that you do not
fall under judgment.

13 Is anyone among you suffering? *Then* he must pray.
Is anyone cheerful? He is to sing praises. **14** Is anyone
among you sick? *Then* he must call for the elders of
the church and they are to pray over him, anointing
him with oil in the name of the Lord; **15** and the prayer of

faith will 'restore the one who is sick, and the Lord will raise him up, and if he has committed sins, they will be forgiven him. [16] Therefore, confess your sins to one another, and pray for one another so that you may be healed. A prayer of a righteous person, when it is 'brought about, can accomplish much. [17] Elijah was a man with a nature like ours, and he prayed earnestly that it would not rain, and it did not rain on the earth for three years and six months. [18] Then he prayed again, and the sky poured rain and the earth produced its fruit.

[19] My brothers *and sisters,* if anyone among you strays from the truth and someone turns him back, [20] let him know that the one who has turned a sinner from the error of his way will save his soul from death and cover a multitude of sins.

5:15 [1] Lit *save*   5:16 [1] I.e., granted by God

The First Letter of
PETER

A Living Hope and a Sure Salvation

1 Peter, an apostle of Jesus Christ,
To those who reside as strangers, scattered throughout Pontus, Galatia, Cappadocia, Asia, and Bithynia, who are chosen 2 according to the foreknowledge of God the Father, by the sanctifying work of the Spirit, to obey Jesus Christ and be sprinkled with His blood: May grace and peace be multiplied to you.

3 Blessed be the God and Father of our Lord Jesus Christ, who according to His great mercy has caused us to be born again to a living hope through the resurrection of Jesus Christ from the dead, 4 to *obtain* an inheritance *which is* imperishable, undefiled, and will not fade away, reserved in heaven for you, 5 who are protected by the power of God through faith for a salvation ready to be revealed in *the* last time. 6 In this you greatly rejoice, even though now for a little while, if necessary, you have been distressed by various trials, 7 so that the proof of your faith, *being* more precious than gold which perishes though tested by fire, may be found to result in praise, glory, and honor at the revelation of Jesus Christ; 8 and though you have not seen Him, you love Him, and though you do not see Him now, but believe in Him, you greatly rejoice with joy inexpressible and full of glory, 9 obtaining as the outcome of your faith, the salvation of 'your souls.

10 As to this salvation, the prophets who prophesied of the grace that *would come* to you made careful searches and inquiries, 11 seeking to know what person or time the Spirit of Christ within them was indicating as He predicted the sufferings of Christ and the glories to follow. 12 It was revealed to them that they were not serving themselves, but you, in these things which now have been announced to you through those who preached the gospel to you by the Holy Spirit sent from heaven—things into which angels long to look.

13 Therefore, prepare your minds for action, keep

---

sober *in spirit,* set your hope completely on the grace to be brought to you at the revelation of Jesus Christ. **14** As obedient children, do not be conformed to the former lusts *which were yours* in your ignorance, **15** but like the Holy One who called you, be holy yourselves also in all *your* behavior; **16** because it is written: "YOU SHALL BE HOLY, FOR I AM HOLY."

17 If you address as Father the One who impartially judges according to each one's work, conduct yourselves in fear during the time of your stay *on earth;* **18** knowing that you were not redeemed with perishable things like silver or gold from your futile way of life inherited from your forefathers, **19** but with precious blood, as of a lamb unblemished and spotless, *the blood* of Christ. **20** For He was foreknown before the foundation of the world, but has appeared in these last times for the sake of you **21** who through Him are believers in God, who raised Him from the dead and gave Him glory, so that your faith and hope are in God.

22 Since you have purified your souls in obedience to the truth for a sincere love of the brothers *and* sisters, fervently love one another from ¹the heart, **23** for you have been born again not of seed which is perishable, but imperishable, *that is,* through the living and enduring word of God. **24** For,

"ALL FLESH IS LIKE GRASS,
   AND ALL ITS GLORY IS LIKE THE FLOWER OF GRASS.
   THE GRASS WITHERS,
   AND THE FLOWER FALLS OFF,
25   BUT THE WORD OF THE LORD ENDURES FOREVER."

And this is the word which was preached to you.

As Newborn Babes

2 Therefore, rid *yourselves* of all malice and all deceit and hypocrisy and envy and all slander, **2** and like newborn babies, long for the pure milk of the word, so that by it you may grow in respect to salvation, **3** if you have tasted the kindness of the Lord.

As Living Stones

4 And coming to Him as to a living stone which has been rejected by people, but is choice and precious in

---

1:22 ¹Two early mss *a pure heart*

the sight of God, 5 you also, as living stones, are being built up as a spiritual house for a holy priesthood, to offer spiritual sacrifices that are acceptable to God through Jesus Christ. 6 For *this* is contained in Scripture:

"BEHOLD, I AM LAYING IN ZION A CHOICE STONE, A PRECIOUS
    CORNERSTONE,
AND THE ONE WHO BELIEVES IN HIM WILL NOT BE PUT TO
    SHAME."

7 This precious value, then, is for you who believe; but for unbelievers,

"A STONE WHICH THE BUILDERS REJECTED,
THIS BECAME THE CHIEF CORNERSTONE,"

8 and,

"A STONE OF STUMBLING AND A ROCK OF OFFENSE";

for they stumble because they are disobedient to the word, and to this they were also appointed.

9 But you are A CHOSEN PEOPLE, A royal PRIESTHOOD, A HOLY NATION, A PEOPLE FOR *GOD'S* OWN POSSESSION, so that you may proclaim the excellencies of Him who has called you out of darkness into His marvelous light; 10 for you once were NOT A PEOPLE, but now you are THE PEOPLE OF GOD; you had NOT RECEIVED MERCY, but now you have RECEIVED MERCY.

11 Beloved, I urge *you* as foreigners and strangers to abstain from fleshly lusts, which wage war against the soul. 12 Keep your behavior excellent among the Gentiles, so that in the thing in which they slander you as evildoers, they may because of your good deeds, as they observe *them,* glorify God on the day of ¹visitation.

Honor Authority

13 Submit yourselves for the Lord's sake to every human institution, whether to a king as the one in authority, 14 or to governors as sent by him for the punishment of evildoers and the praise of those who do right. 15 For such is the will of God, that by doing right you silence the ignorance of foolish people. 16 *Act* as free people, and do not use your freedom as a covering for evil, but *use it* as bond-servants of God. 17 Honor all people, love the brotherhood, fear God, honor the king.

18 Servants, be subject to your masters with all respect, not only to those who are good and gentle, but also to

---

2:12 ¹I.e., Christ's coming again in judgment

those who are harsh. ¹⁹For this *finds* favor, if for the sake of conscience toward God a person endures grief when suffering unjustly. ²⁰For what credit is there if, when you sin and are harshly treated, you endure it with patience? But if when you do what is right and suffer *for it* you patiently endure it, this *finds* favor with God.

Christ Is Our Example

²¹For you have been called for this purpose, because Christ also suffered for you, leaving you an example, so that you would follow in His steps, ²²HE WHO COMMITTED NO sin, NOR WAS ANY DECEIT found IN HIS MOUTH; ²³and while being abusively insulted, He did not insult in return; while suffering, He did not threaten, but kept entrusting *Himself* to Him who judges righteously; ²⁴and He Himself brought our sins in His body up on the 'cross, so that we might die to sin and live for righteousness; by His wounds you were healed. ²⁵For you were continually straying like sheep, but now you have returned to the Shepherd and Guardian of your souls.

Godly Living

3 In the same way, you wives, be subject to your own husbands so that even if any *of them* are disobedient to the word, they may be won over without a word by the behavior of their wives, ²as they observe your pure and respectful behavior. ³Your adornment must not be *merely* the external—braiding the hair, wearing gold *jewelry,* or putting on apparel; ⁴but *it should be* the hidden person of the heart, with the imperishable *quality* of a gentle and quiet spirit, which is precious in the sight of God. ⁵For in this way the holy women of former times, who hoped in God, also used to adorn themselves, being subject to their own husbands, ⁶just as Sarah obeyed Abraham, calling him lord; and you have proved to be her children if you do what is right without being frightened by any fear.

⁷You husbands in the same way, live with *your wives* in an understanding way, as with someone weaker, *since she is* a woman; and show her honor as a fellow heir of

---

2:24 ¹Lit *wood;* see Deut 21:23

the grace of life, so that your prayers will not be hindered.

8 To sum up, all *of you* be harmonious, sympathetic, ¹loving, compassionate, *and* humble; 9 not returning evil for evil or insult for insult, but giving a blessing instead; for you were called for the very purpose that you would inherit a blessing. 10 For,

"THE ONE WHO DESIRES LIFE, TO LOVE AND SEE GOOD DAYS,
    MUST KEEP HIS TONGUE FROM EVIL AND HIS LIPS FROM
        SPEAKING DECEIT.

11 "HE MUST TURN AWAY FROM EVIL AND DO GOOD;
    HE MUST SEEK PEACE AND PURSUE IT.

12 "FOR THE EYES OF THE LORD ARE TOWARD THE RIGHTEOUS,
    AND HIS EARS ATTEND TO THEIR PRAYER,
    BUT THE FACE OF THE LORD IS AGAINST EVILDOERS."

13 And who is there to harm you if you prove zealous for what is good? 14 But even if you should suffer for the sake of righteousness, you are blessed. AND DO NOT FEAR THEIR INTIMIDATION, AND DO NOT BE IN DREAD, 15 but ¹sanctify Christ as Lord in your hearts, always *being* ready to make a defense to everyone who asks you to give an account for the hope that is in you, but with gentleness and respect; 16 and keep a good conscience so that in the thing in which you are slandered, those who disparage your good behavior in Christ will be put to shame. 17 For it is better, if God should will it *so,* that you suffer for doing what is right rather than for doing what is wrong. 18 For Christ also suffered for sins once for all *time, the* just for *the* unjust, so that He might bring us to God, having been put to death in the flesh, but made alive in the spirit; 19 in which He also went and made proclamation to the spirits in prison, 20 who once were disobedient when the patience of God kept waiting in the days of Noah, during the construction of the ark, in which a few, that is, eight persons, were brought safely through *the* water. 21 Corresponding to that, baptism now saves you—not the removal of dirt from the flesh, but an appeal to God for a good conscience—through the resurrection of Jesus Christ, 22 who is at the right hand of God, having gone into heaven, after angels and authorities and powers had been subjected to Him.

3:8 ¹I.e., as brothers and sisters
3:15 ¹I.e., set apart

Keep Fervent in Your Love

4 Therefore, since Christ has [1]suffered in the flesh, arm yourselves also with the same purpose, because the one who has suffered in the flesh has ceased from sin, 2 so as to live the rest of the time in the flesh no longer for human lusts, but for the will of God. 3 For the time already past is sufficient *for you* to have carried out the desire of the Gentiles, having pursued a course of indecent behavior, lusts, drunkenness, carousing, drinking parties, and wanton idolatries. 4 In *all* this, they are surprised that you do not run with *them* in the same excesses of debauchery, and they slander *you;* 5 but they will give an account to Him who is ready to judge the living and the dead. 6 For the gospel has for this purpose been preached even to those who are dead, that though they are judged in the flesh as people, they may live in the spirit according to *the will of* God.

7 The end of all things is near; therefore, be of sound judgment and sober *spirit* for the purpose of prayer. 8 Above all, keep fervent in your love for one another, because love covers a multitude of sins. 9 Be hospitable to one another without complaint. 10 As each one has received a *special* gift, employ it in serving one another as good stewards of the multifaceted grace of God. 11 Whoever speaks *is to do so* as *one who is speaking* actual words of God; whoever serves *is to do so* as *one who is serving* by the strength which God supplies; so that in all things God may be glorified through Jesus Christ, to whom belongs the glory and dominion forever and ever. Amen.

Share the Sufferings of Christ

12 Beloved, do not be surprised at the fiery ordeal among you, which comes upon you for your testing, as though *something* strange were happening to you; 13 but to the degree that you share the sufferings of Christ, keep on rejoicing, so that at the revelation of His glory you may also rejoice and be overjoyed. 14 If you are insulted for the name of Christ, you are blessed, because the Spirit of glory, and of God, rests upon you. 15 Make sure that none of you suffers as a murderer, or thief, or evildoer, or a troublesome meddler; 16 but if *anyone*

4:1 [1] I.e., suffered death

suffers as a Christian, he is not to be ashamed, but is to glorify God in this name. [17] For *it is* time for judgment to begin with the household of God; and if *it begins* with us first, what *will be* the outcome for those who do not obey the gospel of God? [18] AND IF IT IS WITH DIFFICULTY THAT THE RIGHTEOUS IS SAVED, WHAT WILL BECOME OF THE GODLESS MAN AND THE SINNER? [19] Therefore, those also who suffer according to the will of God are to entrust their souls to a faithful Creator in doing what is right.

Serve God Willingly

5 Therefore, I urge elders among you, as *your* fellow elder and a witness of the sufferings of Christ, *and* one who is also a fellow partaker of the glory that is to be revealed: [2] shepherd the flock of God among you, exercising oversight, not under compulsion but voluntarily, according to *the will of* God; and not with greed but with eagerness; [3] nor yet as domineering over those assigned to your care, but by proving to be examples to the flock. [4] And when the Chief Shepherd appears, you will receive the unfading crown of glory. [5] You [1]younger men, likewise, be subject to *your* elders; and all of you, clothe yourselves with humility toward one another, because GOD IS OPPOSED TO THE PROUD, BUT HE GIVES GRACE TO THE HUMBLE.

[6] Therefore humble yourselves under the mighty hand of God, so that He may exalt you at the proper time, [7] having cast all your anxiety on Him, because He cares about you. [8] Be of sober *spirit,* be on the alert. Your adversary, the devil, prowls around like a roaring lion, seeking someone to devour. [9] So resist him, firm in *your* faith, knowing that the same experiences of suffering are being accomplished by your [1]brothers and sisters who are in the world. [10] After you have suffered for a little while, the God of all grace, who called you to His eternal glory in Christ, will Himself perfect, confirm, strengthen, *and* establish *you.* [11] To Him *be* dominion forever and ever. Amen.

[12] Through Silvanus, our faithful brother (for so I regard *him*), I have written to you briefly, [1]exhorting and testifying that this is the true grace of God. Stand firm in it! [13] She who is in Babylon, chosen together with *you,*

5:5 [1]Or *young people*   5:9 [1]Lit *fellowship*   5:12 [1]Or *encouraging*

sends you greetings, and *so does* my son, Mark. [14] Greet one another with a kiss of love.

Peace be to you all who are in Christ.

The Second Letter of
PETER

Growth in Christian Virtue

1 Simon Peter, a bond-servant and apostle of Jesus Christ,

To those who have received a faith of the same kind as ours, by the righteousness of our God and Savior, Jesus Christ: [2] Grace and peace be multiplied to you in the knowledge of God and of Jesus our Lord, [3] for His divine power has granted to us everything pertaining to life and godliness, through the true knowledge of Him who called us by His own glory and excellence. [4] Through these He has granted to us His precious and magnificent promises, so that by them you may become partakers of *the* divine nature, having escaped the corruption that is in the world on account of lust. [5] Now for this very reason also, applying all diligence, in your faith supply moral [1]excellence, and in *your* moral excellence, knowledge, [6] and in *your* knowledge, self-control, and in *your* self-control, perseverance, and in *your* perseverance, godliness, [7] and in *your* godliness, brotherly kindness, and in *your* brotherly kindness, love. [8] For if these *qualities* are yours and are increasing, they do not make you useless nor unproductive in the true knowledge of our Lord Jesus Christ. [9] For the one who lacks these *qualities* is blind *or* short-sighted, having forgotten *his* purification from his former sins. [10] Therefore, brothers *and sisters,* be all the more diligent to make certain about His calling and choice of you; for as long as you practice these things, you will never stumble; [11] for in this way the entrance into the eternal kingdom of our Lord and Savior Jesus Christ will be abundantly supplied to you.

[12] Therefore, I will always be ready to remind you of these things, even though you *already* know *them* and have been established in the truth which is present with *you.* [13] I consider it right, as long as I am in this *earthly* [1]dwelling, to stir you up by way of reminder, [14] knowing that the laying aside of my *earthly* dwelling is imminent,

---

1:5 [1]Or *virtue*   1:13 [1]I.e., human body

as also our Lord Jesus Christ has made clear to me. [15] And I will also be diligent that at any time after my departure you will be able to call these things to mind.

Eyewitnesses

[16] For we did not follow cleverly devised tales when we made known to you the power and coming of our Lord Jesus Christ, but we were eyewitnesses of His majesty. [17] For when He received honor and glory from God the Father, such a declaration as this was made to Him by the Majestic Glory: "This is My beloved Son with whom I am well pleased"— [18] and we ourselves heard this declaration made from heaven when we were with Him on the holy mountain.

[19] And *so* we have the prophetic word *made* more sure, to which you do well to pay attention as to a lamp shining in a dark place, until the day dawns and the morning star arises in your hearts. [20] *But* know this first *of all,* that no prophecy of Scripture becomes *a matter* of *someone's* own interpretation, [21] for no prophecy was ever made by an act of human will, but men moved by the Holy Spirit spoke from God.

The Appearance of False Prophets

2 But false prophets also appeared among the people, just as there will also be false teachers among you, who will secretly introduce destructive heresies, even denying the Master who bought them, bringing swift destruction upon themselves. [2] Many will follow their indecent behavior, and because of them the way of the truth will be maligned; [3] and in *their* greed they will exploit you with false words; their judgment from long ago is not idle, and their destruction is not asleep.

[4] For if God did not spare angels when they sinned, but cast them into [1]hell and committed them to [2]pits of darkness, held for judgment; [5] and did not spare the ancient world, but protected Noah, a preacher of righteousness, with seven others, when He brought a flood upon the world of the ungodly; [6] and *if* He condemned the cities of Sodom and Gomorrah to destruction by reducing *them* to ashes, having made

---

2:4 [1] Gr *Tartarus,* a name used as a reference to the netherworld (hell)
2:4 [2] One early ms *chains of darkness*

them an example of what is coming for the ungodly; 7 and *if* He rescued righteous Lot, *who was* oppressed by the perverted conduct of unscrupulous people 8 (for by what he saw and heard *that* righteous man, while living among them, felt *his* righteous soul tormented day after day by *their* lawless deeds), 9 *then* the Lord knows how to rescue the godly from a trial, and to keep the unrighteous under punishment for the day of judgment, 10 and especially those who indulge the flesh in *its* corrupt passion, and despise authority.

Reckless, self-centered, they speak abusively of *angelic* majesties without trembling, 11 whereas angels who are greater in might and power do not bring a demeaning judgment against them before the Lord. 12 But these, like unreasoning animals, born as creatures of instinct to be captured and killed, using abusive speech where they have no knowledge, will in the destruction of those creatures also be destroyed, 13 suffering wrong as the wages of doing wrong. They count it a pleasure to revel in the daytime. They are stains and blemishes, reveling in their ¹deceptions as they feast with you, 14 having eyes full of adultery that never cease from sin, enticing unstable souls, having hearts trained in greed, accursed children; 15 abandoning the right way, they have gone astray, having followed the way of Balaam, the *son* of Beor, who loved the reward of unrighteousness; 16 but he received a rebuke for his own offense, *for* a mute donkey, speaking with a human voice, restrained the insanity of the prophet.

17 These are springs without water and mists driven by a storm, for whom the black darkness has been reserved. 18 For, while speaking out arrogant *words* of no value they entice by fleshly desires, by indecent behavior, those who barely escape from the ones who live in error, 19 promising them freedom while they themselves are slaves of corruption; for by what anyone is overcome, by this he is enslaved. 20 For if, after they have escaped the defilements of the world by the knowledge of the Lord and Savior Jesus Christ, they are again entangled in them and are overcome, the last state has become worse for them than the first. 21 For it would be better for them not to have known the way of righteousness, than having

---

known it, to turn away from the holy commandment handed on to them. [22] It has happened to them according to the true proverb, "A DOG RETURNS TO ITS OWN VOMIT," and, "A sow, after washing, *returns* to wallowing in the mire."

Purpose of This Letter

3 Beloved, this is now the second letter I am writing to you in which I am stirring up your sincere mind by way of a reminder, [2] to remember the words spoken beforehand by the holy prophets and the commandment of the Lord and Savior *spoken* by your apostles.

The Coming Day of the Lord

[3] Know this first *of all,* that in the last days mockers will come with *their* mocking, following after their own lusts, [4] and saying, "Where is the promise of His coming? For *ever* since the fathers [1]fell asleep, all things continue just as *they were* from the beginning of creation." [5] For when they maintain this, it escapes their notice that by the word of God *the* heavens existed long ago and *the* earth was formed out of water and by water, [6] through which the world at that time was destroyed by being flooded with water. [7] But by His word the present heavens and earth are being reserved for fire, kept for the day of judgment and destruction of ungodly people.

[8] But do not let this one *fact* escape your notice, beloved, that with the Lord one day is like a thousand years, and a thousand years like one day. [9] The Lord is not slow about His promise, as some count slowness, but is patient toward you, not willing for any to perish, but for all to come to repentance.

A New Heaven and Earth

[10] But the day of the Lord will come like a thief, in which the heavens will pass away with a roar and the elements will be destroyed with intense heat, and the earth and its works will be [1]discovered.

[11] Since all these things are to be destroyed in this way, what sort of people ought you to be in holy conduct and godliness, [12] looking for and hastening the coming of the day of God, because of which the heavens will be

---

3:4 [1]I.e., died   3:10 [1]I.e., as worthless; late mss *burned up*

destroyed by burning, and the elements will melt with
intense heat! **13** But according to His promise we are
looking for new heavens and a new earth, in which
righteousness dwells.

14 Therefore, beloved, since you look for these things,
be diligent to be found spotless and blameless by Him, at
peace, **15** and regard the patience of our Lord *as* salvation;
just as also our beloved brother Paul, according to the
wisdom given him, wrote to you, **16** as also in all *his*
letters, speaking in them of these things, in which there
are some things that are hard to understand, which the
untaught and unstable distort, as *they do* also the rest of
the Scriptures, to their own destruction. **17** You therefore,
beloved, knowing this beforehand, be on your guard so
that you are not carried away by the error of
unscrupulous people and lose your own firm commitment, **18** but grow in the grace and knowledge of our Lord
and Savior Jesus Christ. To Him *be* the glory, both now
and to the day of eternity. Amen.

The First Letter of
JOHN

The Incarnate Word

1 What was from the beginning, what we have heard, what we have seen with our eyes, what we have looked at and touched with our hands, concerning the Word of Life—2 and the life was revealed, and we have seen and testify and proclaim to you the eternal life, which was with the Father and was revealed to us— 3 what we have seen and heard we proclaim to you also, so that you too may have fellowship with us; and indeed our fellowship is with the Father, and with His Son Jesus Christ. 4 These things we write, so that our joy may be made complete.

God Is Light

5 This is the message we have heard from Him and announce to you, that God is Light, and in Him there is no darkness at all. 6 If we say that we have fellowship with Him and *yet* walk in the darkness, we lie and do not practice the truth; 7 but if we walk in the Light as He Himself is in the Light, we have fellowship with one another, and the blood of Jesus His Son cleanses us from all sin. 8 If we say that we have no sin, we are deceiving ourselves and the truth is not in us. 9 If we confess our sins, He is faithful and righteous, so that He will forgive us our sins and cleanse us from all unrighteousness. 10 If we say that we have not sinned, we make Him a liar and His word is not in us.

Christ Is Our Advocate

2 My little children, I am writing these things to you so that you may not sin. And if anyone sins, we have an ¹Advocate with the Father, Jesus Christ the righteous; 2 and He Himself is the ¹propitiation for our sins; and not for ours only, but also for *the sins of* the whole world.

3 By this we know that we have come to know Him, if we keep His commandments. 4 The one who says,

---

2:1 ¹ Or *Intercessor*   2:2 ¹ I.e., means of reconciliation with God by atoning for sins; or *sin-offering*

"I have come to know Him," and does not keep His commandments, is a liar, and the truth is not in him; **5** but whoever follows His word, in him the love of God has truly been perfected. By this we know that we are in Him: **6** the one who says that he remains in Him ought, himself also, walk just as He walked.

7 Beloved, I am not writing a new commandment to you, but an old commandment which you have had from the beginning; the old commandment is the word which you have heard. **8** On the other hand, I am writing a new commandment to you, which is true in Him and in you, because the darkness is passing away and the true Light is already shining. **9** The one who says that he is in the Light and *yet* hates his brother *or sister* is in the darkness until now. **10** The one who loves his brother *and sister* remains in the Light, and there is nothing in him to cause stumbling. **11** But the one who hates his brother *or sister* is in the darkness and walks in the darkness, and does not know where he is going because the darkness has blinded his eyes.

12 I am writing to you, little children, because your sins have been forgiven you on account of His name. **13** I am writing to you, fathers, because you know Him who has been from the beginning. I am writing to you, young men, because you have overcome the evil one. I have written to you, children, because you know the Father. **14** I have written to you, fathers, because you know Him who has been from the beginning. I have written to you, young men, because you are strong, and the word of God remains in you, and you have overcome the evil one.

Do Not Love the World

15 Do not love the world nor the things in the world. If anyone loves the world, the love of the Father is not in him. **16** For all that is in the world, the lust of the flesh and the lust of the eyes and the boastful pride of life, is not from the Father, but is from the world. **17** The world is passing away and *also* its lusts; but the one who does the will of God continues *to live* forever.

18 Children, it is the last hour; and just as you heard that antichrist is coming, even now many antichrists have appeared; from this we know that it is the last hour. **19** They went out from us, but they were not *really* of us; for if they had been of us, they would have remained with us; but *they went out,* so that it would be evident that they all are not of us. **20** But you have an anointing from the Holy One, and you all know. **21** I have not written to you because you do not know the truth, but because you do know it, and because no lie is of the truth. **22** Who is the liar except the one who denies that Jesus is the Christ? This is the antichrist, the one who denies the Father and the Son. **23** Whoever denies the Son does not have the Father; the one who confesses the Son has the Father also. **24** *As for* you, *see that* what you heard from the beginning remains in you. If what you heard from the beginning remains in you, you also will remain in the Son and in the Father.

The Promise Is Eternal Life

25 This is the promise which He Himself made to us: eternal life.

26 These things I have written to you concerning those who are *trying to* deceive you. **27** And *as for* you, the anointing which you received from Him remains in you, and you have no need for anyone to teach you; but as His anointing teaches you about all things, and is true and is not a lie, and just as it has taught you, you remain in Him.

28 Now, little children, remain in Him, so that when He appears, we may have confidence and not draw back from Him in shame at His coming. **29** If you know that He is righteous, you know that everyone who practices righteousness also has been born of Him.

Children of God Love One Another

3 See how great a love the Father has given us, that we would be called children of God; and *in fact* we are. For this reason the world does not know us: because it did not know Him. **2** Beloved, now we are children of God, and it has not appeared as yet what we will be. We know that when He appears, we will be like Him, because we will see Him just as He is. **3** And everyone who has this hope *set* on Him purifies himself, just as He is pure.

4 Everyone who practices sin also practices lawlessness; and sin is lawlessness. **5** You know that He appeared in order to take away sins; and in Him there is no sin. **6** No one who remains in Him sins *continually;* no one who sins *continually* has seen Him or knows Him. **7** Little children, make sure no one deceives you; the one who practices righteousness is righteous, just as He is righteous; **8** the one who practices sin is of the devil; for the devil has been sinning from the beginning. The Son of God appeared for this purpose, to destroy the works of the devil. **9** No one who has been born of God practices sin, because His seed remains in him; and he cannot sin *continually,* because he has been born of God. **10** By this the children of God and the children of the devil are obvious: anyone who does not practice righteousness is not of God, nor the one who does not love his brother *and sister.*

11 For this is the message which you have heard from the beginning, that we are to love one another; **12** not as Cain, *who* was of the evil one and murdered his brother. And for what reason did he murder him? Because his *own* deeds were evil, but his brother's were righteous.

13 Do not be surprised, brothers *and sisters,* if the world hates you. **14** We know that we have passed out of death into life, because we love the brothers *and sisters.* The one who does not love remains in death. **15** Everyone who hates his brother *or sister* is a murderer, and you know that no murderer has eternal life remaining in him. **16** We know love by this, that He laid down His life for us; and we ought to lay down our lives for the brothers *and sisters.* **17** But whoever has worldly goods and sees his brother *or sister* in need, and closes his heart against him, how does the love of God remain in him? **18** Little children, let's not love with word or with tongue, but in deed and truth. **19** We will know by this that we are of the truth, and will set our heart at ease before Him, **20** that if our heart condemns us, that God is greater than our heart, and He knows all things. **21** Beloved, if our heart does not condemn us, we have confidence before God; **22** and whatever we ask, we receive from Him, because we keep His commandments and do the things that are pleasing in His sight.

23 This is His commandment, that we believe in the name of His Son Jesus Christ, and love one another, just as He commanded us. **24** The one who keeps His commandments remains in Him, and He in him. We know by this that He remains in us, by the Spirit whom He has given us.

Testing the Spirits

4 Beloved, do not believe every spirit, but test the spirits to see whether they are from God, because many false prophets have gone out into the world. **2** By this you know the Spirit of God: every spirit that confesses that Jesus Christ has come in the flesh is from God; **3** and every spirit that does not confess Jesus is not from God; this is the *spirit* of the antichrist, which you have heard is coming, and now it is already in the world. **4** You are from God, little children, and have overcome them; because greater is He who is in you than he who is in the world. **5** They are from the world, therefore they speak *as* from the world, and the world listens to them. **6** We are from God. The one who knows God listens to us; the one who is not from God does not listen to us. By this we know the spirit of truth and the spirit of error.

God Is Love

7 Beloved, let's love one another; for love is from God, and everyone who loves has been born of God and knows God. **8** The one who does not love does not know God, because God is love. **9** By this the love of God was revealed in us, that God has sent His only Son into the world so that we may live through Him. **10** In this is love, not that we loved God, but that He loved us and sent His Son *to be* the †propitiation for our sins. **11** Beloved, if God so loved us, we also ought to love one another. **12** No one has ever seen God; if we love one another, God remains in us, and His love is perfected in us. **13** By this we know that we remain in Him and He in us, because He has given to us of His Spirit. **14** We have seen and testify that the Father has sent the Son *to be* the Savior of the world.

15 Whoever confesses that Jesus is the Son of God, God remains in him, and he in God. **16** We have come to know and have believed the love which God has for us. God is love, and the one who remains in love remains in God, and God remains in him. **17** By this, love is perfected with us, so that we may have confidence in the day of judgment; because as He is, we also are in this world. **18** There is no fear in love, but perfect love drives out fear, because fear involves punishment, and the one who

---

4:10 †I.e., means of reconciliation with God by atoning for sins; or *sin-offering*

fears is not perfected in love. **19** We love, because He first loved us. **20** If someone says, "I love God," and *yet* he hates his brother *or sister,* he is a liar; for the one who does not love his brother *and sister* whom he has seen, cannot love God, whom he has not seen. **21** And this commandment we have from Him, that the one who loves God must also love his brother *and sister.*

Overcoming the World

5 Everyone who believes that Jesus is the Christ has been born of God, and everyone who loves the Father loves the *child* born of Him. **2** By this we know that we love the children of God, when we love God and follow His commandments. **3** For this is the love of God, that we keep His commandments; and His commandments are not burdensome. **4** For whoever has been born of God overcomes the world; and this is the victory that has overcome the world: our faith.

5 Who is the one who overcomes the world, but the one who believes that Jesus is the Son of God? **6** This is the One who came by water and blood, Jesus Christ; not with the water only, but with the water and with the blood. It is the Spirit who testifies, because the Spirit is the truth. **7** For there are three that testify: **8** the Spirit and the water and the blood; and the three are ¹in agreement. **9** If we receive the testimony of people, the testimony of God is greater; for the testimony of God is this, that He has testified concerning His Son. **10** The one who believes in the Son of God has the testimony in himself; the one who does not believe God has made Him a liar, because he has not believed in the testimony that God has given concerning His Son. **11** And the testimony is this, that God has given us eternal life, and this life is in His Son. **12** The one who has the Son has the life; the one who does not have the Son of God does not have the life.

This Is Written That You May Know

13 These things I have written to you who believe in the name of the Son of God, so that you may know that you have eternal life. **14** This is the confidence which we have before Him, that, if we ask anything according to His will, He hears us. **15** And if we know that He hears us

---

5:8 ¹Lit *for the one thing*

in whatever we ask, we know that we have the requests which we have asked from Him.

16 If anyone sees his brother *or sister* committing a sin not *leading* to death, he shall ask and *God* will, for him, give life to those who commit sin not *leading* to death. There is sin *leading* to death; I am not saying that he should ask about that. **17** All unrighteousness is sin, and there is sin not *leading* to death.

18 We know that no one who has been born of God sins; but He who was born of God keeps him, and the evil one does not touch him. **19** We know that we are of God, and that the whole world lies in *the power of* the evil one. **20** And we know that the Son of God has come, and has given us understanding so that we may know Him who is true; and we are in Him who is true, in His Son Jesus Christ. This is the true God and eternal life.

21 Little children, guard yourselves from idols.

The Second Letter of

JOHN

Walk According to His Commandments

1 The elder to the chosen lady and her children, whom I love in truth; and not only I, but also all who know the truth, **2** because of the truth which remains in us and will be with us forever: **3** Grace, mercy, *and* peace will be with us, from God the Father and from Jesus Christ, the Son of the Father, in truth and love.

4 I was overjoyed to find *some* of your children walking in truth, just as we have received a commandment *to do* from the Father. **5** Now I ask you, lady, not as though *I were* writing to you a new commandment, but the one which we have had from the beginning, that we love one another. **6** And this is love, that we walk according to His commandments. This is the commandment, just as you have heard from the beginning, that you are to walk in it.

7 For many deceivers have gone out into the world, those who do not acknowledge Jesus Christ *as* coming in the flesh. This is the deceiver and the antichrist. **8** Watch yourselves, that you do not lose what we have accomplished, but *that* you may receive a full reward. **9** Anyone who goes too far and does not remain in the teaching of Christ, does not have God; the one who remains in the teaching has both the Father and the Son. **10** If anyone comes to you and does not bring this teaching, do not receive him into *your* house, and do not give him a greeting; **11** for the one who gives him a greeting participates in his evil deeds.

12 Though I have many things to write to you, I do not want to *do so* with paper and ink; but I hope to come to you and speak face to face, so that your joy may be made complete.

13 The children of your chosen sister greet you.

The Third Letter of

JOHN

A Good Report

1 The elder to the beloved Gaius, whom I love in truth.

2 Beloved, I pray that in all respects you may prosper and be in good health, just as your soul prospers. 3 For I was overjoyed when brothers came and testified to your truth, *that is,* how you are walking in truth. 4 I have no greater joy than this, to hear of my children walking in the truth.

5 Beloved, you are acting faithfully in whatever you accomplish for the brothers *and sisters,* and especially *when they are* strangers; 6 and they have testified to your love before the church. You will do well to send them on their way in a manner worthy of God. 7 For they went out for the sake of the Name, accepting nothing from the Gentiles. 8 Therefore we ought to support such people, so that we may prove to be fellow workers with the truth.

9 I wrote something to the church; but Diotrephes, who loves to be first among them, does not accept what we say. 10 For this reason, if I come, I will call attention to his deeds which he does, unjustly accusing us with malicious words; and not satisfied with this, he himself does not receive the brothers either, and he forbids those who want *to do so* and puts *them* out of the church.

11 Beloved, do not imitate what is evil, but what is good. The one who does what is good is of God; the one who does what is evil has not seen God. 12 Demetrius has received a *good* testimony from everyone, and from the truth itself; and we testify too, and you know that our testimony is true.

13 I had many things to write to you, but I do not want to write to you with pen and ink; 14 but I hope to see you shortly, and we will speak face to face.

15 Peace *be* to you. The friends greet you. Greet the friends by name.

The Letter of
JUDE

The Warnings of History to the Ungodly

1 Jude, a bond-servant of Jesus Christ and brother of James,

To those who are the called, beloved in God the Father, and kept for Jesus Christ: 2 May mercy, peace, and love be multiplied to you.

3 Beloved, while I was making every effort to write you about our common salvation, I felt the necessity to write to you appealing that you contend earnestly for the faith that was once for all *time* handed down to the saints. 4 For certain people have crept in unnoticed, those who were long beforehand marked out for this condemnation, ungodly persons who turn the grace of our God into indecent behavior and deny our only Master and Lord, Jesus Christ.

5 Now I want to remind you, though you know everything once *and* for all, that [1]the Lord, after saving a people out of the land of Egypt, subsequently destroyed those who did not believe. 6 And angels who did not keep their own domain but abandoned their proper dwelling place, *these* He has kept in eternal restraints under darkness for the judgment of the great day, 7 just as Sodom and Gomorrah and the cities around them, since they in the same way as these *angels* indulged in sexual perversion and went after strange flesh, are exhibited as an example in undergoing the punishment of eternal fire.

8 Yet in the same way these people also, dreaming, defile the flesh, reject authority, and speak abusively of *angelic* majesties. 9 But Michael the archangel, when he disputed with the devil and argued about the body of Moses, did not dare pronounce against him an abusive judgment, but said, "The Lord rebuke you!" 10 But these people disparage all the things that they do not understand; and all the things that they know by instinct, like unreasoning animals, by these things they are destroyed. 11 Woe to them! For they have gone the way of Cain, and

for pay they have given themselves up to the error of
Balaam, and perished in the rebellion of Korah. **12** These
are the ones who are hidden reefs in your love feasts
when they feast with you without fear, *like shepherds*
caring *only* for themselves; clouds without water, carried
along by winds; autumn trees without fruit, doubly dead,
uprooted; **13** wild waves of the sea, churning up their
own shameful deeds like *dirty* foam; wandering stars, for
whom the gloom of darkness has been reserved forever.

14 *It was* also about these people *that* Enoch, *in the*
seventh *generation* from Adam, prophesied, saying,
"Behold, the Lord has come with many thousands of His
holy ones, **15** to execute judgment upon all, and to convict
all the ungodly of all their ungodly deeds which they
have done in an ungodly way, and of all the harsh things
which ungodly sinners have spoken against Him."
16 These are grumblers, finding fault, following after their
own lusts; they speak arrogantly, flattering people for the
sake of *gaining an* advantage.

Keep Yourselves in the Love of God

17 But you, beloved, ought to remember the words that
were spoken beforehand by the apostles of our Lord
Jesus Christ, **18** that they were saying to you, "In the last
time there will be mockers, following after their own
ungodly lusts." **19** These are the ones who cause
divisions, worldly-minded, devoid of the Spirit. **20** But
you, beloved, building yourselves up on your most holy
faith, praying in the Holy Spirit, **21** keep yourselves in the
love of God, looking forward to the mercy of our Lord
Jesus Christ to eternal life. **22** And have mercy on some,
who are doubting; **23** save others, snatching them out of
the fire; and on some have mercy with fear, hating even
the garment polluted by the flesh.

24 Now to Him who is able to protect you from stumbling, and to make you stand in the presence of His
glory, blameless with great joy, **25** to the only God our
Savior, through Jesus Christ our Lord, *be* glory, majesty,
dominion, and authority before all time and now and
forever. Amen.

THE REVELATION
to John

The Revelation of Jesus Christ

1 The Revelation of Jesus Christ, which God gave Him to show to His bond-servants, the things which must soon take place; and He sent and communicated *it* by His angel to His bond-servant John, **2** who testified to the word of God and to the testimony of Jesus Christ, everything that he saw. **3** Blessed is the one who reads, and those who hear the words of the prophecy and keep the things which are written in it; for the time is near.

Message to the Seven Churches

4 John to the seven churches that are in Asia: Grace to you and peace from Him who is, and who was, and who is to come, and from the *ʼseven spirits who are before His throne, **5** and from Jesus Christ, the faithful witness, the firstborn of the dead, and the ruler of the kings of the earth. To Him who loves us and released us from our sins by His blood—**6** and He made us *into* a kingdom, priests to His God and Father—to Him *be* the glory and the dominion forever and ever. Amen. **7** BEHOLD, HE IS COMING WITH THE CLOUDS, and every eye will see Him, even those who pierced Him; and all the tribes of the earth will mourn over Him. So it is to be. Amen.

8 "I am the Alpha and the Omega," says the Lord God, "who is and who was and who is to come, the Almighty."

The Patmos Vision

9 I, John, your brother and fellow participant in the tribulation and kingdom and perseverance in Jesus, was on the island called Patmos because of the word of God and the testimony of Jesus. **10** I was in *the* ʼSpirit on the Lord's day, and I heard behind me a loud voice like *the sound* of a trumpet, **11** saying, "Write on a scroll what you see, and send *it* to the seven churches: to Ephesus,

---

1:4 ʼPossibly a symbolic reference to the Holy Spirit in His fullness, or to seven key angels   1:10 ʼOr *spirit*

Smyrna, Pergamum, Thyatira, Sardis, Philadelphia, and Laodicea."

12 Then I turned to see the voice that was speaking with me. And after turning I saw seven golden lampstands; 13 and in the middle of the lampstands *I saw* one like [1]a son of man, clothed in a robe reaching to the feet, and wrapped around the chest with a golden sash. 14 His head and His hair were white like white wool, like snow; and His eyes were like a flame of fire. 15 His feet were like burnished bronze when it has been heated to a glow in a furnace, and His voice was like the sound of many waters. 16 In His right hand He held seven stars, and out of His mouth came a sharp two-edged sword; and His face was like the sun shining in its strength.

17 When I saw Him, I fell at His feet like a dead man. And He placed His right hand on me, saying, "Do not be afraid; I am the first and the last, 18 and the living One; and I was dead, and behold, I am alive forevermore, and I have the keys of death and of Hades. 19 Therefore write the things which you have seen, and the things which are, and the things which will take place after these things. 20 *As for* the mystery of the seven stars which you saw in My right hand, and the seven golden lampstands: the seven stars are the angels of the seven churches, and the seven lampstands are the seven churches.

Message to Ephesus

2 "To the angel of the church in Ephesus write:
The One who holds the seven stars in His right hand, the One who walks among the seven golden lampstands, says this:

2 'I know your deeds and your labor and perseverance, and that you cannot tolerate evil people, and you have put those who call themselves apostles to the test, and they are not, and you found them *to be* false; 3 and you have perseverance and have endured on account of My name, and have not become weary. 4 But I have *this* against you, that you have left your first love. 5 Therefore, remember from where you have fallen, and repent, and do the deeds you did at first; or else I am coming to you and I will remove your lampstand from its place—unless you repent. 6 But you have this, that you hate the deeds

---

of the Nicolaitans, which I also hate. 7 The one who has an ear, let him hear what the Spirit says to the churches. To the one who overcomes, I will grant to eat from the tree of life, which is in the Paradise of God.'

Message to Smyrna

8 "And to the angel of the church in Smyrna write:

The first and the last, who was dead, and has come to life, says this:

9 'I know your tribulation and your poverty (but you are rich), and the slander by those who say they are Jews, and are not, but are a synagogue of Satan. 10 Do not fear what you are about to suffer. Behold, the devil is about to throw some of you into prison, so that you will be tested, and you will have tribulation for ten days. Be faithful until death, and I will give you the crown of life. 11 The one who has an ear, let him hear what the Spirit says to the churches. The one who overcomes will not be hurt by the second death.'

Message to Pergamum

12 "And to the angel of the church in Pergamum write:

The One who has the sharp two-edged sword says this:

13 'I know where you dwell, where Satan's throne is; and you hold firmly to My name, and did not deny My faith even in the days of Antipas, My witness, My faithful one, who was killed among you, where Satan dwells. 14 But I have a few things against you, because you have *some* there who hold the teaching of Balaam, who kept teaching Balak to put a stumbling block before the sons of Israel, to eat things sacrificed to idols and to commit sexual immorality. 15 So you too, have some who in the same way hold to the teaching of the Nicolaitans. 16 Therefore repent; or else I am coming to you quickly, and I will wage war against them with the sword of My mouth. 17 The one who has an ear, let him hear what the Spirit says to the churches. To the one who overcomes, I will give *some* of the hidden manna, and I will give him a white stone, and a new name written on the stone which no one knows except the one who receives *it.'*

Message to Thyatira

18 "And to the angel of the church in Thyatira write:

The Son of God, who has eyes like a flame of fire, and feet like burnished bronze, says this:

19 'I know your deeds, and your love and faith, and service and perseverance, and that your deeds of late are greater than at first. **20** But I have *this* against you, that you tolerate the woman Jezebel, who calls herself a prophetess, and she teaches and leads My bond-servants astray so that they commit sexual immorality and eat things sacrificed to idols. **21** I gave her time to repent, and she does not want to repent of her sexual immorality. **22** Behold, I will throw her on a bed *of sickness,* and those who commit adultery with her into great tribulation, unless they repent of ¹her deeds. **23** And I will kill her children with ¹plague, and all the churches will know that I am He who searches the minds and hearts; and I will give to each one of you according to your deeds. **24** But I say to you, the rest who are in Thyatira, who do not hold this teaching, who have not known the deep things of Satan, as they call them—I place no other burden on you. **25** Nevertheless what you have, hold firmly until I come. **26** The one who overcomes, and the one who keeps My deeds until the end, I will give him authority over the nations; **27** AND HE SHALL RULE THEM WITH A ROD OF IRON, AS THE VESSELS OF THE POTTER ARE SHATTERED, as I also have received *authority* from My Father; **28** and I will give him the morning star. **29** The one who has an ear, let him hear what the Spirit says to the churches.'

Message to Sardis

3 "To the angel of the church in Sardis write: He who has the seven spirits of God and the seven stars, says this: 'I know your deeds, that you have a name that you are alive, and *yet* you are dead. **2** Be constantly alert, and strengthen the things that remain, which were about to die; for I have not found your deeds completed in the sight of My God. **3** So remember what you have received and heard; and keep *it,* and repent. Then if you are not alert, I will come like a thief, and you will not know at what hour I will come to you. **4** But you have a few people in Sardis who have not soiled their

---

2:22 ¹ One early ms *their*   2:23 ¹ Lit *death;* i.e., a particular kind of death

garments; and they will walk with Me in white, for they are worthy. **5** The one who overcomes will be clothed the same way, in white garments; and I will not erase his name from the book of life, and I will confess his name before My Father and before His angels. **6** The one who has an ear, let him hear what the Spirit says to the churches.'

Message to Philadelphia

7 "And to the angel of the church in Philadelphia write:

He who is holy, who is true, who has the key of David, who opens and no one will shut, and who shuts and no one opens, says this:

8 'I know your deeds. Behold, I have put before you an open door which no one can shut, because you have a little power, and have followed My word, and have not denied My name. **9** Behold, I will make *those* of the synagogue of Satan, who say that they are Jews and are not, but lie—I will make them come and bow down before your feet, and *make them* know that I have loved you. **10** Because you have kept My word of perseverance, I also will keep you from the hour of the testing, that *hour* which is about to come upon the whole world, to test those who live on the earth. **11** I am coming quickly; hold firmly to what you have, so that no one will take your crown. **12** The one who overcomes, I will make him a pillar in the temple of My God, and he will not go out from it anymore; and I will write on him the name of My God, and the name of the city of My God, the new Jerusalem, which comes down out of heaven from My God, and My new name. **13** The one who has an ear, let him hear what the Spirit says to the churches.'

Message to Laodicea

14 "To the angel of the church in Laodicea write:

The Amen, the faithful and true Witness, the Origin of the creation of God, says this:

15 'I know your deeds, that you are neither cold nor hot; I wish that you were cold or hot. **16** So because you are lukewarm, and neither hot nor cold, I will vomit you out of My mouth. **17** Because you say, "I am rich, and have become wealthy, and have no need of anything," and you do not know that you are wretched, miserable, poor, blind, and naked, ¹⁸ I advise you to buy from Me gold refined by fire so that you may become rich, and white garments so that you may clothe yourself and the shame of your nakedness will not be revealed; and eye salve to apply to your eyes so that you may see. ¹⁹ Those whom I love, I rebuke and discipline; therefore be zealous and repent. ²⁰ Behold, I stand at the door and knock; if anyone hears My voice and opens the door, I will come in to him and will dine with him, and he with Me. ²¹ The one who overcomes, I will grant to him to sit with Me on My throne, as I also overcame and sat with My Father on His throne. ²² The one who has an ear, let him hear what the Spirit says to the churches.' "

Scene in Heaven

4 After these things I looked, and behold, a door *standing* open in heaven, and the first voice which I had heard, like *the sound* of a trumpet speaking with me, said, "Come up here, and I will show you what must take place after these things." ² Immediately I was in *the* 'Spirit; and behold, a throne was standing in heaven, and *someone was* sitting on the throne. ³ And He who was sitting *was* like a jasper stone and a sardius in appearance; and *there was* a rainbow around the throne, like an emerald in appearance. ⁴ Around the throne *were* twenty-four thrones; and upon the thrones *I saw* twenty-four elders sitting, clothed in white garments, and golden crowns on their heads.

The Throne and Worship of the Creator

⁵ Out from the throne *came flashes of lightning and sounds and peals of thunder. And *there were* seven lamps of fire burning before the throne, which are the seven spirits of God; ⁶ and before the throne *there was something* like a sea of glass, like crystal; and in the center and around the throne, four living creatures full of eyes in front and behind. ⁷ The first living creature *was* like a lion, the second creature like a calf, the third creature had a face like that of a man, and the fourth creature *was* like a flying eagle. ⁸ And the four living creatures, each one of them having six wings, are full of

eyes around and within; and day and night they do not cease to say,

"HOLY, HOLY, HOLY *IS* THE LORD GOD, THE ALMIGHTY, who was and who is and is to come."

9 And when the living creatures give glory, honor, and thanks to Him who sits on the throne, to Him who lives forever and ever, 10 the twenty-four elders will fall down before Him who sits on the throne, and they will worship Him who lives forever and ever, and will cast their crowns before the throne, saying,

11 "Worthy are You, our Lord and our God, to receive glory and honor and power; for You created all things, and because of Your will they existed, and were created."

The Scroll with Seven Seals

5 I saw in the right hand of Him who sat on the throne a scroll written inside and on the back, sealed up with seven seals. 2 And I saw a strong angel proclaiming with a loud voice, "Who is worthy to open the scroll and to break its seals?" 3 And no one in heaven or on the earth or under the earth was able to open the scroll or to look into it. 4 Then I *began* to weep greatly because no one was found worthy to open the scroll or to look into it. 5 And one of the elders *said to me, "Stop weeping; behold, the Lion that is from the tribe of Judah, the Root of David, has overcome *so as to be able* to open the scroll and its seven seals."

6 And I saw 1between the throne (with the four living creatures) and the elders a Lamb standing, as if slaughtered, having seven horns and seven eyes, which are the seven spirits of God sent out into all the earth. 7 And He came and took *the scroll* out of the right hand of Him who sat on the throne. 8 When He had taken the scroll, the four living creatures and the twenty-four elders fell down before the Lamb, each one holding a harp and golden bowls full of incense, which are the prayers of the saints. 9 And they *sang a new song, saying,

"Worthy are You to take the scroll and to break its seals; for You were slaughtered, and You purchased *people* for God with Your blood from every tribe,

---

5:6 1 Lit *in the middle of the throne and of the four living creatures, and in the middle of the elders*

language, people, and nation. **10** You have made them *into* a kingdom and priests to our God, and they will reign upon the earth."

Angels Exalt the Lamb

11 Then I looked, and I heard the voices of many angels around the throne and the living creatures and the elders; and the number of them was ¹myriads of myriads, and thousands of thousands, **12** saying with a loud voice,

"Worthy is the Lamb that was slaughtered to receive power, wealth, wisdom, might, honor, glory, and blessing."

13 And I heard every created thing which is in heaven, or on the earth, or under the earth, or on the sea, and all the things in them, saying,

"To Him who sits on the throne and to the Lamb *be* the blessing, the honor, the glory, and the dominion forever and ever."

14 And the four living creatures were saying, "Amen." And the elders fell down and worshiped.

The First Seal: Conqueror on a White Horse

6 Then I saw when the Lamb broke one of the seven seals, and I heard one of the four living creatures saying as *with* a voice of thunder, "Come!" **2** I looked, and behold, a white horse, and the one who sat on it had a bow; and a crown was given to him, and he went out conquering and to conquer.

The Second Seal: War

3 When He broke the second seal, I heard the second living creature saying, "Come!" **4** And another, a red horse, went out; and to him who sat on it, it was granted to take peace from the earth, and that *people* would kill one another; and a large sword was given to him.

The Third Seal: Famine

5 When He broke the third seal, I heard the third living creature saying, "Come!" I looked, and behold, a black horse, and the one who sat on it had a pair of scales in his hand. **6** And I heard *something* like a voice in the center of the four living creatures saying,

"A ¹quart of wheat for a ²denarius, and three quarts of barley for a denarius; and do not damage the oil and the wine."

The Fourth Seal: Death

7 When *the Lamb* broke the fourth seal, I heard the voice of the fourth living creature saying, "Come!" **8** I looked, and behold, an ashen horse; and the one who sat on it had the name Death, and Hades was following with him. Authority was given to them over a fourth of the earth, to kill with sword, and famine, and ¹plague, and by the wild animals of the earth.

The Fifth Seal: Martyrs

9 When *the Lamb* broke the fifth seal, I saw underneath the altar the souls of those who had been killed because of the word of God, and because of the testimony which they had maintained; **10** and they cried out with a loud voice, saying, "How long, O Lord, holy and true, will You refrain from judging and avenging our blood on those who live on the earth?" **11** And a white robe was given to each of them; and they were told that they were to rest for a little while longer, until *the number of* their fellow servants and their brothers *and sisters* who were to be killed even as they *had been,* was completed also.

The Sixth Seal: Terror

12 And I looked when He broke the sixth seal, and there was a great earthquake; and the sun became as black as sackcloth made of hair, and the whole moon became like blood; **13** and the stars of the sky fell to the earth, as a fig tree drops its unripe figs when shaken by a great wind. **14** The sky was split apart like a scroll when it is rolled up, and every mountain and island was removed from its place. **15** Then the kings of the earth and the eminent people, and the commanders and the wealthy and the strong, and every slave and free person hid themselves in the caves and among the rocks of the mountains; **16** and they *said to the mountains and the

---

6:6 ¹Gr *choenix;* i.e., a dry measure almost equal to a qt.   6:6 ²The denarius was a day's wages for a laborer   6:8 ¹Lit *death;* i.e., a particular kind of death

rocks, "Fall on us and hide us from the sight of Him who sits on the throne, and from the wrath of the Lamb; **17** for the great day of Their wrath has come, and who is able to stand?"

An Interlude

7 After this I saw four angels standing at the four corners of the earth, holding back the four winds of the earth so that no wind would blow on the earth, or on the sea, or on any tree. **2** And I saw another angel ascending from the rising of the sun, holding the seal of the living God; and he called out with a loud voice to the four angels to whom it was granted to harm the earth and the sea, **3** saying, "Do not harm the earth, or the sea, or the trees until we have sealed the bond-servants of our God on their foreheads."

The 144,000

4 And I heard the number of those who were sealed: 144,000, sealed from every tribe of the sons of Israel:

5 from the tribe of Judah, twelve thousand *were* sealed, from the tribe of Reuben twelve thousand, from the tribe of Gad twelve thousand,

6 from the tribe of Asher twelve thousand, from the tribe of Naphtali twelve thousand, from the tribe of Manasseh twelve thousand,

7 from the tribe of Simeon twelve thousand, from the tribe of Levi twelve thousand, from the tribe of Issachar twelve thousand,

8 from the tribe of Zebulun twelve thousand, from the tribe of Joseph twelve thousand, *and* from the tribe of Benjamin, twelve thousand *were* sealed.

A Multitude from the Tribulation

9 After these things I looked, and behold, a great multitude which no one could count, from every nation and *all the* tribes, peoples, and languages, standing before the throne and before the Lamb, clothed in white robes, and palm branches *were* in their hands; **10** and they *cried out with a loud voice, saying,

"**S**alvation *belongs* to our God who sits on the throne, and to the Lamb."

11 And all the angels were standing around the throne and *around* the elders and the four living creatures; and they fell on their faces before the throne and worshiped God, **12**saying,

"**A**men, blessing, glory, wisdom, thanksgiving, honor, power, and might *belong* to our God forever and ever. Amen."

13Then one of the elders responded, saying to me, "These who are clothed in the white robes, who are they, and where have they come from?" **14**I said to him, "My lord, you know." And he said to me, "These are the ones who come out of the great tribulation, and they have washed their robes and made them white in the blood of the Lamb. **15**For this reason they are before the throne of God, and they serve Him day and night in His temple; and He who sits on the throne will spread His tabernacle over them. **16**They will no longer hunger nor thirst, nor will the sun beat down on them, nor any scorching heat; **17**for the Lamb in the center of the throne will be their shepherd, and will guide them to springs of the water of life; and God will wipe every tear from their eyes."

The Seventh Seal: Trumpets

8When *the Lamb* broke the seventh seal, there was silence in heaven for about half an hour. **2**And I saw the seven angels who stand before God, and seven trumpets were given to them.

3Another angel came and stood at the altar, holding a golden censer; and much incense was given to him, so that he might add it to the prayers of all the saints on the golden altar which was before the throne. **4**And the smoke of the incense ascended from the angel's hand with the prayers of the saints before God. **5**Then the angel took the ¹censer and filled it with the fire of the altar, and hurled it to the earth; and there were peals of thunder and sounds, and flashes of lightning and an earthquake.

6And the seven angels who had the seven trumpets prepared themselves to sound them.

7The first sounded, and there was hail and fire mixed with blood, and it was hurled to the earth; and a third of the earth was burned up, and a third of the trees were burned up, and all the green grass was burned up.

8:5 ¹I.e., container to burn incense

8 The second angel sounded, and *something* like a great mountain burning with fire was hurled into the sea; and a third of the sea became blood, 9 and a third of the creatures which were in the sea and had life, died; and a third of the ships were destroyed.

10 The third angel sounded, and a great star fell from heaven, burning like a torch, and it fell on a third of the rivers and on the springs of waters. 11 The star is named Wormwood; and a third of the waters became wormwood; and many people died from the waters because they were made bitter.

12 The fourth angel sounded, and a third of the sun, a third of the moon, and a third of the stars were struck, so that a third of them would be darkened and the day would not shine for a third of it, and the night in the same way.

13 Then I looked, and I heard an eagle flying in midheaven, saying with a loud voice, "Woe, woe, woe to those who live on the earth, because of the remaining blasts of the trumpet of the three angels who are about to sound!"

The Fifth Trumpet: Shaft of the Abyss

9 Then the fifth angel sounded, and I saw a star from heaven which had fallen to the earth; and the key to the shaft of the abyss was given to him. 2 He opened the shaft of the abyss, and smoke ascended out of the shaft like the smoke of a great furnace; and the sun and the air were darkened from the smoke of the shaft. 3 Then out of the smoke came locusts upon the earth, and power was given them, as the scorpions of the earth have power. 4 They were told not to hurt the grass of the earth, nor any green thing, nor any tree, but only the people who do not have the seal of God on their foreheads. 5 And they were not permitted to kill anyone, but to torment for five months; and their torment was like the torment of a scorpion when it stings a person. 6 And in those days people will seek death and will not find it; they will long to die, and death will flee from them!

7 The appearance of the locusts was like horses prepared for battle; and on their heads appeared to be crowns like gold, and their faces were like human faces. 8 They had hair like the hair of women, and their teeth were like *the teeth* of lions. 9 They had breastplates like

breastplates of iron; and the sound of their wings was like the sound of chariots, of many horses rushing to battle. **10** They have tails like scorpions, and stings; and in their tails is their power to hurt people for five months. **11** They have as king over them, the angel of the abyss; his name in Hebrew is *1*Abaddon, and in the Greek he has the name Apollyon.

12 The first woe has passed; behold, two woes are still coming after these things.

The Sixth Trumpet: Army from the East

13 Then the sixth angel sounded, and I heard a voice from the *1*four horns of the golden altar which is before God, **14** saying to the sixth angel who had the trumpet, "Release the four angels who are bound at the great river Euphrates." **15** And the four angels, who had been prepared for the hour and day and month and year, were released, so that they would kill a third of mankind. **16** The number of the armies of the horsemen was two hundred million; I heard the number of them. **17** And this is how I saw in my vision the horses and those who sat on them: *the riders* had breastplates *the color* of fire, of hyacinth, and of *1*brimstone; and the heads of the horses are like the heads of lions; and out of their mouths *came fire and smoke and *2*brimstone. **18** A third of mankind was killed by these three plagues, by the fire, the smoke, and the brimstone which came out of their mouths. **19** For the power of the horses is in their mouths and in their tails; for their tails are like serpents and have heads, and with them they do harm.

20 The rest of mankind, who were not killed by these plagues, did not repent of the works of their hands so as not to worship demons and the idols of gold, silver, brass, stone, and wood, which can neither see nor hear nor walk; **21** and they did not repent of their murders, nor of their witchcraft, nor of their sexual immorality, nor of their thefts.

The Angel and the Little Scroll

10 I saw another strong angel coming down from heaven, clothed with a cloud; and the rainbow was

---

9:11 *1*I.e., destruction   9:13 *1*Two early mss do not contain *four*
9:17 *1*I.e., burning sulfur   9:17 *2*I.e., burning sulfur

on his head, and his face was like the sun, and his feet like pillars of fire; 2 and he had in his hand a little scroll, which was open. He placed his right foot on the sea and his left on the land; 3 and he cried out with a loud voice, as when a lion roars; and when he had cried out, the seven peals of thunder uttered their voices. 4 When the seven peals of thunder had spoken, I was about to write; and I heard a voice from heaven, saying, "Seal up the things which the seven peals of thunder have spoken, and do not write them." 5 Then the angel whom I saw standing on the sea and on the land raised his right hand to heaven, 6 and swore by Him who lives forever and ever, who created heaven and the things in it, and the earth and the things in it, and the sea and the things in it, that there will no longer be a delay, 7 but in the days of the voice of the seventh angel, when he is about to sound, then the mystery of God is finished, as He announced to His servants the prophets.

8 Then the voice which I heard from heaven, *I heard* again speaking with me, and saying, "Go, take the scroll which is open in the hand of the angel who stands on the sea and on the land." 9 And I went to the angel, telling him to give me the little scroll. And he *said to me, "Take it and eat it; it will make your stomach bitter, but in your mouth it will be sweet as honey." 10 I took the little scroll from the angel's hand and ate it, and in my mouth it was sweet as honey; and when I had eaten it, my stomach was made bitter. 11 And they *said to me, "You must prophesy again concerning many peoples, nations, languages, and kings."

The Two Witnesses

11 Then there was given to me a measuring rod like a staff; and someone said, "Get up and measure the temple of God and the altar, and those who worship in it. 2 Leave out the courtyard which is outside the temple and do not measure it, because it has been given to the nations; and they will trample the holy city for forty-two months. 3 And I will grant *authority* to my two witnesses, and they will prophesy for 1,260 days, clothed in sackcloth." 4 These are the two olive trees and the two lampstands that stand before the Lord of the earth. 5 And if anyone wants to harm them, fire flows out of

their mouth and devours their enemies; and *so* if anyone wants to harm them, he must be killed in this way. **6** These have the power to shut up the sky, so that rain will not fall during the days of their prophesying; and they have power over the waters to turn them into blood, and to strike the earth with every plague, as often as they desire.

7 When they have finished their testimony, the beast that comes up out of the abyss will make war with them, and overcome them and kill them. **8** And their dead bodies *will lie* on the street of the great city which ¹spiritually is called Sodom and Egypt, where also their Lord was crucified. **9** Those from the peoples, tribes, languages, and nations *will* look at their dead bodies for three and a half days, and will not allow their dead bodies to be laid in a tomb. **10** And those who live on the earth *will* rejoice over them and celebrate; and they will send gifts to one another, because these two prophets tormented those who live on the earth.

11 And after the three and a half days, the breath of life from God came into them, and they stood on their feet; and great fear fell upon those who were watching them. **12** And they heard a loud voice from heaven saying to them, "Come up here." And they went up into heaven in the cloud, and their enemies watched them. **13** And at that time there was a great earthquake, and a tenth of the city fell; seven thousand people were killed in the earthquake, and the rest were terrified and gave glory to the God of heaven.

14 The second woe has passed; behold, the third woe is coming quickly.

The Seventh Trumpet: Christ's Reign Foreseen

15 Then the seventh angel sounded; and there were loud voices in heaven, saying,

"**T**he kingdom of the world has become *the kingdom* of our Lord and of His Christ; and He will reign forever and ever." **16** And the twenty-four elders, who sit on their thrones before God, fell on their faces and worshiped God, **17** saying,

"**W**e give You thanks, Lord God, the Almighty, the One who is and who was, because You have taken Your

---

11:8 ¹I.e., from the viewpoint of the Holy Spirit

great power and have begun to reign. 18 And the nations were enraged, and Your wrath came, and the time *came* for the dead to be judged, and *the time* to reward Your bond-servants the prophets and the saints and those who fear Your name, the small and the great, and to destroy those who destroy the earth."

19 And the temple of God which is in heaven was opened; and the ark of His covenant appeared in His temple, and there were flashes of lightning and sounds and peals of thunder, and an earthquake, and a great hailstorm.

The Woman, Israel

12 A great sign appeared in heaven: a woman clothed with the sun, and the moon under her feet, and on her head a crown of twelve stars; 2 and she was pregnant and she *cried out, being in labor and in pain to give birth.

The Red Dragon, Satan

3 Then another sign appeared in heaven: and behold, a great red dragon having seven heads and ten horns, and on his heads *were* seven crowns. 4 And his tail *swept away a third of the stars of heaven and hurled them to the earth. And the dragon stood before the woman who was about to give birth, so that when she gave birth he might devour her Child.

The Male Child, Christ

5 And she gave birth to a Son, a male, who is going to rule all the nations with a rod of iron; and her Child was caught up to God and to His throne. 6 Then the woman fled into the wilderness where she *had a place prepared by God, so that there she would be nourished for 1,260 days.

The Angel, Michael

7 And there was war in heaven, Michael and his angels waging war with the dragon. The dragon and his angels waged war, 8 and they did not prevail, and there was no longer a place found for them in heaven. 9 And the great dragon was thrown down, the serpent of old who is called the devil and Satan, who deceives the whole world; he was thrown down to the earth, and his angels

were thrown down with him. 10 Then I heard a loud voice in heaven, saying,

"Now the salvation, and the power, and the kingdom of our God and the authority of His Christ have come, for the accuser of our brothers *and sisters* has been thrown down, the one who accuses them before our God day and night. 11 And they overcame him because of the blood of the Lamb and because of the word of their testimony, and they did not love their life *even* when faced with death. 12 For this reason, rejoice, you heavens and you who dwell in them. Woe to the earth and the sea, because the devil has come down to you with great wrath, knowing that he has *only* a short time."

13 And when the dragon saw that he was thrown down to the earth, he persecuted the woman who gave birth to the male *Child*. 14 But the two wings of the great eagle were given to the woman, so that she could fly into the wilderness to her place, where she *was nourished for a time, times, and half a time, away from the presence of the serpent. 15 And the serpent hurled water like a river out of his mouth after the woman, so that he might cause her to be swept away with the flood. 16 But the earth helped the woman, and the earth opened its mouth and drank up the river which the dragon had hurled out of his mouth. 17 So the dragon was enraged with the woman, and went off to make war with the rest of her children, who keep the commandments of God and hold to the testimony of Jesus.

The Beast from the Sea

13 And *the dragon* stood on the sand of the seashore.

Then I saw a beast coming up out of the sea, having ten horns and seven heads, and on his horns *were* ten crowns, and on his heads *were* blasphemous names. 2 And the beast that I saw was like a leopard, and his feet were like *those* of a bear, and his mouth like the mouth of a lion. And the dragon gave him his power and his throne, and great authority. 3 *I saw* one of his heads as if it had been fatally wounded, and his fatal wound was healed. And the whole earth was amazed *and followed* after the beast; 4 they worshiped the dragon because he gave his authority to the beast; and they worshiped the beast, saying, "Who is like the beast, and who is able to wage war with him?" **5** A mouth was given to him speaking arrogant words and blasphemies, and authority to act for forty-two months was given to him. **6** And he opened his mouth in blasphemies against God, to blaspheme His name and His tabernacle, *that is,* those who dwell in heaven.

7 It was also given to him to make war with the saints and to overcome them, and authority was given to him over every tribe, people, language, and nation. **8** All who live on the earth will worship him, *everyone* whose name has not been written since the foundation of the world in the book of life of the Lamb who has been slaughtered. **9** If anyone has an ear, let him hear. **10** If anyone *is destined* for captivity, to captivity he goes; if anyone kills with the sword, with the sword he must be killed. Here is the perseverance and the faith of the saints.

The Beast from the Earth

11 Then I saw another beast coming up out of the earth; and he had two horns like a lamb, and he spoke as a dragon. **12** He exercises all the authority of the first beast in his presence. And he makes the earth and those who live on it worship the first beast, whose fatal wound was healed. **13** He performs great signs, so that he even makes fire come down out of the sky to the earth in the presence of people. **14** And he deceives those who live on the earth because of the signs which it was given him to perform in the presence of the beast, telling those who live on the earth to make an image to the beast who *had the wound of the sword and has come to life. **15** And it was given to him to give breath to the image of the beast, so that the image of the beast would even ¹speak and cause all who do not worship the image of the beast to be killed. **16** And he causes all, the small and the great, the rich and the poor, and the free and the slaves, to be given a mark on their right hands or on their foreheads, **17** and *he decrees* that no one will be able to buy or to sell, except the one who has the mark, *either* the name of the beast or the number of his name. **18** Here is wisdom. Let him who has understanding calculate the number of the beast, for the

---

13:15 ¹One early ms *speak, and he will cause*

number is that of a ¹man; and his number is ²six hundred and sixty-six.

The Lamb and the 144,000 on Mount Zion

14 Then I looked, and behold, the Lamb *was* standing on Mount Zion, and with Him 144,000 who had His name and the name of His Father written on their foreheads. ²And I heard a voice from heaven, like the sound of many waters and like the sound of loud thunder, and the voice which I heard *was* like *the sound* of harpists playing on their harps. ³And they *sang a new song before the throne and before the four living creatures and the elders; and no one was able to learn the song except the 144,000 who had been purchased from the earth. ⁴These are the ones who have not defiled themselves with women, for they are celibate. These *are* the ones who follow the Lamb wherever He goes. These have been purchased from mankind as first fruits to God and to the Lamb. ⁵And no lie was found in their mouths; they are blameless.

Vision of the Angel with the Gospel

⁶And I saw another angel flying in midheaven with an eternal gospel to preach to those who live on the earth, and to every nation, tribe, language, and people; ⁷and he said with a loud voice, "Fear God and give Him glory, because the hour of His judgment has come; worship Him who made the heaven and the earth, and sea and springs of waters."

⁸And another angel, a second one, followed, saying, "Fallen, fallen is Babylon the great, she who has made all the nations drink of the wine of the passion of her sexual immorality."

Doom for Worshipers of the Beast

⁹Then another angel, a third one, followed them, saying with a loud voice, "If anyone worships the beast and his image, and receives a mark on his forehead or on his hand, ¹⁰he also will drink of the wine of the wrath of God, which is mixed in full strength in the cup of His anger; and he will be tormented with fire and brimstone

---

13:18 ¹Or *human*   13:18 ²I.e., spelled out in Gr as 600 + 60 + 6; one early ms has the letters for *616*

in the presence of the holy angels and in the presence of the Lamb. [11] And the smoke of their torment ascends forever and ever; they have no rest day and night, those who worship the beast and his image, and whoever receives the mark of his name." [12] Here is the perseverance of the saints who keep the commandments of God and their faith in Jesus.

[13] And I heard a voice from heaven, saying, "Write: 'Blessed are the dead who die in the Lord from now on!'" "Yes," says the Spirit, "so that they may rest from their labors, for their deeds follow with them."

The Harvest

[14] Then I looked, and behold, a white cloud, and sitting on the cloud *was* one like [1]a son of man, with a golden crown on His head and a sharp sickle in His hand. [15] And another angel came out of the temple, calling out with a loud voice to Him who sat on the cloud, "Put in your sickle and reap, for the hour to reap has come, because the harvest of the earth is ripe." [16] Then He who sat on the cloud swung His sickle over the earth, and the earth was reaped.

[17] And another angel came out of the temple which is in heaven, and he also had a sharp sickle. [18] Then another angel, the one who has power over fire, came out from the altar; and he called with a loud voice to him who had the sharp sickle, saying, "Put in your sharp sickle and gather the clusters from the vine of the earth, because her grapes are ripe." [19] So the angel swung his sickle to the earth and gathered *the clusters from* the vine of the earth, and threw *them* into the great wine press of the wrath of God. [20] And the wine press was trampled outside the city, and blood came out from the wine press, up to the horses' bridles, for a distance of [1]1,600 stadia.

A Scene of Heaven

15 Then I saw another sign in heaven, great and marvelous, seven angels who had seven plagues, *which are* the last, because in them the wrath of God is finished.

14:14 [1] Or *the Son of Man*   14:20 [1] Possibly about 184 miles or 296 km; a Roman stadion perhaps averaged 607 ft. or 185 m

2 And I saw *something* like a sea of glass mixed with fire, and those who were victorious over the beast and his image and the number of his name, standing on the sea of glass, holding harps of God. 3 And they *sang the song of Moses, the bond-servant of God, and the song of the Lamb, saying,

"**G**reat and marvelous are Your works,
    Lord God, the Almighty;
    Righteous and true are Your ways,
    King of the [1]nations!
4   "Who will not fear You, Lord, and glorify Your name?
    For You alone are holy;
    For ALL THE NATIONS WILL COME AND WORSHIP BEFORE YOU,
    For Your righteous acts have been revealed."

5 After these things I looked, and the temple of the tabernacle of testimony in heaven was opened, 6 and the seven angels who had the seven plagues came out of the temple, clothed in [1]linen, clean *and* bright, and their chests wrapped with golden sashes. 7 And one of the four living creatures gave the seven angels seven golden bowls full of the wrath of God, who lives forever and ever. 8 And the temple was filled with smoke from the glory of God and from His power; and no one was able to enter the temple until the seven plagues of the seven angels were finished.

The Bowls of Wrath

16 Then I heard a loud voice from the temple, saying to the seven angels, "Go and pour out on the earth the seven bowls of the wrath of God."

2 So the first *angel* went and poured out his bowl on the earth; and a harmful and painful sore afflicted the people who had the mark of the beast and who worshiped his image.

3 The second *angel* poured out his bowl into the sea, and it became blood like *that* of a dead man; and every living [1]thing in the sea died.

4 Then the third *angel* poured out his bowl into the rivers and the springs of waters; and they became blood. 5 And I heard the angel of the waters saying, "Righteous are You, the One who is and who was, O Holy One, because You judged these things; 6 for they poured out

---

15:3 [1] Two early mss *ages*   15:6 [1] One early ms *stone*   16:3 [1] Lit *soul*

the blood of saints and prophets, and You have given them blood to drink. They deserve it." **7** And I heard the altar saying, "Yes, Lord God, the Almighty, true and righteous are Your judgments."

8 And the fourth *angel* poured out his bowl upon the sun, and it was given *power* to scorch people with fire. **9** And the people were scorched with fierce heat; and they blasphemed the name of God who has the power over these plagues, and they did not repent so as to give Him glory.

10 And the fifth *angel* poured out his bowl on the throne of the beast, and his kingdom became darkened; and they gnawed their tongues because of pain, **11** and they blasphemed the God of heaven because of their pain and their sores; and they did not repent of their deeds.

12 The sixth *angel* poured out his bowl on the great river, the Euphrates; and its water was dried up, so that the way would be prepared for the kings from the east.

Har-Magedon (Armageddon)

13 And I saw *coming* out of the mouth of the dragon, and out of the mouth of the beast, and out of the mouth of the false prophet, three unclean spirits like frogs; **14** for they are spirits of demons, performing signs, which go out to the kings of the entire world, to gather them together for the war of the great day of God, the Almighty. **15** ("Behold, I am coming like a thief. Blessed is the one who stays awake and keeps his clothes, so that he will not walk about naked and *people* will not see his shame.") **16** And they gathered them together to the place which in Hebrew is called Har-Magedon.

The Seventh Bowl of Wrath

17 Then the seventh *angel* poured out his bowl upon the air, and a loud voice came out of the temple from the throne, saying, "It is done." **18** And there were flashes of lightning and sounds and peals of thunder; and there was a great earthquake, such as there had not been since mankind came to be upon the earth, so great an earthquake *was it, and* so mighty. **19** The great city was split into three parts, and the cities of the nations fell. Babylon the great was remembered in the sight of God, to give her the cup of the wine of His fierce wrath.

20 And every island fled, and no mountains were found.
21 And huge hailstones, weighing about ¹a talent each,
*came down from heaven upon people; and people blas-
phemed God because of the plague of the hail, because
the hailstone plague *was extremely severe.

The Doom of Babylon

17 Then one of the seven angels who had the seven
bowls came and spoke with me, saying, "Come
here, I will show you the judgment of the great
prostitute who sits on many waters, 2 with whom the
kings of the earth committed *acts of* sexual immorality,
and those who live on the earth became drunk with the
wine of her sexual immorality." 3 And he carried me
away ¹in the Spirit into a wilderness; and I saw a woman
sitting on a scarlet beast, full of blasphemous names,
having seven heads and ten horns. 4 The woman was
clothed in purple and scarlet, and adorned with gold,
precious stones, and pearls, holding in her hand a gold
cup full of abominations and of the unclean things of her
sexual immorality, 5 and on her forehead a name *was*
written, a mystery: "BABYLON THE GREAT, THE
MOTHER OF PROSTITUTES AND OF THE ABOM-
INATIONS OF THE EARTH." 6 And I saw the woman
drunk with the blood of the saints, and with the blood of
the witnesses of Jesus. When I saw her, I wondered
greatly. 7 And the angel said to me, "Why do you wonder?
I will tell you the mystery of the woman and of the beast
that carries her, which has the seven heads and the ten
horns.

8 "The beast that you saw was, and is not, and is about
to come up out of the abyss and ¹go to destruction. And
those who live on the earth, whose names have not been
written in the book of life from the foundation of the
world, will wonder when they see the beast, that he
was, and is not, and will come. 9 Here is the mind which
has wisdom. The seven heads are seven mountains upon
which the woman sits, 10 and they are seven kings; five
have fallen, one is, the other has not yet come; and
when he comes, he must remain a little while. 11 The
beast which was, and is not, is himself also an eighth and

16:21 ¹I.e., as a measure of weight about 100 lb. or 45 kg   17:3 ¹Or
in spirit   17:8 ¹One early ms *is going*

is *one* of the seven, and he goes to destruction. ¹²The ten horns which you saw are ten kings who have not yet received a kingdom, but they receive authority as kings with the beast for one hour. ¹³These have one purpose, and they give their power and authority to the beast.

Victory for the Lamb

¹⁴These will wage war against the Lamb, and the Lamb will overcome them because He is Lord of lords and King of kings; and those who are with Him *are the* called and chosen and faithful."

¹⁵And he *said to me, "The waters which you saw where the prostitute sits are peoples and multitudes, and nations and languages. ¹⁶And the ten horns which you saw, and the beast, these will hate the prostitute and will make her desolate and naked, and will eat her flesh and will burn her up with fire. ¹⁷For God has put it in their hearts to execute His purpose by having a common purpose, and by giving their kingdom to the beast, until the words of God will be fulfilled. ¹⁸The woman whom you saw is the great city, which reigns over the kings of the earth."

Babylon Is Fallen

18 After these things I saw another angel coming down from heaven, having great authority, and the earth was illuminated from his glory. ²And he cried out with a mighty voice, saying, "Fallen, fallen is Babylon the great! She has become a dwelling place of demons and a prison of every unclean spirit, and a prison of every unclean and hateful bird. ³For all the nations have fallen because of the wine of the passion of her sexual immorality, and the kings of the earth have committed *acts of* sexual immorality with her, and the merchants of the earth have become rich from the excessive wealth of her luxury."

⁴I heard another voice from heaven, saying, "Come out of her, my people, so that you will not participate in her sins and receive *any* of her plagues; ⁵for her sins have piled up as high as heaven, and God has remembered her offenses. ⁶Pay her back even as she has paid, and give back *to her* double according to her deeds; in the cup which she has mixed, mix twice as much for her. ⁷To the extent that she glorified herself and lived

luxuriously, to the same extent give her torment and mourning; for she says in her heart, 'I sit *as* a queen and I am not a widow, and will never see mourning.' 8 For this reason in one day her plagues will come, ¹plague and mourning and famine, and she will be burned up with fire; for the Lord God who judges her is strong.

Grief over Babylon

9 "And the kings of the earth, who committed *acts of* sexual immorality and lived luxuriously with her, will weep and mourn over her when they see the smoke of her burning, 10 standing at a distance because of the fear of her torment, saying, 'Woe, woe, the great city, Babylon, the strong city! For in one hour your judgment has come.'

11 "And the merchants of the earth weep and mourn over her, because no one buys their cargo any more— 12 cargo of gold, silver, precious stones, and pearls; fine linen, purple, silk, and scarlet; every *kind of* citron wood, every article of ivory, and every article *made* from very valuable wood, bronze, iron, and marble; 13 cinnamon, spice, incense, perfume, frankincense, wine, olive oil, fine flour, wheat, cattle, sheep, and *cargo* of horses, carriages, slaves, and human lives. 14 The fruit you long for has left you, and all things that were luxurious and splendid have passed away from you and *people* will no longer find them. 15 The merchants of these things, who became rich from her, will stand at a distance because of the fear of her torment, weeping and mourning, 16 saying, 'Woe, woe, the great city, she who was clothed in fine linen and purple and scarlet, and adorned with gold, precious stones, and pearls; 17 for in one hour such great wealth has been laid waste!' And every shipmaster and every passenger and sailor, and all who make their living by the sea, stood at a distance, 18 and were crying out as they saw the smoke of her burning, saying, 'What *city* is like the great city?' 19 And they threw dust on their heads and were crying out, weeping and mourning, saying, 'Woe, woe, the great city, in which all who had ships at sea became rich from her prosperity, for in one hour she has been laid waste!'

18:8 ¹ Lit *death;* i.e., a particular kind of death

20 Rejoice over her, O heaven, and you saints and apostles and prophets, because God has pronounced judgment for you against her."

21 Then a strong angel picked up a stone like a great millstone and threw it into the sea, saying, "So will Babylon, the great city, be thrown down with violence, and will never be found again. **22** And the sound of harpists, musicians, flute players, and trumpeters will never be heard in you again; and no craftsman of any craft will ever be found in you again; and the sound of a mill will never be heard in you again; **23** and the light of a lamp will never shine in you again; and the voice of the groom and bride will never be heard in you again; for your merchants were the powerful people of the earth, because all the nations were deceived by your witchcraft. **24** And in her was found the blood of prophets and of saints, and of all who have been slaughtered on the earth."

The Fourfold Hallelujah

19 After these things I heard *something* like a loud voice of a great multitude in heaven, saying,

"**H**allelujah! Salvation, glory, and power belong to our God, **2** BECAUSE HIS JUDGMENTS ARE TRUE AND RIGHTEOUS; for He has judged the great prostitute who was corrupting the earth with her sexual immorality, and HE HAS AVENGED THE BLOOD OF HIS BOND-SERVANTS ON HER." **3** And a second time they said, "Hallelujah! HER SMOKE RISES FOREVER AND EVER." **4** And the twenty-four elders and the four living creatures fell down and worshiped God who sits on the throne, saying, "Amen. Hallelujah!" **5** And a voice came from the throne, saying,

"**G**ive praise to our God, all you His bond-servants, you who fear Him, the small and the great." **6** Then I heard *something* like the voice of a great multitude and like the sound of many waters, and like the sound of mighty peals of thunder, saying,

"**H**allelujah! For the Lord our God, the Almighty, reigns.

Marriage of the Lamb

7 Let's rejoice and be glad and give the glory to Him, because the marriage of the Lamb has come, and His bride has prepared herself." **8** It was given to her to clothe herself in fine linen, bright *and* clean; for the fine linen is the righteous acts of the saints.

⁹ Then he *said to me, "Write: 'Blessed are those who are invited to the wedding feast of the Lamb.' " And he *said to me, "These are the true words of God." ¹⁰ Then I fell at his feet to worship him. But he *said to me, "Do not do that; I am a fellow servant of yours and your brothers *and sisters* who hold the testimony of Jesus; worship God! For the testimony of Jesus is the spirit of prophecy."

The Coming of Christ

¹¹ And I saw heaven opened, and behold, a white horse, and He who sat on it *is* called Faithful and True, and in righteousness He judges and wages war. ¹² His eyes *are* a flame of fire, and on His head *are* many crowns; and He has a name written *on Him* which no one knows except Himself. ¹³ *He is* clothed with a robe dipped in blood, and His name is called The Word of God. ¹⁴ And the armies which are in heaven, clothed in fine linen, white *and* clean, were following Him on white horses. ¹⁵ From His mouth comes a sharp sword, so that with it He may strike down the nations, and He will rule them with a rod of iron; and He treads the wine press of the fierce wrath of God, the Almighty. ¹⁶ And on His robe and on His thigh He has a name written: "KING OF KINGS, AND LORD OF LORDS."

¹⁷ Then I saw an angel standing in the sun, and he cried out with a loud voice, saying to all the birds that fly in midheaven, "Come, assemble for the great feast of God, ¹⁸ so that you may eat the flesh of kings and the flesh of commanders, the flesh of mighty men, the flesh of horses and of those who sit on them, and the flesh of all people, both free and slaves, and small and great."

¹⁹ And I saw the beast and the kings of the earth and their armies, assembled to make war against Him who sat on the horse, and against His army.

Doom of the Beast and False Prophet

²⁰ And the beast was seized, and with him the false prophet who performed the signs in his presence, by which he deceived those who had received the mark of the beast and those who worshiped his image; these two were thrown alive into the lake of fire, which burns with

brimstone. 21 And the rest were killed with the sword which came from the mouth of Him who sat on the horse, and all the birds were filled with their flesh.

Satan Bound

20 Then I saw an angel coming down from heaven, holding the key of the abyss and a great chain in his hand. 2 And he took hold of the dragon, the serpent of old, who is the devil and Satan, and bound him for a thousand years; 3 and he threw him into the abyss and shut *it* and sealed *it* over him, so that he would not deceive the nations any longer, until the thousand years were completed; after these things he must be released for a short time.

4 Then I saw thrones, and they sat on them, and judgment was given to them. And *I saw* the souls of those who had been beheaded because of their testimony of Jesus and because of the word of God, and those who had not worshiped the beast or his image, and had not received the mark on their foreheads and on their hands; and they came to life and reigned with Christ for a thousand years. 5 The rest of the dead did not come to life until the thousand years were completed. This is the first resurrection. 6 Blessed and holy is the one who has a part in the first resurrection; over these the second death has no power, but they will be priests of God and of Christ, and will reign with Him for a thousand years.

Satan Freed and Doomed

7 When the thousand years are completed, Satan will be released from his prison, 8 and will come out to deceive the nations which are at the four corners of the earth, Gog and Magog, to gather them together for the war; the number of them is like the sand of the seashore. 9 And they came up on the broad plain of the earth and surrounded the camp of the saints and the beloved city, and fire came down from heaven and devoured them. 10 And the devil who deceived them was thrown into the lake of fire and 'brimstone, where the beast and the false prophet *are* also; and they will be tormented day and night forever and ever.

20:10 1 I.e., burning sulfur

Judgment at the Throne of God

11 Then I saw a great white throne and Him who sat upon it, from whose presence earth and heaven fled, and no place was found for them. **12** And I saw the dead, the great and the small, standing before the throne, and books were opened; and another book was opened, which is *the book* of life; and the dead were judged from the things which were written in the books, according to their deeds. **13** And the sea gave up the dead who were in it, and Death and Hades gave up the dead who were in them; and they were judged, each one *of them* according to their deeds. **14** Then Death and Hades were thrown into the lake of fire. This is the second death, the lake of fire. **15** And if anyone's name was not found written in the book of life, he was thrown into the lake of fire.

The New Heaven and Earth

21 Then I saw a new heaven and a new earth; for the first heaven and the first earth passed away, and there is no longer *any* sea. **2** And I saw the holy city, new Jerusalem, coming down out of heaven from God, prepared as a bride adorned for her husband. **3** And I heard a loud voice from the throne, saying, "Behold, the tabernacle of God is among the people, and He will dwell among them, and they shall be His people, and God Himself will be among them[1], **4** and He will wipe away every tear from their eyes; and there will no longer be *any* death; there will no longer be *any* mourning, or crying, or pain; the first things have passed away."

5 And He who sits on the throne said, "Behold, I am making all things new." And He *said, "Write, for these words are faithful and true." **6** Then He said to me, "It is done. I am the Alpha and the Omega, the beginning and the end. I will give *water* to the one who thirsts from the spring of the water of life, without cost. **7** The one who overcomes will inherit these things, and I will be his God and he will be My son. **8** But for the cowardly, and unbelieving, and abominable, and murderers, and sexually immoral persons, and sorcerers, and idolaters, and all liars, their part *will be* in the lake that burns with fire and brimstone, which is the second death."

9 Then one of the seven angels who had the seven

21:3 [1] One early ms adds, as *their God*

bowls, full of the seven last plagues, came and spoke with me, saying, "Come here, I will show you the bride, the wife of the Lamb."

The New Jerusalem

10 And he carried me away [1]in *the* Spirit to a great and high mountain, and showed me the holy city, Jerusalem, coming down out of heaven from God, **11** having the glory of God. Her brilliance was like a very valuable stone, like a stone of crystal-clear jasper. **12** It had a great and high wall, with twelve gates, and at the gates twelve angels; and names *were* written on *the gates,* which are *the names* of the twelve tribes of the sons of Israel. **13** *There were* three gates on the east, three gates on the north, three gates on the south, and three gates on the west. **14** And the wall of the city had twelve foundation stones, and on them *were the* twelve names of the twelve apostles of the Lamb.

15 The one who spoke with me had a gold measuring rod to measure the city, its gates, and its wall. **16** The city is laid out as a square, and its length is as great as the width; and he measured the city with the rod, [1]twelve thousand stadia; its length, width, and height are equal. **17** And he measured its wall, [1]144 cubits, *by* human measurements, which are *also* angelic *measurements.* **18** The material of the wall was jasper; and the city was pure gold, like clear glass. **19** The foundation stones of the city wall were decorated with every kind of precious stone. The first foundation stone was jasper; the second, sapphire; the third, chalcedony; the fourth, emerald; **20** the fifth, sardonyx; the sixth, sardius; the seventh, chrysolite; the eighth, beryl; the ninth, topaz; the tenth, chrysoprase; the eleventh, jacinth; the twelfth, amethyst. **21** And the twelve gates were twelve pearls; each one of the gates was a single pearl. And the street of the city was pure gold, like transparent glass.

22 I saw no temple in it, for the Lord God the Almighty and the Lamb are its temple. **23** And the city has no need of the sun or of the moon to shine on it, for the glory of God has illuminated it, and its lamp *is* the Lamb. **24** The

---

21:10 [1]Or *in spirit*   21:16 [1]Possibly about 1,380 miles or 2,220 km; a Roman stadion perhaps averaged 607 ft. or 185 m   21:17 [1]Possibly about 216 ft. or 65 m; a cubit is about 18 in. or 45 cm

nations will walk by its light, and the kings of the earth will bring their glory into it. 25 In the daytime (for there will be no night there) its gates will never be closed; 26 and they will bring the glory and the honor of the nations into it; 27 and nothing unclean, and no one who practices abomination and lying, shall ever come into it, but only those whose names are written in the Lamb's book of life.

The River and the Tree of Life

22 And he showed me a river of the water of life, clear as crystal, coming from the throne of God and of 'the Lamb, 2 in the middle of its street. On either side of the river *was* the tree of life, bearing twelve *kinds of* fruit, yielding its fruit every month; and the leaves of the tree *were* for the healing of the nations. 3 There will no longer be any curse; and the throne of God and of the Lamb will be in it, and His bond-servants will serve Him; 4 they will see His face, and His name *will be* on their foreheads. 5 And there will no longer be *any* night; and they will not have need of the light of a lamp nor the light of the sun, because the Lord God will illuminate them; and they will reign forever and ever.

6 And he said to me, "These words are faithful and true"; and the Lord, the God of the spirits of the prophets, sent His angel to show His bond-servants the things which must soon take place.

7 "And behold, I am coming quickly. Blessed is the one who keeps the words of the prophecy of this book."

8 I, John, am the one who heard and saw these things. And when I heard and saw *them,* I fell down to worship at the feet of the angel who showed me these things. 9 And he *said to me, "Do not do that; I am a fellow servant of yours and of your brothers the prophets, and of those who keep the words of this book. Worship God!"

The Final Message

10 And he *said to me, "Do not seal up the words of the prophecy of this book, for the time is near. 11 Let the one who does wrong still do wrong, and the one who is

---

22:1 1 Or *the Lamb. In the middle of its street, and on either side of the river, was*

filthy still be filthy; and let the one who is righteous still practice righteousness, and the one who is holy still keep himself holy."

12 "Behold, I am coming quickly, and My reward *is* with Me, to reward each one as his work deserves. **13** I am the Alpha and the Omega, the first and the last, the beginning and the end."

14 Blessed are those who wash their robes, so that they will have the right to the tree of life, and may enter the city by the gates. **15** Outside are the dogs, the sorcerers, the sexually immoral persons, the murderers, the idolaters, and everyone who loves and practices lying.

16 "I, Jesus, have sent My angel to testify to you of these things for the churches. I am the root and the descendant of David, the bright morning star."

17 The Spirit and the bride say, "Come." And let the one who hears say, "Come." And let the one who is thirsty come; let the one who desires, take the water of life without cost.

18 I testify to everyone who hears the words of the prophecy of this book: if anyone adds to them, God will add to him the plagues that are written in this book; **19** and if anyone takes away from the words of the book of this prophecy, God will take away his part from the tree of life and from the holy city, which are written in this book.

20 He who testifies to these things says, "Yes, I am coming quickly." Amen. Come, Lord Jesus.

21 The grace of the Lord Jesus be with ¹all. Amen.

22:21 ¹One early ms *the saints*

INTRODUCTIONS
to the
NEW TESTAMENT

THE GOSPELS, THE GOOD NEWS, contain divinely inspired accounts of the life of Jesus Christ, the Messiah, the eternal Son of God. The Gospels take us from Old Testament Law, given by Moses, to New Testament Grace through the message of the cross—the sacrifice of Jesus Christ, the spotless, perfect, sinless, blood offering.

MATTHEW, one of the twelve apostles, accepted Jesus as the Christ (Messiah), the eternal Son of God, and left his job in Capernaum as a tax collector for the Romans to follow Him. Matthew records the birth and life of Jesus, His crucifixion, resurrection, and ascension. This Gospel sets forth the distinction between law and grace. Jesus is the eternal High Priest and gives Himself as the spotless, perfect blood sacrifice for all sinners, once for all time. Matthew tells us of conflicts between Jesus and the Jewish religious authorities, and he records five great discourses by Jesus, including the Sermon on the Mount.

MARK: The Gospel of Mark is a fast-moving narrative of the life of Jesus as the Servant King and His divine authority over illness, demon activity, and the created world as evidenced by twenty-one miracles! Mark gives us an account of God's Servant, Jesus Christ, atoning for our sins by His crucifixion, and His resurrection. Mark concludes with the great commandment of Jesus, the Christ, the Messiah, to His followers to be His witnesses throughout the world (16:15).

LUKE was a physician and a Gentile who recorded the birth, ministry, death, resurrection, and ascension of Christ. Luke tells us of Jesus the Messiah, who provides redemption for all believers. Prayer and praise dominate the Gospel of Luke, and twenty-seven parables spoken by

Jesus are recorded. The Gospel of Luke is a constant source of joy to all who first learn, or are reminded of God's grace through His Messiah, the Redeemer—Jesus Christ who purchased salvation for all who trust Christ's shed blood and thereby become recipients of eternal life!

JOHN was an eye-witness of Jesus Christ throughout His earthly ministry, and he rejoiced to see the risen Christ the very day of the resurrection. The Gospel of John emphasizes Jesus Christ as God. Its purpose is to bring people to faith in Christ as Savior and Lord so that they will have eternal life. John records nine discourses given by Jesus and eight miracles. John wants us to know that Jesus is God, the Bread of Life, the Light of the world, the Door, the Good Shepherd, the Resurrection and the Life, the Way, the Truth and the Life, and the True Vine.

ACTS: The Book of Acts is the record by Luke the physician of the power of the Holy Spirit and His work through the apostles of Jesus. Luke was an eye-witness of many of the events, and he provides details about the activities of key leaders in the early church and emphasizes the supernatural character of the Christian faith. The Book of Acts provides the historic background for ten of Paul's letters and documents nine sermons each by Peter and Paul. It reveals God's leadership of His church through His chosen servants, the apostles.

ROMANS: The righteousness of God is revealed in Romans by the Apostle Paul, writing under the inspiration of the Holy Spirit. Romans is the key to understanding Paul's teachings throughout the New Testament. The first man, Adam, sinned by disobeying God and the result is that all people are sinners, doomed to eternal death. But God provides salvation by His grace (unmerited favor) through faith alone; it cannot be earned by human effort of any kind. Justification and righteousness (right standing before God) are provided in and through Christ to all who accept Him as Lord and Savior. Paul emphasizes that salvation is directly available to all mankind, both Jews and Gentiles. He also discusses various responsibilities of those who accept and believe in Christ Jesus: they are to be subject to civil authorities, they are to serve one another, and in general are to become like Christ in their values and personal conduct.

FIRST CORINTHIANS: The Apostle Paul addresses divisions and dissension in the church, problems of immorality, unethical behavior, and more. The wisdom of God is contrasted with the wisdom of the world. Paul answers several questions about marriage and teaches the proper use of Christian liberty. He describes worship that honors the Lord, teaches the proper use of spiritual gifts, and gives instruction on the resurrection and the collection for needy believers in Jerusalem.

SECOND CORINTHIANS: The Apostle Paul again deals with the continuing tension, divisions, and strife in the Church at Corinth. False teachers had crept in, and some of the members were refusing to repent of sinful behavior. Also, Paul's personal integrity and authority as an apostle were being challenged by his opponents. He writes this letter in part to defend his apostleship, while at the same time showing his concern and love for the readers. Paul explains his ministry in detail, and describes his feelings, desires, obligations, and responsibilities to the church.

GALATIANS: The Apostle Paul again proclaims the gospel to the church at Galatia. Jewish Christians erroneously insisted that the Gentile converts to Christianity abide by certain Old Testament laws and rituals, especially circumcision. But Paul sternly corrects his readers and explains again that a person is saved solely by the grace of God (God's unmerited favor) through faith in Jesus Christ, the Messiah. Believers are to be led by the Holy Spirit, not by the law, and the leading of the Spirit will be evidenced by good attitudes and behavior toward others.

EPHESIANS: The Apostle Paul writes this letter to the church in Ephesus while imprisoned in Rome. Paul proclaims salvation by grace through faith in Jesus Christ, not by good deeds, not by being a good person. There is to be unity among believers, made possible by the Holy Spirit. The church is the body of Christ, and Christ is the head of the church. Believers are to be imitators of God and to live in love under control of the Holy Spirit. In that regard, Paul provides a number of admonitions and offers encouragement for setting a good Christian example in a variety of challenging situations.

PHILIPPIANS: Paul speaks of unity among Christians and reminds them that God's abundant grace brings Christians joy even in the midst of adversity and suffering. The ultimate example of the joy of service is that of Christ's own humility and exaltation (2:1-11). Paul tells of salvation's joy for believers, cautions about those who advocate good works as a substitute for righteousness received through faith in Christ, and reveals the source of peace and serenity.

COLOSSIANS: Paul warns his readers of heresy and gives the Biblical view of the person and work of Christ as refutation of it. Paul teaches that understanding the grace of God motivates Christians to allow Christ first place in all things. He explains how this principle should be applied at home, work, prayer, and with unbelievers.

FIRST THESSALONIANS: In this book Paul offers his readers encouragement and hope for dealing with the loss of departed loved ones who have died believing in Christ. He also instructs them to practice moral purity, brotherly love, good work ethics, and to comfort those who have deceased loved ones. He assures believers of deliverance from the coming judgment of the Day of the Lord, and urges them to be watchful and orderly at all times.

SECOND THESSALONIANS: Paul reveals some of the signs and events leading to the Day of the Lord, the second coming of Jesus Christ, the Messiah. There will be persecution of believers, increased lawlessness, and apostasy (denunciation of the faith). The man of lawlessness, the Antichrist, will be revealed and worshiped; he will enter the temple of God and proclaim that he himself is God. But Christians need not fear—the Lord Jesus is in control and He will destroy the Antichrist. Paul encourages his readers not to get tired of doing good, and to discipline those among them who become rebellious.

FIRST TIMOTHY: Paul extols fighting the good fight (1:18), keeping faith, and maintaining a good conscience. He urges prayers, petitions to God, and giving thanks on behalf of all people. He gives instructions for public worship and sets forth qualifications for overseers and deacons. Paul warns against heretics and those who see ministry as a source of financial gain.

SECOND TIMOTHY: The Apostle Paul was awaiting his execution by the Romans when he wrote this letter to Timothy. In the letter, he tells Timothy to be strong in the grace that is in Christ Jesus, and to suffer hardship as a good soldier of Christ. He warns that difficult times will come and orders Timothy to "preach the word." In closing, Paul states, "I have fought the good fight, I have finished the course, I have kept the faith" (4:7).

TITUS: God desires that Christians be a credit to their faith in Christ in the church, at home, and in the world. Paul writes to Titus the Greek, who ministers on the island of Crete. Paul instructs him how to appoint the right kind of leaders in the church. He is to teach Christians, regardless of age or status, how to demonstrate their faith in the home and family. Titus is to warn the believers about those beliefs and behaviors that detract from their Christian testimony to the world.

PHILEMON: This brief letter is a masterpiece of Christian diplomacy, setting the example in how to deal with a serious conflict between brothers and sisters in

Christ. During Paul's house arrest in Rome, Onesimus, a runaway slave, came into contact with Paul and was brought to faith in Christ by him. The two of them agreed that Onesimus should return to his master, Philemon. In the letter, Paul leaves it to Philemon to decide whether to retain Onesimus or to return him to Paul; he maintains that God's pardoning grace provides sufficient motive to forgive Onesimus and accept him into fellowship as a Christian brother. He does not address slavery as an issue, which indicates that Onesimus was in this position to make restitution for an unpaid debt, or a robbery or embezzlement committed against Philemon. Scripture does not record the result of Paul's request, but according to tradition, Onesimus was freed. There is a strong comparison to the New Covenant: the Master, the disobedience of people, and an everlasting guarantee (redemption and salvation from sin and eternal punishment).

HEBREWS: The people to whom Hebrews was written were steeped in Jewish law and tradition, but they had heard the gospel and had witnessed miracles. While they had grasped basic spiritual principles, their deficiencies included an unresponsive attitude to sound teaching and a reluctance to practice what they knew to be right. There were some committed Christians, including converted Jewish priests, who endured suffering for their faith. Others had been intellectually persuaded about Christianity but remained uncommitted in terms of their personal relationships with Christ, and some were not yet convinced of the truth of the gospel. This letter of exhortation reminds the Jewish converts and others of God's provision of a perfect priest and sacrifice for sin, in Jesus Christ.

JAMES: This letter by the half-brother of our Lord Jesus is a handbook of practical Christianity. It is a lesson in contrasts, like genuine and counterfeit wisdom, and true and false faith. The challenge to all Christians, is "If you possess genuine faith in Christ for salvation, demonstrate it!" Christians are to endure suffering with joy and to render service as a natural result of their faith. The best evidence of genuine faith is found in the way one lives.

FIRST PETER: The Apostle Peter describes people as living in spiritual ignorance and darkness until they accept Jesus as the Christ, High Priest, and Lord. God is the source of confidence to every believer who experiences trials and suffering. The proper conduct for a believer is illustrated by the suffering of Christ. Christians are to love and serve one another by using their spiritual gifts. Spiritual leaders are to edify those in their care, and all believers are to be vigilant in the fight against the devil.

SECOND PETER: In this letter the Apostle Peter is admonishing Christians who are being bombarded with false teaching in contrast to the truth. Peter warns them that false teachers promise counterfeit freedom and are motivated by personal gain. The antidote for false teaching is full and true spiritual knowledge. The divine realities of the Christian faith are highlighted for the instruction of the readers. Peter wishes for all his readers to continue growing both in grace and in the knowledge of the Lord Jesus.

FIRST JOHN: The Apostle John speaks to Christians as children in the family of God. John wants them to know that they really are in God's family, so he outlines several confirmations of the new birth. He also warns them that false prophets and opponents of Christ have joined forces to deceive Christians and draw them away from the truth. Love is an important aspect of John's teaching, and it is mentioned over fifty times in this short letter.

SECOND JOHN: In this letter, the Apostle John states the essentials of Christian conduct for the believer in Christ, and gives further warning about false teachers and heresies. As in John's day, believers always need to be wary of spiritual leaders who attempt to modify sound Biblical teaching.

THIRD JOHN: This letter condemns a man named Diotrephes, who had repudiated the Apostle John's authority by rejecting his letter to the church in which Diotrephes was a leader. Not only had he maligned John; he also refused to receive workers approved by John, and removed those who did receive them from the church. This brief letter encourages all believers to show hospitality to their fellow servants of Christ.

JUDE: The letter of Jude warns us about false teachers who creep in among those who truly believe in Jesus Christ. Jude characterizes ungodly leaders so that they can be identified and confronted. There is need for the renewal of spiritual fervor for the faith, and for rescue of those who are falling prey to ungodliness.

REVELATION: The apostle John was exiled to the island of Patmos in the Mediterranean (Aegean) Sea. While there, he received divine visions of things past, things present, and things future. Among other things, the book of Revelation tells us of the Second Coming of Jesus Christ (as King and Judge), the great tribulation, the millennium (a thousand years), the battle of Armageddon, the great white throne of judgment, and the New Jerusalem. Revelation was written in response to the direct command of the Lord, and there is a promise of blessing to all who read or hear its words.